Address in Portuguese and Spanish

Address in Portuguese and Spanish

Studies in Diachrony and Diachronic Reconstruction

Edited by
Martin Hummel and Célia dos Santos Lopes

DE GRUYTER

Veröffentlicht mit Unterstützung des Austrian Science Fund (FWF): PUB 611-G30.

Gedruckt mit Unterstützung der Prof. Dr. Hugo-Schuchardt'schen Malvinenstiftung

ISBN 978-3-11-069026-2
e-ISBN (PDF) 978-3-11-070123-4
e-ISBN (EPUB) 978-3-11-070185-2
DOI https://doi.org/10.1515/9783110701234

Library of Congress Control Number: 2020935642

Bibliographic information published by the Deutsche Nationalbibliothek
The Deutsche Nationalbibliothek lists this publication in the Deutsche Nationalbibliografie;
detailed bibliographic data are available on the Internet at http://dnb.dnb.de.

Typesetting: Integra Software Services Pvt. Ltd.
Printing and binding: CPI books GmbH, Leck

www.degruyter.com

Contents

Célia dos Santos Lopes and Martin Hummel
Introduction —— 1

Martin Hummel
Diachronic research on address in Portuguese and Spanish —— 7

Víctor Lara Bermejo
Forms of address in the south-western *Sprachbund* of the Iberian Peninsula:
One hundred years of evolution in western Andalusian Spanish and European
Portuguese —— 71

Célia Regina dos Santos Lopes, Leonardo Lennertz Marcotulio and Thiago
Laurentino de Oliveira
Forms of address from the Ibero-Romance perspective: A brief history of
Brazilian *voceamento* —— 111

Izete Lehmkuhl Coelho and Christiane Maria Nunes de Souza
Variation and change in the second person singular pronouns *tu* and *você*
in Santa Catarina (Brazil) —— 155

Vanessa Martins do Monte
Forms of address in São Paulo: A historical approach —— 207

Márcia Cristina de Brito Rumeu
Variation in the paradigms of *tu* and *você*: Subject and complements in letters
from Minas Gerais, Brazil, 1860–1989 —— 227

Gunther Hammermüller
Retracing the historical evolution of the Portuguese address pronoun *você*
using synchronic variationist data —— 251

Virginia Bertolotti
The loss of *vosotros* in American Spanish —— 291

Philipp Dankel and Miguel Gutiérrez Maté
Vuestra atención, por favor 'your attention, please'. Some remarks on the usage
and history of plural *vuestro/a* in Cusco Spanish (Peru) —— 317

María Marta García Negroni and Silvia Ramírez Gelbes
Prescriptive and descriptive norms in second person singular forms of address in Argentinean Spanish: *vos, usted, tú* —— 361

María Eugenia Vázquez Laslop
Addressing in two presidential election debates in Mexico (1994 and 2012): Forms and functions —— 385

Calderón Campos, Miguel and María Teresa García-Godoy
The European roots of the present-day Americanism *su merced* —— 413

Isabel Molina Martos
Linguistic change and social transformation: The spread of *tuteo* in Restoration Spain and the Second Republic (1875–1939) —— 443

Célia dos Santos Lopes and Martin Hummel

Introduction

The volume *Address in Portuguese and Spanish: Studies in Diachrony and Diachronic Reconstruction* provides the first systematic contrastive approach to the history of forms of address in Portuguese and Spanish in their European and American varieties. It brings together the most relevant and significant authors on this topic. From a methodological point of view, the volume is innovative as it links historical linguistics with diachronic reconstruction based on synchronic variation. It includes theoretical reflections as well as fine-grained empirical studies. Since nearly all studies on address in Portuguese and Spanish have been published in languages other than English, this collection will allow the international scientific community to become more familiar with the field.

The Portuguese and Spanish languages are intimately related, especially in the case of address. Crucial moments in the diachrony of address are situated in shared political and geographic contexts (e.g., the personal union of Philipp II of Spain and Philipp I of Portugal; the parallel colonization of the Americas by Portugal and Spain; the long-term transformation from a feudal to a democratic system). Consequently, the dialogue between research on Portuguese and on Spanish promises new insights (see also Rebollo Couto & Santos Lopes 2011). To give one example, empirical data show that the puzzling late spread of Sp. *usted* 'you (formal, polite)' and Pt. *você* 'you' (see below on glossing problems) across America can be explained for both languages by the role of the political and military colonial administration.

It should be added that this volume has its own remarkable history. It is part of a long-term effort designed to stimulate and coordinate research on address in Spanish and Portuguese. It continues and complements the volume *Formas y fórmulas de tratamiento en el mundo hispánico* published in 2010 by Hummel, Kluge & Vázquez Laslop, which resulted from the first *Congreso sobre Formas y Fórmulas de Tratamiento en el mundo hispánico* (CFFT1) held at the University of Graz in 2006. The conference was intended to bring together, for the first time, what was then very active but widely dispersed research on address in Spanish in the New and the Old Worlds. The call for papers was received with great enthusiasm, and the 13 reviews of the volume published in journals around the world reflected that the time had come to bring together the diverse strands of research in this field. The volume has become a major reference in studies on address.

However, the success of this first phase could not hide the shortcomings of the state of research at the time. First, the diachronic dimension of research was clearly underrepresented. Second, bringing together Spanish-speaking America and Europe certainly had merit, but the linguistic, cultural, and above all historical links between Spanish and Portuguese had not been a focus. Consequently, the ambition of CFFT2, held in Graz in 2016, was to create a space for researchers on both languages to meet and exchange. Consequently, Célia dos Santos Lopes was invited to join the organizing team of CFFT2. In the resulting conference, the participants made an impressive effort to provide parallel versions of the handouts in the complementary language (Spanish or Portuguese) or in English. This new approach was very positively received, and had the desired effect of stimulating dialogue among participants. It was repeated at the ALFAL conference in Bogotá in 2017 in a session we organized on *Formas y fórmulas de tratamiento del español y del portugués/Formas e fórmulas de tratamento do português e do espanhol.*

The present volume is the fruit of this long-term linguistic effort. It includes studies directly comparing Portuguese and Spanish, or dealing with one of the languages, always from a diachronic perspective, not only in a traditional chronological sense, but also in terms of diachronic reconstruction from synchronic variationist data.

Given the complexity of address in Portuguese, the glosses and translations to English of the different terms used for address can only be tentative. The inventory of the Portuguese and Spanish forms of address is longer than in English, and linguistic variation accounts for different meanings and functions of the same pronoun. Thus Pt. *você* originally was a formal and polite form of address, albeit not as formal as its etymological forerunner *vossa mercê* 'Your Honor/Grace'. In present-day Portugal, *você* is situated in between formal *o senhor/a senhor* 'Mr/Mrs.' and informal *tu*. It may also be negatively connoted by the speakers if used in asymmetrical personal relations, e.g. between employer and employee. By contrast, in Brazil *você* comes close to Engl. *you*, being indifferent regarding (in)formality. In some varieties, Sp. *usted* is used in the same way for both formal and informal contexts, while it is still highly formal in Spain, even more so than in the past. In order to more closely match reality, we use the indices T (informal) and V (formal) with Engl. *you*. Hence, *you*$_T$ refers to informal (close relationship) address, and *you*$_V$ to formal (distant, polite) relations expressed by the Portuguese or Spanish form of address. Since (European) Portuguese and Spanish are *pro-drop* languages (tending to not overtly express the subject pronoun), the personal relationship is usually expressed with the verb only. In such cases, the notations *come*$_T$ or *come*$_V$ may be used. Intermediate terms may also figure, e.g., *you*$_{VT}$.

Glossing follows the Leipzig Glossing Rules. However, in the running text, outside the glosses, the Leipzig abbreviations "1 = first person", "2 = second person", etc. would not be clear (e.g. *"the verb is used in 1"). In this case, 1P = first person, 2P = second person, etc. are used. In cases where "person" is followed by "singular" and "plural" the glossing rules are clear also in the running text, so 1SG = first person singular, 2SG = second person singular, etc. are adopted. In the running text normal capital letters are used, in the glosses small caps.

Discussions with colleagues from the *International Network on Address Research* (INAR) made us aware of the fact that Portuguese and Spanish may well be the best studied languages in the domain of address. This is reflected by the more than 1,500 entries in the newly updated online bibliography created by Mauro Fernández and Katharina Gerhalter (2017). However, almost no bibliographic references are available in English. Consequently, the international reception of these studies is very limited. For this reason, we have chosen English as the sole language of the collection. This will facilitate links between the research presented here and the efforts that have been undertaken in parallel by INAR, especially through its conferences in Berlin 2013, Hildesheim 2014, College Station/Texas 2015, and Helsinki 2017 (see Visman 2015).

Meanwhile, a third conference, the CFFT3, has crossed the Atlantic to Florianópolis, Brazil, where the conference was held in May 2018. The conference links with previous efforts in Brazil to promote research on address, in particular the *I Simpósio do LaborHistórico: História dos Pronomes de tratamento* (Rio de Janeiro 2015) (see Marcotulio et al. 2015).

The volume is structured into three parts that reflect the challenge of bringing together research on Portuguese and Spanish in the Old and New Worlds in the domains of historical linguistics and diachronic reconstruction.

Part I consists of three contributions that directly tackle the comparison of Portuguese and Spanish. **Martin Hummel** provides a critical overview, pointing out the advantages and shortcomings of different approaches to the topic. **Víctor Lara** presents the first empirical study comparing the use of forms of address in European Spanish and Portuguese. The study claims that western Andalusian Spanish and southern Portuguese constitute a *Sprachbund* (linguistic area build by different languages) by sharing a series of salient linguistic features including address. The results are likely to stimulate discussion about the impact of this *Sprachbund* on the general history of Portuguese and Spanish in the Americas. **Célia Regina dos Santos Lopes, Leonardo Lennertz Marcotulio & Thiago Laurentino de Oliveira** outline the major axes of the diachronic development of forms of address in the complex diatopic landscape of Brazil, summing up the results of two decades of empirical research within the framework of the over-arching project *Projeto Para uma História do Português Brasileiro* (PHPB).

Part II comprises four chapters on the historical sociolinguistics of European and Brazilian Portuguese. Combining synchronic and diachronic data displaying linguistic variation, the contribution by **Izete Lehmkuhl Coelho & Christiane Maria Nunes de Souza** provides insights into historical, social and migrational contexts to explain the specific present-day distribution of *tu* and *você* in the State of Santa Catarina, Brazil. **Vanessa Martins do Monte** examines private letters written in the *Capitania* of São Paulo, Brazil, from 1870 to 1950, the period when *você* started to compete with *tu*. At present, *você* prevails, with some remarkable regional differences, especially in the port town of Santos. She also shows that, while *tu* is generally not overtly expressed in the subject position, following the *pro-drop* tendency, *você* tends to be used overtly, probably inheriting this property from its nominal origin *vossa mercê* ('Your Honor/Grace'). The chapter thus also contributes to the widely discussed *anti-pro-drop* tendency of present-day Brazilian Portuguese. In the same vein, **Márcia Cristina de Brito Rumeu** explores letters written in the Brazilian State of Minas Gerais between 1840 and 1990. She focuses on the repercussions of the changes in the subject position on the syntactic functions that may agree with the subject, such as direct/indirect objects, possessives, and prepositional complements. **Gunther Hammermüller** uncovers and analyzes for the first time the rich dialect archives of Manuel de Paiva Boléo (University of Coimbra, Portugal) who, supported by his students, collected data on rural European Portuguese between the 1940s and 1960s. Data from more than 3,000 interviews provide insights into the synchronic variation during that period, which Hammermüller uses in the diachronic reconstruction of *você*. Each village in Portugal seems to have had a particular and highly differentiated address system and practice.

Part III deals with the diachrony of Spanish, and in particular the related history of European and American Spanish. The first two contributions deal with the neglected history of plural forms. **Virginia Bertolotti** investigates the unknown reasons for the loss of *vosotros* in the Spanishes of the Americas (with the exception of its use in highly ceremonial and formulaic contexts). Criticizing the common bias of considering *Modern* European Spanish as the original variety, she shows that the loss of *vosotros* starts earlier than assumed, in the 18th century, probably as a consequence of the fact that plural distinctions never rooted in American Spanish in the domain of pronominal address. **Philipp Dankel & Miguel Gutiérrez Maté** analyze the particular phenomenon of ongoing usage of the possessive *vuestro* 'your$_V$ (plural, polite)' in the Spanish of Cusco in Peru. While ceremonial *vuestro* may occur in many varieties of American Spanish, the productive and strategic use for marking social identity in the in-group/out-group context created by the heritage of Quechua is unique to this region. The authors explain this specific phenomenon as a consequence of linguistic and cultural contact with Quechua. Using data from 1960 and 2015, **María Marta García Negroni & Silvia Ramírez Gelbes** study the breakdown of prescriptive norms created in order to impose the usage of *tú* and *usted* on the descriptive norm of using simple *vos* in Argentinean Spanish. According to the authors, the values of social proximity and symbolic identity have guided this process. **María Eugenia Vázquez Laslop** examines two presidential debates in Mexico that took place in 1994 and 2012. The analysis shows a considerable difference between the two debates, with a more informal relationship with the audience in 2012. Address forms play a strategic role in this type of communication which is highly oriented to achieving specific goals. A long-term analysis of future debates will test the hypothesis that this type of variation is a diachronic change, ruling out the specific context of the debate.

Miguel Calderón Campos & Mª Teresa García-Godoy examine new corpora in order to test hypotheses about the diachrony of the alleged Americanism *su merced* 'his grace' – a variant of *vuestra merced* which may be used for informal address in some present-day varieties of Spanish. The data provide evidence for the shortcomings of literary corpora that have suggested a diachrony related to the language of African slaves in the Caribbean. The authors show that the first occurrences of *su merced* in America are not restricted to the zones where slavery was common. The data indicate instead that *su merced* orginated from European Spanish, where its use was kept to delocutive reference in third person. However, the development of second person address in both formal and informal contexts is indeed a specificity of American Spanish. Finally, **Isabel Molina Martos** explores the sociohistorical background(s) of the well-known expansion of informal *tuteo* (that is, the use of informal *you*) in Spain in the period of drastic political and social changes between 1875 and 1939. Mutual *tuteo* started as a pointed upper-class behavior producing top-down imitation, which ended up joining the parallel and independent development of mutual *tú* among the lower classes. In the first half of the 20th century, not only did progressive intellectuals adopt the popular usage of mutual *tú*, but so did the fascist and communist ideologies trying to mobilize the masses. The author documents the complexity of this process through the analysis of letters written by people belonging to different social classes and ideologies.

It may surprise that the volume does not include a general index of relevant names and topics, but the open access digital version allows free individual parsing in a way that largely exceeds the necessarily limited list of items included in a printed index.

The volume thus provides thorough theoretical, methodological, and empirical insights into the multifaceted aspects of historical linguistics and diachronic reconstruction. Nevertheless, there is clearly scope for further investigation. We want to draw attention to two areas that remain underrepresented in research.

The first area is the lack of investigation into the history of European Portuguese in the research landscape of Portugal. As a probable consequence of the dominance of Generative Linguistics in Portugal over a number of decades, the study of address has been undertaken only by foreign researchers (Sandi

Michele de Oliveira, Gunther Hammermüller, Víctor Lara, Leonardo Lennertz Marcotulio). Whereas in Spanish the investigation of the origins and the history of address has a long tradition culminating in the current systematic corpus-based efforts, in Portuguese the last landmark study on the diachrony of address written by a Portuguese author is almost 50 years old (Cintra 1972). For this reason, the Brazilian PHPB project, which does not tackle data older than the 18th century, lacks a solid historical ground: the European origins of address. These origins and their development during the first century of Portuguese have to be investigated on solid empirical grounds.

Future research should also tackle the Latin–Romance transition, e.g., in translations, as well as the comparative study of address in all Romance languages and varieties. The contributions of this volume provide multiple evidence for the linguistic and cultural relationships that tie the Romance languages together. However, this dimension of address has not been systematically investigated. It would be a good topic for one of the next CFFT conferences.

Finally, we express our gratitude to the organizations that provided the funding for travel costs for colleagues to CFFT1 and CFFT2: the Hugo Schuchardt Foundation, the Styrian Government, and the Arts and Humanities Faculty of the University of Graz. Last but not least, the Austrian Science Fund FWF financed this open access publication. We also feel grateful to the editors of the *Topics in Address Research* series for making helpful comments. The volume could finally not be published in that series. The English version has been carefully revised, first by individual native reviews of each paper, then Jane Warren checked the complete volume.

References

Cintra, Luís F. Lindley. 1972. *Sobre "formas de tratamento" na língua portuguesa*. Lisbon: Livros Horizonte.

Fernández, Mauro & Katharina Gerhalter. 2017. Pronombres de segunda persona y fórmulas de tratamiento en español: Una nueva bibliografía (1867 – 2016). *Lingüística en la Red* (25.3.2017). http://www.linred.es/informacion_pdf/LR_informacion20_20170219.pdf.

Marcotulio, Leonardo Lennertz, Célia Regina dos Santos Lopes & Silvia Regina de Oliveira Cavalcante (eds.). 2015. *História dos pronomes de tratamento no português brasileiro*, special issue of *LaborHistórico* 1,1.

Rebollo Couto, Leticia & Célia Regina dos Santos Lopes (eds.). 2011. *As formas de tratamento em português e em espanhol. Variação, mudança e funções conversacionais/Las formas de tratamiento en español y en portugués. Variación, cambio y funciones conversacionales*. Niterói: Editora da UFF.

Vismans, Roel. 2015. INAR 3. http://languagesatsheffield.blogspot.co.uk/2015/11/inar-3.html.

Martin Hummel
Diachronic research on address in Portuguese and Spanish

Abstract: This chapter provides a critical synopsis of the current state of research on address in Portuguese and Spanish.[1] The comparative approach, using two typologically and culturally related languages, provides evidence for the value of contrastive methodologies, especially if grounded in cross-linguistic functions or concepts. The chapter therefore analyses the consequences of the typological discussion of *pro-drop* languages for addressing, and vice versa. Variation plays a major role in both the synchronic dynamics and the diachronic change of language. In this context, permanent *crisis* is pointed out as a major property that distinguishes address from other linguistic domains. From a diachronic point of view, a pluralistic approach is proposed that integrates the study of visible diachrony, language elaboration, effects of norms and education, as well as diachronic reconstruction.

Keywords: address, diachrony, discourse tradition, education bias, Portuguese, (*anti*) *pro-drop* tendencies, reconstruction, Romance languages, Spanish, *Sprachausbau*, standardization, *voseo*, crisis

1 Introduction

The majority of the work on the synchrony and diachrony of address systems in Portuguese and Spanish deals with specific aspects, such as sets of texts (corpora), single items or paradigms (e.g., subject pronouns; or one such pronoun), and certain periods. This is unavoidable since the sociolinguistic complexity of address in synchrony and diachrony requires an extensive and differentiated documentation in comparison to other research domains. Gaps in documentation must therefore be filled before we can seriously tackle a synthesis of the diachrony of address based on linguistic variation. This research activity should not exclude, however, the discussion and further development of theoretical and methodological reflection. In this respect, the chapter's bibliography produces

---

1 This chapter is part of the project FFI201346207 "Oralia diacrónica del español (ODE)", funded by the Spanish Ministerio de Economía y Competitividad and the European Regional Development Fund (FEDER).

an overall impression that theoretical and methodological reflection is limited or lacking. Major hypotheses guiding research on diachronic change in address systems of Romance languages are crucially missing (see also Tuten 2008). This chapter outlines theoretical and methodological aspects that may guide research in the future. Consequently, the arguments developed here are not meant to be an endpoint but a reference to start discussion.

Cross-linguistic comparison provides a powerful method for the identification of general features of address that may be used in turn to formulate theoretical frameworks. Not surprisingly, one of the major advances in address research, Brown & Gilman's 1960 study on "power and solidarity", has such a contrastive methodological basis. Their article provides a general hypothesis that has guided research to the present day. However, power and solidarity are not necessarily decisive for linguistic behavior in a situation where a young man addresses an old woman, a relation which may be solidary and respectful at the same time. Lopes & Rumeu (2015: 23) classify the relation "son-mother" as asymmetrical, while Martins et al. (2015: 31) consider the same relation as symmetrical and rather solidary. Moreover, asymmetry of power does not exclude mutual *tu* or *você*. Roughly speaking, the terms do not necessarily match the relations, feelings and attitudes of speakers in the complex diversity of situations, nor does power necessarily determine address. It is obviously the speakers' attitudes and communicative goals that guide their linguistic behavior when using or not using socially established patterns. Furthermore, relations of the "father/mother-son" type are not intrinsically only asymmetrical (power) or only solidary/symmetrical. This depends on the practice of each family and each situation, which may or may not activate the parents' power. Hence, it is hard to assume a general determinism of address by objective social relations.

Moreover, the paradigms and the principles of address of the languages analyzed by Brown & Gilman are very similar from a general cross-linguistic standpoint. Nevertheless, this does not invalidate the fruitfulness of Brown and Gilman's general theoretical reflections. The long-term background of their hypothesis should not be forgotten when applying the hypothesis to situational behavior, nor should we forget that Brown & Gilman dedicated their last section to "pronouns of address as expressions of transient attitudes" expressing a "momentary shift of mood". This means that the authors were aware of the theoretical limitations. Hence, the problems mainly arise when this theory is uncritically applied to a set of data.

Contrastive approaches are under-represented in research, at least in Romance, possibly because linguistic address is a complex phenomenon whose manifold interfaces require an intimate knowledge of many research issues. In addition, the tradition of Romance linguistics dealing with several Romance languages has often been replaced by linguistics dealing with single Romance languages. While Germanic countries conserve the former tradition in Romance linguistics, it has become rare in countries of the Romance language family. Research on address has to reactivate contrastive approaches. It should therefore be linked to existing projects adopting a general typological point of view, for example, the current Melbourne MAPET project (Hajek et al. 2013).

First, however, cross-linguistic studies on Romance are required. While the typological perspective tends to exclude common cultural traditions in order to provide evidence for universal or widespread features of address, general political developments such as the interrelated ruling monarchic dynasties in former Europe, as well as democracy and communism in modern times, entail the necessity of placing the diachronic development of address in broader political and cultural contexts shared by several languages. Hence, broader cultural perspectives have to be added to typological ones, similar to research in the domain of politeness. More specifically, Romance languages share a long linguistic *and* cultural tradition ascending to the Roman Empire and Latin. The colonization of the New World, for example, concerns Portuguese, French, and Spanish, including creolization, where the usage of *bos* 'you' (< Pt./Sp. *vós/vos*) provides further insights into linguistic practices during colonization. To sum up, several contrastive frameworks should be explored.

This is one of the reasons why the main objective of the conference *Formas y fórmulas de tratamiento en el mundo hispánico y luso-brasileño* (CFFT II, Graz 2016) was to bring together linguists working on closely related Portuguese and Spanish. A draft version of this chapter was already available as a reference for discussion during the conference. The diachrony of address in these languages is indeed objectively related and often comparable, if not transferable. While reading this chapter, one may even feel that the diachronies of Spanish and Portuguese get mixed up at times. This may be problematic. Nevertheless, if we want to stimulate reflection and provide hypotheses, each fact we know about one of these languages may be used as an orientation or hypothesis for the other.

In the following, I shall first question the possibility of defining a linguistic theory of the address system and the use of forms of address (Section 2). Sections 3 and 4 center on the fact that *crisis* is a characteristic feature in both everyday language (situations of address) and in the paradigm of forms of address (system of address). Crisis is considered a major source of permanent linguistic change in this domain. As an outcome of crisis, new models of address and subsequent linguistic variation, *cultures of addressing,* and *discourse traditions* have been developed and undergo changes in diachrony. Section 5 considers the main methods of diachronic research.

2 Towards a modular theory of address

No purely linguistic theory will be able to cover the domain of address, given that address is socially and culturally embedded. However, a modular approach with theories concerning certain domains seems to be possible. For this purpose, it is crucial to be aware of the limitations of each such approach. In the following, I will discuss the methodological advantages and short-comings of various approaches, regardless of the fact that the authors I refer to usually include complementary considerations that compensate for some of the shortcomings. I thus do not aim to criticize the authors, above all because it is obviously legitimate and even advisable to choose a methodologically well-defined approach. I simply intend to promote a methodological discussion.

2.1 Grammaticalization theory

Grammaticalization theory provides insights into the diachronic development of nominal Sp. *vuestra merced* 'respectful and reverential address (lit. *Your Mercy*)' to pronominal (grammaticalized) *usted* 'you', 'respectful address' (see, e.g., de Jonge 2005; de Jonge & Nieuwenhuijsen 2009; Sáez Rivera 2006, 2014a, 2014b). However, it does not provide opportunities to take into account the impact of language policy, e.g., the 16th century Laws of Courtesy (see 5.3.2), nor does the prevailing tendency to provide one-dimensional clines of grammaticalization consider linguistic variation, for example regional variation, or the interplay of orality and literacy. Moreover, the diachrony of writing reflected by a corpus is often supposed to be equivalent to the diachrony of the whole language without discussing the orality-literacy interface.[2] Obviously, grammaticalization theory can be developed towards a more differentiated analysis. In this sense, Sáez Rivera (2006, 2013, 2014a, 2014b) analyzes whole texts, takes into account all variants, suggests studies on dialects,[3] and includes, as far as possible, the differentiation of oral and written traditions. But only a metalinguistic commentary from the beginning of the 18th century provides the insight that *usted* had become the spoken variant for written *v.m.*, the abbreviation of *vuestra merced* (Sáez Rivera 2006: 2904). Fortunately, the complexity of address seems to stimulate more differentiated analyses on grammaticalization than in other linguistic domains.

---

2 See the critical analysis of these general aspects with regard to the interface of spoken and written language and variationist diachrony in Hummel (2012: 329–404).
3 A contrastive dialectological study on Andalusian Spanish and European Portuguese has recently been carried out by Lara Bermejo (2015, and in this volume). See also Obediente (2010).

The inclusion of variationist aspects into grammaticalization theory is a step forward, but there are still more profound limits due to the theory itself, which considers diachrony as a genuinely intralinguistic process obeying certain principles and paths. The theory suggests a descriptive explanation of processes leading from nominal forms of address to pronouns. This semasiological[4] perspective only concerns an isolated aspect of the address system. Paradigmatic relations underlying diachronic selection (onomasiology) are not under scrutiny. The tendency of Brazilian Portuguese to substitute oblique cases such as the dative pronoun *lhe* 'him/her' with the more explicit prepositional phrases *para ele/ela* 'for him/her' or, in the case of address, with *para você (para o senhor/a senhora)* 'for you (sir/madam)', is not really a process of *degrammaticalization*, since *lhe* and other such pronouns do not change but are *substituted* by more explicit constructions. This tendency has been related to tendencies from synthetic to analytic grammar, and even to embryonic creolization at early stages of Brazilian Portuguese (Holm 2004; Noll 2008: 183–218). In this sense, the semasiological approach of grammaticalization theory requires an onomasiological complement in order to seize all items covering a given linguistic function, for example, the function of addressing in general or, more specifically, respectful address. All the items sharing work in such a functional domain are crucial for the understanding of address. The onomasiological approach is particularly valuable for closely related languages such as Portuguese and Spanish. It permits the contrastive analysis of diachronic paths consisting of etymologically unrelated units that are used in the same functional domain.

For the sake of example, I discuss a case of etymologically unrelated diachrony. Usually, linguistic analyses semasiologically discuss etymologically related diachronies such as Pt. *vossa mercê* > *você*. By contrast, present-day Pt. *o senhor* does not stem from *vossa mercê*, and *vossa mercê* does not stem from *vós*. However, if we onomasiologically consider the forms of address that convey the conceptual domains of [+ respect] and [+ reverence] in diachrony, the diachronic sequence Pt. *vós* > *vossa mercê* > *o senhor/a senhora*[5] *(roughly: you* (respectful) > *Your Mercy* > *Mr./Mrs.*) mirrors the following crucial fact: while the linguistic items used to express respect and reverence have undergone successive replacement, the conceptual background has remained rather unchanged. In other words, the linguistic function is a long-term fact, while the life period of the lexical items

---

4 In Romance, the terms *semasiology* and *onomasiology* refer to complementary methods: the former considers the meaning and function of a given linguistic item, the latter considers all alternative linguistic expressions that are used for the same functional or conceptual domain, e.g. all terms used to address a single person.

5 For the sake of simplicity, here and elsewhere I only refer to the singular form.

that express this function is comparatively short. The linguistic expression of these semantic-pragmatic features being a permanent communicative goal of speakers in diachrony, the relevant linguistic explanation cannot be formulated in terms of grammaticalization or semasiological development, but only in terms of selection, that is, the choice of linguistic items for fulfilling these communicative functions. In this semantic-pragmatic path, first *vós* loses the feature [+ reverence], being replaced by *vossa mercê* for this function; then, the same happens with *vossa mercê*, which maintains this function for some time, while one of its variants, *você*, loses [+ reverence], *vossa mercê* being newly replaced by *o senhor/a senhora* for the expression of [+ reverence]. Only the secondary path *vossemecê > você* can be described in terms of grammaticalization. Hence, grammaticalization fails to explain the whole process. The underlying function of the chain, [+ respectful] between equals, and [+ reverential] in hierarchical relations, has been conserved over time, while the units occupying this function were constantly replaced in order to renew the deferential-reverential power of address (see Section 5.2). In more general terms, innovation and selection according to underlying conceptual patterns are more relevant for the diachrony of terms of address than the development of etymologically related items according to semasiological clines. Moreover, a consistent onomasiological approach might offer a solution for the extreme variation of address in America, also because from an overall American Spanish perspective the systems of address and their practices still share a common basis.

Finally, the features of respect and reverence possibly turn out to be diachronic invariants as specific instances of the parameter "distance". "Distance" will then be opposed to "proximity" with further subcategorizations ("trust", "intimacy", "informality"). This suggests creating a theory that integrates these features. The combination of both approaches allows for a more flexible and adequate explanation of address selection, for example, *tuteo* in the relationship between Sancho and Don Quijote as an instance of proximity overruling power, but also the option of a situational change of address as a correlate of power (see Section 3.1).

2.2 Variationist approaches

Variationist approaches that are onomasiologically related to communicative functions therefore seem to be promising as an alternative to monolithic visions of language, especially in a domain where diachrony provides overwhelming evidence for diverging developments, even more so than in other linguistic domains. To mention just one of the many bibliographical references, the landmark study conducted by Rona (1967) displays the geolinguistic variation of Sp. *voseo*[6] in Hispanic America. This valuable approach necessarily neglects alternatives and the respective communicative functions of the whole paradigm, not to speak of relevance in terms of frequency. To sum up, variationist approaches need an adequate onomasiological basis.

Variationist approaches belong to the abstract inventory of structural linguistics created in order to analyze the inner structure of paradigms and the distribution of linguistic items. Traditional sociolinguistic approaches try to relate variationist features to extralinguistic features such as age, gender, and socio-economic background, but strategic individual choice in communication is not a relevant issue as far as it is not *determined* by these features. Variationist approaches thus tend to perceive the speaker not as a subject but as an object of variation. This entails fundamental limitations in variationist approaches, which do not capture the fact that speakers are not subject to variation but strategically use forms of address and negotiate their use in interaction (see e.g., Moreno 2002; André 2010; Hummel 2010a; Helincks 2016). If we look at real communication, we have to reject the assumption that speakers "vary" (in the sense of being subject to variation) when they communicate, especially in the case of address, since forms of address are consciously and often strategically or playfully selected. This is also the case in literary texts, where the notion of (individual, genre, epoch) *style* has to be investigated and possibly related to *discourse traditions* (see sections 2.4 and 5.3.5). Strategic situational choice, style, and respect for or development of discourse traditions have to be taken into account in order to counterbalance the biases entailed by structural variationist approaches.

2.3 Retractable and non-retractable systems?

Jucker & Taavitsainen (2003: 14–15) distinguish non-retractable systems, where address is stable, from retractable systems, where address switching is common. However, this is not a matter of the linguistic system, but a matter of culture, since any system itself allows for switching, if more than one option is provided. Jucker & Taavitsainen mention American Spanish as an example of a retractable

---

6 *Voseo* is the use of the etymological second person plural pronoun *vos* and/or the corresponding second person plural verb forms for addressing a single person, similar to the diachrony of Engl. *you*, but including the complete loss of the plural functions. In America, plural address is primarily realized by *ustedes* and/or the corresponding verb forms, while standard European Spanish distinguishes informal plural *vosotros* from respectful *ustedes*. Nominal forms of address are used to further differentiate this practice.

system,[7] as opposed to non-retractable European Spanish. However, if we take into account the nominal forms of address, it will be hard to find a non-retractable language. The very notion of "retraction" seems to be quite "Germanic". In German, it is sometimes difficult to switch from respectful *Sie* to informal-confidential *Du*. This change may require rituals such as sharing a glass of wine.[8] *Retraction* is a serious, conventionalized act which is expressed by the expression *das Du entziehen* 'to retract T'. The negatively connoted notion "retraction" is not adequate for traditions where playfully switching address is an everyday practice. Respectful *usted* in intimacy (*usted de cariño*) has nothing to do with the retraction of *tú*. Brazilian friends simply addressing me with *Hummel*, do not retract anything, but instead convey a high degree of trust and sympathy in that moment.

In Portuguese and Spanish, retraction is generally restricted to initial negotiation (see also Section 3.3). Hummel (2002) relates the reaction of a Portuguese middle-class woman in her sixties who refused to be addressed with *você* in a supermarket, saying *De onde a senhora me conhece?* ('Where do you know me from, senhora?'). Virginia Bertolotti reports a similar case in Uruguay, where *tú* was rejected in the same terms: *¿Nos conocemos?* (personal communication). Address rituals are more likely to happen when intimacy (Mexican "romper el turrón") or respect ("compadrazgo") are upgraded.

2.4 Discourse traditions

Koch (2008) suggests applying the theory of *discourse traditions* to the analysis of address. This approach makes sense when applied to linguistic practices of social groups, types of texts, and so on (see Lopes 2011; García-Godoy 2015), but not with regard to phenomena belonging to general language. Once the use of a phenomenon is generalized, its connection with a discourse tradition gets lost. Again, these limitations do not exclude the utility of this approach for certain issues, for example, the diachrony of address in commercial letters. Koch (2008; see also Gutiérrez Maté 2012) himself chooses the discourse-tradition

---

7 One can obviously question the assumption of American Spanish being a single system in the domain of address. American Spanish has developed a complex culture of variation in discourse directed to one and the same person, thus facilitating address switching.
8 Jucker & Taavitsainen (2003: 14). The *Du > Sie* transition in German is certainly easier than it was in former times (Clyne et al. 2009: 48–49), but it is still far away from the liberal address switching in the American varieties of Portuguese and Spanish.

approach in order to analyze the diachrony of Sp. *vuestra merced* > *usted* (see Section 4.2.4).

Another scenario for discourse traditions can be identified for Sp. *tú*. It would obviously make no sense to describe this standard form of address in Spain in terms of a discourse tradition, but it has been shown that in the early 20th century "progressive" university students changed from usual *usted* to innovative *tú* for in-group communication (Molina Martin, in this volume). Similarly, "academic *tú*" is a relevant discourse tradition in present-day Chile (Hummel 2002) and Uruguay (*tuteo magisterial* 'tu used by teachers', see Bertolotti 2015: 73, 269). It would be interesting to investigate whether the academic traditions are related. Note also that these discourse traditions concern leading social groups.

The social stigmatization of *usted* and the preference for using *tú* in Cuba can be interpreted as a discourse tradition in the political context of communism. However, reducing the analysis to a discourse tradition results in serious limitations, insofar as the sociocultural background has to be taken into account. Combining the theory of discourse tradition with sociolinguistic theory would not be sufficient for an analysis in this case, because politics and ideology have also to be considered. An interesting case is It. *lei* 'usted', which was first used in its original function as an anaphoric feminine subject pronoun replacing the nominal address *Vostra Signoria (Vossignoria)* in discourse. Interestingly, the nominal having been introduced, according to some, during the two centuries of Spanish domination, "foreign" *lei* was banned under fascism in the early 20th century in favor of "traditional" *voi* (from Latin *vos*), a measure which in turn played again in favor of *lei* after the Second World War (Renzi et al. 2001: 350–375).

2.5 Cognitive approaches

Cognitive approaches are rather marginal in address research, but plural forms used for addressing a single person (e.g., Sp. *vos*, Pt. *vós* (out of use in standard),[9] Fr. *vous*, It. *voi* (most persistent in Southern Italian), Ger. *Ihr* (old-fashioned)/*Sie*) have been explained in terms of metaphorization (Listen 1999: 40–49). However, this approach concerns a detail in the larger domain of strategies used to avoid direct linguistic items for direct address, preferring indirect deictics for direct address (e.g., third person singular Sp. *él/ella*, Ger. *er/sie/es*). Consequently,

---

9 Correia (1954) relates regional instances of *vós* still being used in Portugal in the 1950s. See also Hammermüller (1993, and in this volume), and, for present-day use, Lara, in this volume, as well as for Brazil, e.g., Martins et al. (2015).

possible functions of metaphor must be placed into the more general theoretical framework of indirect address. The fact that the plural is transposed from its source domain to a new target domain is rather banal. The case provides evidence for the problems of simply applying a meta-theory to linguistic phenomena. Research may take relevant aspects into account, but there will be no simply cognitive linguistic or simply sociolinguistic explanation of address. The only domain where cognitive linguistics could possibly provide more insights is understanding the cognitive background of underlying conceptual patterns deriving from general human behavior, which could provide a coherent basis for the above-mentioned onomasiological approach.

2.6 Social and grammatical determinism

Social determinism is one of the most frequently applied theories in the domain of address research. The groundbreaking work of Brown & Gilman (1960) suggests that the long-term transformation of feudal society to democracy explains the expansion of T-forms for informal address at the expense of V-forms for respectful address. It has been noted that complex linguistic systems of address, as in the case of Portuguese and many areas of American Spanish, cannot be reduced to a binary type of determinism (de Oliveira 2005). Determinism also conflicts with the culture of switching forms of address with the same person in American Spanish. However, it should be noted that Brown & Gilman focus on long-term tendencies rather than grammatical rules for the use of forms of address in communicative situations, even if such situations are used for empirical evidence. As pointed out in Section 1, this theory needs complementary theories dealing with attitudes, situations, and communicative strategies.

Traditional *grammatical rules* such as "mutual *tú* in family communication in present-day European Spanish" only work up to a certain degree. The culture of switching address in American Spanish conflicts with this traditional approach (e.g., Hummel 2010a, Quesada Pacheco 2010; Gutiérrez Maté 2013: 229). It is interesting, however, that grammatical rules work much better in the European varieties of Romance languages. This could be the outcome of stronger standardization and normalization in the history of the Old World. The simplistic point of view adopted by the T-V model of Brown & Gilman can possibly be related to the rather simple systems of address in most of the European languages. This aspect will be discussed as "education bias" in Section 5.3.6. European Portuguese may be seen as an exception because of the rich varieties of address in use, but one can also discuss it as a more fine-tuned type of normalization.

2.7 Pragmatics

In view of these problems, one may be tempted to argue that pragmatics could do the job. Pragmatics often appears to be an attractive alternative to the shortcomings of traditional linguistic approaches. But then we have the same problem as in pragmatics in general: there is no general pragmatic theory, but several theoretical modules. The reason for this is just the same as for the address system. If we abandon the (limited) structural linguistic analysis, language necessarily produces interfaces with non-linguistic parameters such as interaction, situation, culture, society, communicative strategy, ideology, etc. Consequently, theory is necessarily modular, each module being adapted to its domain.

If we disregard the above-mentioned limitations, *pragmatic linguistic approaches* are certainly crucial for the analysis of the great variety of effects that are observed in specific situations. *Face theory* provides useful analytical tools for the study of situational behavior. As Bertolotti (2015) repeatedly shows, *face* relates further to in-group vs. out-group behavior, including groups such as "age", and "gender". The very morphosemantics of Sp. *nosotros* 'lit. we others' and *vosotros* 'lit. you others' provides evidence for the relevance of this feature (see also Dankel & Maté, this volume).

Another crucial feature is the opposition of private and public communication. A striking fact is the repeatedly observed change of frequency in the case of BPt. *tu* vs. *você*. While *você* clearly prevails in situations where the informant knows that s/he is being recorded, *tu* is more frequent than *você* in secret recordings. Thus, the proportion of *você/tu* in overtly recorded vs. secretly recorded discourse reverses from, roughly speaking, 2:1 to 1:2 in Santos (Santos, SP) and 3:1 to 1:3 in Bahia (see Nogueira 2013: 33, 43–43).

Quite often, it is not the function or meaning of the form of address that changes from one situation to another, but the same meaning produces different communicative effects depending on the situation's configuration. In Portugal, *você* is problematic only when in a given situation the personal relation is felt to be asymmetrical, while it is rather unproblematic for symmetrical relations in informal contexts. A greater emphasis on *subjectivity* would also be informative. A sociolinguist may classify a speaker as a member of a group according to his/her real age, but this speaker may subjectively feel young, matching his/her linguistic behavior to this perception or pretension (while younger people may simultaneously reject his/her strategy, perceiving it as intrusive). This points to *negotiation* as a relevant feature of situational behavior, including tension and conflict.

2.8 Politeness

Lebsanft (1990) suggests compensating for the limitations of Brown & Gilman's determinism by adding a theory of *politeness*. However, the dichotomy "polite/ impolite" cannot be applied to all types of interaction (Jucker & Taavitsainen 2003: 11), not only because dichotomies are inadequate, if we do not take them as simple heuristic devices. As an example, in a football team communication is simple and direct. In this context, neither lauding nor offensive nominal forms of address can be analyzed in terms of (im)politeness, which is simply not an issue. Addressing a teammate with a dirty word that in another context would be a serious insult may express a high degree of respect and recognition in a given situation (e.g., Sp. *cabrón* 'lit. cuckold', possible translation *bastard*). Politeness may come into play in out-group behavior with another team, together with rude behavior. Similarly, the prevailing feature of Sp. *usted* is not politeness but formal respect (e.g., King 2010: 539–541). The formal (distant) semantic-pragmatic feature may even be used for rather impolite address, e.g., *usted de enojo* ('*usted* of anger', see Hummel 2010a). But a father addressing his child with *usted de enojo* is not impolite. Politeness is not relevant here. Consequently, the concept of *(im)politeness* should not be taken as a basic instrument of analysis. Politeness needs itself to be analyzed with more basic categories (e.g., *face*, general imperatives of interpersonal behavior).

2.9 Conclusion

This brief and essayistic overview is meant neither to be complete and developed in detail, nor to minimize the value of the approaches. What I do claim is that we need a pluralistic theoretical and methodological approach in order to coherently describe and explain what happens with address in language. As already argued, and partly put into practice in Hummel (2010a), synthesis in terms of explanatory coherence helps overcome the limits of single approaches. What we can do is explore domains, develop theoretical modules, and try to formulate major research questions and hypotheses guiding future research in order to achieve a coherent explanation. The result could be a modular theory of address.

3 Address is crisis

Unlike in most linguistic domains, *crisis* is an everyday feature of address. Every time people meet, address is a latent problem that requires a solution. Crisis also affects the very system of address, that is, the verbal, pronominal, and nominal paradigms, especially the (subject) pronominal paradigm, as we shall see in Section 4. As a consequence, morphological paradigms tend to vary and change (if standardization does not act against variation; see Section 5.3.4). This is at least the case for languages such as Portuguese and Spanish where colonial expansion favored local differences. The term *crisis* is certainly rather suggestive and negatively connoted, but it might fruitfully stimulate the discussion, as has been the case for the suggestive terms *power* and *solidarity*.

3.1 Situational crisis...

Theatre plays and literature in general provide a large amount of probably exaggerated evidence for the manifold types of crisis in specific situations. At work, hierarchy crucially cuts across gender, inasmuch as female secretaries sometimes prefer using V-forms although their male boss invites them to use the informal T-form, for example, *tú* rather than *usted* (Hummel 2002). But Martínez Sariego (2006: 550) refers to the case of a man also using *usted* as a shield. This not only holds for pronouns, as in Sp. *tú/usted*, but also for nominal forms such as Ger. *Liebe Frau Maier* ('dear Mrs. Maier' or 'dear + first name, e.g. *dear Jane*'; boss to secretary) and Ger. *Sehr geehrter Herr Müller* ('Mr. Müller'; secretary to boss), which would be quite usual in Austria. Hummel (2002) quotes the surprise of a Chilean speaker employing V-forms with unknown people, when confronted with general *tuteo* in Cuba. There is no need to add more examples since every speaker knows such critical situations. Speakers generally remember them, which is certainly less the case in other domains. Questionnaires therefore successfully use such questions (Hummel 2010a). On a broader scale, the Laws of Courtesy reflect a widespread social awareness of crisis in the 16th century (see Section 5.3.2).

3.2 ... and techniques for contextual reparation ...

As a consequence of situational crisis, techniques of contextual reparation (neutralization) constitute a prominent domain of research. Sp. *usted* is respectful and distant at the same time. Hence it primarily preserves the *negative face* of the interlocutor. In some contexts, this is felt as not being polite enough. *Positive facework* is required. The addition of a *reverential* form provides an adequate solution:

(1)   — *Disculpe* la hora, pero necesito conversar unas palabritas con *usted*,
      señora, si *fuera* tan amable [...]
      (Ampuero 1998: 146; my italics)

   'Sorry for being late, but I need to talk to *you, Madam*, if I may'

In this literary example from Chilean Spanish quoted by Hummel (2010a), *usted* preserves the negative face of the interlocutor, a strategy to which *señora* adds a positive, face-flattering element. The underlying general principle is that context and situation can neutralize single semantic features of a form of address. In the example, *señora* does not neutralize the formal politeness conveyed by *usted* because it contains the same feature, but it compensates the effect of distance and emotional coldness conveyed by *usted*, adding reverence (see Calderón Campos 2010; Rigatuso 1988–1989). By contrast, the feature "distance" conveyed by *usted* or Ger. *Sehr geehrter Herr* 'Dear Sir' is used as an arm or *shield* by the female employees mentioned in Section 3.1.

European Pt. *você* is traditionally avoided by middle-class speakers, especially by those who are older, because of its downgrading social connotation in out-group communication. However, *você* is a situational variant, not only for young people allegedly influenced by Brazilian usage, but also for other people who know each other in a way that excludes this negative connotation (see also Hammermüller 1980, 1992). Hence, *você* may be used for in-group communication if the speakers want to use a more respectful, but still rather intimate, form of address than *tu*. A similar effect can be achieved in French, combining respectful *vous* with the first name. Inserted in a culture of playful switches of address, the *principle of contextual neutralization/reparation* explains situational variation and catalyzes the development of systematic patterns for this purpose (see already Meier 1951, on *Ausgleich* ('compensation') in European Portuguese). Both would be an interesting topic for systematic research. According to recent data, the use of *você* has become widespread in Portugal, but systematic avoidance persists in idiolects as a deliberate option (Melo e Abreu 2013: 280). It is noteworthy that in French the avoidance of addressing or being addressed with *tu* is attested as an occasional idiolectal feature (Havu 2013: 87). In such cases, *vous* is the only pronoun in the idiolect. In more general terms, *vous* can be analyzed as the default of address in French, a fact that calls to mind the pronoun *vos* in Old Spanish.

3.3 ... and negotiation

The *negotiation of address* or the playful multiplication of terms of address directed to the same person also correlate with crisis. In a broader sense, negotiation may be considered as a technique for the construction of individual identity and the definition of personal relations (see de Oliveira 2009; Raymond 2016; Kluge 2016). It should be noted that the goals and effects of negotiation exceed the domain of *face*, insofar as personal relations are concerned as a whole (e.g., the employee-boss relation). This is a serious limitation of *face theory*. *Negotiation* is also a problematic notion, inasmuch as the common meaning of the term presupposes a specific outcome, that is, a form of address being temporarily or definitively established between persons. This cannot account for playful address switching. Hence, the very idea of negotiation may be seen as a projection of European standards onto other cultures. It further presupposes a very individualistic perception of address, which may hold for loosely stratified and democratic European societies but not, or much less so, for hierarchical ones.

3.4 Migration

Recurrent situations of crisis achieving a social dimension seem to be a major aspect related to both diachronic change and synchronic variation. As an outcome of social crisis, new models of address, and subsequent linguistic variation, *cultures of addressing* and *discourse traditions* may be developed diachronically and undergo changes. In a small village in Portugal the complex system of pronominal and nominal address works because everybody knows everybody (see de Oliveira 2009: 420). Mass migration and individual professional mobility have repeatedly affected this situation, for example, the colonial migration of Europeans to America, the migration of rural populations to urban agglomerations during the 20th century, and the migration of Hispanics to the USA. In Mexican families living in the United States, parents often try to conserve asymmetrical address patterns with their children, but the rather informal tradition of using *you* in the surrounding anglophone world provokes crises, for example, when children overtly challenge the tradition of using *usted* to address their parents (see Hummel 2010b).

In modern Western civilizations, people often change the company they work for or they work in different locations for the same company. Internationalization may additionally play a role. The struggle for equal rights and treatment in the domain of gender also affects linguistic address. The increase in the social prestige of youth and "young behavior" during the 20th century has affected the conditions of linguistic change to the disadvantage of changes initiated by groups with a high level of social prestige ("change from above"). Good examples of this are salutation formulae initially linked to T-forms such as Ger. *tschüss*, Fr. *à plus*, It. *ciao*, all of which have considerably increased in frequency. These forms may also be used for mitigation or reparation, insofar as Ger. *tschüss* reduces formality in V-communication. Migration and mobility in general also affect and question the forms of address. Television encourages national standardization and globalization, for example, the spread of *você* among the younger generation in Portugal. This fact is generally attributed to the influence of Brazilian TV productions, but no empirical evidence has been provided for the moment. Be that as it may, language contact certainly includes crisis. All these processes may change the usage of address formulas and thus create conflicts with people attached to tradition.

3.5 Domain-specific neutralization

In established varieties, the national or cultural context can play a similar role of neutralization as in situational contexts. In this sense, the usage of *usted* has been generalized in Mérida (Venezuela) as the unmarked form of address of this variety. At the same time, *usted* consciously marks regional identity against prevailing *tú* in Caracas (Obediente 2009). Similarly, the general usage of *voseo* in Córdoba (Costa Rica) conveys in-group solidarity and coherence, also as opposed to prevailing *usted* in the capital, San José. Weyers (2016) observes an increased prestige of vernacular *voseo* in Medellín (Colombia). In the same vein, Argentinian *vos* expresses national identity, being historically related to the attempt to create the Argentinian language, which is unique in the Spanish-speaking world, and also to the political victory of the lower classes during the 20th century. Other striking cases are politically motivated *tuteo* in Cuba, *usted* being considered as politically incorrect and socially stigmatized, and the generalization of *du* in Swedish in the second half of the 20th century as the counterpart of political and social equality. Hence, the construction of identity by linguistic address and the definition of relations is not only an individual process, as shown in Section 3.3, but also a social process marking in-group and out-group identity. Social or political identity reinforces the frequency of the identitary form of address, which may secondarily reduce the relevance of its opposition to other forms. If *vos* is used as a marker of identity, this not only affects the alternative form *tú*, but also *usted*. *Vos* may thus turn out to be the only form of address for in-group communication, becoming neutral.

Neutralization of features that compose the meaning of a form of address is not only a matter of regional varieties. It also occurs in routinized situational patterns. The use of respectful *usted* in intimate situations of love and personal concern for addressing a beloved person is an established pattern in many parts of Hispanic America. The expression of love is thus combined with high respect.

A similar process accompanies the celebration of *compadrazgo* between men, a sort of fraternization by means of integration into one's extended family (Vázquez & Orozco 2010), whereby people who always used *tú* or *vos* establish *usted* as the standard formula between *compadres*. *Usted* is thus meant to express the highest degree of mutual respect. It has been reported to me that two sisters living in the Dominican Republic started to use *usted* instead of mutual *tú* from the moment one sister witnessed the marriage of the other. In these cases, the new personal relation neutralizes the distance feature of *usted*. Uber (1985: 390) refers to a non-institutional case of replacement in female communication in Colombia:

(2) When I first arrived in Bogotá, the family I lived with and their friends all used *usted* with me. But after I had been there for a few months, the people I had become closest to began to use *tú* with me. Similarly, if one becomes intimate with someone with whom he/she has been using *tú*, he/she may switch to the *usted* of solidarity for that person.

3.6 Conclusion

The topic of this section may have appeared to be thoroughly well-known. This is certainly right insofar as the examples for critical situations stand for an over-whelming bulk of evidence in the literature. However, I claim that "crisis" is an interesting approach in order to bring together all these phenomena. Crisis is a major feature that distinguishes address from most or all other linguistic items or functions. "Crisis" means "searching for solutions". These solutions appear in contexts that include situational pragmatics, regional differentiation, linguistic patterns, personal and social identity. As far as colonial Spain and Portugal are concerned, the expansion to the New World acted in a critical way on traditions of addressing people.

Crisis is an important feature of individual and collective use of forms of address. Interestingly, variation driven by crisis may mostly be described in terms of recurrent features such as [+/− respectful], [+/− reverential], [+/− distant-formal], [in-group/out-group], and [public/private]. These features may be osten-tatiously reinforced, mitigated or neutralized, at either the individual or the social level. The fact that forms of address have a compositional semantic struc-ture seems to allow a componential type of analysis such as the one suggested by Gaglia & Rivadeneira (2014). The factors in play are possibly too complex for formalizations in the recent theoretical framework of Optimality Theory (Prince & Smolensky 2004), but a matrix of features might provide a useful onomasiological basis for diachronic analyses, at least if applied to languages that share the same cultural tradition. Wierzbicka (2016) suggests a still more radical approach to address based on cross-linguistic semantic components, which have been tested for European languages only. We should therefore bear in mind that Braun's broad cross-linguistic analysis did not bring to light any universal feature, except one: "address is differentiated in any language" (1988: 304).

4 Crisis in the linguistic address system: typology and paradigmatic relations

The permanent crisis of address in the linguistic system itself is a striking fact, if compared to other systems or paradigms. In addition, research on linguistic address intersects with a prominent typological topic: the "omission/deletion" or "insertion" of subject pronouns in so-called *pro-drop/non-pro-drop* languages, a discussion mainly stimulated by the diachronic development in Brazilian Portuguese in the 19th and 20th centuries (sections 4.1 and 4.2). However, the use of subject pronouns for address cannot exclusively be explained with *pro-drop* features. In particular, the fact that negative connotations and effects prevail in quantitative terms over positive ones requires an explanation that includes nominal forms of address (Section 4.3). In addition, the denominal diachrony of Pt. *você* and Sp. *usted* causes problems for simply analyzing the properties of their use in terms of subject pronouns. Pt. *vossa mercê* and Sp. *vuestra merced* were obviously created for overt usage. Hence, their successors, *você* and *usted*, may have simply inherited this property at least for a certain time. On the other hand, they may have promoted the overt usage of traditional subject pronouns.

4.1 *Personal pronouns in* pro-drop *languages*

Personal pronouns (*I, you, he, she*, etc.) are deictic items, that is, they strengthen the operation of reference, being devices for pointing to someone. As a consequence of this, they are potentially face-threatening if the denoted person shares the same situational context. This is particularly true for *I* and *you* since they point directly to one of the interlocutors, while *s/he* points to a third person not directly involved in the conversation. In *pro-drop* languages such as Spanish and European Portuguese, where the T-form or V-form can be simply marked by the verb once the addressee is known in the text or situation, the explicit use of a subject pronoun is unavoidably a syntactically and pragmatically marked feature which reinforces the deixis of addressing. This amplifies the pronoun's face-threatening force.

In present-day European Spanish, most people feel uncomfortable about the personal distance created by *usted* and consequently avoid using it. This is not the case for informal *tú*, but its explicit use is not frequent. Explicitness becomes more frequent when conversation turns out to be aggressive: *¿Y tú quieres darme lecciones de ética?* 'And you want to teach me ethics?'. In Chilean Spanish, the *vo(s) de insulto* ('offensive *vo(s)*') consists of explicitly using *vo(s)*, while the corresponding verb forms do not have this effect; they are simply marked as substandard (*voseo tradicional*) or youth language (*voseo culto*; see Torrejón 1986). Note that *vos* had this offensive function in older European Spanish texts as well (e.g., in the Golden Age, see Moreno 2002: 39). In European Portuguese, for many speakers *você* is aggressive and pejorative in asymmetrical out-group communication. The corresponding third person verb forms could not convey this pragmatic effect since they also combine with respectful or reverential *o senhor, a senhora*. According to Argentinian informants, the explicit use of *usted* is systematic with the *usted de enojo* ('*usted* of annoyance'), but rather unusual with the *usted de cariño* ('loving and caring *usted*'). Both patterns vary in the same type of relation, according to a situation's emotional loading (parents to children, teachers to children, a couple). These examples suggest that the explicit use of the subject pronouns tends to convey negative connotations. This means that the usage of pronominal forms of address in *pro-drop* Romance languages is particularly susceptible to crisis.

Interestingly, the plural forms are never problematic: Sp. *vosotros* (informal), *ustedes* (formal), Pt. *vocês* (plural of *você*). In southern varieties of German the informal plural *ihr* (T-form) is often accepted for addressing a group of persons, even if the individual address is formal *Sie* (V-form). The plural seems to be perceived as less direct, at least with regard to the individuals who compose the group. Addressing an individual is certainly more face-threatening than addressing a group or an individual as a member of a group. *What are you guys going to do?* may well be directed to a single person, but it foregrounds group membership, which in turn transfers a part of the individual responsibility to the group. In view of general claims of pragmatic theory, indirectness is a universal feature of avoidance strategies (see also Brown & Levinson 1987: 198–203, Hammermüller 2010: 510). Plural forms of address mitigate the face-threatening potential of the deictic act.

It is possible that the plural also neutralizes the upgrading reverential features of the singular form. This could have played a role in the expansion of the plural *ustedes* in Andalusia and America. In line with this, Morgan & Schwenter (2016) claim that European *vosotros* tends to be used as a generalized plural for both *tú* and *usted*. This means that it also compensates for possible downgrading effects of familiar *tú*. Hence, there are universal pragmatic reasons for a general tendency of making fewer distinctions in plural address. Is there, then, a general or universal neutralizing force of the plural from a structural linguistic point of view? I believe instead that the crucial point is that the plural is less relevant for both face-threatening and face-flattering effects. This is confirmed by the fact that both Sp. *vosotros* and its German equivalent *ihr* conserve their informal nature. Consequently, informality or, if one prefers, solidarity, is better accepted for plural than for singular address forms. Diachronically, *vosotros* was a suppletive plural of *vos* used for singular address. Hence, *tú* had no plural of its own, even at times when *vos* was used for respectful address.

By contrast, *usted* has developed a plural form. Diachronically, *ustedes* is the plural of formal *usted*. De Jonge & Nieuwenhuijsen (2009: 1641) consider the plural as an innovation which was possible once *vuestra merced* was grammaticalized to *usted* (plural *ustedes*). However, the nominal plural *vuestras mercedes* also existed. It consequently appears in contracted forms. In the Algarve, Pt. *vossemecê(s)* (< *vossa mercê*) has both singular and plural forms (see also Basto 1931; Ali 1975: 95). Hence, we have to distinguish the functional possibility of forming the plural, which holds for all variants, from the empirical issue of diachronic attestation. The plural Sp. *vuestras mercedes* is indeed documented (de Jonge & Nieuwenhuijsen 2009: 1646), as is Pt. *vossas mercês* (Basto 1931: 184). Possibly, the dynamics of language elaboration (see Section 5.3.3) plays a role as well in that, for pragmatic reasons, elaboration may primarily aim at introducing singular forms of address, which will consequently be more prominent than their (potential) plurals. Similarly, innovation first yields subject pronouns and only secondarily affects the oblique ones, producing mixed systems (e.g., *a vuestra merced os digo* 'formal *Your Mercy* combines with informal/neutral *you*'; *a vos te digo* 'informal *vos* combines with informal *tú*'). Hence, it would come as no surprise that innovative *vuestra merced* was integrated into a mixed system where *vosotros* was conserved for the plural, at least in terms of frequency (see also García 1994; Calderón Campos in press).

Using third person pronouns is another technique for indirect addressing. In dialects of German, third person pronouns are used for second person address, including the neuter pronoun *es* for female children: *Was macht Er/Sie/Es denn?* 'But what is s/he (= are you) doing?'. A similar technique has been observed in the diachrony of Spanish, where it probably compensated for some time for the loss of prestige of *vos* (see also Bentivoglio 2003: 178):

(3) — ¿Y *él* no habla nada? ¿Y *ella* es soltera o casada?

"'And *he*, doesn't *he* say anything? And *she*, is *she* unmarried or married?'"
(Tirso de Molina, *apud* Hammermüller 2010: 514; my italics)

The same strategy is transposed to nominal forms of address used with the article in Pt. *o senhor/a senhora* or in Ger. *der Herr, die Dame, die Herrschaften* '(What does/do) *the gentleman, the lady, the gentlemen* (desire)'. The latter sound old-fashioned but are still used today by people serving in smart restaurants, hotels, and similar situations. Consequently, subject pronouns of address are particularly face relevant, but the paradigm also offers solutions for the mitigation of face-threatening risks. The risks concentrate on the direct forms of address for both the T-form and the V-form. These are also the forms that tend to be newly introduced, thus potentially triggering further changes and crisis in the paradigm.

4.2 Personal pronouns in non-pro-drop languages

Romance varieties marked by a so-called *non-pro-drop* tendency, which would be better termed a *pro-insert* tendency, do not develop face-threatening risks using singular forms for direct address. In French, *tu* and *vous* are not face-threatening at all, if they are appropriatetly used. The same holds for Brazilian Portuguese, not only for generalized *você* but also for *tu*, which may be marked as substandard or simply informal, for example, in Rio de Janeiro (see Lopes et al. 2009; Silva 2011; see also Pöll 2015), but not as insulting. Unlike French, Brazilian Portuguese has not completely lost its *pro-drop* nature, inasmuch as the subject pronoun is often absent once the referent has been introduced (some authors use the term *semi-pro-drop*; see also Gutiérrez Maté 2013: 116–120). This notwithstanding, Brazilian Portuguese has a clear tendency to frequently use overt subject pronouns (Duarte 1993; see also Duarte 2012). In the 19th and 20th centuries, however, the pronoun *tu* was not explicit in all occurrences of *tuteio* in a corpus of letters written in the Northeast (Bahia) (Martins et al. 2015: 32). This means that at that time *tuteio* was simply realized as a combination of nominal forms of address (e.g., Christian names) and the *tuteio* form of the verb. It would consequently be problematic to assume a leading role of *tu* for the pro-insert tendency.

Since the diachrony *vossa mercê* > *você* and the subsequent usage of third person verb forms for address functionally presupposes the explicit use of the nominal, at least at a first stage of development, we may instead assume a pioneering role of this nominal pronoun for using explicit subject pronouns. In the Bahia corpus, the rate of explicit use indeed increases with *vosmecê* (100%) and *você* (56%). This means that the nominal address was the driving force of the *pro-insert* tendency. The fact that the nominal address was progressively grammaticalized as a pronoun has led to the present-day *pro-insert* tendency. A similar corpus of letters from the southern state of Santa Catarina displays a very similar situation (de Souza & Coelho 2015).

It is noteworthy that in the diachrony of Caribbean Spanish the explicit use of subject pronouns is (i) particularly frequent with second person pronouns (unlike first person, etc.) and (ii) within second person pronouns it is increasingly favored according to the hierarchy *vuestra merced > usted > tú* (Gutiérrez Maté 2013: 282–283). In other words, *tú* favors the explicit usage more than, for example, first person *yo*, but the *pro-insert tendency* is still more favored by *vuestra merced*. Newall (2016: 165–166) observes the following hierarchy of explicit subject pronoun use in Colombian Spanish (Cali): *tú > vos > usted*, with *vos* almost as frequent in raw figures as *usted*. Newall draws attention to the fact that the "subject expression rate of *voseo* was high despite its low verbal ambiguity", that is, there is no functional need for using the pronoun. In the same vein, Bertolotti (2010, 2011) provides evidence for higher overt usage rates of *usted*, compared to *tú* and *vos*, in 19th century Uruguayan Spanish. The fact that the rates of explicit *usted* decline over time, without however reaching the low levels of *tú* and *vos*, supports the hypothesis of "diachronic memory", that is, the persistence of subsequent effects tracing back to the nominal origin of *usted*. Bertolotti further shows that the functions of *usted* qualitatively differ from *tú* and *vos*, to the degree that *usted* is not fully integrated into the subject pronoun paradigm. Sánchez López (1993) goes as far as to consider *usted* an anomaly in the Spanish pronominal system.

In sum, *pro-insert* is related with address in general (second person) and with the nominal origin of *usted* in particular. All this obviously does not explain why the *pro-insert* tendency appears in Caribbean Spanish, but not in European Spanish. In the case of European Portuguese, the introduction of respectful *o senhor/a senhora* and the negative connotation of *você* are likely to explain why overt pronoun usage is less frequent than in Brazil.

Contrastive analyses of Pt. *tu* vs. *você* usage confirm the pioneering role of the reduced nominal *você*. In 19th century Rio de Janeiro, the degree of explicit use was higher for *você* compared to *tu* (Lopes & Machado 2005; Rumeu 2013). This was probably a heritage from *vossa mercê* for expressing respect-reverence. This would also mean that the overt use of *você* is not a consequence of a development from a *pro-drop* to a *pro-insert* language, especially because this was not the case for *tu* (Rumeu 2013: 277). The heritage of *você* could have been the basis for this pronoun promoting the *pro-insert* tendency. However, the fact that in Spanish *vuestra merced > usted* did not produce a *pro-insert* tendency in the long run shows that the same diachrony does not necessarily produce the same tendency. Be this as it may, the tendency to explicitly use all personal pronouns has become a major feature of present-day Brazilian Portuguese.

In Argentina, *vos* is also often explicitly used. The case of Argentinian Spanish is different, however, inasmuch as it is a *pro-drop* language where the use of *vos* has been developed for reasons of national and social identity, not to speak of the fact that the economic and political context has long been in the hands of rural elites. *Voseo* was commonplace in the whole Río de la Plata region (Bertolotti 2016). Using *vos* as a symbol was welcome, albeit not for all social classes, and was rejected particularly in the education system (see García Negroni & Ramírez Gelbes, this volume). In spite of distinct historical contexts, the fact that Pt. *vossa mercê* > *você* and ArgSp. *vos* show individual prestige in the first case and ideological prestige in the second, provides evidence for the fact that positive valorization strongly favors explicit usage. We may possibly relate it in more general terms with the specific feature [+ reverence].

4.3 Nominal forms of address and communication culture

The fact that negative connotations and effects of subject pronouns prevail in quantitative terms over positive effects cannot be explained by *pro-drop* features. The decisive factor is probably a paradigmatic one: the preference for nominal forms of address for reverential address, especially in European Portuguese (Meier 1951), but also in Spanish (Calderón Campos 2010). One of the distortions created by the grammatical and linguistic description of Romance traces back to the fact that the focus of analysis and teaching concentrates on pronouns. We say that *tú* or *usted* is used, while in most cases it is simply the verb that marks the person. In fact, the prevailing type of address is using a nominal form, generally the first name, at least at the beginning of a conversation, continuing with verb forms without using explicit pronouns. It is noteworthy that singular forms for nominal address largely prevail over plural forms. This deficit in plural nominal forms suggests the hypothesis that the explicit use of pronouns could be relatively more frequent in plural than in singular, for example, Sp. *vosotros* or *ustedes*. Nevertheless, nominal forms of address are favored in communications between several speakers because they permit individual differentiation (André 2010), while plural pronouns only serve for collective address. Vocatives should also be taken into account (see Sonnenhauser & Noel 2013). Portuguese marks the vocative with the morpheme *ó*: *Ó Carlos!* 'Hey Charles!' vs. *o Carlos* 'lit. the Charles', the latter being used for both nominal address and simple denotation of a third person.

A second bias has recently joined the linguistic tradition of preferentially studying pronouns. The method of exploring digitalized corpora for research, for example, for the analysis of grammaticalization paths, tends to misguide research since nominals and verb forms are generally overlooked. Whereas the latter causes problems such as morphological ambiguity due to diachronic syncretism, nominal forms of address are of concern because they are an open paradigm. Given the huge number of nominals, the parsing of corpora will at best attest the nominals we look for and which have been previously identified, but an exhaustive analysis would require the reading of the texts, not to speak of the bulk of nicknames used in spoken language. Consequently, most work concentrates on pronouns or selected nominal forms. It is probable that the discussion on the "retraction" of address (see Section 2.3) suffers from a "pronominal bias" as well, insofar as nominals and plural may be playfully used. The study of nominal forms is therefore a major area for research.

According to Cintra (1972: 15), the nominal forms of address in Portuguese constitute the *level of courtesy*, an expression I would replace by *level of reverence*. Consequently, the other levels (first level: pronouns, second level: verb forms) are not the levels of reverence. In European Portuguese, the nominal system is used whenever the knowledge about a person allows for it. Cintra distinguishes four components at the level of nominal courtesy: (1) differentiation of gender (and number) in formal politeness: *o senhor, a senhora* (to add: *os senhores, as senhoras)*; (2) social or professional differentiation: *o senhor dr., a senhora dra.*, etc.; (3) kinship: *pai* 'father', *mãe* 'mother'; and (4) the name: *o Antônio, o Manuel, a Carolina, a D. Carolina* [= *a Dona Carolina*]. Every adult speaker is likely to use all these four types several times per day. The list of available nominals fills pages (see de Oliveira 2005). In European Spanish, only the fourth domain is systematically used, and sometimes the second (e.g., *Emilio, professor*), generally without title. Nevertheless, address usually starts with the first name. Hence, the nominal paradigm of Spanish is less differentiated than that of Portuguese, but both languages share the fact that nominals dominate addressing, secondarily allowing for their replacement by pronouns or simple verb forms. If the preferred solution for positive facework is a nominal form of address, pronouns are likely to be perceived as less positive markers, which is already a negative connotation.

In line with Cintra, Jucker & Taavitsainen (2003: 11) allude to "positive politeness". This is, however, a simple fact of usage in a society and in situations where politeness is an imperative. In functional terms, nominals are simply more explicit, which includes "positive rudeness/discourtesy". Face-threatening nominal vocatives such as Sp. *cabrón* or Chilean Sp. *huevón* 'insult such as, e.g. bastard' can be discussed as a counterargument to the above-mentioned tendency (see also Gutiérrez-Rivas 2016). As a matter of fact, Cintra's ascription of nominals to the level of courtesy represents only one side of the coin. So why does the use of pronouns favor negative markedness? This is probably due to the fact that respectful address prevails in communication, being generally expected by the interlocutors. Explicit nominal address best serves full respect. In other words, our *communication culture* favors respectful and reverential nominals. Consequently, the tendency of pronouns to convey negative connotations corresponds to our communication culture.

The notion of *communication culture* seems to be useful because one easily conceives that Brazilian Portuguese has a communication culture that favors address switching as a means of positive facework and personal attention. Even the surname may be used as an affective variant of address (*Hummel*, also with the vocative *ó Hummel*), while it would be offensive in German or Spanish. This culture is much less developed in Europe, with European Portuguese being the most advanced in this context (see above *D. Carolina* as a respectful and even tender form of address). In a similar way, positive facework with nominals is more developed in Austrian German than in Germany (e.g., *Herr Doktor*, *Herr Professor*, *Herr Direktor*, etc., are currently used in everyday communication). While the notion of *discourse tradition* has a limited scope for research on address (see sections 2.4 and 5.3.5), the broader term of *communication culture* seems to provide a necessary element for understanding the pragmatics of address. As is obvious, the term contains a diachronic dimension in the sense of *communication traditions*. *Communication culture* is a necessary counterpart to situational face theory since the interaction depends also on cultural patterns.

4.4 Do subject (pro)nominals control the verb and the oblique pronouns?

An interesting domain of research is the relation between pronominal and nominal forms of address and verb inflection. It is generally assumed that the second person singular pronoun triggers the corresponding second person verb form. However, this principle basically reflects standardized norms of writing. Following this principle, the introduction of Sp. *vuestra merced* instead of *vos* went hand in hand with a change from the second person plural form of the verb (used for second person singular address) to third person singular (Old Sp. *vos cantades* vs. *vuestra merced canta*). But *vuestra merced* has long been used with second person plural (see below). Subsequently, the grammaticalization *vuestra merced > usted* conserved the third person verb form for deferential address. Hence, nominals used for address do not control the verb as directly as nominal subjects in other types of utterance (see Lara, this volume, on nominal used as topics vs. subjects).

4.4.1 Pronouns controlling the verb?

Syntax is scarcely taken into account by research on address. It plays a marginal role in de Jonge & Nieuwenhuijsen (2009), which is a coherent and differentiated study from other points of view. According to Hammermüller (2010: 522), syntax is however a decisive factor in the diachronic process that replaces the pronoun *vos* by the pronoun *usted*, changing the verb form from second person singular to third person singular:

(4)   *¿Vos cantáis, vuestra merced? > ¿vuestra merced, vos cantáis?*
      > ¿vuestra merced, cantáis? > ¿vuestra merced, canta?
      > ¿vuesa merced, canta? > ¿usted canta?

'Do you$_{v2}$ sing$_{v2}$, Your Grace? > Your Grace, do you$_{v2}$ sing$_{v2}$?
Your Grace sing$_{v2}$? > Your Grace sings$_{v3}$?
Your Grace [shortened] sings$_{v3}$? > Usted [still more shortened] sings$_{v3}$'
[the indices "v2" and "v3" refer to polite Sp. 2nd person plural referring to a single person and 3rd person singular, respectively, M.H.]

According to this simplified path of grammaticalization, the initially postposed nominal form *vuestra merced*, used as an apposition, conquers first the intial topic position, then the subject position, replacing the pronoun *vos*. It consequently starts to control the verb, which adopts the third person (but not in all varieties; see Lara, this volume). Finally, phonetic reduction leads to a series of opaque morphemes, such as *vuesa*, which converge to the grammaticalized pronoun *usted*. In other words, the general claim of grammaticalization theory that foregrounds the role of "local context(s)" for grammaticalization implies the crucial role of the specific syntactic context. Changes mostly start by local syntax imposing a new function to an item. Only syntax explains how *vuestra merced* was enabled to control the verb. It is noteworthy that research on address needs a broader definition of "local context" than most other types of grammaticalization. In a given text, nominal forms of address are needed in order to license the subsequent use of pronouns or verb forms as a place holder. In discourse, nominal forms of address and the first occurrence of a pronominal place holder or the bare verb forms may be separated by several utterances, especially in *pro-drop* languages, since the *pro-drop* effect holds for both the noun-verb and the pronoun-verb relations. This considerably enlarges what should be considered as the pertinent "local context". Complementarily, Bertolotti (2017) draws attention to the role played by the internal syntax of noun phrases used for address in diachrony.

This notwithstanding, the scenarios evoked in the phrases at (4) above concern the narrow local context. *Vos* and *vuestra merced* were not exclusive in the beginning but complementary. According to the first item and the example quoted by de Jonge & Nieuwenhuijsen (2009: 1640), *vuestra merced* played the same role as *señora* in the Chilean example quoted in 3.2; that is, it added the feature [+ reverential] to the feature [+ respectful] conveyed by *vos* (see also Calderón Campos 2006).

According to this pattern, *vuestra señoría* 'Your Honor', *vuestra excelencia* 'Your Excellency', *vuestra alteza* 'Your Highness', *vuestra majestad* 'Your Majesty' (see Section 5.2.3) were added to express scales of reverence. In more general terms, *vuestra merced* assumed the function nominal forms of address have up to the present day. This analysis also provides evidence for the fact that *vos* and *vuestra merced* were competing in the same context. In terms of hypothesis, this could explain why *usted* and possibly Pt. *você* replaced contextually co-occurring *vos/vós* in areas such as Mérida (Colombia) or Brazil, without relevant competition from *tú/tu*, while later colonization involves increasing relevance of the latter as a consequence of changes located in Europe. In other areas such as Costa Rica, *usted* still competes with *vos*, with new liberal attitudes favoring the latter (see Section 5.5).

In the case of Brazilian Portuguese, however, it seems that the partial erosion of the verbal paradigm (with the exception of the first person singular) is prior to or independent of the rise in use of the correspondent subject pronoun. The usage of the unmarked verb form with *tu* in regions such as Maranhão, where *tu* is traditionally used, might confirm this hypothesis, insofar as the loss of the second person morpheme -*s* cannot be explained by the replacement of *tu* by third person pronouns, since these never came into use in a significant way (Alves & Scherre 2015). The process of morphological simplification is often seen as an instance of creolization (see Holm 2004: 80–83), but this term has to be taken in a very broad sense, close to language contact in general and linguistic restructuring provoked by crisis. This discussion is certainly thought provoking, but, clearly, it has to be set on more solid empirical grounds.

At present, the following pronouns combine or may combine with third person singular verb forms in Brazilian Portuguese, such as the verb *fazer* 'to do':

(5) *tu*   (you.2SG)   *faz*   (do.3SG.PRS.IND)
    você   (you.2SG)   *faz*   (do.3SG.PRS.IND)
    nós   (we.1PL)   *faz*   (do.3SG.PRS.IND)
    a gente (the people.3SG(1PL)) *faz*   (do.3SG.PRS.IND)

This situation can again be diachronically compared to French where *je, tu, il/elle*, *ils/elles* combine with verb forms that only differ in spelling, not in their oral realization, as in the following examples of the verb *chanter* 'to sing': *chante, chantes, chante, chantent*. In both languages, the tendency to replace the first person plural by generic Pt. *a gente* or Fr. *on* is very strong in oral communication, also with third person singular (Fr. *on fait*). Both pronouns favor the use of the singular verb form (but in Europe Pt. *a gente fazemos* (do.1PL.PRS.IND) is used as well).

Note also that in both Brazilian Portuguese and French explicit subjects are often repeated by the pronoun, even in abstract topics such as discourse on syntax:

O sujeito, ele vem antes do verbo. Le sujet, il vient avant le verbe (lit. 'The subject, it stands before the verb'). Since mutual influence of French and Brazilian Portuguese can be excluded for historical reasons, the analogies support the relevance of typological factors (*pro-insert* tendencies). This holds also for the usage of subject pronouns to replace oblique pronouns (BPt. *vejo você* 'I see you', see below).

4.4.2 Subject pronouns controlling oblique pronouns?

The controlling force of subject pronouns on oblique pronouns is rather weak in the domain of address in American Spanish and Portuguese. Sp. *vos* (second person singular) generally combines with accusative-dative *te* morphologically corresponding to *tú*. Similarly, Brazilian *você* may combine with both *te* (T-form) and the V-forms for accusative *o/a* (masc./fem. 'him/her') and dative *lhe* 'to/for him', the latter being rarely used. Innovative dynamics have started to replace these pronouns with the subject pronoun in the case of accusative (BPt. *vejo você* 'I see you') and a prepositional phrase for dative (*Dou isso para você* 'I give this to you'), with still more variants, but the traditional accusative-dative pronoun *te* still prevails. A similar tendency can be observed for Argentinian and Uruguayan Sp. *vos* and corresponding usage of *a vos/para vos*. This is obviously not due to creolization but to restructuring

The direct object corresponding to BPt. *você* or *tu* may be realized as *te*, *você*, *o/a*, zero, *tu*. It is possible that the recent increase in use of *tu* in the urban substandard variety of Rio de Janeiro simply follows the path made by *você* (see also Lopes et al. 2009):

(6) *Você faz. Eu vejo você. Digo a você. Faço para você. Dou para você.*

'lit. You do. I see you. I tell to you. I make (it) for you. I give (it) to you'

(7) *Tu faz. Eu vejo tu. Faço para tu. Dou para tu.*

'lit. You do. I see you. I make (it) for you. I give (it) to you'[10]

The variants in (6) are also used for writing, whereas those in (7) are from informal spoken language. It is noteworthy that *Faço para tu/você* and *Dou para tu/você*

---

10 The translation into English is the same in both cases since either *você* or *tu* may be used with the same pragmatic range as Engl. *you*, as if English had a second pronoun for the same functions.

include the previously mentioned zero realization of the direct object pronoun (see also canonical European Pt. *Faço-o para ti* or *faço-to*; *dou-lho*).[11]

For both historical and synchronic-variationist reasons, variation seems to be more basic for language than the "one-correct-solution" model. The rather systematic usage of etymological oblique pronouns in European Portuguese and Spanish therefore suggests an explanation based on stronger standardization in Europe. The linguists' canonical vision of control does not match with more playful combinations in the present and in former times. In fact, standardization does not act against complexity, as shown by the differentiated address system in standard European Portuguese, but it certainly restrains switching and morphological variation.

4.5 Conclusion

According to my purpose of suggesting general hypotheses, this chapter has singled out the relevance of typological features and questioned the canonical view of subjects controlling the predicate and the oblique pronouns. Typological approaches are widespread for the cross-linguistic analysis of subject pronouns, as in the discussion on *pro-drop* vs. *pro-insert* languages, but address research has not thoroughly integrated and questioned this approach. In addition, nominal forms of address are crucially relevant for the usage and the functions of pronouns. The paradigmatic relations between both should therefore be taken into account. Finally, syntactic relations including oblique pronouns and prepositional solutions have to be integrated, not to speak of more general aspects of communication culture.

5 From synchrony to diachrony to synchrony

5.1 "Downstream" and "upstream" diachrony

The history of a language is almost always conceived as a diachronic process from its beginnings up to the present. Consequently, research follows time. In truth, this method only provides the history of the written language since only written

---

11 See Rumeu & de Oliveira (2016) on the diachrony of non-subject *você* (bibliographic overview and new data).

texts are available for diachronic research, except for very recent times. Hence, there is a serious written language bias (see, e.g., Maas 2010; Kabatek 2012). The shortcomings of this approach cannot be identified within a methodology relying on the analysis of written sources.

All accessible present-day language data, including orality and dialects, are results of diachrony. Hence, it is legitimate to investigate the history of these data. Doing this, we quickly find out that not all existing data have their history documented in written texts. Some are not documented at all. This is obviously the case for pronunciation, where indirect evidence such as rime or orthography has to be considered. Others are underrepresented. This is the case for typically oral discourse markers, which are scarcely documented (Ocampo 2006) or seem to appear abruptly, for example because literature starts to dig out substandard registers in order to more objectively document the surrounding world. A good example is the Chilean slang discourse marker *cachái* 'you understand?, got it?, right?' Most people and linguists suggest an explanation as an Anglicism (< *to catch*). This has been convincingly refuted by Gille (2015), who started from present-day trying to retrieve data supporting its genuine Spanish etymology. In the domain of address, problems would probably appear if one wanted to retrieve the history of richly used nicknames in *barrios* or urban neighborhoods of Hispanic American cities (see Placencia 2010). In the same vein, the variants in (7) are unlikely to be found in written texts. They will at least be very underrepresented compared to spoken language. This situation can be extrapolated to the past, that is, written texts must not be confounded with the language as such. These arguments are a strong claim for combining *downstream diachrony* (following the timeline) with *upstream diachrony* (tracing back along the timeline).

Methodologically, a combination of approaches is needed in order to counterbalance written language bias. The first approach is the traditional documentation of *visible diachrony* according to the available written texts (see Section 5.2). It can be argued that certain text types such as private letters provide a window to spoken communication in the past. The second is the study of *language elaboration* (*Sprachausbau*) (see Section 5.3). It is important to know how the written language transforms underlying spoken practice if the linguist wants to separate both. In other words, the question *What is oral?* requires the complementary one *What is written?* The third approach is *diachronic reconstruction* on the basis of synchronic variation (see Section 5.4). Diachrony develops from past synchronies and synchronies result from diachrony. Hence, we have to ask for the most probable diachrony of present-day oral data and for what they may tell us about history. All three approaches have shortcomings and include speculation. The best way forward is therefore to combine them in order to provide mutual control. The synthesis of the approaches provides the ultimate means of methodological control (see 5.5).

5.2 Visible diachrony in written texts

5.2.1 Incomplete documentation and the risk of generalization

Simon (2003b) provides an example of how misleading documentation may be. The three available 13th century manuscripts of the German *Nibelungen* saga diverge to the point that the same protagonists use different forms of address depending on the manuscript. This shows that standardization had not yet been achieved. In addition, one easily imagines what would happen if only one manuscript had been conserved, as is often the case in the earliest period of language, and if these data had been extrapolated to common usage. The results would create a false picture of uniformity. Moreover, linguists are likely to accept this because they expect it. Europeans (and the educated in general) are accustomed to standardized languages and thus tend to expect similar situations in other cultures and epochs. As a consequence, the extrapolation of a simple, non-representative situation found in one text is likely to cause less surprise than complex but more representative situations (see Section 5.3). Witness Díaz Collazos (2015: 276) referring to the "sense of chaos" caused by the use of address in the Golden Age, and León (2008: 1910) alluding to "socio-communicative anarchy", as if this would have been tolerated in the 16th century. These all are reactions of speaker-linguists accustomed to rule guided standards. Again, the data in (6) and (7) show that rich variation is possibly a more fundamental feature of language than rule guided uniformity. In other words, we linguists have to be aware of our own "bias of the educated".

5.2.2 Analyzing texts supposed to closely reflect orality

In universal terms, written texts available for diachronic research do not directly represent practices of oral communication. In particular, the visible diachrony of written texts tends to reflect the colonial linguistic standard promoted by Portugal or Spain, with Brazil more radically drifting apart since the beginning of the 20th century. Therefore, the retrieval of the oral tradition is highly relevant for the development of the Spanishes in America and Brazilian Portuguese. For this reason, linguists pay special attention to texts supposed to best reflect orality such as private letters, theatre plays, and court proceedings documenting oral testimonies.

Research on address, especially by Fontanella de Weinberg in the late 1960s (see synthesis in Fontanella 1999), was a precursor in this domain long before general interest in writing the history of American Spanish began to increase during more recent decades. Following this tradition, theatre plays are systematically used for describing oral practice in the Spanish Golden Age (e.g., King 2010; Moreno 2002). The Brazilian research group on the diachrony of address from the 19th century to the present, coordinated by Célia dos Santos Lopes, uses data based on private letters. Similarly, the *pro-insert* tendency of Brazilian Portuguese was developed by Duarte on the basis of theatre plays (Duarte 1993; see also Duarte 2012). On the one hand, theatre plays and letters are indeed among the most valuable sources for analyzing the diachrony of spoken language with written documents. On the other hand, any transcription of informal oral communication in present-day communications shows that plays and letters do not directly reflect orality. Systematic studies on how orality is transformed by written texts are crucially lacking. Retrieving traces of spoken language in written texts therefore remains intuitive rather than systematic.

For reasons of genre and style, theatre plays tend to use asymmetrical forms of address excessively in order to increase social and personal tensions, aiming to create suspense or to mark or stigmatize characters, for example, Sp. *él/ella* as a feature of the servants' discourse in Golden Age theatre (Ly 2001; see also Eberenz 2000; Anipa 2001). Playful innovations such as *uced* and *usasted* are only documented in such sources. Do they reflect orality or are we dealing with inventions in literature? Similarly, in an analysis of just five contemporary Chilean novels, Hummel (2002) finds a rich variety of different patterns of address. Conflict, irony, and humor frequently accompany address. The corresponding address patterns provide evidence for possible functions and conventionalized scenarios but they do not represent everyday practices in terms of relevance or frequency. In this sense, *uced* and *usasted* certainly testify to a situation of speakers being uncertain about the pronunciation. However, we cannot be sure that they really have been used – except if they could be found in several texts. At any rate, reality has been selectively amplified in the rhetoric of theatre plays.

Letters are no less determined by imperatives of genre, at least in former times. However, letters written by semi-literate writers may provide evidence for everyday practices. Individual style may help as well. Rumeu (2013: 284) quotes an explicit commentary from 1904, where the author of the correspondence under scrutiny affirms not to "grammatically control his sentences" and "to mix up *tu* and *você* as he always used to do". This may be considered an early testimony to the liberal attitude of Brazilians with regard to norm in oral communication, which is currently a major feature. Although the general tendency of written texts is that they may not directly match the spoken language, the example shows that there are texts reflecting innovative oral practices, even if this holds more for type than for token frequency. In this sense, the documented replacement of direct and indirect object pronouns (*vejo-o* 'I see you', *dizer-lhe* 'say to you') in 1908 by the subject pronoun (*vejo você* 'I see you' or *dizer a você* 'say to you') (Lopes et al. 2011: 334, 340–341, de Oliveira 2015[12]) and explicit commentaries on the preferential usage of the latter in Rio de Janeiro in the 1940s (Nascentes 1949–1950: 68) clearly document an oral practice in recent history.

The written documentation of testimonies giving oral evidence in court has been fruitfully used for detecting traces of orality, as in Company Company's *Sintaxis histórica* (see also de Jonge & Nieuwenhuijsen 2009). According to García Godoy (2015), *usted* is documented in the discourse of witnesses as early as the 17th century, while its first attestation in letters occurs a century later. Hence, the diachrony of *vuestra merced/usted* appears to vary according to the type of sources. This means that we have to be cautious when using standard corpora such as the diachronic corpus of Spanish CORDE. However, the fact that Gutiérrez Maté (2013: 245) attests the use of *usted* in a letter from Santo Domingo written in 1661 shows that incomplete documentation crucially biases our conclusions. Considering that the written language tends to be restrictive with regard to traditions and innovations of the spoken language, I would argue that the sporadic documentation of *usted* reflects an advanced stage of using *usted* and similar variants in spoken Spanish.

In sum, in spite of the unavoidable limitations of methods using written texts for uncovering oral practices, the combination of several sources and the internal richness of the texts provides some evidence for the diachrony of spoken language.

5.2.3 Semasiological and onomasiological diachrony

In the introduction, I have argued in favor of onomasiological approaches to diachrony as a means to link etymologically unrelated but diachronically conected items. I have also argued that semantic-pragmatic features such as "reverence", "respect", "informality" seem to have long-term relevance, even if their social relevance may change in terms of token frequency, as in the case of "reverence". Since these features seem to have cross-linguistic relevance, the onomasiological approach is particularly valuable for contrastive analyses. Simon (2003a) stresses the cross-linguistic value of the category "respect". However, for the reasons exposed in Section 1, I will not follow Simon's analysis of "respect" as a subcategory of "politeness".

---

12 Again, these are the same variants we find in French: *je vous vois*; *je vous le dis, je le dis à vous* (marked variant).

In order to illustrate this type of analysis, Figure 1 places the relevant forms of address in a tentative onomasiological schema based on the concepts of reverence, respect and trust, following the diachrony for both Portuguese and Spanish.

Century		14th	15th	16th	19th	21st
Reverence			Pt. *vossa mercê*	*vossa excelência, senhoria,* etc.		
			Sp. *vuestra merced*	*vuestra excelência, señoría,* etc.		
				vossa mercê		
				vuestra merced		
					Pt. *o senhor/a senhora*	
Respect				*você*	Pt. *o senhor/a senhora*	
				usted		
		Pt. *vós*			*você*	
		Sp. *vos*			*usted*	*usted*
Confidence					*você*	
			Pt. *vós*			
			Sp. *vos*			
		Pt. *tu*			EPt. *tu*	BPt. *você*
		Sp. *tú*			Sp. *tú*	
						BPt. *tu*
						ASp. *vos*

Figure 1: Onomasiological outline of the diachronic development in the domain of address.

In the 14th century, even the king was addressed by Sp./Pt. *vos/vós,* and he himself used it with his vassals, if there was no intimate relation justifying *tú/ tu.*[13] To take the case of Portuguese, *Vossa Mercê* starts to be sporadically used in the 14th century, and *Vossa Alteza/Vossa Senhoria* in the 15th, with the first examples being placed in the discourse of foreigners (diplomats), by Castilians

---

13 I use the modern orthography.

(*Vossa Mercê*) and Italians (*Vossa Alteza/Vossa Senhoria*). These are increasingly used from the second half of the 15th century, first directed to the king (also *vós*) and to high nobility. In 1460, *Vossa mercê* was the most usual form of address for the king (Cintra 1972: 22). This supports the assumption that it was not used to any significant degree outside the court. However, the reverential power of the nominal form *vossa mercê/vuestra merced* diminished as a consequence of other newly introduced, more prestigious variants of the same pattern "*vossa/vuestra* + other honorifics than *mercê/merced*". Hence, there was a permanent top-down pressure that negatively affected the upgrading features expressed by items situated at a lower level.

As shown in (4), *vossa mercê/vuestra merced* could be added to the respectful subject pronoun *vós/vos*. This shows that local syntax directly activated the opposition of the features "reverence" and "respect", which obviously favored the implicature of "(only) respectful, not reverential". In a process starting in the 16th century, these nominal forms, which were themselves pushed down, progressively replaced the pronouns as a means of expressing respect. Consequently, *vós/vos* were downgraded from the domain of respect to the domain of confidence, while nominal forms started a twofold diachrony. The bleaching of the reverential feature of *vossa mercê/vuestra merced* was particularly strong with their phonetically reduced variants *você/usted*. It was the latter that finally replaced *vós/vos* in the domain of respect. Unlike Spanish, Pt. *o senhor/a senhora* replaced the "*vossa* + honorific" pattern in the 19th century. While respect was still a feature of using *você* in 18th century colonial Brazil (Marcotulio 2010), in the long run *você* underwent further attenuation towards a rather neutral or informal form of address in current Brazilian Portuguese. Present-day usage of European Pt. *você* shares the features of downgrading out-group members and respectful confidential treatment of in-group members with Sp. *vos*, as long as this pronoun was competing with *vuestra merced*, roughly speaking until the end of the Spanish Golden Age, that is, until the last decades of the 17th century (see synthesis by Bertolotti 2015: 96–103, 114, de Jonge & Nieuwenhuijsen 2009). This similarity could be due to general (universal?) properties of in-group vs. out-group behavior, which are not reflected in Figure 1. Figure 1 only claims that the forms of address contain semantic-pragmatic features. These features may produce different effects, for example, according to in-group or out-group behavior.

In sum, we may hypothesize two processes. First, a general diachronic tendency (diachronic invariant?) of reorganizing the address system according to the (universal?) socio-pragmatic parameters of respectful plus reverential and respectful minus reverential address in the context of distinctive in-group vs. out-group behavior. Second, the transmission or inheritance of features such as "respect" from one morphological form of address to another.

5.3 Sprachausbau *(language elaboration)*

5.3.1 General aspects

The theory of *Sprachausbau* (Kloss 1967, 1978), that is, the "elaboration of language for specific purposes" such as writing, provides a general framework for the study of languages in relation to cultures, which aim at developing the spoken language for socially relevant, new types of communication (e.g. writing in general, telegrams, short messages, twitter, braille). *Discourse tradition* may also be related to such efforts. In Section 2, I have argued that innovation and selection are major features of diachrony. *Sprachausbau* takes into account the fact that the diachrony of many languages is marked by efforts deployed in order to enrich, purify, standardize, and teach the language. In more general terms, Kloss holds that there are languages that naturally differ by their inherent typological distance, but there are others which differ essentially as a consequence of cultural "elaboration". To give an example, during the last decades empirical research has shown that the main reason why Latin *varieties* split into Neolatin *languages* was the development of area specific traditions of writing with subsequent standardization (Wright 1983, 2002, 2011; Herman 2006). Hence, the Romance languages are far from simply having developed from regional varieties of Latin. Reading any medieval Spanish text it becomes apparent that some constructions no longer in use in standard Spanish continue to be of common currency in standard Portuguese. In America, the deans of linguistic policy, Andrés Bello (1781–1865) and José Rufino Cuervo (1844–1911), made efforts to avoid the splitting of American Spanish into different languages, as had happened with Latin. Consequently, they acted in favor of creating a common American Spanish standard of educated speaking and writing. However, illiteracy in Ibero-America restricted the impact of such efforts compared to Europe. In contrast to Spanish, the tendency of creating their own national norms accompanies the recent history of Portugal and Brazil, as well as efforts to avoid the two norms drifting apart, such as in orthography.

It comes as no surprise that language elaboration is exactly one of the points where the New and the Old World drift apart. In most cases, research questions ask how a particular idiosyncrasy of the American varieties came into use, such as *voseo* in the domain of address. However, the question should often be put the other way round. Hummel (2013) shows that the normative movements of 17th century purism (e.g., foundation of academies), 18th century rationalism (e.g., preference for rules), and 19th and 20th century schooling (e.g., manuals) were quite successful in eliminating certain variants by virtue of maxims such as *bon usage* 'good use', *génie de la langue* 'genius of the language', *clarté et logique* 'clarity and logic', 'speak as you write (e.g., whole sentences)'. Since the impact of these movements was less strong or less profound in the American varieties, many traditional variants have more continuity in use than in Europe. In the same vein, Noll (2008) discusses many cases where the innovation has to be attributed to Portugal, not to Brazil. This is of methodological interest, since American usage may be used for the reconstruction of oral diachrony in the European varieties.

5.3.2 The Laws of Courtesy

In the domain of research on address, a relevant effort to elaborate and normalize the system has been deployed by Philip II of Spain. The extra-linguistic historical context was the Empire of the Habsburg Charles V (1500–1558; Holy Roman Empire of the German Nation). Charles V's son, Philip II of Spain (1527–1598), promoted the so-called *Leyes de Cortesía*, also named *Pragmática de tratamiento y cortesía* 'Laws of Courtesy' (1586). He did this not only for Spain but also for Portugal (1597), since Portugal was under the same crown from 1580 to 1640, Philip II of Spain being also called Philip I of Portugal. He followed the tradition initiated by his father Charles V, who introduced the *uso de Borgoña* ('etiquette of Burgundy') in 1548. The law tried to put an end to the confusion caused by the people's desire to negotiate the usage of forms marked for higher social positions, which was apparently felt as a violation of social norms by the ruling class. Table 1 sets out what the law prescribed for both Portugal and Spain, according to the pattern "possessive corresponding to *vos/vós* + honorific nominal", documented since the 13th century (Moreno 2002: 16–17). The use of *Vossa Mercê* was not fixed by law, and it could therefore be freely used.

Table 1: Honorifics in 16th century Portugal and Spain.

Portuguese	Spanish	Adressees
Vossa Majestade	*Vuestra Majestad*	King, queen
Vossa Alteza	*Vuestra Alteza*	Princes, princesses, royal family
Vossa Excelência	*Vuestra Excelencia*	Legitimate sons and daughters of princes and princesses
Vossa Senhoria	*Vuestra Señoría*	High nobility and clergy, high charges in administration
------------social demarcation line for the upper class----------------------------------		
Vossa Mercê	*Vuestra Merced*	not fixed by law

In 1739, John V of Portugal newly fixed the nominal forms of address with regard to social hierarchy (*Vossa Senhoria, Vossa Excelência*; see Cintra 1972: 31–33). He reacted against the struggle of the rising classes to also be addressed with *Vossa Senhoria* or *Vossa Excelência* during the 17th and 18th centuries (Cintra 1972: 34–35). This meant that they did not want to be addressed with *Vossa Mercê* (see demarcation line in Table 1). This is certainly the origin of the pejorative value later assumed by *você* (< *vossa mercê*). At any rate, the Laws of Courtesy contributed to the increase in prestige of nominal forms of address. This prepared the territory for the use of the present-day V-form *o Senhor/a Senhora* during the 19th century, once civil society replaced aristocratic society (Cintra 1972: 38). To put it another way, the struggle for nominal forms of address in the domain of politeness implicated the loss of prestige of simple *vós*. Secondarily, despite once having been the prestigious form to address the king, *Vossa Mercê* was excluded from the prestigious forms, first by the laws of Philipp I/II, and later again by John V.

5.3.3 Sprachausbau *and underlying oral traditions*

In view of the complex present-day system, Cintra (1972: 16–17) draws attention to the fact that Portuguese nominal forms of address are practically inexistent in the oldest texts (14th and 15th centuries). In a similar way to present-day French *tu* and *vous* (and traditional It. *tu/voi*, still largely used in southern Italy), intimate *tu* and deferential *vós* were used for singular, while *vós* covered both functions in plural. Hence, according to Cintra, the nominal part of the address system was an innovation. This is certainly true for the "*vossa* + nominal" pattern. However, a closer look at old texts reveals familiar nominal forms of address such as *filho*, *mãe*, *tia*, ('son', 'mother', 'aunt'), which are still in use today, in both Portugal and Brazil (Luz 1958–1959; Cook 1994–1995; Biderman 1972–1973). Therefore, a differentiated analysis is required that takes into account two traditions: the genuine tradition of using familiar nominals in the private domain, and the constantly elaborated tradition of using honorific nominals in the public domain of formal courtesy in order to express reverence. It is noteworthy that the terms *courtesy* or *politeness* do not fit with the familiar series of nominals. Respect may play a role, but not courtesy.

The fact that French continues to use a very simple T-V system can possibly be related to the historical fact that the relevant part of its present-day territory did not belong to the empire of Charles V and Philip II (Guiter 1959). The equivalents Sp. *vuestra merced*, Pt. *vossa mercê*, It. *Vostra Grazia*, Ger. *Euer Gnaden* are indicators of a common tradition in the domains ruled by the Habsburg dynasty (see also Hammermüller 2010: 525–526; Maas 2012: 199). It still should be explained why we also find Engl. *Your Grace* (see Cook 1994–95: 81; Hammermüller 2010: 526). All this would be an interesting topic of research within the theoretical framework of *Sprachausbau*.

5.3.4 Standardization

Figure 1 does not single out the impact of standardization. While the Laws of Courtesy (Table 1) concerned a restricted domain of language, even with regard to address, the usage of address was also affected by the general standardization process, such as the orthography of Sp. *usted*. Standardization also favored the usage of *tú*, up to the point that in America the impact of Sp. *tú* generally reflects the influence of the European standard and education. Chilean Spanish is a good example of how normative efforts were made in order to normalize the language via schooling. Generalized education only started in the 19th century with national independence. The elimination of *voseo* was a major issue in this context. In the final decades of the 20th century, rebellious urban youth language promoted the so-called *voseo culto* 'vos used by the educated' (Torrejón 1986). Today, the general decrease in normative pressure facilitates the revival of the *voseo*. In Argentina, schoolbooks only recently gave up prescribing *tú* as the correct form instead of the generally used *vos* (García Negroni & Ramírez Gelbes 2010).

Figure 2 presents Simon's (2003b) synopsis of the diachronic development of address in German, which shows a similar situation of elaboration and reduction.

The reduction of the number of units entering the pronominal paradigm of address is not necessarily related to standardization. If a society needs a differentiated system, there is no principled obstacle for its standardization (see European Portuguese). Brown & Gilman's hypothesis, which holds that changes in social structure are decisive for the patterns of address in a long-term perspective, also offers a valuable explanation, if we disregard the dichotomous T-V simplification. In the case of Portuguese and Spanish, there can indeed be no doubt that the nominals defined by the Laws of Courtesy no longer correspond to the present-day political and social hierarchy. However, this does not automatically exclude an additional impact of elaboration and standardization. In particular, Brown & Gilman's deterministic approach runs short of explaining stage I where only Ger. *du* was in use. Was society even more equitable than in stage VI, which refers to present-day usage? That is hard to believe. And what about nominal forms of address? Brown & Gilman's hypothesis would claim a similar development. This has to be empirically tested.

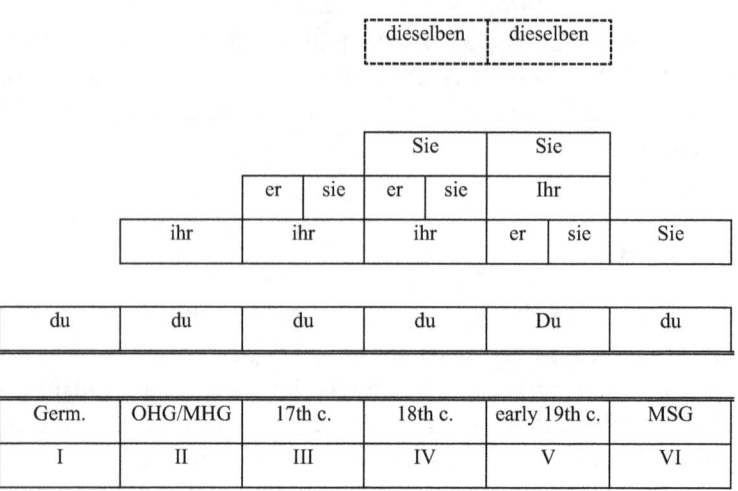

Figure 2: Diachrony of German pronouns used for addressing a single person[14].

5.3.5 Discourse tradition and diachronic change[15]

One of the most puzzling questions is the generalization of *vuestra merced* > *usted* to the whole domain of American Spanish long after colonization had started. Still more puzzling is the fact that the same happens with Pt. *vossa mercê* > *você*. The latter is the generalized unmarked form of address in Brazilian Portuguese, while its use in European Portuguese is restricted. This means that the process of expansion of *você* to colonial Brazil has been even stronger than for Spanish *usted*. The topic obviously suggests a contrastive approach.

Do Monte (2015a, 2015b) shows that Pt. *vossa mercê* (> *você*) was the general respectful form of address used in the official correspondence and public communication of the 18th century colonial civil and military administration in the district (*capitania*) of São Paulo, even in isolated parts of the territory. This is clearly a discourse tradition related to a specific social domain of communication. This social practice fulfills the conditions of relatedness with Portugal and of spanning across the whole empire. The contemporary documents analyzed by this author provide evidence for local people adopting this practice in everyday

---

14 Germ. = Germanic, OHG = Old High German, MHG = Middle High German, MSG = Modern Standard German.

15 Discourse traditions could be treated in a section called 'communication culture', rather than in a section on *Sprachausbau* (see also Kabatek 2007). However, as the examples show, discourse traditions are not independent of the elaboration process.

life. Apparently, this discourse tradition worked as a model that was taken on by local people claiming the same respectful address. In the long run, the expansion of this discourse tradition was so strong that we cannot detect it any more as such in present-day usage, since it has simply become the prevailing common language form of address. As mentioned above, the grammaticalized variant *você* drifted away from fully transparent *vossa mercê*, in the same way as Sp. *usted* with regard to *vuestra merced* – both reduced forms losing the reverential feature (18th century; see Lopes & Machado 2005; García-Godoy 2012, 2015). In other words, the former morphologically derived from the latter, but both forms coexisted and underwent a process of functional pragmatic differentiation, whereby only the fully transparent variant *vuestra merced* conserved the reverential feature. The process was shared by Portuguese and Spanish.

The fact that, in the case of Spanish, the expansion of Sp. *vuestra señoría* (> *usía*) and *vuestra excelencia* (directed to higher ranks) has also been related to their military and administrative usage (Sáez Rivera 2013, 2014b; see also García-Godoy 2019) provides additional evidence for this way of diffusion. Castillo Mathieu (1982) mentions that *vuestra merced* was the way a soldier addressed his captain in 17th century Columbia, documenting as well its expansion to everyday life (*vuesamerced*). It seems obvious that the official hierarchical organizations respected and transmitted the official usage of nominal forms of address according to the patterns Sp. "*vuestra* + noun" and Pt. "*vossa* + noun", parts of which were regulated by the Laws of Courtesy for Portugal and Spain under the same king. This common discourse tradition and social practice continued in both languages, providing different local results.

5.3.6 The education bias

As Maas (2012: 25) points out, high levels of formal education make speakers inclined to assume their standardized views of language are shared by the entire population. This means that, as linguists, we are all intuitively inclined to take our standardized vision of language for granted. Extreme examples are schoolmasters who explain the dialects they want to eradicate as results of "linguistic corruption", as if the people in the region had used standard language at some time in the past. Andrés Bello's[16] attitude to Chilean Spanish followed

---

16 This Venezuelan linguist created and supervised Chile's national education system in the 19th century. His grammar and his linguistic comments deeply rooted in teaching until recent times.

this line (even if he also acted in defense of American Spanish varieties). Examples provide rich evidence for this education bias.[17] The educated deplore the decline of the subjunctive mood in spoken language (often referring to the outgroup of young people), not seeing that the historical development of a written culture favoring hypotaxis unilaterally favored this mood in a process of *Sprachausbau* driving away from orality. Hence, it is not necessarily the oral tradition that changed, but possibly the written one. The *pro-drop* discussion takes the educational ideal of "complete sentences" for granted, but Romance languages are clearly *pro-insert* in nature, that is, they insert a subject pronoun when this is required. No speaker drops a subject, and sentences without overt subject are not syntactically "incomplete". In the domain under scrutiny, we should not ask why and how *voseo* became widespread in America, in contrast to Spain. The more appropriate question is why and how it disappeared in Spain during the Golden Age (King 2010: 535). However, many people tend to perceive present-day European Spanish as the genuine traditional Spanish. Consequently, American Spanish is felt to have drifted away from Europe.

In the same vein, we should probably not ask why linguistic variation and cultures of address switching "have become common" in America, but why the European countries have adopted simpler and more rule-guided practices of address. To provide a further example, it is generally believed that the substandard second person past tense verb form *tú cantastes*, *hicistes*, etc. (canonical: *cantaste*, *hiciste*, etc.) is an innovation caused by analogy with recurrent *-s* as a second person marker (present tense: *tú cantas*, *haces*). Most linguists adopt this interpretation. However, we only need to open *Don Quijote de la Mancha* to find *vos pedistes y suplicastes* or *vos pagastes* (Miguel de Cervantes 2015: 5, 69). Hence, diachronic evidence points to *voseo* and not to analogy with *tuteo*. This case is not an instance of innovation but of maintenance. The educated tend to confound norm and standard with linguistic origin. *Tú pedistes* is considered substandard, and consequently, we tend to perceive it as a case of corruption starting off from *tú pediste*. The fact is that *vos cantastes* was the prior form, *vos* being replaced by *tú*. *Tuteo* was superimposed on *voseo*, but the replacement was more successful for the subject pronoun than for the verb form. Informal language conserved the traditional second person form *cantastes* (also in European Portuguese). The educated reinterpreted this form as an analogy to *tuteo -s*. This is obviously also a fact, but the diachronic interpretation is incorrect.

---

17 The following and other examples are analyzed in detail by Hummel (2014a). See also Bertolotti (2015: 105) about the tendency "to see the past with our eyes".

All these historical reconstructions can also be seen as the survival of a "colonial perspective" systematically reducing American varieties to the status of "exceptions" or "deviations". However, the acquisition of linguistic standards via education seems to be the main factor, since the examples do not simply stand for a European vision. Americans generally put the questions the same way ("Where do the peculiarities of the American variety stem from?"),[18] even if the interpretation of the facts may separate Europeans and Americans (e.g., the discussion on the *Andalusian hypothesis*). The decisive fact is that, at least in the case of Spanish, the standards of writing in different areas are very close. Consequently, linguists from both sides of the Atlantic Ocean have a similar educational bias. They tend to formulate research questions in the same way.

It is noteworthy that standardization and linguistic norms tend to be synchronically perceived as restricting, conservative forces acting against variation and innovation. However, from the diachronic point of view, the development of a culture of writing based on standardization is *the* major innovation in the languages under scrutiny. The fact that we intuitively consider norms as conservative forces reinforces the tendency of projecting our patterns back on the past. As in the discussion on the decline of the subjunctive mood, present-day norms are believed to represent the genuine tradition. Bertolotti (2015: 100–101, 105) rightly argues that we have to pay more attention to variation and to critically view our own convictions. This presupposes that we actively tackle diachrony from the point of view of *Sprachausbau*.

5.4 Diachronic reconstruction

In view of the shortcomings of visible diachrony based on written texts (Section 5.2), the methodology of *diachronic reconstruction* merits more interest. This approach uses data from synchronic linguistic variation in order to hypothesize their origin.[19] In particular, present-day synchrony is the only way to directly access spoken language. The corresponding data are definitively a result of oral diachrony. Hence, present-day data should be used as a starting point for the retrieval of the older usages they stem from. Even if reconstruction is never free from speculation (Labov 1994), it may help in formulating hypotheses for text-based diachronic research. If we know what we are looking for, the analysis of

---

18 I would be glad to see one day the publication of a book entitled *Curiosities and deviations of European Spanish*.
19 See Mühlhäusler & Harré's (1990: 269–277) general reflections on the historical reconstruction of personal pronouns.

written texts will provide better results. To give an example, early documents of Romance convey a very incomplete view of language in use. Reconstruction allows for interpreting a single occurrence of an item as a fact that probably stood for an already common phenomenon in spoken language (see, e.g., Hummel 2013 on 8th century *solamente*). On the one hand, such a single occurrence helps reconstruction to be less speculative. On the other, reconstruction helps to better interpret the scarce data found in visible diachrony. Using synchronic variation for *diachronic reconstruction* is therefore an interesting method in order to counterbalance the written language bias and to better understand oral traditions. Consequently, diachronic analyses based on written documents and reconstruction based on synchronic variation should be combined in order to ensure a mutual methodological control.

Reconstruction presupposes a contrastive methodology applied to variation and variety inside the same language. The comparison of languages sharing a common tradition may provide additional evidence in the tradition of historical-comparative linguistics. In the case of Romance and Indo-European in general, linguistics traditionally uses the historical comparison of languages and varieties for reconstruction. These efforts are generally devoted to the oral tradition. In line with this, Lara Bermejo (2015, and this volume) studies address in Andalusia and Portugal using variationist data to suggest hypotheses about the diachronic origin of the present-day situation. However, common features may also derive from shared cultural traditions, for example, the written tradition. *Language elaboration* is not necessarily an isolated phenomenon. The development of linguistic standards in Europe was culturally embedded in the Greco-Roman metalinguistic tradition. As shown by Hummel (2014b), it was the shared metalinguistic cultural context that made English and Romance favor the usage of the adverbial suffixes Engl. *-ly* and Romance *-ment(e)* during the process of standardization. This means that shared features that are methodologically identified by contrastive analyses do not necessarily point to oral traditions but may reflect close cultural contexts. The latter is obviously more important in the domain of address than, for example, in phonetics.

The rich variety of forms and usages in Hispanic America, which are related to a communicative culture of address switching, contrasts with a rather simple, non-switching linguistic reality in Spain. Recently, Helincks (2016) has documented the Chilean practice of address switching on a broad empirical basis. It clearly comes out that address switching is not a marginal phenomenon but an every-day practice which can be empirically accessed and used for quantitative analyses. In terms of reconstruction, we may ask ourselves how the culture of address switching has developed in America. This is indeed the way the problem is generally stated, especially by Europeans. To answer this question, we have to bear in mind that American Spanish is, historically, an extension of the Castilian dialect. Consequently, the secondary or tertiary dialects produced by these movements are much more homogeneous than dialects in England or Germany. This historical background makes the rich variety of forms and usages of address in Ibero-America rather exceptional and surprising. But if we assume on the contrary that in 15th century Spain a similar culture of liberal and playful usage existed before standardization minimized this tradition, the present-day reality of American Spanish becomes natural. Despite its many innovations due to the very tradition of playfully using address in a huge territory, American Spanish seems to have conserved an old, liberal tradition. This is indeed the reconstructionist hypothesis we have to suggest for diachronic studies on the basis of present-day variation. An old tradition of variation naturally explains what we observe at present. Hence, the question is not how variation developed in America. Putting the question this way is biased because it carries the implicit assumption that uniformity and regularity were the "normal" or "basic" starting point in diachrony. The right question asks how Europe reduced variation.

Intersubjective validation is an important element in research. In this sense, it is noteworthy that in the presentation that followed my own at the 2015 Munich Conference, where I first presented the value of reconstruction, Calderón Campos (2015) used modern Chilean examples in order to illustrate the communication culture of the 16th century. This does not mean that Chileans talk like people in that century, only that they have conserved a rich usage of nominals and the tradition of address switching. Calderón considered the Chilean usage to be closer to the Spanish Golden Age than present day European Spanish.

The heuristic value of reconstructionist hypotheses consists also in opening our eyes to existing data. In terms of personal experience, I may adduce that after having formulated, at the Munich conference, the hypothesis of address switch being diachronically prior to standardized uniformity, I paid more attention to this point. The following two observations stem from this new awareness.

The first observation concerns the fact that a similar situation of address switching has been occasionally mentioned for Old and Middle French (in addition to the evidence provided by Simon for German in Section 5.3.4; see also Lebsanft 1987):

Dans l'ancienne langue, aucune règle fixe ne délimitait l'emploi de *tu* et celui du *vous* de politesse; souvent même les deux pronoms alternaient dans un même passage. C'est au XVIIe siècle que l'influence de la cour fit prévaloir le *vous* de politesse. Sous l'Ancien Régime, les "honnêtes gens" ne se tutoyaient pas entre eux, mais ils tutoyaient l'homme du peuple. La République établit en l'an II le tutoiement général, mais on en revint sous l'Empire à l'usage d'avant la Révolution.

[...]

En anc. fr. [ancien français], on passait couramment – et sans aucune raison d'ordre affec-
tif – du *tu* au *vous* et vice versa:

Pren la corone, si seraz coronez	Prends$_T$ la couronne, et tu seras$_T$ couronné
O se ce non, filz, laissiez la ester	Ou sinon, fils, laissez$_V$-la là
Je vos defent que vos n'i adesez	Je vous défends que vous y touchiez$_V$

(*Couronnement de Louis*) (Grevisse & Goosse 2016: 915–916)

'In the old language, no rule guided the use of *tu* and *polite* vous; they even frequently
alternated in the same passage. It was the influence of the Royal Court in the 17th century
that acted in favor of polite *vous*. During the *Ancien Régime*, "decent people" did not use *tu*
to address themselves, but they used it to address the common people. In Year II, the French
Revolution established generalized *tu*, but under the Empire people went back to the usage
before the Revolution.

[...]

In Old French, people commonly – and for no emotional reason - switched from *tu* to *vous*
and *vice versa* [the indices "T" and "V" refer to Fr. *tu* and polite *vous* respectively, M.H.]:
Take$_T$ the crown, and you$_T$ will be crowned
If not, son, leave$_V$ it there
I prohibit you$_V$ to touch it'

The column on the right-hand side is the Modern French version of the Old French
original on the left (12th century). The Modern Spanish translation would be:
'Acepta la corona, y serás coronado/Si no la acepta, hijo, déjela donde está/Yo le
prohibo tocarla'. This means that French has also changed from a switching type
practice of address in Old and Middle French to a standardized one in Modern
French. This diachronic process is roughly summarized in the first part of the
quotation. As in many other domains, the 17th century appears to be crucial for
the diachronic change in terms of standardization reducing variation.

The second observation concerns *power and solidarity*. If the practice of
address switching was common until the 15th century, roughly speaking, Brown
& Gilman's (1960) theory of *power and solidarity* encounters serious problems.
Reading their study again, one discovers that they do not fully feel at ease with
the medieval practice. Instead of explaining the medieval usage of address as a
consequence of social and political structures, they simply assume that "medieval European societies were not so finely structured" (Brown & Gilman 1960: 256).
Since they do not provide any objective evidence for this fact (why should "power"
have been less important in the Middle Ages?), it seems that they somehow adapt
their vision of society to their knowledge of the practice of address at that time,
which was a simple one (see Figure 1). Instead of deducing the explanation of
address from the available knowledge about the structure of medieval society,
they invent a social structure that fits with the practice of address. In particular, they state that "there was much inexplicable fluctuation between *T* and *V* in

Old French, Spanish, Italian, and Portuguese [...], and in Middle English" (1960: 255). If this is the case, the scope of their theory is rather restricted to the transition from aristocratic to civil society within the periods covered by the terms *modern English*, *modern Spanish*, and so on. Furthermore, they completely overlook the role of standardization in the transformations of address practice. It is noteworthy that standardization is a common cultural background of the type mentioned at the beginning of Section 5.4. Standardization is characteristic not only of Romance but also of other European languages. It comes as no surprise, then, that the reduction in liberal variation is also observed in English.

In her landmark studies on the diachrony of *voseo*, Fontanella de Weinberg sees the complexity of address in the 16th century as a source of instability (see overview in Fontanella de Weinberg 1999: 1413). The regional diversity of the address systems in present-day Ibero-America is consequently explained as a result of crisis offering several solutions. This is obviously possible, in particular because the new element in the system, *vuestra merced*, was generally used. In other words, its frequency had come to a critical point for its coexistence with *vos*. However, there might be an educational bias and a theory bias (structuralism) in this interpretation of the past, insofar as complex systems are seen as intrinsically problematic. In my view, the competition of *vuestra merced* and *vos* is a historical and cultural fact. This competition is not due to the immanent problems of a linguistic system. Address systems simply match what is needed or wanted for communication. Hence, the causes, if I may say, are not systematic and structural in nature. The fact that a reduced system is perceived as the best one is biased by education tied to the present-day standard. The assumption of inherent instability of systems has also been favored by contemporary structural linguistic theory. The extreme complexity of the current European Portuguese address system invalidates this hypothesis. It is also hard to imagine how complexity could have increased in Spain from the 12th to the 16th century if the natural tendency is simplicity. Even the close competition of plural *vos* with *vosotros* is not intrinsically conflictual but complementary, if the *contrast* "first person (singular/plural = speaker) to second person (= the others)" is relevant. Then the addition of *otros* may appear as a means to underline this contrast (see García et al. 1990; de Jonge & Nieuwenhuijsen 2009: 1598–1600, 1607–1614; see also Simon 2005).

5.5 *Towards synthesis: the interplay of* voseo, tuteo *and* usted

To say that something is trivial does not mean that it is not true and useful. In this sense, trying to bring together all the many details brought to light by research is an interesting methodology as well. Efforts of synthesis are a powerful heuristic device which uses explanatory coherence as a means to clearly determine the role of all the single components coming together. On the other hand, synthesis certainly tends to overgeneralize and to sacrifice the heuristic value of some details on the altar of coherence (hopefully not in this chapter). But tidy syntheses might be considered useful provocations that encourage future research. In the following, I will therefore try to join up the loose ends, well knowing that this effort remains tentative.

American Spanish *voseo* is an interesting case. As already suggested, the question should not (only) be formulated in the traditional way of how this peculiarity appeared in America, but also of how it disappeared in Europe. Until the 14th century, *vos* had a reverential (e.g., addressing the king) or respectful (between nobles) function, before it was negatively connoted and suffered sharp decline (de Jonge & Nieuwenhuijsen 2009: 1636; see also Lapesa 2000: 322–329). At the end of the Golden Age, it was almost out of use in European Spanish, at least according to written texts. Its decline coincided with the rise of reverential *vuestra merced* in the 14th century, whose generalization in the 16th century again parallels the decline of *vos* (de Jonge & Nieuwenhuijsen 2009: 1638–1641).

In America, the decline of *vos* was areaspecific. In the first thorough study on the diachrony of address in America, Bertolotti (2015) concludes against other hypotheses that the usage of canonical second person *tú* can best be explained as a result of *educational pressure*, that is, a process acting against preexisting *vos*. In Chile, *tú* is still a symbol of education. In their analysis of historical documents, Gaglia & Rivadeneira (2015) show that the subject pronoun *tú* starts being used as late as the 17th century. In the case of *tú*, educational pressure overlaid *colonial pressure*, that is, the transmission of a system where *vos* was progressively missing. The fact that the main vice-kingdoms representing Spain in America, Mexico and Peru, as well as the bridgehead Cuba, almost completely replaced *vos* by *tú* provides convincing evidence for the colonial influence (see Lapesa 2000: 682). In the political periphery, that is, Argentina, Chile, Uruguay, Central America, interior of Columbia, the colonial pressure was weak because colonization came later and the process was generally not driven by people coming directly from Europe (see the case study on Chile by Sweeney 2005). In these areas, *tuteo* was a matter of educational pressure, that is, a process starting later. In fact, the evidence for educational pressure basically stems from the colonial political periphery. The new model for respectful address, *usted* (about *1629), seems to have been created in Spain (252 cases in the 17th century), the first American attestations having been found in Mexico, Peru, and Paraguay (8 cases) (Hammermüller 2010: 523, de Jonge 2005). This corroborates the "colonial diachrony": metropolitan Spain > vice-kingdoms (Peru, Mexico) > general usage. Colonial pressure preceded educational pressure, as education only became a major issue for larger parts of the population in the new independent nations (19th century).

These layering processes entail the assumption that *voseo* was the dominant second person address in colonial America. European colonial pressure "from above" and educational pressure "from above" acted as superstrata which won where the colonial and/or educational impact was strong, while they remained secondary or were left to specific geographic or social domains where this type of pressure was weak. Crucially, in the periphery educational pressure specifically implemented *tuteo* amongst the educated, in sharp contrast to surrounding *voseo*. Since nowadays both colonial and educational pressures give way to more liberal attitudes, *voseo* revives, especially as a symbol for social identity (*voseo culto* of young people in Chile, Torrejón 1986), regional identity (Córdoba in Costa Rica) or as a general tendency (Costa Rica: Michnowicz et al. 2016; Chile: Rivadeneira Valenzuela 2016). We might thus assume the acting of present-day *liberal pressure*. This term may be felt as contradictory, but teachers attached to traditional norms clearly feel phenomena such as Chilean *voseo culto* as a threat for good Spanish. Hence, liberalism may be felt as negative pressure by traditionalists. In her detailed diachronic sociolinguistic study of the Andean region of Colombia, the first one of this type, Díaz Collazos (2015) convincingly traces *voseo* back to the beginnings of colonization, having persisted until today against pressures from outside. Liberal attitudes favoring regional identity reinforce the identitary *regional pressure* in several regions of the Spanish speaking world.

From the reconstructionist point of view, all this can be interpreted as an indicator of generalized *voseo* in spoken European Spanish in times when colonization began. The types of pressure outlined above acted against this status quo. Since official documents and literary texts are more in touch with individual and social hierarchy, as well as with trends of language elaboration, the available written documents make linguists underestimate the real extension of *voseo* in informal oral communication, and especially its persistence at the time when the Laws of Courtesy became effective. From the point of view of intersubjective validation, it is noteworthy that King (2010), an author working with Golden Age documents, shows himself skeptical about the representativeness of theatre plays, concluding that the commonly used unmarked form of address was probably *vos* and the corresponding verb forms (also Moreno 2002: 44; see also another case of literary bias in the history of *su merced* in Calderón Campos & García-Godoy, this volume). In the same vein, Hammermüller (2010: 525) alludes to a "*vos* casi universal". This means in turn that the abundantly documented pejorative function of *vos* in 16th-17th century plays (King 2010: 535) possibly reflected an advanced stage in a movement of change from above which at that time had not been taken on to the same degree by the lower classes. At least, we can assume the persistence of respectful *vos* in the variationist landscape of Spain in the beginnings of the 16th century, as shown by Calderón Campos (2002).

More recently, Boluda Rodríguez (2016) provides evidence for the widespread usage of *vos* by the lower classes according to oral testimonies transcribed in witchcraft trials from 1602. This matches the widespread use of *vos* in informal oral communication all over present-day American Spanish, as well as in the Spanish lexified creole *palenquero* (Gutiérrez Maté 2019). In his pioneering study, Castillo Mathieu (1982) concludes that *vuestra merced* and *vos* were used at the same respectful-reverential level in America until the middle of the 16th century. According to Bentivoglio's (2003) analysis of private letters sent from America to Andalusia, *vos* was still highly preferred over *vuestra merced* in the second half of the 16th century, the latter being reserved for formal contexts such as requests or complaints. This points to a generalized usage of *vos* in everyday life, except for marked situations. From the methodological point of view, this is a case where the likeliest diachrony formulated by reconstruction meets the complementary assumption independently formulated by linguists working on historical texts, with the awareness that theatre plays do not really reflect the most common practices of addressing, which are the less interesting ones for dramaturgy.

Portuguese provides additional evidence for the assumption that *vós* was part of the genuine oral tradition. As shown in Figure 1, Portuguese started from a simple *tu/vós* system. Familiar nominals such as *pai* 'father' or *tia* 'aunt' were probably used as well, but typical honorifics such as *vossa mercê* were later introduced "from above". The fact that France, where the loss of Burgundy in 1477 was cruelly felt, did not follow the etiquette of Burgundy adopted by the Habsburgs, supports the hypothesis that the French system was the traditional one in Romance. The above-mentioned usage of It. *tu/voi* provides additional evidence for these pronouns building a common basis in Romance.

The hypothesis assuming a widespread unmarked usage of *vos* in the 16th century conflicts with another hypothesis claiming the expansion of *voseo* by change from above via *hidalguización* 'aristocratization' (see also overview in de Jonge & Nieuwenhuijsen 2009: 1654; Díaz Collazos 2015: 263). This hypothesis is fully convincing in the case of the honorifics *vuestra + majestad/alteza/excelencia/señoría/merced* (see details in García-Godoy 2019). It also fits perfectly with the role of the colonial civil and military administration observed in Section 5.3.5, including Portuguese. Example (8) shows that the Spanish governor in 18th century colonial Colombia insisted on being addressed as *Señoría*:

(8) Quizá debido al enfrentamiento que ya se perfilaba por esa época entre criollos y chapetones, o tal vez por el creciente recelo con que la nobleza criolla miraba los avata-
res de la política borbónica, el nuevo gobernador mandó arrestar al científico español
Antonio de Ulloa simplemente porque éste le llamó *Vuesa Merced* en lugar de llamarle
Señoría. (Lafuente & Mazuecos 1992: 114–115, *apud* Castro-Gómez 2005: 241).

'It possibly was due to the then looming confrontation between *criollos* 'Spaniards already rooted in America' and *chapetones* 'newly arriving Spaniards', or because the local Spanish aristocracy was more and more concerned by the Borbonian policy, the new governor ordered the Spanish scientist Antonio de Ulloa to be arrested, simply because he addressed him as *Vuesa Merced* 'Your Grace' instead of *Señoría* ('Your Honor').'

However, the application of the aristoticratization hypothesis to the pronoun *vos* requires further investigation. According to this hypothesis, the high percentage of noblemen in the beginnings of colonization was responsible for the expansion of *vos* as a marker of aristocratic address. However, at the end of the 15th century, *vos* was the default address in use, at least for communication in public. Why should the elite ostentatiously use this pronoun in the New World, while aristocrats in Europe struggled for the use of the above-mentioned honorifics? What should lower-class speakers have used? Did they only use *tú*? Why, then, did Hispanic America not turn out to become a *tuteo* zone? Inversely, we could argue that the formation of an upper class of local *criollos* played against the colonial pressure of increasingly using honorifics, even at the level of upper class behavior, and especially in public discourse, insofar as the creole elite claimed to defend the local population during their struggle for more autonomy and independence. This discourse must have favored the usage of shared forms of address, while it is not convincing at all that this group should have followed the process of aristocratization, which entails identification with the colonial system. Hence, there would have been an *anti-colonial pressure* as well, which is indeed a fact in terms of American history in general. It comes as no surprise that there is empirical evidence for the ostentatious maintenance of *vos* in the upper class until educational pressure came into play, consciously ignoring the norms of the educated (see Sweeney 2005, about Chile). This coincides with the major role of this class in the long process leading to national independence in the 19th century.

In sum, the maintenance of *vos* in the upper class leading the process of independence provides a coherent hypothesis. However, this does not necessarily mean that the other classes did not also traditionally use *vos*. As I will show below, *vos* might have simply been the only relevant pronoun for respectful address in public in the oral tradition of Spanish (and Portuguese). Hence, the usage of the *criollos* would have been just the same as everyone else, in contrast to the innovations imported by colonial pressure. This conclusion, grounded in reconstruction, matches with Eberenz' (2000: 89–102) analysis of the social groups using *vos* in the 15th century, on the eve of colonization, *tú* prevailing only in texts following the model of Classical Latin and religious discourse addressing god. Eberenz goes on to explain the apparently sudden rise of *vos* as an effect of documentation, that is, a phenomenon due to visible diachrony, thus assuming a covert widespread usage of *vos*, even before the 15th century (Eberenz 2000: 89, 112–113). The fast expansion in the European lower classes of the plural *vosotros* as a substitute for plural *vos* provides indirect evidence for the underlying generalization of singular *vos* used to respectfully address a single person (Eberenz 2000: 74–83).

In sum, both American and European history should be explained in terms of *voseo* being pushed back. While this process was successful in Europe, its marginalization was more or less successful in America, according to the local conditions. This explains part of the manifold regional and social variation in present-day language.

The competing or complementary forms of address, *tú* and *usted*, were newly favored or later introduced through processes initiated in Spain. Hence, it is clear that there has been a layering process whereby *usted* and *tú* were superposed and interacted with the tradition of using *vos* for oral communication, which was the relevant fact, since only a few people were literate. All this does not mean, however, that the extension of *voseo* in everyday life was the same in Spain and its colony. Migration and social melting may have specifically favored generalized *voseo* (see also Moreno 2002: 17), at least if we assume that its negative connotation had not permeated the relevant social groups. In line with this, Eberenz (2000: 90) notes that *vos* was used in the 15th century for addressing unknown persons. The fact that people migrating to the New World abandoned their villages and their families, where address might have been very differentiated, could have reinforced the usage of *vos* as a good candidate for address in a social melting pot where many people must have felt a sense of belonging to their own group, while rarely knowing the others. This is an interesting topic for future research in the linguistics of migration. In what follows, I try to identify the types of pressure exerted on *vos* and other address terms.

The long-term persistence of *voseo* is the major distinctive feature of the colonial periphery. This fact is also crucial for the development of respectful *usted*, inasmuch as this pronoun did not compete with *tú*, as in the colonial political center, but with *vos*. Until the Golden Age, *tú* was used for intimate relations, whereas *vos* was more relevant for respectful address in intimate relations and public communication between persons of equal status. Consequently, theory has to add the opposition of the *familiar domain* and the *public domain* to the opposition of the *in-group* and *out-group domains* (see Section 2). *Usted* came into use as the respectful, somehow less reverential son or daughter of *vuestra merced*. It consequently competed with public and generally deferential *vos* in the colonial periphery. The present-day situation reflects all the possible results of this competition. In Chile, *vo(s)* went to substandard, secondarily undergoing the educational pressure of *tú*. In this case, educational pressure can directly be related to the influence of Andrés Bello, the spiritual father and rector of the education system in the new nation. This process was probably similar in Argentina (see the landmark study by Fontanella 1971: 495, 506), but in the 19th century national affirmation and the power of rural elites created a situation again favoring *vos* as a distinctive symbol. Significantly, education resisted this influence longest (García Negroni & Ramírez Gelbes 2010). We might say that in this case *national pressure* layered onto preceding colonial and subsequent educational pressure. In fact, in all new nations, national pressure came into play. In contrast to colonial and educational pressure, this pressure was area-specific.

In Central America, *usted* often became the public respectful and *vos* the confidential familiar form. It probably conserved a more respectful component if compared to *tú*. In Mérida (Venezuela), *usted* fully replaced *vos* for both of its traditional functions, that is, the public and familiar, still rather respectful usage. Since *usted* is used in Mérida as a marker of regional identity, as opposed to Caracas (*tuteo*), we can add *regional pressure* as another factor eventually occurring as a reaction against *national pressure* identified with the capital. In a similar way to Brazilian *você*, *usted* never adopts the directness of *tú* as it is used in Europe.[20] In the colonial center (Antilles, Mexico, Peru), descending from *vuestra merced*, *usted* easily shared labor with the traditionally familiar and direct *tú*, possibly replacing *su merced*. There was no risk of conflict or confusion. Hence, the main difference between the colonial center and the periphery was the early absence of competition in the former[21] and the long-term competition of *usted* with *vos* in the latter. Importantly, the *family domain* should not be overlooked. Families often behave conservatively, including hostile attitudes against social pressure, for example, Hispanics in present-day United States (Hummel 2010b). Power asymmetries are not only a property of society, but a frequent correlate of power related to generations, age, and gender in hierarchically organized families. Such families may be responsible for the long-term availability of socially out-dated types of address. Other families may progressively follow trends, for example, address models from other countries (e.g., Fr. *papa, maman* providing Sp. *papá, mamá* and BPt. *papa/papai, mamã/mamãe*; see López Vallejo 2010).

In the case of Brazilian Portuguese, the layering process of *vossa mercê* (replacing *vós*) > *você* (progressively replacing *tu*), whereby *você* became the generalized unmarked form of address in most regions and the standard (see bibliographical

---

20 *Vos* was used for respectful but not distant in-group behavior in colonial Spain (Bertolotti 2015: 104).

21 See however the remnants of *voseo* in Cuba (Román Fernández 1991, Hummel 2010c).

overview in Marcotulio 2010: 19–34 and the geolinguistic overview by Rumeu 2013: 35–52), requires further investigation. Although a considerable collective effort is currently underway in order to bring to light the internal variationist diachrony of Brazilian Portuguese since the independence of Brazil, the diachrony of European Portuguese and its influence on Brazil, as well as reactions against colonial and educational pressure, have been neglected by research. The data analyzed by de Souza & Coelho (2015) point to educational pressure in favor of *tuteio* to the detriment of *você*, but this pressure did not produce a systematic variationist feature in present-day Brazilian Portuguese, where *tu* is often considered substandard (in varieties where *você* prevails). The demarcation line seems to separate the traditional use of *tu* plus agreeing second person verb form, which is canonized by school education, from *tu* plus third person verb form, which violates the normative principle of agreement, being consequently considered a substandard variant. More than in Spanish, the layering process of innovative *vossa mercê* and later *você* is particularly visible with oblique pronouns and possessives used with the same subject pronoun (Lopes et al. 2011). The widespread usage of *vossa mercê* (do Monte 2015a) seems to have been the diachronic basis for the later development of *você*, which first somehow conserved the reverential function of *vossa mercê* (Lopes & Rumeu 2015) before it became a common term of informal address.

6 Conclusion

I have argued in favor of a multifaceted theoretical and methodological approach to linguistic address, deliberately choosing a contrastive analysis of Portuguese and Spanish because this methodology is appropriate for singling out common and specific features of language. The shortcomings of previous work in address research have been systematically pointed out. This is not intended as a critique, if seen negatively, but as an argument in favor of complementary modular approaches. In fact, we cannot criticize an excellent study for the limitations entailed by the theory, the method, or the data that have been chosen for this purpose. I am more than aware of the fact that my own analysis is risky, insofar as a better knowledge of local contexts is often required. I consciously run this risk because I feel that there is a lack of general hypotheses that may guide case studies and promote discussion.

The first point in the paper is "crisis". This may be considered a rather smooth, non-rigorous approach. The main reason for this suggestion is the fact that crisis is a distinctive feature of address when compared to other linguistic domains. Crisis allows for integrating a countless number of scenarios. It further includes a dynamic perspective since it entails reparation strategies, which are salient features of address, including systematic patterns such as use of plural, third person, combinations of pronouns with nominals, and avoidance strategies (e.g., verb form only in *pro-drop* languages, neutral Sp./Pt. *se* (Hummel 2010a), Fr. *on/nous*, Ger. *man*).

The second point is that of typology. Typological tendencies directly affect the possibilities of using forms of address. The similarities between French and Brazilian Portuguese provide evidence for the fact that analogous typological tendencies entail similar processes of adaptation. However, shared cultural traditions, as is the case for Portuguese and Spanish, but also for Romance in general, have also to be taken into account.

The third point concerns the interpretation of the data. I have suggested analytically separating the following two approaches, before their results can be used for synthesis.

The first consists of analyzing the available written texts covering diachrony. The limitations of such analyses are clear: they only partially cover what happened in language, especially in the spoken modality, which was crucial for the development of Portuguese and Spanish in America. This approach to *visible diachrony* is the one we traditionally use. But even in this framework, we should consider approaches that reverse the perspective, asking for the origin of present-day data, especially oral data (e.g., dialects). The combination of downstream and upstream perspectives necessarily brings to light the gap that separates visible diachrony from invisible or less visible diachrony. "Less visible" is a major point at this stage, since the present-day relevance of a feature allows for a better evaluation of poorly represented diachronic data, that is, data that were possibly more frequent in the spoken language than is witnessed by written texts. Certainly, oral traces in written texts are often discussed in work on visible diachrony. However, this discussion is rather intuitive, including assumptions such as theatre plays and letters being closer to orality. Every transcription of an informal oral present-day communication shows that this is highly problematic.

Obviously, the domain under scrutiny interlinks with history in general. Consequently, the internal development of language entails a narrowed vision of diachrony. Research on address is aware of this, but some possible instruments of analysis have been neglected. One of these, *Sprachausbau*, is completely lacking in address research. In fact, only a thorough comprehension of the processes involved in the elaboration of a culture and a standard of writing, which are major innovations in diachrony, allow for a better discrimination of what is oral and what is written in a given text. In the domain of address research, change from above is crucial. It is clearly related to attempts to normalize language situated in sociolinguistic contexts.

The second complementary approach, reconstruction, is traditionally used for etymology and historical-comparative approaches in general, but it has not been systematically used for research on address. We find arguments based on reconstruction in many analyses, but what I claim is that this approach should be systematically developed, including the awareness that it entails speculation. Being placed under the label of "reconstruction", it is legitimate to push the hypotheses to the extreme by extrapolation to the past. It is not claimed that things indeed have been as it is assumed, but that there is evidence that they could have been so. In this sense, I have extrapolated the present-day culture of address switching in Hispanic America to a similar practice in Old Spanish.

The underlying idea is that the combination of downstream and upstream visible diachrony with the theory of *Sprachausbau* and the reconstruction of oral traditions provides better results since it ensures a higher degree of methodological control, leading to descriptive and explanatory synthesis.

References

Ali, M. Said. 1975. *Investigações filológicas*. Rio de Janeiro: Grifo & Mec.

Alves, Cibelle Corrêa Béliche & Maria Marta Pereira Scherre. 2015. Pronomes de segunda pessoa no espaço maranhense. Paper read at the *I Simpósio do LaborHistórico: História dos Pronomes de tratamento* (Rio de Janeiro 2015).

Ampuero, Roberto. 1998. *Boleros en La Habana*. Santiago: Planeta Chilena.

André, Virginie. 2010. Emploi stratégique des formes nominales d'adresse au sein de réunions de travail. In Catherine Kerbrat-Orecchioni (ed.), *S'adresser à autrui. Les formes nominales d'adresse en français*, 63–87. Chambéry: Université de Savoie.

Anipa, Kormi. 2001. Address formulae. In Kormi Anipa (ed.), *A critical examination of linguistic variation in Golden-Age Spanish*, 187–288. New York: Peter Lang.

Basto, Cláudio. 1931. Formas de tratamento, em português. *Revista Lusitana* 29. 183–202.

Bentivoglio, Paola. 2003. Spanish forms of address in the sixteenth century. In Jucker & Taavitsainen (eds.), 177–191.

Bertolotti, Virginia. 2010. La gramaticalización de *usted*: un cambio lingüístico en proceso. Evidencias en el Uruguay del siglo XIX. *Filologia Linguística Portuguesa* 12,1. 149–177.

Bertolotti, Virginia. 2011. Semántica y pragmática de los usos de *usted*, *tú* y *vos* como sujeto en el siglo XIX en Uruguay. In Rebollo & Lopes (eds.), 349–379.

Bertolotti, Virginia. 2015. A mí de vos no me trata ni usted ni nadie. *Sistemas e historia de las formas de tratamiento en la lengua española en América*. Mexico City: UNAM/Universidad de la República de Uruguay.

Bertolotti, Virginia. 2016. *Voseo* and *tuteo*, the countryside and the city. *Voseo* in Río de la Plata Spanish at the beginning of the 19th century. In Moyna & Rivera-Mills (eds.), 15–33.

Bertolotti, Virginia. 2017. Formas de tratamiento con posesivo en el español. In Concepción Company Company & Norohella Huerta Flores (eds.), *La posesión en la lengua española*, 297–324. Madrid: CSIC (*Revista de Filología Española*, Anejo 105).

Biderman, Maria Tereza Camargo. 1972–1973. Formas de tratamento e estruturas sociais. *Alfa* 18–19. 339–381.

Boluda Rodríguez, María Dolores. 2016. Análisis de las fórmulas de tratamiento pronominales de segunda persona (*vos-yú* [sic]) en un pleito por brujería de 1602. *Revista de Investigación Lingüística* 19. 133–171.

Braun, Friederike. 1988. *Terms of address. Problems of patterns and usage in various languages and cultures*. Berlin, etc.: Mouton de Gruyter.

Brown, Roger & Albert Gilman. 1960. The pronouns of power and solidarity. In Thomas A. Sebeok (ed.), *Style in language*, 253–276. Cambridge: MIT Press.

Brown, Penelope & Stephen C. Levinson. 1987. *Politeness. Some universals in language usage*. Cambridge: Cambridge University Press.

Calderón Campos, Miguel. 2002. Fórmulas de tratamiento en las cartas del Conde de Tendilla (1504–1506). In *Actas del V Congreso Internacional de Historia de la Lengua Española* (Valencia 2000), 477–487. Madrid: Gredos.

Calderón Campos, Miguel. 2006. El desgaste pronominal y verbal de *vos* en la primera mitad del siglo XVI. In José Jesús de Bustos Tovar et al. (eds.), *Actas del VI Congreso Internacional de Historia de la Lengua Española* (Madrid 2003), 557–568. Madrid: Arco Libros.

Calderón Campos, Miguel. 2010. Los elementos nominales en el sistema de tratamiento del español de Andalucía durante la restauración (1875–1931). In Hummel et al. (eds.), 551–570.

Calderón Campos, Miguel. 2015. Estilo directo y tratamientos en el CORDEREGRA. Paper presented at *Evolución y variación de las formas de tratamiento en español*, Munich (3.7.2015).

Calderón Campos, Miguel. In press. "A vuestras mercedes pido que veades esta carta". Concordancia gramatical y concordancia pragmática en las cartas de estilo cortesano. In Viorica Codita & Mariela de la Torre (eds.), *Tendencias y perspectivas en el estudio de la morfosintaxis histórica hispanoamericana*, 45–56. Madrid/Frankfurt: Iberoamericana/Vervuert.

Castillo Mathieu, Nicolás del. 1982. Testimonios del uso de *vuestra merced*, *vos* y *tú* en América (1500–1650). *Thesaurus* 37. 602–644.

Castro-Gómez, Santiago. 2005. *La hybris del punto cero. Ciencia, raza e ilustración en la Nueva Granada (1750–1816)*. Bogotá: Editorial Pontificia Universidad Javeriana.

Cintra, Luís F. Lindley. 1972. *Sobre "formas de tratamento" na língua portuguesa*. Lisbon: Livros Horizonte.

Clyne, Michael, Catrin Norrby & Jane Warren. 2009. *Language and human relations. Styles of address in contemporary language*. Cambridge: Cambridge University Press.

Cook, Manuela. 1994–1995. On the Portuguese forms of address: from *vossa mercê* to *você*. *Portuguese Studies Review* 3,2. 78–89.

CORDE [= Corpus Diacrónico del Español], Real Academia Española. http://www.rae.es/recursos/banco-de-datos/corde.

Correia, João de Araújo. 1954. Do tratamento de *vós*. *Boletim da Casa Regional da Beira Douro* 3,6. 166–168.

Couto, Leticia Rebollo (see Rebollo).

de Cervantes, Miguel. 2015. *Don Quijote de la Mancha*, edited by Instituto Cervantes (1605, 1615, 2015), edition directed by Francisco Rico, vol. 1. Madrid: Real Academia Española.

de Jonge, Bob. 2005. El desarrollo de las variantes de *vuesa merced* a *usted*. *Estudios de Lingüística del Español (EliEs)* 22. www.elies.rediris.es/elies22/cap.7.htm.

de Jonge, Bob & Dorien Nieuwenhuijsen. 2009. Formación del paradigma pronominal de las formas de tratamiento. In Concepción Company Company (ed.), *Sintaxis histórica de la lengua española. Segunda parte: La frase nominal*, vol. 2, 1595–1671. México DF: UNAM/ Fondo de Cultura Económica.

de Oliveira, Sandi Michele. 2005. A retrospective on address in Portugal (1982–2002). Rethinking power and solidarity. *Journal of Historical Pragmatics* 6,2. 308–333.

de Oliveira, Sandi Michele. 2009. Negotiating identity, conflict, and cooperation within a strategic model of address. In Ann Denis & Devorah Kalekin-Fishman (eds.), *Contemporary sociology. Conflict, competition, cooperation*, 416–432. Los Angeles, etc.: Sage.

de Oliveira, Thiago Laurentino. 2015. Os pronomes dativos de 2ª pessoa na escrita episcolar carioca. *LaborHistórico* 1,1. 81–98.

de Souza, Christiane Maria Nunes & Izete Lehmkuhl Coelho. 2015. Caminhos para a investigação da alternância de pronomes de segunda pessoa em Santa Catarina. In Marcotullio et al. (eds.), 49–61.

Díaz Collazos, Ana María. 2015. *Desarrollo sociolingüístico del voseo en la región andina de Colombia* (1555–1976). Berlin/Boston: De Gruyter.

do Monte, Vanessa Martins. 2015a. *Correspondências Paulistas: as formas de tratamento em cartas de circulação pública (1765–1775)*. São Paulo: Fapesp, Humanitas.

do Monte, Vanessa Martins. 2015b. A categoria socioprofissional: uma proposta de abordagem para o estudo das formas de tratamento. *LaborHistórico* 1,1. 116–131.

Duarte, Maria Eugênia Lamoglia. 1993. Do pronome nulo ao pronome pleno: a trajetória do sujeito no português do Brasil. In Ian Roberts & Mary A. Kato (eds.), *Português brasileiro. Uma viajem diacrónica*, 107–128. Campinas, São Paulo: Editora da Unicamp.

Duarte, Maria Eugênia Lamoglia (ed.). 2012. *O sujeito em peças de teatro (1833–1992). Estudos diacrônicos*. São Paulo: Parábola.

Eberenz, Rolf. 2000. *El español en el otoño de la Edad Media. Sobre el artículo y los pronombres*. Madrid: Gredos.

Fontanella de Weinberg, Beatriz. 1971. El voseo en Buenos Aires en las dos primeras décadas del siglo XIX. *Thesaurus* 26. 495–514.

Fontanella de Weinberg, Beatriz. 1999. Sistemas pronominales de tratamiento usados en el mundo hispanoamericano. In Ignacio Bosque & Violeta Demonte (eds.), *Gramática descriptiva de la lengua española*, vol. 1, 1399–1425. Madrid: Espasa.

Gaglia, Sascha & Marcela Rivadeneira. 2014. Las formas de tratamiento en Chile: entre la teoría y la empiria. Aplicación del modelo de la *geometría de los rasgos* en un corpus oral. Paper read at ALFAL 2014, João Pessoa (Brazil).

Gaglia, Sascha & Rivadeneira, Marcela. 2015. *A vos questays presente*. Aspectos diacrónicos del voseo chileno: Una aproximación cuantitativa. Paper read at the congress SOCHIL 2015 (Sociedad Chilena de Lingüística), Temuco (Chile).

García, Erica. 1994. Una casilla vacía en el paradigma pronominal del voseo: *convusco*. In Jens Lüdtke (ed.), *El español de América en el siglo XVI*, 13–38. Frankfurt: Vervuert.

García, Erica, Robert de Jonge, Dorien Nieuwenhuijsen & Carlos Lechner. 1990. *(V)os – (otros)*: ¿Dos y el mismo cambio? *Nueva Revista de Filología Hispánica* 38. 63–132.

García-Godoy, María Teresa. 2012. El tratamiento de *merced* en el español del siglo XVIII. In María Teresa García-Godoy (ed.), *El español del siglo XVIII. Cambios diacrónicos en el primer español moderno*, 111–152. Bern, etc.: Peter Lang.

García-Godoy, María Teresa. 2015. El cambio *vuestra merced > usted* desde la documentación archivística. In Juan Pedro Sánchez Méndez, Mariela de la Torre & Viorica Codita (eds.),

Temas, problemas y métodos para la edición y el studio de documentos hispánicos antiguos, 661–694. Valencia: Tirant Humanidades.

García-Godoy, María Teresa. 2019. El tratamiento indirecto en el español colonial. Los títulos honoríficos. In Juan Pedro Sánchez Méndez, Antonio Corredor Aveledo & Elena Padrón Castilla (eds.), *Estudios de morfosintaxis histórica hispanoamericana*, vol. 1: *El pronombre*, 219–262. Valencia: Tirant Humanidades.

García Negroni, María Marta & Silvia Ramírez Gelbes. 2010. Acerca del voseo en los manuales escolares argentinos (1970–2004). In Hummel et al. (eds.), 1013–1032.

Gille, Johan. 2015. On the development of the Chilean discourse marker *cachái*. *Revue Romane* 50,1. 3–29.

Girón Alconchel, José Luis & Daniel M. Sáez Rivera (eds.). 2014. *Procesos de gramaticalización en la historia del español*. Madrid/Frankfurt: Iberoamericana/Vervuert.

Grevisse, Maurice & André Goosse. 2016. *Le bon usage*. 16th ed. Bruxelles: De Boeck.

Guiter, Henri. 1959. L'extension successive des formes de politesse. In *Actes du Congrès International de Linguistique et de Philologie Romanes* (Lisbonne 1959) (= *Boletim de Filologia* 18), vol. 1, 195–202.

Gutiérrez Maté, Miguel. 2012. El pronombre *usted* en el español de Cartagena de Indias del siglo XVII y su "divergencia" de *vuestra merced*. In Emilio Montero Cartelle (ed.), *Actas del VIII Congreso Internacional de Historia de la Lengua Española*, 1889–1904. Santiago de Compostela: Meubook.

Gutiérrez Maté, Miguel. 2013. *Pronombres personales sujeto en el español del Caribe. Variación e historia*. PhD thesis. Universidad de Valladolid.

Gutiérrez Maté, Miguel. 2019. Palenquero (Colombia): The grammar of second person pronouns and the pragmatics of address switching. In Bettina Kluge & María Irene Moyna (eds.), *It's not all about* you. *New perspectives on address research*, 162–190. Amsterdam/ Philadelphia: John Benjamins.

Gutiérrez-Rivas, Carolina. 2016. La palabra *marico* como nueva forma de tratamiento nominal anticortés en el habla de jóvenes universitarios de Caracas: un estudio desde la perspectiva de los hablantes. *Logos* 26,1: 3–22. DOI: 10.15443/RL2601.

Hajek, John, Heinz L. Kretzenbacher & Robert Lagerberg. 2013. Towards a linguistic typology of address pronouns in Europe – past and present. In John Henderson, Marie-Eve Ritz & Celeste Rodríguez Louro (eds.), *Proceedings of the 2012 Conference of the Australian Linguistic Society*. www.als.asn.au.

Hammermüller, Gunther. 1980. Você é estrubaria? *Iberoromania* 12. 30–40.

Hammermüller, Gunther. 1993. *Die Anrede im Portugiesischen*. Chemnitz: Neuer Verlag.

Hammermüller, Gunther. 1992. O tratamento de *vós* em Rio de Onor. In Jürgen Schmidt-Radefeldt (ed.), *Semiótica e linguística portuguesa e românica*, 43–54. Tübingen: Gunter Narr.

Hammermüller, Gunther. 2010. Evolución de las formas de tratamiento del español medieval hasta el siglo XVI. In Hummel et al. (eds.), 507–529.

Havu, Eva. 2013. L'emploi des pronoms d'adresse dans un corpus français. In Suomela-Härmä et al. (eds.), 69–87.

Helincks, Kris. 2016. *Variation and discursive shifting of address forms in Chilean Spanish. Formal, socio-situational and pragmatic analysis of spontaneous conversation*. PhD thesis. University of Gent.

Herman, József. 2006. *Du latin aux langues romanes II*. Tübingen: Niemeyer.

Holm, John. 2004. *Languages in contact. The partial restructuring of vernaculars,* Cambridge: Cambridge University Press.

História dos pronomes de tratamento no português brasileiro, see Marcotulio et al. (2015).

Hummel, Martin. 2002. Formen der Anrede im Spanischen Chiles. In Alberto Gil & Christian Schmitt (eds.), *Gramática y pragmática del español,* 179–228. Bonn: Romanistischer Verlag.

Hummel, Martin. 2010a. Reflexiones metodológicas y teóricas sobre el estudio de las formas de tratamiento en el mundo hispanohablante. In Hummel et al. (eds.), 101–162.

Hummel, Martin. 2010b. La investigación de las formas y fórmulas de tratamiento en la diversidad sociolingüística del español en los Estados Unidos de América: una tarea pendiente. In Hummel et al. (eds.), 483–504.

Hummel, Martin. 2010c. El estudio de las formas de tratamiento en las Antillas hispanohablantes. In Hummel et al. (eds.), 293–323.

Hummel, Martin. 2012. *Polifuncionalidad, polisemia y estrategia retórica.* Berlin/Boston: De Gruyter.

Hummel, Martin. 2013. Attribution in Romance: Reconstructing the oral and written tradition. *Folia Linguistica Historica* 34. 1–42.

Hummel, Martin. 2014a. La reconstrucción diacrónica entre oralidad y escritura. El caso de los marcadores discursivos *claro, entonces* y *total.* In María Marta García Negroni (ed.), *Marcadores del discurso. Perspectivas y contrastes,* 35–61. Buenos Aires: Santiago Arcos.

Hummel, Martin. 2014b. The adjective-adverb interface in Romance and English. In Petra Sleeman, Freek Van de Velde & Harry Perridon (eds.), *Adjectives in Germanic and Romance,* 35–71. Amsterdam/Philadelphia: John Benjamins.

Hummel, Martin, Bettina Kluge & María Eugenia Vázquez Laslop (eds.). 2010. *Formas y fórmulas de tratamiento en el mundo hispánico,* México DF: El Colegio de México/ Universität Graz.

Jucker, Andreas & Irma Taavitsainen. 2003. Diachronic perspectives on address term systems. Introduction. In Taavitsainen & Jucker (eds.), 1–25.

Kabatek, Johannes. 2007. Las tradiciones discursivas entre conservación e innovación. *Rivista di Filologia e Letterature ispaniche* 10. 331–345.

Kabatek, Johannes. 2012. Corpus histórico, oralidad y oralización. In Victoria Béguelin-Argimón, Garbriela Cordone & Mariela de La Torre (eds.), *En pos de la palabra viva: huellas de oralidad en textos antiguos,* 37–50. Bern, etc.: Peter Lang.

King, Jeremy. 2010. Ceremonia y cortesía en la literatura del Siglo de Oro: un estudio de las formas de tratamiento en español. In Hummel et al. (eds.), 531–550.

Kluge, Bettina. 2016. Forms of address and community identity. In Moyna & Rivera-Mills (eds.), 325–333.

Kloss, Heinz. 1967. "Abstand languages" and "Ausbau languages". *Anthropological Linguistics* 9. 29–41.

Kloss, Heinz. 1978. *Die Entwicklung neuer germanischer Kultursprachen seit 1800.* Düsseldorf: Schwann.

Koch, Peter. 2008. Tradiciones discursivas y cambio lingüístico: el ejemplo del tratamiento *vuestra merced* en español. In Johannes Kabatek (ed.), *Sintaxis histórica del español y cambio lingüístico,* 53–87. Madrid/Frankfurt: Iberoamericana/Vervuert.

Labov, William. 1994. The use of the present to explain the past. In William Labov, *Principles of linguistic change,* vol. 1: *Internal factors,* 9–27. Oxford: Blackwell.

Lafuente, Antonio & Antonio Mazuecos. 1992. *Los caballeros del punto fijo. Ciencia, política y aventura en la expedición geodésica hispanofrancesa al virreinato del Perú en el siglo XVIII*. Quito: Abya Yala.

Lapesa, Rafael. 2000. *Estudios de morfosintaxis histórica del español*, 2 vols. Madrid: Gredos.

Lara Bermejo, Víctor. 2015. *Los tratamientos de 2pl en Andalucía occidental y Portugal: estudio geo- y sociolingüístico de un proceso de gramaticalización*. PhD thesis. Universidad Autónoma de Madrid.

Lebsanft, Franz. 1987. Le problème du mélange du "tu" et du "vous" en ancien français. *Romania* 108,429. 1–19.

Lebsanft, Franz. 1990. Die Anredeforschung und das Spanische. *Zeitschrift für Romanische Philologie* 106. 147–165.

León, Ana Emilia. 2008. Decadencia socio-comunicativa de *vos* en el ámbito peninsular (siglos XVI y XVII), parte 1. In Concepción Company Company & José G. Moreno de Alba (eds.), *Actas del VII Congreso Internacional de Historia de la Lengua Española*, Mérida (Yucatán) (2006), 1905–1918. Madrid: Arco Libros.

Listen, Paul H. 1999. *The emergence of German polite* Sie. *Cognitive and sociolinguistic parameters*. Bern, etc.: Peter Lang.

Lopes, Célia Regina dos Santos. 2011. Tradição discursiva e mudança no sistema de tratamento do português brasileiro: definindo perfis comportamentais no início do século XX. *Alfa* 55,2. 361–392.

Lopes, Célia dos Santos & Ana Carolina Morito Machado. 2005. Tradição e inovação: indícios do sincretismo entre a segunda e a terceira pessoas nas cartas dos avós. In Célia dos Santos Lopes (ed.), *A norma brasileira em construção. Fatos lingüísticos em cartas pessoais do século 19*, 45–66. Rio de Janeiro: UFRJ.

Lopes, Célia Regina dos Santos et al. 2009. Quem está do outro lado do túnel? *Tu* e *você* na cena urbana carioca. *Neue Romania* 39. 49–66.

Lopes, Célia Regina dos Santos, Márcia Cristina de Brito Rumeu & Leonardo Lennertz Marcotulio. 2011. O tratamento em bilhetes amorosos no início do século XX: do condicionamento estrutural ao sociopragmático. In Rebollo Couto & Lopes (eds.), 315–348.

Lopes, Célia Regina dos Santos & Márcia Cristina de Brito Rumeu. 2015. A difusão do *você* pelas estruturas sociais carioca e mineira dos séculos XIX e XX. *LaborHistórico* 1,1. 12–25.

López Vallejo, María Á. 2010. Algunas fórmulas de tratamiento del ámbito familiar en los repertorios lexicográficos. In Hummel et al. (eds.), 571–594.

Ly, Nadine. 2001. La interlocución en el teatro del Siglo de Oro: una poética de la interferencia, *Criticón* 81–82. 11–28.

Luz, Marilina dos Santos. 1958–1959. Fórmulas de tratamento no português arcaico. *Revista Portuguesa de Filologia* 9,1–2. 55–281.

Maas, Utz. 2010. Literat und orat. Grundbegriffe der Analyse geschriebener und gesprochener Sprache. *Grazer Linguistische Studien* 73. 21–150.

Maas, Utz. 2012. *Was ist deutsch? Die Entwicklung der sprachlichen Verhältnisse in Deutschland*. Munich: Fink.

Marcotulio, Leonardo Lennertz. 2010. *Língua e história. O 2º marquês do Lavradio e as estratégias linguísticas no Brasil Colonial*. Rio de Janeiro: Ítaca.

Marcotulio, Leonardo Lennertz, Célia Regina dos Santos Lopes & Silvia Regina de Oliveira Cavalcante (eds.). 2015. *História dos pronomes de tratamento no português brasileiro*, special issue, *LaborHistórico* 1,1.

Martínez Sariego, Mónica María. 2006. Fórmulas de tratamiento pronominal en la relación preceptor-alumna en el seno de familias artistocráticas: El caso de Apolonio (s. XIII). In Javier Rodríguez Molina & Daniel M. Sáez Rivera (eds.), *Diacronía, lengua española y lingüística*, 541–556. Madrid: Síntesis.

Martins, Marco Antoni et al. 2015. Para um panorama sócio-diacrônico das formas de tratamento na função de sujeito na região Nordeste. *LaborHistórico* 1,1. 26–48.

Meier, Harri. 1951. Die Syntax der Anrede im Portugiesischen. *Romanische Forschungen* 63. 95–124.

Melo e Abreu, Liisa. 2013. *Há soluções de reforma que mudam contigo, aliás, consigo, perdão, com o senhor* – resultados do *case-study* sobre o uso das formas de tratamento no Português europeu. In Suomela-Härmä, Härmä & Havu (eds.), 257–283.

Michnovicz, Jim, J. Scott Despain & Rebecca Gorham. 2016. The changing system of Costa Rica pronouns of address. In Moyna & Rivera-Mills (eds.), 243–265.

Moreno, María Cristobalina. 2002. The address system in the Spanish of the Golden Age. *Journal of Pragmatics* 34. 15–47.

Morgan, Terrell A. & Scott A. Schwenter. 2016. *Vosotros, ustedes*, and the myth of the symmetrical Castilian pronoun system. In Alejandro Cuza, Lori Czerwionka & Daniel Olson (eds.), *Inquiries in Hispanic linguistics: From theory to empirical evidence*, 263–280. Amsterdam/Philadelphia: John Benjamins.

Moyna, María Irene & Susana Rivera-Mills (eds.). 2016. *Forms of address in the Spanish of the Americas*. Amsterdam/Philadelphia: John Benjamins.

Mühlhäusler, Peter & Rom Harré. 1990. *The linguistic construction of social and personal identity*, Oxford: Basil Blackwell.

Nascentes, Antenor. 1949–1950. Fórmulas de tratamento no Brasil nos séculos XIX e XX. *Revista Portuguesa de Filologia* 3. 52–68.

Newall, Gregory M. 2016. Second person singular forms in Cali Colombian Spanish. In Moyna & Rivera-Mills (eds.), 149–169.

Nogueira, Francieli Motta da Silva Barbosa. 2013. *Como os falantes de Feira de Santana e Salvador tratam o seu interlocutor?* Master's thesis. Universidade Federal da Bahia.

Noll, Volker. 2008. *O português brasileiro*. São Paulo: Globo.

Obediente Sosa, Enrique. 2009. Formas de tratamiento en Mérida (Venezuela) durante el siglo XVIII. *Boletín de Lingüística* 21,31. 86–107.

Obediente Sosa, Enrique. 2010. Visión diacrónica y dialectal de las formas de tratamiento en los Andes venezolanos. In Claudia Borgonovo, Manuel Español Echevarría & Philippe Prévost (eds.). *Selected proceedings of the 12th Hispanistic Linguistics Symposium*, 87–96. Somerville, MA: Cascadilla Proceedings Project.

Ocampo, Francisco. 2006. La evolución de *bueno* de adjetivo a partícula discursiva. Un proceso de discursivización. *Oralia* 9. 231–257.

Placencia, María Elena. 2010. *¿Qué dice flaco?* Algunos aspectos de la práctica social de apodar. In Hummel et al. (eds.), 965–992.

Pöll, Bernhard. 2015. Caribbean Spanish = Brazilian Portuguese? Some comparative thoughts on the loss of *pro-drop*. *Studies in Hispanophone and Lusophone Linguistics* 8,2. 317–354.

Prince, Alan & Paul Smolensky. 2004. *Optimality Theory: Constraint interaction in Generative Grammar*. Oxford: Wiley-Blackwell Publishers.

Quesada Pacheco, Miguel Ángel. 2010. Formas de tratamiento en Costa Rica y su evolución (1561–2000). In Hummel et al. (eds.), 649–669.

Raymond, Chase Wesley. 2016. Reconceptualizing identity and context in the deployment of forms of address. In Moyna & Rivera-Mills (eds.), 267–288.

Rebollo Couto, Leticia & Célia Regina dos Santos Lopes (eds.). 2011. *As formas de tratamento em português e em espanhol. Variação, mudança e funções conversacionais/Las formas de tratamiento en español y en português. Variación, cambio y funciones conversacionales*. Niterói: Editora da UFF.

Renzi, Lorenzo, Giampaolo Salvi & Anna Cardinaletti (eds.). 2001. *Grande grammatica italiana di consultazione*, vol. 3. Bologna: il Mulino.

Rigatuso, Elizabeth M. 1988–1989. Fórmulas de tratamiento sociales en el español bonaerense de mediados del siglo XIX. *Cuadernos del Sur* 21–22. 65–93.

Rivadeneira Valenzuela, Marcela. 2016. Sociolinguistic variation and change in Chilean *voseo*. In Moyna & Rivera-Mills (eds.), 87–117.

Román Fernández, Mercedes. 1991. Formas pronominales de tratamiento en el español dominicano del siglo XVIII. In César Hernández et al. (eds.), *El español de América*, 341–354. Valladolid: Junta de Castilla y León.

Rona, José Pedro. 1967. *Geografía y morfología del voseo*. Pôrto Alegre: Pontifícia Universidade Católica do Rio Grande do Sul.

Rumeu, Márcia Cristina de Brito. 2013. *Língua e sociedade. A história do pronome* você *no português brasileiro*. Rio de Janeiro: Ítaca.

Rumeu, Márcia Cristina de Brito. 2015. *Tu* ou *você*, *te* ou *lhe*?: a correlação entre as funções de sujeito e complemento verbal de 2ª pessoa. *Lingüística* 31,2. 83–109.

Rumeu, Márcia Cristina de Brito & Thiago Laurentino de Oliveira. 2016. A expressão da 2ª pessoa do singular em contextos de complementação e de adjunção: retratos do encaixamento estrutural e social. *Lingüística* 32,2. 25–46.

Sáez Rivera, Daniel M. 2006. *Vuestra merced > usted:* nuevos datos y perspectivas. In José Jesús de Bustos Tovar & José Luis Girón Alconchel (eds.), *Actas del VI Congreso Internacional de Historia de la Lengua Española*, vol. 3, 2899–2911. Madrid: Arco/Libros.

Sáez Rivera, Daniel M. 2013. Formación e historia de *vuecencia* en español como proceso de rutinización lingüística. *Ibero* 77. 108–129.

Sáez Rivera, Daniel M. 2014a. Procesos de lexicalización/gramaticalización en la formación e historia de *usía* en español. In Girón Alconchel & Saéz Rivera (eds.), 159–186.

Sáez Rivera, Daniel M. 2014b. The interplay of object clitic doubling and the grammaticalization of address forms in the genre of collections of letters in Spanish (Peliger 1599, Páez 1630, Sobrino 1720). In Girón Alconchel & Saéz Rivera (eds.), 321–360.

Sánchez López, Cristina. 1993. Una anomalía del sistema pronominal del español. *Dicenda* 11. 259–284.

Silva, Vera Lúcia Paredes Silva. 2011. Notícias recentes da presença do pronome *tu* no quadro dos pronomes do português falado no Rio de Janeiro. In Rebollo Couto & Lopes (eds.), 245–262.

Simon, Horst. 2003a. *Für eine grammatische Kategorie "Respekt" im Deutschen. Synchronie, Diachronie und Typologie der deutschen Anredepronomina*. Tübingen: Niemeyer.

Simon, Horst J. 2003b. From pragmatics to grammar. Tracing the development of respect in the history of the German pronouns of address. In Taavitsainen & Jucker (eds.), 85–123.

Simon Horst. 2005. Only *you*? Philological investigations into the alleged inclusive-exclusive distinction in the second person plural. In Elena Filimonova (ed.), *Clusivity. Typology and case studies of the inclusive-exclusive distinction*, 113–150. Amsterdam/Philadelphia: John Benjamins.

Sonnenhauser, Barbara & Patrizia Noel Aziz Hanna (eds.). 2013. *Vocative. Addressing between system and performance*. Berlin/Boston: De Gruyter.

Suomela-Härmä, Elina, Juhani Härmä & Eva Havu (eds.). 2013. *Représentations des formes d'adresse dans les langues romanes*. Helsinki: Société Néophilologique.

Sweeney, Patricia. 2005. *El voseo en Chile: factores histórico-morfológicos que explican su aparición y mantenimiento*. PhD thesis. Albany State University.

Taavitsainen, Irma & Andreas Jucker (eds.). 2003. *Diachronic perspectives on address term systems*. Amsterdam/Philadelphia: John Benjamins.

Torrejón, Alfredo. 1986. Acerca del voseo culto de Chile. *Hispania* 69. 677–683.

Tuten, Donald N. 2008. Factores socioculturales en el desarrollo de *vuestra merced/usted*. In Concepción Company Company & José G. Moreno de Alba (eds.), *Actas del VII Congreso Internacional de Historia de la Lengua Española*, vol. 2, 2189–2199. Madrid: Arco/Libros.

Uber, Diane Ringer. 1985. The dual function of *usted*: Forms of address in Bogotá, Colombia. *Hispania* 68. 388–392.

Vázquez Laslop, María Eugenia & Leonor Orozco. 2010. Formas de tratamiento del español en México. In Hummel et al. (eds.), 247–269.

Weyers, Joseph R. 2016. Making the case for increased prestige of the vernacular. In Moyna & Rivera-Mills (eds.), 289–304.

Wierzbicka, Anna. 2016. Making sense of terms of address in European languages through the Natural Semantic Metalanguage (NMS). *Intercultural Pragmatics* 13,4. 499–527.

Wright, Roger. 1983. Unity and diversity among the Romance languages. *Transactions of the Philological society* 81. 1–22.

Wright, Roger. 2002. *A sociophilological study of Late Latin*. Turnhout: Brepols.

Wright, Roger. 2011. Romance languages as a source for spoken Latin. In James Clackson (ed.), *A companion to the Latin language*, 59–79. Oxford: Wiley-Blackwell.

Víctor Lara Bermejo

Forms of address in the south-western *Sprachbund* of the Iberian Peninsula

One hundred years of evolution in western Andalusian Spanish and European Portuguese

Abstract: South-western Peninsular Spanish (Andalusian) and European Portuguese rely on a single plural pronoun to address a group of people (*ustedes/vocês* respectively). However, this can induce two different agreements in the verb, in the object pronouns and in the possessive: (i) second person plural (2PL) and (ii) third person plural (3PL). This chapter studies the linguistic spread of these agreement patterns during the last hundred years as well as the theoretical aspects that led to this variation in use, and it also confirms the *Sprachbund* theory that has been recently put forward regarding western Andalusian and southern European Portuguese, since both varieties share a series of linguistic behaviours and developments in phonetics, lexicon and morpho-syntax.

Keywords: agreement, Andalusian Spanish, European Portuguese, person, case, *Sprachbund*

1 Introduction

The evolution of the plural systems of address throughout the Iberian Peninsula has undergone quite a similar process in all its Romance languages. Catalan, Galician and Spanish have two different pronouns: one for informality (*vosaltres, vosoutros, vosotros* respectively) and another one, for formality (*vostès, vostedes, ustedes* respectively) (Wheeler et al. 1999; Álvarez & Xove 2002; RAE-ASALE 2009: § 16.3). Standard European Portuguese, on the contrary, possesses a single pronoun to address a group of people both in an informal and a formal context (*vocês*). However, the northern part still maintains an older system based on the dichotomy of two pronouns: *vós* for informality and *vocês* for formality; *vós* is also resorted to in Church or military speech all throughout the country (Raposo et al. 2013). The levelling attested in standard European Portuguese extends throughout southern and central areas of Portugal and coincides with an analogous levelling in the Spanish of western Andalusia (in southern Spain). This region has eliminated the opposition *vosotros – ustedes* by favouring the use of *ustedes* both for formal and informal contexts. The fact that these two instances of levelling occur in the same area in which other linguistic features emerge as a consequence of the geographical proximity of Andalusian Spanish and southern European Portuguese has led scholars to put forward the existence of a *Sprachbund*, that is, a group of languages (in this case, Spanish and Portuguese) spoken within a specific area sharing several linguistic features as a consequence of their geographical proximity. Map 1 depicts the *Sprachbund* in the domain of plural forms of address.

Map 1: Geographical extension of the levelling in *ustedes* and *vocês* in the Iberian Peninsula.

This proximity is also attested in other phenomena regarding lexicon and phonetics. According to Fernández-Ordóñez (2011), the word *borrego* 'lamb' to refer to the baby sheep is found throughout the west-southern area of the Spanish Peninsula and spreads to the centre-southern part of Portugal, to the detriment of the northern word *cordeiro*. Furthermore, the word *chivo* 'goat' is also attested uninterruptedly in western Peninsular Spanish and in the centre and the south of Portugal (*chibo*), as is the term *mazorca – maçaroca* 'corncob' which shares a similar geographical distribution. It is noteworthy that these words do not simply mirror lexical variation: they belong to agriculture and cattle breeding and, consequently, reflect a close cultural proximity. Cintra (1961, 1962) splits the centre-north and the centre-south of Portugal, following the origin of the differences between the words *ordeñar* 'to milk' or *ubre* 'udder', among others, and he notes that the southern area possesses a certain tendency to diffuse innovations although not systematically. As for phonetics, Cintra (1971) establishes the distinction centre-north and centre-south when he compares the realisation of the sibilant that corresponds to the spellings <s> and <ss>. According to the author, the northern pronunciation is apical-alveolar, whereas the southern one is pre-dorso-dental. It is precisely the southern pronunciation that coincides with the *seseo* pronunciation (the non-distinction between the phonemes [s] and [θ] by favouring the former) of western Andalusia.

In Section 2, I detail the evolution of Peninsular Spanish and European Portuguese regarding their plural forms of address system and the information available up to now about the situation in the abovementioned *Sprachbund*. Later in Section 3, I describe the methodology employed to elicit the study's data. Afterwards, I describe the results firstly from a synchronic perspective (4.1) and then from a diachronic view (4.2). In the following (4.3), I analyse the results from a theoretical point of view. I then discuss the historical evolution of forms of address in Portuguese and Spanish, (4.4), and in Section 5 I present the study's conclusions.

2 Development of the forms of address system in the *Sprachbund*

2.1 Spanish

Standard Peninsular Spanish possesses four pronouns of address: two for informal contexts (*tú* and *vosotros*, singular and plural respectively) and two for formal contexts (*usted* and *ustedes*, singular and plural respectively). Formality is expressed through the third person while informality chooses the second one (Table 1).

Table 1: Forms of address system in standard Peninsular Spanish.

	Informality	Formality
Singular	*tú* + 2SG	*usted* + 3SG
Plural	*vosotros* + 2PL	*ustedes* + 3PL

However, the western part of Andalusia (in southern Spain) eliminated this distinction around the 18th century (Fernández 2012) and levelled any plural form of address in the pronoun *ustedes*. Nevertheless, despite the fact that the syntax requires the elements that refer to *ustedes* to agree in 3PL, it induces both 2PL and 3PL inflections (Alvar 1996; Cano 2004, 2008; Carrasco Santana 2002; De Jonge et al. 2012; Lapesa 1981; Menéndez Pidal 2005; Penny 2004 or RAE-ASALE 2009). This situation is identical to the one attested in the Spanish spoken in Latin America, with the difference that in Latin America *ustedes* systematically agrees in 3PL (Fontanella de Weinberg 1999). The disappearance of *vosotros* in Latin America is said to have occurred around the 19th century, when *vosotros* was relegated to rhetoric, the army and the church (Vázquez Laslop 2010; Bertolotti, this volume).

Regarding western Andalusian, the available data (especially the studies by Alvar et al. 1961–1965; Carricaburo 1997; Lapesa 2000; Hummel et al. 2010) only suggest that the reflexive pronoun and the verbs in the past simple adopt the 3PL whereas the rest of the elements adopts the 2PL, except the possessive, which in principle is construed with the prepositional phrase *de ustedes* (Table 2). Notice that the subject form and the form inside a prepositional phrase are identical in Spanish; this is why I use stressed pronoun to refer to both elements.

Table 2: Agreements in the levelling of *ustedes*.

Agreeing item	Stressed pronoun	Reflexive pronoun	Past simple	Other tenses	Objects pronouns	Possessive
Type of Agreement	*ustedes* (3PL)	3PL	3PL	2PL	2PL	*de ustedes*

Thanks to the data of the *Linguistic atlas of the Iberian Peninsula* (ALPI), collected between 1931 and 1954, Lara (2012) has shown that the levelling in *ustedes* ran throughout the Andalusian provinces of Huelva, Seville, Cádiz, Málaga (except the most eastern part) and Córdoba (except the most northern part) and that it could induce either the 3PL or the 2PL, based on the hierarchy represented in (i).

(i)   Stressed pronoun > reflexive > accusative > embedded verb

The continuum set out in (i) shows the extension of the 3PL throughout the different elements that refer to *ustedes*: if the 3PL emerges in the accusative (*los*), it also arises in the reflexive (*se*) and the stressed pronoun (*ustedes*), but not yet in the embedded verb. In (1 a – d) the evolution of the agreement is shown based on the ALPI data.

(1) a. Ustedes   no   os   disteis cuenta de   cuándo   os
         You.3PL   NEG   REFL.2PL.   notice.2PL.PAST.   when   ACC.2PL.
         vieron   mientras   caminabais.
         see.3PL.PAST   while   walk.2PL.IMP.
         'You did not notice that they saw you while you were walking'

b. Ustedes   no   se   disteis cuenta de   cuándo os
    You.3PL   NEG   REFL.3PL.   notice.2PL.PAST. when   ACC.2PL.
    vieron   mientras caminabais.
    see.3PL.PAST while   walk.2PL.IMP.
    'You did not notice that they saw you while you were walking'

c. Ustedes   no   se   disteis cuenta de cuándo los
    You.3PL   NEG   REFL.3PL.   notice.2PL.PAST. when   ACC.3PL.
    vieron   mientras caminabais.
    see.3PL.PAST while   walk.2PL.IMP.
    'You did not notice that they saw you while you were walking'

d. Ustedes   no   se disteis cuenta de cuándo los
    You.3PL   NEG REFL.3PL.   notice.2PL.PAST.   when   ACC.3PL.
    vieron   mientras caminaban.
    see.3PL.PAST. while   walk.3PL.IMP.
    'You did not notice that they saw you while you were walking'

These examples show that the 3PL gradually spreads throughout the syntax. While (1b) only induces the 3PL in the stressed pronoun and the reflexive pronoun, (1d) already adopts the 3PL in the accusative pronoun and the verb of the embedded sentence, as (i) illustrates.

The methodology employed in the ALPI, based on a questionnaire with pre-established sentences and words that the informants had to repeat in their vernacular varieties, did not provide information about the agreement of all the syntactic elements governed by *ustedes*, since there were no questions eliciting the dative, the possessive or other verb tenses. Likewise, this atlas has limited quantitative data, for it only collected one response per sentence and informant (who was always male, non-mobile, rural, with a limited educational background and over fifty years old) (Sanchís Guarner 1962).

2.2 Portuguese

European Portuguese exhibits an analogous case to the Andalusian one. Before the 18th century, the whole area possessed the opposition of two different pronouns, *vós* and *vocês*, that expressed informality and formality, respectively (Table 3).

However, nowadays, the standard plural address pattern is levelled in *vocês* although it relies on a great many noun phrases that express kinship or social and professional differentiation in order to be more polite (Braun 1988; Carreira 2003). Amongst all the nominal formulas, the most common and least marked

Table 3: Plural address system in European
Portuguese before the 18th century.

Informality	Formality
vós + 2PL	vocês + 3PL

construction corresponds to *os senhores/as senhoras* 'sirs', 'madams' and, like *vocês*, it must agree in 3PL (Table 4).

Table 4: Plural address system in current European Portuguese.

Informality	Formality	Distance
vocês	vocês	os senhores/as senhoras

Nonetheless, the standard norm requires that certain elements take 3PL inflections and other elements 2PL inflections. So, the reflexive and any verb tense receive 3PL whereas object pronouns and possessives agree in 2PL (Table 5) (Cunha & Cintra 1992; Brito et al. 2006; Raposo et al. 2013).

Table 5: Agreements in the levelling of *vocês* in European Portuguese.

	Stressed pronoun	Reflexive pronoun	Verb	Objects pronouns	Possessive
Agreement	vocês (3PL)	3PL	3PL	2PL	2PL

Again, Lara (2012) identified this phenomenon in the ALPI and realised that the standard system was only attested in the southern half of Portugal (Faro, Setúbal, Beja, Évora, Portalegre, Santarém, Lisbon, Coimbra and Leiria) while the northern half still maintained the previous system, represented in Table 3. This means that the paradigm of Table 3 was still valid in the northern region at least until the first half of the 20th century. With regard to the agreement of the levelling in *vocês*, as the Andalusian, the 3PL spread hierarchically based on (ii).

(ii) Stressed pronoun/reflexive/verb > accusative

In other words, the hierarchy shows that if the 3PL is attested in the accusative, it is necessarily attested in the verb, the reflexive and the stressed pronoun (2a – b).

(2) a. Vocês   não   se   aperceberam   de quando vos
        You.2PL no   REFL.3PL   realise.3PL.PST. of when   ACC.2PL.
        viram.
        ver.3PL.PST
        'You did not realise when they saw you'

    b. Vocês   não   se   aperceberam   de quando os
        You.2PL no   REFL.3PL   realise.3PL.PST. of when   ACC.3PL.
        viram.
        ver.3PL.PST
        'You did not realise when they saw you'

As illustrated in examples (1a – d), example (2b) shows that the 3PL already emerged in the stressed pronoun, the reflexive pronoun and the accusative pronoun, while in (2a) it had not reached the accusative pronoun.

The ALPI data do not provide information about the situation of the dative and the possessive, as has been explained above. Moreover, the methodology of this atlas does not allow for the quantitative analysis of a given phenomenon, and the *modus operandi* could have tainted the informants' responses. Thus, the data collected in the ALPI have to be evaluated taking into account its methodological limitations.

3 Corpus and methodology

With the aim of investigating the social and linguistic reality of both levellings and compensating the shortcomings of other methods, I carried out fieldwork throughout western Andalusia and the centre-southern part of Portugal in 2012 and 2013. Such fieldwork consisted of a series of interviews in which the informants had to watch several scenes (without the audio track) of two famous sitcoms that usually show a character addressing a group of people. After watching them, the informants had to become the character and dub the scene. The scenes were chosen in a way to ensure that many tokens of 2PL/3PL would have to be produced. The informants were recorded while they carried out the activity and, later, the audio recordings were transcribed (Lara, 2016). Any occurrence that included a second person plural was classified on the basis of its syntax (subject, reflexive, direct object, indirect object, possessive, verb) and on the informants' extra-linguistic features (gender, age, educational background, origin, number of inhabitants of the place of origin). Moreover, within the category of verb, a distinction was made based on tense, mood, modality or the type of sentence (main or embedded). Lastly, the selection of the scenes was chosen, by taking into account different kinds of interlocutors (friends, family, strangers, elderly people, etc.) with the aim of finding possible pragmatic differences expressed in the agreement. Altogether, over 250 informants were surveyed and approximately 4,900 occurrences were obtained.

Two statistical tests were applied to the results: Pearson's *chi squared* and a logistic regression. The former gives the real significance of an independent variable (gender, age, etc.) and the latter orders the degree of affectedness of every significant variable. In the studied phenomena, the *chi squared* results highlighted the importance of the factors age, educational background and size of the population of the municipality. Hence, both in the Spanish and Portuguese areas, the tendency toward adopting the standard pattern (the distinction between *vosotros* and *ustedes* in Spanish, and the levelling in *vocês* in Portuguese) is usually related to middle-aged informants with a higher education background who, at the same time, live in urban environments (Lara 2015). However, the goal of this chapter is to account for the linguistic extension of the agreement throughout all the elements that refer to *ustedes* and *vocês*.

4 Results

Below, I show the results of my fieldwork. In the first place, in 4.1 I discuss the data from a synchronic perspective; later in 4.2, I deal with both phenomena from a diachronic view; then, I analyse them theoretically in 4.3; finally, I compare the common evolution of Spanish and Portuguese over time in 4.4.

4.1 Synchronicity

4.1.1 Subject and verb agreement

Independently of the social situations (that will not be analysed here), the levellings in Spanish and Portuguese (*ustedes* and *vocês*) are characterised by their exhibiting an identical syntactic behaviour. Let us begin with Spanish.

The use of *ustedes* has produced three geographical areas based on the frequency of the levelling and its grammatical behaviour (Map 2).

Map 2 shows that the centre-northern area of Córdoba and the most eastern area of Málaga are characterised by a low or null use of *ustedes* as the single plural address term. In other words, the areas with < 33%, either follow the

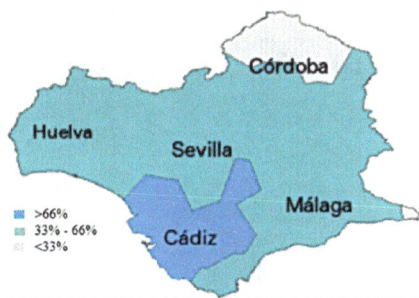

Map 2: Current geographical extension of the levelling in *ustedes*.

standard pattern, or have a low proportion of speakers that choose the vernacular response. On the opposite side, we find the territory comprised of southern Seville and all of Cádiz, with > 66% of use of the levelling in *ustedes*. In these areas, the virtual totality of speakers selects a single pronoun and only a few of them tend to employ the normative pattern. In an intermediate position, there is the area with 33%–66% of use of the levelling. That is to say, this last area possesses the same proportion of speakers that choose the standard paradigm as the number of informants that maintain the vernacular model.

From the grammatical point of view, the three areas present different behaviours regarding the agreement between *ustedes* and the verb. While the area with < 33% is characterised by a strong disagreement (virtually all verbs adopt the 2PL) (3 – 4), the area with > 66% has widely made regular the 3PL in the verb (5 – 6). Again, the area with 33%-66% shows an intermediate behaviour, where the 3PL is more numerous than in the area with < 33%, but it is not yet consistent (7 – 9).

(3) Ustedes,   no   tenéis   nómina.
    You-3PL,   no   have-2PL.PRES.IND   salary
    'You do not have any salary'

(4) Ustedes,   habéis   desorganizado   mi   casa.
    You-3PL,   have-2PL-PRES.IND   mess up-PCP   my   house
    'You have messed up my house'

In examples (3 – 4), there are several occurrences in which the informants belonging to the area with < 33% have expressed a pause between the pronoun *ustedes* and the verb, which is inflected in 2PL; this is why the comma is written.

Within the area 33%-66%, we find a higher proportion of agreement in 3PL although it is still low. Furthermore, we attest the concatenation of the 2PL and 3PL inflections materialised in unstressed pronouns and verbal morphology (5 – 6).

(5) Se   os   queréis   ir.
     REFL-3PL   REFL-2PL   want-2PL.PRES.IND   leave-INF
     'You want to leave'

(6) Intentarois   entrar.
     Try-3PL+2PL.PERFC.IND   come in-INF
     'You tried to come in'

Lastly, the area with > 66% exhibits an overwhelming use of *ustedes* and so is the agreement in 3pl, as can be observed in the examples (7 – 9).

(7) Ustedes,   ¿no   estarían   cotilleando?
     You-3PL,   no   be-3PL.COND   gossip-GER
     'Wouldn't you be gossiping?'

(8) Son   ustedes   las que   entraron   en   mi
     Be-3PL.PRES.IND   you-3PL   who   enter-3PL.PERF.IND   in   my
     piso.
     apartment
     'You were the ones who entered my apartment'

(9) Ustedes   me   han   pedido   un   crédito.
     You-3PL   DAT.1SG   have-3PL.PRES.IND   ask-PCP   a   loan
     'You have asked me for a loan'

In the case of Portuguese, I have not found disagreements between *vocês* and the verb, as the following instances show.

(10) A   que   horas   se   levantaram   vocês?
      To   what   time   REFL.3PL   wake up-3PL.PRET.IND.   you-3PL
      'What time did you get up?'

(11) Vocês   não   venham   tarde   para   casa.
      You-3PL no   come-3PL.PRES.SUBJ.   late   to   house
      'Don't come home late'

Examples (10 – 11) illustrate that whenever *vocês* is chosen, the reflexive and the verb are inflected in 3PL, as its syntax induces.

4.1.2 Clitics and possessives agreement

Let us begin with the analysis of the unstressed pronouns or clitics (Figure 1).

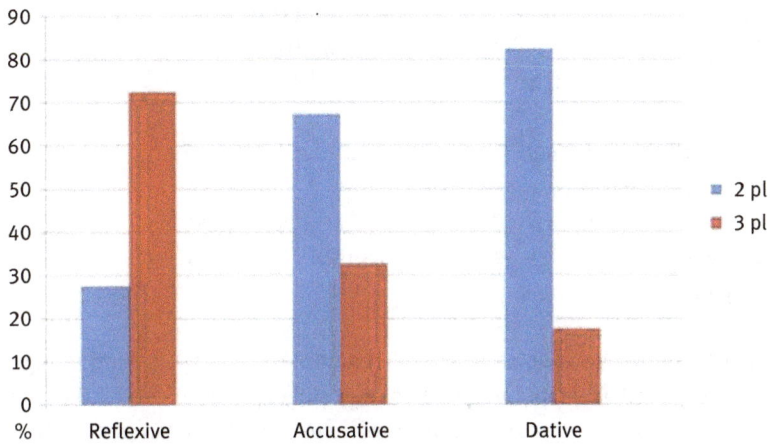

Figure 1: Agreement of clitics (*ustedes*).

As can be seen in Figure 1, the clitic likelier to adopt the 3PL is the reflexive, followed by the accusative and, then, the dative. Based on these data, three phases can be identified in (12 – 14).

(12) a. Ustedes se   van   de viaje.
          You   REFL.3PL go-3PL.PRES.IND. on trip
          'You are going on a trip'
      b. [A   ustedes] os   vi   ayer.
          [To you]   ACC.2PL. see-1SG.PRES.IND. yesterday
          'To you, I saw you yesterday'
      c. [A   ustedes] os   doy   las llaves.
          [To you]   DAT.2PL give-1SG.PRES.IND. the keys
          'To you, I give you the keys'

(13) a. Ustedes se   van   de viaje.
          You   REFL.3PL go-3PL.PRES.IND. on trip
          'You are going on a trip'
      b. [A   ustedes] los   vi   ayer.
          [To you]   ACC.3PL. see-1SG.PRES.IND. yesterday
          'To you, I saw you yesterday'

    c. [A   ustedes] os   doy   las llaves.
       [To you]   DAT.2PL give-1SG.PRES.IND. the keys
      'To you, I give you the keys'

(14) a. Ustedes se   van   de viaje.
        You   REFL.3PL go-3PL.PRES.IND. on trip
        'You are going on a trip'
    b. [A   ustedes] los   vi   ayer.
       [To you]   ACC.3PL. see-1SG.PRES.IND. yesterday
      'To you, I saw you yesterday'
    c. [A   ustedes] les   doy   las llaves.
       [To you]   DAT.3PL give-1SG.PRES.IND. the keys
      'To you, I give you the keys'

In a first stage, the reflexive adopts the 3PL (352 examples out of 490), even though object pronouns are still inflected in 2PL. In a later stage, the accusative takes the 3PL (74 out of 190 cases) whereas the dative prefers to keep the *vosotros* morphology. In an ulterior phase, the dative starts agreeing in 3PL (59 out of 349 cases), and this is why all unstressed pronouns end up receiving the agreement induced by *ustedes*. Let us analyse the behaviour of Portuguese to this respect (Figure 2).

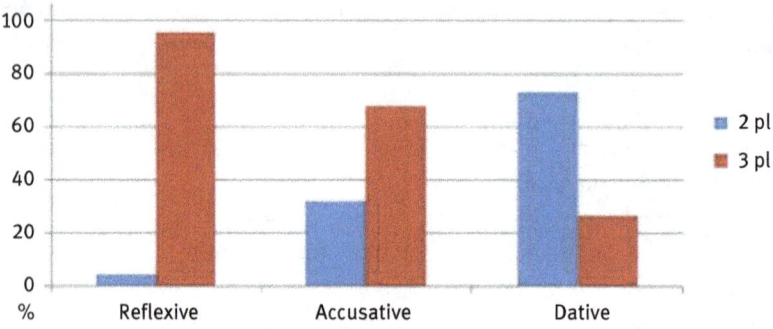

Figure 2: Agreement in clitics (*vocês*).

In Figure 2, which encompasses the percentage of use of either the 2PL or the 3PL in clitics, we see that, again, the reflexive is widely inflected in 3PL (62 out of 65 instances), followed by the accusative (whose alternative in 2PL increases up to 35%: 42 out of 62 occurrences have adopted the 3PL) and, the dative, which presents a wide percentage of tokens in 2PL (15 – 16) (14 out of 52 occurrences). In the case of the reflexive, the few examples of 2PL referred to the pronoun *vós* in areas where the previous diaphasic distinction between *vós* and *vocês* still remains, so I have not collected disagreements between *vocês* and the reflexive.

(15) a. Ontem   não os   vi.
          Yesterday no   ACC.3PL. see.3PL.PST
          'Yesterday I did not see you'
      b. A   mãe   tem-vos   contado   alguma
          The mother have.3PL.PRS.+DAT.2PL. tell.PCP.   some
          historia?
          story
          'Has your mother told you any story?'

(16) a. Ontem   não os   vi.
          Yesterday no   ACC.3PL. see.3PL.PST
          'I did not see you yesterday'
      b. A   mãe   tem-lhes   contado
          The mother have.3PL.PRS.+DAT.3PL. tell.PCP.
          alguma   história?
          some   story
          'Has your mother told you any story?'

The agreement patterns throughout the clitics show that, once *ustedes* and *vocês* become full subjects (I will refer to this later), they start spreading their syntactic agreement (3PL) throughout all the elements that refer to them. This process is gradual and progressive.

Let us end by looking at the situation of the possessive. Figure 3 shows that the prepositional phrase *de ustedes* is hardly attested and it is outnumbered by the choice in 2PL, *vuestro,* or the standard third person form, *su,* with an occurrence of 20%.

It is precisely in the area where the 3PL has extended until the dative (area with >66%) where the possessive begins to agree in 3PL; hence, it is the last element in the chain to adapt to the new agreement (out of 155 examples, only 6 correspond to *de ustedes*; 31 to *su*; and 118 to *vuestro*) (see examples 17 to 20).

(17) Irse   a   sus   casas.
      Go.INF+REFL.3PL.   to   POSS.3PL houses
      'Go home'

(18) Meterse   en   la   vida de
      Get   into.3PL.INF.+REFL.3PL. in   the   life   of

ustedes.
you.3PL.
'Mind your business'

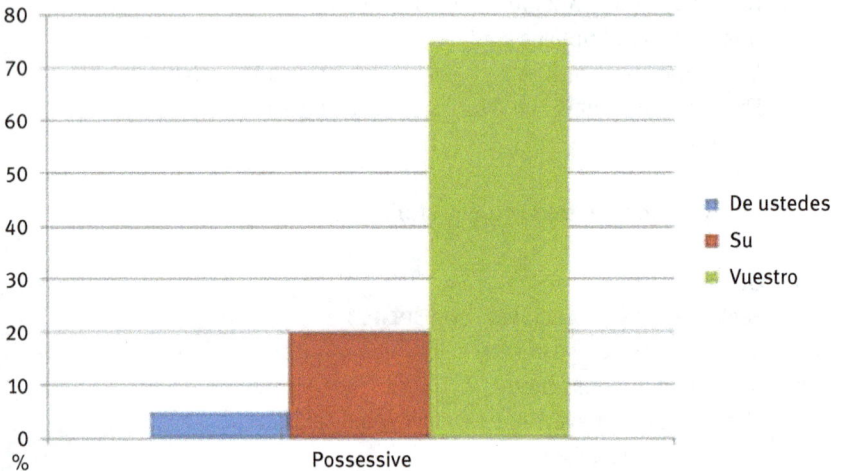

Figure 3: Possessive (*ustedes*).

(19) Meteros   en   vuestros   asuntos.
      Get into.3PL.INF.+REFL.2PL. in   POSS.2PL. affairs
      'Mind your business'

(20) Os   vais   a   vuestra   casa.
      REFL.2PL   go.2PL.PRES.   to   POSS.2PL   house
      'Go home'

In the case of Portuguese, the possessive starts being inflected in 3PL although
the geographical space of this stage is only attested in the most south-eastern
part of Portugal, on the border with western Andalusia, where there is the levelling to *ustedes* (out of 50 examples recorded, only 9 were in 3PL). These stages are
exemplified in (21 – 22) (Figure 4).

(21) Como   estão   os vossos   pais?
      How   be.3PL.PRS.   POSS.2PL   parents
      'How are your parents?'

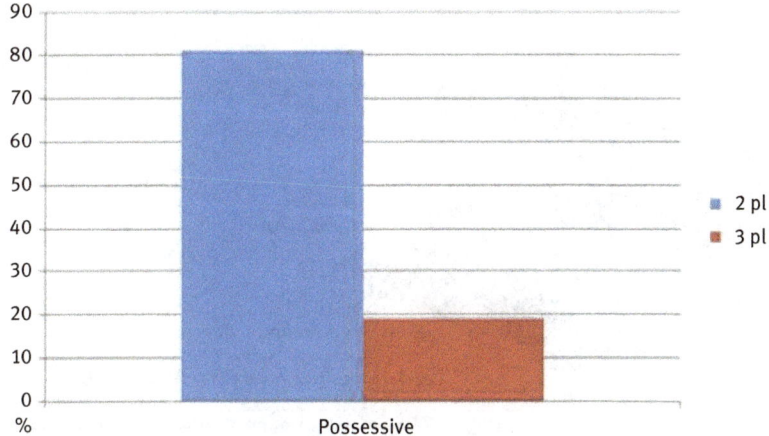

Figure 4: Possessive (*vocês*).

(22) Como estão os   pais   de   vocês?
      How   be.3PL.PRS. the parents of   you.3PL
      'How are your parents?'

4.2 Diachrony

If we synthesise the result presented above, we can observe a diachronic path both in Portuguese and Andalusian Spanish. Let us begin with the latter.

Map 2 shows the three different areas that have resulted from the agreement patterns: < 33%, 33%-66% and > 66%. Based on this classification, the area characterised by > 66% presents systematic agreement in 3PL with *ustedes*. In principle, this leads us to put forward that this zone was the one in which the levelling originated. As a matter of fact, if we compare the current results to the ones attested almost one century ago in the ALPI (Map 3), and already described and analysed in Lara (2012), we observe that the same area of > 66% presented the most evolved stage nearly one hundred years ago.

However, the 3PL in the verb had not completely generalised and it started emerging every now and then. Nowadays, it exhibits complete agreement in 3PL. Likewise, the area classified as 33%-66%, which presents an intermediate percentage of 3PL agreement with *ustedes* coincides with the area in which the 3PL only arose in reflexives and stressed pronouns. Lastly, the zone < 33%, which nowadays presents a low percentage of agreement in 3PL exhibited no agreement in 3PL with any syntactic element almost one hundred years ago. In fact, it only construed the stressed pronoun in 3PL. Therefore, the grammatical situation

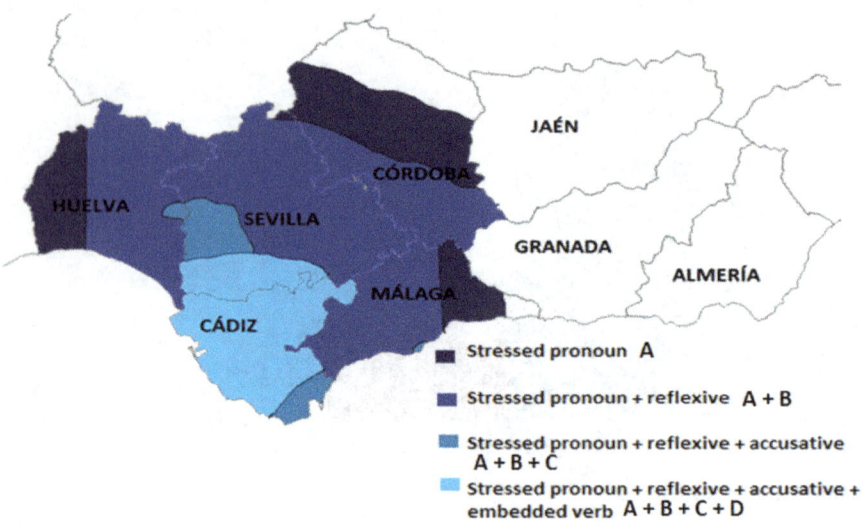

Stressed pronoun **A**

Stressed pronoun + reflexive **A + B**

Stressed pronoun + reflexive + accusative
A + B + C

Stressed pronoun + reflexive + accusative +
embedded verb **A + B + C + D**

Map 3: ALPI's geographical and grammatical extension of the levelling in *ustedes*.

has changed during at least the last 75 years. Again, it is the area >66% the most innovative one, by spreading the 3PL throughout more syntactic elements than the rest of geographical areas. Hence, it is in this zone where the levelling commenced and was later diffused toward its outlying areas until reaching almost all of western Andalusia. In sum, the area > 66% only agreed in 3PL the stressed pronoun and the reflexive in the first half of the 20th century and sometimes the verb, but now it induces 3PL to all verbs, apart from reflexives and stressed pronouns. The area 33%–66% could only agree in 3PL reflexives and stressed pronouns previously, but now it also starts doing so in verbs, though not systematically. Finally, the area < 33% only inflected in 3PL the stressed pronoun in the last century, but now it also induces it in reflexives and in an extremely low proportion in verbs.

In the case of European Portuguese, the data analysed in Lara (2012) regarding the extension of the levelling as well as the grammatical agreement shows that at least two stages can be observed (Map 4).

In the first stage, the 3PL agreed with the subject, the reflexive and the verb, while the second one had extended the 3PL also onto the accusative pronoun. Map 4 can be compared to the current linguistic situation illustrated in Map 5.

Map 5 shows that nowadays European Portuguese presents four stages. In phase 1, the pronoun *vocês* has displaced *vós* as an informal address and has generalised the 3PL in the verb and the reflexive (23 – 24).

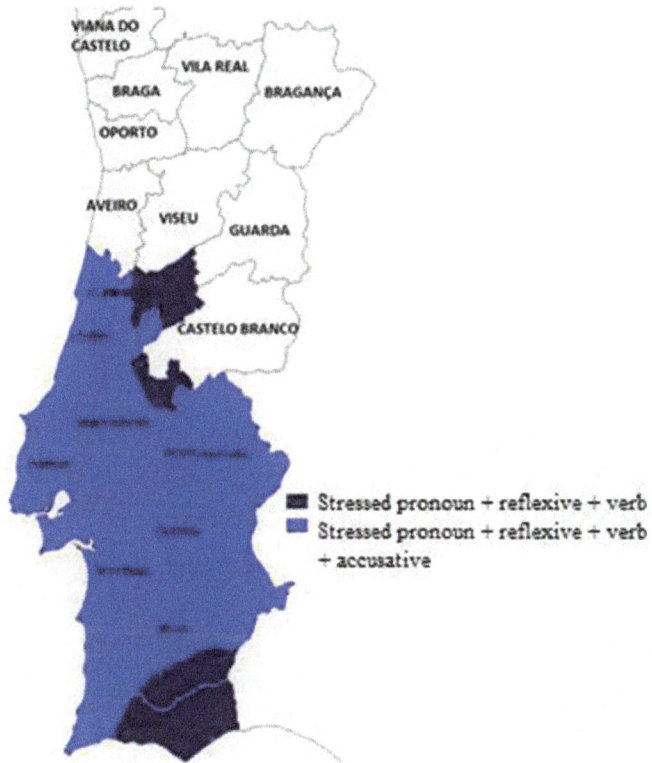

Map 4: ALPI's geographical and grammatical extension of the levelling in *vocês*.

(23) Onde   é   que   vocês   se   conheceram?
      Where be.3PL.PRS. that you.3PL REFL.3PL   meet.3PL.PST
      'Where did you meet?'

(24) Vocês   estão   a   falar   mal de
      You.3PL be.3PL.PRS. to   talk.INF bad about
      alguém.
      somebody
      'You are criticising somebody'

The second stage implies the adoption of the 3PL in the accusative, despite the fact that the standard does not induce 3PL inflections in object clitics. This phase is attested in rural environments of south-eastern Alentejo and all Algarve. Immediately afterwards, the dative adopts the 3PL though its extension is even less than that of the accusative.

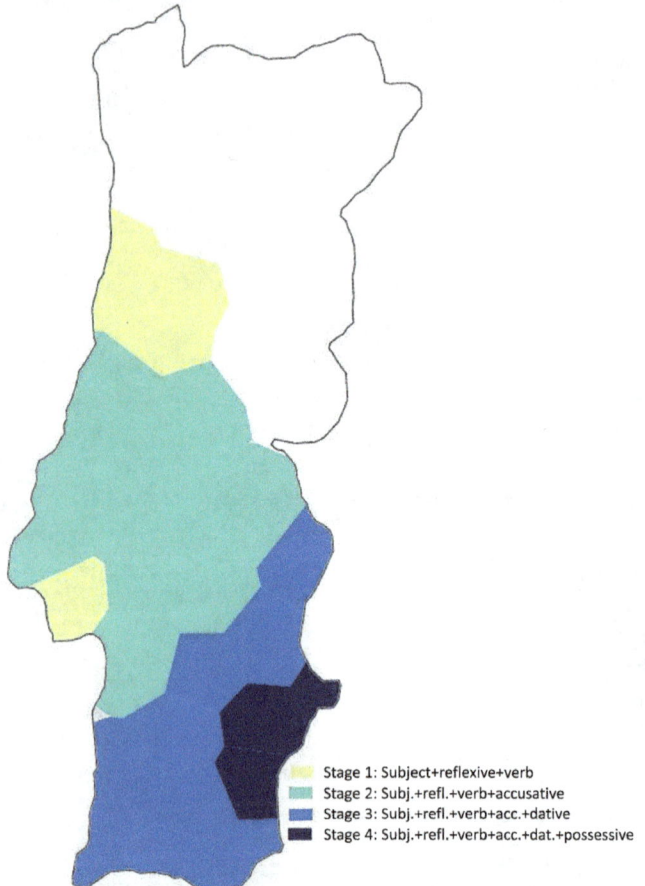

Map 5: Current geographical extension of the levelling in *vocês*.

Lastly, the possessive starts being construed in 3PL although the geographical space of this phase is only documented in the most south-eastern part of Portugal, on the border with the Andalusian phenomenon of the levelling to *ustedes*. The single area that has remained isolated to the successive innovative waves of the *vocês* phenomenon has been the city of Lisbon, whose status of urban, cultural, social and political centre has caused it to stay faithful to the standard pattern that does not allow the 3PL to generalise further than in the reflexive and the verb.

As has been remarked for the Andalusian levelling, the most advanced areas in terms of the extension of the 3PL in the *vocês* phenomenon in the first half of the 20th century are now again the most innovative one, since the 3PL has even spread throughout all the syntactic elements that refer to *vocês*. We cannot know what agreement datives or possessives adopted in the last century, because there were no occurrences about these elements in the available corpora, but virtually all the area characterised by inducing 3PL in the accusative has remained in the same stage or has furthered by spreading the 3PL to the dative and, to a lesser extent, to the possessive. The areas that presented fewer cases of 3PL extension have either maintained the stage attested last century or adopted the 3PL in the accusative too. Lastly, there are new areas affected by the levelling; these only agree in 3PL the subject, the reflexive and the verb, as the first stage attested in the data from one hundred years ago. The only region that does not show any kind of change in terms of the extension of the 3PL is the city of Lisbon. As in the data analysed in Lara (2012), it only inflects the subject, the reflexive and the verb in 3PL, but prefers the 2PL for object pronouns and possessives. Though the singularity of Lisbon has been repeatedly referred to,[1] such as in the case of the phonetic change of /e/ to /a/ before palatal consonant (Teyssier 1982), or the uvular pronunciation of /r/ (Barbosa 1983) or even the maintenance of the diphthong /ei/ despite the southern tendency of converting it into the monophthong /e/ (Cintra 1983), it is *a priori* more convenient to suggest that the conservative behaviour of Lisbon responds to its demography. As has been demonstrated by Wolfram & Schilling – Estes (2003) or Chambers & Trudgill (1980), urban centres gather the political, economic and social power of a given territory and this power regularly imposes the standard variety (Joseph 1987). The non-adoption of the 3PL in object pronouns and possessives in the levelling of *vocês* in Lisbon would only be an attitude inclined to the standard pattern (it must be remembered that the 2PL is the norm in these syntactic contexts) at the expense of vernacular innovations from more rural areas. Lisbon simply follows the standard model imposed by itself (Lara 2017).

4.3 Theoretical analysis

I have pointed out that Andalusian induced person mismatches between the subject and the verb. These person mismatches are not anomalous in Spanish nor are they in many other languages, as has been researched by Ackema & Neeleman (2013), Choi (2013) and Höhn (2016). As a matter of fact, Ordóñez & Treviño (1999) or Fábregas (2008) (for Spanish) and Papangeli (2000) (for Greek)

---

1 In fact, Leite de Vasconcelos (1897) and (1929) distinguished the Lisbon variety within the *estremenho* subdialect, while placing it in the southern dialect; also Vázquez Cuesta and Mendes da Luz (1971), who consider it a variety in and of itself which also functions as the standard pattern.

have investigated the employment of a verbal agreement different to that of the subject, such as in (25) and (26).

(25) Los estudiantes somos jóvenes.
     The students be-1PL.PRES.IND young
     'We students are young'

(26) La gente somos muy curiosos.
     The people be-1PL.PRES.IND very curious
     'We, the people, are very curious'

Though a vast amount of literature has been devoted to the study of noun phrases (mainly in the plural), there have been a few studies on the lack of agreement between personal pronouns and verb tenses that depend on them. In fact, one of the most remarkable phenomena in Spanish regarding pronoun disagreement is *voseo*, whose agreement swings between that of *vos* and that of *tú*. Abadía de Quant (1992), Bertolotti & Coll (2003) and Fontanella de Weinberg (1979) argue that the use of *vos* starts in the stressed pronoun and, later, it induces its agreement gradually: firstly, in imperatives; secondly, in the present of the indicative; and, eventually, in the present of the subjunctive and the past simple. Currently, the rest of verbal tenses, as well as clitics and possessives, are built with *tú* and not *vos* morphology.

Bosque & Gutiérrez Rexach (2009) explain that person disagreement is the result of topicalisation, in which the element that is located in the left periphery is not really the subject that must agree with the verb, but the topic. Precisely, the characteristics of the latter are its position outside the clause, its autonomy and the obligation to be recovered anaphorically within the sentence; additionally, this anaphor is not forced to receive obligatorily the same syntactic features as those of the topic.

Topic constructions have led to deep linguistic changes in Spanish and in many other languages. Elvira (1993, 1996) and Fernández Ordóñez (2009) argue that the current word order in Spanish (SVO) is due to the frequency in the Middle Ages of placing the subject in a topical position; according to Adams (1987), old French behaved as a V2 language, but the tendency to place the subject in a topical position prompted the current order and the obligation of making it explicit. Italian exhibits nowadays three third person pronouns (*lui*, *lei*, *loro*) which, at one time, were oblique. Their frequent placing in a topical position triggered the displacement of the older normative subject pronouns (*egli*, *essa*, *essi*) and the imposition of the oblique pronoun as new subject third person pronouns (Rohlfs 1968; Ernst et al. 2008).

One of the particularities of Spanish is its *pro-drop* character; this is why the expression of the subject emerges in contrastive and disambiguating readings. Therefore, the above mentioned examples (3 – 6) lack a syntactically 2PL pronoun (*vosotros*) because it is omitted. To this respect, RAE-ASALE (2009) affirms that the western part of Andalusia presents records in which two 2PL person pronouns are concatenated, as reproduced in (27).

(27) Ustedes   vosotros   sois   hermanos.
      You-3PL.   you-2PL.   be-2PL.PRES.IND.   siblings
      'You you are siblings'

Example (27) effectively shows that the expression of both pronouns within the same sentence exists and that *vosotros* is still present, at least, in a certain area of western Andalusia. Although my corpus does not include concurrent occurrences of both stressed pronouns, it has recorded the concatenation of these pronouns in other grammatical contexts (28 – 30).

(28) Se   os   queréis   ir.
      REFL-3PL   REFL-2PL   want-2PL.PRES.IND   leave-INF
      'You want to leave'

(29) Intentarois   entrar.
      Try-3PL+2PL.PERFC.IND   come in-INF
      'You tried to come in'

(30) Me   abrierois   los   grifos.
      DAT-1SG   open-3PL+2PL.PERFC.IND   the   taps
      'You opened the taps of my house'

As can be seen in (28 – 30), the overt use of the two pronouns in the same sentence is vernacularly possible (32 examples were collected). In the first case, the informants produce the reflexive in 3PL and, then, in 2PL. Even the verbal inflection shows in its hybrid form the emergence of both agreements: *-ro* in 3PL and *-is* in 2PL (40 examples of this case). It is precisely in the area with 33%-66% where these tokens have been recorded: the area in which the use of *ustedes* is intermediate and the syntactic agreement in 3PL is higher than in the area with < 33%. However, it is not as consistent as it is in the area with > 66% (in fact, from 270 examples of *ustedes* + verb, 147 adopt 3PL, and 123, 2PL). These instances point out that the concatenation of the stressed pronouns (*ustedes* + *vosotros*) exists, but it is uncommon due to the *pro-drop* parameter of Spanish. The no need to express the subject (*vosotros*) leaves the topic (*ustedes*) as the single explicit pronoun. *Ustedes* is followed by a verb in 2PL, which really agrees with *vosotros* and not with *ustedes*.

The existence of two different forms that refer to the same entity within the same sentence has also been documented in Italian. Again, in the development of the pronouns *lui*, *lei* and *loro* at the expense of *egli*, *essa*, *essi*, it has been observed that, in a certain period of this development, both pronouns coexisted within the same phrase (31 – 33) (Ernst et al. 2008).

(31) Lui, egli sa ogni cosa.
    3SG. 3SG. know-3SG.PRS every thing
    lit. 'Him, he knows everything'

(32) Lui e' sa ogni cosa.
    3SG. 3SG know-3SG.PRS every thing
    lit. 'Him he knows everything'

(33) Lui sa ogni cosa.
    3SG. know-3SG.PRS every thing
    lit. 'He knows everything'

As can be seen, the use of *lui* begins in topical constructions and it is recovered by an anaphor (*egli*). With time, the topic starts being reinterpreted as the subject although it does not possess all the features that a topic has and it coexists in the same sentence with the old pronoun (that loses phonic weight) which the new one wants to oust. Lastly, *lui* ends up being imposed and displacing completely the old use, which disappears. This last phase is exactly what one can find in Andalusian, within the area with > 66%, where the use of *ustedes* is hegemonic and so is the agreement in 3PL, as can be observed in the examples (34 – 37) (out of 151 cases, 134 adopted the 3PL in the verb and the rest, the 2PL).

(34) Ustedes, ¿no estarían cotilleando?
    You-3PL, no be-3PL.COND gossip-GER
    'Wouldn't you be gossiping?'

(35) Ustedes me han pedido un crédito
    You-3PL DAT.1SG have-3PL.PRES.IND ask-PCP a loan
    'You have asked me for a loan'

(36) A   ustedes,   ¿qué   les   importa?
     To   you-3PL,   what   DAT.3PL   matter-3SG.PRES.IND
     'Mind your own business'

(37) Inundaron   el   piso.
     Flood-3PL.PFC.IND   the   apartment
     'You flooded the apartment'

The occurrences show an automatic agreement in 3PL due to the subject status that *ustedes* possesses in this area, since it has stopped being a topic. Even in sentences where *ustedes* is made explicit as a topic (34 and 36), the 3PL arises because the subject is the same as the topic. It is in this area where *vosotros* does not exist anymore and *ustedes* has completely displaced the old 2PL informal pronoun. In Table 6, the development of *ustedes* and the agreement with the verb is synthesised.

Table 6: Development of *ustedes* from topic to subject.

	Ustedes	Vosotros	Agreement
Phase 1 (< 33%)	Topic	Subject	2PL
Phase 2 (33%-66%)	Topic-subject	Subject	3PL + 2PL
Phase 3 (> 66%)	Subject	Eliminated	3PL

This conversion from topic into subject is widely documented cross-linguistically. Hopper & Traugott (2003) argue that subjects are basically reanalysed topics and the latter tend to become subjects because they are usually placed in positions prototypically held by them (the left periphery). Givón (1975, 1990) is one of the best exponents of the change from topic into subject. According to the author, the development of a topic into a subject undergoes three different stages. In the first one (38), there is a topical construction, where the topic is inserted in the left periphery, followed by a comma that marks the prosodic pause with the rest of the sentence. In addition, the sentence contains an anaphor that refers to such topic and which really behaves as the true subject of the sentences.

(38) The man, he came.

The frequency of the construction (38) makes speakers reanalyse the element positioned on the left as the subject, since it occupies its prototypical position. Nevertheless, before being completely reinterpreted as the subject, the topic undergoes an intermediate phase in which it does not possess all the elements of a topic (the pause disappears and it is inserted inside the sentence), but it does not receive either the features of a subject (it still needs to be referred to by an anaphor), as shown in example (39).

(39) The man he came.

The last stage in this development is accomplished when the speakers completely reinterpret the old topic as the subject of the sentence, prompting the disappearance of the anaphor (40).

(40) The man came.

If this process is applied to the levelling of *ustedes*, the stage exemplified in (38) corresponds to the one documented in the area with < 33%, where *ustedes* acts as the topic and it is recovered by an anaphor (*vosotros*) which is *silent* (not produced phonetically) due to the *pro-drop* parameter in Spanish. Next, the stage illustrated in (39) is attested in the area with 33%-66%, since we observe the emergence of occurrences where the two forms are expressed (*se os, intentarois*): one of them refers to the topic and the other to the true subject. In this phase, the topic coexists with the still-subject, but it does not enjoy yet the status of the latter, as it needs to be anchored by an anaphor. The cases in which the form that refers to the true subject does not emerge are simply *silent*. Lastly, the stage reproduced in (40) is attested in the area with > 66%, where *ustedes* is definitely a subject and, therefore, it induces the verb to the 3PL.

The apparent person mismatches, as has been explained, are due to non-explicit elements. The existence of these phonetically covert elements has also been widely researched. According to Kayne (2003, 2005, 2007), French and Italian have constructions that contravene the norm or that show an apparent disagreement. If we take into account example (41) from dialectal Italian on reflexive constructions, it is clear that the reflexive does not agree with the subject.

(41) Noi altri se   lavemo   le   man.
      1PL.   REFL.3SG. wash.1PL.PRS. the hands
      'We wash our hands'

According to Kayne, these sentences contain a *silent* element that indicates the feature of person, but which is simply not expressed phonetically. So, (41) really corresponds to (42).

(42) Noi altri ne   se   lavemo   le   man.
     1PL.   REFL.1PL. REFL.3SG. wash.1PL.PRS. the hand
     'We wash our hands'

Likewise, French is inclined to topical constructions, whose topic is recovered by an anaphor. However, there exist counterexamples as the ones compared in (43 – 46).

(43) Lui (,)   (il)   a   téléphoné.
     3SG.MASC   (3SG.MASC.CLIT)   have-3SG.PRES.IND phone-PCP
     'He has phoned'

(44) Eux (,)   (ils)   ont   téléphoné.
     3PL.MASC   (3PL.MASC.CLIT)   have-3PL.PRES.IND phone-PCP
     'They have phoned'

(45) Moi,   *(j')   ai   téléphoné.
     1SG   (1SG. CLIT)   have-1SG.PRES.IND phone-PCP
     'I have phoned'

(46) Toi,   *(tu)   as   téléphoné.
     2SG   (2SG. CLIT)   have-2SG.PRES.IND phone-PCP
     'You have phoned'

Based on (43) and (44), third person stressed pronouns allow the non explicitness of the subject, unlike the rest of persons, where it is obligatory (45 and 46). The explanation for this, according to Kayne, is the presence of an element that is simply not expressed. As has been mentioned above, I have not found disagreements between *vocês* and the verb in European Portuguese, so I infer that *vocês* behaves as a true subject and not a topic.

Once the term of address has become the subject and does not work any longer as a topic, the 3PL starts spreading throughout the rest of syntactic elements that refer to *ustedes* or *vocês*. In the case of Andalusian Spanish, this extension follows a hierarchy that can be synthesised in (iii).

(iii) Subject > reflexive > verb > accusative > dative > possessive

Based on this continuum, if the 3PL emerges in the dative, it also appears in the accusative, the verb, the reflexive and the subject. The spread of the 3PL runs the continuum from left to right through implicational phases.

For European Portuguese, the agreement also follows the same continuum, though in a slightly different way (iv).

(iv) Subject/reflexive/verb > accusative > dative > possessive

The continuum indicates that if the 3PL emerges in the accusative, it also appears in the elements on the left, but not yet on the right.

From a grammatical point of view, the main question now is why the extension of the 3PL follows this pattern and not a different one. According to Corbett (2006), the agreement depends on various factors: in the first place, on the opposition between *controller* and *target*. While the former is the element that induces the agreement, the latter is the element that receives it. So, if a *controller* induces two different agreements, the *target* will acquire one of the two based on two parameters. One of them refers to the position that both the *controller* and the *target* hold within the sentence. This means that the further away the *controller* and the *target* are from each other, the more independence the *target* has to select the agreement. Let us analyse the following example (47), taken from Corbett (2006).

(47) The committee has decided to pass the law but they have been discussing the whole night.

In (47), the *controller* (*committee*) induces singular agreement as the verb shows, despite the fact that it is semantically plural. Nonetheless, its reference is again recovered in the adversative sentence through a plural pronoun and a verb that agrees in the plural with this pronoun. The employment of *they* is the image of a higher independence, because the *target* is found far away from the *controller*; in fact, it is found in a different sentence. Thus, in this instance, its preference is the semantic agreement (plural) and not the syntactic choice (singular).

The other element on which the adoption of the agreement also depends refers to the status that the *target* may have in a hierarchy, represented in (v).

(v) Personal pronoun > relative pronoun > predicate > attributive

Based on the continuum, the further we move rightwards in the hierarchy, the likelier it will be for the target to choose syntactic agreement; while the further we move leftwards, the likelier it will be for the semantic agreement to emerge. Let us analyse example (48).

(48) Sus   excelentísimas   majestades están
      POSS.3PL.   excellent.FEM.PL.   majesties   be.3PL.PRES.IND.
      muy   satisfechos   con   la   noticia.
      very   satisfied.MASC.PL.   with   the   news
      'Their majesties are very satisfied with the news'

In (48) we observe that, although *majestades* is feminine, it refers to an inclusive masculine. The two adjectives that agree with *majestades* adopt both the masculine and the feminine, but its choice depends on the stage within the continuum in (v). Whereas *excelentísimas* behaves as the attributive, *satisfechos* belongs to the environment of the predicate and, therefore, based on the hierarchy, it is closer to the semantic agreement than the attributive. A proof of this alternating quality is found in the mass neuter.[2] Fernández-Ordóñez (2006, 2007) explains that the part of the Iberian Peninsula where the mass neuter is reported presents an agreement extension that coincides with the hierarchy of Corbett, since the syntactic agreement emerges in the attributive and spreads gradually over to the pronoun. This continuum runs from the centre-east of Asturias (where the syntactic agreement is more rooted) up to the centre-west part of Castile, where the semantic agreement is higher.

Hence, in the case of *ustedes* and *vocês*, the verb and the reflexive adopt first the syntactic agreement, because their proximity and dependence with respect to the *controller* is quite close; only when the inductor pronoun behaves as a topic, does the agreement tend to be semantic, for the *controller* is no longer found in the same sentence. Object pronouns rely on a higher autonomy owing to the fact that they do not possess any *controller* that previously induces them an agreement, but they are the first reference to the entity within the sentence (except in topicalisation or double-clitic constructions). So, they take more time to access the 3PL, followed by the possessive, which also has enough autonomy (even deeper than for objects) so as to adopt an agreement not induced by any *controller*.

Despite the precious study by Corbett, his research is circumscribed to the syntactic and semantic difference mainly in gender and number, so the conflict of the grammatical person (2PL versus 3PL) is not resolved in his investigation. The work by Wechsler & Zlatic (2000, 2003) deals more in depth with the agreement conflicts and for this they distinguish two terms: *index* and *concord*. The *index* agreement is that which is established between subject and predicate and it is subjected to the features of person, number, gender (and sometimes, case);

---

2 The agreement induced by uncountable nouns in a number of vernacular varieties of Peninsular Spanish.

concord works with the agreement in the environment of a noun phrase and it usually responds to the features of case, gender and number.

However, as Wechsler & Hahm (2011) discuss, the pronouns of address are sometimes characterised by a totally independent behaviour, as can be seen in examples (49 – 52).

(49) Vous   êtes   loyal.
      You   be.2PL.PRS.   loyal.SG.MASC.
      'You are loyal'

(50) Vous   êtes   loyale.
      You   be.2PL.PRS.   loyal.SG.FEM.
      'You are loyal'

(51) Vous   êtes   loyaux.
      You   be.2PL.PRS.   loyal.PL.MASC.
      'You are loyal'

(52) Vous   êtes   loyales.
      You   be.2PL.PRS.   loyal.PL.FEM.
      'You are loyal'

Though all *vous* cases induce plural, part of the *index* behaviour chooses the singular as the only way to disambiguate the referent. In spite of the fact that *ustedes* and *vocês* are forms of address, the agreement they induce do seem to fulfil the principles of Wechsler & Zlatic (2000, 2003). Therefore, according to these authors, the reflexive and the verb must accept the features of agreement that the subject sends them, this is why *ustedes* and *vocês*, when reanalysed as subjects, have to induce the 3PL in both elements, as the *index* agreement establishes and this forces the subject to agree with the predicate. Otherwise, object clitics behave more independently. They are not usually governed by an entity that is previously expressed such as in double-clitic constructions. They nearly always present for the first time the reference in the sentence. As objects are not obliged to agree with anything else within the sentence, they are not obliged to adopt *index* agreement. The possessive however is usually built in the noun phrase, so it is the element with the least pressure to adopt the person marker (since its agreement is *concord* and not *index*).

Irrespective of the type of agreement adopted by the syntactic elements that refer to *ustedes* and *vocês* (syntactic – semantic, *index* – *concord*), both are ruled by the same pattern in the grammatical cases (Table 7).

Table 7: Agreement extension in *ustedes* and *vocês*.

	Subject	Reflexive	Verb	Accusative	Dative	Possessive
Stage 1	3PL	2PL/3PL	2PL/3PL	2PL	2PL	2PL
Stage 2	3PL	3PL	2PL/3PL	2PL	2PL	2PL
Stage 3	3PL	3PL	3PL	2PL	2PL	2PL
Stage 4	3PL	3PL	3PL	3PL	2PL	2PL
Stage 5	3PL	3PL	3PL	3PL	3PL	2PL
Stage 6	3PL	3PL	3PL	3PL	3PL	3PL

Table 7 shows that the first element to agree is the subject (and the prepositional phrase analogously, as it is the same form for both syntactic contexts) and those closely-related to the subject: reflexive and verb (in the case of Spanish, we observe that the reflexive agrees firstly and, later, with the verb; Portuguese has not offered cases of disagreements between subject, verb and reflexive). This means that the syntactic contexts typically held by the nominative or that refer to it are the first ones to adopt the 3PL. They are followed by the accusative, the dative and the genitive, whose marker is usually represented by the possessive. This order does not seem random, as can be observed in (vi).

(vi)   Nominative > accusative > dative > ablative > genitive

According to Pinkster (1985, 1990), the usual order in Latin in case inflections followed a hierarchy that corresponded to the one reproduced in (vi). It is exactly the same by which the extension of the agreement is ruled (remember that the subject and the prepositional phrase are homophonous, so both adopt the 3PL at the same time; consequently, the ablative stage must be disregarded in this case). Moreover, such case hierarchy coincides with the hierarchy of syntactic contexts to which many languages obey. Let us analyse (vii).

(vii)   Subject > direct object > indirect object > oblique

The continuum reproduced in (vii) shows, according to Blake (2004), that most languages follow a non-marked order based on this hierarchy. Even the possibility to produce a passive sentence follows this pattern. While Spanish and Portuguese only have the possibility to passivise the direct object (53a – b), English does so with indirect objects too and, as a consequence, it implies that it produces a direct object passive (54a – b).

(53) a. El   dinero   te   fue   dado.
        The   money   DAT.2PL   be.3SG.PST. give.PCP
        'The money was given to you'
     b. *Tú   fuiste   dado   el   dinero.
        You   be.2SG.PST. give.PCP. the   money
        *'You were given the money'

(54) a. The money was given to you.
     b. You were given the money.

This distinction on the basis of the case marker can also be attested in other cross-linguistic phenomena. Keenan & Comrie (1977) remark that the ability to relativise an element depends on its case function. So, there are languages capable of relativising only the subject, while others can do so with the subject and the direct object; others can do so with the subject, the direct object and the indirect object. However, no language is able to relativise the indirect object but not the direct object and the subject. Consequently, based on (vii), every language able to relativise an oblique object can do so with the elements on the left. But even the change of the argument structure responds to this criterion. Comrie (1976, 1989) argues that causativisation in Turkish follows this hierarchy in adding valency. For instance, if one more valency is added to an intransitive sentence, the former subject becomes the direct object, and the new valency becomes the subject; if one more is added, the direct object turns into the indirect object, the former subject becomes the direct object and the new valency is the new subject and so on (55 – 56).

(55) a. Hasan   öl-dü.
        Hasan.NOM   die-PST.
        'Hasan has died'
     b. Ali   Hasan-ı   öl-dür-dü.
        Ali.NOM   Hasan.ACC die.CAUS.PST.
        'Ali has killed Hasan'

(56) a. Müdür   mektub-u   imzala-dı.
        director.NOM   letter.ACC   sign.PST
        'The director signed the letter'

b. Ali   mektub-u   müdür-e   imzala-t-tı.
   Ali.NOM   letter.ACC   director.DAT sign.CAUS.PST
   'Ali has made the director sign the letter'

As a result, if the analysis carried out by Blake (2004) or Keenan & Comrie (1977) in their investigations are applied to the extension of the 3PL, we notice that it is firstly attested in the subjects or the elements that depend on it or refer to it (reflexive and verb); later, it moves onto the direct object (a function prototypically held by the accusative), then onto the indirect object (the common case of datives) and in the last place, onto the possessive (usually the genitive). Even though Blake explains that the oblique case appears before the genitive in the hierarchy, *ustedes* and *vocês* have the same form for the subject and the oblique case, which is why once the 3PL is attested in the subject, the oblique case automatically adopts the 3PL.

4.4 Sprachbund and the Americas

The data analysed in the previous sections account for the fact that the development of the Portuguese and Spanish levellings have undergone an identical pathway regarding their grammatical evolution as well as they have definitely established themselves throughout the south-western part of the Iberian Peninsula. However, this is not the first time they end up developing a common strategy with regard to politeness.

The emergence of various noun phrases in the late Middle Ages occurred contemporaneously and both languages evolved into the same system: *vuestra merced/vossa mercê* became the least marked polite strategy, *vuestra majestad/ vossa majestade* was employed to address the monarch, *vuestra excelencia/ vossa excelência* was reserved for gentry and clergy (Menon 2006; Menéndez Pidal 2005). In the case of the former (*vuestra merced/vossa mercê*), the two of them underwent the same grammaticalisation process. In fact, Lara (2012) shows occurrences of old stages in the grammaticalisation of *vossa mercê* to *você*, since the ALPI data provide evidences of *vossemecê* or *vomecê*. These two alternatives coincide with intermediate phases of the evolution from *vuestra merced* to *usted* in Spanish, such as in *vuested* or *vuesasted* (Menon 2006; Pla Cárceles 1923). From a grammatical point of view, the path has repeated itself on several occasions. I have put forward the topical character of *ustedes* one hundred years ago and its tendency toward becoming a subject. According to Hammermüller (2010), the imposition of *vuestra merced* over *vós* followed the same process. It was firstly expressed as a vocative and, therefore, out of the sentence. The verb was inflected in 2PL because its agreement was induced by the pronoun *vós*. As Spanish is *pro-drop*, the production of *vós* had to be low in comparison to the likelihood of expression of the vocative or topic (*vuestra merced*). Once the construction became more and more frequent, *vuestra merced* was reinterpreted as the subject and, as a consequence, the verb started to agree in 3SG. In fact, according to Menon (2006), Menéndez Pidal (2005) and Cano (2008), the first uses of *vuestra merced/vossa mercê* alternated with 2PL and 3SG agreements.

Nevertheless, the most remarkable feature to be analysed concerning the forms of address system in both languages takes place in the abovementioned *Sprachbund*. The levellings are restricted to the south-western part of the Iberian Peninsula (although in the case of Portugal it starts spreading northwards because it represents the standard). Even though the best known *Sprachbünde* are the ones attested in the Balkans and the South Asian area of linguistic convergence (and even a major one in Europe, Haspelmath 2001), the Iberian region in which these levellings are witnessed is characterised by sharing a common development irrespective of the historical period. For instance, the pre-Roman language Tartessian, spoken throughout the Iberian Peninsula before the conquest by the Roman Empire extended virtually throughout the most south-western part of the *Sprachbund*, that is, the area in which the grammatical agreement is complete. However, the period of time in which such a geographical zone shared more exchange was the time after the discovery of America and the division of the world between the crowns of Spain and Portugal.

During the following centuries until the independence of the Spanish and Portuguese colonies in America, the south-western region of the Iberian Peninsula was the area from which the diverse expeditions departed and from which trade was carried out with the American continent. And, as in European Portuguese and western Andalusia, we see the same levellings in the American varieties of these two languages. The influence between both sides of the Atlantic to this respect has not been studied in depth. I do not wish to discuss the Andalusian influence in the Latin American varieties, since it represents a controversial topic, but somehow they have conditioned each other even in post-colonial era. I have already commented that the elimination of *vosotros* in Andalusia began in the 1700's, when Spain was still an empire. By the 19th century, *ustedes* was generalised (Fernández 2012; García Godoy 2012). Likewise, *vosotros* is said to have completely disappeared from the American varieties in the late 19th century (Bertolotti 2015 and this volume). Portuguese exhibits the same pattern. Just like for Spanish, I will not discuss the influence of southern European Portuguese on the Brazilian variety, but the levelling in *vocês*, which also started in the 18th century (Cintra 1972; Faraco 1996), has spread throughout Brazil and has represented the only informal pronoun in the plural for more than two centuries (Menon 2006).

Nonetheless, in the singular, it is possible to attest analogous developments on both sides of the Atlantic. Currently, the formal pronoun *usted* in Spanish is perceived as informal and even affectionate in certain American regions, especially in Central America and the Caribbean (Hummel et al. 2010). Its use is shared with traditional informal pronouns *tú* and *vos*, since the three of them can be resorted to in informal and intimacy contexts. García Godoy (2012) and Calderón Campos (2010) state that *usted* as informal or affectionate could be used in Andalusian Spanish during the late colonial period, that is, at the time in which Latin American started adopting it for informality too. Again, the levelling in singular *usted* at the expense of *tú* originates in south-western Peninsular Spanish and is later exported to the American varieties. This also seems to be the case in the plural.

The situation of Portuguese is better documented. In the plural, Brazilian Portuguese does not possess *vós* for informality as 2PL and neither does southern European Portuguese. Likewise, *vocês* is informal and *os senhores* is the most common formal strategy to address a group. In the singular, *você* has ousted *tu* in almost all of Brazil (Lopes & Cavalcante 2011) and in southern European Portuguese, *você* can be attested as an informal pronoun too (Lara & Guilherme 2015). Furthermore, similarities also arise in the 1PL: the Brazilian spread of *a gente* 'the people' instead of the traditional *nós* 'we' for the 1PL is spatially attested in southern Portugal, but not in the north (Lara & Díez del Corral 2015). Notice that all these phenomena originate in the Iberian *Sprachbund* and then start being witnessed in the American varieties, both in Portuguese and Spanish.

The similarities in phonetics, morpho-syntax and the forms of address systems in American and the south-western region of the Peninsula are attested in the areas where the trade ports were established. The geographical closeness in the case of western Andalusia and southern Portugal as well as their common historical development led to a shared local paradigm that can be still attested. As has been pointed out, the own development with regard to the forms of address of the south-western region of the Iberian Peninsula and its extension throughout Latin America can only be justified because of the intense exchange during centuries. The relations among Seville, Cádiz, Lisbon and Algarve with the American colonies produced the levellings attested up to now, in comparison to other major ports elsewhere in the Peninsula, which maintained other linguistic features. If only the ports had been the reason, we would expect Porto or Bilbao to have developed similar features. But Porto and Bilbao received commodities from elsewhere and did not foster much exchange with the American colonies (O'Flanagan 2008). Their independence made the opposition between *vós – vocês* and *vosotros – ustedes* survive; on the contrary, the interdependence of the south-western ports among each other (Pike 1972) and with their American counterparts provoked a shared local development which can be observed in the lexical and phonetic features commented above, but mainly in the forms of address systems and their evolution until the present day.

In terms of pragmatics, the levellings studied in the south-western region go in line with the diachronic evolution of forms of address systems in Spanish and Portuguese on both sides of the Atlantic. As Molina Martos (this volume) puts forward, the increase of informal *tú* in the late 19th-century Spain was triggered by upper-class members and it was later spread by lower classes too. Similarly, the use of former polite *você* in Portugal as informal is related to the upper class and was later adopted by the rest of the social spectrum. And the same applies for the plural. Fernández (2012) confirms that the diffusion of informal *vosotros* to contexts where *ustedes* was the norm in the 18th century is also a change from above. It is exactly what Faraco (1996) remarks about *vocês* in Portugal at the same period of time.

5 Conclusion

My fieldwork has allowed for the detailed analysis of the parallel linguistic levellings towards *ustedes*, in Spanish, and *vocês*, in Portuguese, as well as a comparison of results with those from the first half of the 20th century. Based on these data, the two phenomena are characterised by an analogous behaviour. Nearly one century ago, the levellings were spread throughout western Andalusia and the Portuguese districts of Faro, Lisbon, Setúbal, Beja, Santarém, Évora, Portalegre, Coimbra and Leiria. Nowadays, the Spanish case is attested in the same Andalusian area (although it is declining) and the Portuguese case has also established itself in the districts of Aveiro, Viseu and part of Castelo Branco.

From a grammatical point of view, *ustedes* and *vocês* are topics reanalysed as subjects and this is why there are apparent disagreements. This transformation allows for two different agreement patterns to emerge every now and then, as has been observed cross-linguistically. As soon as *ustedes* and *vocês* are reinterpreted as subjects, the 3PL spreads hierarchically throughout the rest of elements in this order: the reflexive and the verb are the first one to adopt it (in the case of Spanish), followed by the direct object, the indirect object and the possessive. For Corbett (2006), the adoption of either agreement depends, among other things, on the independence that the *target* has with respect to its *controller*. In our case, the verb and the reflexive depend directly on the subject, so their independence from their *controller* is very limited and, therefore, they are more inclined to the 3PL. Objects and possessives, on the other hand, do not depend on an inducing element, but they are, as a whole, the first reference given of an entity, and this grants them enough autonomy not to agree with *ustedes* or *vocês* automatically. According to Wechsler & Zlatic (2003), the verb and the reflexive adopt the 3PL earlier because they follow *index* agreement and they have to receive the features of person, gender and number of the subject; objects do not depend on the subject or any other inductor, so they are not obliged to be built under the same parameters as the verb and the reflexive, while the possessive responds to the features of case, gender and number, since it is usually inserted in noun phrases and, as a consequence, it is characterised by *concord* agreement. Finally, we notice that the extension coincides with the studies carried out by Blake (2004) regarding case-marking and syntactic contexts, as many linguistic phenomena obey the hierarchy exemplified throughout the chapter: from relativisation to passivisation or the unmarked word order.

Finally, the utility of the type of research conducted here brings together different data and analytical approaches to understand how shared address patterns in an understudied *Sprachbund* came to be.

References

Abadía de Quant, Inés. 1992. La relación pronominal-verbal de segunda persona singular en el español de Corrientes durante el siglo XIX, su comparación con la situación en Buenos Aires. *Revista Argentina de Lingüística* 8. 31–46.

Ackema, Peter & Ad Neeleman. 2013. Subset controllers in agreement relations. *Morphology* 23. 291–323.

Adams, Marianne. 1987. From old French to the theory of pro-drop. *Natural Language and Linguistic Theory* 5. 1–32.

ALPI, see García Mouton et al. 2016.

Alvar, Manuel. 1996. *Manual de dialectología hispánica*. Barcelona: Ariel.

Alvar, Manuel et al. 1961–1965. *Atlas lingüístico y etnográfico de Andalucía (ALEA)*. Granada: Universidad de Granada.

Álvarez, Rosario & Xosé Xove. 2002. *Gramática da língua galega*. Vigo: Galaxia.

Barbosa, Jorge Morais. 1983. *Études de phonologie portugaise*. Évora: Universidade de Évora.

Bertolotti, Virginia & Magdalena Coll. 2003. A synchronical and historical view of the *tú/vos* option in the Spanish of Montevideo. In Silvina Montrul & Francisco Ordóñez (eds.), *Linguistic theory and language development in Hispanic languages*, 1–12. Somerville: Cascadilla Press.

Bertolotti, Virginia. 2015. *A mí de vos no me trata ni usted ni nadie*. Montevideo: Universidad de la República.

Blake, Barry. 1994. *Case*. Cambridge: Cambridge University Press.

Bosque, Ignacio & Javier Gutiérrez-Rexach. 2009. *Fundamentos de sintaxis formal*. Madrid: Akal.

Braun, Friederike. 1988. *Terms of address. Problems of patterns and usage in various languages and cultures*. Berlin: Mouton de Gruyter.

Brito, Ana Maria et al. *Gramática da língua portuguesa*. Lisbon: Caminho.

Calderón Campos, Miguel. 2010. Los elementos nominales en el sistema de tratamiento del español de Andalucía durante la Restauración (1875–1931). In Hummel et al. (eds.), 551–570.

Cano, Rafael. 2004. *Historia de la lengua española*. Barcelona: Ariel.

Cano, Rafael. 2008. *El español a través de los tiempos*. Madrid: Arco Libros.

Carrasco Santana, Antonio. 2002. *Los tratamientos en español*. Salamanca: Ediciones Colegio de España.

Carreira, Maria Helena Araújo. 2003. Les formes allocutives en portugais européen: évolution, valeurs et fonctionnements discursifs. *Franco-British Studies* 33–34. 35–45.

Carricaburo, Norma. 1997. *Las fórmulas de tratamiento en el español actual*. Madrid: Arco Libros.

Chambers, John K. & Peter Trudgill. 1980. *Dialectology*. Cambridge: Cambridge University Press.

Choi, Jaehoon. 2013. Pro-drop in pronoun-noun constructions. In Stefan Keine & Shayne Sloggett (eds.), *NELS 42: Proceedings of the 42nd meeting of the North East Linguistic Society*, 119–128. Amherst: GLSA.

Cintra, Luís Felipe Lindley. 1961. Une frontière lexicale et phonétique dans le domaine linguistique portugais. *Boletim de filologia* 20. 31–38.

Cintra, Luís Felipe Lindley. 1962. Áreas lexicais no território português. *Boletim de filologia* 20. 273–307.

Cintra, Luís Felipe Lindley. 1971. Nova proposta de classificação dos dialectos galego-portugueses. *Boletim de Filologia* 22. 81–118.

Cintra, Luís Felipe Lindley. 1972. *Sobre "formas de tratamento" na língua portuguesa*. Lisbon: Horizonte.

Cintra, Luís Felipe Lindley. 1983. *Estudos de dialectologia portuguesa*. Lisbon: Sá da Costa.

Comrie, Bernard. 1976. The syntax of causative constructions: cross-language similarities and divergences. In Masayoshi Shibatani (ed.), *The grammar of causative constructions (Syntax and Semantics 6)*, 261–312. New York: Academic Press.

Comrie, Bernard. 1989. *Language universals and linguistic typology*. Oxford: Blackwell.

Corbett, Greville. 2006. *Agreement*. Cambridge: Cambridge University Press.

Cunha, Celso & Luís Felipe Lindley Cintra. 1992. *Nova gramática do português contemporâneo*. Lisbon: Sá da Costa.

de Jonge, Bob & Dorien Nieuwenhuijsen. 2012. Forms of address. In José Ignacio Hualde et al. (eds.), *The handbook of Hispanic linguistics*, 247–262. Malden: Blackwell.

Elvira, Javier. 1993. La función cohesiva de la posición inicial de frase en la prosa alfonsí. *Cahiers de linguistique hispanique médiévale* 18/19. 243–278.

Elvira, Javier. 1996. La organización del párrafo alfonsí. *Cahiers de linguistique hispanique médiévale*. 21. 325–342.

Ernst, Gerhard et al. 2008. *Romanische Sprachgeschichte*. Berlin/New York: Mouton de Gruyter.

Fábregas, Antonio. 2008. Variación en forma morfológica de los pronombres de primera y segunda persona del plural. *Revista Española de Lingüística* 38. 155–184.

Faraco, Carlos Alberto. 1996. O tratamento *você* em português: uma abordagem histórica. *Fragmenta* 13. 51–82.

Fernández-Ordóñez, Inés. 2006. Del Cantábrico a Toledo: el neutro de materia hispánico en un contexto románico y tipológico (I). *Revista de Historia de la Lengua Española* 1. 67–118.

Fernández-Ordóñez, Inés. 2007. Del Cantábrico a Toledo: el neutro de materia hispánico en un contexto románico y tipológico (II). *Revista de Historia de la Lengua Española* 2. 29–81.

Fernández-Ordóñez, Inés. 2009. Orden de palabras, tópicos y focos en la prosa alfonsí. *Alcanate* 6. 139 – 172.

Fernández-Ordóñez, Inés. 2011. *La lengua de Castilla y la formación del español*. Madrid: Real Academia Española.

Fernández Martín, Elisabeth. 2012. *La oposición* vosotros/ustedes *en la historia del español peninsular (1700–1931)*. Granada: Universidad de Granada.

Fontanella de Weinberg, Beatriz. 1979. La oposición *cantes/cantés* en el español de Buenos Aires. *Thesaurus* 34. 72–83.

Fontanella de Weinberg, Beatriz. 1999. Sistemas pronominales de tratamiento usados en el mundo hispánico. In Ignacio Bosque & Violeta Demonte (eds.), *Gramática descriptiva de la lengua española*, 3 vols. 1399–1425. Madrid: Espasa.

García Godoy, María Teresa. 2012. El tratamiento de *merced* en el español del siglo xvIII. In María Teresa García Godoy (ed.), *El español del siglo xvIII. Cambios diacrónicos en el primer español moderno*, 111–152. Bern: Peter Lang.

García Mouton, Pilar et al. (eds.). 2016. *Atlas Lingüístico de la Península Ibérica (ALPI-CSIC)*. Madrid: CSIC. www.alpi.csic.es.

Givón, Talmy. 1975. Topic, pronoun and grammatical agreement. In Charles Li (ed.), *Subject and topic*, 149–188. New York: Academic Press.

Givón, Talmy. 1990. *Syntax, a functional-typological introduction*. Amsterdam/Philadelphia: John Benjamins.

Hammermüller, Gunther. 2010. Evolución de las formas de tratamiento del español medieval hasta el siglo xvi. In Hummel et al. (eds.), 507–529.

Haspelmath, Martin. 2001. *Language typology and language universals*. Berlin: Mouton de Gruyter.

Höhn, Georg. 2016. Unagreement is an illusion: Apparent person mismatches and nominal structure. *Natural Language and Linguistic Theory* 34,2. 543–592.

Hopper, Paul & Elizabeth Traugott. 2003. *Grammaticalization*. Cambridge: Cambridge University Press.

Hummel, Martin, Bettina Kluge & María Eugenia Vázquez Laslop (eds.). 2010. *Formas y fórmulas de tratamiento en el mundo hispánico*. México DF: El Colegio de México/ Karl-Franzens-Universität Graz.

Joseph, John Earl. 1987. *Eloquence and power: the rise of language standards and standard languages*. London: Blackwell.

Kayne, Richard. 2003. Person morphemes and reflexives in Italian, French and related languages. In Christina Tortora (ed.), *The syntax of Italian dialects*, 102–136. Oxford: Oxford University Press.

Kayne, Richard. 2005. *Movement and silence*. Oxford: Oxford University Press.

Kayne, Richard. 2007. *Some silent first person plurals*. New York: New York University.

Keenan, Edward & Bernard Comrie. 1977. Noun phrase accessibility and universal grammar. *Linguistic Inquiry* 8. 63–99.

Lapesa, Rafael. 1981. *Historia de la lengua española*. Madrid: Gredos.

Lapesa, Rafael. 2000. *Estudios de morfosintaxis histórica del español*. Madrid: Gredos.

Lara, Víctor. 2012. *Ustedes* instead of *vosotros* and *vocês* instead of *vós*: an analysis through the Linguistic Atlas of the Iberian Peninsula (ALPI). *Dialectologia* Special Issue 3. 57–93.

Lara, Víctor. 2015. Allocutive pronouns in Andalusia and their tendency toward standardisation. *Dialectologia* Special Issue 5. 241–260.

Lara, Víctor. 2016. Spontaneous dubbing as a tool for eliciting linguistic data: the case of second person plural inflections in Andalusian Spanish. In John Nerbonne et al. (eds.), *The future of dialects: selected papers from Methods XV*, 261–281. Berlin: Language Science Press.

Lara, Víctor. 2017. La generalización de *vocês* en el portugués europeo continental y su patrón de difusión geográfica. *Hispanic Research Journal* 18,2. 93–117.

Lara, Víctor & Elena Díez del Corral. 2015. Los clíticos de primera persona del plural en las lenguas peninsulares: una visión dialectal. *Zeitschrift für Romanische Philologie* 131,4. 950–977.

Lara, Víctor & Ana Guilherme. 2015. *Quão cortês é você?* O pronome de tratamento *você* em Português Europeu. *Labor Histórico* 1,2. 167–180.

Lopes, Célia Regina dos Santos & Sílvia Regina de Oliveira Cavalcante. 2011. A cronologia do voceamento no português brasileiro: expansão de *você*-sujeito e retenção do clítico *-te*. *Lingüística* 25. 30–65.

Menéndez Pidal, Ramón. 2005. *Historia de la lengua española*. Madrid: RAE/Fundación Menéndez Pidal.

Menon, Odete Pereira da Silva. 2006. A história de *você*. In Maria Guedes et al. (eds.), *Teoria e análise lingüísticas: novas trilhas*, 99–160. Araraquara (São Paulo): Cult. Acadêmica.

O'Flanagan, Patrick. 2008. *Port cities of Atlantic Iberia c. 1500 – 1900*. Aldershot: Ashgate.

Ordóñez, Francisco & Esthela Treviño. 1999. Left dislocated subjects and the pro drop parameter: a case study of Spanish. *Lingua* 107. 39–68.

Papangeli, Dimitra. 2000. Clitic doubling in Modern Greek: a head-complement relation. In Corinne Iten & Ad Neeleman (eds.), *UCL Working Papers in Linguistics 12*, 473–497. London: University College London.

Penny, Ralph. 2004. *Variación y cambio en español*. Madrid: Gredos.

Pike, Ruth. 1972. *Aristocrats and traders. Sevillian society in the sixteenth century*. Cornell: Cornell University Press.

Pinkster, Harm. 1985. Latin cases and valency grammar: some problems. In Christian Touratier (ed.), *Syntaxe et latin: Actes du IIème Congrès International de Linguistique Latine*, 163–90. Aix-en-Provence: Université de Provence.

Pinkster, Harm. 1990. *Latin syntax and semantics*. London: Routledge.

Pla Cárceles, José. 1923. La evolución del tratamiento *vuestra merced*. *Revista de Filología Española* 10. 245–280.

Raposo, Eduardo Buzaglo Paiva et al. 2013. *Gramática do português*, 2 vols. Lisbon: Fundação Calouste Gulbenkian.

RAE-ASALE, Real Academia Española & Asociación de Academias de la Lengua Española. 2009. *Nueva gramática de la lengua española*, 2 vols. Madrid: Espasa.

Rohlfs, Gerhard. 1968. *Grammatica storica della lingua italiana e dei suoi dialetti*. Turin: Einaudi.

Sanchís Guarner, Manuel. 1962. El Atlas Lingüístico de la Península Ibérica (ALPI). In *Trabajos, problemas y métodos. Actas del IX Congreso Internacional de Lingüística y de Filología Románica*, 113–120. Lisbon: Universidade de Lisboa.

Teyssier, Paul. 1982. *História da língua portuguesa*. Lisbon: Sá da Costa.

Vasconcelos, José Leite de. 1897. Mapa dialectológico do continente português. In Manuel António Ferreira-Deusdado (ed.), *Corografia de Portugal*, 510. Lisbon: Guillard, Aillaud et Cª.

Vasconcelos, José Leite de. 1929. Mapa dialectológico português. *Opúsculos* IV. 791–796. Coimbra: Universidade de Coimbra.

Vázquez, Pilar & Maria Albertina Mendes da Luz. 1971. *Gramática portuguesa*. Madrid: Gredos.

Vázquez Laslop, María Eugenia. 2010. Formas de tratamiento en el español de México. In Hummel et al. (eds.), 247–269.

Wechsler, Stephen & Hyun-Jong Hahm. 2011. Polite plurals and adjective agreement. *Morphology* 21. 247–281.

Wechsler, Stephen & Larissa Zlatic. 2000. A theory of agreement and its application to Serbo-Croatian. *Language* 76. 799–832.

Wechsler, Stephen & Larissa Zlatic. 2003. *The many faces of agreement*. Stanford: CSLI Publications.

Wheeler, Max et al. 1999. *Catalan: a comprehensive grammar*. London: Routledge.

Wolfram, Walt & Natalie Schilling-Estes. 2003. Dialectology and linguistic diffusion. In Brian Joseph & Robert Janda (eds.), *The handbook of historical linguistics*, 713–735. Malden: Blackwell.

Célia Regina dos Santos Lopes, Leonardo Lennertz Marcotulio
and Thiago Laurentino de Oliveira

Forms of address from the Ibero-Romance perspective

A brief history of Brazilian *voceamento*

Abstract: The objective of this chapter is to map how the new (sub)systems of second person singular address in Brazilian Portuguese (BP) became organized, examining how address forms in subject position correlate with forms in the other positions (accusative, dative, oblique, genitive). We analyze samples of personal letters written by Brazilians in the 19th and 20th centuries from two regions of the country (Southeast and Northeast). In subject position, the results evidence a gradual loss in use of the pronoun *tu* 'you' to the benefit of the new form *você* 'you', starting in the first half of the 20th century. In the other morphosyntactic contexts, we found a very irregular distribution of the innovative form *você*.

Keywords: Brazilian Portuguese, address system, subject position, nominative, accusative, genitive, dative, oblique

1 Introduction

Ibero-Romance languages such as Portuguese and Spanish historically share parallel processes of change to their address systems that can be compared and contrasted. Having a known common predecessor, inherited from Vulgar Latin, these languages had, by the end of the Middle Ages, the address triad (Pt./Sp.) *tu/tú* 'you-SG', *vós/vos* ('you-PL', used to address a singular interlocutor with deference) and *vossa mercê/vuestra merced* 'lit. Your Mercy', which was then transferred to America. We discuss the grammatical repercussions resulting from these changes in the pronominal system for the second person singular in Brazilian Portuguese (BP), triggered by the inclusion of the new pronoun *você* 'you' (*voceamento*[1]), resulting from *vossa mercê*. While we acknowledge the relatively similar

---

1 *Voceamento* refers to the system in Brazilian Portuguese that uses the *você* pronoun of address as a form of intimacy.

origins, we do not intend to focus on a discussion of the pragmatic differences between the forms from Europe and from various areas in America.

Therefore, the purpose of this chapter is to present, in broad terms, the results from diachronic studies carried out thus far by a large team of researchers from the Project for the History of Brazilian Portuguese (PHPB,[2] acronym in Portuguese). The objective is to present the reorganization in the pronominal system for the second person singular in BP, from a geolinguistic and diachronic perspective, based on an analysis of the forms of address found in personal letters written in different locations in the most populous regions of Brazil during the 19th and 20th centuries: the Southeast and the Northeast.

To that end, this chapter is organized as follows. In Section 2, we provide a simple and broad review of the historical evolution of forms of address in Portuguese, arriving at more recent proposals on the development of the subsystems of address in modern BP. We then compare this development to that of Hispanic American *voseo*[3], discussed in Rona (1967), Fontanella de Weinberg (1992), Carricaburo (1997), as well as in Hummel et al. (2010) and Bertolotti (2015). Our purpose is simply to illustrate a certain parallelism in terms of the positions occupied by forms from each paradigm in the new pronominal systems for the second person in BP and in Hispanic American *voseo*. In Section 3, we present the description of the corpus of letters used in this study and, in Section 4, we discuss the reorganizations that took place in subject position in BP. In Section 5, we describe the other grammatical relations, such as the accusative, dative, oblique and genitive. Finally, we map the results obtained, which will serve as a brief and explanatory foundation for future studies, although this is not the case of the proposal advanced here.

---

2 UFRJ (Universidade Federal do Rio de Janeiro): Célia Lopes, Leonardo Marcotulio, Thiago Oliveira, Rachel Lucena, Janaina Souza, Camila Souza; UFMG (Universidade Federal de Minas Gerais): Márcia Rumeu; UFRN (Universidade Federal do Rio Grande do Norte): Marco Martins, Kássia Moura; UFRPE (Universidade Federal Rural de Pernambuco): Valéria Gomes; UEFS (Universidade Estadual de Feira de Santana): Zenaide Carneiro; Mariana Oliveira, Aroldo Andrade, among others.

3 *Voseo* refers to the pronoun *vos* in Hispanic American Spanish as a form of address in the second person singular used in contexts of intimacy.

2 The Ibero-Romance dynamics of Brazilian *voceamento* and Hispanic *voseo*: a brief review

In order to understand the development of the new second person pronominal system in modern Brazilian Portuguese (BP), we provide a summarized review of the successive changes that took place in the formal and informal address systems over the course of the history of Portuguese. As we aim to show, certain pronominal forms fell into disuse while the new nominal forms began to take on roles typical of the class of pronouns – a process which provoked a major reconfiguration on the level of formality as well as informality. Table 1 sets out the four stages in the evolution of formal (V) and informal (T) second person in subject position.

Table 1: System of address for the formal (V) and informal (T) second person in subject position in Portuguese: four evolutionary stages.

STAGES	I	II	III	IV
CENTURIES	Up to 14th/15th	15th to 18th/19th	End of 19th to first quarter of 20th	During the 20th/21st
Intimacy [– formal] (T)	*tu*	*tu*	*tu*	*tu* / *você*
Politeness [+ formal] (V)	*vós*	*vós* / *vossa mercê*	*você*	*o/a senhor(a)*

Similarly to other Romance languages such as Spanish and French, Portuguese inherited from Vulgar Latin a system with two forms of address for the second person singular: the original pronoun *tu* for the level of informality/proximity and the (primarily plural) pronoun *vós* for the level of formality/distance (*T* and *V*, respectively, according to Brown & Gilman 1960), as we see in stage I. These forms are distinguished on pragmatic grounds: while the former (T) was used in more informal contexts between equals and in relations from superior to inferior, the latter (V) was a formal address form.

Due to the spread of the *vós* form to the less privileged strata of society and its consequent pragmatic bleaching, the address system in Portuguese became more complex by the end of the medieval period, with the introduction of new forms in the realm of formality, as is the case of *vossa mercê* (Faraco 1996), among other nominal forms not mentioned here due to the objectives of this chapter. This new form of address in the second person was originally a noun phrase – therefore, a third person form – which was reanalyzed as a form of address in the second person (Marcotulio 2015). For this reason, due to its nominal origin, the new form of address conforms with the entire verbal and pronominal paradigm of the third person.

It is worth noting that, in stage II in Table 1, the Portuguese system had uniform paradigms for the different syntactic functions: nominative (subject), accusative (direct object), dative (indirect object), oblique (verb and noun complements or adjuncts) and genitive (possessive). In other words, the *tu*, *vós* and *vossa mercê* (after *você*) paradigms were regular and symmetrical. For the *tu* paradigm, we have, respectively, *te*, prep. + *ti, contigo, teu(s)/tua(s)*. For *vós*, we have *vos*, "prep. + *vós*", *convosco, vosso*; and, finally; for *vossa mercê* > *você* we have *o/a, lhe, você*, "prep. + *vossa mercê/você*", *seu(s)/sua(s)*.

In a similar way to what happened with the formal address pronoun *vós*, the new form, *vossa mercê*, also gradually underwent semantic bleaching in its formality/deference feature. At the end of the 15th century, the use of *vossa mercê* was not limited only to addressing the Portuguese king, broadening its scope to other social spheres such as dukes and heirs, then, noblemen and, in the 16th century, bourgeois who had been on the rise since the 12th century. As a result of a grammaticalization process, from the 17th century on, there were already occurrences of the *você* form (Rumeu 2013; Faraco 1996), also evidencing an accelerated phonetic deterioration of the original *vossa mercê*. However, in pragmatic terms, *você* behaved like a multifunctional address form, since it still had features of (V) address until the beginning of the 20th century, occupying the realm of formality on its own. This is due to the fact that the old *vós* was in the process of becoming archaic and was consequently abandoned in the 18th century (Cintra 1972; Faraco 1996), as observed in stage III.

The new grammaticalized pronoun *você* had kept its use as a formal address pronoun in European Portuguese (EP), though its pragmatic value had shifted after the inclusion of new nominal forms such as *o senhor/a senhora* ('Sir/ Madam'). However, *você* in Brazilian Portuguese (BP) has taken a different path. From the first quarter of the 20th century, as a consequence of a faster grammaticalization process (compared to EP), we observe a shift of *você* to the realm of informality in BP (Rumeu 2013). The loss of the *T/V* pragmatic opposition starts to become increasingly clear in Brazilian documents in the 20th century, in which the *tu* and *você* forms coexist as subjects (Rumeu 2013, Souza 2012) in more intimate contexts (stage IV).

In fact, with this overview, we intend to arrive at a single point: to show that the emergence of *você* did not lead to the disappearance of the older pronoun (*tu*), but generated a coexistence of different subsystems of pronominal address in Brazil with geographical, sociolinguistic and pragmatic variations. Despite the indication that, in stage IV, *tu* and *você* would be variants on the level of intimacy, this situation is not exactly the same all over Brazil. Whether *você* is more or less intimate really depends on the presence of *tu*, which is not always present across the country.

Some proposals, such as the one provided by Scherre et al. (2009, 2015) based on research carried out with oral data, have aimed to describe the distribution of the *tu* and *você* forms of address in Brazil. Based on various studies carried out until 2012, the authors propose the existence of six subsystems of address in BP, taking into account the agreement patterns noted between the subject pronoun and the verb. In addition to canonical patterns of agreement (*tu cantas*, *você canta* 'you sing'), the absence of verbal marking for the second person singular (morpheme *-s* in this case) with the *tu* subject is also possible in Brazil: *tu canta∅*. In other words, this is a pattern that points to the absence of markings of canonical agreement or, for some authors, agreement with the verb in the third person. The six subsystems are divided as follows:

1) *Você*: exclusive use of *você* with its reduced variants *ocê* and *cê*. The *você* subsystem, with the verb consistently in the third person singular, is predominantly concentrated in the central area of Brazil. In the Midwestern region, with the exception of Brasília, it has been identified in the states of Goiás, Mato Grosso and Mato Grosso do Sul. In the Southeastern region, it has been identified in Minas Gerais (with the exception of São João da Ponte) and São Paulo (with the exception of Santos). In the Northeastern region, it appears mostly in the capital of Bahia (Salvador). In the Northern region, it has been found thus far in Tocantins. In the Southern region, it has been found in Paraná.

2) *Tu with low verbal agreement*: the prevalence of *tu* is over 60%, with second person verbal agreement (*tu cantas*) below 10%, preferring *tu canta*. This subsystem appears in two regions: North (Amazonas) and South (Rio Grande do Sul).

3) *Tu with high verbal agreement*: the prevalence of *tu* is over 60%, with agreement between 40% and 60%. It also appears at the geographical extremes: North (Pará) and South (Santa Catarina).

4) *Tu/você with low verbal agreement*: moderate use of *tu* below 60%, with agreement below 10%. Identified in the Northeast (Maranhão) and South (Santa Catarina).

5) *Tu/você with average verbal agreement*: moderate use of *tu* below 60%, with agreement between 10% and 39%. It occurs in various states of the Northeastern Region (Maranhão, Piauí, Ceará, Paraíba, Pernambuco), in the Northern Region (Amazonas) and in the Southern Region (Santa Catarina).

6) *Você/tu without agreement*: the use of *tu* ranges from 1% to 90%. Identified in all regions of Brazil, except in the Southern Region: Midwest (Federal District), Southeast (Rio de Janeiro and São Paulo, particularly in Santos), Minas Gerais (in the rural area); Northeast (Maranhão, Tocantins, Bahia outside of the capital); North (Rondônia, Acre, Tocantins).

Map 1 provides a general overview of the subsystems described above.

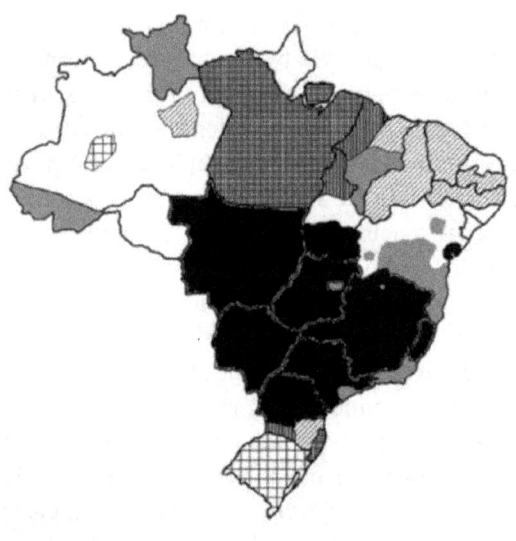

◼ 1 - only *você*, with *você/cê/ocê* variants

▦ 2 - more *tu* (> 60%) and low agreement with *tu* (< 10%)

▦ 3 - more *tu* (> 60%) and high agreement with *tu* (from 40% to 60%)

▥ 4 - *tu/você* (*tu* < 60%) and low agreement with *tu* (<10%)

▨ 5 - *tu/você* (*tu* < 60%) and moderate agreement with *tu* (from 10% to 39%)

▢ 6 - *você/tu* – *tu* from 1% to 90% without agreement

Map 1: Six systems with the second person pronouns *você* and *tu* in Brazilian Portuguese (source: Scherre et al. 2015: 142).

For the discussion that we propose in this chapter, we have reduced the six subsystems in Scherre et al. (2015) to only three because, at this point, we do not intend to take into account the issue of verbal agreement. Therefore, we have three subsystems: (i) *você*, (ii) *tu* and (iii) *você/tu* (Lopes & Cavalcante 2011). This amalgam is especially pertinent for historical studies, since they are based on written texts and the inflectional second person markings appear in most cases. In this sense, we have determined that the following pertain to (i) the *você* subsystem – the individuals/writers who used the *você* pronoun mostly or exclusively in addressing the interlocutor, as exemplified in example (1); (ii) the *tu* subsystem – the individuals/writers who used the *tu* form of address with or without agreement markings, as in example (2); and finally (iii) the *você/tu* subsystem – there is variable use on the part of the individuals/writers, using two forms of address in reference to the interlocutor, as in example (3).

(1)   a nave que *você pilota* há de erguer vôo seguro elevando você às alturas. [first half of the 20th century, MG]

the craft that you pilot has to take flight safe elevating you to the heights.

'the craft that you pilot has to take flight safely lifting you high up'

(2)   Eu soube que *tu vinhas* do dia 4 de Setembro. *pediste* que tua mãe foste te buscar [first half of the 20th century, RJ]

I heard that you came from the day 4 of September. Ø *asked* that your mother went to you get

'I heard that you were coming on the 4th of September. [You] asked your mother to pick you up'

(3)   *Você vê* minha amizade por meu irmão. Quando visite o tumulo de nossa santa mãe não te Ø *esqueças* de pedir pelas minhas intenções. [1first half of the 20th century, RJ]

You see my friendship for my brother. When visit the tomb of our holy mother not you Ø forget to ask for my intentions.

'You see my friendship with my brother. When [you] visit the tomb of our holy mother, do not forget to ask for my intentions'

We must still take into account that the process of change triggered by the inclusion of the grammaticalized pronoun *você* as a subject together with *tu* led to important consequences for the rest of the pronominal paradigm. Table 2 sets out the various forms for *tu* and *você* as part of a symmetrical and uniform paradigm.

However, we argue that the table presented, along the lines proposed, is restricted to normative descriptions and is not representative of address usage of BP speakers. Though the *você* form in the role of subject has become, in most of

Table 2: Symmetrical second person system of address in the various functions.

Nominative (Subject)	Accusative (Non-prepositional complement)	Dative (Complement not necessarily prepositioned)	Oblique (Prepositional complement)	Genitive (Possessive)
tu	*te*	*te, a/para ti*	*prep. + ti, contigo*	*teu(s)/tua(s)*
você	*o/a, você*	*lhe, a/para você*	*prep. + você*	*seu(s)/sua(s)*

Brazil, a variant of *tu* on the level of intimacy, in the other grammatical functions, this use has not developed in the same way. This means that forms from the *tu* paradigm have not completely disappeared, and they are indeed still frequently used in some functions as we intend to show. The new second person paradigm that was established in BP allows, for example, the use of *você* in the role of subject together with the clitic *te* (accusative or dative), as in (4a) and (4b), respectively:

(4) a. *Você₁ sabe que eu te₁ amo.*
         You know that I *you* love
         'You know that I love you'
     b. *Você₁ disse que eu te₁ dei o livro.*
         You said that I *you* gave the book
         'You said that I gave you the book'

Table 3 illustrates all the possibilities of the new second person singular (2SG) paradigm in BP. We highlight the most frequent forms from the two paradigms as we will explain below.

Table 3: Development of a new second person paradigm.

Nominative (Subject)	Accusative (Non-prepositional complement)	Dative (Complement not necessarily prepositioned)	Oblique (Prepositional complement)	Genitive (Possessive)
você/tu	*você, lhe, o/a, te*	*lhe, a/para você, te, a/para ti*	*prep. + você, prep. + ti, contigo*	*seu(s)/sua(s), teu(s)/tua(s)*

Considering the historical background, briefly illustrated in Table 1, the first working hypothesis is that the pronoun *você* was included more quickly into the pronominal system as a new form of reference to 2SG only in subject role. In the other grammatical relations, this pronoun could be found only in some specific positions, such as prepositional complement and genitive (in some contexts and regional areas). Therefore, one of the objectives of this chapter is to diachronically map how the new 2SG (sub)systems of address in BP were established, comparing the subject position with the other positions (accusative, dative, oblique, genitive) (see Section 5). Another hypothesis that will guide this study is based on the similarities of this new paradigm in Brazilian Portuguese with some subsystems of address from Hispanic *voseo* as we intend to briefly show next. These similarities are not related necessarily to the variant forms themselves, but to the places in the pronominal table in which forms from one or the other paradigm were established.

Within a broader contrastive perspective, the two languages had, during the medieval period, (i) come in contact with the system inherited directly from Vulgar Latin in which there were two forms of address distinguished pragmatically for a single interlocutor: (Sp./Pt.) *tú/tu* and *vos/vós*; (ii) included a new nominal form *Vuestra Merced/Vossa mercê*; and finally (iii) undergone a desemanticization of the old address form for deference (*vos/vós*).[4] Unlike Spanish, Portuguese did not experience a shift of *vós* to the realm of intimacy with a consequent loss of the *tu/vós* opposition. Though it deteriorated pragmatically after the inclusion of *Vossa mercê*, *vós* continued to be a form of distancing throughout the medieval period (Domingos 2001; Marcotulio 2014), surviving until the 18th century (at least) as an address form of non-solidarity, when it then underwent a process towards becoming "archaic", in the terms of Cintra (1972) and Faraco (1996), at least in most varieties of Portuguese including the standard forms. The shift from one level to the other that occurs in Portuguese takes place based on the *você* form (resulting from the grammaticalization of *Vossa mercê*), which began to occupy the sphere of intimacy, dissolving the old pragmatic *tu/você* opposition. If, in BP, there is *você* and *tu* and, in Sp. *voseo*, there is *vos* and *tú*, what do these two systems have in common?

It is necessary to have in mind that the processes of implementing forms of distance within the realm of intimacy, triggered initially by issues of a pragmatic nature, can lead to similar repercussions on the grammatical level, specifically with respect to the forms from one paradigm or another that have been established in the address system. What do we mean by this?

There is no single type of *voseo* used across all of Hispanic America. This is due to regional and sociopragmatic differences and the various possible combinations in verbal-pronominal terms – *voseante* pronominal forms combined with *tuteante* verbal forms (*vos cantas*) and vice versa (*tu cantás*). However, as

---

4 The later developments in the various subsystems in Hispanic America are very complex and will not be addressed here due to the specific objective of this chapter. For more details, see, among others, Hummel et al. (2010), and, more recently, Bertolotti (2015).

Bertolotti (2015: 31) points out, "in the *voseante* modalities, the integration of the *vos* paradigm with the object pronouns and original possessives from the *tú* paradigm" is very general. In BP, the same occurs: *você* is more general as a subject and as a prepositional complement (prep. + *você*), while the forms from the *tu* paradigm have been kept as object pronouns (*te* in the accusative and dative). The difference is in the possessive, since *seu* – as well as inflections – from the *você* paradigm predominates, not the *tu* forms (*teu* and inflections).

Bertolotti's study (2015) is very revealing in showing the complexities of the Spanish that arrived in America over the centuries. The author claims that forms of address referred to as *pure* and *mixed* forms coexisted. Table 4 summarizes the distinction: the *pure* forms for each of the existing paradigms are in lines 1, 2 and 3, and the forms *mixed* "by combining elements from lines 1 and 2 or 1 and 3" respectively, are in lines 4 and 5.

Table 4: *Pure* and *mixed* pronominal and verbal forms organized according to their paradigm (adapted from Bertolotti 2015: 152).

	Subject	Clitic complement	Complement of preposition	Possessive	Verb
1.	*vos*	*os*	*vos*	*vuestro/a(s)*	*voseante* (diphthong or monophthong, with or without ending in -*d*)
2.	*tú*	*te*	*ti*	*tu/tuyo/a(s)*	*tuteante*
3.	*usted < vuestra merced*	*lo/la/le*	*usted < vuestra merced*	*su/suyo/a(s)*	in morphological third person
4.	*vos*	*te*	*vos/ti*	*tu/tuyo/a(s)*	*voseante* or *tuteante*
5.	*usted*	*os*	*usted*	*vuestro*	*voseante* or in morphological third person

Bertolotti (2015) attempts to provide an explanation for these new so-called *mixed* forms (for lack of a better term). The author claims that the mix of forms in line 4 of Table 3 does not indicate a *fusion of paradigms* because of the loss of contrast between *vos* and *tú*, as argued by Fontanella de Weinberg (1992: 185). One of the reasons is the fact that the *mix* of forms found in the documents is prior to the desemanticization of *vos* as an address term of trust and deference. Another possible explanation for the establishment of the clitic (*te*) and the possessive *tu/tuyo(a(s)* in the *vos* paradigm (line 4) could be systemic in order to distinguish the singular forms from the plural. However, we consider these arguments to be insufficient in providing an explanation.

The pragmatic and structural motivations to explain the development of the mixed *voseo* paradigm in Hispanic America and the *você* paradigm in BP are fundamental for understanding the processes of change. Nevertheless, our intention here is not to present an explanatory proposal for the phenomenon. For now, we limit ourselves to examining whether the identical positions of the mix of forms in both paradigms are truly coincidental.

What stands out is that in the two paradigms[5] (BP and Sp. *voseo*) the differences almost always occur in the same place: *você/vos* is in the role of subject and prepositional complement (prep. + *você*/prep. + *vos*), but *te/te* is a non-prepositional complement (see Table 5). This non-coincidence occurs in the possessives: *seu/sua/a(s)* in BP and *tu/tuyo/a(s)* in Sp. *voseo*.

Table 5: Comparison of BP and Hispanic American *voseo*: coinciding positions in the second person singular system (2SG).

	Subject	Non-prepositional complement	Prepositional complement	Possessive
PB	*você*	*te*	prep. + *você*	*seu/sua/a(s)*
Hispanic *voseo*	*vos*	*te*	prep. + *vos/ti*	*tu/tuyo/a(s)*

In sum, while Brazilian Portuguese does not yet have a complete descriptive mapping of the current status of its pronominal address system, unlike Hispanic America,[6] it is undeniable that *você* generalized in BP as a subject pronoun together with a more limited presence of *tu* in some geographical areas. In the same way as occurs in various Hispanic America types of *voseo*, specific studies on BP show that the system based on *você* seems to have kept, in some regions in Brazil, the clitic *te* (from the *tu* paradigm) as a direct and indirect object (accusative and dative, respectively), even when the speaker/writer uses *você* in subject position (Oliveira 2014; Souza 2014). The prepositional complements also seem to favor the forms from the *você* paradigm (prep. + *você*) and not those from the *tu* paradigm (prep. + *ti*), similarly to what occurs in the Hispanic *voseante* system, in which "prep. + *vos*" is more frequent than "prep. + *ti*".

We therefore intend to show in this chapter that the symmetrical and uniform systems (*tu-te-ti-contigo-teu*) or (*você-o/a-lhe-* prep. + *você-seu*) are virtually unused in Brazilian Portuguese. We claim that the introduction of *você* in the

---

5 We point out the most frequent forms and not the only possibilities, as we will show in the description of the results for BP.
6 See also Carricaburo (1997: 12–13), Fontanella de Weinberg (1992: 140), Bertolotti (2015: 71), among others.

pronominal system in BP did not occur in the same way in the entire pronominal paradigm. Therefore, we aim to examine the rate at which the changes in the development of the address systems in BP took place. To this end, we will map the results from two Brazilian regions (Southeast and Northeast), representing the relation between subject (nominative) position and the other positions (accusative, dative, oblique and genitive) based on data from letters written by Brazilians at the end of the 19th century and over the course of the 20th century. The intention, as Conde Silvestre (2007: 150) claims, is to determine the stages of the changes in the pronominal structure in the linguistic system, determining the changes that took place more quickly or more slowly.

3 The corpus

To historically rebuild the subsystems of address in Brazil, following the spread of *você* between the end of the 19th century and over the course of the 20th century, we used part of the National PHBP corpus – *Project for the History of Brazilian Portuguese*. The partial studies we used analyzed a total of 1,332 personal letters written by people who belonged to different groups of prominent and non-prominent families. The letters from the Southeastern[7] region total 522: 366 from Rio de Janeiro (1870–1979); 89 from Minas Gerais (1850–1989); and 67 from São Paulo (1870–1930). For the Northeast,[8] the material is slightly broader in scope. There are 810 letters: 383 from Bahia (1810–1990); 123 from Pernambuco (1869–1969); and 304 from Rio Grande do Norte (1916–1925). Although the distribution is not completely balanced, the sample allows us to outline a broad and diversified profile of the community studied. Since the study of forms of address depends on interactive situations, we chose letters of a rather personal nature, such as messages exchanged between family members, friends and couples.

In order to offer an overview that could serve as a foundation for the representation of Brazilian Portuguese, our choice of the two regions analyzed – the Southeast and Northeast – was not random. These regions currently represent 70% of the population of the country (ESTIMATIVAS 2015). Due to the coloniza-

---

7 We will use the following abbreviations for the Southeastern states: RJ (Rio de Janeiro), MG (Minas Gerais) and SP (São Paulo).
8 Similarly, we will use BA (Bahia), PE (Pernambuco) and RN (Rio Grande do Norte) for the Northeastern states.

tion process, the highest population concentration is in coastal areas, particularly in the Southeastern region and in the so-called Northeastern *Zona da Mata*.[9] The Southeastern region, which is the most populous, has more than 85 million inhabitants (42%) and the Northeastern region has more than 56 million (28%). The Southeastern region also has the three most populous metropolitan areas in the country according to the last census in 2010 (São Paulo-SP, with 21,242,939 inhabitants; Rio de Janeiro-RJ, in second place, with 12,330,186; and Belo Horizonte-MG, third, with 5,873,841 inhabitants). Salvador-BA and Recife-PE, in the Northeastern region, are, respectively, the seventh and eighth most populous regions, while Natal-RN is in 19th place (Demografia 2018).

If we go back to the time when the first letters analyzed here were written (1870), we can determine that the two regions studied were the most populous, though with an inverse population density. Some areas of the Northeast, such as Pernambuco, had a higher number of inhabitants than the most populous state in Brazil today (São Paulo). Consequently, the first demographic census in Brazil, carried out in 1872, during the imperial period, indicated that the Northeastern region was the most populous in the country. Brazil had 9,930,478 inhabitants and four of the eight most populous provinces were in the Northeast. The two regions together contained 87.2% of the Brazilian population.

Map 2 illustrates the growth of the main Brazilian capitals from 1872 (Censo demográfico do Brasil from 1872, 2018) until the 2000s. The shading in the colored circles, from lighter to darker shades, shows the locations that had almost 300 thousand inhabitants at the end of the 19th century. In this case, they are São Paulo-SP, Rio de Janeiro-RJ, Salvador-BA and Recife-PE. The size of the circle indicates the size of the population concentration over the course of more than 100 years.

In conclusion, this brief overview of the Brazilian demographics aims to show that the areas selected are representative because they concentrate the largest part of the country's population in the course of more than a century. However, we cannot ignore that we are analyzing texts written by a population with a low literacy rate from the beginning (in the 19th century, less than 40% of the population was literate). This means that the results obtained can only be indicators of the path of change in progress.

---

9 This refers to a narrow, coastal plain that runs along the Northeastern edge of the country and has a tropical climate.

Crescimento das capitais

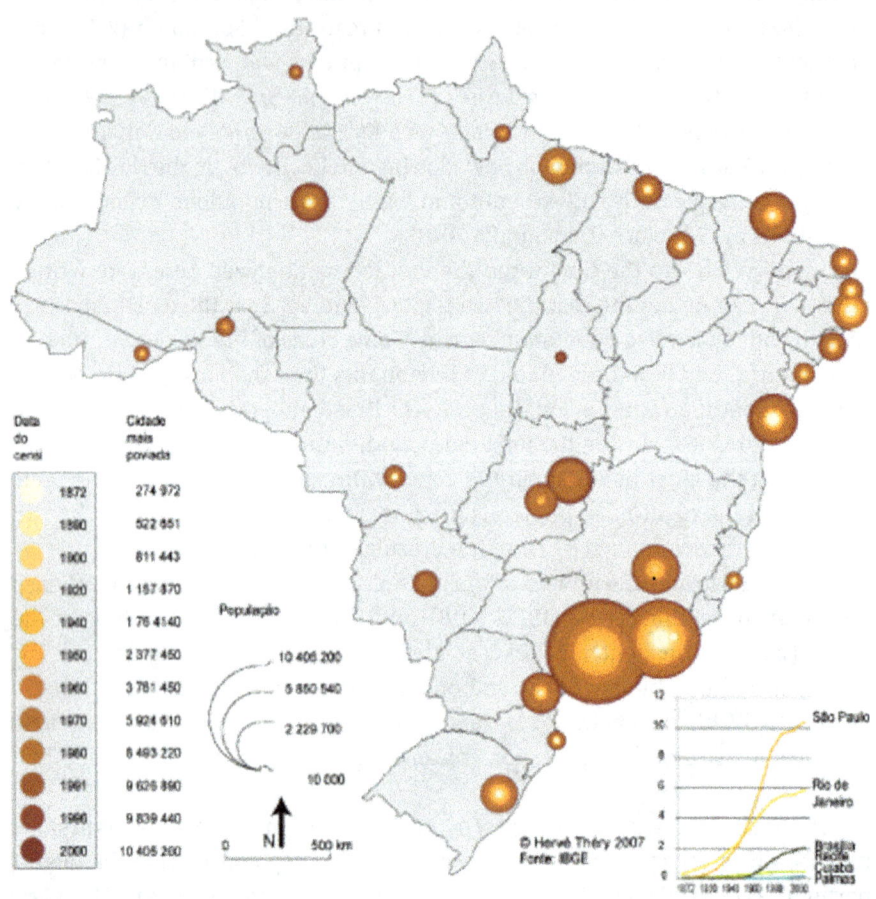

Map 2: Growth of the main Brazilian capitals from 1872 to 2000 (source: *Wikimedia Commons, the free media repository*. 25 Feb 2014, 21 Sept. 2018, https://commons.wikimedia.org/w/index.php?title=File:ARCHELLA_E_THERY_Img_07.png&oldid=117330012).

4 The subject position

4.1 *Você* and *tu* in subject position in letters from the 19th and 20th centuries: Southeastern region

Synchronic studies based on oral data point out that the Southeastern region is not homogeneous in its use of subsystems of address in subject position. On the one hand, there is a mixed subsystem (*você~tu*) in the more coastal area, represented here by Rio de Janeiro (Paredes 1996; Santos 2012). On the other hand, there is the almost absolute predominance of *você* and its variants (*ocê*, *cê*, etc.) in the more interior states, such as São Paulo and Minas Gerais (Scherre et al. 2015; Peres 2006: 131; Mota 2008).

The establishment of this current system in the Southeastern region needs to be mapped in socio-historical terms. The various analyses carried out, based on the letters produced by residents in Rio de Janeiro, São Paulo and Minas Gerais, between the end of the 19th century and over the course of the 20th century, show that the presence of the two variant forms is very old. In the documents analyzed, we can clearly see senders using only *você*, only *tu*, or the two forms in variation in the same letter for their recipients. Graph 1 brings together the results from these three locations in the Southeastern region, adapted from Lopes & Souza (2018), Rumeu, Cruz & Cardos (2018) and Balsalobre & Monte (2018).

The graph presents the historical behavior of the use of *você* in relation to the *tu* pronoun in subject position in three locations in the Southeastern region.[10] As we mentioned, the sample of letters analyzed here is not entirely comparable if we take into account, for example, that the sample of letters for São Paulo only goes up to 1930. Nevertheless, we can still comment on the dissemination of *você* in subject position in the letters from this region.

Although the path of each line in Graph 1 is different, we can see that from the end of the 19th century (1870–1879) until the mid-20th century – approximately 1940 – the use of second person forms of address in the letters from Rio de Janeiro and São Paulo was equivalent, as distinct from what was observed in the letters from Minas Gerais. While in the former two regions *você* address was very little used – more so in the letters from Rio de Janeiro[11] than in those from São Paulo – the letters

---

10 Since Graph 1 only shows the results of *você*, the data regarding *tu* can be understood in a complementary way. For example, 31% of *você* means that there is a 69% rate of *tu* at the same time.
11 The historical explanations for the more frequent use of *tu* in Rio de Janeiro are very complex and are usually associated with the establishment of the Portuguese Court in the 19th century and the constant arrival of Portuguese to the then capital of the country.

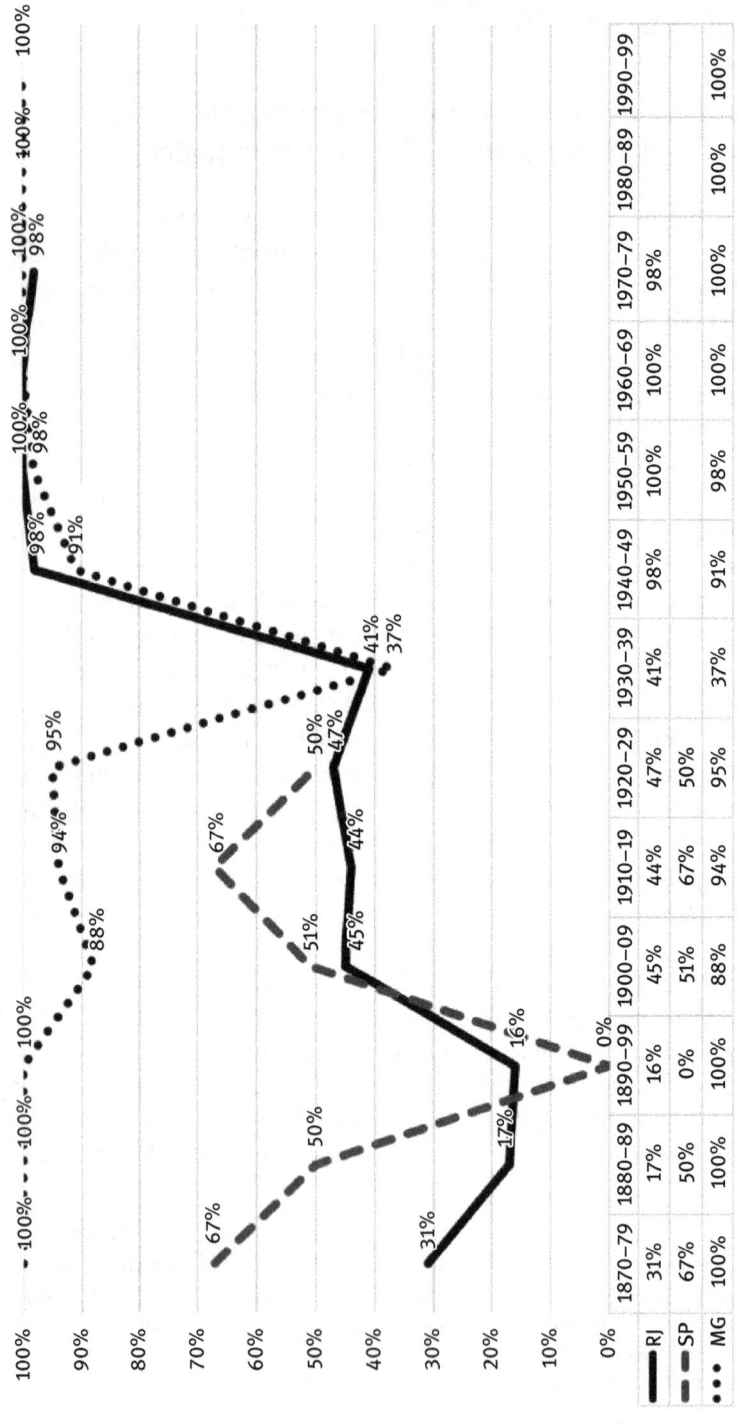

	1870–79	1880–89	1890–99	1900–09	1910–19	1920–29	1930–39	1940–49	1950–59	1960–69	1970–79	1980–89	1990–99
RJ	31%	17%	16%	45%	44%	47%	41%	98%	100%	100%	98%	100%	
SP	67%	50%	0%	51%	67%	50%	37%	91%	98%	100%	98%	100%	
MG	100%	100%	100%	88%	94%	95%	37%	91%		100%	100%	100%	100%

Graph 1: *Você* in subject position: Southeastern region.

from the Minas Gerais writers indicate an almost exclusive use of *você* with rates very close to 100%. The point of intersection seems to be in the years 1930–40, in which the curves of Rio de Janeiro and Minas Gerais overlap with low rates of *você* in the two locations and they continue to overlap from then on, revealing, however, a generalization of *você* in the two locations with frequencies closer to 100%.

Lopes & Souza (2018) clearly point out the rate at which *você* spread by identifying different behaviors of the innovative pronominal form over time. At the end of the 19th century, the use of *você* was more frequent than *tu* in asymmetrical and less intimate relations between writers, maintaining the politeness features from *vossa mercê*. The use of *você* served as an attenuation strategy in favor of linguistic politeness and for marking greater distance, which guaranteed a less invasive tone in the interaction, as shown in example (5).

(5) Peço-te pois *intenderes* com <u>elle</u> esperando qelleasuma ao <u>meo</u> pedido, pelo <u>q</u> mui agradecido. Podia <u>tambem</u> escrever a seoPae, e <u>Dr</u> J. P. <u>porem</u> entendo não ser <u>necessario</u> só basta <u>q</u> *você* <u>si</u> interessou. [1st half of the 20th century, RJ]

[I] ask-you since *to-understand* with him waiting that he accept to my request, for that very grateful. Could also to-write to your Father, and Dr. J.P. though [I] understand not to-be necessary only enough that you yourself interested.

'I ask that you come to an understanding with him hoping that he accepts my request, for which I am very grateful. I could also write to your father, and Dr. J.P., though I understand that it is not necessary, only that you are interested'

In example (5), we see a motivated use of *você*. The sender gives an indirect order in a request, which favors the use of an attenuating address form. In the letter, in which (null) *tu* predominates almost categorically, the intruder *você* is not a pronominal variant, but a form of address that minimizes the request made. The uncle claims that it was not necessary to make the request to the father of the receiver, who was an important politician, since he was interested in solving the problem in question.

At the beginning of the 20th century, the use of *você* could still mark a certain deference, mainly in letters by women, as in example (6). Among men, even though there was asymmetry between them, *tu* prevailed, which was not common or adequate for women, as illustrated in example (7).

(6) Afonsinho Saude te desejo e a todos os seus. Vamos indo sem novidade, E. tem melhorado da tosse. *Vossé* querendo me favoreçer, compra para vossé. Não quero te caçetear, dê um beijo nos pequenos e com M. aceite um abraço

saudoso de Sua tia e ama cinçera A. Não repare a letra q estou muito sem vista. (aunt-nephew) [1st half of the 20th century, RS]

Afonsinho Health you [I]wish and to all of yours. [We]go going without news, E. has improved of-the cough. *You* wanting me to favor, buy for you. Not [I]want you upset, give a kiss in-the little-ones and with M. accept a hug missing of Your aunt and love sincere A. Not notice the letter that I am very much without seeing

'Afonsinho I wish health to you and yours. We have had no news. E.'s cough has improved. You are trying to help me, buy it for yourself. I don't want to upset you, give a kiss to the little ones and with M. accept a beloved hug from your aunt and sincere love A. Ignore my writing since my sight has been greatly lacking'

(7) Pela tua carta de 1º vejo os motivos que *tens* para não *escreveres* todos os dias o que me pareciam justos. *Escrevas* quando *puderes*, ao menos uma vez por semana. (father-son) [2nd half of the 19th century, RJ]

For your letter of 1st [I]see the motives that *[you]have* to not *[you]write* all the days the that me seem fair. *[You]write* when *[you]can*, at least one time a week.

'From your letter, I can already see the reasons you have for not writing every day, which seems fair to me. You write when you can, at least once a week'

Gradually, the *você* form started to be used in the same functional contexts as *tu*, including more informal and intimate contexts – see example (8). The *você* form also began to take the place of *tu* in symmetrical relations: a functional space that was assumed gradually.

(8) Pode *você* bem calcular o vasio infinito que se fez na minha vida. [1st half of the 20th century, RJ]

Can *you* well to-calculate the empty infinite that is done in my life

'You can easily calculate the infinite void that you have left in my life'

The spread of *você* over the course of the 20th century is related mainly to the dissemination of its use in egalitarian relations, as in example (9). At the end of the 20th century, the *você* pronoun replaced the older strategy with its expansion to contexts typical of *tu*. As a strategy of neutral reference, the *você* pronoun became a versatile strategy for the new social roles of contemporary societies.

(9) São três e meia da manhã de domingo acabei de chegar do samba e ao subir me entregaram sua carta que em poucas linhas disse muitas coisas bonitas coisas que *você* sabe que sinto mas que não consigo passar para o papel. [2nd half of the 20th century, RJ]

Are three and half of morning of Sunday [I]ended of to-arrive of-the samba and to to-go up me [they]delivered your letter that in few lines said many things pretty things that *you* know that [I]feel but that no [I]can to-pass to the paper

'It is three-thirty on Sunday morning and I have just arrived from the samba and when I went up, they gave me your letter, which in a few lines said many things, beautiful things that you know that I feel, but I cannot put on paper'

In conclusion, the results obtained from the letters written in the Southeastern region show that the spread of *você* took place mainly from the mid-20th century on. With rates of frequency fluctuating a great deal in each location, we determined the presence of *tu* at the end of the 19th century and at the beginning of the 20th century, mainly in Rio de Janeiro, due to the strong movement of Lusitanian influence that occurred upon the arrival of the Portuguese Court in the beginning of the 19th century and the constant arrival of the Portuguese until the 1940s. The letters from Minas Gerais reveal very consistent behavior over the course of the entire period analyzed, with widespread and regular use of *você*.

4.2 *Você* and *tu* in subject position in letters from the 19th and 20th centuries: Northeastern region

The situation in the Northeastern region is very complex, with variation between *você* and *tu* in most of the states. The regional distinctions in the Northeast are limited to the presence or absence of agreement with the *tu* pronoun, which does not exceed 40%, according to Scherre et al. (2015). As in the Southeast, there are areas with predominant use of *você*, as is the case of the capital of Bahia (Salvador). In the rest of the state, and in the others analyzed (Pernambuco and Rio Grande do Norte) the subsystem is mixed: *você~tu* (Lucchesi et al. 2009: 83–95; Almeida 2012; Amor Divino 2008; Sette 1980: 148–168; Coelho da Silva 2015).

The results from letters written at the end of the 19th century and over the course of the 20th century are presented in the Graph 2. They were taken from the studies by Andrade, Oliveira & Carneiro (2018); Gomes & Lopes (2018) and Moura & Martins (2018).

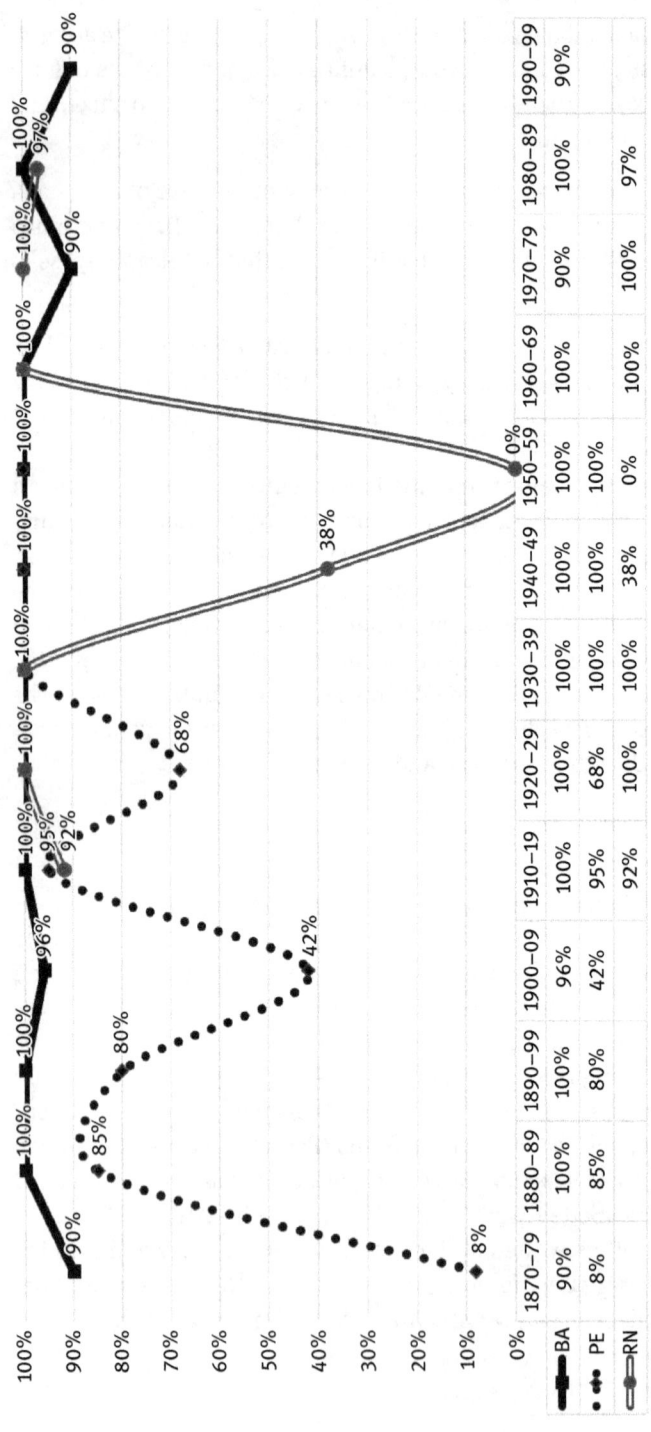

	1870–79	1880–89	1890–99	1900–09	1910–19	1920–29	1930–39	1940–49	1950–59	1960–69	1970–79	1980–89	1990–99
BA	90%	100%	100%	96%	100%	100%	100%	100%	100%	100%	90%	100%	90%
PE	8%	85%	80%	42%	95%	68%	100%	100%	100%	100%			
RN					92%	100%	100%	38%	0%	100%	100%	97%	

Graph 2: *Você* and *tu* in subject position: Northeastern region.

As in Graph 1 representing the Southeast, Graph 2 reveals the spread of *você* in the Northeast starting mainly in the second half of the 20th century. In comparative terms, the behavior of the three Northeastern locations is not the same, with areas of strong variation between *tu* and *você*, as observed in Pernambuco, and areas of stability, such as in the letters from Bahia. The results from Rio Grande do Norte span practically the entire 20th century. As seen in the graph of the Southeastern region, here we also observe an abrupt and rapid decline in the 1950s. Nevertheless, Graph 2 with data from the letters from the Northeast indicates greater stability in the use of *você* over the course of the period analyzed when compared to what was observed in the Southeast.

Finally, in the written samples from the two regions, in general, a gradual loss of the *tu* pronoun took place in favor of the new grammaticalized *você* form. This loss was observed mostly in the first half of the 20th century. The use of these forms, however, presents a quantitative distribution in geographical terms. As Lopes et al. (2017) argue, the results point to the multifunctional behavior of *você*, since the new pronominal form loses the semantics of power, preserved from the original *vossa mercê*, moving into the space of solidarity.

Map 3 illustrates the changes in the use of *você* at three moments in time across the Brazilian territory as a whole, and demonstrates the gradual and continuous generalization of *você* in the main areas of the two regions studied. The colour scale used goes from black to light gray: the darker the color, the greater the use of *tu*, and the lighter the color, the higher the rates of use of the *você* pronoun.

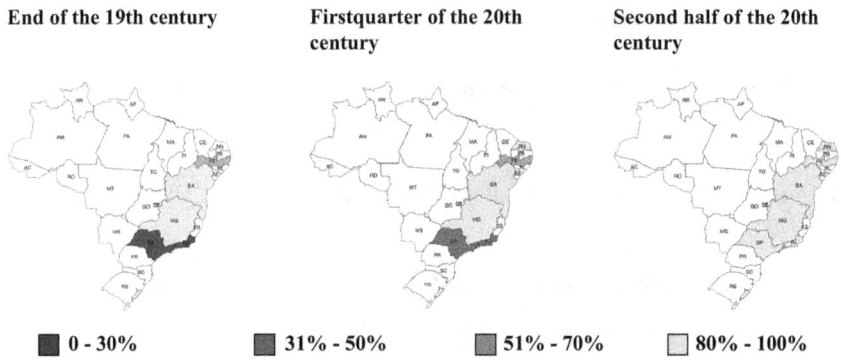

End of the 19th century **First quarter of the 20th century** **Second half of the 20th century**

■ 0 - 30%   ■ 31% - 50%   ■ 51% - 70%   □ 80% - 100%

Map 3: The second person subject position in BP: rates of use of *você* at three moments in time.

The maps illustrate the dissemination of *você* in relation to *tu* in subject position in the recent history of BP and indicate its expansion into the Southeast and Northeast regions. We observe the rise of the frequencies of *você* between the end of the 19th century and the first quarter of the 20th century, spreading with greater intensity in the second half of the 20th century.

To a certain extent, the subsystems of address seen from a diachronic perspective correspond to the current existing subsystems in BP, such as those outlined by Scherre et al. (2009, 2015). The letters from writers in Bahia – predominantly a *você* subsystem – reveal a consistent use of this form over the course of the period analyzed. This behavior is very similar to that seen in Minas Gerais in Graph 1. The results from Pernambuco – currently a *você/tu* subsystem – are similar to those seen in Rio de Janeiro, with alternation between the two variant forms until the mid-20th century.

In addition to the general results from each location, it is also worth separately investigating the data found in the letters in which writers use the *você* form exclusively in subject position. To this end, we consider three possibilities as the criteria for analyzing the data:

a) *exclusive tu*: the cases in which the sender used only the *tu* pronoun (null or overt) as a subject in their letters, as in example (10):

(10) **tu** resolverás como entenderes, meu querido anjo, e, eu cegamente cumprirei o que **tu** ordenares. [1st half of the 19th century, RJ]

you will resolve as [you]understand, my dear angel, and, I blindly will-fulfill what **you** order

'you will sort it out the way you think is best, my dear angel, and, I will blindly do what you wish'

b) *exclusive você*: the cases in which the sender used only *você* as a subject in the letters analyzed:

(11) **Você** não imagina como Marília está levada. [2nd half of the 20th century, MG]

You not imagine as Marília is naughty

'You cannot believe how naughty Marília is'

c) *mixed tu/você*: the cases in which the sender used both forms in the same letter in subject position:

(12) **Tu** não deves pensar em bobagens ... **você** sabe perfeitamente que só ati é que eu amo. [1st half of the 20th century, RJ]

You not should to-think in nonsense ... *you* know perfectly that only to-you that I love.

'You should not think about nonsense (...) you know perfectly well that I only love you'

If the writer used *você* in the role of subject, what forms can be found in the other grammatical relations? Are there differences across regions? Which forms constitute the Brazilian *voceamento* system? We will discuss these questions in the following section.

5 The behavior of other second person functions in Brazilian letters from the 19th and 20th centuries: accusative, dative, oblique and genitive

The objective of this section is to present the consequences of the spread of *você* on second person verbal complement relations (accusative, dative and oblique), traditionally known as "oblique pronouns" (tonic and atonic), and on possessive pronouns (genitive relation). Although there is not complete correspondence between the Portuguese and Latin pronominal forms, considering the variation of case, we will adopt the following terminology for the verbal complements and the second person possessives:

a. *accusative (AC)* – complement or direct object (DO);
b. *dative (DAT)* – complement or indirect object (IO), realized as a clitic or as a prepositional phrase. In this latter case, there is also the possibility of cliticization using *lhe*;
c. *oblique (OBL)* – prepositional phrase complement, which cannot be substituted by a clitic;
d. *genitive (GEN)* – complement or nominal adjunct, represented by a possessive pronoun.

If, as we have seen, the *você* pronoun was incorporated over time into the BP address system as a variant of the older *tu* pronoun, what happened in the other syntactic positions? Did the forms from the *você* paradigm start being used in all of the syntactic functions at the same rate that it was used in subject position? After the inclusion of *você*, how did the *voceante* system in BP develop in the rest of the pronominal system?

5.1 The variants of second person accusative complements in Brazilian letters from the 19th and 20th centuries

We consider accusatives to be the second person pronominal forms that take on the role of direct object. In the traditional perspective of maintaining the same paradigm or "uniformity of address", the original second person form in the accusative case would only be the clitic *te*. However, upon the inclusion of *você* in the system, there are other variants in BP that belong to the *você* paradigm. In this case, they are the *você* form itself and the clitics from this paradigm, *o/a* and *lhe*.

The variation of accusative forms associated with the *você* paradigm is more diversified due to the origin of this form and to the alterations within the pronominal paradigm. Resulting from a nominal expression (*vossa mercê*), which required the verb to be in the third person singular, the *você* form kept some of the morpho-syntactic properties of its original form – even though its semantic-discursive interpretation became a second person reference. Unlike the original second person pronoun *tu*, the grammaticalized form (*você*) can appear in all of the syntactic positions without altering its form. Consequently, the *você* pronoun brings to the second person pronominal system forms originally from the third person system.

In the accusative function, the following can occur: the tonic form *você*, the original third person clitic – *o(s)/a(s)* – in addition to the third person dative clitic (*lhe*), which also began to function as an accusative in reference to the second person.

In sum, if there was symmetry or a maintenance of forms from the same paradigm, the clitic *te* (example (13)) would be used with the *tu* pronoun in subject position. However, if the writer addresses their interlocutor with *você*, in this case, they would use the forms corresponding to the *você* paradigm, originally in the third person: lexical pronoun *você* (example (14)), the clitics *o/a* (example (15)), the clitic *lhe* (example (16)) and, even the null object (example (17)), which is very rare in this role.

(13) No momento mais triste de minha vida **te** <u>encontrei</u>. [1st half of the 20th century, RJ]

In-the moment most sad of my life **you** [I]found

'At the saddest moment in my life, I found you'

(14) a nave que você pilota há de erguer voo seguro <u>elevando</u> **você**. [1st half of the 20th century, MG]

the craft that you pilot has to take flight safe elevating *you* to the heights

'the craft that you pilot has to take flight safely lifting you high up'

(15) Percizava v*ello* para sentar as couzas milhor. [2nd half of the 19th century, BA]

Needed see-*you* to sit the things better

'I had to see you to settle things better'

(16) Com affecto *lhe* abraço e sou sua irmã. [2nd half of the 19th century, RJ]

With affection *you* [I]hug and [I]am your sister

'With affection, I hug you and I am your sister'

(17) tu sabes como me sinto, cada vez mais cego, e cada vez querendo Ø *amar* mais. [1st half of the 20th century, RJ]

you know how me [I]feel, each time more blind, and each time wanting Ø *to-love* more

'you know how I feel, increasingly blind, and increasingly wanting to love you more'

Table 6 presents the distribution of the variant accusative forms in the personal letters from the locations studied in the two regions.

Table 6: Distribution of second person accusative variants in Brazilian letters by region (19th-20th centuries).

Accusative		*te*	*você*	*lhe*	*o/a*	Ø	Total
Southeast	Rio de Janeiro (RJ)	337/433 78%	29/433 7%	17/433 4%	40/433 9%	10/433 2%	443/829 53%
	Minas Gerais (MG)	21/42 50%	3/42 7%	3/42 7%	15/42 35%		42/829 5%
	São Paulo (SP)	15/34 44%	2/34 6%	6/34 18%	11/34 32%		34/829 4%
Northeast	Bahia (BA)	7/62 9%	1/62 1%	28/62 38%	26/62 35%		62/829 7%
	Pernambuco (PE)	14/45 31%	6/45 13%	6/45 14%	19/45 42%		45/829 5%
	Rio Grande do Norte (RN)	151/213 71%	18/213 8%	40/213 19%	4/213 02%		213/829 25%
Total		530/829 64%	59/829 7%	100/829 12%	127/829 15%	10/829 1%	829

In terms of the overall results, the clitic *te* was the most frequent accusative strategy in the sample, in 530 of a total of 829 occurrences (approximately 65% of the corpus). The second and third most frequent strategies, respectively, were well under 20%. They are, in this case, the accusative clitic *o/a* with 15% and *lhe* with 12%.

Considering the partial results, by region, *te* predominated in the Southeastern region and in one Northeastern state (RN). In the others, there was more frequent use of specific forms from the *você* paradigm, as in Bahia, in which *lhe* (38%) and *o/a* (35%) were more frequent, and in Pernambuco, with 42% using *o/a*. It is worth noting as well that in none of the locations studied in our analysis did the *você* form, used itself in the accusative role, register a frequency higher than 10%. In the majority of the states, the accusative *você* was the third most used strategy, amounting to only a few occurrences.

We must also mention some rarer occurrences, as in the case of the zero identified in the letters from Rio de Janeiro. Most of the time, the zero accusative occurs in coordinated structures of the type (*te estima e Ø adora* 'esteem you and adore Ø).

In order for us to determine how the *voceante* paradigm developed in BP, we will now analyze the variant forms of the accusative that occurred only when the writer used the *você* pronoun as the exclusive subject in their letters. In principle, if the system of address were symmetrical, we would expect the accusative clitic *te* to occur only in letters with the *tu* subject. Similarly, accusative forms from the *você* paradigm (*você/lhe/o,a*) would occur with the *você* subject. Table 7 sets out the results.

Table 7: Distribution of second person accusative variants in letters with the *você* subject, by Brazilian region (19th-20th centuries).

Accusative		2P Accusative forms and the use of the *você* subject				
		te	*você*	*lhe*	*o/a*	*Ø*
Southeast	Rio de Janeiro	60/118 51%	19/118 16%	10/118 9%	26/118 22%	3/118 2%
	Minas Gerais	15/29 51%	5/29 17%		9/29 31%	
	São Paulo	1/3 33.3%	1/3 33.3%		1/3 33.3%	
Northeast	Bahia	2/47 4%	1/47 2%	24/47 51%	20/47 43%	
	Pernambuco	1/29 3%	5/29 17%	6/29 21%	17/29 59%	
	Rio Grande do Norte			3/3 100%		
Total		79/229 35%	31/229 13%	43/229 19%	73 32%	3/229 1%

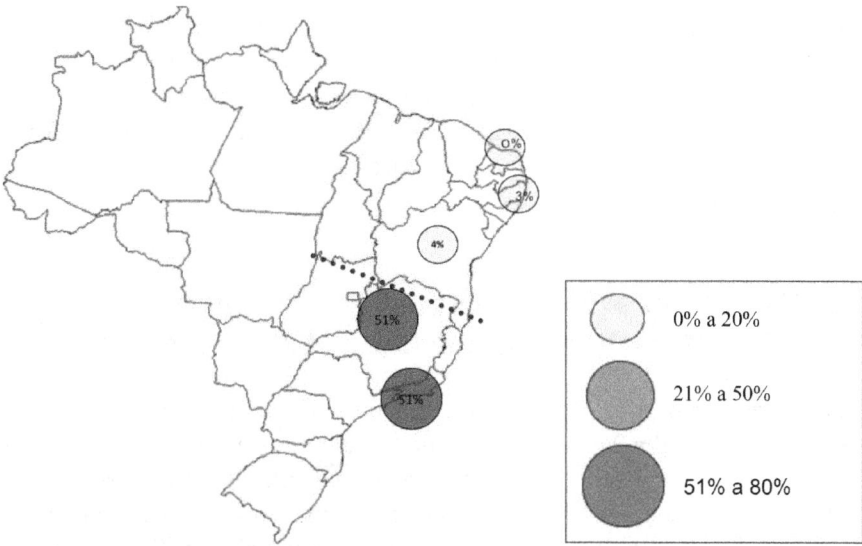

Map 4: The clitic accusative *te* in letters with the *você* subject (19th-20th centuries)[12].

As can be seen in Table 7, the results obtained based on cross-referencing the exclusive use of *você* in subject position and the accusative second person forms reveal that the clitic *te* (from the *tu* paradigm) was used as the most frequent strategy, at 35%. This predominance of *te* did not occur in both regions: only in the letters from the Southeast were there rates over 50% in Rio de Janeiro and Minas Gerais. In the Northeastern region, the behavior differed, since the forms belonging to the *você* paradigm predominated with differences regarding the frequencies of each strategy. While the letters from Bahia and Rio Grande do Norte revealed the use of *lhe* with respective frequencies of 51% and 100%, in Pernambuco, the *o/a* clitic was the most frequently used, at 59%. Finally, the letters from São Paulo had the lowest number of occurrences (only three), which does not provide robust results. In this location, there was only a single occurrence of *te*, *você* and *o/a*.

The coexistence of the *tu* and *você* subsystems of address led to the development of a paradigm towards Brazilian *voceamento*: *você* began to be used in subject role, but the clitic *te* was kept as an accusative complement, most frequently used in the most populous region of Brazil (Southeast), as set out in Map 4.

---

12 We have not mentioned the results from São Paulo on the map due to the low number of occurrences (three occurrences of accusative forms in letters with *você*).

The regional differences in Brazil evidence the speed with which this change took place in the second person pronominal system at a time in which we can identify distinct systems in the Brazilian geographical space. Regarding the accusative, we observed a faster implementation of forms from the *você* paradigm in the Northeast than in the Southeast, which most frequently used the original clitic *te*.

5.2 The variants of second person dative complements in Brazilian letters from the 19th and 20th centuries

We analyzed as datives the internal arguments of transitive and ditransitive verbs that receive the thematic role of *target* or *source* of an action. Datives, differently from accusatives, prototypically represent entities with the [+animate] feature. In representing the second person singular in Brazilian Portuguese, we can find datives in the form of clitics, prepositional phrases (in most cases, with the prepositions *a* or *para*[13]) and also with no phonetic realization (null dative).

Originally, the second person dative in Portuguese was represented by forms from the *tu* paradigm: the clitic *te* (example (18)) and the prepositional phrase *a/para ti* (example (19)). With the emergence of the new *você* pronoun, however, new forms became licensed for the dative, like the clitic *lhe* (example (20)) and the prepositional phrase *a/para você* (examples (21) and (22)). In the following examples, we illustrate the variants of the dative with data taken from the corpus under analysis, to which we add the possibility of a null dative (example (22)).

(18)   O Tito vai bem, hoje vai *te* <u>escrever</u>, elle gostou muito do Rio. [1st half of the 20th century, RJ]

The Tito goes well, today go **you** to-write, he liked much of Rio

'Tito is doing well, today he will write to you, he liked Rio very much'

---

13 There are few cases in which the dative can be introduced by a different preposition. For example, when this argument receives the thematic role of *source* from the verb, it is more natural (if not the only possibility) for it to be introduced by the preposition *de*, especially in BP: *O João tomou a carta **de** você* ('John took the letter from you') – *O João **lhe** tomou a carta* ('John you took the letter'); *A Maria roubou **de** ti um beijo* ('Maria stole from you a kiss') > *A Maria **te** roubou um beijo* ('Maria you stole a kiss').

(19) se não fosse isso seria capaz de ficar a noite toda <u>escrevendo</u> *para ti*. [1st half of the 20th century, RJ]

if not were this would-be capable of to-stay the night all writing *to you*

'if it weren't for this, I could stay up all night writing to you'

(20) Hontem telegraphei a # Velloso para *lhe* <u>dar</u> mais dinheiro. [1st half of the 20th century, PE]

Yesterday [I]telegraphed to # Velloso to *you* to-give more money

'Yesterday I telegraphed Velloso to give you more money'

(21) Muito <u>agradeço</u> *a você*, mamãe. [1st half of the 20th century, MG]

Much [I]thank *to you*, mom

'Thank you very much, mom'

(22) Lucinha, <u>mandei</u> uma foto *prá você*. [2nd half of the 20th century, RN]

Lucinha, [I]sent a photo *to you*

'Lucinha, I sent a photo to you'

(23) Fora o que já ø <u>contei</u>, não tenho feito nada de extraordinariamente interessante. [2nd half of the 20th century, RJ]

Out of what already ø [I]told, not [I]have done nothing of extraordinarily interesting

'Except for what I've already told you, I haven't done anything extraordinarily interesting'

As we have already discussed in relation to the accusative, the main objective of this investigation is to determine to what extent the forms related to the *você* paradigm accompanied the new subject pronoun. Moreover, we pose another question: does the implementation of the innovative forms take place in a generalized way in Brazilian Portuguese or is it possible to find dialectical differences? In Table 8, we present the distribution of the variant forms of the dative identified in the corpus of personal letters.

Overall, we can see that the dative clitics *te* (from the *tu* paradigm) and *lhe* (from the *você* paradigm) were the most frequent variants in the entire sample: together, these forms correspond to more than 70% of the occurrences observed. The third most

Table 8: Distribution of second person dative variants in Brazilian letters by region (19th-20th centuries).

Dative		te	lhe	a/para ti	a/para você	prep. + você	Ø	Total
Southeast	Rio de Janeiro	464/811 58%	92/811 11%	25/811 3%	49/811 6%		181/811 22%	811/1694 48%
	Minas Gerais	41/136 30%	63/136 46%		13/136 10%		19/136 14%	136/1694 8%
	São Paulo	53/90 59%	33/90 36%		4/90 5%			90/1694 5%
Northeast	Bahia	15/251 06%	188/251 75%		7/251 3%		41/251 16%	251/1694 15%
	Pernambuco	32/214 15%	158/214 73%	8/214 4%	16/214 8%			214/1694 13%
	Rio Grande do Norte	60/192 31%	93/192 48%	3/192 2%	25/192 13%	11/192 6%		192/1694 11%
Total		665/1694 39%	627/1694 37%	36/1694 2%	114/1694 7%	11/1694 1%	241/1694 14%	1694

frequent variant was the null dative (14%), which did not occur in all of the letters in the sample. In relation to prepositional phrases, we observe that the prepositional phrase *a/para você* was the most frequent (7% – 114/1694) in the two regions, in comparison to *a/para ti* (2% – 36/1694), which was very sporadic in the letters analyzed.

We see a clear difference between the two regions regarding the most frequent dative strategies. This enables us to outline an isogloss to determine the forms in competition, with areas of transition. On the one hand, in the Northeastern region, the clitic *lhe* was predominant in the three states analyzed. On the other, in the Southeastern region, the clitic *te* predominated in most of them (Rio de Janeiro and São Paulo), with the exception of Minas Gerais, in which *lhe* overlaps with the clitic dative *te*. It is worth noting that the state of Minas Gerais shares a geographical border with each region.

Adopting the same perspective used for the analysis of the accusative, we now examine the consequences for the second person dative in a more *voceante* paradigm. Therefore, in Table 9, we chose only those occurrences of the second person dative in the letters in which the author exclusively used the *você* pronoun in subject position.

Table 9: Distribution of the second person dative variants in letters with the *você* subject, by Brazilian region (19th-20th centuries).

Dative		2P Dative forms and the use of the *você* subject					
		te	*lhe*	*a/para ti*	*a/para você*	*prep. + você*	*Ø*
Southeast	Rio de Janeiro	85/275 31%	75/275 27%	1/275 1%	34/275 12%		80/275 29%
	Minas Gerais	19/107 18%	62/107 58%		11/107 10%		15/107 14%
	São Paulo	7/16 44%	07/16 44%		2/16 12%		
Northeast	Bahia	4/206 2%	164/206 80%		7/206 3%		31/206 15%
	Pernambuco		134/149 90%		13/149 10%		
	Rio Grande do Norte		42/49 86%		7/49 14%		

The results seen here are not so different from those in Table 8 with all of the data. In the data taken from the samples from the Southeastern region, we observe that even in the letters in which the sender uses only *você* in subject position, we find fairly high rates of the *te* clitic: 44% in the SP sample, 31% in the RJ sample and 18% in the MG sample. By contrast, the data collected in the samples from the Northeastern region suggest a more significative implementation of the *lhe* clitic, associated with the use of the *você* subject: 80% in the BA sample, 90% in the PE sample and 86% in the RN sample.

In conclusion, we can say that there is variation in the use of second person dative clitics that is directly correlated with the geographical variable: *lhe* in the Northeastern region and *te* in the Southeastern region, with the state of Minas Gerais marking an area of transition, at least, in the letters analyzed (Map 5).

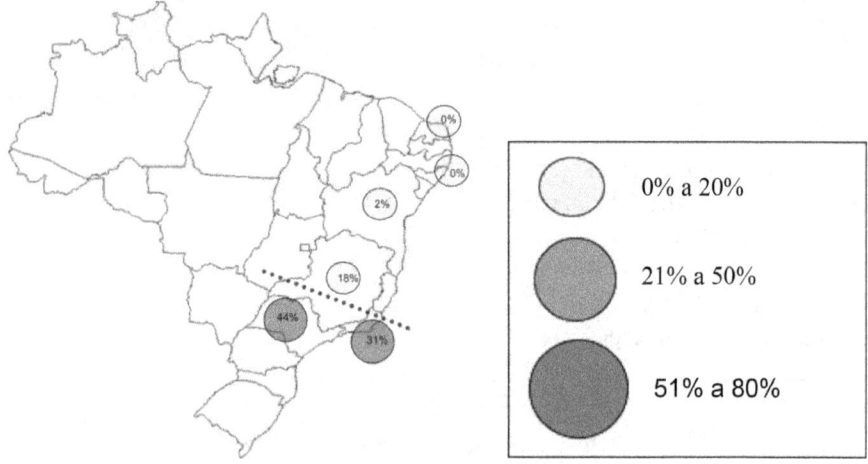

Map 5: The dative clitic *te* in letters with the *você* subject (19th-20th centuries).

These regional differences disappear when we focus on the prepositional variants: the variant *a~para você* was the most frequent in the two regions in comparison to the *a~para ti* variant. There was only one occurrence of the latter, in the RJ sample. This result reveals that the *a~para você* variant seems to have followed the implementation of *você* in subject position more intensely, in detriment to the *a~para ti* variant, which tends to disappear to the extent that the *tu* pronoun is no longer used in subject position.

Contrasting these results with what is seen in the Spanish *voseo* system, we have shown that the Southeastern region – this time excluding Minas Gerais – reveals behavior that is similar to the *voseante* regions, since the *te* clitic was the most frequently used strategy. On the other hand, considering the use of prepositional phrases for expressing the dative, the *voseante* and *voceante* systems coincide, in which the innovative variant prep.+ *vos/você* occupies the position of prepositional complement.

5.3 The variants of second person oblique complements in Brazilian letters from the 19th and 20th centuries

In addition to accusatives and datives, we also consider other constituents that can act as complements for some verbs, namely, obliques. Obliques are characterized by a wide variety of forms and semantic nuances that they can take on; they are always tonic and introduced obligatorily by a preposition[14] (for example, *com*, *de*, *em*, *sem*, *por* 'with, of, in, without, by'). Another characteristic of obliques is the fact that they cannot be substituted by a clitic pronoun (for example: *todas as noites, eu sonho* com você 'every night I dream *with you*' > * *todas as noites eu* lhe *sonho* '*every night I *you* dream').

With respect to the second person, there are three variant forms of the oblique in Brazilian Portuguese: "prep. + *ti*" (examples (24) and (25)), related to the paradigm of the *tu* pronoun; *contigo* (< *com* + *tigo* < *tecum*) (example (26)), related to the *tu* pronoun; and "prep. + *você*", related to the paradigm of the *você* pronoun (examples (27) to (29)).

(24) tu mereces muito mais minha flor, *sem ti* <u>morrerei</u>. [1st half of the 20th century, RJ]

you deserve much more my flower, *without you* [I]will-die

'you deserve much more my flower, without you, I will die'

(25) porque *em ti* <u>reside</u> a creatura que me dá toda a alegria. [1st half of the 20th century, RJ]

because *in you* resides the creature that me gives all the happiness

'because in you resides the creature that gives me all the happiness'

(26) quero beijar-te loucamente, furiosamente, como quem deseja sorver-te em beijos e em beijos <u>finar-se</u> *comtigo*. [1st half of the 20th century, PE]

[I]want to-kiss-you crazily, furiously, with who desires devour-you in kisses and in kisses faint *with you*

'I want to kiss you crazily, furiously, as if I wanted to cover you in kisses and in kisses faint with you'

---

14 The exception is the form *contigo*, the result of a specific evolutionary process: Latin *te cum* > archaic Portuguese *tigo* > *com tigo* > modern Portuguese *contigo*. As we can see, in the archaic phase of Portuguese, this form was also prepositional, before the preposition *com* became agglutinated to the archaic pronoun *tigo*.

(27) eu <u>confio</u> muito *em você*. [2nd half of the 20th century, RN]

    I trust much *in you*

    'I trust you very much'

(28) tendo <u>perguntado</u> *por você* com muito interesse. [1st half of the 20th century, MG]

    having asked **for you** with much interest

    'having asked about you with much interest'

(29) eu sempre <u>simpatizei</u> *com você*. [1st half of the 20th century, RN]

    I always sympathized *with you*

    'I have always liked you'

The previous questions, raised during the presentation of the accusative and dative data, also apply to the oblique: can we say that the oblique forms related to *você* follow the emergence of this pronoun in subject position? Does the emergence of these forms occur generally in Brazilian Portuguese or variably, according to the dialectical differences already presented? To this end, we will discuss these questions for obliques, based on Table 10, which presents the distribution of the variant oblique forms taken from the corpus of personal letters.

Table 10: Distribution of second person oblique variants in Brazilian letters by region (19th-20th centuries).

Oblique		*contigo*	*prep. + ti*	*prep. + você*	Total
Southeast	Rio de Janeiro	40/380 11%	172/380 45%	168/380 44%	380/511 74%
	Minas Gerais		2/16 12%	14/16 88%	15/511 3%
	São Paulo			1/1 100%	1/511 <1%
Northeast	Bahia			10/10 100%	10/511 2%
	Pernambuco		12/32 38%	20/32 62%	32/511 6%
	Rio Grande do Norte			72/72 100%	72/511 14%
Total		40/511 8%	186/511 36%	285/511 56%	511

In general, we can say that the overall results for obliques suggest a usage that is very different for these constituents in comparison to what we observed for accusatives and datives. The oblique forms related to the *você* paradigm predominated over the forms related to the *tu* paradigm, independently of the location of the sample analyzed. Altogether, the results showed 56% prep. + *você* against 36% prep. + *ti*. The only exception was the sample from RJ, in which we observed a certain balance between the variants related to *você* (prep. + *você* with 44%) and the variants related to *tu* (prep. + *ti* with 45%). The occurrences of *contigo* only appeared in the sample from RJ: 8% of the overall data. The only occurrence in the SP sample was precisely with the preposition followed by *você*, as seen in example (30).

(30) e que ahi <u>esteve</u> *com Você* ficando Você de entrar com os restantes 40:300$000. [1st half of the 20th century, SP]

and that there was *with you* staying you of to-enter with the remaining 40: 300$000

'and there he was with you, and you were to enter with the remaining 40: 300$000'

In Table 11, we present the distribution of obliques in letters with the exclusive use of *você* in subject position.

Table 11: Distribution of the second person oblique variants in letters with the *você* subject, by Brazilian region (19th-20th centuries).

Oblique		2P Oblique forms and the use of the *você* subject		
		contigo	prep. + *ti*	prep. + *você*
Southeast	Rio de Janeiro		9/59 15%	50/59 85%
	Minas Gerais			11/11 100%
Northeast	Bahia			9/9 100%
	Pernambuco			17/17 100%
	Rio Grande do Norte			1/1 100%

This overview based on letters with the exclusive use of *você* in subject position confirms that, in the oblique role, *voceamento* spread more extensively in the BP system than in the other functions (accusative and dative). In both regions, with the exception of Rio de Janeiro, which made use of the *você-tu* subsystem, the use of prepositional phrases with *você* is practically categorical (100%). Considering these results, it seems logical to claim that the emergence of the *você* pronoun in subject position is reflected, to a great extent, in the use of second person obliques: in the six Brazilian locations studied, the oblique forms related to *você* were predominant. These results constitute a meeting point between Brazilian *voceamento* and Hispanic *voseo*, in which we observe the *vos* form as a prepositional complement, in constituents with the oblique function.

Regarding the oblique forms related to the *tu* pronoun, the data from the corpus of personal letters allow us to claim that these variants have not been kept in the system given the presence of *você* in subject position. While, in the overall results, they only occurred in the samples from RJ and PE, in the results with the exclusive use of the *você*-subject, we only find *prep. + ti* with a percentage of 15% in the RJ sample.

5.4 The variants of the second person (genitive) possessive in Brazilian letters from the 19th and 20th centuries

Finally, we also considered the possessive forms in the second person singular resulting from the original *tu* (*teu/tua/teus/tuas*) and *você* (*seu/sua/seus/suas*) paradigms. The possessive pronoun, also called the genitive, is traditionally a constituent belonging to the noun phrase, which carries information about person. Moreover, the possessive is a genitive argument of the noun with which it establishes a thematic relation (Castro 2006), which, among others, can be that of possession. We point out that possession is not the only thematic relation fulfilled by the possessive, established between the possessor and the object possessed. This is why we do not define possessives here by a single criterion that privileges exclusively the semantic expression of possession.

Historically, the possessive *seu* and its variants, in the early stages of Portuguese, only made reference to the new third person (*ele/ela*) forms coming from the Latin demonstrative *ille*. With the inclusion of *Vossa mercê* in the system, around the 15th century, the original third person possessive started to appear in the system of the second person forms of address, due to the remaining properties of class origin in the noun phrase, which is involved in this pronominalization process. Therefore, in the medieval period, *seu*, related to the nominal forms *Vossa mercê*, *Vossa Senhoria* and *Vossa Excelência*, became a variant of *vosso*,

Table 12: Distribution of second person genitive variants in Brazilian letters by region (19th-20th centuries).

Genitive		*teu*	*seu*	Total
Southeast	Rio de Janeiro	1002/1300 77%	298/1300 23%	1300/2225 58%
	Minas Gerais	29/146 20%	117/146 80%	146/2225 6%
	São Paulo	46/108 43%	62/108 57%	108/2225 5%
Northeast	Bahia	1/105 1%	104/105 99%	105/2225 5%
	Pernambuco	67/249 27%	182/249 73%	249/2225 11%
	Rio Grande do Norte	119/317 37%	198/317 63%	317/2225 14%
	Total	1264/2225 57%	961/2225 43%	2225

a genitive corresponding to *vós*, expressing deference, in the field of linguistic politeness to the interlocutor. With the grammaticalization of *Vossa mercê > você*, starting from the moment in which *você* moved into the realm of intimacy, the possessive *seu*, originally from *você*, started to coexist with the possessive *teu*, originally from the intimate pronoun *tu*.

Table 12 shows the overall distribution of *teu* and *seu*, according to the analysis of the corpus of personal letters used in this study, considering different Brazilian locations.

Although the possessive from of the *tu* paradigm (*teu*) is more frequent than that of *você* (*seu*) with 57% against 43%, basically due to the predominance of the data from the Rio de Janeiro sample, the possessive *seu* is used more often in five of the six locations from both regions. These results on the possessive in geographic terms are very similar to what we have seen with oblique complements: predominance of the genitive form *seu* belonging to the *você* paradigm in the Northeastern and Southeastern regions, with the exception again of Rio de Janeiro in which the *teu* form from the *tu* paradigm dominates. Examples (31) to (34) illustrate the range of possessive forms.

(31)   Quando será a *tua* vinda a S. Paulo? [1st half of the 20th century, MG]

   When will-be the *your* arrival to S. Paulo

   'When will you arrive in S. Paulo?'

(32) Já logrei o *teu* perdão. [1st half of the 20th century, PE]

Already [I]obtained the *your* pardon

'I have already earned your forgiveness'

(33) Mas vai preparando o *seu* espírito. [1st half of the 20th century, MG]

But go preparing the *your* spirit

'But start preparing your spirit'

(34) Recebi duas cartinha *suas* e respondo-as. [1st half of the 20th century, PE]

[I]received two letter *yours* and [I]respond-them

'I have received two of your letters and I am answering them'

Next, we set out in Table 13 the results regarding the second person possessives in letters with the exclusive use of *você* in subject position to analyze the *voceante* paradigm.

Table 13: Distribution of the second person genitive variants in letters with the *você* subject, by Brazilian region (19th-20th centuries).

Genitive		2P Genitive forms and the use of the *você* subject	
		teu	*seu*
Southeast	Rio de Janeiro	35/269 21%	234/269 79%
	Minas Gerais		107/107 100%
	São Paulo	3/25 12%	22/25 88%
Northeast	Bahia		37/37 100%
	Pernambuco	2/157 1%	155/157 99%
	Rio de Janeiro	10/78 13%	68/78 87%

The results of the second person possessive variants in letters with the *você* subject show the more frequently used *seu* in all locations/regions. This predominance does not, however, prove the categorical use of *seu*, since the variant *teu* (from *tu*), though less frequent, still occurred in some locations in the two regions: in the Southeast, in letters from Rio de Janeiro (21%) and São Paulo (12%); in the Northeast, in letters from Pernambuco (1%) and Rio Grande do Norte (13%).

In contrast to the other grammatical relations, there is a point of divergence between Brazilian *voceamento* and Hispanic American *voseo* regarding possessives: while in the latter the original possessive *tu/tuyo* is chosen, in the former, we see the preferred option is the innovative form *seu*, from the *você* paradigm.

Comparing the results obtained for the genitive with the results presented in the previous sections for the positions of accusative, dative and oblique, we provide evidence that, regarding the implementation of forms from the *você* paradigm following the inclusion of this form in subject position, the behavior of the genitive relation seems to be similar to that of the oblique, due to the high frequency of *seu* and *prep. + você*, respectively. In the accusative and dative relations, however, the presence of forms from the *tu* paradigm is shown to be more salient.

6 Conclusion

The inclusion of the grammaticalized pronoun *você* in the realm of intimacy, previously occupied exclusively by the original *tu* form, triggered a series of reorganizations in the Portuguese pronominal system. Initially in subject position, we observed a coexistence between the *tu* and *você* forms. The other grammatical relations were not immune to the spread of *você*: third person pronominal forms, revealing the nominal origin *Vossa mercê*, start to become a part of the second person singular system, in the positions of accusative, dative, oblique and genitive, to a greater or lesser degree of inclusion and distribution. As a result, we have a new paradigm in Brazilian Portuguese, set out in Table 14.

Table 14: Development of a new suppletive second person paradigm.

PB	NOM	AC	DAT	OBL	GEN
Paradigm 1 (original)	*tu*	*te*	*te* a/para ti	*contigo* prep. + ti	*teu*
Paradigm 2 (resulting from *v.m.* > *você*)	*você*	a/o *você*	*lhe* a/para *você*	prep. + *você*	*seu*
Paradigm 3 (new suppletive paradigm)	*tu* *você*	*te* *lhe* *você*	*te* *lhe* a/para *você*	*contigo* prep. + *ti* prep. + *você*	*teu* *seu*

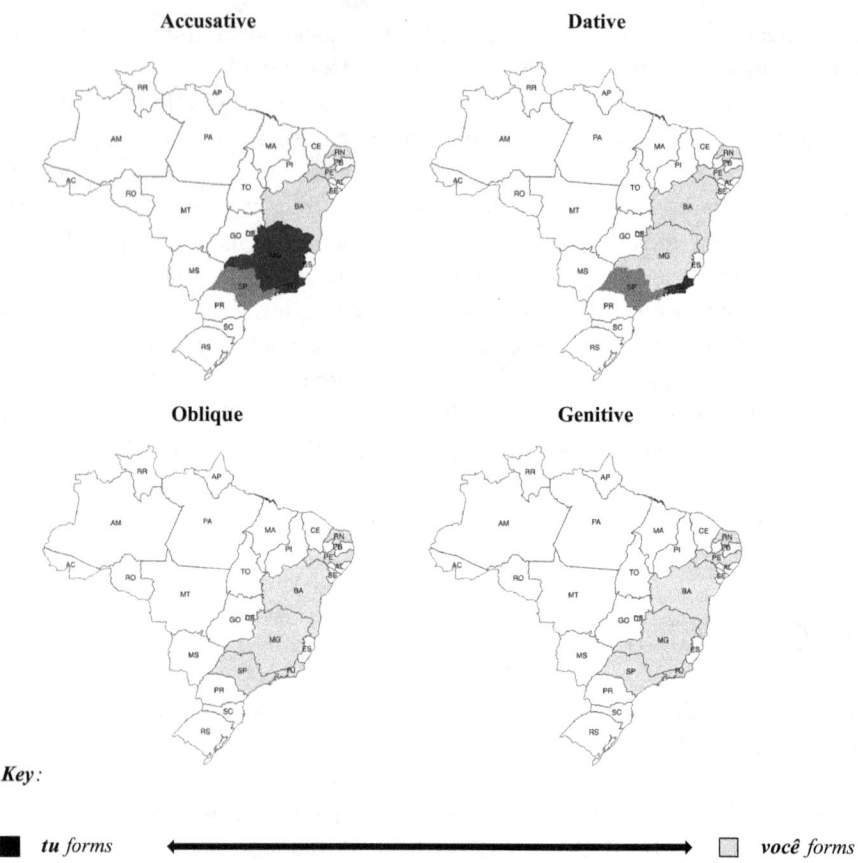

Map 6: Development of Brazilian *voceamento* (19th-20th centuries): original vs. innovative forms.

These changes of keeping original forms and implementing new forms can be better visualized in Map 6, in which the lighter shade refers to the innovative forms of the *voceante* system (*você* paradigm) and the darker shade refers to the original forms specific to the *tu* paradigm. Regarding the accusative relation, we observed a faster implementation of forms from the *você* paradigm in the Northeast than in the Southeast, where the original clitic *te* is most frequently used. The linguistic frontier is somewhat different for the dative variants. Minas Gerais, which lies in the Southeast of Brazil, behaves similarly to the Northeast region with greater use of the *você* forms. The regional differences disappear when we focus on the prepositional variants and genitive. In these grammatical relations, it is possible to observe the implementation of forms from the *você* paradigm.

As can be seen, after the inclusion of *você* in subject position, the implementation of forms from its paradigm in other syntactic contexts did not occur in the same way, or at the same rate, in all regions of Brazil. Consequently, our results confirm the following observation by Conde Silvestre (2007: 143):

> Changes do not usually affect all speakers of a language evenly, but they are the result of processes of generalization over prolonged periods of time, during which their spread through the system and community progresses at a different rate according to the stage in which the affected variable is found.

The sociopragmatic values and the structural contexts of the variant forms need to be more thoroughly analyzed in future studies. In this chapter, we have presented a starting point of a descriptive nature that should and must be reviewed with new data samples and with theoretical-explanatory proposals that shed more light on the issue. The correlation with Hispanic American *voseo* also requires further development, but we have, for now, a starting point for the discussion of common Ibero-American changes in terms of the second person address systems.

References

Almeida, Norma Lucia F. de. 2012. Urbanização, escolarização e variação linguística em Feira de Santana-Bahia (século XX). *Tabuleiro de Letras* 4. 71–85.

Amor Divino, Ludinalva Santos do. 2008. *Como trato meu receptor?* A propósito do uso de *tu/ você* em Santo Antônio de Jesus-BA. M.A. thesis. Federal University of Bahia.

Andrade, Aroldo Leal de, Mariana Fagundes de Oliveira & Zenaide de Oliveira Novais Carneiro. 2018. Formas de tratamento em cartas da Bahia. In Lopes (ed.), 107–117.

Balsalobre, Sabrina Rodrigues Garcia & Vanessa Martins do Monte. 2018. Formas de tratamento em cartas de São Paulo. In Lopes (ed.), 78–90.

Bertolotti, Virginia. 2015. A mí de vos no me trata ni usted ni nadie. *Sistemas e historia de las formas de tratamiento en la lengua española en América*. Mexico City: UNAM/Universidad de la República de Uruguay.

Brown, Roger & Albert Gilman. 1960. The pronouns of power and solidarity. In T.A. Sebeok (ed.), *Style in language*, 253–276. Cambridge-Mass: MIT Press.

Carricaburo, Norma. 1997. *El voseo en la literatura argentina*. Madrid: Arco/Libros.

Castro, Ana. 2006. *On possessives in Portuguese*. PhD dissertation: Universidade Nova de Lisboa.

Censo demográfico do Brasil de 1872. *Wikipédia, a enciclopédia livre*. https://pt.wikipedia. org/w/index.php?title=Censo_demogr%C3%A1fico_do_Brasil_de_1872&oldid=52729284 (23 July, 2018).

Cintra, Luís F. Lindley. 1972. *Sobre "formas de tratamento" na língua portuguesa*. Lisbon: Livros Horizonte.

Coelho da Silva, Francielly. 2015. *Variação entre os pronomes tu e você na função de sujeito na fala de Natal (RN): uma abordagem sociofuncionalista.* M.A. thesis. Federal University of Rio Grande do Norte.

Conde Silvestre, Juán Camilo. 2007. *Sociolingüística histórica.* Madrid: Gredos.

Demografia do Brasil. *Wikipédia, a enciclopédia livre.* https://pt.wikipedia.org/w/index. php?title=Demografia_do_Brasil&oldid=53116893 (12 September, 2018).

Domingos, Tânia Regina Eduardo. 2001. *Pronomes de tratamento do português do século XVI: uma gramática de uso.* São Paulo: Annablume.

ESTIMATIVAS da população residente no Brasil e unidades da Federação com data de referência em 1º de julho de 2015. Rio de Janeiro: IBGE. ftp://ftp.ibge.gov.br/Estimativas_de_ Populacao/Estimativas_2015/estimativa_dou_2015_20150915.pdf (12 September, 2017).

Faraco, Carlos Alberto. 1996. O tratamento *você* em português: uma bordagem histórica. *Fragmenta* 13. 51–82.

Fontanella de Weinberg, María Beatriz. 1992. La evolución de los usos americanos de segunda persona singular. *Lingüística* 4. 7–25.

Fontanella de Weinberg, María Beatriz. 1977. La constitución del paradigma pronominal del voseo. *Thesaurus* 32,2. 227–241.

Gomes, Valéria Severina. 2018. Formas de tratamento em cartas de Pernambuco. In Lopes (ed.), 118–128.

Hummel, Martin, Bettina Kluge & María Eugenia Vázquez Laslop (eds.). 2010. *Formas y fórmulas de tratamiento en el mundo hispánico.* México DF/Graz: El Colegio de México/ Karl-Franzens-Universität Graz.

Lapesa, Rafael. 2000. *Estudios de morfosintaxis histórica del español.* Madrid: Gredos.

Lopes, Célia Regina dos Santos (ed.). 2018. *Mudança sintática das classes de palavra: perspectiva funcionalista – História do Português Brasileiro,* vol. 4. São Paulo: Editora Contexto.

Lopes, Célia Regina dos Santos & Janaina Pedreira Fernandes Souza. 2018. Formas de tratamento em cartas do Rio de Janeiro. In Lopes (ed.), 46–66.

Lopes, Célia Regina dos Santos & Silvia R. Cavalcante. 2011. A cronologia do voceamento no português brasileiro: expansão de *você*-sujeito e retenção do clítico *-te. Lingüística* 25. 30–65.

Lucchesi, Dante, Alan Baxter & Ilza Ribeiro (eds.). 2009. *O português afro-brasileiro.* Salvador: Editora da Universidade Federal da Bahia.

Luz, Marilina dos Santos. 1958. Fórmulas de tratamento no português arcaico – subsídios para o seu estudo. *Revista Portuguesa de Filologia* 9. 55–144.

Marcotulio, Leonardo Lennertz. 2015. Sobre la génesis de "Vossa Mercê" en el portugués medieval. *Lingüística* 31,1. 61–79.

Marcotulio, Leonardo Lennertz. 2014. Formas de tratamento no português arcaico: contribuições do teatro português quinhentista. *Confluência* 46. 157–200.

Marcotulio, Leonardo Lennertz. 2010. *Língua e História: o 2º marquês do Lavradio e as estratégias linguísticas da escrita no Brasil Colonial.* Rio de Janeiro: Ítaca Comunicações.

Moser, Karolin. 2010. San José (Costa Rica): desde los significados pragmáticos del ustedeo en el registro coloquial actual hacia sus primeras manifestaciones en el Valle Central (siglo XVIII). In Hummel et al. (eds.), 671–713.

Mota, Maria Alice. 2008. A variação dos pronomes *tu* e *você* no português oral de São João da Ponte (MG). M.A. thesis. Federal University of Minas Gerais.

Oliveira, Thiago. 2014. Entre o linguístico e o social: complementos dativos de 2a pessoa em cartas cariocas (1880–1980). Master's thesis. Federal University of Rio de Janeiro.

Paredes Silva, Vera Lúcia Pereira. 1996. A variação *você/tu* na fala carioca. Paper presented in *1º Encontro de Variação Linguística do Cone Sul*. Federal University of Rio Grande do Sul.

Peres, Edenize Ponzo. 2006. O uso do *você, ocê, cê* em Belo Horizonte – um estudo em tempo aparente e em tempo real. Ph.D. Dissertation: Federal University of Minas Gerais.

Placencia, María Elena. 2010. El estudio de formas de tratamiento en Colombia y Ecuador. In Hummel et al. (eds.), 341–373.

Rona, José Pedro. 1967. *Geografía y morfología del voseo*. Pôrto Alegre: Pontifícia Universidade Católica do Rio Grande do Sul.

Rumeu, Márcia Cristina de Brito, Iracema Aguiar da Cruz & Nayara Domingues Cardoso. 2018. Formas de tratamento em cartas de Minas Gerais. In Lopes (ed.), 67–77.

Rumeu, Márcia Cristina de Brito. 2004. *Para uma história do português no Brasil: formas pronominais e nominais de tratamento em cartas setecentistas e oitocentistas*. M.A. thesis. Federal University of Rio de Janeiro.

Rumeu, Márcia Cristina de Brito. 2013. *Língua e sociedade: a história do pronome 'você' no português brasileiro*. Rio de Janeiro: Ítaca.

Santos, Viviane Maia dos. 2012. "*Tu* vai para onde?... *Você* vai para onde": manifestações da segunda pessoa na fala carioca. M.A. thesis. Federal University of Rio de Janeiro.

Scherre, Maria Marta Pereira et al. 2009. Usos dos pronomes *você* e *tu* no português brasileiro. Comunicação apresentada no *II SIMELP – II Simpósio Mundial de Estudos de Língua Portuguesa*: Universidade de Évora.

Scherre, Maria Marta Pereira, Edilene Patrícia Andrade Dias, Carolina Andrade & Germano Ferreira Martins. 2015. Usos dos pronomes *você* e *tu*. In Marco Antônio Martins & Jussara Abraçado. *Mapeamento sociolinguístico do português brasileiro*, 133–172. São Paulo: Editora Contexto.

Sette, Neide Durães. 1980. *Formas de tratamento no português coloquial*. M.A. thesis. Federal University of Pernambuco.

Souza, Camila. 2014. *Eu te amo, eu lhe adoro, eu quero você*: a variação das formas de acusativo de 2a pessoa em cartas pessoais (1880–1980). Master's thesis. Federal University of Rio de Janeiro.

Souza, Janaína. 2012. Mapeando a entrada do *você* no quadro pronominal: análise de cartas familiares dos séculos XIX–XX. Master's thesis. Federal University of Rio de Janeiro.

Izete Lehmkuhl Coelho and Christiane Maria Nunes de Souza

Variation and change in the second person singular pronouns *tu* and *você* in Santa Catarina (Brazil)

Abstract: This chapter aims to provide an overview regarding variation and change between *tu* and *você* pronouns in six samples of personal letters from the PHPB-SC, covering the period between 1870s and 1990s. Considering samples examined in this study, some tendencies may be signalized: (i) in the 19th century *tu* is largely used, while in the 20th century variation between *tu* and *você* is observed; (ii) *tu* is mostly correlated to null subjects, and *você* is mostly correlated to explicit subjects; (iii) *tu* seems to be associated to personal issues and *você* seems to be associated to professional issues; (iv) *tu* is used most in Greater Florianópolis mesoregion, while *você* is the most productive pronoun in the Planalto Serrano, Vale do Itajaí and Nourthern Santa Catarina mesoregions, and these preferences appears to have some relation to the colonization of these cities. These results are discussed based on the field of historical sociolinguistics and may contribute to the second person singular pronouns description concerning written Portuguese in Brazil and in Santa Catarina specifically.

Keywords: second person singular pronouns, personal letters, diachrony, Florianópolis

1 Introduction

In this chapter, we propose a mapping of the process of variation and change in the use of informal second person singular pronouns *tu* and *você* in the Portuguese of Florianópolis, capital of the state of Santa Catarina, located in Southern Brazil. The investigation of this linguistic phenomenon in Florianópolis is particularly interesting because the city's patterns of use are distinct from patterns found in other regions of Brazil, where *você* has replaced *tu* as the informal second person singular pronoun.

In Florianópolis, *tu* – the oldest second person singular pronoun in the pronominal pool of the Portuguese language, and a Latin inheritance – still persists and even flourishes, as studies by Loregian-Penkal (2004), Rocha (2012), Davet (2013), among others have shown. This may be due to the Azorean colonization of the region in the middle of the 18th century (Furlan 1989; Oliveira 2004; Coelho & Görski 2011) and to the geographic isolation of the Island of Santa Catarina, which persisted until the early decades of the 20th century, when the first bridge connecting the island to the mainland was constructed (Nunes de Souza 2011; 2015; Nunes de Souza & Coelho 2015).[1]

Based on these assumptions, this study describes variation and change in the pronouns *tu* and *você* in Florianópolis, investigating the following areas: (i) pronoun distribution in the Portuguese currently spoken in Florianópolis, in contrast with that spoken in other cities of Santa Catarina; (ii) the rate of use of both pronouns in personal letters written by *Catarinenses*[2] in the 19th and 20th centuries; and (iii) the group of internal and external factors that may be correlated to the process of variation and change in the pronominal forms. This study leads us to reflect on (i) differences and similarities concerning the use of the pronouns *tu* and *você* in different parts of the state of Santa Catarina and the evaluation of this use; (ii) evidence of linguistic change or stability; (iii) patterns of variation and change; and (iv) aspects of the social history of the state which may help explain this pronominal variation/change process. The chapter begins with an overview of studies investigating the distribution of second person singular pronouns in Florianópolis and in other cities of Santa Catarina at the end of the 20th and the beginning of the 21st centuries.

1.1 Present-day variation

Let us first consider the present-day situation. Examples (1) to (4) are taken from speech data from the city of Florianópolis, extracted from Rocha (2012) and Davet (2013), and illustrate the use of different variants of second person singular in the subject position. In example (1), we observe the use of the null pronoun *tu*, with second person singular agreement expressed on the verb. In example (2), *tu* is present and followed by a verb unmarked for person.[3] Example (3) illustrates

---

1 The territory of Florianópolis is mainly situated on an island, but also extends to a small area of the mainland.

2 *Catarinense* is the term used to refer to those born in the state of Santa Catarina. In this chapter, the term will be used both as a noun, and as an adjective meaning 'from' or 'of' Santa Catarina. Other Brazilian state terms like *Paulista* (from São Paulo), *Gaúcho* (from Rio Grande do Sul) and *Paranaense* (from Paraná) are also kept in their original Portuguese form.

3 In Portuguese, third person singular subject pronouns *ele/ela* ('he/she') are followed exclusively by a verb unmarked for person (for example, *ele/ela falaØ* – *he/she speakØ*). As distinct from Angolan Portuguese, for example, in Brazilian Portuguese second person singular subject pronoun *você*, like pronouns *ele/ela*, only precedes an unmarked verb (*você falaØ* – *you*

the use of *você*, which in Brazilian Portuguese is categorically combined with a verb with no morphemic person marking. Finally, example (4) shows both overt *tu* with second person singular agreement expressed on the verb and the pronoun *você*.

(1) eu tinha até uma professora que já era viúva...
/I had even a teacher who already was widow.../
já era uma mulher,
/[she] already was a woman,/
e ela assim: ai, *vais casar*
/and she like: yikes, **Ø.2sg go.pres.2sg marry.inf⁴**/
com operário,
/with factory worker,/
e eu ficava quieta...
/and I would remain silent.../

'I even had a teacher who was already a widow... she was already a woman, and she would go like: yikes, are you going to marry a factory worker, and I would remain silent...' (Floripa Sample, 2010s)⁵

(2) ee daí me cercaram e falaram assim:
/and then they me surrounded and said like:/
'ou *tu dá* o troco do pão ou
/'either **you.2sg give.pres.3sg** [us] the change for the bread or/
a gente vai levar o teu relógio'
/we will take the your watch/'

'and then they surrounded me and said: "either you give us change for the bread or we will take your watch"' (Floripa Sample, 2010s)

---

*speak*Ø). As seen in examples (1), (2), and (4), *tu* is followed by a verb with varying behavior that may or may not take the second person singular morphemic mark *-s* (*tu fala*Ø or *tu falas*). Once it is traditionally associated with third person, the unmarked verb is referred to (here and in other texts) as third person verbal morphology or verb in 3P, even when coupled with a second person pronoun.

4 The glosses provide POS transcription for the italicized phrase in the original text.

5 The samples are described in Section 4.1.

(3) Às vezes *você toma* uma atitude
/Sometimes **you.2sg take.pres.3sg** an action/
que não deveria ser aquela,
/that not should be that,/
mas depois você pode ficar
/but later **you.2sg may.pres.3sgstay.inf**/
com a consciência pesada.
/with a conscience heavy./

'Sometimes you take an action that you shouldn't, and later you may have a heavy conscience' (VARSUL Sample, 1990s)

(4) *Tu não me vens* com Luciano do Vale
/You.2sg not to me come.pres.2sg [with] Luciano do Vale/
que também ele pode entender muito
/that as well he may know a lot/
lá dos comentários dele lá.
/[there] about the comments of his, there./
Como *você sabe* o filho dele joga futebol.
/As **you.2sg know.pres.3sg** the son of his plays soccer./

'Don't come talking to me about Luciano do Vale, because he may know a lot about those comments of his as well. As you know, his son plays soccer' (VARSUL Sample, 1990s)

Even though the topic of this chapter is variation in second person singular pronominal forms *tu* and *você* in the subject position, it is important to explain the verbal morphology that accompanies *tu* for readers who are not familiar with Brazilian Portuguese. In examples (1) and (4), *tu*, both null and overt, is followed by a verb with the distinctive second person singular morpheme *-s* (third person *vai* 'go' becomes second person *vais*, for example). In example (2), the verb that follows *tu* does not have the distinctive second person (2P) morpheme (*dá* Ø 'give' instead of *dás*).

Moreover, it is also possible to use a distinctive second person morpheme *-sse*, known as "assimilated", in the past tense indicative (see Loregian-Penkal 2004; Davet 2013), although the morpheme is not present among the variants depicted in the examples. This results in three verbal morphology configurations which can be combined with *tu* in the past tense indicative: (1) the presence of the morpheme defining second person singular *-ste* (*tu falaste* 'you spoke', for example); (2) the absence of a specific morpheme to distinguish the person (*tu falou* 'you spoke', for example); and (3) the presence of the assimilated second person singular morpheme *-sse* (*tu falasse* 'you spoke').

1.2 Focusing on a diachronic perspective

The diachronic data central to this study are from six samples of personal letters by *Catarinenses* dating from 1880 to 1992. The varying second person singular forms found are the same as those identified in speech data samples from the late 20th and early 21st centuries, as illustrated in examples (5) to (8), which means that diachrony is still 'alive' in the present-day use of Portuguese in Florianópolis. Example (5) illustrates the use of null pronoun *tu*, identified through the distinctive second person singular morpheme -*s* on the verb that follows it. Example (6) shows the use of overt *tu* coupled with a verb with no distinctive morpheme for person. In example (7), we can observe the use of *você*, which, as previously mentioned, in Brazilian Portuguese is only used alongside a verb unmarked for person. Finally, example (8) displays the variants identified in examples (5) and (7), and the use of overt *tu*, followed by a verb marked for second person singular.

(5) comquanto passassemos tanto tempo sem nos communicar
     /even though it takes so long without us communicate/
     por meio da escripta,
     /by means of the writing,/
     continúas a ser meu maior amigo,
     /Ø.2sg remain.pres.2sg [to be] my greatest friend,/
     o mais altamente sincero e dedicado; [...]
     /the most highly sincere and dedicated; [...]/

     'even though it takes us so long to communicate through writing, you remain my greatest friend, the most highly sincere and dedicated' (CS Sample, 1890s)

(6) Tudo era triste...!
     /Everything was sad...!/
     E eis que derepente *tu surge*,
     /And then, [that] suddenly **you.2sgappear.pres.3sg**,/
     em uma tarde inesquecível,
     /in one afternoon unforgettable,/
     talves ao encontro de um alguém [...]
     /maybe by meeting of a someone [...]/

     'Everything was sad...! And then, suddenly, you appear in one unforgettable afternoon, maybe to meet someone' (VL Sample, 1960s)

(7) Mas ontem a B me telefonou
/But yesterday the B me called/
e disse que *você* já *comprou.*
/and said that **you.2sg** already **have.3sg buy.past** [them]/
Tudo bem. Não se afogue com estas
/Everything alright. Not yourself go choking with these/
balinhas e maçãs. Acho que era só isto.
/candies and apples. [I] think that [it] was all./

'But yesterday B called me and said that you have already bought them.
That's alright. Don't go choking yourself on these candies and apples. I think
that was all' (MD Sample, 1980s)

(8) Não importa-me dançar!
/Not care to-me dancing!/
Compreendes, a não ser que
/**Ø.2sg understand.pres.2sg**, unless [that]/
você pedisse! do contrário ficarei
/**you.2sg ask.past.3sg**!/ otherwise [I] would spend/
a noite inteira apreciando [rasura] tu tocares! Adoro!
/the night all watching   **you.2sg play.pres.2sg**! [I] love it!/

'I do not care about dancing! You understand, unless you asked me to! Otherwise I would spend all night watching you play! I love it!' (VL Sample, 1960s)

Putting to one side the morphological idiosyncrasies of the verbs that follow the
second person singular pronouns – which were not part of the criteria used in
the selection of the analyzed variable – and observing only the variation between
tu and *você*, the eight examples illustrate three patterns of use of second person
singular pronouns: (i) exclusive use of *tu* (examples (1), (2), (5) and (6)); (ii)
exclusive use of *você* (examples (3) and (7)); and (iii) alternation of *tu* and *você* in
the same text (examples (4) and (8)).

1.3 Questions and hypotheses

Based on these observations, the following questions arise: (i) What diachronic
path can be noted regarding variation and change in the use of pronouns *tu* and
você? (ii) Which linguistic and extralinguistic factors influence the distribution of
the pronouns *tu* and *você*? (iii) Is it possible to affirm that *você* has made its way

into the *Catarinense* variety of Portuguese as early as the end of the 20th century? (iv) What is the social and linguistic history of the presence of the new form *você* in *Catarinense* samples?

We seek to answer these questions by examining the phenomenon in personal letters, limiting the analysis to the subject position. Our main hypothesis, supported by previous studies, is that, even though the innovative pronoun *você* was widespread in Brazilian Portuguese, it was not yet very frequent in personal letters by *Catarinenses* at the end of the 20th century (when our latest sample was produced), with a predominance of the earliest form *tu*.

Further hypotheses lead on logically from the first: (i) *tu* is highly frequent in both centuries as null subject of second person (2P) verbal morphology in more informal contexts, especially in symmetrical relations between lovers, friends and family members; (ii) the new pronoun *você* makes its entry in the early 20th century, combined with third person (3P) verbal morphology, bearing traces of the formality conveyed by *Vossa Mercê* ('lit. Your Mercy'), the address form that preceded innovative *você*; (iii) people begin employing the form *você*, in the middle of the 20th century, in the same discourse contexts as those for *tu* (informal situations such as the symmetrical relations between lovers, friends and family members); and (iv) *você* does not supplant *tu* in the analyzed sample.

1.4 Theoretical background

This investigation is situated in the field of historical sociolinguistics (see Conde Silvestre 2007), which is grounded in the principles of the theory of variation and change (see Weinreich, Labov & Herzog 2006 [1968]). We seek to understand and explain processes of variation and change in written documents from the past, spread across different moments of the 19th and 20th centuries. In so doing, we start from the following principles: (i) variation is inherent to language systems; (ii) structured variability therefore characterizes the normal use of the language; (iii) language change is gradual; (iv) processes of language variation/change are connected to social and linguistic factors; (v) quantitative procedures may help explain linguistic variation and change.

From this theoretical point of view, we understand that as change develops, we must assume the existence of systematic heterogeneity, whether in data from the present or from the past. Our investigation starts with the varying forms found in the present, which allows us to observe, in documents written in the past, at which moment and through which paths the new form enters the language. We believe that, in accordance with the principle of linguistic uniformity,[6] the linguistic factors that favor language change in the present are not absolutely different from those in motion in the past. It is possible to assume that, from the moment *você* begins competing with pronoun *tu,* the linguistic variation between the two pronouns in the past was structured in the same way as it is in the present. Our starting point is therefore the results from speech samples, which will be discussed in Section 4.

In addition, personal letters have been analyzed in order to ascertain the varying uses of the pronouns *tu* and *você* in written documents. We believe that letters are texts "that translate into the written genre, communicative exchanges that occurred or could occur in oral speech" (Conde Silvestre 2007: 45). This type of text is likely to manifest a greater degree of variation since it shows, in a way, written records that can reproduce the vernacular of different epochs. It therefore allows for a tighter correlation between linguistic and social factors, the latter including, as far as possible, the personal circumstances reflected in the relationship between senders and their addressees. In letters, the influence of the recipient is likely to be present in the choices the writer makes between the varying forms.

In addition to reconstructing the pronominal system of the past through the lens of the present, we will observe whether it is possible to reconstruct the social contexts of the past from the different styles reflected in the historical documents. Following the observations made by Conde Silvestre (2007) of the stylistic-social continuum theorized by Labov (1966; 1972), we assume that differences in style may, to some extent, be related to social differences. In other words, variants used in more informal contexts correspond to those more frequently used by people towards the lower end of the socioeconomic hierarchy, whereas variants present in formal contexts correspond, to a certain extent, to the forms more frequently used by those towards the top of the hierarchy. The more formal variants found in the speech of higher status speakers are better evaluated, whereas the forms that are more frequent in the speech of lower status speakers have less prestige or can even be stigmatized.

Throughout our discussion, we will focus on the realization of the pronominal subject, a variation phenomenon much debated by those dedicated to investigating changes in Brazilian Portuguese. We depart from reflections by Duarte

---

6 According to Milroy (1992, cited in Conde Silvestre 2007: 41), "in its sociolinguistic contemporary formulation, this principle prescribes seeing variability as an inherent trait of languages, from past to present and understanding that, in the same way that different languages display this characteristic nowadays, we can assume they were subject to variability in their historical development".

(1993, 1995), Duarte et al. (2012) and Gravina (2008, 2014) about the use of the subject in the Southern Region of Brazil, observing the behavior of this variable in the samples investigated here.

1.5 Organization of the chapter

Section 2 presents the socio-historical context of the state of Santa Catarina and its capital, Florianópolis. Section 3 is dedicated to studies that examine the variation of *tu* and *você* in speech samples by *Catarinenses* in recent decades. Section 4 presents the methodology, including a description of the six samples of personal letters written by *Catarinenses* in the 19th and 20th centuries and the *tu* and *você* controlled variables. It also presents statistical results of the use (or lack thereof) of the pronominal subject in the letter samples. Section 5 discusses the results in relation to our hypothesis that linguistic change in the use of second person pronominal forms is a slow process in the letters by *Catarinenses*. Finally, we present our conclusions based on the study's findings.

2 Socio-historical context

In order to contextualize the social history of the state of Santa Catarina (see Map 1 below), we turn our attention to pioneer studies by Furlan (1989) and Koch (2000), as well as hypotheses on the appearance of pronouns *tu* and *você* in Santa Catarina through contact during different historical moments in the 18th century.

According to Furlan (1989), the linguistic history of the coastal areas becomes particularly interesting during the mid-18th century, as the Portuguese government offered incentives for Azoreans to emigrate to the coast of Santa Catarina (from São Francisco to the north down to Laguna in the south, including the Island of Santa Catarina) seeking to expand the settlement of the state. Between 1748 and 1756, about 1,000 Madeirans and 5,000 Azoreans were transferred from the Archipelagos of Madeira and The Azores to populate Santa Catarina.[7] This would have resulted in a population increase of more than 100%. The immigrants were, in general, illiterate, and their culture was associated with the conservative practices and values of the 15th and 16th centuries. Historians' accounts claim

---

7 According to Mosimann (2010), some have argued that the ship bringing the largest number of Madeiran immigrants in 1759 may well have sunk and, in fact, only 59 Madeirans arrived on the *Catarinense* shore.

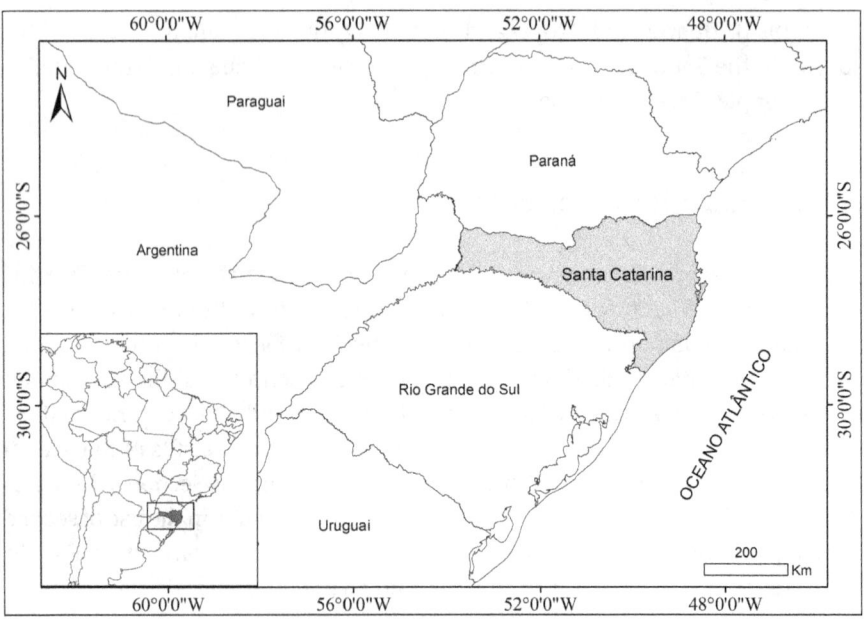

Map 1: Map of Santa Catarina (Brazil).

that the Azoreans who arrived in the south of Brazil, up until that point, would have been living in a feudal socioeconomic system (see also Mosimann 2010). According to Furlan (1989), these immigrants brought with them the pronouns *tu* (as an informal address form) and *vós* and *Vossa Mercê* (for polite address), in addition to the palatalized /s/, which is still present in the region. In the 19th century, the building of a new harbor on the island was responsible for the development of commercial and administrative activities in the capital. However, access to the Island of Santa Catarina was only made easy in the 1920s, with the construction of the Hercílio Luz Bridge. From that point on, a significant growth in population was evident, as schools and other public buildings were built.

In the same period, the Planalto Serrano region, where the city of Lages is located, developed as a result of another flow of migration, known as the *Tropeiros* route, where cattlemen from the states of São Paulo and Minas Gerais would leave Sorocaba (São Paulo) and the neighboring area, headed to Vacaria in the state of Rio Grande do Sul. On their way south, they would bring a number of goods and, on their way back, they would take back cattle raised in Rio Grande do Sul. This movement guaranteed supply for the population of the Planalto Serrano region, and that section of the route became known as the *Lages path*. It is said that the first people to populate the region were precisely the inhabitants of São

Paulo engaged in travels back and forth along the *Tropeiros* route. It is important to highlight that Lages, up until 1820, was part of the São Paulo captaincy, from where it possibly inherited the retroflex /r/ and the second person pronoun *você*.

According to Nunes de Souza (2015), historians have provided information that helps to interpret these uses: there is consensus among scholars that the *Paulistas* were the first to settle in Lages. Even though cattlemen from São Paulo, Minas Gerais and Rio Grande do Sul all crossed the city of Lages, the *Gaúchos* (from Rio Grande do Sul) had to pay fees to spend the night, which consequently made the place more welcoming for cattlemen from the Southeastern Region than from the Southern Region. In the 20th century, however, a second wave of settlers from Rio Grande do Sul arrived in Lages, and thus guaranteed the city's ties with countless traits of the *Gaúcho* tradition.

Still in Santa Catarina, one other type of colonization left important linguistic traces. This process became known as "late colonization", due to the migration flow of Germans and Italians at the beginning of the 19th century. The Germans arrived in Southern Brazil, especially in the states of Rio Grande do Sul and Santa Catarina, from 1824 onwards. The Italian immigration happened later, starting in 1887. In the areas occupied by German and Italian immigrants, "bilingualism was one of the most expressive, if not the most meaningful, characteristic of the linguistic landscape of Southern Brazil" (Altenhofen 2002: 131). The northern and western portions of Santa Catarina are considered multilingual contact zones, noticeably German (in Blumenau) and Italian (in Chapecó).

The Germans who arrived in the 19th century and overpowered the Indigenous peoples (the Xokleng tribe) had a prominent role in the colonization of Blumenau. The majority of German migrants were Protestants, a religion that was different from the one practiced in Brazil. The religious divergence, alongside other linguistic and cultural aspects, contributed to their continued isolation, preserving their language and their culture. It is an acknowledged fact that, at the beginning of the 20th century, due to nationalist policies, Portuguese was made compulsory in schools of Blumenau, thereby imposing the language on native speakers of German. During this period, according to Büchler (1914, as cited in Vandresen 2008), the pronominal paradigm found in schoolbooks that were used to teach Portuguese as a second language did not include the pronouns *tu* and *vós*. We can therefore conclude that the second person singular pronoun learned at schools in Blumenau – whose people spoke Portuguese as a second language – was *você*, not *tu*.

The colonization of Chapecó, now a major city in the west of Santa Catarina, also underwent the influence of two main flows of migration. The first settlers, in 1838, were cattlemen from São Paulo who traveled along the path known as *Estrada das Missões*, connecting Guarapuava, in Paraná, to Cruz Alta, in Rio Grande do Sul, cutting through Chapecó. The second wave of settlers arrived around 1917, from Italy. The Italians who colonized Chapecó migrated within the country, creating what has been known in history as New Colonies. Margotti (2004) asserts that after the War of *Contestado* (1916) the government decided to populate the west of the state. To enable this, plots of land would be sold to German and Italian settlers from Rio Grande do Sul. Even though Chapecó had its origins in the clash between *Paulistas* and the local Indigenous peoples, and later in the territorial dispute between Paraná and Santa Catarina, from 1917 onwards it received a significant number of migrants, mostly Italians from Rio Grande do Sul. This had a huge influence on the present-day characteristics of the area, both in economic terms – the presence of agro-industries – and in cultural terms, with clear affinities shared by the inhabitants of Chapecó and Gaúcho culture in areas such as cuisine, soccer, and language.

According to Margotti (2004), when the Italians arrived in Southern Brazil the Germans had already been there for about 50 years, which influenced the power relations between the two groups. However, unlike the Germans, whose language and culture were significantly different from those of the Portuguese, the Italians were Catholic – the official religion in Brazil – and their language was one of the Romance languages and therefore more similar to Portuguese than German. The varieties of Portuguese that have evolved from these contacts present traits associated with the presence of the German and Italian languages at different linguistic levels.

This socio-historical contextualization is explained in detail in Koch (2000) and Altenhofen (2002), based on dialectological studies from the *Atlas Linguístico Etnográfico da Região Sul do Brasil* (ALERS[8]) project. According to Koch (2000: 59), the Southern Region can be divided into two main linguistic areas: the *Paranaense* and the *Gaúcho*. In this division, the state of Santa Catarina is considered an area of transition, which the author names the *Catarinense* spectrum, with the following factors playing a role in linguistic variation:
1. The presence of Azoreans in the east of Santa Catarina;
2. Political borders with Spanish-speaking countries on the southernmost border and consequent Portuguese-Spanish contact;
3. Contact between *Paulistas* and *Gaúchos* in two opposing migration flows and the role of the *Tropeiro* routes in cattle trade;

---

8 ALERS is an interinstitutional project initiated in the 1980s that researches an ethnography of special variation in the three states of the Southern Region (Paraná, Santa Catarina and Rio Grande do Sul). Its research method consists of systematic questionnaires with speakers from the different rural areas of the region.

4. The existence of noticeable bilingual areas, created in the 20th century through the settlement of non-Portuguese-speaking European immigrants in the (old) forest zones.

For Koch, this division is probably a reflex of two moments of colonization in opposite directions. The first was towards the southwest, starting from what he calls old Paraná and the south across Lages and Curitibanos, with *Paulista-Paranaense* traces. The second was towards the west, as a result of extending the colonization of the northwestern region of Rio Grande do Sul (the Missions), where a majority of German, Italian and Polish descendants are situated, outside the so-called old colonies.

Complementing the detailed analysis presented by Koch (2000), Altenhofen (2002) lists the following geolinguistic scenarios for the Portuguese spoken in rural areas of the Southern Region of Brazil, based on data mapped by ALERS, which are set out in Map 2:

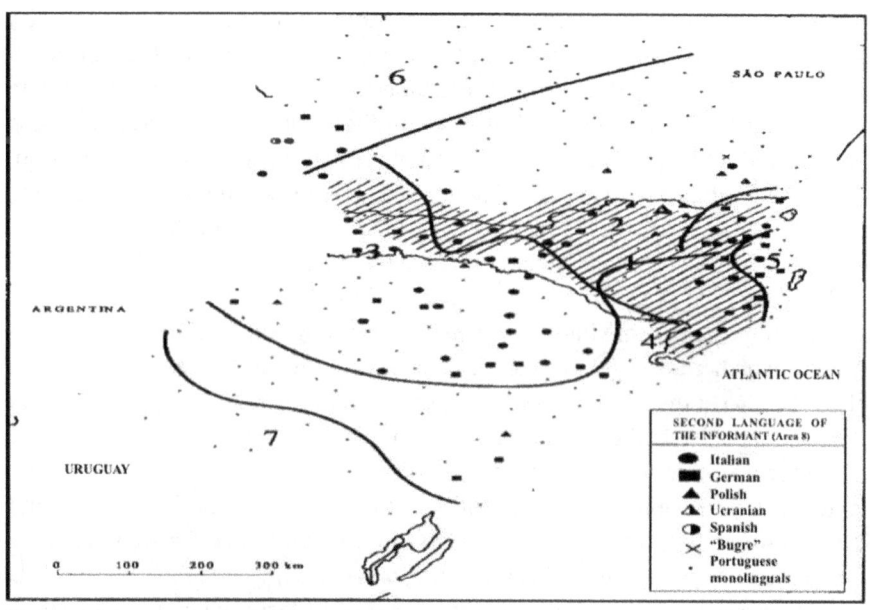

Map 2: Linguistic areas of the Southern Region (see Map 1) based on data from ALERS (**Source:** Altenhofen 2002: 133).

1. Santa Catarina is an area of transition (the *Catarinense* spectrum postulated by Koch 2000) between Rio Grande do Sul and Paraná;
2. The central route towards Paraná has the shape of a wedge, with the migration routes of the *Paulistas*;

3. The western pathway towards Rio Grande do Sul is an area under the influence of European immigrants;
4. The eastern route headed to Rio Grande do Sul (*Gaúcho* cluster, according to Koch 2000) is an area that portrays the occupation of the Campos de Cima da Serra and Lages;
5. The lateral Azorean-*Catarinense* zone ranges from Laguna to São Francisco do Sul;
6. The lateral zone in the North of Paraná (*Paranaense* cluster, according to Koch 2000) is related to the form of colonization;
7. The lateral zone of the foreign border of Rio Grande do Sul is related to traces of the contact between Portuguese and Spanish.

The present study is particularly concerned with the first five areas identified in Map 2, looking at Santa Catarina as an area of transition between Rio Grande do Sul and Paraná. In the central route towards Paraná we can note the migration routes of *Paulistas* in the cattle trade and the influence they left in Lages. In the western pathway towards Rio Grande do Sul, we can see the traces left by the *Gaúcho* Italian descendants in Chapecó. In the Eastern route headed to Rio Grande do Sul, the Gaúcho influence on the colonization of Lages can also be observed. The lateral zone experienced Azorean (and Madeiran) colonization, along the *Catarinense* coast, from Laguna to São Francisco do Sul, including the Island of Santa Catarina. These areas in particular account for the colonization of the Planalto Serrano region and the coast (see Margotti 2004 and Rocha 2012), and are particularly relevant to the discussions that follow.

In order to illustrate the *Catarinense* spectrum, we now turn to a map from ALERS, which shows the answers by speakers from rural areas to a question about the use of the second person singular pronoun. The set of questions about the second person in the questionnaire took into account the linguistic sensibility of the speakers regarding symmetrical and asymmetrical relations between interlocutors, for example brother-to-brother, parent-to-child, child-to-parent, and friend-to-friend. The results are presented in Map 3, and show the second person forms used by speakers to address a sibling or neighbor.

The areas marked with squares represent the places where speakers from rural areas interviewed by ALERS used the pronoun *você* to address a sibling or neighbor. This use is predominant in the state of Paraná (mostly in green to the north) but can also be found in some small regions of Santa Catarina (centre) and Rio Grande do Sul (south). These regions coincide with the *Tropeiros* route, identified by Altenhofen (2002) as the central route projected towards Paraná. The areas with black circles identify the places where rural speakers used the pronoun *tu* to speak to a sibling or neighbor. We can observe that this use is

ATLAS LINGÜÍSTICO-ETNOGRÁFICO DA REGIÃO SUL DO BRASIL (ALERS)

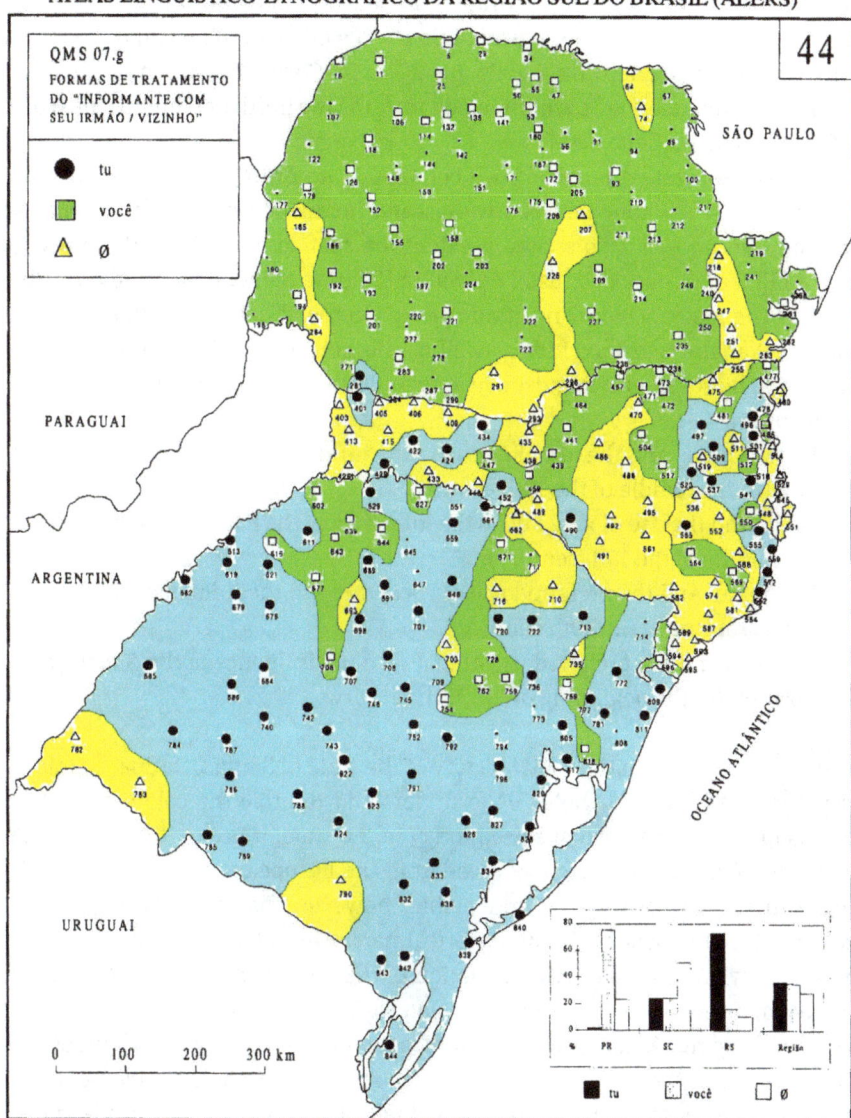

Map 3: Address form used by informants with a sibling/neighbor.
(**Source:** ALERS 2002, adapted by Rocha 2012: 53).

predominant in the state of Rio Grande do Sul. In Santa Catarina, the pronoun *tu* is found especially in the coastal regions, as well as in the north of the state. Looking at the map, according to Rocha (2012: 54), "we are given the impression that *tu* ascends from the Southern region towards the north and bumps into *você*, definitely in Santa Catarina".[9]

The generalization proposed by Koch (2000), according to which Santa Catarina is a transition zone between two greater linguistic areas – the *Paranaense* and the *Gaúcho* – can, to a certain extent, be seen at work. With these results from ALERS and the social history of Santa Catarina alone, it is already possible to relate the factor "colonizing ethnic group" to the variety found in the coastal and the Planalto Serrano cities as well as the northern and western regions of the state. The social and linguistic history of these areas allow us to correlate the following:

- Florianópolis and the use of *tu* due to the influence of the Azorean colonization (in the middle of the 18th century);
- Lages and the use of *você* due to the influence of the *Paulista* colonization (in the middle of the 18th century);
- Blumenau and the preferred use of *você*, through the influence of school (at the beginning of the 20th century);
- Chapecó and the preferred use of *tu* due to the influence of the *Gaúcho* colonization (at the beginning of the 20th century).

In spite of the fact that the social history of the state of Santa Catarina, as told by historians and linguists, helps us to understand the role the colonizing ethnic groups played in the language used today in the state, it is easy to perceive that some ethnic groups – especially those from the European continent – are privileged in this narrative. It is undeniable, however, that other ethnic groups, frequently made invisible in the historical narrative as told by Europeans, have significantly contributed to the formation of the *Catarinense*, and consequently, to the language spoken by them. Some noteworthy examples are the roles played by the Kaingang, Xokleng and Guarani peoples, who still inhabit (though in small numbers) the state of Santa Catarina. In addition, the *Catarinense* are, to a considerable degree, made up of individuals of African descent. This is mainly due to the centuries of slavery to which Africans and African descendants were

---

9 The triangles in the yellow areas indicate the places where speakers did not use a pronoun. These results will not be taken into account in this analysis, since the research did not control whether the null pronoun was *tu* (Ø *Sabes que horas são?* – 'Do Ø know what time it is?') or *você*, which is often called neutral as it is not marked for person in the subject or verb morphology (Ø *sabe que horas são?* – 'Ø know the time?').

subjected on Brazilian territory. About 15% of the *Catarinense* population self-declared as "Black" in the 2010 census conducted by the Brazilian Institute of Geography and Statistics (IBGE). Few studies examine the influence of Indigenous and African peoples on the language spoken in the state and those that exist tend to focus on lexical aspects (Altenhofen 2002). In spite of this, we believe that "the" socio-historical context that we have presented here is an important factor in explaining the use of second person pronouns by *Catarinenses*, which will be discussed in the next sections.

3 The use of the present to explain the past

The description of the alternation between second person pronouns *tu* and *você* in spoken Portuguese, not only in Santa Catarina, but also in the remaining two states of the Southern Region, was greatly aided by the creation in the 1990s of the VARSUL[10] (Linguistic Variation in Southern Brazil) database. The initial sample from Santa Catarina was complemented by samples consisting of sociolinguistic interviews that were similar in form to those of the initial data collection model used by VARSUL. These additional interviews contribute above all to the description of the Portuguese language spoken in the capital, which was, consequently, the preferred location for the subsequent sample collections.

Due to the update of the VARSUL database with data collected in subsequent decades, it is possible to make a comparison between the use of the pronouns in the 1990s, 2000s and 2010s in the city of Florianópolis. In order to conduct the comparison, we looked at studies by (a) Loregian-Penkal (2004), who analyzed the initial VARSUL sample and the Brescancini Sample;[11] (b) Rocha (2012),

---

10 "VARSUL (Linguistic Variation in the Southern Brazil) is a research nucleus that contains different data samples. In the Base Sample, there are 288 interviews conducted in the Southern Region in the 1990s. In each of the three states, the capitals and three other cities were chosen, the latter representative of different ethnicities and settlements: in Paraná, the cities of Curitiba, Irati, Londrina and Pato Branco; in Santa Catarina, the cities of Florianópolis, Chapecó, Lages and Blumenau; and in Rio Grande do Sul, the cities of Porto Alegre, Flores da Cunha, São Borja and Panambi. In each city, 24 interviews were carried out with informants stratified according to the variables gender, schooling and age group. More information on VARSUL can be found on their webpage: <www.varsul.org.br>" (Nunes de Souza 2015: 77).

11 "The Brescancini Sample consists of 12 interviews conducted by researcher Cláudia Regina Brescancini in the 1990s, for her master's thesis. The informants of this sample are residents of the Ribeirão da Ilha neighbourhood – the second oldest district in the capital of Santa Catarina, far from Downtown, where cultural characteristics (cuisine, architecture, economy) of the who cross-analyzed interviews from the initial VARSUL sample, the Monguilhott Sample[12] and the Floripa Sample; and (c) Davet (2013), who studied the Floripa Sample.[13] These studies present results about the alternation between the second person pronouns *tu* and *você* in the subject position, the varying realization of the verb agreement with the pronoun *tu,* and the correlation between pronouns used as subjects and pronouns used in other morphosyntactic contexts. These results are summarized in Table 1.

Table 1: Trends in the use of *tu* in speech data from Florianópolis in the 1990s and 2006–2012 (adapted from Loregian-Penkal 2004; Rocha 2012; and Davet 2013).

Variable	Controls	Trends in use	
		1990s	2006–2012
Second person singular subject pronoun	Preferred pronoun	*Tu*	*Tu*
	Social contexts	The young	The young
		Better educated	Better educated
		Women	Women
		Urban area	Urban area
		–	Symmetrical, asymmetrical and hierarchically descending relations
	Linguistic contexts	Determinate subject	–
		Pronoun is absent (null subject)	Pronoun is present (overt subject)

Loregian-Penkal's study (2004) takes into account both the linguistic behavior attributed to the community and the linguistic behavior found in individual anal-

Azorean settlers are preserved – and were equally divided by gender and schooling, on the basis of the VARSUL Sample-base, but not by age group" (Nunes de Souza 2015: 75).

12 "The Monguilhott Sample consists of 32 interviews, 16 of which were collected in Florianópolis and 16 in Lisbon during the years 2006 and 2007. On that occasion, the researcher Isabel de Oliveira e Silva Monguilhott collected the data for her doctoral thesis, defended in 2009. She was concerned with contemplating more and less urban areas in each of the cities, as well as informants of different educational levels and age groups, disregarding the variable 'gender'." (Nunes de Souza 2015: 76).

13 "The Floripa Sample consists of interviews conducted by students of the discipline Socio-linguistics and Dialectology, offered by the PPGLg (*Programa de Pós-Graduação em Linguística*) at UFSC (*Universidade Federal de Santa Catarina*), between 2009 and 2012, and includes a less urban area in the city of Florianópolis" (Nunes de Souza 2015: 76).

yses. She begins her investigation by presenting a chart indicating the individual preferences of the participants. Of the 24 interviewees in the urban areas of Florianópolis in the 1990s, 13 used only the pronoun *tu*, one used only *você*, and the remaining 10 alternated between the two pronouns. Of the 11 informants from Ribeirão da Ilha (a less urbanized neighborhood) in the same decade, seven used only the pronoun *tu* and four alternated between the two forms. In other words, none of the informants exclusively used *você* in Ribeirão da Ilha.

In her conclusion, Loregian-Penkal (2004) points to the predominance of pronoun *tu* over *você* both in urbanized Florianópolis and in Ribeirão da Ilha. In the initial VARSUL sample, in turn, the informants make use of *tu* in the subject position in 585 of the 767 occurrences of 2P (76%). In the Brescancini Sample (collected in Ribeirão da Ilha), this number becomes larger as the informants utilize the older pronoun in 445 of the 462 occurrences of 2P (96%), which reveals a more widespread use of *tu* in the less urbanized area in contrast with the more urbanized area of the *Catarinense* capital.

In the correlation between the dependent variable and the extralinguistic factor groups, a similarity can be perceived between the two locations investigated by the author. As far as the age of the informants is concerned, no significant statistical difference was found between age groups, but both locations show greater use of *tu* among informants aged between 25 and 49 than among those over 50. Regarding school instruction, both in Ribeirão da Ilha and in the urban areas the more educated speakers use *tu* more frequently than those with fewer years of schooling. Finally, although the difference in men's and women's use of *tu* is marked in the urban areas and minimal in the non-urban neighborhood, women appear to be leading the use of *tu* as opposed to *você* in both areas.

Loregian-Penkal (2004) also identifies contexts where the pronoun *tu* is more likely to occur in each location. In the more urbanized area of Florianópolis, the extralinguistic variables "gender" and "school instruction" are significant as they point to the same trends found in the frequencies: women and the more educated speakers tend to use the older pronoun *tu*. The linguistic variables "discourse determination"[14] and "overt *vs.* null-subject pronouns" are significant, with determinate discourse and the absence of the pronoun (null subject) favoring the

---

14 In the study by Loregian-Penkal (2004), the variable "discourse determination" refers to (in) determination of the pronoun referent. If the referent is recoverable, it is categorized as determinate; if there is no way to retrieve the referent, it is categorized as indeterminate. Among the examples offered by the author are the following: (i) when I came here the manager told me: *"É, Alemão, tu não é fácil"* ('Yes, German, you are not easy') (determinate); and (ii) *"pra entrá no hospital tu precisa dá uma entrada, senão eles não aceitam"* ('to enter the hospital you need to pay in advance, otherwise they will not take you in') (indeterminate).

use of *tu*. In Ribeirão da Ilha, in contrast, no extralinguistic variables are selected as significant. However, one linguistic variable is significant – "discourse determination", with determinate discourse favoring *tu*, which follows the pattern of use in the more urbanized area of the *Catarinense* capital.

Rocha (2012), in turn, investigates the distribution of the pronouns *tu*, *você*, and *o senhor* in subject position in 28 interviews. Four of the interviews were conducted in the 1990s, and the others between 2006 and 2009. Participants came from urban zones – the City Center and the Ingleses neighborhood – and less urban zones – the neighborhoods of Ribeirão da Ilha, Costa da Lagoa, Santo Antônio de Lisboa and Ratones. Rocha's results show that, of the 28 informants, 17 utilized *tu* categorically and 11 alternated between *tu* and *você* – no informants used the form *você* exclusively.

Rocha's findings (2012) correspond to those presented by Loregian-Penkal (2004): *tu* is favored by young, more educated, female speakers, and those who live in less urbanized urban zones. Rocha also found morphosyntactic correlations pointing towards symmetry in the use of clitics and possessives, with forms associated with the pronoun *tu* (*te*, *teu/tua*) being used in parallel with subject pronoun *tu*. Furthermore, The author identified a decrease in the rate of use of verbal agreement with *tu*, at 19%, contrasting to Loregian-Penkal's (2004) results of 43% in the central area and 60% in Ribeirão da Ilha.

It is worthwhile mentioning that Rocha (2012) correlated the alternation between *tu* and *você* with using or dropping the pronoun. His results regarding the linguistic variable "overt *vs.* null subject pronouns" show that both the use of the pronoun *tu* and the use of the pronoun *você* are related to a greater use of the subject pronoun, and possibly for that reason, the variable was not selected as significant. Of the 440 uses of *tu*, 349 (79%) are overt, and of the 99 uses of *você*, 77 (78%) are overt. We believe that the high rate of use of pronoun *tu* is associated with dropping the agreement morpheme, given that once the identification of the subject can no longer be rendered by verbal morphology, the use of the pronominal subject becomes necessary. This association will be further discussed in the following section, where we explore the variable "using the subject pronoun".

In a more recent study, Davet (2013) analyzed the verbal agreement with pronoun *tu* in more urbanized zones (Ingleses and City Center) and in less urbanized zones (Ribeirão da Ilha and Costa da Lagoa) of Florianópolis, using the Floripa Sample, collected between 2009 and 2012. Davet begins her investigation by mapping individual use of second person singular pronouns in the subject position. In the 31 interviews she examined, 22 informants made categorical use of *tu*, one informant used *você* exclusively, six informants alternated between the two forms, and two informants did not use any form of 2P pronouns. Of particular relevance to our analysis, the 959 occurrences of second person pronouns found by Davet comprise 147 uses of *você* (15%) and 812 of *tu* (85%). This indicates that the high rates of use of the pronoun *tu* in Florianópolis speech data from the beginning of the 21st century have been maintained.

Other studies of Florianópolis speech have explored individual attitudes towards second person singular pronouns. Part of the study conducted by Ramos (1989) was dedicated to interviewing 36 informants, born and living in urban areas of the city, about their attitudes towards the pronouns *tu* and *você*. The results are presented in Figure 1.

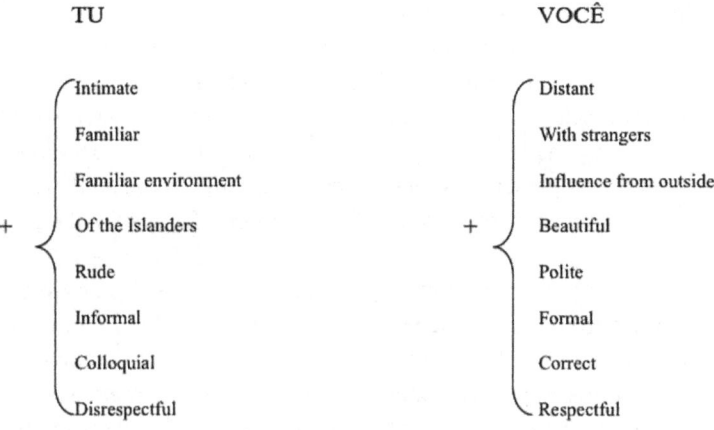

Figure 1: Attitudes towards pronouns *tu* and *você* in Florianópolis. (adapted from Ramos 1989: 46)

4 reveals that Ramos's (1989) informants evaluate the pronoun *tu* in a varied manner, attributing to the form both positive or neutral values like "intimate", "familiar", "of the islanders", "informal" and "colloquial", and negative values, such as "rude" and "disrespectful". On the other hand, *você* is associated with mostly positive or neutral values, such as "beautiful", "correct", or "influence from outside" – even though outsider influence is not always welcome by the residents of the island, as noted by Pagotto (2004). A closer look into the appendices of Ramos's (1989) dissertation, however, shows that pronoun *você* is, at times, evaluated by her participants as "snobbish", a negative value. This evaluation is confirmed in non-systematic observations of spontaneous conversations by Florianópolis residents.

Rocha (2012) also conducted attitudinal tests with 40 speakers from Florianópolis. When asked which form they considered more beautiful, 11% of the informants chose *tu*, 40% chose *você*, 28% chose *senhor* and 12% selected none.

When asked which form they considered ugly or bad, 34% answered *tu*, 4% chose *você*, 2% chose *senhor* and 60% picked none of the options. Although the two studies are 23 years apart, their results seem to reveal the prestige of the form *você* and a certain stigma associated with *tu*, even though, in terms of use, the islanders prefer *tu*, as repeatedly indicated by Loregian-Penkal (2004), Rocha (2012), and Davet (2013).

In order to understand the distinctiveness of second person singular pronoun distribution in the city of Florianópolis, it is useful to compare studies conducted in the capital with studies examining speech data from other locations in Santa Catarina. We believe that the differences found among the cities may in great part be due to their different socio-historical contexts.

Hausen (2000) sought to investigate two variables, the alternation between the 2P pronouns and the varying marking of verbal agreement with pronoun *tu*, starting with the initial VARSUL sample of the cities of Blumenau, Chapecó and Lages. Generally speaking, as far as the distribution of pronouns is concerned, the cities of Santa Catarina present distinct patterns, although some similarities can be pointed out in relation to the groups of conditioning factors for the pronoun's distribution.

Hausen (2000) begins the mapping of pronoun distribution by observing whether there is co-occurrence of *tu* and *você* in the subject position in the same sociolinguistic interview. In 53 of the 72 interviews analyzed, there is variation between the two pronouns. However, some categorical behaviors are observed: (i) three speakers from Blumenau and two from Chapecó use only *tu* during the interview; (ii) two informants from Blumenau, five from Chapecó and six from Lages make categorical use of the pronoun você; (iii) one informant from Blumenau does not use any second person singular pronouns: and (iv) no informants from Lages make categorical use of the pronoun *tu*.

The overall pronoun distribution, presented in Table 2, indicates that *você* is more widely used than *tu*, which is different from the distribution in the capital Florianópolis.

Despite the preponderance of *você* in the corpus (74%, or 1,587 of 2,148 uses), some particularities in the use of *tu* (26%, or 561 of the 2,148 uses) in the subject position deserve attention. The first is related to the distribution of variants across localities. Both in Blumenau and Lages, there is a minority use of *tu* (23% and 26% respectively); in Chapecó, on the other hand, the distribution of the two variants is evenly balanced at 50% each.

This preference for *você* can be explained by the socio-historical context of the state. The history of the cities investigated by Hausen (2000) is different from that of the capital, colonized by Azoreans in the 18th century. As we saw in Section 2, Lages was a checkpoint for *Mineiro* and *Paulista* cattlemen in the 18th

Table 2: Use of *tu* as opposed to *você* in the subject position in Blumenau, Chapecó and Lages according to informants' social characteristics (adapted from Hausen 2000: 69).

Social characteristics		BLUMENAU		CHAPECÓ		LAGES		TOTAL	
		Tu/ Total	%	*Tu/* Total	%	*Tu/* Total	%	*Tu/* Total	%
Age	25–50	97/ 321	30%	199/ 316	63%	155/ 806	19%	451/ 1.443	31%
	>50	16/ 178	9%	64/ 205	31%	30/ 322	9%	110/ 705	16%
School Instruction[15]	Elementary	41/1 47	28%	46/ 123	37%	17/ 228	07%	104/ 498	21%
	Middle School	28/ 146	19%	110/ 173	64%	68/ 415	16%	206/ 734	28%
	High School	44/ 206	21%	107/ 225	48%	100/ 485	21%	251/ 916	27%
Gender	Female	82/ 172	48%	148/ 245	60%	109/ 478	23%	339/ 895	38%
	Male	31/ 327	09%	115/ 276	42%	76/ 650	12%	222/ 1.253	18%
	Total	113/ 499	23%	263/ 521	50%	185/ 1.128	16%	561/ 2.148	26%

century[16] and was part of the captaincy of São Paulo until 1820. Nowadays, we can observe that the form *você* and its reduced variants *ocê* and *cê* are the most frequent 2P pronouns in the states of Minas Gerais and São Paulo. This observation allows us to establish a relationship between the "colonizing ethnicity" factor and the variation demonstrated in the Planalto Serrano city.

---

15 In the Brazilian school system, the three stages correspond to the first 5, 9 and 12 years of formal education, respectively.

16 As observed in the previous section, cattlemen from Rio Grande do Sul (*Gaúchos*) also crossed Lages, and later new Gauchos arrived at the locality, so that residents of the Planalto Serrano of Santa Catarina still conserve many habits common to the *Gaúchos*. However, although one might suppose that the influence of Rio Grande do Sul in Lages also affected the use of 2P pronouns, this is not what the studies by Hausen (2000) and Loregian-Penkal (2004) indicate. They point to a prevalence of *você* in Lages and a preference for the pronoun *tu* in the four Rio Grande do Sul cities that make up the initial VARSUL sample. These results are in line with what the social history of the region indicates. Although the Southeastern and Southern cattlemen crossed Santa Catarina's Planalto Serrano, the latter had to pay to stay overnight at the checkpoint located in Lages.

Similarly, explanations for the pronoun distribution in Blumenau can be drawn from social history. In this location, Portuguese was learned from the beginning of the 20th century at school, as a second language, where the form *você* was privileged through its presence in schoolbooks. Regarding Western Santa Catarina, Chapecó is the city with the highest rate of *tu* use (50%), as well as the lowest rate of distinctive second person singular morphemes on the verb that accompanies the pronoun (3%, or 5/161). This combination resembles the variety spoken in Rio Grande do Sul, where rates of *tu* use are quite high – exceeding 90% – and agreement with this pronoun is rare (commonly below 10%), according to Loregian-Penkal (2004)[17] and Amaral (2003).[18] Such similarities are certainly not due to chance and can be explained via social history, as emphasized in Section 2.

Table 2 also shows that, in spite of the general preferences for one or the other variant in each locality, the speakers of the younger age group are the ones who more frequently use the pronoun *tu*, with 30% of occurrences in Blumenau (as opposed to 9% for older speakers), 63% in Chapecó (as opposed to 31% for older speakers) and 19% in Lages (as opposed to 9% for older speakers). Likewise, female informants use the variant *tu* more often than male informants in all cities investigated by Hausen (2000), regardless of whether the general preference in the locality is *tu* or *você*. In Blumenau, women use *tu* in 48% of cases (men, in only 9%); in Chapecó women use *tu* in 60% of cases (42% for men); and in Lages women use *tu* in 23% of cases (18% for men).

However, there does not seem to be a direct relationship between the use of *tu* and level of school instruction – at least not one shared by the three cities in question. In Blumenau, the least educated informants more often employ the pronoun *tu* (28%, compared to 19% of those with middle school education and 21% with high school education), whereas in Chapecó it is the speakers with middle school education who more frequently use pronoun *tu* (64%, compared to the less educated with 37%, and those with most schooling, with 48%). In Lages, *tu* is favored by those with high school education (21%, compared to the less educated with 7%, and to those with middle school education, with 16%).

Hausen (2000) also examined linguistic contexts that could correlate to the distribution of second person pronouns. When the variant form *tu* is used to refer directly to an interlocutor – in a dialogue with the interviewer (29% of occur-

---

17 In his thesis, Loregian-Penkal (2004) analyzed the alternation between the pronouns *tu* and *você* and the verbal agreement with pronoun *tu* in VARSUL Base Sample data from the four cities of Santa Catarina and the four cities of Rio Grande do Sul covered by the database.

18 Amaral (2003) analyzed sociolinguistic interviews conducted in the city of Pelotas (RS) between 2000 and 2001, belonging to the Sociolinguistic Data Base per Social Class (VarX).

rences), with a phatic function (59%), in reported speech from others (33%), in self-reported speech (46%), and with third parties during the interview (50%), it is used more often than with an indeterminate referent (22%). This seems to point to the fact that *você*, among the second person singular pronouns, is the favored form with indeterminate referents, which reveals traces of its non-pronominal origins.

The results of these studies that examine variation between *tu* and *você* in speech in Santa Catarina indicate some trends in pronoun use. Among the four cities investigated, the pronoun *tu* is used most, in percentage terms, in Florianópolis, followed by Chapecó, Blumenau, and Lages, in that order. The social history of these various locations provides clues to understanding these trends.

In all localities, in spite of the general preference for one or the other variant, *tu* is used more by the young than by the elderly, more by women than by men, and more frequently employed with determinate than with indeterminate reference. In Florianópolis and Lages, the better educated lead the use of *tu*, even though, in the capital, the older pronoun is preferred and, in the city of Planalto Serrano, speakers prefer the more innovative pronoun. As far as Florianópolis is concerned, *tu* is associated with less urbanized areas, symmetrical relations and descending asymmetrical relations, as well as with overt subjects. The form *você*, which is not favored in the capital, is evaluated more highly than the form *tu*.

We consider that these most recent analyses of data on the distribution of second person singular pronouns in Santa Catarina should provide evidence of the varying use of pronominal forms in the past. In the same way, in the personal letter samples, evidence is sought that may corroborate the hypotheses proposed for the interpretation of current linguistic uses based on the social history of the state of Santa Catarina. Due to the limitations of the material gathered so far, the analysis focusses mainly on data from the Greater Florianópolis area, but a counterpoint can be established with the city of Lages (and, on a smaller scale, with the city of Blumenau) when dealing with data from the second half of the 20th century.

4 From past to present: epistolary writing of the 19th and 20th centuries

This section examines the distribution of pronouns *tu* and *você* in the subject position in six samples of letters from the PHPB-SC,[19] covering the period between

---

[19] Projeto Para a História do Português Brasileiro – Santa Catarina (Project for the History of Brazilian Portuguese in Santa Catarina).

the 1870s and the 1990s. Although the letters are relatively homogeneous, they differ from one another and display idiosyncrasies. There are also disparities in the quantity and quality of these historical texts left for posterity, which, in the words of Conde Silvestre (2007: 36), are "survivors by chance".

The following sections set out similarities and differences between the letters. The analysis takes into account linguistic (internal) variables – the factors that control the pronoun in subject position – and extralinguistic (external) variables – when the letters were written, the gender of sender and recipient, the relationship between sender and recipient, and the topic of the letters. This is followed by an analysis of pronominal alternation in the corpus, with a focus on letters from the city of Florianópolis. Given that this is a diachronic study, the analysis includes a reconstruction of the social context, both at a macro-sociological level and at a level closer to the specific context in which the letters were written.

4.1 Letter samples

CS Sample: consists of 35 love and friendship letters written during the 1870s, 1880s and 1890s. The protagonist of the sample (CS), at times the sender, at times the recipient, is a renowned poet of the Symbolist literary school in Brazil. Although the phrase "public figure" could be attributed to the sample, given the poet's public life and literary production, it is important to emphasize that the writer only became acknowledged after his death. The contents of these letters are linked to the relation between sender and recipient. There are love letters from the poet to his fiancée; letters addressed to the poet written by two friends, who were also writers (VV and AF) and who were politically active in Desterro, talking about friendship and the social context of the time; and letters sent by the poet's father, whose contents involve family themes.

JB Sample: is composed of 15 letters of friendship, written by six senders to the politician and intellectual JB between the 1880s and 1930s. Among the senders is the writer VV, who also kept in constant communication with CS. The other senders – RF, UC, VK, TC and EF – seem to have been friends with JB, although, to a certain extent, there is a political slant. Sample JB was created during the lifetime of the JB (1865–1934) and LB (1880–1966) siblings. JB was born in Desterro and founded the Law School there, as well as the Historical-Geographical Institute of Santa Catarina and the Academy of Letters of Santa Catarina (Cunha 2008). He can, therefore, be considered a "public figure" recipient.

MS Sample: consists of 68 letters to friends sent by the writer MS (1904–1991) to five recipients – four men and one woman – in the 1960s, 1970s, 1980s, and 1990s. The men are all writers and the only female recipient is responsible for the MS "folder" at the Academy of Letters of Santa Catarina. The missives range from updates on the writer's personal life to information about the Brazilian literary universe, with special attention to Santa Catarina, and were largely sent from the city of Rio de Janeiro, where the writer lived after her divorce at a young age. Born in Florianópolis, MS is considered a "public figure" because she was the first woman to hold a chair at an Academy of Letters in Brazil. In addition, she wrote several books, and had a recognized public life. The writer was also involved in feminist and environmental causes and is often portrayed as "a woman ahead of her time" (see Schroeder 1997).

HL Sample: is composed of 93 friendship letters sent by *Catarinense* writer HL to his translator and friend CC during the 1980s and 1990s. Born in Tijucas, in the Greater Florianópolis, HL is considered to be a "public figure", since he has a well-known public life, and his letters to CC deal with both professional and personal matters. The letters document the relationship between writer and translator, which grows over the years, and although the subjects of the letters contemplate questions related to translation and publication of books, it is especially dedicated to narratives concerning the friendship between sender and recipient (Nunes de Souza 2015; Grando 2016).

DS/MD Samples: consist of a combination of two samples, DS and MD, and include 23 love and friendship letters, written by different letter writers. The DS Sample consists of six love letters written by men, addressing women, in the 1950s and one love letter written by a man to a woman in the 1970s. The MD Sample consists of 16 letters from female friends and family members written in the 1980s to a single female addressee. Little is known about the interlocutors of the DS Sample besides their love relationships, which can be inferred from the content of the missives. The MD Sample has the social profile of its known interlocutors. This sample consists of letters sent to a student, in the health care area, by her mother, cousins, and friend while she was away in Florianópolis pursuing higher education. The letters contain updates on school and social life in their hometown in the case of the letters written by the younger letter writers, and instructions for the payment of bills and purchase of books, besides parents' news, in the letters written by the mother.

The two samples were combined due to the limited number of letters in the DS Sample, the theme and temporal proximity of the samples, and, above all, the fact that the two samples are written not only by "private individuals", but also by non-natives of the capital of Santa Catarina. The interlocutors are from the region of Lages, whose social history differs from that of the coastal regions, where the capital is located. Lages was a checkpoint on the *Tropeiros* route, as previously mentioned, which seems to have contributed to its economic, cultural, and linguistic structure.

VL Sample: is composed of 41 love and friendship letters written by 15 young women to the same addressee in Vale do Itajaí, in the 1960s. The senders were born in Santa Catarina and lived in the Greater Florianópolis area, in Vale do Itajaí, in the Planalto Serrano, and in the north of the state. They write to the same recipient, a young male Portuguese teacher who was also a musician and who traveled with his band to many cities in the state. Most of the senders give signals of being romantically interested in the musician, but the letters also talk about friendship. Overall, the sample is interesting as it consists of letter writers from different localities in Santa Catarina, thus shedding light on the distribution of second person singular pronouns in different regions of the state. Moreover, the senders may be considered "private individuals" and, since they are young, it is inferred that they have not yet finished high school, which means that the sample is composed of more vernacular characteristics than those composed of letters written by "public figure" senders.

4.2 Description of second person singular pronouns in letters by Catarinenses

Table 3 presents information about the six samples, detailing the sender-recipient dyads, the gender of the interlocutors, and preferences for the use of the second person singular pronouns in the subject position in each sample, based on number of occurrences.

Table 3 shows that the oldest letters – the CS Sample (1870/1880/1890) – contain only the subject-pronoun *tu*. From the JB Sample (1880/1910/1920/1930) onwards, pronouns *tu* and *você* begin to be used interchangeably as subject. In the JB sample, a preference for *você* can be noticed, and is repeated, to a greater or lesser extent, in the MS (1960/1970/1980/1990), DS/MD (1850/1970/1980) and VL (1960) Samples. Only in the HL Sample (1980/1990) is *tu* the preferred form.

General preferences for *tu* or *você* in the samples, at first glance, do not seem to clearly follow a regular pattern. Knowing that the new form is *você*, it could be expected that, in the course of more than a century of epistolary writing, the old form *tu* would lose space to its competitor. That prediction is only partially met, since diachronically there is a transition from the categorical use of *tu* to an alternating use of *tu* and *você*. However, focusing on the letters from the capital, more robust patterns of use of the second person singular pronouns can be discerned, especially between different localities and different styles. In the analysis, therefore, we seek to explain the uses of *tu* and *você* according to four dimensions: the historical/diachronic, the social, the geographical and the stylistic.

Table 3: General characterization of sender-recipient dyads within the samples and occurrence of second person singular subject pronouns.

Total letters by sample and period	Sender(s)	Recipient(s)	Gender (sender-recipient)	Subject Pronoun	
				Tu	*Você*
CS Sample	CS	Fiancée G.	M – F	28	–
35 letters	VV	CS	M – M	36	–
(Florianópolis)	AF	CS	M – M	33	–
1870–1890	CS's father	CS	M – M	13	–
		Total		110/110 (100%)	0/110 (0%)
JB Sample	RF	JB	M – M	2	–
15 letters	VV	JB	M – M	2	2
(Florianópolis)	UC	JB	M – M	–	1
1880–1930	VK	JB	M – M	–	3
	TC	JB	M – M	–	1
	EF	JB	M – M	–	4[20]
		Total		4/15 (26%)	11/15 (74%)
MS Sample	MS	N	F – M	6	146
68 letters	MS	P	F – M	20	–
(Florianópolis)	MS	S	F – F	2	5
1960–1990	MS	C	F – M	30	17
	MS	Z	F – M	11	–
		Total		69/237 (29%)	168/237 (71%)
HL Sample	HL	CC	M – F	316	29
93 letters		Total		316/345 (92%)	29/345 (8%)
(Florianópolis)					
1980–1990					

(continued)

---

20 The sender remarks that his daughter is writing the letter because he is ill at that moment.

Table 3: (continued)

DS and MD	S	J	F – F	–	33
Samples	F	J	F – F	1	11
(Lages)	B	J	F – F	–	3
23 letters	R	J	F – F	–	7
1950–1980	W	X	M – F	13	9
	A	X	M – F	1	28
			Total	15/106 (15%)	91/106 (85%)
VL Sample	A	N	F – M	10	2
41 letters	B	N	F – M	4	1
(different	C	N	F – M	5	-
localities)	D	N	F – M	6	41
1960	E	N	F – M	4	8
	J	N	F – M	15	1
	L	N	F – M	1	5
	M	N	F – M	5	-
	N	N	F – M	1	13
	O	N	F – M	40	4
	R	N	F – M	1	21
	T	N	F – M	2	2
	V	N	F – M	–	5
	Y	N	F – M	2	4
	Z	N	F – M	2	1
			Total	98/206 (48%)	108/206 (52%)

Considering the historical/diachronic dimension, the 19th century shows stability (with a categorical use of *tu*), whereas the 20th century is more unstable (with variation between the forms *tu~você*). In order to better understand the instability of the 20th century, Table 4 highlights patterns of use in a subset of samples that have a robust dataset and greater variation between the 2P pronouns.

Table 4: Distribution of 2P pronouns in Samples MS, DS/MD and VL.

Samples	Sender	Recipient	Gender	Tu	Você
MS	MS	N	F–M	6	146
(29% *tu* and 71% *você*)	MS	P	F–M	20	–
	MS	C	F–M	30	17

Table 4 (continued)

Samples	Sender	Recipient	Gender	*Tu*	*Você*
DS and MD	S	J	F–F	–	33
(15% *tu* and 85% *você*)	W	A	M–F	13	9
	A	T	M–F	1	29
VL	D	N	F–M	6	41
(48% *tu* and 52% *você*)	O	N	F–M	40	4

This subset of samples, located between the 1950s and the 1980s, generally indicates that the form *você* is more productive than the alternative *tu*, with 71% *você* in the MS Sample, 85% in the DS and MD Samples, and 52% in the VL Sample. It is not a coincidence that, among the three samples with the greatest variation, two involve writers who are not considered public figures: this may be evidence that better educated people tend to show less variation in their writing, which would, consequently, reveal a relationship between pronominal variation and the social dimension of language.

Similarly, the linguistic behavior of sender W from Samples DS/MD appears to be, to some extent, associated with social factors. Even though in the three samples singled out here the form *você* prevails, W prefers to use *tu*. A quick examination of W's letters reveals that, among the letter writers included in this section, W is the one who least mastered writing (See Nunes de Souza 2015). Examples (9), (10) and (11) illustrate W's linguistic behavior. In examples (10) and (11), in addition, we note how insecure W is about his writing.

(9)   Bem *deves saber que intereçei /*
      Well **Ø.2sg should.pres.2sgknow.inf** that [I] was interested/
      que vosse se acertasse com o J novamente
      /that **you.2sgmake up.pres.3sg** with J again/
      muinto conselho dei a ele
      /many pieces of advice [I]did give to him,/
      não sei se viz – bem ou mal
      /not know if [I] did [it] – well or bad/
      o outro rapaz também *não éra mau*
      /the other lad also not was bad,/
      mais estava muito errado em debochar o outro por isto
      /but [he] was very wrong in mocking the other for this,/
      e eu era comtra, fiquei satisfeito quando sube
      /and I was against [it], [I]was pleased to know/
      que vosse estava bem com o J [...]
      /that **you.2sg be.imperf.2sg** good with J [...]/

'You should well know that I was interested in seeing you and J make up again. I did give him many pieces of advice. I don't know if I have done well or not. The other lad wasn't bad either, but he was very wrong in mocking the other for such a thing, and I was against it. I was pleased to know that you were on good terms with J' (W, 195-)

(10) Nesta pesso desculpar as faltas
/In this [I] ask to apologize for faults,/
pois a minha inteligecia não é igual a *tua*
/as my intelligence not is match for **yours.2sg.poss**/
muito falta-me para comparar
/much lacks me to compare [to you],/
por isso não mantenho legível.
/therefore [I] not remain readable./
Aceite um forte adeusinho
/**Accept.imp.2sg** a strong so long/

'This is to apologize for my faults, as my intelligence is no match for yours. I have a long way to go before I can compare to you, therefore I remain unreadable. Accept a strong "so long"' (W, 1952)

(11) Sempre lembrada Minhas saudades Hoje neste feliz momento/
Forever remembered My longing Today in this happy moment/
e que dirijo-me a indereçar-*te*
/and that [I]bring myself to addressing **you.2sg.dat**/
estas mal escritas...
/these poorly written.../

'Forever remembered my longing today in this happy moment that I bring myself to addressing you these poorly written [lines]' (W, 195-)

Table 4 only highlights letter writers who have a considerable number of letters. By singling these letters out, two cells reveal categorical behaviors: one with exclusive use of *tu* (sender MS – recipient N) and another with categorical use of *você* (sender S – recipient N). The letters written by S show individual stability in the use of *você*. In the letters by MS, however, the use of pronouns varies if we consider the entire sample. Depending on who the interlocutor is, the sender uses *tu* (to recipients P and C) or *você* (to recipient N). As the content of the letters is similar for all recipients, it is the relationship between writer and recipient, which is unknown to us, and the period in which the letters were written, which can influence pronoun use, as will be discussed below.

Turning to the geographical dimension, the results presented in Section 3 from studies that, to a considerable extent, had the *VARSUL* database as corpus, point to regional differences in the use of second person singular pronouns in Santa Catarina. The *VARSUL* Base Sample was formed based on a socio-historical hypothesis, namely that different types of colonization would lead to different linguistic behaviors. In our letter samples, there are only a limited number of letters from the 20th century whose writers' birthplace is known. It is therefore not possible to map the linguistic behaviors of all six of what are known as the mesoregions of Santa Catarina (the Greater Florianópolis Area, Northern Santa Catarina, Western Santa Catarina, Planalto Serrano, Southern Santa Catarina and Vale do Itajaí).[21] However, we can point to different pronoun preferences by comparing senders from the Greater Florianópolis area with senders from other mesoregions of the state (see Map 4 below).

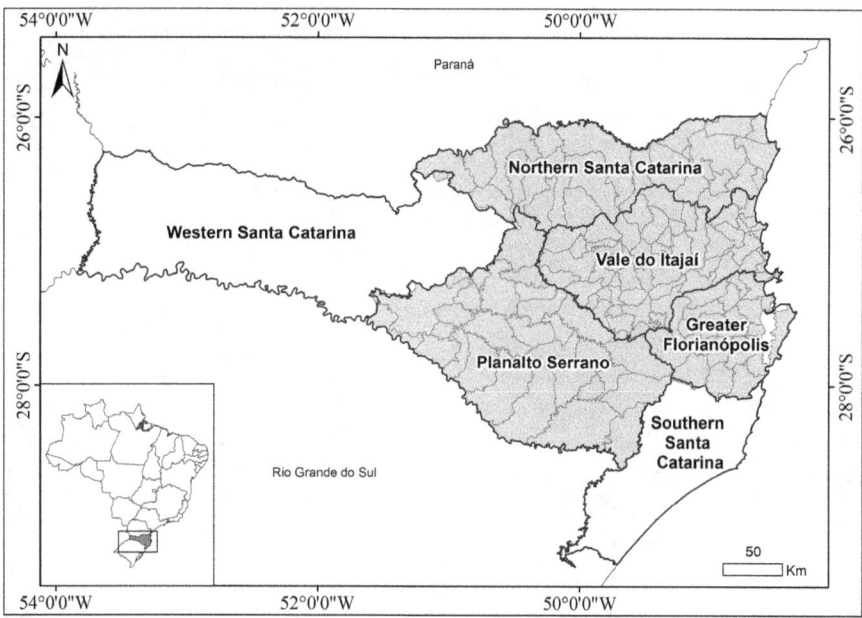

Map 4: Map of the mesoregions of Santa Catarina (Brazil).

---

21 A mesoregion in Brazil is a subdivision of a state that groups together municipalities that are geographically close and share common characteristics. It should be noted that the state of Santa Catarina is divided into mesoregions by strictly geographical criteria, not by colonizing ethnical group or economic activity, although there is in many cases an overlapping of these characteristics. Taking the Greater Florianópolis as an example, it is observed that the colonizing ethnic group is predominantly Azorean, but the municipality of Angelina, colonized by Germans, for example, is part of that mesoregion.

Table 5: Use of *tu* and *você* in the subject position in the 20th century, by senders' mesoregion.

	Personal letters by *Catarinenses* in the 20th century			
Mesoregion	Status	Letter writer	*Tu*	*Você*
Greater Florianópolis	Private individual	A	10	2
	Private individual	B	4	1
	Private individual	C	5	0
	Private individual	E	4	8
	Private individual	L	1	5
	Private individual	O	40	4
	Private individual	T	2	2
	Private individual	Z	1	1
	Subtotal		68 (75%)	23 (25%)
	Public figure	MS	69	168
	Public figure	HL	316	29
	Subtotal		385 (66%)	197 (34%)
	Total		453 (67%)	220 (33%)
Planalto Serrano	Private individual	S	0	33
	Private individual	F	1	11
	Private individual	B	0	3
	Private individual	R	0	7
	Private individual	W	13	9
	Private individual	A	1	28
	Private individual	Y	2	4
	Total		17 (15%)	95 (85%)
Vale do Itajaí	Private individual	J	15	1
	Private individual	N	1	13
	Private individual	R	1	21
	Private individual	V	0	5
	Total		17 (30%)	40 (70%)
Northern Santa Catarina	Private individual	D	6	41
	Total		6 (13%)	41 (87%)

The Table 5 presents letter writers classified according to their geographical origin and status (public figure/private individual), and no longer references the samples of which they are part.

Beginning with the public figures from the Greater Florianópolis mesoregion (MS is from Florianópolis and HL was born in Tijucas), their preferences seem more dependent on individual choice than on a pattern followed by the community. While HL mostly makes use of pronoun *tu*, MS prefers the form *você*. The period in which MS writes may help us interpret the linguistic uses made by the writer, as we discuss in the following sections.

For the private writers, even though, individually, some contradict the general pattern exhibited by mesoregion, the difference overall between the Greater Florianópolis area and other localities is evident. Writers from the Greater Florianópolis area use *tu* in 75% of cases, whereas those from the Planalto Serrano mesoregion use *tu* in only 15% of cases. Similarly, writers from the Vale do Itajaí mesoregion (which has an outlet to the sea like Florianópolis, but unlike the capital was mainly colonized by Germans and Italians) use the form *você* 70% of the time, and those from the North use *você* 87% of the time (with the caveat that the North is represented in the sample by a single letter writer). We can draw a parallel between Blumenau and the cities such as Lages whose data were analyzed (see Section 2). Blumenau, which shows a low rate of *tu* usage in speech data, is also located in Vale do Itajaí; the city of Lages, also preferring the form *você* in speech, is in the Planalto Serrano mesoregion. These results corroborate the strong correlation established between colonizing ethnic group and choice of 2P pronoun.

Moreover, important considerations about the use of *tu* and *você* by decade can be drawn from Table 5. Even though each sample displays preferences for one or the other 2P pronoun, in the MS Sample the supremacy of pronoun *você* in the 1960s and 1970s gives way to a homogeneous distribution of pronouns *tu* and *você* in the 1980s. Once *você* was the novel form, its decreasing usage was unexpected. A thorough analysis of the writer's letters, however, reveals an explanation for this behavior.

In the letters from the 1980s, MS announces the beginning of her retirement. In the same decade the author begins to express dissatisfaction with her illnesses and those of her partner, and with small domestic accidents which seem to steal away her focus on her writing. This is hinted at in examples (12) to (15).

(12)   Cousin vai dar à Achiamé inéditos vários
       /Cousin will give to Achiamé *unpublished* many/
       (contos, crônicas, ensaios, reedição)
       /(short stories, chronicles, essays, new editions)/
       mas eu não darei mais nada, pois ele, me deixou mais doente –
       /but I not will give anything else, since he me made more ill –/
       e eu fiquei há 5 anos com o corpo e alma abalados,
       /and I have been for 5 years with body and soul shaken,/
       como você sabe.
       /as **you.2sg know.pres.3sg**./

'Cousin will give Achiamé many unseen [works] (short stories, chronicles, essays, new editions) but I won't give anything else, since he made me more ill – and I have spent five years with my body and soul shaken, as you know' (MS, 1984)

(13)   Querido, vamos muito conversar pessoalmente,
       /Dear, [we] are going much to speak in person,/
       mas, se *puderes*,
       /but if Ø.2sgcan.past.2sg, /
       fala nos dois assuntos de que falei
       /talk about the two subjects of which [I] have spoken/
       nestas mal traçadas.
        in these badly written./

'Darling, we are going to speak a great deal in person, but if you can, talk about the two subjects I have spoken of in these badly written [lines]' (MS, 1987)

(14)   Não quis escrever para não deixar a respiração na carta
       /[I] Not want to write to not let [my] breathing in the letter/
       e não pude telefonar de novo
       /and [I] not could telephone again/
       porque a voz não permitia.[...]
       /because the voice not would allow [it] [...]/
       Eu quero dizer-*te* que o frio está uma loucura aqui,
       /I want to let **you.2sg.dat** know that the cold is a madness here,/
       estou com os dedos duros e roxos
       /[I] have [my] fingers hardened and purple/
       e ainda queimei o polegar direito
       /and on top of that [I]have burned [my] right thumb/
       na cozinha.
       /in the kitchen./

'I did not want to write so as not to breathe on [*sic*] the letter and I could not telephone again because my voice would not allow it [...]. I want to let you know the cold is crazy here, my fingers are hardened and purple and on top of that I have burned my right thumb in the kitchen' (MS, 1987)

(15)   Piorei muito da gripe forte –
       /[I]became much worse from the flu strong –/
       e por isso não *te* telefonei nem *te* escrevi.

/and because of that not **you.2sg.dat** ring or **you.2sg.dat** wrote./
Melhorei um pouco e aqui *te* mando estes garranchos,
/[I]got a little better and here [I] **you.2sg.dat** send these scribbles,/
que peço que *rasgues.*
/which [I] **ask** [that] **Ø.2sg tear apart.pres.2sg**./
Se eu morrer, peço que sejas muito amigo de Cousin.
/If I die, [I] ask that **Ø.2sg be.pres.2sg** friends with Cousin./
Ele está aflito.
/He is distressed./

'I became much worse from the strong flu – and because of that I have not called or written. I feel a little better now and I send you these scribbles, which I ask you to tear up. If I die, I ask that you be friends with Cousin. He is distressed' (MS, 1988)

These examples suggest a relation between the amount of attention dedicated to writing and the choice between one or the other pronoun, with the higher rates of *tu* occurring when MS appears less focused. This behavior allows us to draw a conclusion regarding the stylistic dimension mentioned earlier: when both 2P pronouns are part of a speaker's linguistic repertoire, the pronouns are used in different discourse contexts. This observation is further supported by sender E, from the VL Sample, who reveals to her recipient that she prefers to use *tu* in oral speech (normally considered more informal than writing) and with close relations, while opting for *você* in writing, as shown in example (16).

(16)   *Você* também *deve* ter *notado*
/**You.2sg** also **might.pres.3sghave.infnotice.pp**/
a diferença de tratamento que *lhe* dispensei.
/the difference of treatment that [I] **you.2sg.dat** give/
Vou explicar-*lhe*:
/[I] will explain **you.2sg.dat**:/
considero o tratamento "você" muito impessoal por isso
/[I] consider the form of address "você" very impersonal, therefore/
prefiro-o para cartas ou para pessoas totalmente desconhecidas.
/[I] prefer it to letters or to people completely strangers./
O mais costumo usar "tu".
/Elsewhere [I] normally use "tu"./
Como vê, a gramática e eu não nos damos.
/As **Ø.2sg see.pres.3sg**, the grammar and I not get along well./

'You might have also noticed the different manner in which I addressed you. I shall explain: I consider the form of address "você" very impersonal, therefore I prefer to use it in letters or with complete strangers. Elsewhere I normally use "tu". As you see, grammar and I do not get along well' (E, 1965)

4.3 Variable subject use

We now turn to the topic of variable subject use. Current Brazilian Portuguese (BP) shows high rates of overt pronominal subject use, especially in the first and second person, according to Duarte (1993, 1995), Duarte et al. (2012), Kato & Duarte (2008) and Gravina (2008, 2014), who analyse data from the Southeast. In the third person, the change is greatly influenced by the [+animated] trace of the antecedent. The [-animated] trace of the antecedent is more resistant to the use of overt referential subjects.

We depart from studies on the representation of the subject in BP that point to a change in the *pro-drop* parameter. The generative literature in the 1980s associated the languages that were marked with the null subject parameter as having a set of properties that distinguishes them from the languages that are negatively marked for this parameter. In a language like Portuguese, two features are described as characterizing a null subject: (i) subject omission and (ii) "free" inversion of simple sentences.

Duarte's (1993) pioneering studies, based on a sample of plays written in Rio de Janeiro in the 19th and 20th centuries, reveal that first and second person show a steep decrease in the use of null subject from one century to the next. The studies make the connection between this decrease and changes in use of pronouns *tu*, *você* and *a gente* 'we'. Firstly, the fall in the null second person subject (dropping from 69% in 1918 to 25% in 1937–1938, and following the same downward trend in 1955, 1975–1986 and 1990–1992) is related to the decrease in use of pronoun *tu* and the increase in the use of *você* at the beginning of the 20th century. Secondly, the fall in the use of the null first person plural subject (decreasing from 56% in 1955 to 32% in 1975–1986 and 18% in 1990–1992) is related to the entry of the pronoun *a gente* in the pronominal paradigm in the 1950s. Both pronouns (*você* and *a gente*) agree with a 3P verb form, since that form does not mark person (*você/a gente amaØ* – 'you/we love'). Therefore, simplifications in the inflection paradigm and overt subject seem to be associated.

According to Duarte (1993, 1995), from 1930 on, BP has been transitioning from being a *pro-drop* language to a *non-pro-drop* language. The author shows that the loss in functionality of the verb inflection paradigm in BP, caused mainly by the use of *você/vocês* and *a gente* at the expense of pronouns *tu/vós* and *nós* ('we'), respectively, could help explain the ongoing change of the *pro-drop* parameter in this language. The third person is the only one that does not seem to be affected by the reduction in the paradigm, since the third person subject remains attached to the option allowed in *pro-drop* languages.

The initially proposed binary marking of the null subject (*pro-drop* and *non-pro-drop* languages) was, to a certain extent, abandoned by generative studies, once many languages showed specific conditions and contexts both for the occurrence and absence of null subject, being denominated "partial null-subject" languages. Currently, due to occasionally diverging theoretical approaches, some authors (see Kato & Duarte 2008; Gravina 2008, 2014, among others) have described the changes in the null subject parameter as evidence that BP could be included in the group of partial null-subject languages.

In general, these studies have shown that the null subject is restricted to determined syntactic environments. The empty category in the place of subject may have a diverse nature, interpreted not (only) by verb inflection, where personal pronouns are expressed by verb inflection, but by an antecedent expressed in syntactic, discourse, and pragmatic contexts. Our analysis observes the behavior of overt use of second person singular subject in samples from 19th and 20th century Santa Catarina in different decades, and does not take into account discussion on the third person.

In the set properties that compose the null-subject parameter, the verb-subject order (VS) has an important role, as can be observed in Romance languages like Italian and Spanish. Results of diachronic studies dealing with the phenomenon of order point to the 20th century as a period marked by a system with no VS syntactic restrictions (Berlinck 1988, 1995; Coelho 2006; Berlinck & Coelho 2018; among others), in contrast with the system of the 20th century, especially after the 1930s, with VS being progressively more restricted to contexts of unaccusative verbs. The fall of both VS order and the null subject seem to follow the same direction.

For the purposes of this study, it is relevant to seek evidence that (i) in 19th century *Catarinense* Portuguese, the second person pronominal subject (*tu*) was mostly null, since it could be identified by the morphemic mark on the verb (as happens in Italian and Spanish); and (ii) in 20th century *Catarinense* Portuguese, the second person pronominal subject (*tu~você*) was null especially when identified by the second person morphemic mark in the verb (2P) and was overt when combined with third person (3P) verb morphology.

Table 6 shows the correlation between pronominal alternation and the use of an overt pronominal subject, two phenomena undergoing variation/change in Brazilian Portuguese. The results presented take into account the external

Table 6: Overt versus null second person singular pronominal subject in the analyzed samples, organized by time period (**source:** the authors, including adaptations from Grando 2016: 46–47).

Sample	Decade	*Tu*		*Você*	
		Null	Overt	Null	Overt
CS	1870	4/5 80%	1/5 20%	–	–
	1880	27/35 78%	8/35 22%	–	–
	1890	56/70 80%	14/70 20%	–	–
	Total	**87/110** **79%**	**23/110** **21%**	–	–
JB	1880 and 1890	4/4 100%	0/4 0%	–	–
	20	–	–	7/11 64%	4/11 36%
	Total	**4/4** **100%**	**0/4** **0%**	**7/11** **64%**	**4/11** **36%**
MS	1960 and 1970	1/1 100%	0/1 0%	32/91 35%	59/91 65%
	1980 and 1990	65/68 96%	3/68 4%	34/77 44%	43/77 56%
	Total	**66/69** **96%**	**3/69** **4%**	**66/168** **40%**	**102/168** **60%**
HL	1980	177/190 93%	13/190 7%	13/26 50%	13/26 50%
	1990	112/126 89%	14/126 11%	0/3 0%	3/3 100%
	Total	**289/316** **91%**	**27/316** **9%**	**13/29** **45%**	**16/29** **55%**
DS and MD	1950	10/13 77%	3/13 23%	6/9 66%	3/9 34%
	1970	0/1 0%	1/1 100%	15/28 54%	13/28 46%
	1980	1/1 100%	0/1 0%	22/54 41%	32/54 59%
	Total	**11/15** **74%**	**4/15** **26%**	**43/91** **47%**	**48/91** **53%**
VL	1960 (Total)	92/98 **93%**	6/98 **7%**	31/108 **28%**	77/108 **72%**

variable of the period when the letter was written, and the internal variable of the use of an overt pronominal subject.

The results of the 19th century, represented predominantly by the CS sample, for the variable "overt *versus* null subject" reveal an impressive rate of null second person subject *tu* (79%), against a mere 21% of full subject. It is important to make the following observations about this sample. Firstly, all occurrences of pronoun *tu*, be they null or overt, are accompanied by verbs with distinctive 2P endings. The second person subject is expressed on the verb (see Kato & Duarte 2008). Secondly, when overt, the subject is accompanied by additional information for emphasis or contrast. In these cases, in general, the pronoun could not be omitted. Examples (17) and (18) illustrate this strategy.

(17) Só *tu és* merecedôra
      /Only **you.2sg be.pres.2sg** deserving/
      de que eu *te* ame muito, como *te* amo,
      /of that I **you.2sg.acc** love a lot, as I **you.2sg.acc** love,/
      muito, muito, muito, e cada vez mais, com mais firmeza,
      /a lot, a lot, a lot, and always more, with more steadfastness,/
      sempre fiél, sempre teu escravo bom e
      /*always faithful, always your slave good and*/
      agradecido, fazendo de ti, minha estrella, a esposa santa,
      /grateful, making of **you.2sg.obl**, my star, my wife sacred/
      adorada companheira dos meus dias.
      /beloved companion to my days./

      'Only you are deserving of my love, as I love you very much, very much, very much and always more, with more steadfastness, always faithful, always your good and grateful slave, making of you, my star, my sacred wife, beloved companion to my days' (CS Sample, 1890)

(18) *Tu*, G., não me *conheces* ainda bem,
      /**You.2sg**, G., not me **know.pres.2sg** yet well,/
      não *sabes* que amor eterno eu tenho
      /**Ø.2sg**not **know.pres.2sg** that love eternal I have/
      no coração por *ti*,
      /in heart for **you.2sg.obl**,/
      como eu adóro os *teus* olhos que me dão alegria,
      /how I love the **your.2sg.poss** eyes that me bring joy,/
      as *tuas* graças de mulher nova, de moça,
      /the **your.2sg.poss** charms of woman young, of girl,/

carinhosa e amiga de sua boa mãe.
/affectionate and friend of her good mother./

'You, G., do not know me well yet, you don't know the eternal love I have in my heart for you, how I love your eyes, that bring me joy, your charms of a young woman, of a girl who is affectionate and a friend to her good mother' (CS Sample, 1890s)

Thirdly three of the occurrences with overt pronominal subject *tu* are in VS order, as seen in example (19).

(19) *Escreve*-me *tu* extensamente,
      /**Write.imp.2sg** me **you.2sg** extensively,/
      como ás veses *costumas*,
      /as sometimes **Ø.2sg.be used to.pres.2sg**,/
      tens tempo pra isso.
      /**Ø.2sg.have.pres.2sg** time for that./

'Write me extensively, as sometimes you used to do. You have time for that' (CS Sample, 1880s)

On the other hand, in the samples from the 20th century, regardless of the choice of pronoun, it is clear that *tu* appears preferably as null subject and that *você* is preferably overt. Furthermore, there may be a connection between this use and some syntactic-semantic properties. Firstly, *tu* is mostly combined with a verb in 2P form. In this case, the subject is null in 80% of occurrences, keeping a rate of null subjects that is close to that found in the 19th century. Analyzing the contexts of use, however, the inflection of the verb alone no longer guarantees recognition of the subject. Two of the ten occurrences from the DS and MD Sample, one of the 65 occurrences from the MS Sample, and one occurrence from the VL Sample are examples of full *tu* combined with a verb in 3P, as shown in example (6), presented again in example (20).

(20) Tudo era triste...!
      /Everything was sad...!/
      E eis que derepente *tu surge*,
      /And then, [that] suddenly **you.2sg appear.pres.3sg**,/
      em uma tarde inesquecível,
      /in one afternoon unforgettable,/
      talves ao encontro de um alguém [...]
      /maybe by meeting of a someone [...]/

'Everything was sad...! And then, suddenly, you appear in one
unforgettable afternoon, maybe to meet someone' (VL Sample, 1960s)

Secondly, *você* enters the *Catarinense* system in the 1920s, as null subject. These
occurrences resemble the courtesy implied in *Vossa Mercê* 'lit. Your Mercy' as in
example (21), and remain preferably with a full subject thereafter.

(21) Meu caro Dr. Boiteux, mandei *lhe* um folhete
      /My dear Dr. Boiteux, [I] have sent **you.sg.dat** a leaflet/
      de meu "Programa de Socorro"
      /of my "Program [of] Help"/
      tambem não sei se *recebeu*!
      /[I] also not know if **you.2sg [have] receive.3sg.past** [it]!/
      Victor, como *sabe*, está tambem interessado,
      /Victor, as **Ø.2sg know.pres.3sg**, is too interested,/
      é um grande passo
      /[it] is a big step/
      o *Amigo* ahi com os seus Amigos, ver se é, possível.
      /the **friend.2sg** there with your friends, see if [it] is, possible./

      'My dear Dr. Boiteux, I have sent you a leaflet of my "Help Program". I do
      not know if you have received it! Victor, as you know, is interested too. It is
      a big step. See with your friends if it is possible' (JB Sample, 1920s)

Thirdly, there are two occurrences of VS order in the second person contexts, but
they refer to idiomatic, formulaic constructions, as shown in example (22).

(22) Saudações. Olá meu amor como *vai voce*
      /Greetings. Hello my love how **be.pres.3sg you.2sg**/
      espero que *esteja* com muita saúde
      /[I] hope that **Ø.2sg.be.pres.3sg** [with] much health/
      e felicidades.
      /and happinesses./

      'Greetings. Hello, my love. How are you going? I hope you are very healthy
      and happy' (MD Sample, 1970s)

Finally, the results regarding second person singular indicate that *Catarinense*
writing from the 19th century reveals properties of a null-subject language, with
categorical use of *tu* coupled with verbs in 2P and possibilities of VS order. In
the 20th century, in turn, the two forms, *tu* and *você*, compete. The persistence

of pronoun *tu* is, in most cases, related to properties of a null-subject language, like the distinctive 2P inflection in the verb that follows the pronoun. In parallel with this system, pronoun *você* makes its slow entrance in this variety of Portuguese, but it does not replace *tu*. By comparing these results with Duarte's (1993), it is possible to ascertain that change in *Catarinense* writing, considering the second person singular, is slower than in the spoken language. The difference between Duarte's results for the second person singular and those presented in Table 6, however, may be related to the difference between the discourse genres analyzed by the author and in this study – plays and personal letters, respectively.

We are aware of the limitations of the samples and the analysis that we have carried out here. Nonetheless, in the next section, we make some generalizations departing from the results described here.

5 General patterns of use in the letter samples

This section discusses results judged of particular significance in the process of variation/change of 2P pronouns observed in *Catarinense* letters, in order to identify general patterns. We start by organizing the data by decade, in order to track the course of change, as presented in Graph 1.

The *Catarinense* Portuguese of the 19th century (1870s, 1880s, and 1890s), represented here by the CS Samples and part of the JB Sample, shows stability with categorical rates of the *tuteamento* (addressing with *tu*) system. The trajectory of the address form in the 20th century, on the other hand, portrays instability, which may indicate a change in progress. According to the principles of the theory of variation and change, in order for a linguistic change to occur there needs to be a period of variation (even though not all variation leads to change). In the first decades of the 20th century (1920s, 1930s), we can observe the categorical use of *você* that enters Santa Catarina, bearing the traces of courtesy implied by *Vossa Mercê*. In the JB Sample, seven of the 11 occurrences of *você* observed are null subject, which, combined with the absence of pronominal person marking on the verb, may convey neutrality in the treatment of the interlocutor. From the 1950s and 1960s onwards, pronouns *tu* and *você* are used alternately, with peaks of almost exclusive use of *você* (in the 1970s) and almost categorical use of *tu* (in the 1990s). As shown in Section 4, all the evidence points to a connection between this varying use of the pronouns and the personal preferences of the letter writers, which are conditioned by the writers' place of origin.

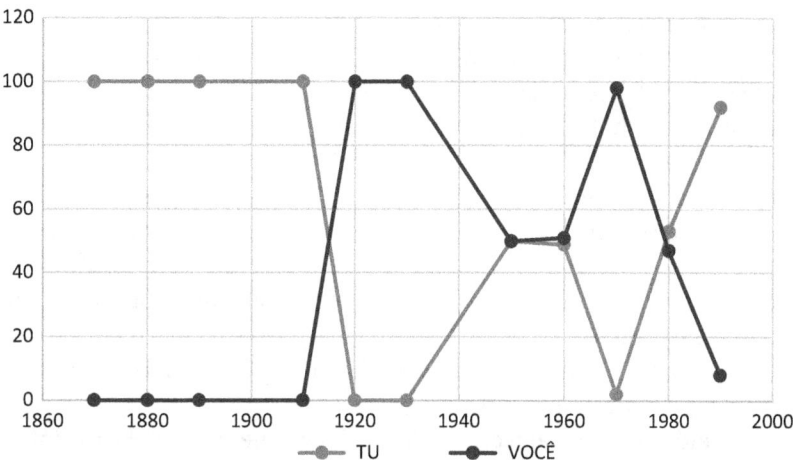

Graph 1: Frequency of use of *tu* and *você* by decade in the six samples of letters by *Catarinenses*.

Table 7 presents the overall numbers of private individual letter writers by mesoregion.

Table 7: Frequency of use of *tu*/*você* by mesoregion in letters by private *Catarinenses* of the 20th century.

Personal letters by private *Catarinenses* of the 20th century		
Mesoregion	*TU*	*VOCÊ*
Greater Florianópolis	68 (75%)	23 (25%)
Planalto Serrano	17 (15%)	95 (85%)
Vale do Itajaí	17 (30%)	40 (70%)
Northern	6 (13%)	41 (87%)

Considering these rates of usage, there is a clear difference between letter writers from the Greater Florianópolis area (with 75% use of *tu*) and correspondents from other mesoregions, especially the Planalto Serrano mesoregion (with 85% use of *você*), whose letters contain more occurrences and thus allow for more accurate and robust comparisons. The social and linguistic history of the Greater Florianópolis area and the Planalto Serrano allows us to associate the second person forms with the process of colonization of the two mesoregions of Santa Catarina by Azoreans and *Paulistas*, respectively. In the case of the Vale do Itajaí and the Northern mesoregions, which were predominantly colonized by Germans, the prevalence of the form *você* (70% and 87%) may be a reflection of the Portuguese learned at school as a second language, where textbooks presented the new form as the standard second person singular pronoun. These results reflect the speech results found in the linguistic atlas research conducted by ALERS and in the studies by Loregian-Penkal (2004), Rocha (2012) and Davet (2013), conducted on VARSUL data. We therefore argue that "colonizing ethnicity" is a key factor in 2P pronoun usage in the coastal, Planalto and Northern middle-regions,[22] as follows:

1. Greater Florianópolis and the preferred use of pronoun *tu*: influenced by the Azorean colonization;
2. Planalto Serrano mesoregion (Lages) and use of the pronoun *você*: influenced by the *Paulista* colonization;
3. Northern and Vale do Itajaí mesoregions and the preferred use of *você*: influenced by schooling.

In addition to the influences of the colonizing ethnic group, which seem to explain the instability at the level of the community, there is instability at the individual level, depending on the relationship between the letter writer and the recipient or on the topic of the letter. In Section 4, data from the MS Sample and the VL Sample served to illustrate how, depending on the situation, the same letter writer makes use of *tu* or *você*. The letters of HL are a further indication of how the variation in 2P pronoun use reflects stylistic variation. This is demonstrated by Grando (2016) who analysed the address forms used as a vocative in the HL Sample, where the letter writer takes two paths:

1. Increasing familiarity: HL begins to exchange letters with her translator (CC) at the beginning of the 1980s, addressing her as Dear Madam CC (letter from 1984), Dearest Mrs. CC (letter from 1986), and Dearest Mme. CC (letter from 1987). Starting at the end of 1987, the letter writer begins employing familiar vocatives with CC, like My dear C. (letter from 1987), Dear C. (Letter from 1988), Dear C-y (diminutive) (1988), Dearest C. (1989), *Chère* C. (1990), C., *ma fleur* (letter from 1992). The change in vocative forms reflects the evolution of their relationship from a more professional to a more friendly and close one, from writer-translator to friend-friend, in the course of two decades. This evolution is consequently accompanied by changes in pronominal forms from *você* to *tu* (as subject and complement). This strategy maintains the dyad

---

22 In the sets of samples used in this study, there are no personal letters from the middle-region of Western Santa Catarina, where the city of Chapecó, a town colonized by Gaúchos, mostly of Italian descent, is located. We believe that in this case there would be significant use of *tu*, reflecting the speech data results by ALERS and VARSUL.

formality-informality, conserving the asymmetrical relation between the pronouns of power (V) and those of solidarity (T).

2. From a professional to a personal topic: the same change in pronominal forms observed in the move from a formal to an informal relationship is found in the topic of the letter. There is a clear link between professional topics and the use of *você* (example (23)) and between personal subjects and the use of *tu* (example (24)). Depending on the topic these uses may vary within the same letter.

Professional topic

(23) Eis um belo título para o futuro livro,
/That is a beautiful title for the upcoming book,/
pois acredito que a palavra é
/for [I] believe that the word is/
bastante sonora em francês
/very well sounded in French/
e que talvez não exista na língua francesa,
/and that perhaps [it] not exist in the language French,/
Mas, naturalmente, *você pode sugerir* outro.
/But, naturally, **you.2sg may.3sg suggest.inf** another./

'That is a beautiful title for the upcoming book, for I believe that the word sounds fine in French and that, perhaps, it does not exist in the French language, but naturally you may suggest another one' (HL, 1987)

Personal theme

(24) Um beijo em retribuição àquele furtivo
/A kiss in retribution for the furtive one/
que me *deste* uma noite em que eu
/that me **Ø.2sg give.past.2sg** one night when I/
estava em minha mesa de trabalho e tu ias dormir.
/was at my desk of work and **you.2sg be.imperf.2sg sleep.inf**./

'A kiss in retribution for the furtive one you gave me one night when I was at my desk and you were going to bed' (HL, 1989)

The distribution between pronoun *tu* associated with more informal vocatives and personal topics, and pronoun *você* associated with more formal vocatives and more professional topics can be also seen in the letters by the public figures

JB and MS. In these cases, we argue that it is possible to regard the forms *tu* and *você* as variants or forms under strict variation.

Beyond the evidence that second person pronouns in Santa Catarina bear traces of the colonizer and of the dual system of power and solidarity (terms from Brown & Gilman 2003 [1960]), we are led to believe that the use of null or overt subjects in the *Catarinense* linguistic system is also conservative: pronoun *tu* is null across time, as shown in Graph 2.

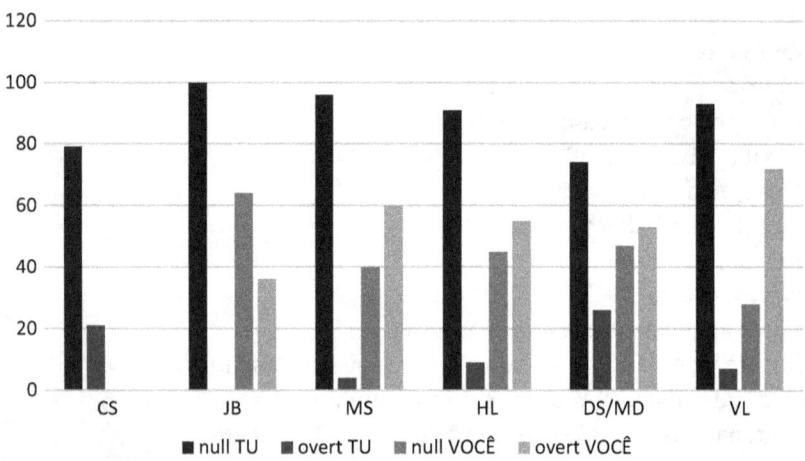

Graph 2: Percentage of use of tu/*você*, according to the variable use of pronouns in the 19th and 20th centuries.

Graph 2 shows that *Catarinense* Portuguese from the 19th century shows stability, with categorical rates of the use of *tu* and null subject, the overt subject being, in this case, used especially as a strategy for emphasis or contrast when trying to solve ambiguity problems (see subsection 4.2). This stability in the behavior of null subject *tu* can also be observed in the writing by public 20th century letter writers. Pronoun *você*, in turn, follows the changes in the pronominal system of other regions of Brazil: it appears as null subject in samples JB, MD, and HL – as if maintaining a strategy for neutrality or formality – and stabilizes as overt subject when competing with the form *tu*, as observed in samples DS/MD and VL.

Considering only the letters of the private individuals (samples DS/MD, and VL), the following trends are evident:
1. Pronouns *tu* and *você* compete as variants of the same variable when they are used as a strategy for informality.
2. The null pronoun *tu* tends to be identified by verbal inflection.

3. Cases of overt *tu* coupled with a verb in 3P are scarce, but they already indicate that verb inflection is no longer a guarantee of subject identification.
4. Pronoun *você* is combined with a verb in 3P and is preferably overt.

To sum up, the results relating to the second person singular allow us to say that, in the 19th century, the Portuguese spoken in Santa Catarina shows properties relevant to the null subject parameter. In the 20th century, in turn, the variation between *tu* and *você,* with significant rates of preferentially null *tu* and preferably overt *você,* shows that there are specific conditions and contexts for a null subject. This seems to indicate two systems at play: the *tuteamento,* with the personal pronoun *tu* marked by verb inflection (see Kato & Duarte 2008), and the *voceamento* (addressing with *você*) system, with no distinctive verbal ending and full subject *você.*

These results provide some indication of the persistence, over time, of null pronoun *tu,* coupled with a verb in 2P, and of the slow evolution of *você* in the pronominal system of *Catarinense* Portuguese. It is likely that social circumstances, such as the colonization and isolation of the island, were motivating factors in the generally conservative system found in *Catarinense* samples of the 20th century.

6 Conclusion

Click here to enter text.

The main questions that this study sought to answer were: (i) What diachronic path can be noted regarding variation and change in the use of pronouns *tu* and *você*? (ii) Which linguistic and extralinguistic factors influence the distribution of the pronouns *tu* and *você*? (iii) Is it possible to affirm that *você* has made its way into the *Catarinense* variety of Portuguese as early as the end of the 20th century? (iv) What is the social and linguistic history of the presence of the new form *você* in *Catarinense* samples?

Regarding the six samples analyzed, our results reveal that, in the 19th century, *tu* is the only pronoun used by letter writers to refer to the second person singular. In the 20th century, in contrast, *tu* and *você* compete against each other. The analysis of differences and similarities in the use of the two pronouns indicates that:

1. Pronoun *tu* is used most in coastal areas and *você* is used in the Planalto Serrano mesoregion. These differences in usage must be related to the colonization of these regions by Azoreans and *Paulistas*, respectively. In regions of German colonization, *você* is the predominant form, which can be explained

as a strategy learned at school, in Portuguese as a second language classes. This indicates that aspects of Santa Catarina social history related to the "colonizing ethnicity" can explain the process of pronominal change/variation observed in the samples.

2. Pronoun *você* enters *Catarinense* writing in the early 20th century, bearing traces of the courtesy imparted by *Vossa Mercê*, the form of address that gave rise to the innovative pronoun *você*. This formality is perceived especially in the samples of public senders (JB, MS and HL). In private individuals' samples (DS/MD and VL), *tu* and *você* compete as variants of the same variable, as *você* is used with the same function as *tu*, that is, in more informal contexts.

3. There is evidence of linguistic change or linguistic instability in the community when observing private writers from the Greater Florianópolis area and the Planalto Serrano mesoregion who use the two pronouns *tu* and *você* as variants of the same variable. If, on the one hand, the letter writers of the coastal regions – mostly users of *tu* – adopt (albeit on a small scale) the pronoun of the Planalto (*você*), on the other hand, the writers from the latter, mainly using *você*, adopt (although on a small scale) the pronoun of the coast (*tu*).

4. The use of null or overt pronouns in the *Catarinense* linguistic system is conservative: pronoun *tu* appears in both centuries, especially as a null subject, coupled with second person (2P) verbal morphology, while pronoun *você* (although related to the null subject at the beginning of the 20th century) is more often used as an overt subject, combined with third person (3P) verbal morphology.

Based on the empirical evidence presented here – from present to past and from past to present – it is not possible to assert that the form *você* arrived in the *Catarinense* variety of Portuguese as early as the end of the 19th century. *Você* does not supplant the form *tu* in this study's corpus. The social history of the colonization of the coast and the mountain plateau is quite revealing of the linguistic history of these pronouns. *Tu* reveals traces of the Azorean colonizers, and *você*, of the colonists from São Paulo. The isolation of the island prior to the beginning of the 20th century may be responsible for the preservation of the Latin form *tu* and the resistance to the entry of *você* in the writing and speech of people from coastal Santa Catarina.

References

ALERS, see fn. 7.
Altenhofen, Cléo Vilson. 2002. Áreas linguísticas do português falado no sul do Brasil: Um balanço das fotografias geolinguísticas do ALERS. In Paulino Vandresen (ed.). *Variação e mudança no português da Região Sul*, 115–145. Pelotas: EDUCAT.

Amaral, Luis Isaías Centeno do. 2003. *A concordância verbal de segunda pessoa do singular em Pelotas e suas implicações lingüísticas e sociais.* PhD thesis. Porto Alegre: Universidade Federal do Rio Grande do Sul.

Berlinck, Rosane de Andrade. 1988. *A ordem V SN no português do Brasil: Sincronia e diacronia.* MA thesis. Campinas, SP: Universidade Estadual de Campinas.

Berlinck, Rosane de Andrade. 1995. *La position du sujet en portugais: Etude diachronique des variétés brésilienne et européenne.* PhD thesis. Leuven: Katholieke Universiteit Leuven.

Berlinck, Rosane de Andrade & Izete Lehmkuhl Coelho. 2018. A ordem do sujeito em construções declarativas na história do português brasileiro. In Sônia Cyrino & Maria Aparecida Torres Morais (eds.). *História do português brasileiro*, vol. 4: *Mudança sintática do português brasileiro: perspectiva gerativista*, 308–381. São Paulo: Contexto.

Brown, Roger & Albert Gilman. 2003 [1960]. The pronouns of power and solidarity. In Christina Bratt Paulston & Richard G. Tucker (eds.). *Sociolinguistics – The essential readings*, 156–176. Oxford: Blackwell.

Coelho, Izete Lehmkuhl. 2006. Variação na sintaxe: estudo da ordem do sujeito no PB. In Jânia Martins Ramos (ed.). *Estudos sociolinguísticos: Quatro vértices do GT da ANPOLL*, 84–99. Belo Horizonte: FALE & Editora da UFMG.

Coelho, Izete Lehmkuhl & Edair Maria Görski. 2011. A variação no uso dos pronomes *tu* e *você* em Santa Catarina. In Célia Regina dos Santos Lopes & Letícia Rebollo Couto (eds.). *Formas de tratamento em português e espanhol: Variação, mudança e funções conversacionais,* 263–287. Niterói: Editora da UFF.

Conde Silvestre, Juan Camilo .2007. *Sociolingüística histórica.* Madrid: Gredos.

Cunha, Maria Teresa Santos. 2008. Assa coisa de guardar... Homens de letras e acervos pessoais. *História da Educação* 12,25. 109–130.

Davet, Julie Cristiane Teixeira. 2013. *Estudo da concordância verbal de segunda pessoa do singular em Florianópolis-SC: Algumas implicações identitárias.* MA thesis. Florianópolis, SC: Universidade Federal de Santa Catarina.

Duarte, Maria Eugênia Lamoglia. 1993. Do pronome nulo ao pleno: a trajetória do sujeito no Português do Brasil. In Mary Kato & Ian Roberts. (eds.). *Português Brasileiro: Uma viagem diacrônica,* 107–128. Campinas, SP: Editora da Unicamp.

Duarte, Maria Eugênia Lamoglia. 1995. *A perda do princípio "evite pronome" no português brasileiro.* PhD thesis. Campinas, SP: Universidade Estadual de Campinas.

Duarte, Maria Eugênia Lamoglia, Gabriela Costa Mourão & Heitor Mendonça Santos. 2012. Os sujeitos de 3ª pessoa: revisitando Duarte 1993. In Maria Eugênia Lamoglia Duarte (ed.). *O sujeito em peças de teatro (1833–1992): Estudos diacrônicos*, 21–44. São Paulo: Parábola.

Furlan, Oswaldo Antônio. 1989. *Influência açoriana no português do Brasil em Santa Catarina.* Florianópolis: EdUFSC.

Gravina, Aline Peixoto. 2008. *A natureza do sujeito nulo na diacronia do PB: Estudo de um corpus mineiro.* MA thesis. Campinas, SP: Universidade Estadual de Campinas.

Gravina, Aline Peixoto. 2014. *Sujeito nulo e ordem VS no Português Brasileiro.* PhD thesis. Campinas, SP: Universidade Estadual de Campinas.

Grando, Vanessa. 2016. *Formas de tratamento nas cartas de Harry Laus para Claire Cayron: Uma análise sociolinguística.* BA thesis. Florianópolis, SC: Universidade Federal de Santa Catarina.

Hausen, Telma Acacia Pacheco. 2000. *Concordância verbal do pronome "tu" no interior do estado de Santa Catarina.* MA thesis. Curitiba, PR: Universidade Federal do Paraná.

Kato, Mary Aizawa & Maria Eugênia Lamoglia Duarte. 2008. Mudança paramétrica e orientação para o discurso. *XXIV Encontro Nacional da Associação Portuguesa de Linguística* (ms.).

Koch, Walter. 2000. O povoamento do território e a formação de áreas linguísticas. In Eberhard Gärtner, Christine Hundt & Axel Schönberger (eds.), *Estudos de geolingüística do português Americano*, 55–69. Frankfurt: TFM.

Labov, William. 2006 [1966]. *The social stratification of English in New York City*. Cambridge: Cambridge University Press.

Labov, William. 1972. *Sociolinguistic patterns*. Philadelphia: University of Pennsylvania Press.

Loregian-Penkal, Loremi. 2004. *Re(análise) da referência de segunda pessoa na fala da Região Sul*. PhD thesis. Curitiba, PR: Universidade Federal do Paraná.

Margotti, Felício Wessling. 2004. *Difusão sócio-geográfica do português em contato com o italiano no sul do Brasil*. PhD thesis. Porto Alegre, RS: Universidade Federal do Rio Grande do Sul.

Mosimann, João Carlos. 2010. *Catarinenses: Gênese e história*. Florianópolis: Edição do autor.

Nunes de Souza, Christiane Maria. 2011. *Poder e solidariedade no teatro florianopolitano dos séculos XIX e XX: Uma análise sociolinguística das formas de tratamento*. MA thesis. Florianópolis, SC: Universidade Federal de Santa Catarina.

Nunes de Souza, Christiane Maria. 2015. *A alternância entre tu e você na correspondência de florianopolitanos ilustres no decorrer de um século*. PhD thesis. Florianópolis, SC: Universidade Federal de Santa Catarina.

Nunes de Souza, Christiane Maria & Izete Lehmkuhl Coelho. 2015. Caminhos para a investigação da alternância de pronomes de segunda pessoa em Santa Catarina. *LaborHistórico* 1,1. 49–61.

Oliveira, Gilvan Müller. 2004. *Política lingüística, Política historiográfica: Epistemologia e escrita da história da(s) língua(s) a propósito da língua portuguesa no Brasil Meridional (1754–1830)*. PhD thesis. Campinas, SP: Universidade Estadual de Campinas.

Pagotto, Emílio Gozze. 2004. *Variação e(é) identidade*. Maceió: ED/UFAL e EDUFBA.

Ramos, Myriam Pereira Botelho. 1989. *Formas de tratamento no falar de Florianópolis*. MA thesis. Florianópolis, SC: Universidade Federal de Santa Catarina.

Rocha, Patrícia Graciela da. 2012. *O sistema de tratamento do português de Florianópolis: Um estudo sincrônico*. PhD thesis. Florianópolis, SC: Universidade Federal de Santa Catarina.

Schroeder, Rosa Maria Steiner. 1997. Uma mulher além de seu tempo: *Maura de Senna Pereira*. MA thesis. Florianópolis, SC: Universidade Federal de Santa Catarina.

Vandresen, Paulino. 2008. Sociolinguística e ensino: O sistema pronominal e a concordância verbal no português falado na Região Sul. In Mailce Borges Mota Fortkamp & Lêda Maria Braga Tomitch (eds.). *Aspectos da linguística aplicada: Estudos em homenagem ao professor Hilário Inácio Bohn*, 229–242. Second edition. Florianópolis: Insular.

VARSUL, see fn. 9.

Weinreich, Uriel, William Labov & Marvin Herzog. 2006 [1968]. *Fundamentos empíricos para uma teoria da mudança linguística*. Translation by Marcos Bagno. Rev. Carlos Alberto Faraco. São Paulo: Parábola.

Vanessa Martins do Monte

Forms of address in São Paulo

A historical approach

Abstract: This chapter[1] presents a study of the forms of address found in databases of letters written in São Paulo during the 18th, 19th and 20th centuries. The data are analyzed qualitatively and quantitatively, considering aspects such as the gender of those involved in the epistolary relationship, date, exclusive or mixed use of a form, relationship between sender and recipient, as well as pragmatics. In the 18th century correspondence, there is widespread use of *vossa mercê* (lit. 'Your Mercy') precisely in the region which later on will be characterized by the exclusive use of *você*. In the 19th and 20th century letters, *você* shows up with greater frequency than *tu*. The results show a higher frequency of *você* in the period studied here, foreshadowing the subsystem of address forms currently used in the state of São Paulo.

Keywords: forms of address, *vossa mercê*, historical linguistics, philology

1 Introduction

The history of forms of address in Portuguese is particularly interesting because of the widespread use of the form *você*, especially in Brazil. Much recent research focuses on the geographical distribution of *você* across the vast Brazilian territory (Lopes et al. 2018; Scherre et al. 2015). In the regions historically influenced by the Captaincy of São Paulo, *você* occurs practically alone as the unique second person pronoun (Monte 2015). Even in localities in which *você* competes with *tu*, *você* is also becoming the preferred form. In these places, it seems that *tu* has become prevalent during certain periods for socio-historical reasons.

The collective efforts to research the history of Brazilian Portuguese have had many positive outcomes, including a common methodology for the diachronic

---

1 The research for this chapter was partially supported by Karl-Franzens-Universität Graz, which financed my participation at the II Congress of Forms and Formulas of Address, in Graz, June 2016. I thank the photographer Flávio Morbach Portella for the images in Figures 2 and 3, which he generously made available to be used in this chapter. I am grateful to my colleague Maria Clara Paixão de Sousa for an extensive review of the English used in this chapter. All remaining errors are my responsibility.

investigation of address forms. Thanks to recent studies, it is possible today to compare data on this topic in several different Brazilian states. These studies are enabling us to develop a comprehensive historical narrative of address forms in Brazil, from at least the 18th century to the present day (Lopes et al. 2018). In this chapter, we adopt this common research methodology, generating comparable data regarding a broader history, not only related to São Paulo, but to Brazil more widely. Starting from reliable scholarly editions of letters, we analyze the period from 1870 to 1949.

Investigating the history behind the spread of *você* in Portuguese America[2] may help elucidate the Brazilian Portuguese pronoun system, which differs considerably from that of European Portuguese.

The first obstacle to this historical approach lies in the source material. The form *vossa mercê* (lit. 'Your Mercy')[3] and its correlated phonological reductions (such as *vossemecê, vosmecê, vossuncê, vossancê*) are rarely documented in old texts, where we find that *vossa mercê*, more often than not, is abbreviated. There is a large list of possible abbreviations, using only the initials (V. M.) or the initials combined with the other letters (V. M^ce.), as we will see later (it is also important to mention that the use of capital letters as initials was not mandatory at that time, so that it is very common to find forms of address written entirely in lowercase letters).[4] The conventional editorial approach in the semi-diplomatic editions is to insert full forms into the abbreviations used in the original manuscripts, as part of the editors' efforts to amend and elucidate the originals – a technique that is used not only in the corpus under study here (to be described below), but also in all corpora used for research on address forms that we are aware of.[5] In this

---

2 Portuguese America refers to the area colonized by the Portuguese from 1500 to 1822.

3 In this chapter we prefer to use the literal translation *Your Mercy*, for two main reasons: (1) this translation is frequent in the specialized literature about forms of address (e.g. Pharies 2015 and Hualde, Olarrea & O'Rourke 2012); (2) the expression was used in Middle English (e.g. Barratt 2010: 240 and *Middle English Dictionary* 2014) with the exact same value that it had in Medieval Portuguese, from which it specialized as a form of address. In English, though, the preferred form was "Your Grace".

4 In this chapter, we opted to write forms of address using lowercase, unless the capital letters were used by the original manuscript's scribe.

5 "Semi-diplomatic" is a format of scholarly edition that seeks to reproduce most of the features of an original (spelling, punctuation, etc.), while changing a few aspects, such as the abbreviations. Although they differ from "diplomatic" editions in a few aspects – notably, abbreviations are not developed by the editor in diplomatic transcriptions – semi-diplomatic editions are still considered conservative approaches to the original text, and constitute the most widely used format of scholarly edition for corpora that are destined for historical linguistic studies, at least within Portuguese historical linguistics.

approach, importantly, the full forms inserted (for example, V<*ossa*> M<*ercê* > where an original scribe used V.M. or V. M^{ce}) are mere conventions by the editors of the texts, derived from their philological criteria. Crucially, this means that it is almost impossible to pursue the written history of the form that, according to previous research, gave rise to the pronoun *você*.

This chapter intends to investigate the forms of address found in letters produced between the 18th and 20th centuries in São Paulo. The research includes three historical periods of the current "Estado de São Paulo":

- Letters from 1722 to 1809: Captaincy of São Paulo (Colonial period)
- Letters from 1844 to 1889: Province of São Paulo (Imperial period)
- Letters from 1890 to 1953: Estado de São Paulo (Republic of Brazil period)

Based on philological editions of letters from the 18th to the 20th centuries, this chapter aims to answer the following questions: (a) how were the forms *tu* and *você* distributed in São Paulo?; (b) was the form *você* always the most frequent?; and (c) how do the results compare to those of other studies of Brazilian letters from other parts of the country? The chapter is organized as follows: Section 2 describes the *corpora*, and Sections 3 and 4 present the data analysis according to century, followed by a discussion of the results.

2 The corpora

Letters are one of the most common types of texts for researching forms of address from a diachronic perspective (Lopes 2012, Marcotulio 2010, Rumeu 2013). They are documents in which one can easily identify the interlocution process in which the linguistic forms are used. Among these forms, it is very usual to find specific forms of address. Besides their constitutive characteristics, letters also offer the possibility of investigating the sender and recipient relationship, and, depending on the data available, it is possible to gather some sociolinguistic information, which adds to the analysis of the forms of address.

Recently, there have been several initiatives to prepare scholarly editions based on documents produced in Portuguese America (1500–1822) and in Brazil (after 1822), as a result of comprehensive projects about the history of Brazilian Portuguese. The first initiative, started during the 1990s, was the Project for the History of Brazilian Portuguese (also known as PHPB), later subdivided into a series of regional projects, such as the Project for the History of Paulista Portuguese (also known as PHPP). The editions used in this chapter are all outcomes from the PHPP and are published on the project website (http://phpp.fflch.usp.br/corpus).

The *corpus* used for this chapter is composed as follows:

(1) From the 18th century and the first decade of 19th century, there are two series of documents:
- Letters from Public Administration: 1765–1775 (Monte 2015)
- Indigenous settlement: 1722–1809 (Kewitz & Simões 2006)[6]

There are several challenges when dealing with documents of this period. The first is the difficulty of establishing the private or public context of the letters – we will come to the other challenges in Section 3. Considering the rich socio-historical context of Portuguese America, where relations could be public and private simultaneously, the public circulation of documents is a key element in determining their more or less public status (Barbosa 1999).

The Public Administration letters from the period of Morgado de Mateus' government in the Captaincy of São Paulo (1765–1775) circulated publicly. They involve aspects of the public administration of the territory, such as crime (defense, complaint, investigation or caution), financial topics (tax collection, debt or account settling) and conscription. The majority of the letters were written by army officers and soldiers, and local administration officials in diverse captaincies. In most cases, the soldiers wrote to one another or to the local administrators. Monte (2015) made an in-depth study of the senders and found that at least 32 documents (out of 81) were written, or dictated, by men born in Portuguese America, mainly in the São Paulo Captaincy. We are thus able to assume that the documents are authentic records of the language that would later give rise to Brazilian Portuguese.

The letters relating to the creation of villages for the Indigenous peoples, where they could be controlled and exploited by the metropole, were written by priests to their superiors or to the army officers. The topics range from the enlistment of Indigenous people to particular episodes that occurred in the villages, which were all close to São Paulo. These letters are considered to pertain to private administration. Their semi-diplomatic edition was prepared and published by Kewitz & Simões (2006).

(2) The 19th century includes three series of private documentation:
- Correspondence received by Washington Luís: 1897–1900 (Kewitz & Simões 2005/2006)
- Collection of "Clube Republicano": 1883–1889 (Simões 2007)
- Private correspondence of the Rafael Tobias de Aguiar archive: 1844–1890 (Módolo & Marques 2010)

---

6 This series also includes four letters from the 19th century, dated 1801, 1804 and 1809. These letters were included in the 18th century period, as the letters from the 19th century all dated from the last quarter of the century.

Washington Luís was the last Brazilian president (1926–1930) of the period known as the Old Republic. Despite being born in the city of Macaé (in Rio de Janeiro), he spent most of his life in São Paulo, where he held many public positions. In 1900, Washington Luís married Sophia Oliveira de Barros, a member of a wealthy family from São Paulo. The letters in this collection involve his mother-in-law, brothers-in-law and sisters-in-law, as well as other important people from São Paulo. The semi-diplomatic edition of the letters, followed by an in-depth historical study, was prepared by Kewitz & Simões (2006).

The missives in the Collection of "Clube Republicano" were written between 1883 and 1889 by important politicians from the Province of São Paulo. They are samples of private correspondence, and are part of the corpus that Simões analyzed in his PhD thesis (2007).

The private correspondence of the Rafael Tobias de Aguiar archive includes letters edited by Módolo & Marques (2010), addressed to him. All the letters were produced in the cities of São Paulo and Santos.

(3) From the 20th century, the following sets of documentation were used:
   - Family Letters of Washington Luís: 1901–1950 (Kewitz 2016)
   - Correspondence of Fernando and Julio Prestes de Albuquerque to Washington Luís: 1909–1932 (Kewitz, Ferreira & Albuquerque 2015)
   - Correspondence of the Junqueira Family: 1900–1953.

The first set involves the same people as the 19th century set to Washington Luís, Despite being written in a familiar register, they also deal with business, since most of the family was also involved in politics.

The second set involves Fernando Prestes and his son, Julio Prestes, who were two important figures in the history of São Paulo, and were exiled to Europe with Washington Luís after 1930. The letters and postcards were all written by Fernando and Julio to Washington. They are considered to be private administration letters and the scholarly edition was published by Kewitz, Ferreira & Albuquerque (2015).

The third set, which is not yet published, contains some family letters and private administration missives from a very important family called Junqueira, from Ribeirão Preto (São Paulo). Besides the letters sent within the family, we also find interesting letters written by the farm administration to the owner.[7]

The following sections provide an analysis of data from each time period.

---

7 The edition of these letters is being prepared by the author of this chapter.

3 18th century: The history of an abbreviation

When dealing with letters written by famous people from the past, it is straightforward to gather data about them. From a diachronic perspective, public letters written by well-known people use honorific address forms, such as *vossa excelência* ('Your Excellency') and *vossa senhoria* ('Your Lordship/ Ladyship'). We are interested in changes in pronominal address, and the form that we are looking for is *vossa mercê*, which probably gave rise to the present-day form *você* via grammaticalization. The letters sent to less eminent people are more likely to have this less honorific form. Besides the difficulty of getting information about ordinary people living in Portuguese America (such as birthplace, birthdate, level of education), it is also harder to find these kinds of documents. They were considered less important and therefore less likely to be conserved than documents that circulated within high administration.

After extensive searches in Brazilian and European archives and with the precious documentation in hand, our research of address forms, mainly *vossa mercê*, meets its second challenge. The full form is not attested, which means that we are researching an abbreviation, commonly *v.m.* or *v.m^e*. The supposed grammaticalized forms, the phonological reductions *vossemecê* and *vassuncê*, were mentioned by researchers at the beginning of 20th century (Basto 1931; Nogueira 1927; Amaral 1955), and they seem to have not been used in earlier written documents.

The development of the *v.m.* abbreviation is a convention. The full form is generally *vossa mercê* (following a quite general rule of using italics for the letters omitted in the manuscript). However, it is important to remember that we are studying an abbreviation of an address form, not the whole address form in the manuscript. This observation necessarily leads to a philological approach to the topic.

Identifying an abbreviation correctly is not always a simple task. It requires accurate paleographical observation of the handwriting to detect the letters used by the scribe. Monte (2015) has shown some similarities between the abbreviation of *vossa senhoria* and that of *vossa mercê*. The images in Figure 1 illustrate two abbreviations found on letters dating from the 18th century.

The abbreviation in (1a) is clearly an abbreviation of the form *vossa mercê*, since one easily identifies the capital letters "V" and "M", which were drawn without taking the quill pen off the paper. The second abbreviation, in (1b), by contrast, is harder to identify. At a first glance, it seems to have three letters: a "v", probably an "S", which is followed by an "e". If we read it like this, we will

(a)   (b)

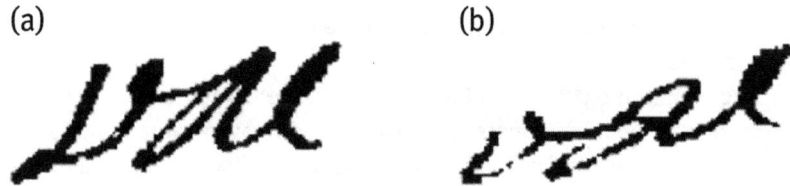

Figure 1: Abbreviations of forms of address.

probably interpret it as an abbreviation of the form *vossa senhoria*. However, after an accurate paleographical analysis, Monte (2015: 236) proves that what appears to be the letters "S" and "e" are actually the capital letter "M", which was badly drawn by the scribe. It is clear, then, that problems can arise from a misinterpretation of an abbreviated form of address, and great care is needed in correctly identifying them.

In the 105 letters[8] dating from the 18th century, we found an expressive use of *vossa mercê*, in both symmetrical and asymmetrical relationships. Table 1

Table 1: Forms of address in letters from 1722 to 1809.

Forms of address	Number of letters	Percentage
vossa mercê	68	65%
vossa excelência	25	24%
vossa senhoria	8	7%
vossa reverendíssima ('Your Most Reverend')	3	3%
vossa majestade ('Your Majesty')	1	1%
Total	**105 letters**	**100%**

shows that the frequency of *vossa mercê* is very high (65%). Its use is related to the socio-professional category of the recipient (Monte 2015). The form is used in almost all situations inside the military hierarchy: when a soldier writes to his superior, when he writes to another soldier and when the superior writes to the soldier. It is important to note that the forms are abbreviated in 100% of cases.

---

8 We also included two documents that have a structure very similar to a letter, but their proper diplomatic classification is official letter and mandate (Monte 2015).

Using their full forms is a general convention, based on the edition criteria commonly used in Brazil.

According to Marcilio (1974) and Bacelar (2009), the Captaincy of São Paulo was made up of poor people, farmers, businessmen with low resources, and artisans. In the 18th century, rural property was used for establishing people's social condition. It was only the men with land who were of interest to the metropole administration, as they were the ones who held military rank. The most elevated military positions were occupied by men who had more land and preferably had been born in the village. These local people address their equals in the letters with vossa mercê.

Based on the hypothesis of a socio-professional constraint on the choice of address forms, Monte (2015) developed the framework shown in Table 2.

Table 2: Socio-professional categories and their preferred forms of address.

Socio-professional category	Preferred form of address
Local administration Military people Common clergymen (priests)	vossa mercê
General administration (high status)	vossa excelência and vossa senhoria vossa majestade (king)
Clergymen – high positions	vossa excelência (reverendíssima) vossa senhoria vossa reverendíssima

The local administrators were all men of the countryside, born in Portuguese America. They occupied positions as local judges, chief guards and other officials. The military staff and the priests were also local people, normally born in the colonial villages of the São Paulo Captaincy. When addressing their equals in writing, they would choose the form vossa mercê, regardless of the position they occupied within the hierarchy.

The general administration, composed almost entirely of Portuguese, was normally designated by those administrators very close to the monarch. They were both addressed and addressed their equals with the more honorific forms vossa excelência and vossa senhoria. In the only letter addressed to the king, the form exclusively used was vossa majestade.

The high positions occupied by clergymen were always marked with highly honorific forms, varying from vossa reverendíssima and its variations (vossa excelência reverendíssima) to the use of vossa excelência.

As the data show, at this time there was a solid socio-professional constraint that seems to regulate the choice of address forms. The documents from this period circulated publicly, so we do not have samples of intimate communication, which explains the complete absence of the second person pronoun *tu*.

4 19th and 20th centuries: competition between *tu* and *você* and the victory of *você*

The period under scrutiny in this section is 1870 to 1949.[9] In the documents listed in Section 2 for this period, the following aspects were analyzed: a) the form of address in subject position; b) the sender's gender; c) social relations.

4.1 Subject position

Regarding the subject position data, we find a clear prevalence of *você*, as shown in Table 3.

Table 3: Forms of address in subject position.

Form of address in subject position	Number and %
tu	75/244 – 31%
você	142/244 – 58%
o senhor 'sir'	22/244 – 9%
vossa senhoria	3/244 – 1%
vossa excelência	2/244 – 1%

The majority of the occurrences concern the form *você* (58%), which may appear abbreviated by "V." or developed, as we can see in Figures 2, 3 and 4.

---

9 The last decade of the 19th century (1890–1899) is represented by only two letters, which may affect the results, as we will discuss later.

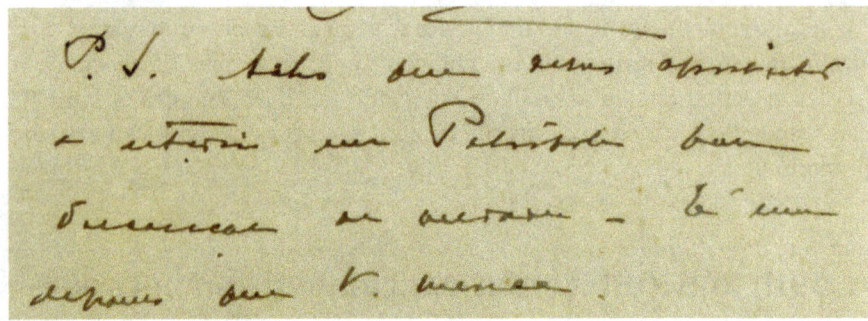

Figure 2: Letter from João Alves de Lima to Washington Luís (10 February 1927).
Transcription made by Verena Kewitz and Cássio de Albuquerque (Kewitz 2016 – Letter 157):
P.S. Acho que deves aproveitar
a estadia em Petropolis para
descançar de verdade - É´ um
repouso que *Voce* merece.
'I think [you] should take advantage of [your] stay in Petropolis to rest properly – it is a repose
you deserve'

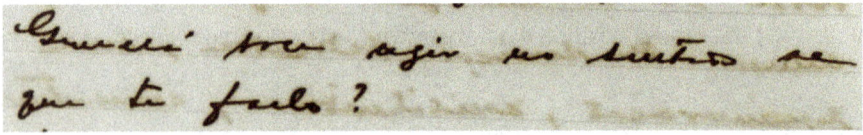

Figure 3: Letter from João Alves de Lima to Washington Luís (10 January 1929).
Transcription made by Verena Kewitz and Cássio de Albuquerque (Kewitz 2016 – Letter 154):
Quererá voce agir no sentido de
que te fallo?
'Will you wish to act in the way [I] speak of to you?'

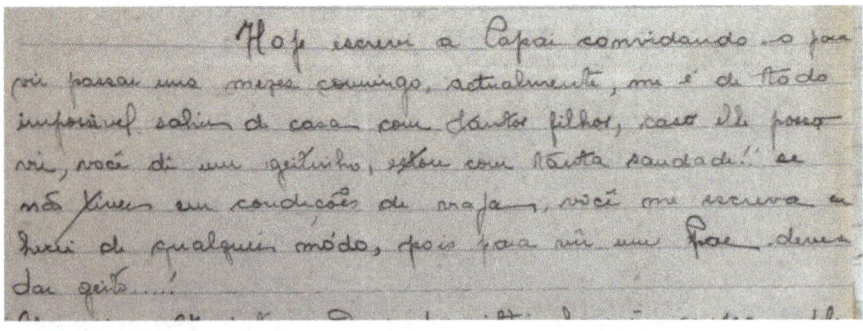

Figure 4: Letter to Mario Pereira Lima from his sister (19 January 1932).

figure 4 (continued)

Transcription:
Hoje escrevi a Papai convidando-o para
vir passar uns mezes commigo, actualmente, me é de todo
impossivel sahir de casa com tantos filhos, caso elle poss[a]
vir, você dê um geitinho, estou com tanta saudade!! se
não tiver em condições de viajar, você me escreva eu
hirei de qualquér módo, pois para vêr um Pae devese
dar geito...!
'Today [I] wrote to Daddy inviting him to come spend a few months with me, currently, it is
entirely impossible for me to get out of the house with so many children, in case he can come,
will you find a way, [I] miss him so much!! If [he] is not able to travel, will you write to me, I will
go somehow, since to see a father one must find a way...!'

Figures 2 and 3 possibly concern two letters written by the same sender, João Alves de Lima. In one missive, he uses the abbreviated form "V.", and in the other one, he opts for the whole form "voce". This sender has used both abbreviated and whole forms in his letters, but when he uses the whole form, he does not include the accent, which is why it is transcribed without it. Figure 4, a letter written by Mario Pereira Lima's sister, documents the extensive use of the developed form *você* in the first paragraph.

Tu is used in around a third of cases (31%) – just over half the occurrences of *você*. The form *o senhor* was found 22 times, representing 9% of the total forms of address in the subject position. *Vossa senhoria* and *vossa excelência*, as expected, appeared only five times, in very particular cases where the relationship between the sender and the recipient was not close.

Compared to the results presented by Lopes & Souza (2012) for letters from Rio de Janeiro, we have a very different scenario for the same period (1870–1949). While in Rio the most frequent form was *tu*, with 62%, followed by *você*, with 38%, our results for letters from São Paulo show the opposite pattern. These two scenarios may indicate that in São Paulo the form *você* had penetrated earlier in the pronominal framework compared to Rio de Janeiro.[10]

When investigating the occurrence of null subject versus non-null subjects, we find a very impressive number of non-null subjects with the form *você*: 82% versus 18% of null subjects,[11] as shown in Table 4.

---

10 After 1930, in Rio de Janeiro, the use of the form *você* outstrips the use of the form *tu* (cf. Lopes & Souza 2012; Duarte 1993).
11 Corresponding to the form *você*, we consider only the letters using exclusively the form *você*.

Table 4: Non-null subjects and null subjects.

	Non-null subjects	Null subjects
tu	–	75/75 – 100%
você	117/142 – 82%	25/142 – 18%
o senhor	20/22 – 91%	2/22 – 9%
vossa senhoria	2/3 – 67%	1/3 – 33%
vossa excelência	2/2 – 100%	–

There were no occurrences of the overt form *tu*, that is, the non-null form, in the subject position in the São Paulo letters. This form was identified only by its verbal morpheme (*-s*). In missives from Rio de Janeiro, in contrast, Lopes & Souza (2012) found 25% of overt subject pronoun *tu* compared with 75% of null subjects corresponding to the form *tu*. The forms *o senhor* and *vossa excelência* tend to appear overtly. There was only one occurrence of non-overt *vossa senhoria* in a letter where the recipient was referred to as *vossa senhoria* during the whole text.

We also compared missives with mixed usage, in which the sender uses a combination of two different forms of address, to letters exclusively using a single form of address. The results are set out in Table 5.

Table 5: Mixed usage and single form letters.

	tu	você	o(a) senhor(a)	vossa senhoria	vossa excelência
tu only (18 letters)	32/32 – 100%	–	–	–	–
você only (43 letters)	–	91/91 – 100%	–	–	–
tu/você (6 letters)	42/68 – 62%	26/68 – 38%	–	–	–
o(a) senhor(a) only (3 letters)	–	–	13/13 – 100%	–	–
você/o(a) senhor(a) (4 letters)	–	23/32 – 72%	9/32 – 28%	–	–
vossa senhoria only (1 letter)	–	–	–	2/2 – 100%	–

Table 5 (continued)

	tu	você	o(a) senhor(a)	vossa senhoria	vossa excelência
vossa excelência only (1 letter)	–	–	–	–	2/2 – 100%
no addressee reference (3 letters)	–	2/3 – 67%	–	1/3 – 33%	–

The most remarkable result is the high number of letters exclusively using the form *você*: 43 of a total of 104 letters (41%). There are 18 missives where the form *tu* was used exclusively. Only six letters use both *tu* and *você*, with *tu* the most frequent – 42 out of a total of 68 occurrences. Consequently, it appears that the most frequent pattern is the combination of instances of null subjects with the verb inflected for the second person singular (i.e. with the verbal morpheme -*s*, corresponding to the second person singular pronoun, *tu*), and instances of overt subjects with the form *você* (accompanied by the verb with the zero morpheme). This mixed usage also includes letters that combine the more honorific form *o(a) senhor(a)* with *você*. The forms *vossa senhoria* and *vossa excelência* are never mixed with other forms.

Graph 1 shows the use of the forms *você* and *tu* in the letters from São Paulo by decade during the period 1870 to 1949. The consistent rise of *você* over *tu* begins in the second decade of the 20th century (1910–1919). Before this, the forms are either equally distributed (1880–1889 and 1900–1909) or one form is predominant: *você* in 1870–1879 and *tu* in 1890–1899.

It is significant that we have only two letters from 1890–1899, which may explain the unexpected absence of the form *você* in this decade. The exclusive use of the form *tu* in these letters is associated with socio-geographical factors. According to the literature (cf. Lopes et al. 2018), Rio de Janeiro is a state where we identify significant use of *tu* during the 19th century and similar frequencies of *você* and *tu* from 1900 to 1939. One of these missives was written by Homem de Mello, who, despite being born in São Paulo, lived for a long time in Rio de Janeiro, where he wrote the letter. The other letter was written by a brother-in-law of Washington Luís, João de Oliveira Barros, who was from São Paulo. It is essential to locate more letters representative of this decade to ensure a more robust result.

Whereas in the missives from São Paulo, the predominance of *você* over *tu* starts in the years 1910-1919, in Rio de Janeiro, this change is observed 20 years later, during the decade 1930–1939 (Lopes & Souza 2012).

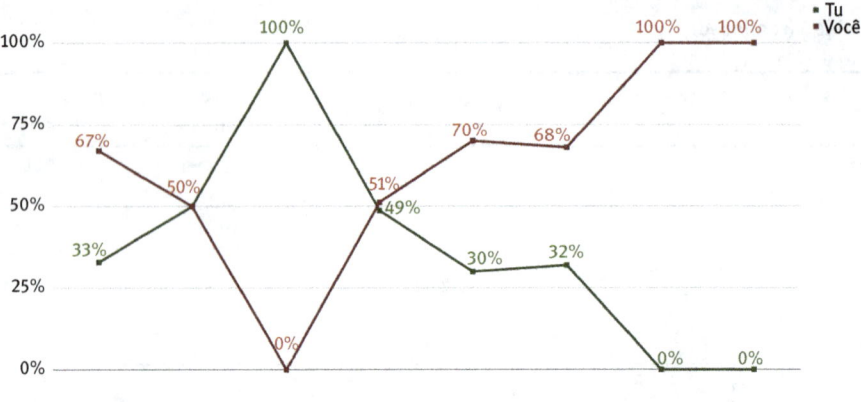

Graph 1: *Tu* and *você* in subject position from 1870 to 1949, by decade.

4.2 Gender

There are nine letters written by women. As expected (cf. Lopes & Souza 2012 and Labov 1994, among others), the use of innovative forms correlates with female speakers. An analysis of the senders' gender shows that women use the form *você* almost exclusively (89%). The recipients of these letters were other women and Washington Luís, who received many letters from his mother-in-law. There is only one case of the form *tu*, in a mixed usage letter. The other form found in missives written by women is the more courteous form *o senhor*, used twice. The results are set out in Table 6.

Table 6: Forms of address in letters written by women.

Forms of address	Number and %
tu	1/27 – 4%
você	24/27 – 89%
o senhor	2/27 – 7%

4.3 Social relations

The last element of analysis concerns the social relations between sender and recipient, to investigate the distribution of address forms according to symmetrical and asymmetrical relationships (see Table 7). The results show that the form *você* is productive in all three types of relations examined: symmetrical (between friends: 69%), asymmetrical inferior-superior (son > mother: 72%) and asymmetrical superior-inferior (mother-in-law > son-in-law: 76% / uncle > nephew: 100%). The only type of relationship in which the frequency of the form *tu* appears to be close to that of the form *você* is the solidary relation between cousins: the forms *tu* and *você* are equally distributed.

Table 7: Symmetrical/asymmetrical social relations and use of address forms.

	Social relations	tu		você		o senhor/ a senhora		vossa senhoria		vossa excelência	
Symmetrical relations	between cousins	18/36	50%	18/36	50%	–	–	–	–	–	–
	between brothers-in-law	45/99	45%	54/99	55%	–	–	–	–	–	–
	between friends	7/35	20%	24/35	69%	1/35	3%	3/35	9%	–	–
	between sisters	–	–	6/6	100%	–	–	–	–	–	–
Asymmetrical relations	son > mother	–	–	23/32	72%	9/32	28%	–	–	–	–
	mother/father-in-law > son-in-law	5/21	24%	16/21	76%	–	–	–	–	–	–
	uncle > nephew	–	–	1/1	100%	–	–	–	–	–	–
	nephew/niece > uncle	–	–	–	–	12/14	86%	–	–	2/14	14%

The forms *o senhor* and *vossa senhoria* are used between friends, while the more honorific *vossa excelência* is documented only between nephew and uncle. The feminine form *a senhora* is used by a son writing to his mother.

Examples (1) to (5) are extracts from the corpus letters and they show that, in these letters from São Paulo, the form *você* was so well-established that it had already spread into accusative positions as well. Example (1) documents this use of *você* as an accusative.

(1) Eis o que agora penso, submetto a seu criterio, e julgado util por todos os interessados, que no caso sao os meus filhos, autorizo *você* a agir por minha parte.
'This is what [I] think now, [I] submit it to your appreciation, and if all interested parts deem it useful, in this case my children, I allow you to act on my behalf' (Letter n. 177, 1 August 1937, Washington Luís)

In the letters written by Mariquinha, 2nd Baroness of Piracicaba, who exclusively uses the form *você* in subject position, the clitics *o/a* (related to *você*)[12] are very productive, as seen in examples (2) and (3). Example (2) is from a letter written by Mariquinha in 1912, where she uses the possessive *tua*, related to the form *tu*.

(2)   Queira aceitar muitas saudades de *tua* mãe que muito *o* estima e considera.
       'lit. Please accept many vows of missing you from your mother who very much esteems and values you'
          (Letter n. 08, 3 December 1912, 2.ª Baronesa de Piracicaba – Mariquinha)

(3)   Desculpe *encommodal_o*, junto remeto essa carta, de minha Sobrinha fasendo esse pedido [...]
       '[I] am sorry to bother you, enclosed [I] send this letter, from my niece making that request'
          (Letter n. 55, 27 August 1921, 2.ª Baronesa de Piracicaba – Mariquinha)

Example (4) is from a letter in which the sender, João Oliveira de Barros, is addressing the recipient with the form *você* throughout the entire missive, but at the very end, uses the form *tu*, identified by the ending of the verb *poder* (*podes*). The expression *podes crêr* (lit. '(you) can believe', or more idiomatically, 'believe you me') is an idiomatic phrase, still very much used nowadays in more informal situations. The use of *tu* here could be understood as part of this fixed expression and not a conscious choice on the part of the writer. The same letter contains both *você* in the accusative ("que pode esclarecer voce" 'that may enlighten you') and *você* with a preposition (dative case) ("que <p>uder ser util a você" 'that may be useful to you').[13]

---

12 In Portuguese, accusative (i.e. object) pronouns appear in the form of clitics (i.e. weak forms), with the following paradigm:
1SG, subject pronoun: *Eu* – object clitic: *me*;
2SG, subject pronoun: *Tu* – object clitic: *te*;
3SG, subject pronoun: *Ele/Ela* – object clitic *a/o*;
1PL, subject pronoun: *Nós* – object clitic: *nos*;
2PL, subject pronoun: *Vós* – object clitic: *vos*;
3PL, subject pronoun: *Eles/Elas* – object clitic *os/as*.
13 The symbol <..> in the transcription indicates the editor's emendations – so, in <p>uder, the "p" was inserted by the manuscript's editor, and was either absent or barely legible in the original.

(4) no tempo que elle foi inspector ou antes fiscal do governo junto a Ingleza, elle collecionou muita cousa que pode esclarecer *voce* sobre a situação da Ingleza Em tudo que <p>uder ser util *a voce, podes crêr* que terei muito prazer.

'at the time when he was the inspector or rather government auditor at the Ingleza, he collected many things that may enlighten you about the situation at the Ingleza [...] In all that may be useful to you, [you] can believe [I] will be much obliged'   (Letter n. 138, 4 July 1927, João Oliveira de Barros)

Example (5) shows an exclusive *você* letter with the use of the clitic *o*. Unlike examples (2) and (3), where the use of the clitic appears to be conditioned by fixed expressions, in this case the clitic appears in a random sentence ("pois nada resolveremos sem ouvi-lo"), In fact, standard grammar recommends that the clitic is placed just after *sem* 'without'.

(5)   Qualquer proposta viavel mandaremos telegramma, pois nada resolveremos sem ouvil-*o*.
       'Any viable proposal [we] will send a telegram, as [we] shall decide nothing without hearing from you'.
                              (Letter n. 180, 7 August 1946, Álvaro de Souza Queirós)

5 Conclusion

The analysis of letters written in São Paulo from the period 1870 to 1949 shows that the form *tu* is used exclusively as a null subject. It is therefore only possible to identify its use by verb endings. This finding differs from that for letters written in Rio de Janeiro, in which the form *tu* explicitly appears in 25% of cases (Lopes & Souza 2012). Another difference between letters from São Paulo and Rio de Janeiro is the higher frequency of the form *você* in São Paulo (58%), compared with the more frequent use of *tu* in Rio de Janeiro (62%).

In São Paulo, *você* is used more frequently than *tu* in the 1910s, whereas in Rio de Janeiro this occurs only in the 1930s. Lopes & Souza (2012) found *você* as an accusative only in letters from Rio de Janeiro which presented innovative structures, with mixed forms of address, whereas in missives from São Paulo, the accusative positions with clitics *o/a* related to the form *você* appear in letters in which *você* is used exclusively. The fact that the form *você* is very productive in all types of social relations, both symmetrical and asymmetrical, associated with the fact that the form appears frequently in accusative positions, probably shows that *você* had become part of the pronominal framework of São Paulo before this occurred in Rio de Janeiro.

Bearing in mind that the corpora only shed a selective light on the diachrony under scrutiny, the results show that the spread of *você* in the Capitaincy of São Paulo happened before the spread of *você* in Rio de Janeiro. As we suggested, a higher frequency of *você* would represent the foreshadowing of the current subsystem of address forms used in the state of São Paulo. More specifically, because the rate of overt usage in the subject position is higher with *você*, and actually zero with *tu*, this supports the hypothesis of *você* leading the present-day tendency of high use of overt pronominal subjects in Brazilian Portuguese as compared with European Portuguese. In this regard, our results may be revealing for the history of *você*, although the domain of intimacy, privacy and orality (where *tu* might have been more frequent) is underrepresented in the corpus.

References

Amaral, Amadeu do. 1955. *O dialeto caipira*. São Paulo: Hucitec. http://www.dominiopublico. gov.br/pesquisa/DetalheObraForm.do?select_action=&co_obra=7381 (13 February, 2017).
Bacelar, Carlos de Almeida Prado. 2009. O processo de povoamento do território paulista nos séculos XVI a XX. In Ataliba Teixeira de Castilho (ed.), *História do Português Paulista*, vol. 1, 137–147. Campinas: UNICAMP/Publicações IEL.
Barbosa, Afranio Gonçalves. 1999. *Para uma história do português colonial: aspectos lingüísticos em cartas de comércio*. PhD thesis. Rio de Janeiro, RJ: Universidade Federal do Rio de Janeiro.
Barratt, Alexandra. 2010. *Women's writing in Middle English*. Oxford/New York: Routledge.
Basto, Claudio. 1931. Formas de tratamento em português. *Revista Lusitana* 29. 183–202.
Duarte, Maria Eugênia Lamoglia. 1993. Do pronome nulo ao pleno: a trajetória do sujeito no Português do Brasil. In Mary Kato & Ian Roberts (eds.), *Português Brasileiro: Uma viagem diacrônica*, 107–128. Campinas, SP: Editora da Unicamp.
Hualde, José Ignacio, Antxon Olarrea & Erin O'Rourke (eds.). 2012. *The handbook of Hispanic linguistics*. Oxford: Blackwell.
Kewitz, Verena. 2016. *Cartas Familiares: em torno de Washington Luís*. São Paulo: Faculdade de Filosofia, Letras e Ciências Humanas, Universidade de São Paulo (USP).
Kewitz, Verena & José da Silva Simões. 2005/2006. *Edição da correspondência passiva de Washington Luiz – Século XIX*. São Paulo: Humanitas.
Kewitz, Verena & José da Silva Simões. 2006. *Cartas paulistas dos séculos XVIII e XIX*. São Paulo: Humanitas.
Kewitz, Verena, Rafael Rodrigo Ferreira & Cássio de Albuquerque. 2015. *Edição semidiplomática da correspondência de Fernando e Julio Prestes de Albuquerque a Washington Luís*. São Paulo: Faculdade de Filosofia, Letras e Ciências Humanas, Universidade de São Paulo (USP).
Labov, William. 1994. *Principles of linguistic change: internal factors*. Oxford: Blackwell.

Lopes, Célia Regina dos Santos. 2012. Tradição textual e mudança linguística: aplicação metodológica em cartas de sincronias passadas. In Marco Antonio Martins & Maria Alice Tavares (eds.). *História do Português Brasileiro no Rio Grande do Norte: análise linguística e textual da correspondência de Luís Câmara Cascudo a Mário de Andrade – 1924 a 1944*, 17–54. Natal: EDUFRN. http://www.letras.ufrj.br/laborhistorico/producao/UFRN.pdf (13 February, 2017).

Lopes, Célia Regina dos Santos et al. 2018. A reorganização do sistema pronominal de 2ª pessoa na história do português brasileiro: a posição de sujeito. In Célia Regina dos Santos Lopes (ed.). *História do português brasileiro: mudança sintática das classes de palavra: perspectiva funcionalista*, 24–141. São Paulo: Contexto.

Lopes, Célia Regina dos Santos & Janaina P. F. Souza. 2012. Os caminhos trilhados por *você...* em cartas cariocas (século XIX-XX). In Tânia Lobo et al. (eds.). *ROSAE: Linguística histórica, história das línguas e outras histórias*. Salvador: EDUFBA. http://www.letras.ufrj.br/laborhistorico/producao/rosae.pdf (13 February, 2017).

Marcilio, Maria Luiza. 1974. *A cidade de São Paulo: povoamento e população, 1750–1850*. São Paulo: Pioneira/EDUSP.

Marcotulio, Leonardo Lennertz. 2010. *Língua e história: o 2º marquês de Lavradio e as estratégias linguísticas no Brasil Colonial*. Rio de Janeiro: Ítaca.

Middle English Dictionary. University of Michigan, 2001–2014. http://quod.lib.umich.edu/cgi/m/mec/med-idx?type=id&id=MED27400 (21 October, 2018).

Módolo, Marcelo & Alexandra de Souza Marques. 2010. *Correspondências particulares do fundo Rafael Tobias de Aguiar – Museu Paulista*. São Paulo, FFLCH, USP.

Monte, Vanessa Martins do. 2015. *Correspondências paulistas: as formas de tratamento em cartas de circulação pública (1765–1775)*. São Paulo: Humanitas/FAPESP.

Nogueira, Rodrigo de Sá. 1927. A psicologia vista através da filologia. *Revista Alma Nova* 2,5. http://hemerotecadigital.cm-lisboa.pt/Periodicos/AlmaNova/5Serie/N02/N02_master/AlmaNovaN2.pdf (13 February, 2017).

Pharies, David A. 2015. *A brief history of the Spanish language*. Chicago: University of Chicago Press. DOI:10.7208/chicago/9780226134130.001.0001.

Rumeu, Márcia Cristina de Brito. 2013. *Língua e sociedade: a história do pronome* você *no português brasileiro*. Rio de Janeiro: Ítaca.

Scherre, Maria Marta Pereira, Edilene Patrícia Dias, Carolina Queiroz Andrade & Germano Ferreira Martins. 2015. Variação dos pronomes *tu* e *você*. In Marco Antônio Martins & Jussara Braçado (eds.), *Mapeamento sociolinguístico do português brasileiro*, 133–172. São Paulo: Contexto.

Simões, José da Silva. 2007. *Sintaticização, discursivização e semanticização das orações de gerúndio no português brasileiro*. PhD thesis. São Paulo: Universidade de São Paulo. http://www.teses.usp.br/teses/disponiveis/8/8142/tde-04102007-140928/ (13 February, 2017).

Márcia Cristina de Brito Rumeu

Variation in the paradigms of *tu* and *você*

Subject and complements in letters from Minas Gerais, Brazil, 1860–1989

Abstract: This chapter presents a quantitative analysis of the use of Portuguese second person singular (2SG) address pronouns *tu* and *você* in correlation with second person verbal complements (*te, a ti*, prep. + *ti, você, a você, para você*, prep. + *você, lhe, o/a*, zero (Ø)). We analyse the diversity of 2SG verbal complements in accusative, dative and oblique structures in letters written by individuals from the state of Minas Gerais, Brazil, between 1860 and 1989. The results show that oblique verbal complementation functions as a syntactic context that tends to favor the use of *você* (Rumeu & Oliveira 2016), whereas the dative and accusative functions are seen as survival contexts for the clitic pronominal *te*.

Keywords: second person singular, verbal complement structure, personal pronouns

1 Introduction

In present-day Brazil, the pronominal forms *tu* and *você* coexist as forms of the second person singular (2SG) subject. These pronominal forms are distributed geographically in six subsystems of address forms (see Scherre et al. 2015), and also throughout the dynamics of social relations. The six subsystems currently used in Brazilian Portuguese (BP) as described by Scherre et al. (2015) can be further reduced to three subsystems, if subject-verb agreement is not taken into consideration (see Lopes & Cavalcante 2011). *Você* (also present in the variant forms *ocê* and *ce*)[1] is the dominant 2SG form in the city of Belo Horizonte, in the state of Minas Gerais, Brazil.

Given that historically *você* was introduced later than *tu*, the present study tackles the question of how this layering process was realised over time, particularly during the 19th and 20th centuries. In addition, the subsequent layering in

---

[1] According to Peres (2006), in 2002, in the spoken language in Belo Horizonte *cê* amounted to 72.6 percent (10/1453) of the data tokens, followed by *você* with 23.5 percent (342/1453) and *ocê* with 3.9 percent (56/1453).

dependent functions such as direct and indirect object will also be studied. A *corpus* of letters written by individuals from Minas Gerais during the 19th and 20th centuries provides the data for an investigation of the functional potential of new pronominal forms of the *você* paradigm (prep. + *você, você, lhe, o/a*) co-related to the *você* and to the *tu* paradigms (prep. + *ti, te*). Given that the arrival of *você* in the BP address system did not take place to the same degree in all morphosyntactic contexts (see Lopes et al. 2009), this study analyses the diversity of forms of verbal complementation of the 2SG that occur in accusative, dative and oblique contexts of verbal complementation for the period between 1860 and 1989.

This chapter is organised as follows. Section 2 summarises the history of the emergence of *você* in the pronominal system of BP. Section 3 gives an overview of the criteria used to identify accusative, dative and oblique structures of verbal complementation. Section 4 describes the corpus of letters written by individuals from Minas Gerais representative of the evolution of address forms in BP. Section 5 discusses the results of the correlation between the *tu/você* forms functioning as subjects and the 2SG complement pronouns in the corpus. The conclusion summarises the study's findings on the use of 2SG pronominal forms in verbal complementation contexts (accusative, dative and oblique).

2 The emergence of *você* in the pronominal system of BP

Analyses of *tu/você* alternation between the 18th and 20th centuries have been based on different types of text. These include letters (Rumeu 2004; Lopes & Machado 2005; Barcia 2006; Lopes & Marcotulio 2011; Lopes & Cavalcante 2011; Pereira 2012; Silva 2012; Rumeu 2013), notes (Lopes, Marcotulio & Rumeu 2011), theatre plays (Lopes & Duarte 2003; Machado 2006, 2011) and movie scripts (Lopes, Couto & Duarte 2005). These studies have provided evidence that *você*, which originated from the grammaticalisation of *vossa mercê* 'your grace', primarily took on the functions of *subject* and *complement* in the pronominal system of BP. Furthermore, the second quarter of the 20th century, more specifically between 1925 and 1945, was the period when *você* became the most productive, as it took over the 2SG subject function (see Rumeu 2013: 278).

Based on letters written by individuals from the city of Rio de Janeiro (*carioca*) and exchanged during the 19th and 20th centuries (1870–1970), Souza (2012: 90) mapped the emergence of *você* in BP's pronominal system, identifying three clear phases in this process. By the end of the 19th century (1870–1890, phase 1), the pronoun *tu*, which denoted intimacy, was more productive than the form *você*. The latter maintained the semantics of distance/formality, which is typical of its origins in the formal *vossa mercê* as observed by Rumeu (2013). The turn of the century (1900–1930, phase 2) represents a transitional period: as the pronoun *você* began to compete for the same functional space as *tu*, its use extended to relations characterised by informality. From 1940 onwards (1940–1970, phase 3), the pronoun *tu* took the opposite direction to that observed at the end of the 19th century, as *você* began to prevail and *tu* fell into disuse. The widespread use of *você* forced the desemanticisation or bleaching of the term, that is, the loss of distance/formality. This led to a *neutral* form of address, which neither showed distance nor specified intimacy, at least within the scope of the city of Rio de Janeiro society between the end of the 19th century and the beginning of the 20th century (see Souza 2012; Rumeu 2013).

The starting point of the present analysis is the proposal of Scherre et al. (2015) regarding the synchronic productivity of the six subsystems of 2SG subject address forms in current BP, reduced by Lopes & Cavalcante (2011: 39) into three subsystems: (i) the *tu*-only subsystem, (ii) the *você*-only subsystem and (iii) the mixed-*tu*/*você* subsystem, exemplified in examples (1) to (3) respectively from the corpus of Minas Gerais letters.

(1) Letter exclusively using *tu* in subject position:

A., meu presadíssimo filho [...] Bôa saude e satisfação em tudo e por tudo, é o que desejo. Louvando incessantemente a Deus, dou-te os meus sinceros parabens pela tonsura clerical, que a 28 do passado mez te **foste** conferido pelo santo Arcebispo, meu respeitavel e amigo, em Jesus Christo [...] (RAAP. Lagoa Santa, 06.04.1914)[2]

'A., my mostly esteemed child [...] I wish good health and satisfaction in everything and for everything. Incessantly praising the Lord, I give you [*te*] my most sincere congratulations for the clerical tonsure, which you [*te*] **received** on the 28th of the past month by the saintly Archbishop, my respectful and friendly, in Jesus Christ'

(2) Letter exclusively using *você* in subject position:

Minha H. Antes d. hontem te escrevi por um cartão mandando a chave da caixinha que o Comendador-mor A. levou com o serviço do chá. [...] Como é que **você** diz que eu não lembro do nosso bemsinho? [...] e por isso

---

2 The examples are followed by the abbreviated reference to the name of the writer, as well as the place and date of writing of the missives.

lembrando a todo o momento de ti, minha H., eu lembro do nosso bemsinho. (JPS. RJ, 09.11.1890)

'My H. The day before yesterday I wrote you [*te*] a card with the little key to the box that the Supreme Commander A. brought with the tea service [...] How can you [**você**] say that I do not remember our little darling? [...] and for this reason every time I think of you [*de ti*], my H., I think about our little darling'

(3) Letter with mixed-*tu/você* in subject position:

Muito te agradeço a parte que **estás** tomando em meus soffrimentos [...] Tenho fé em Deus que **você** há de ser muito feliz em tua melindrosa carreira sacerdotal [...] (FAP. Caeté, 03.07.1917)

'I thank you [*te*] very much for the sympathy you [*tu **estás***] show towards my suffering. I have faith in God that you [***você***] will be very happy in your [*tua*] sensitive priestly career'

Considering the forms of address currently used in Minas Gerais (*você* in subject position) (see the work by Lopes & Cavalcante 2011, based on Scherre et al. 2015), this chapter describes the extent to which the forms of the *você* paradigm (prep. + *você*, *você*, *lhe*, *o/a*) exemplified in examples (4) to (6), are used in verbal complementation instead of the forms of the *tu* paradigm (prep. + *ti*, *te*), as in examples (7) and (8). Verbal predicates which govern address forms are indicated in bold while the pronouns that accompany them are presented in italics.

(4) **Confio** *em você*, para suprir a orfandande moral da nossa L. (OLR. Bruxelas, 30.07.1959)

'I **trust** you [*em você*] to remedy our L.'s moral orphanage'

(5) Não **convocamos** *Você* para ficar lá conosco porque não há commodo [...] (AR. BH, 07.03.1940)

'We have not **summoned** You [*Você*] to stay with us because there is no chamber'

(6) Você não aparece por estas bandas? Não vem a Paris? Ou só a Itália *o* **tenta**? (OLR. Bruxelas, 29.01.1959)

'Are you [*Você*] not coming [aparece] around? Not coming [vem] to Paris? Or only Italy **tempts** you [*o* tenta]?'

(7) Antes d. hontem *te* **escrevi** por um cartão... Hontem estando a ler deitado na cama jornaes e com o pensamento de *te*-**escrever** [...] (JPS. RJ, 09.11.1890)

'The day before yesterday I **wrote** you [*te*] a card... Yesterday I was reading newspapers while lying on my bed and thought about **writing** to you [*te*-]'

(8) Realmente seria dificil citar as poesias de que mais gostei, tantas são elas, por êste ou aquele motivo: Em infancia pus-me a **lembrar** *de ti*, não tanto em casa a olhar o rio [...] (MJLB. Lambari, 04.08.1941)

'It would be really hard to quote all the poems I liked the most, they are so plentiful, for one reason or the other. As a child, I **remembered** you [*de ti*], not so much as a result of staring at the river'

3 2SG pronominal forms in accusative, dative and oblique verbal complements

This section focuses on describing the pronominal forms of the *você* and *tu* paradigms used in verbal complementation in the accusative (direct object of the verb), dative (indirect object of the verb, whether or not preceded by a preposition) and oblique functions (a non-cliticisable prepositional complement).

3.1 The accusative (direct) object

The accusative (direct) object appears in a verbal predicate with two arguments, that is, subject and direct object (direct transitive verb [SU V **DO**]), three arguments ([SU V **DO** OBL$_{COMPL}$] and ditransitive [SU V **DO** IO]).[3] From a formal perspective, the accusative verbal complement represents the formally cliticisable 2SG direct object in atonic pronominal forms in the *tu* (*te*) and *você* (*o/a*, *lhe*) paradigms. Semantically, the accusative takes the thematic role of a patient or theme. From the perspective of the grammatical tradition, the complement pronoun *te* is the only form to comply with the subject pronoun *tu*, in agreement with a uniform address. However, the emergence of *você* as subject pronoun in the BP pronominal system led to a confusion of paradigms characterised by the coexistence of

---

3 The abreviations are as follows: SU= subject, V= verb, DO= direct object, OBL$_{COMP}$ = oblique complement, IO = indirect object.

forms of the *tu* (*te*) paradigm alongside forms of the *você* (*o/a*,[4] *lhe*) paradigm, as well as by the absence of the direct object (∅ = null 2SG direct object) and by the use of 3rd person possessives linked to *você*, e.g. *seu*. Evidence of accusative pronominal 2SG forms are illustrated in examples (9) to (13).

(9)   Mal você volta ao govêrno, cá estou eu para **chateá**-*lo*. Desculpe. Mas o caso é importante e urgente. O meu irmão G., que *o* está **procurando**, foi nomeado nos últimos dias do govêrno MC [...] (OLR. RJ, 14.02.1951)

‘You [*você*] have barely returned to government and here I am **bothering** you [-*lo*]. I am sorry. But the issue is important and urgent. It is my brother, G., who **is looking for** you [*o*], he was nominated in the last days of the MC government’

(10)   Você deve me mandar, com urgência, os seus elementos [...] Depois **procurarei** *você* para conversarmos. (AG. 20.02.1943)

‘You [*Você*] must urgently send me your [*seus*] elements [...]. **I will look** out for you [*você*] afterwards so that we can talk’

(11)   Da filha que *lhe* **beija** as mãos, H. (HL. RJ, 30.08.1933)

‘From your daughter, who **kisses** your [*lhe*] hands, H.’

(12)   Abraça [tu] por mim a tia Sinhá e as meninas. **Beija**-*te* com carinho e saudades a prima e comadre muito amiga [...] (L. Thebas, 24.01.1925)

‘Give [Abraça (*tu*)] Aunt Sinhá and the girls a hug from my part. Your cousin and friend [comadre] **kisses** you [-*te*] with affection’

(13)   Appareça por aqui. Hoje escrevi para G. para saber suas noticias. Deus que te **abençoe** e ∅ **felicite** [...] (RAAP. BH, 03.04.1925)

‘You should come around [Appareça (*Você*)]. Today I wrote to G. in order to hear news from you [*suas*]. God bless you [*te*] and **greet** ∅’

---

4 Phonologically conditioned variant forms *lo/la* and *no/na* also exist and are subsumed under *o/a* here.

3.2 The dative (indirect) object

The *dative* encompasses syntactic constructions traditionally identified as *indirect object*. These are so named because they are indirectly linked to a verb through a preposition. In the present study, the dative grammatical relation is interpreted as a term which takes a preposition; it is clitisable as *lhe*, and appears in a verbal predicate with two arguments (indirect transitive verbs – [SU V **IO**]), or three arguments (ditransitive verbs [SU V DO **IO**]), see Duarte (2006: 296, 298–299), which refer to the target, the source or the beneficiary of the action with the semantic feature [+animate]. Examples (14) and (15) from the MG corpus illustrate 2SG datives linked to the *tu* (*te*, *a ti*) paradigm, while examples (16) through (19) illustrate them in the *você* (*lhe*, *a você*, *para você*)[5] paradigm. The absence of the dative complement (Ø = null 2SG indirect object) is shown in example (20).

(14) a prova és que ainda não *te* pude **arranjar** nada, nenhuma quantia de din-heiro ainda não *te* pude **mandar** [...] (RAAP. Lagoa Santa, 18.05.1915)

'you are [(*tu*) *és*] the proof that I could not **offer** you [*te*] anything, I could not **send** you [*te*] any sum of money yet'

(15) **Agradeço** *a ti* muito o gentil offerecimento prova segura da amizade que me dedicas. (FAP. Caeté, 19.08.1917)

'I **thank** you [*a ti*] very much for kindly offering a safe proof of the friend-ship you commit [(*tu*) *dedicas*] to me'

(16) Querida H., Promessa é dívida: aqui estou para cumprí-la. Prometi com efeito **mandar-***lhe* uma foto de Jorge Guillén: ei-la. (MM. Roma, 06.12.1961)

'Dear H., a promise made is a debt unpaid: and I am here to pay it. I actually promised to **send** you [-*lhe*] a picture of Jorge Guillén: here it is'

(17) **Mando** *a você* uma cópia do meu livro que pretendo publicar [...] (JAG. 20.02.1943)

'I **send** you [*a você*] a copy of my book that I am planning to publish'

---

5 The choice of separating the prepositions *para* and *a* from other prepositions was motivated by that fact that, in Brazilian Portuguese, the preposition *a* is in process of being replaced by the preposition *para* in dative structures (see Gomes 2007).

(18) Ingrid, que **manda** muitos abraços *para você*, ficou de devolver-me os orig-
inais. (AM. RJ, 01.06.1941)

'Ingrid, who **sends** you [*para você*] many hugs, is yet to send me back the
originals'

(19) Querida Titia [...] Andamos de bicicleta no Parque Novo e depois fomos no
outro parque beber água. Mamãe e papai **mandam** abraços *para você*. Um
abraço para V. (M. Campanha, 30.08.1968)

'Dear Auntie [...] We rode our bikes through the New Park and then we went
to the other park to drink some water. Mommy and Daddy **send** you [*para
você*] hugs. Hugs to V.'

(20) O G. vai fazer a secção de crítica na Folha, a partir de amanhã, domingo.
Foi anunciado. Tenho um palpite de que possa começar a série com a nota
sobre o seu livro. Se assim for, **mandarei** Ø amanhã o recorte. [...] Logo que
Você possa ir ao Vargas, avise. (JCL. MG, Lambari, 21.06.1941)

'G. will be writing the critique section of the *Folha* [newspaper] from tomorrow, Sunday, onwards. It has been announced. I have an intuition that he
might start his series with the note about your [*seu*] book. If this is the case,
I will **send** Ø the newspaper clipping tomorrow. If You [*Você*] are able to go
to Vargas's, let me know'

3.3 The oblique (prepositional) object

The *oblique* form is syntactically linked to a verbal predicate in the form of a
(non-cliticisable) non-dative prepositional phrase, e.g. *comtigo* 'with you (tu)'.
Following Duarte & Brito (2006: 169–170), the oblique is interpreted as the argument that, when linked to a verbal predicate in the form of a non-dative prepositional phrase, is a complement to the verbal predicate in a nuclear (nuclear
oblique) or optional form (non-nuclear oblique).[6] The latter is projected as an
adjunct, while the former is projected as a complement, as discussed by Rumeu &

---

6 According to the Rocha Lima, the *nuclear oblique* can be labelled as a *relative complement*
given that it determines the structure of the complementation (COMP), but also as a result of the
specificity of the argument that provides meaning to its predicator (which is a relative transitive
verb, in the terms of Rocha Lima), usually through two-argument verbs [SU V OBL$_{COMP}$] (see Duarte & Brito 2006).

Oliveira (2016), Cruz (2017) following the works of Duarte & Brito (2016) and Ilari et al. (2015). Examples (21) to (24) provide samples of the nuclear and non-nuclear oblique 2SG structures with pronominal forms of the *tu* and *você* paradigms.

(21) Quando você telefonou, eu estava no banho. Logo em seguida, o H. – que **leva** *sôbre você* a vantagem [...] (OLR. RJ, 02.08.1950)

'I was showering when you [*você*] called. Soon after, H. – who **has** advantage over you [*sobre você*]'

(22) Pudesse eu **viver** isolado *comtigo* e meu filho bem longe d. tudo d. todos e eu teria uma immensa alegria. (JPS. RJ, 15.02.1891)

'If only I could **live** with you [*comtigo*] and my child, isolated, very far away from everything and everyone I would be immensely joyous'

(23) Realmente seria dificil citar as poesias de que mais gostei, tantas são elas, por êste ou aquele motivo: Em infancia pus-me a **lembrar** *de ti*, não tanto em casa a olhar o rio [...] (MJLB. Lambari, 04.08.1941)

'It would be really hard to quote all the poems I liked the most, they are so plentiful, for one reason or the other. As a child, I **remembered** you [*de ti*], not so much as a result of staring at the river'

(24) Encantei-me e **aprendi** muita cousa *com você*, principalmente sobre A. de G. (HL. 29.03.1979)

'I have been mesmerised by and have **learned** a great deal from you [*com você*], especially about A. de G.'

The following section will proceed with the description of historical samples of correspondence written by individuals from the state of Minas Gerais (19th and 20th centuries).

4 Analysing the samples of historical correspondence and the informants

Human languages follow a dynamic of ordered heterogeneity from which linguistic manifestations can be described and analysed from a structural and social perspective (Weinreich, Labov & Herzog 1968; Labov 1994). If the objective is to reconstruct linguistic realities of past synchronies, it is important to bear in mind the possible obstacles to working with historical data, such as those related to the authorship as well as the historical and social validity of historical texts. This has led to the construction of a specific methodology for approaching historical corpora (see Hernández-Campoy & Conde-Silvestre 2014; Conde-Silvestre 2007).

The present study is based on the analysis of two hundred thirty-four personal handwritten letters from the period 1869 to 1989, by individuals born in the state of Minas Gerais in Brazil. These letters reveal the intimacy of love, family, and friendship relationships, see Table 1, through social relations that are informed by various degrees of affective proximity between the sender and the receiver.

Table 1: Types of personal letters.

CORPUS OF PERSONAL LETTERS	
Love letters	04
Family letters	127
Friendship letters	103

The *corpus* consists of love, family and friendship letters written by JPS,[7] a well-known political figure in Minas Gerais, and were produced between 1869 and 1908. The love letters were exchanged between him and his wife H. He also wrote to his uncle (family letters) and other authorities of the state's political scene (friendship letters) (see Luz 2015). There are also letters exchanged by the AP family, dating from 1907 to 1944. The letters were directed to the priest A., and were written by the parents, siblings, a (female) cousin, and a brother-in-law. This correspondence is characterised by a sense of proximity amongst family members. We know that the family members were from Minas Gerais because their biographical details were reconstructed from the letters. Particularly with regard to the father and the brother (the men of the AP family), it is known that they were educated informants as one was a professor of languages and the other a professor of medical pathologies. The intimacy of family relations allows them to express how they miss one another (*saudades*), to exchange news (*notícias*) and to make the most varied requests. In addition, the corpus contains letters written by local poets between 1917 and 1989, which illustrate relations of friendship and family ties.

With the goal of constructing an historical sociolinguistics of BP, a set of methodological steps have been adopted. They work as premises to confirm the

---

7 Only the letter writers' initials are referred to here in order to ensure anonymity.

authorship and historical and social validity of the letters written by well-known or public figures from Minas Gerais. The steps are as follows:

(i)   the reconstruction of the social profile of the letter writers, based on the identification of their origin (nationality and place of birth), gender (sex), age group, schooling background, and social role;

(ii)   the comparison of various letters written by the same person, enabling us to determine the respective authorship of the handwritten letters (love, friendship and family related);

(iii) the conservative editing of letters written by individuals from Minas Gerais, which consists of the facsimile reproduction and transcription of the manuscripts without any intervention by the editor with regards to spelling, punctuation or other textual practices specific to the 19th and 20th centuries.

Following the presentation of these historical samples with regards to writers from Minas Gerais and the subtypes of personal letters (love, family and friendship related), we proceed to the analytical description of accusative, dative and oblique 2SG contexts linked to the subject pronouns *tu* and *você*.

5 Accusative, dative and oblique 2SG verbal complements used with *tu* and *você*

As we have seen, pronominal variant forms of the *tu* and *você* paradigms can be used in accusative, dative and oblique 2SG contexts in BP. The letters in the corpus were controlled for pronouns used in the subject function and for pronouns used in the verbal complement function, as well as for variant forms of the 2SG paradigms. The goal was to quantify the use of variant pronominal forms from the *tu* and *você* paradigms in accusative, dative, and oblique verbal complement structures, and to discover whether these pronominal forms matched the use of *tu* or *você* in subject position.

5.1 The accusative (direct) object

The results show that among the pronominal forms used in the accusative function (present in 26/436 or five per cent of the letters analysed), *te* was the one most frequently used, with levels varying between 80 and 97 per cent of the letters. *Te* shares its functional space mainly with the clitic accusative form *o/a*, which also had productivity levels of over 70 per cent. Figure 1 presents the distribution of

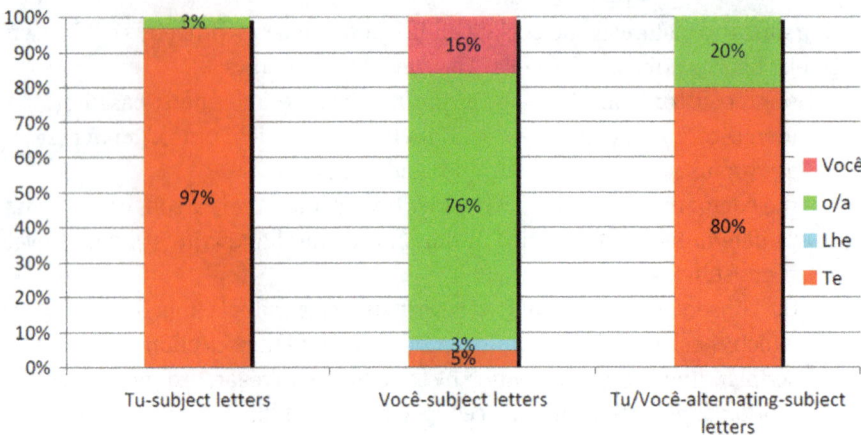

Figure 1: Accusative forms employed with 2SG subject pronouns.

accusative pronominal forms in relation to each specific pronoun used in 2SG subject function (*tu*-only letters, *você*-only letters and mixed-*tu/você* letters).

The *te* form is predominant in *tu*-only missives as well as in letters with mixed-*tu/você* in subject position, as illustrated in examples (25) and (26). These results confirm those of other studies that show that the use of *tu* and *você* is identical in relation to the semantic person they refer to ([-EU][8] = 2SG) (Lopes & Rumeu 2007; Rumeu 2006). Conversely, however, in letters with *você* as the exclusive subject, the direct object clitic *o/a* is prevalent in 76 per cent of the data in reference to 2SG, as illustrated by examples (27) and (28). Given that the accusative clitic *o/a* was etymologically geared towards 3SG, its use in reference to 2SG seems to constitute an innovation in BP, which was already evident in the writing of educated individuals from the state of Minas Gerais between the 19th and 20th centuries.

(25)   *Tu* as exclusive subject:

Não fôras tu, minha terna companheira e a vida para mim seria detestavel! [...] Eu *te*-**conheci**, minha esperança carinhosa, eu *te* **conheci** em São Paulo! [...] (JPS. RJ, 14.02.1891)

'If it were [*(tu) foras*] not for you [*tu*], my dearest partner and life would be detestable to me! [...] I **met** you [*te*], my loving hope, I **met** you [*te*] in São Paulo!'

---

8 This refers to the specific semantic notion of pronominal forms in the second person singular: *tu/você* = "you-sg".

(26) Mixed-*tu*/*você* as subject:

> Muito te agradeço a parte que estás tomando em meus soffrimentos [...] Tenho fé em Deus que você há de ser muito feliz em tua melindrosa carreira sacerdotal [...] Aguardo com ansiedade recebimento de tuas amaveis cartas. **Abraça-***te* apertadamente Teu tio e Amigo grato [...] (FAP. Caeté, 03.07.1917)

> 'I very much thank you [*te*] for the sympathy you show [(*tu*) *estás*] towards my suffering. I have faith in God that you [*você*] will be very happy in your [*tua*] sensitive priestly career [...]. I anxiously await your [*tuas*] lovely letters. I **hug** you [-*te*] tight, Your [*Teu*] uncle and grateful friend'

(27) *Você* as exclusive subject:

> Se você vier antes, espero **reencontrá**-lo aquí depois, após minha volta de Minas [...] (OLR. RJ, 26.07.1951)

> 'If you [*você*] come earlier, I hope to **see** you [-*lo*] here again afterwards, after I have returned from Minas'

(28) *Você* as exclusive subject:

> Fazendo-lhe uma visitinha muito afetuosa venho **convida**-la para assistir à festinha da entrega dos diplomas no próximo dia 30. Terei muito gôsto que você venha. (CLB. Lambari, 25.11.1941)

> 'Paying you [-*lhe*] a short and very affectionate visit, I hereby **invite** you [-*la*] to attend the little party in which we will handle the diplomas on 30th. I will be very pleased should you [*você*] come'

In relation to the context of letters using only *você*, the forms *te*, *lhe* and *você* as direct complements occurred less frequently – see examples (29) to (32).

(29) *Você* as exclusive subject:

> Chegando eu hontem de B. Horizonte encontrei aqui sua preçioza carta a qual me trouçe uma tão bôa notiçia. Deus que *te* **ajude** em tudo e por tudo [...] Joãozinho inda não veio é posivel que você desta vez veja elle [sic] pois até o mez de Junho voçe já está em ferias. (RAP. Caeté, 05.04.1915)

> 'As I arrived yesterday from B. Horizonte I found your [*sua*] precious letter, which brought me such good news. May God **help** you [*te*] in everything and for everything [...]. Joãozinho has not come yet and it is possible that

this time you [*você*] will meet him since you will be [*voçe esta*] on holiday until the month of June'

(30)   *Você* as exclusive subject:

Você recebeu a minha carta em resposta á que me escreveu em Agosto? [...] Basta de **amolar**-*lhe* [...] (MA. Serra Azul, Itaúna, 10.01.1917)

'Have you [*você*] received my letter in response to the letter you wrote [escreveu] me in August? [...] Enough with **bothering** you [-*lhe*]'

(31)   *Você* as exclusive subject:

Está claro que, para mim, seria extraordináriamente simpático e agradável **ter** *Você* como companheiro de exílio. Você me atrai mais a Madrid do que o Museu do Prado [...] (OLR. Bruxelas, 01.12.1958)

'It is clear that, for me, it would be extraordinarily agreeable and pleasant **having** You [*Você*] as my company in exile. You [*você*] are attracting me to Madrid more than the whole of the Prado Museum'

(32)   *Você* as exclusive subject:

Para **distrair** *você* da doença, vou tocando em outros assuntos [...] (AM. RJ, 01.10.1945)

'In order to **distract** you [*você*] from the illness, I will address other topics'

In *tu*-only letters and in mixed-*tu/você* letters, the clitics *te* and *o/a* share the same functional field of reference to the 2SG, as shown in examples (33) and (34) respectively.

(33)   Mixed-*tu/você* as subject:

Por que havia esta desgraçada fatalidade d. *te*-**ferir** assim *a Você*, a tua santa esposa e aos teos filhinhos?! (JPS. Caeté, 29.12.1896)

'Why must this disgraceful tragedy **hurt** you [-*te*-], you [*a você*], your [*tua*] saintly wife and your [*teos*] little children so much?!'

In the original example, it is possible to see evidence of the accusative *a você* in a redoubling structure already present in Minas Gerais writing from the late 19th century. This structure is productive in contemporary Minas Gerais spoken language, as shown by the following examples from Duarte & Diniz (2012: 92). *Eu vou* *te$_i$ levá ocê$_i$ lá* 'I will take you, take you, there'. *Uma coisa eu vou te$_i$ falá com ocê$_i$* 'I will tell you something to you'. *Eu vou te$_i$ contá pro ocê$_i$ um pouquim da minha vida* 'I will tell you something to you a bit about my life'.

(34) Mixed-*tu*/*você* as subject:

E entretanto a minha H. sempre deixa para me escrever quando o Paulo não *a* **deixa** escrever. Se soubesses a aflicção com que espero o correio para ler as tuas cartas [...] Quando eu te telegraphar você manda fazer a mudança [...] (JPS. RJ, 15.02.1891)

'And meanwhile my H. always begin [*(tu) deixa*] to write to me when Paulo does not **let** you [a] write. If you only knew [*(tu) soubesses*] how afflicted I feel while waiting for the post in order to read your [*tuas*] letters [...] When I send you [*te*] a telegraph you [*você*] should send orders to begin with the move'

5.2 The dative (indirect) object

In dative verbal complements (328/436, 77 per cent of the samples), *te* shares its functional contexts with the clitic *lhe*, as well as with the prepositional phrase *a você* and *para você*. The clitics *te* and *lhe* are the most frequently used verbal complement pronominal forms. Figure 2 presents the distribution of these pronominal forms across the subsystems of forms of address in *tu*-only letters, *você*-only letters, and mixed-*tu*/*você* letters.

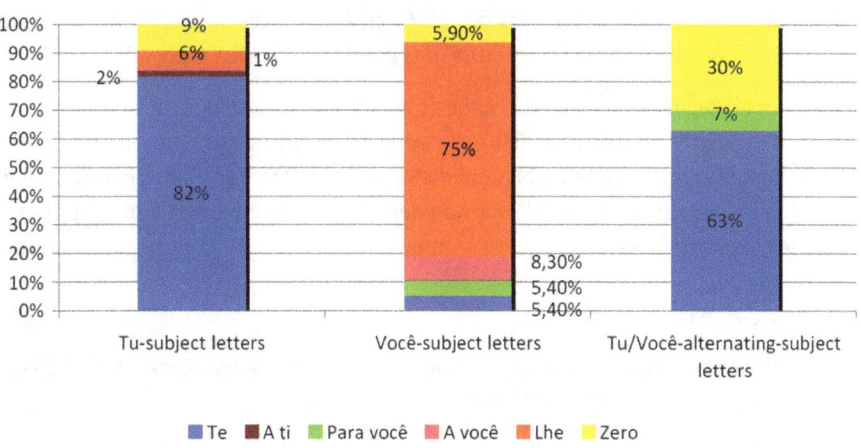

Figure 2: Dative forms employed with 2SG subject pronouns.

Generally speaking, the dative form -*te* is predominant not only in the *tu*-only letters (82 per cent, 80 occurrences), but also in mixed-*tu*/*você* letters (63 per cent, 17 occurrences), as illustrated by examples (35) and (36). On the other hand, *lhe* is the preferred strategy (75 per cent, 152 occurrences) in *você*-only letters, as illustrated by examples (37) and (38). The phrases preceded by prepositions *a você*, *para você*, the clitics *te* and zero (Ø), in turn, are present in the *you*-subject letters with low levels of productivity (8.3 per cent, 5.4 per cent, 5.4 per cent, and 5.9 per cent, respectively). In short, the *você*-only context seems to boost the use of the *lhe*-dative, while the *tu*-only letters and the *você*-only letters are productive contexts for the *te*-dative in letters written by individuals from Minas Gerais.

(35) *Tu* as exclusive subject:

Quanto á escola, é como bem pódes avaliar. Tenho recebido tuas cartas com muito prazer e contentamento; e, si não *te* **escrevo** sempre, **peço**-*te* dar me desconto: pouco ou nenhum tempo para escrever com tranquillidade e socêgo [...] (RAAP. Lagoa Santa, 30.10.1912)

'As to the school, it is as you might [(*tu*) *podes*] evaluate it. I have received your [tuas] letters with much pleasure and satisfaction, and, if I do not **write** to you [*te*] more frequently, I **ask** you [-*te*] not to be so hard on me: I have little to no time to write with tranquillity and quietness'

(36) Mixed-*tu*/*você* as subject:

Adelaide, como sabes, é nervosa em excesso e está em uso de remedios; eu; por minha vez, sou tambem nervoso, a nossa casa é pequena e mal nos comporta; o que has depois fazer?! **Peço**-*te* escreva-me a respeito [...] Você não deixe de vir aqui passar uns dias connosco. (FAP. Caeté, 02.08.1913)

'Adelaide, as you know [(*tu*) *sabes*], is excessively nervous and under medication; I, in my turn, am also a nervous man, our house is small and barely accommodates us, what is there else to do? I **ask** you [-*te*], write me about it [...] Please do not refrain [*Você não deixe*] from coming here and spending a few days with us'

(37) *Você* as exclusive subject:

Sem mais, **peço**-*lhe* velho irmão mui sigilo. Como já *lhe* **disse**, você e o Fernando, sim? (WF. BH, 10.11.1949)

'Without further ado, I **ask** you [-*lhe*] much secrecy, my old brother. As I have **told** you [*lhe*] already, you [*você*] and Fernando, right?'

(38) *Você* as exclusive subject:

Você continua satisfeita com o serviço da Vicentina? [...] Ia esquecendo de **contar**-*lhe* que Marília está cada vez mais parecida com você [...] (MAVP. Campanha, 17.12.1961)

'Are you [*você*] still satisfied with Vicentina's work? [...] I have almost forgotten to **tell** you [-*lhe*] that Marília looks everyday more like yourself [*você*]'

The coexistence of forms of the *tu* (*te*) paradigm and forms of the *você* (*você, lhe* and *o/a*) paradigm, as in example (36), is yet another indication of the fusion of second and third person paradigms since the emergence of *você* in the BP pronominal system.

5.3 The oblique (prepositional) object

In oblique verbal complements (82/436, 18 per cent), pronominal phrases preceded by a preposition (prep. + *ti* and prep. + *você*) had the highest levels of productivity in the contexts of the *tu*-only and *você*-only letters, respectively. This illustrates a symmetry between the pronominal choices used in the 2SG subject and verbal complement positions.

Figure 3 reveals that the subject pronoun seems to determine the oblique 2SG pronominal form, replicating the patterns observed in the accusative and oblique 2SG structures. Consequently, we can assert that the forms that follow a preposition, prep. + *ti* and prep. + *você*, are predominant in *tu*-only letters and in *você*-only letters, respectively, as illustrated in examples (39) and (40).

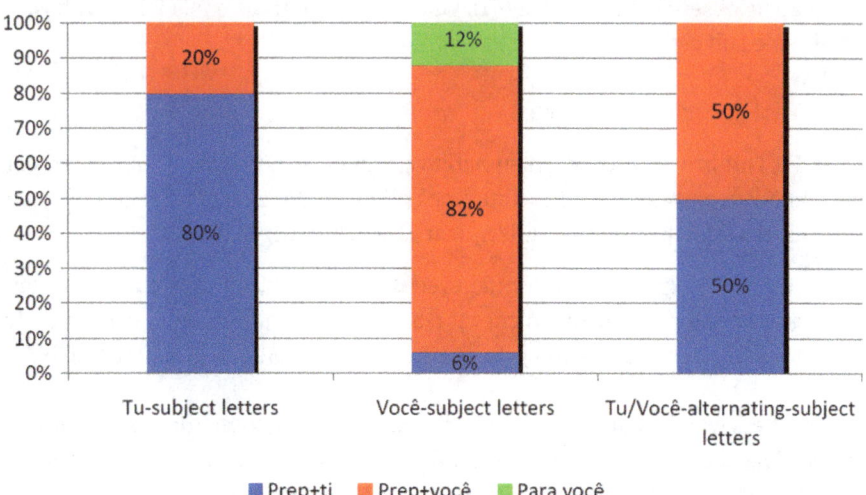

Figure 3: Oblique forms employed with 2SG subject pronouns.

(39)   *Tu* as exclusive subject:

Estou em falta contigo, não tendo ainda agradecido o livro que nos envias-tes [...] Realmente seria difícil citar as poesias de que mais gostei, tantas são elas, por êste ou aquele motivo: Em infancia pus-me a **lembrar** *de ti*, não tanto em casa a olhar o rio [...] (MJLB. Lambari, 04.08.1941)

'I still owe you [*contigo*] for not having thanked you for the book you sent us [*(tu) enviastes*] [...] It would be really hard to quote all the poems I liked the most, they are so plentiful, for one reason or the other. As a child, I **remem-bered** you [*de ti*], not so much as a result of staring at the river'

(40)   *Você* as exclusive subject:

O Astrogildo pediu-me que **obtivesse** *de você* que está ficando famosa no assunto, um pequeno ensaio (de dez a doze páginas) sobre "literatura para criança" [...] Será que você topa, L.? Não quero que se sacrifique [...] (AM. RJ, 18.10.1946)

'Astrogildo told me to **get from** you [*de você*], since you are [*(você) está*] getting famous in this area, a short essay (from ten to twelve pages long) on "children's literature" [...] I wonder if you [*você*] would do it, L.? I do not want you [*(você) se*] to make too much of a sacrifice'

Oblique forms structured with the innovative use of *você* (as in prep. + *você*) have a slight advantage (over prep. + *ti*), which describes the oblique grammatical rela-tion as a more favourable context for pronominal forms than the *você* paradigm. This can be observed in example (41), which shows *para você* in a letter with *você* as the sole subject pronoun.

(41)   *Você* as exclusive subject:

H., **Quebro** *para Você* o meu habito carranca de não felicitar qualquer, por motivo nenhum [...] a nave que você pilota ha de erguer vôo seguro elevan-do você às alturas onde quizer ficar. (JLJ. Lambari, 23.10.1924)

'H., for You (*para Você*) I would even **dispose** of my grumpy custom of con-gratulating no-one, for whichever reason [...] the ship you pilot will certainly take off safely, raising you [*você*] to the heights where you [*você*] want to be'

In the letters where *tu* and *você* coexist in the subject function, the variant form of the *você* paradigm, prep. + *você*, is evident in example (42), although coexisting with the variant form of the *tu* paradigm, prep. + *tu*, as can be seen in example (43).

(42) Mixed-*tu*/*você* as subject:

Pudesse eu **viver** isolado *comtigo* e meu filho [...] Se soubesses a afflicção com que espero o correio para ler as tuas cartas, me mandarias menos cartões! [...] Você não quiz mandar medida para um vestido [...] (JPS. RJ, 15.02.1891)

'If only I could **live** with you [*comtigo*] and my child, isolated [...]. If you only knew [*(tu) soubesses*] how afflicted I feel while waiting for the post in order to read your [*tuas*] letters, you would send [*(tu) mandarias*] me less cards! [...] You [*você*] *didn't* wish to send me your measurements for a dress'

(43) Mixed-*tu*/*você* as subject:

Nem sei, meo infeliz amigo, que palavras d. consolação nesta hora para você tão escura, possa eu descobrir que te levassem o conforto de que precisas. [...] **chorando** com *Você* meo amigo! a tua immensa desgraça! [...] e que você não deixaria também nunca soffrer nunca um filho meo [...] (JPS. Caeté, 29.12.1896)

'I do not even know, my unfortunate friend, which words of solace for you [*para você*] in such a dark hour I could come up with in order to give you [*te*] the comfort you need. [...] **crying** alongside you [*com Você*] my friend! in this immense tragedy of yours [*tua*]! [...] and you [*você*] would never let [*(você) deixaria*] a son of mine suffer'

6 Conclusion

After the analysis of the forms *te*, *a ti*, prep. + *ti*, *a você*, *para você*, prep. + *você*, *lhe*, *o/a*, zero (Ø) in verbal complement structures, it is possible to make some brief generalisations about the use of these pronouns in accusative, datives and oblique structures in letters with *tu*-only used in subject position, *você*-only, and mixed-*tu*/*você*.

Accusative pronominal forms diachronically follow their respective nominative forms, since it was shown that the clitics *te* and *o/a* (corresponding to the pronominal forms of the paradigms *tu* and *você*) are predominant in the *tu*-only and *você*-only letters respectively. In letters where the pronouns *tu* and *você* alternate as subject, accusative *te* also prevails. This indicates the *neutral* character that the clitic *te* has acquired (see the debate by Oliveira 2014 and Cruz 2017 in relation to letters from the states of Rio de Janeiro and Minas Gerais, respectively).

As for 2SG dative structures, pronominal forms also follow their respective nominative options. This is shown by the prevalence of *te* (dative) in *tu*-only missives and of *lhe* (dative) in *você*-only letters. The absence of pronominal forms in 2SG dative structures (zero dative) occurred infrequently, regardless of the pronoun used in the nominative function. On the other hand, the forms *para você* and *a você* in dative structures are evident in limited numbers: contexts of *você*-only and mixed-*tu*/*você* letters. In short, *te* – the pronominal form of the *tu* paradigm – persists in the accusative and dative structures of *tu*-only letters and mixed-*tu*/*você* letters (see Lopes & Cavalcante 2011; Oliveira 2014; Souza 2014; Cardoso 2017).

Two specific characteristics of letters written by individuals from Minas Gerais are related to the fact that *lhe* (originally the third person dative clitic) functioned in dative structures with 2SG reference. This is evidence of the high level of formality between the writers, but also of the innovative role of the clitic *o/a* (originally the third person accusative clitic) in 2SG accusative structures.

As was also observed for accusative and dative structures, oblique structures are guided by the nominative forms (*tu* subject → prep. + *ti*; *você* subject → prep. + *você*). The variant form prep. + *você* is highly productive in oblique structures in the *você*-only letters.

To sum up, these results confirm the hypothesis that the emergence of *você* in the pronominal system of BP has not reached all syntactic contexts to the same degree (Lopes et al. 2009). In the letters written by individuals from Minas Gerais in the 19th and 20th centuries, the oblique grammatical relation of the verbal complement favours the diffusion of *você* (Rumeu & Oliveira 2016), while the dative and accusative grammatical relations are the syntactic contexts where the *tu* is maintained, consolidated through the high productivity of the clitic *te*.

References

Barcia, Lucia Rosado. 2006. *As formas de tratamento em cartas de leitores oitocentistas: peculiaridades do gênero e reflexos da mudança pronominal*. Master's thesis. Rio de Janeiro: Federal University of Rio de Janeiro.

Cardoso, Nayara Domingues. 2017. *As estratégias de dativo de 2ª pessoa em cartas pessoais (séculos XIX e XX)*. Master's thesis. Federal University of Minas Gerais.

Conde-Silvestre, Juan Camilo. 2007. *Sociolingüística histórica*. Madrid: Gredos.

Cruz, Iracema Aguiar da. 2017. *A alternância tu/você em contextos sintáticos de comple-mentação e de adjunção: estudo de cartas pessoais dos séculos XIX e XX*. Master's thesis. Federal University of Minas Gerais.

Duarte, Fábio Bonfim & Carolina Ribeiro Diniz. 2012. Eu te falei para você: redobro de pronomes? In Jânia Martins Ramos & Sueli Coelho (eds.), *Português brasileiro dialetal: temas gramaticais*, 91–102. São Paulo: Mercado de Letras.

Duarte, Inês. 2006. Relações gramaticais, esquemas relacionais e ordem de palavras. In Maria Helena Mira Mateus et al. (eds.), *Gramática da Língua Portuguesa*, 275–321. Lisbon: Caminho.

Duarte, Inês & Ana Maria Brito. 2006. Predicação e classes de predicadores verbais. In Maria Helena Mira Mateus et al. (eds.), *Gramática da língua portuguesa*, 179–203. Lisbon: Caminho.

Charlotte Galves, Juanito Avelar, Dorothy Brito, Danniel Carvalho, Célia Lopes & Leonardo Marcotulio. 2016. Morfossintaxe e uso dos pronomes pessoais na sincronia e na diacronia do português brasileiro. In Marco Antonio Martins & Lucrécio Araújo de Sá Júnior (eds.), *Rumos da linguística brasileira no século XXI: historiografia, gramática e ensino*, 123–154. São Paulo: Blucher.

Gomes, Christina Abreu. 2007. Uso variável do dativo em textos jornalísticos. *Lingüística* 3, 1. 7–19.

Hernández-Campoy, Juan M. & Juan Camilo Conde-Silvestre (eds.). 2012. *The handbook of historical sociolinguistics*. Oxford: Wiley-Blackwell.

Hernández-Campoy, Juan M. & Natalie Schilling. 2012. The application of the quantitative paradigm to historical sociolinguistics: Problems with the generalizability Principle. In Hernàndez-Campoy & Conde-Silvestre (eds.), 63–79.

Ilari, Rodolfo, Ataliba Teixeira de Castilho, Maria Lúcia Leitão, Lou-Ann Kleppa & Renato Miguel Basso. 2015. A preposição. In Rodolfo Ilari (ed.), *Gramática do português culto falado no Brasil: palavras de classe fechada*, 163–310. São Paulo: Contexto.

Labov, William. 1994. *Principles of linguistic change: internal factors*. Oxford: Blackwell.

Lopes, Célia Regina dos Santos & Leonardo Lennertz Marcotulio. 2011. O tratamento a Rui Barbosa. In Dinah Callou & Afranio Barbosa (eds.), *A norma brasileira em construção: cartas a Rui Barbosa (1866 a 1899)*, 265–292. Rio de Janeiro: Fundação Casa de Rui Barbosa.

Lopes, Célia Regina dos Santos, Leonardo Lennertz Marcotulio & Márcia Cristina de Brito Rumeu. 2011. O tratamento em bilhetes amorosos no início do século XX: do condicionamento estrutural ao sociopragmático. In Célia Lopes Regina dos Santos & Letícia Rebollo Couto (eds.), *As formas de tratamento em português e em espanhol: variação, mudança e funções conversacionais*, 315–348. Niterói: Editora da UFF.

Lopes, Célia Regina dos Santos & Sílvia Regina de Oliveira Cavalcante. 2011. A cronologia do voceamento no português brasileiro: expansão de você-sujeito e retenção do clítico -te. *Lingüística* 25, 30–65.

Lopes, Célia Regina dos Santos & Márcia Cristina de Brito Rumeu. 2007. O quadro de pronomes pessoais do português: as mudanças na especificação dos traços intrínsecos. In Ataliba Teixeira de Castilho, Maria Aparecida Torres Morais, Ruth E. Vasconcellos Lopes, Sônia Cyrino (eds.), *Descrição, história e aquisição do português brasileiro – Estudos dedicados a Mary Kato*, 419–435. Campinas: Fapesp/Pontes Editora.

Lopes, Célia Regina dos Santos et al. 2009. Sobre norma e tratamento em cartas a Rui Barbosa. In Vanderci de Andrade Aguilera (eds.), *Para a história do português brasileiro*, 45–92. Londrina: Eduel.

Lopes, Célia Regina dos Santos & Ana Carolina Morito Machado. 2005. Tradição e inovação: indícios do sincretismo entre a segunda e a terceira pessoas nas cartas dos avós. In Célia Regina dos Santos Lopes (eds.), *A norma brasileira em construção. Fatos linguísticos em cartas pessoais do século 19*, 45–66. Rio de Janeiro: Fundação de Amparo à Pesquisa do Estado do Rio de Janeiro.

Lopes, Célia Regina dos Santos, Letícia Rebollo Couto, Maria Eugênia Lamoglia Duarte. 2005. Como as pessoas se tratam no cinema latino-americano: análise de formas de tratamento em roteiros de três países, In Alba Valencia E. (ed.), *Actas do XIV Congresso internacional da ALFAL*, vol. 2, 1–14. Monterrey: Santiago de Chile. https://www.mundoalfal.org/es/content/actas.

Lopes, Célia Regina dos Santos & Maria Eugênia Lamoglia Duarte. 2003. De *Vossa Mercê* a *você*: análise da pronominalização de nominais em peças brasileiras e portuguesas setecentistas e oitocentistas. In Silvia Figueiredo Brandão & Maria Antónia Coelho da Mota (eds.), *Análise contrastiva de variedades do português: primeiros estudos*, 61–76. Rio de Janeiro: In-Folio.

Luz, Ricardo Dias. 2015. *O tratamento na produção epistolar de João Pinheiro da Silva: análise sociopragmática de tu x você e respectivas formas gramaticais*. Master's thesis. Federal University of Ouro Preto.

Machado, Ana Carolina Morito. 2006. *A implementação de você no quadro pronominal: as estratégias de referência ao interlocutor em peças teatrais no século XX*. Master's thesis. Federal University of Rio de Janeiro.

Machado, Ana Carolina Morito. 2011. *As formas de tratamento nos teatros brasileiro e português dos séculos XIX e XX*. PhD thesis. Federal University of Rio de Janeiro.

Mota, Maria Alice. 2008. *A variação dos pronomes tu e você no português oral de São João da Ponte (MG)*. Master's thesis. Federal University of Minas Gerais.

Oliveira, Thiago Laurentino de. 2014. *Entre o linguístico e o social: Complementos dativos de 2ª pessoa em cartas cariocas (1880–1980)*. Master's thesis. Federal University of Rio de Janeiro.

Pereira, Rachel de Oliveira. 2012. *O tratamento em cartas amorosas e familiares da família Penna: um estudo diacrônico*. Master's thesis. Federal University of Rio de Janeiro.

Rocha Lima, Carlos Henrique (ed.). 2001 [1972]. *Gramática normativa da língua portuguesa*. Rio de Janeiro: José Olympio.

Rumeu, Márcia Cristina de Brito. 2004. *Para uma história do português no Brasil: Formas pronominais e nominais de tratamento em cartas setecentistas e oitocentistas*. Master's thesis. Federal University of Rio de Janeiro.

Rumeu, Márcia Cristina de Brito. 2006. Traços formais e semântico-discursivos no processo de gramaticalização de *Vossa Mercê > você*. *Revista do GEL* 3. 67–82.

Rumeu, Márcia Cristina de Brito. 2014. A difusão do *você* pelos contextos sintáticos de complementação e de adjunção. *Revista Portuguesa de Humanidades* 18. 91–114.

Rumeu, Márcia Cristina de Brito. 2015. *Tu ou você, te ou lhe?*: a correlação entre as funções de sujeito e complemento verbal de 2ª pessoa. *Lingüística* 31,2. 83–109.

Rumeu, Márcia Cristina de Brito (ed.). 2013. *Língua e sociedade: a história do pronome você no português brasileiro*. Rio de Janeiro: Ítaca.

Rumeu, Márcia Cristina de Brito & Thiago Laurentino de Oliveira. 2016. A expressão da 2ª pessoa do singular em contextos de complementação e de adjunção: retratos do encaixamento estrutural e social. *Lingüística* 32. 25–46.

Silva, Érica Nascimento. 2012. *Cartas amorosas de 1930: o tratamento e o perfil sociolinguístico de um casal não-ilustre*. PhD thesis. Federal University of Rio de Janeiro.

Souza, Camila Duarte de. 2014. Eu te amo, eu lhe adoro, eu quero você: *a variação das formas de acusativo de 2ª pessoa em cartas pessoais (1880–1980)*. Master's thesis. Federal University of Rio de Janeiro.

Souza, Janaina Pedreira Fernandes de. 2012. *Mapeando a entrada do* você *no quadro pronominal: análise de cartas familiares dos séculos XIX-XX*. Master's thesis. Federal University of Rio de Janeiro.

Scherre, Marta, Edilene Patrícia, Carolina Andrade Dias & Germano Ferreira Martins. 2015. Variação dos pronomes *tu* e *você*. In Marco Antonio Martins & Jussara Abraçado (eds.), *Mapeamento sociolinguístico do português brasileiro*, 133–172. São Paulo: Contexto.

Weinreich, Uriel, William Labov & Marvin I. Herzog. 1968. Empirical foundations for a theory of language change. In Winfried Lehmann & Yakov Malkiel (eds.), *Directions for historical linguistics*, 97–195. Austin: University of Texas Press.

Gunther Hammermüller

Retracing the historical evolution of the Portuguese address pronoun *você* using synchronic variationist data

Abstract: This chapter describes the historical evolution of Portuguese address forms based on regional documents from the *Inquérito Linguístico Boléo* (ILB) recorded from 1942 to 1974 (University of Coimbra). It focuses on regional and social variation of the *vossemecê-você* family of address forms. The analysis leads to a (hypothetical) diachronic pedigree of these pronouns as well as to a survey of regional speakers' evaluations of the forms. It concludes that in Portugal there are numerous many-layered islands of address-norm systems that may be understood as a complex system of *socioglosses*.

Keywords: dialectology, Portugal, diachronic reconstruction, geolinguistic variation, *você*, *vossa mercê*

1 Introduction

This chapter analyzes the diachrony of the *vossemecê-você* 'Your Grace – formal *you*' family of address forms in order to provide a systematic account of regional and social variation in Portuguese. The analysis is based on unpublished dialect data from Portugal from 1942 to 1974 – the *Inquérito Linguístico Boléo* (ILB). Basing the analysis on ILB documents showing synchronic variation, this study aims to make a *diachronic reconstruction* of elements illustrating the development of the series of variants associated with the pronouns *vossemecê* and its reduced variant, *você*, used in the present-day standard variety of Portuguese.

Section 2 discusses some theoretical and terminological issues, followed by the presentation of the the ILB corpus in Section 3. Section 4 examines a representative set of data, and Section 5 outlines the morphological diachrony from Latin VOSTRA MERCED to Portuguese *você* based on the analysis of the ILB corpus data. Section 6 takes the District of Viseu as a representative example of address form choices, and Section 7 outlines a geographical survey of *você* evaluations across Portugal. Finally, Section 8 summarises the results and findings of the study.

Given the complexity of address in Portuguese, the glosses and translations of the different terms used for address can only be tentative. The letters T and V in cases such as *you$_T$* and *you$_V$* refer to the informal (close) or formal (distant, polite) relationship expressed by the form of address. If the personal relationship is expressed with the verb only, notations such as *come$_V$* may be used. Intermediate terms may appear as, e.g. *you$_{VT}$*. In general, the terms are only glossed on their first occurrence.

2 Theoretical considerations

In undertaking an analysis of Portuguese address forms, there are a number of theoretical questions that need to be addressed.

2.1 Basic address conventions

Addressing one another is a universal behavior that is realized interpersonally in a given situation. We make an individual evaluation of the persons in front of us and our relationship with them. These evaluations may be described as positive or negative according to theories of "face" (e.g. Goffman 1959; Brown & Levinson 1987). Either a speaker intuitively classifies an addressee and treats her/ him accordingly, or strategically chooses an address term in order to voluntarily define or negotiate the interpersonal relation. Communities united by language and/or culture may appear to be more or less dynamic in their addressing behavior. The Portuguese address system seems to be a first-rate example of a less static system if we compare it, for example, to the traditional German one, where a change from *Sie* to *Du* among adults is usually controlled by an explicit ceremonial agreement (see Glück & Koch 1998; Clyne, Norrby & Warren 2009). In Portugal, you may increase or reduce perceived interpersonal distance by using *você* instead of *tu* or *o senhor*, etc., or simply by switching from third person to second person, and vice versa (see e.g. de Oliveira 2009 and Hummel, in this volume). The most important forms of address in use are: *tu* 'informal you$_T$', *você* 'respectful but not distant you$_{T/V}$', *vo(sse)mecê* 'forerunner of *você* used in dialects for roughly the same purpose as *você*', *o senhor/a senhora* (very formal *you$_V$*, e.g. *you, Sir*), *amigo/a* 'friend', *camarada* 'comrade, mate', *excelência* 'Your Excellency', third person form of the verb.

2.2 How not to be confused by a third person designating second persons

In Portuguese, the information conveyed by the grammatical person, gender or number (second or third person/feminine or masculine/singular or plural) does not always match the features of the referential person. Thus, a morphological third person form may refer to the direct interlocutor, which is in fact a referential second person (e.g., *O senhor* 'you$_V$'), a morphological feminine may be used to address a man (e.g., *Vossa Senhoria*, a former address of high status persons), and a morphological plural can be used to denote a single person (e.g., archaic or regional *vós* 'sg. you$_V$'). This study therefore establishes a terminological difference between the *person(s) addressed* and the *grammatical forms* used to refer to the person.

The distinction between 1P (first person singular) to 6P (third person plural) as "morphological persons" (*grammatical form*) and P_1 (EGO), P_2 (VIS-À-VIS), P_3 (TRACTATUM) (*person addressed by reference*), etc., as semantic partners in communication, as well as combinations of these, provides unambiguous terms. The terminological set proposed here is based on conceptual deliberations on onomasiology[1] by Klaus Heger, who referred to the ideas of Karl Bühler in particular (see Heger 1965 and Bühler 1967). Table 1 applies this terminology to Portuguese.

Table 1: Addressing persons (n = more persons).

VERBAL FORM (e.g., *ir* 'go')		ACTING PERSON(S)	ADDRESSING
1P	(*eu*) *vou* 'I go'	P_1	P_1 (inner dialogue?)
2P	(*tu*) *vais* 'you go'	P_2	P_2/P_1 (inner dialogue)
3P	(*ela/ele*) *vai* 'she/he goes'	P_3	P_2
4P	(*nós*) *vamos* 'we go'	P_1+2/P_1+3/P_1+2+3	P_1+2+n/P_2 (*vamos!* 'let's go')
5P	(*vós*) *ides* 'you go'	P_2+n	P_2+n/P_2
6P	(*eles/elas*) *vão* 'they go'	P_3+n	P_2+n

---

1 The term *onomasiology* refers to a methodology that looks for linguistic items covering a given conceptual or functional domain, e.g. the lexical fields of 'anger', 'address', and so on.

2.3 "Formas de tratamento" and/or "Fórmulas de tratamento"?

In Portuguese, the distinction between the expressions *formas de tratamento* 'address forms' and *fórmulas de tratamento* 'address formulas' is an interesting one. On the one hand, there are formal differences between so-called *pronominal forms* such as *tu/você/vossemecê*, and on the other hand, the so-called *nominal forms* such as *o senhor/a senhora* or *o Manuel/a Maria*. At the same time, it is clear that the syntactic positions of these elements show at least two patterns: they are to be found in either the subject or object position within a given sentence. Moreover, they may be rendered prominent as appositions as in Pt. *Ó Sr. Manuel, você .../Não se lembra de mim, ti' António?* 'You Mr. Manuel, you$_V$ .../ Don't you remember me, uncle Antonio?' In the linguistic bibliography on Portuguese, the cited nominal address forms may be called *formas* or *fórmulas*, no matter whether they are placed as subjects in normal phrases (*O Manuel quer ...?* 'Manuel, do you$_{T/V}$ want...'), or rather, as their (preceding or following) appositional counterparts (*Ó Senhor Manuel, você ...?* 'You Mr. Manuel, do you$_V$ want...?'). Moreover, this latter type is often labeled as *vocative*,[2] whether it includes a special marker *ó* or not (cf. for an appellative use without a vocative marker: *Dê-me uma codinha, senhora mãe...* 'Please give me a piece of bread, mother...' (Aquilino Ribeiro 2015: 115).

This apparent terminological ambiguity led to the search for a better distinction between basic syntactic types of address constructions, and as a result, the following suggestions have been put forward, most recently in Hammermüller (2010):

A: *Actantial*[3] *elements* – pronouns and nouns in subject (or object, etc.) position
B: *Appositional elements* – pronouns and nouns in adjunctive position
C: *Appositional vocatives* – forms as in B, but with vocative markers like *ó*
The following examples illustrate distinction.

A   Actantial Address Forms
    A-1   Nominal Address   *O Senhor* está bom? 'Are you$_V$ ok, Sir?'
    A-2   Pronominal Address   *Você* está bom? 'Are you$_V$ ok?'
    A-3   Verbal Address   *Estás* bom? 'Are you$_T$ ok?'

---

2 Portuguese has the specific vocative morpheme *ó* (open vowel [ɔ]). It must not be confused with the masculine singular definite article *o* (pronounced [u]). As a consequence, *ó pai* 'You, father/ Hey, father' has to be distinguished from *o pai* 'lit. the father'. Both are used for address. In this chapter, the former is glossed as 'You, father' (vocative), the latter as 'Father' (simple address).
3 Other terminologies would use the term *syntactic arguments* instead of *actantial elements*.

B   Appositional Address Forms (Pt. *apelemas* 'appealing forms')

   B-1   Nominal Appealing Forms   Está tudo bom, *Sr. Fulano*? 'Everything ok, Mr. X?'

   B-2   Pronominal Appealing Forms   *Tu!*, estás bom? 'And you$_T$, are you$_T$ ok?'

   B-3   Verbal Appealing Forms   *Esteja quieto!* 'Be$_V$ quiet' (polite) (imperative)

C   Appositional Vocatives (forms as in B, but with vocative markers like *ó*)

   C-1   Nominal Vocatives   Está tudo bom, *ó Sr. Fulano?*

   C-2   Pronominal Vocatives   *Ó tu!*, estás bom?

   C-3   Verbal Vocatives   *Olá, venha cá! 'Hey, come$_V$ here'

2.4   Elaborating onomasiological tools for specific address studies

For the analysis of the ILB corpus with respect to historical traces of Portuguese address forms, it is necessary to choose the best adapted methodological tools and terminology. The term for address forms in Portuguese is *formas de trata-mento,* literally 'forms of treatment'. Fundamentally, speakers experience verbal address as an immediate and more or less direct treatment by their interlocutor. An addressee can take this treatment positively or negatively, so that – by the speaking self (EGO) – it has to be seen as a more or less immediate access to the other person (VIS-À-VIS). In order to prevent the respective inventory of onomasi-ological concepts from being too near to tautology, valid conceptual instruments are required that represent a special meta-language. The interlingual definitions of these conceptual terms should be able to establish functional *tertia compara-tionis* (that is, a common point of reference that allows comparison) as linguis-tic tools for onomasiological and/or contrastive investigation in the domain of address (and others).

2.5   The concept of RESPECT as an onomasiological tool

Linguistic analysis in the domain of address has led many investigators to dis-cover the relevance of concepts such as "respect", "reverence", "veneration", "courtesy", "politeness", and others (see Hummel, in this volume). These mostly Latin-based philosophical terms have been accepted as being rather universal – at least for an enlarged European context (cf. the keyword *respect* in the *Stanford Encyclopedia of Philosophy*). They seem to have proved helpful for the descrip-tion of the *necessary conditions* regarding address. Trying to establish a useful intercultural *tertium comparationis*, they enable us to evaluate (and to accept or not) the way in which we are addressed. In particular, the widely accepted (because of being less polysemic?) term of *respect* seems to offer itself as first choice for onomasiological research in the field of address forms and conventions, as we shall see below.[4]

Without claiming to have a perfect conceptual hypothesis for the wider field of address, I propose a suitable approximation for the initial analysis of the relevant ILB data. The aim is to discover specific language development implications in the domain of the descendants of late medieval *vossa mercê*. As a first step, it will be useful to distinguish the categories of in-group and out-group addressees (or: *insiders* vs. *outsiders*) as well as those of older and/or higher status addressees. The two types can be compared in order to show possible affinities. Table 2 presents some typical examples (all based on occurrences in the ILB database) used in north-eastern parts of Portugal, but also elsewhere.

Table 2: Respect Matrix (core groups in bold).

Respect Matrix	In-group	Out-group
older people	*ó pai/mãe, você quer …?*	*o Sr./a Sr.a quer …?*
higher status individuals	*ó patrão, você quer …?*	*ó mestre, você quer …?*
children & youth	*tu*	*o/a menino/a*
equals (school/workmates)	*tu, você*	*você, tu*
older (**parents**/godparents)	*ó pai/mãe, você quer …?*	*o Sr./a Sr.a quer …?*
older (without direct kinship)	*vossemecê, vomecê*	*o Sr./a Sr.a quer …?, você*
superiors	*ó patrão, você quer …?*	*ó mestre, você quer …?*
lower status	*tu, você, tiazinha*	*você, santinha, tiazinha*

In order to reduce complexity, I propose a simplification with regard to some basic categories. It might be useful to have special distinctions at least for younger people, equals, and older people outside one's family, as well as a complementary categorization of higher status and lower status addressees. Although this presentation of types of address remains limited, it shows how it is possible to gradually refine onomasiological tools needed for specific purposes.

---

4 Here we may possibly include non-European languages like Turkish, where *saygı* means 'respect, esteem' and is close to 'politeness', as is shown by the derived adjective *saygıyla* 'polite'; found in *Langenscheidt's Online Dictionaries* [accessed 7 July 2017].

3 The *Inquérito Linguístico Boléo (ILB)*

The ILB Archives of the *Faculdade de Letras* at the University of Coimbra consti‐
tute a rich collection of regional language and ethnographic data from all over
Portugal (Boléo 1942/1974). They comprise about 3,100 questionnaires (plus com‐
plementary documents) completed between 1942 and 1974 by Manuel de Paiva
Boléo, Professor of Romance philology and Portuguese linguistics at Coimbra
(see Hammermüller 1995). The documents contain two types of spoken language
data obtained from local native speakers.

The first set of data was produced in 1942. Boléo posted out a huge number
of questionnaires (in total around 15,000 copies were printed) to primary school
teachers and local village priests, with the majority going to the north and the
center of Portugal (Boléo 1942/1974). This first printed version (with 550 items) of
the questionnaire had 1,829 completed returns (Boléo 1974: 322).

A second set of data was collected by Boléo's students after a theoretical and
practical introduction to dialectological methods in the second year's part of
their *Introdução aos estudos de filologia/linguística (2ª parte)* 'Introduction to the
study of philology/linguistics (part II)' (Boléo 1974: 322–323). From 1942 onwards,[5]
Boléo's students were required to undertake fieldwork, using an expanded 1942
questionnaire with up to 757 items (see last edition in 1978 of the 3rd version by
Fátima Matias, University of Aveiro).

The results gathered via questionnaire constitute the *Inquiry* (*Inquérito*).
From 1945 to 1974 (the year Boléo retired from teaching), his students were also
asked to write up a *Relatório*, which described their local experiences and docu‐
mented ethnographic and language facts they found worthwhile recording. Most
of the original copies are still conserved in Coimbra, with a total of approximately
3,100 *Inquéritos* and 1,800 *Relatórios*.

The ILB database can be seen as nothing less than a linguistic (and ethno‐
graphic) bonanza for diachronic reconstruction based on synchronic variation. The
data enable us to analyze oral forms of address conserved by a rural milieu (at least
to a very large extent) which was – up to the second half of the 20th century – still
widely marked by illiteracy. This derives from the fact that in Portugal the general
school system (promoted during teachers' education in *Escolas de Magistério* in
many district capitals) had only slowly been developed from the first half of the 20th
century onwards, as illustrated by the picturesque description of a regional school
by Gibbons (1984). The data thus reproduce the limited literacy of rural, lower status
speakers (and as a product of internal migration, also of urban speakers).

---

5 For 1942, we found at least two *Inquéritos* already completed by students.

4 Address forms (e.g. *você*) and their use in ILB questionnaires

Exploring the ILB data from 1942 onwards, Boléo and collaborators produced more than 160,000 excerpted words on paper sheets and a huge number of published and unpublished memoirs and theses written by their students (cf. Boléo 1971b, 1976, 1979). However, these efforts never led to the realization of Boléo's original idea of producing a *Dicionário do Português Regional* (first in 1959), proposed also as DFPM (*Dicionário dos falares portugueses modernos*) (cf. Boléo 1959, 1971a, 1976: 8; Hammermüller 1995). The following sections present parts of the ILB corpus that shed some light on the geolinguistic remnants of address forms used up to the latter part of the 20th century.

Table 3 provides an abstract map of continental Portugal including the districts used to classify the data (see Hammermüller 2011: § 5.1). The numbers go from north (1) to south (8), including the two archipelagos in the Atlantic Ocean (9), and the names refer to districts (see map of Portugal in Lara, this volume).

Table 3: Districts of Portugal.

North (1) to South (8) plus islands (9)	West	Middle	East
1	VIANA DO CASTELO		BRAGANÇA
2	PORTO	BRAGA	VILA REAL
3	AVEIRO	VISEU	GUARDA
4	COIMBRA		
5	LEIRIA		CASTELO BRANCO
6	LISBOA	SANTARÉM	PORTALEGRE
7	SETÚBAL	ÉVORA	BEJA
8		FARO	
9	AÇORES		MADEIRA

4.1 The questions

This section presents an analysis of ILB summaries of address usage in the third edition modified by Boléo's former student Fátima Matias.[6] Table 4 sets out the questions in the ILB survey dealing with forms of address (see Matias 1978: ILB-§ 371 + § 371b (pages 75/75 A)).[7]

Table 4: Questions about address in the ILB questionnaire.

371	*tratamento*
[1]	Quando os filhos chamam os pais, os avós, os padrinhos, dizem: *ó pai? ó meu pai? ó sr. pai? ó sr. padrinho?*
[2]	Quando se lhes dirigem, como os tratam: por *vossemecê?*
[3]	Quando falam deles na ausência dizem: *a mãe está doente* ou *a minha mãe está doente?*
[4]	Usa-se dizer, em conversa com uma pessoa de condição social superior, *o sr. seu pai, a sr°. sua mãe?*
[5]	É costume tratar o irmão ou irmã mais velha por *mano, mana?*
'371	*address*
[1]	When children call their parents, grandparents, godparents, do they use: *you father? you my father? you senhor father? you senhor godfather?*
[2]	When children address these people, what do they use: *vossemecê?*
[3]	What do children use to refer to these people if the latter are absent: *mother is sick* or *my mother is sick?*
[4]	What is usually chosen in conversations with higher status people, *senhor your father, senhora your mother?*
[5]	Do you usually address your older brother or sister with *mano, mana* (short forms of *irmão* 'brother' and *irmã* 'sister')'

Outras observações: p.ex.: se é costume as crianças pedirem a benção quando encontram o padrinho ou o pároco da terra:

[6]	*deite-me a sua benção, meu padrinho*, e qual a resposta destes
[7]	(*Santinho!, Deus te abençõe*, etc.).

---

6 Matias went back to a second edition by Boléo from 1962 (probably to its reprint in 1963) where the exploration of *tratamento* given in section § 371 had been complemented by another section, § 371b, in order to broaden the inquiry to include extra-familiar address. But, apparently, Boléo had already proposed earlier a longer list of additions when preparing his students for their fieldwork. So § 371b had already appeared before (and was added by hand to the printed text of the 1942 questionnaire as "371–5: Indicar as fórmulas de tratamento para com estranhos (*você, vossemecê, patrãozinho, senhor*, etc.)".

7 For practical reasons numbers from [1] to [7] have been assigned to the questions in § 371.

Table 4 (continued)

'Further observations: e.g. if children ask for a blessing when they meet their godfather or the village priest:
[6]   *may I receive your blessing, my godfather,* and what do they answer
[7]   (*Santinho!* 'Saint + diminutive *-inho*', *God bless you,* etc.)'

371b   Indicar as fórmulas de tratamento para com estranhos: *você* (é ofensivo este tratamento?), *vossemecê, patrãozinho, senhor, santinha,* etc.
'371b   Indicate the forms of address used with strangers: *você* (would this be offensive?), *vossemecê* 'you$_{VT}$', *patrãozinho* 'boss + diminutive', *senhor* 'Mister, Sir', *santinha* (feminine form of *Saint* plus feminine form of the diminutive *-inha*)'

4.2 Questionnaire responses

The ILB summaries refer to several locations within Portuguese districts ordered from north to south. The answers come from different years, and illustrate a variety of address form uses that – at first glance – do not show much regularity concerning geolinguistic, sociolinguistic and transgenerational developments. Rather, it can be observed that the individual locations (mostly consisting of villages) have (or at least had) a social life of their own, using their own system of address accordingly. When looking at the regional distribution of different pronounciations, e.g. the bilabial onset [v-, b-], it must be borne in mind that many of the fieldworkers writing down the file cards, and particularly those inquiries completed by correspondence from 1942, may have preferred to follow the standard spelling, e.g. (standard) initial <v-> orthography.

(1)   Afife (Viana do Castelo)
371:     É curioso em Afife o tratamento quase familiar entre todas as pessoas. Os mais velhos tratam por *tu* todos os mais novos, e os de igual idade, tambem se tratam por *tu.* Os novos tratam os mais velhos por «tios», salvo, é claro, os de certa representação social. Quando os filhos chamam os pais, o padrinho, o avo dizem: <ò mêu pài, ò padriñu, ò mêu abô>*. Quando se lhes dirigem tratam-us por <bòsê>*.

'The striking fact in Afife is the almost familiar treatment of all people. The oldest address the youngest with *tu* 'you$_T$', and people of the same age also use *tu.* Young people address old people with 'uncle', with the obvious exception of higher status people. When the children address their parents, godfather or grandfather, they say: <you my father, you my godfather, you my grandfather>*. When they address them they use <bòsê>* (variant of *você* 'you$_{VT}$')'

371b: < bòsê>* (não sendo ofensivo) e <bòsəməsê>*.

'<bòsê>* (variant of *você* 'you$_{VT}$', which is not offensive) and <bòsəməsê>* (variant of *vossemecé* 'you$_{VT}$')'

Table 5: Forms of address used in Afife (Viana do Castelo).[8]

Categories	<-> young[8]	<->equals	> parents	> older	> strangers	> superiors
appellative			ó meu pai	tio/a		
actantial	tu, 2P	tu, 2P	vo(sse)mecê	vo(sse)mecê		

ILB-0112/64_Afife/Afife/Viana do Castelo/VIANA DO CASTELO [Q ²1962][9]

(2)   Antela (Porto)

371:    o tratamento geral é de *você, ó pai, ó mãe* (*senhor pai* caiu já em desuso)*.

'the general form of address is *você, ó pai* 'you father', *ó mãe* 'you mother' (*senhor pai* has fallen out of use)'

371b: O tratamento de *você* é geral e de modo nenhum ofensivo. É vulgar quando se fala com uma pessoa mais nova, é vulgar tratá-la por *netinho* e se fôr mais velha, <abuziñu>*.

'*Você* is generalized and not offensive at all. It is vulgar to address a younger person with *netinho* 'grandson' and older people with <abuziñu> [= *avô* 'grandfather' + diminutive -*inho*]'

Table 6: Forms of address used in Antela (Porto).

Categories	<-> young	<->equals	> parents	> older	> strangers	> superiors
appellative			ó pai/mãe	tio/a; avozinho		
actantial		você	você	você		

ILB-0863/65_Antela/Lavra/Matosinhos/PORTO [Q ²1962]

---

8 <-> means 'between', < means 'directed to'.

9 This is the ILB identification number. It provides the year of the inquiry after the slash, e.g., ILB-0112/64 equals the year 1964. The identification number is then followed by the indication of "locality/community/canton/DISTRICT", plus the edition of the questionnaire [Q ²1962]. Intentionally omitted parts of recorded responses are marked by [...]. The symbol <...>* (i.e., followed by an asterisk) means a slightly modified reproduction of the original phonetic transcription, where <ò> represents an open vowel and <ô> a closed vowel; <S> corresponds to the Sampa-code for the sibilant [ʃ].

(3)   Nevogilde (Porto)

371:    O tratamento entre iguais é: *bòsê* – *Bocê faça-me isto. Bocê disse aquilo.*

'The address term used between equals is *bòsê* (= *você*) – *Bocê, please do this for me. Bocê, you said those things*'

371b: O tratamento por *você* não é de modo algum depreciativo. *Vossemecê* é um tratamento respeitoso que se dá a pessoas de categoria mais elevada.

'*Você* is not derogatory at all. *Vossemecê* is used to respectfully address higher status people'

Table 7: Forms of address used in Nevogilde (Porto).

Categories	<-> young	<->equals	> parents	> older	> strangers	> superiors
appellative			*ó pai/mãe*	*tio/a*		
actantial		*você*	*você*	*você*	*você*	*vossemecê*

ILB-0867a/49_Nevogilde/Nevogilde/Porto (Foz)/PORTO [Q 1942]

(4)   Foz do Douro (Porto)

371:    Quando se dirigem aos pais ou familiares mais velhos dizem apenas: <Pai ou u pai fieS iStu?>*. Tratam os irmãos mais velhos pelo nome próprio, sem fazer distinção em relação aos mais novos.

'When they address their parents or older relatives, they only say: <*father* or *you father*, have you done this?> They address their older siblings with their first name, without marking any difference regarding the younger ones'

371b: Dizem quando se dirigem a estranhos: <u siñuar>*. A uma mulher mais idosa podem dizer: <sãntiña>*.

'With strangers they use <u siñuar> (= *O senhor* – 'you, Sir'), with an old woman they may use <sãntiña> (= *Santinha* 'Saint + diminutive')'

Table 8: Forms of address used in Foz do Douro (Porto).

Categories	<-> young	<-> equals	> parents	> older	> strangers	> superiors
appellative	name	name	*pai/mãe*	*tio/a*		
actantial		*você*	*o pai/a mãe*	*você*	*o senhor*	*o senhor**

ILB-0870/67_Foz do Douro/FdD/Porto/PORTO [Q ²1962]

(5)   Aveiro (Aveiro)

371:    É uso chamarem: *ó pai! ó bó! ó padrinho!* Há quem use tratar os pais por *você* mas geralmente é só: *ó pai faz-me isto ou aquilo.*

'Usual terms are *ó pai! ó bó!* 'you, grandfather', *ó padrino* 'you, godfather'. Some use *você* for addressing their parents, but normally they say: *you$_T$, father, do$_T$ this or that*'

Table 9: Forms of address used in Aveiro (Aveiro).

Categories	<-> young	<-> equals	> parents	> older	> strangers	> superiors
appellative			ó pai	tio/a		
actantial			o pai/você			

ILB-1069/44_Aveiro/Aveiro/Aveiro/AVEIRO [Q 1942]

(6)   *Corujeira (Viseu)*

371:    hoje chamam *meu pai, minha mãe, meu padrinho* etc. Ha poucos anos ainda era *snr pai, senhora mãi* e, quando falavam a alguem – *o Snr seu pai,* etc. Usam o *vossemecê* quando falam a alguem superior, *você* menos cerimonhoso.

'at present *meu pai, minha mãe, meu padrinho,* etc. are used. A few years ago, *snr pai, senhora mãi,* and, speaking to other people – *o Snr seu pai* 'senhor your$_v$ father', etc., were used. People use *vossemecê* when they speak to higher status persons; *você* is less ceremonial [formal]'

Table 10: Forms of address used in Corujeira (Viseu).

Categories	<-> young	<->equals	> parents	> older	> strangers	> superiors
appellative			meu pai			
actantial			você			vossemecê

ILB-1273/42_Corujeira/Ventosa/Vouzela/VISEU [Q 1942]

(7)   Vilharigues (Viseu)

371:    <meu pai>*. Os ricos dizem <senhor pai>*, <meu padriñu>*. Padrinho de posição social superior: <senhor padriñu>*.

'<my father>. The rich say *<senhor* father>. <my godfather>. If the godfather is a higher status person: *<senhor* godfather>'

371b: *tu* – para os da mesma idade e condição. <bòsê, bòsəməsê> – para as pessoas mais ricas e mais velhas. <səñôra> – para posição social superior.

'you$_T$ – for people of the same age and social condition. <bòsê, bòsəməsê> (= *você, vossemecê*) – for richer and older people. *Senhora* for higher status people'

Table 11: Forms of address used in Vilharigues (Viseu).

Categories	<-> young	<-> equals	> parents	> older	> strangers	> superiors
appellative			*meu pai* *sr. pai* (< ricos)			*senhora*
actantial	*tu*	*tu*	*você*	*você,* *vossemecê*	*vossemecê*	*vossemecê*

ILB-1274/63_Vilharigues/Paços/Vouzela/VISEU [Q ²1962]

(8)   Várzea (Viseu)

371:   Quando os filhos chamam os pais, dizem: *ó sr. pai!, ó senhora mãe*. Quando se lhes dirigem: *Bomecê!*

'Children calling their parents say: *you senhor father, you senhora mother*. Simply addressing them, they use *Bomecê! (Vossemecê!)*'
5) Indicar as fórmulas de tratamento para com estranhos (*você, vossemecê, patrãozinho, senhor*, etc.): *a senhora; patrãozinho; patroa; bomecê*.
'Forms of address used with strangers (*você, vossemecê, patrãozinho, senhor*, etc.): *a senhora; patrãozinho* '(male) boss + diminutive -*(z)inho*)'; *patroa* '(female) boss'; *bomecê*'

Table 12: Forms of address used in Várzea (Viseu).

Categories	<-> young	<-> equals	> parents	> older	> strangers	> superiors
appellative			*ó sr. pai*		*senhora*	*patrão*
actantial			*vomecê*	*vomecê*	*vomecê*	*vomecê*

ILB-1287/59_Várzea/Calde/Viseu/VISEU [Q 1942 + (5)]

(9)   Celas (Coimbra)

371:   ó pai?, você 'you, father, you'

Table 13: Forms of address used in Celas (Coimbra).

Categories	<-> young	<->equals	> parents	> older	> strangers	> superiors
appellative			*ó pai*			
actantial			*você*			

ILB-1685/42_Celas/Olivais/Coimbra/COIMBRA [Q 1942]

(10) Tovim de Baixo (Coimbra)

371-(5): O tratamento mais corrente é por *vossemecê*. Se alguém trata outro com quem não tem grande confiança por *você* levam a mal. De igual modo se se tratar de pessoas a quem por natureza se deve respeito como os pais ou outras pessoas de família. A maneira como esse tratamento lhes repugna aparece com nitidez nesta expressão: *bòsê è iStrubaria!*

'The usual form of address is *vossemecê*. If people do not feel confident, a person addressed with *você* may hold it against the speaker. The same happens addressing people who deserve respect, e.g. the parents or other members of the family. The rejection of this form of address is clearly expressed by the locution *você è estrubaria! 'você* is crap' [that is, connoted with stable and dung, see fn. 9].

Table 14: Forms of address used in Tovim de Baixo (Coimbra).

Categories	<-> young	<->equals	> parents	> older	> strangers	> superiors
appellative						
actantial		*você (?)*	*vossemecê*	*vossemecê*	*vossemecê*	*vossemecê*

ILB-1687/55_Tovim de Baixo/Sto. António dos Olivais/Coimbra/COIMBRA [Q 1942]

(11) Sacavém (Lisbon)

371: Os filhos chamam: *Ó pai! Ó meu pai?* Quando se lhes dirigem tratam-nos por *bòcê* e *bossemecê*. [...] Quando se dirigem a pessoas de categoria dizem: *V. Ex.ᵃ*.

'The children call their parents: *you, father! you, my father?* When simply addressing them, the children use *bòcê* and *bossemecê* (= *você* and *vossemecê*). [...] When they address higher status people: *Vossa Excelência* 'Your Excellency"

Table 15: Forms of address used in Sacavém (Lisbon).

Categories	<-> young	<-> equals	> parents	> older	> strangers	> superiors
appellative			ó (meu) pai			
actantial			vo(sseme)cê			V.Ex.ia

ILB-2090/42_Sacavém/Sacavém/Loures/LISBOA [Q 1942]

(12) Negrais (Lisbon)

371: dizem *ó pai*; *ó velha*, *ó velhinha* (para a avó); *ó sr. padrinho* (para o padrinho). Quando se lhes dirigem tratam-nos por *vossemecê*. [...] É muito vulgar
tratar-se o irmão ou a irmã mais velha por *mano* ou *mana*.

'If they call them, they use *ó pai*; *ó velha* 'you, old lady', *ó velhinha* ('you,
old lady' + feminine diminutive -*inha*; for their grandmother), *ó sr. padrinho* (for their godfather). To simply address them they use *vossemecê*. [...] It
is considered very vulgar to address the older brother or sister with *mano*
or *mana* [shortened forms of *irmão* 'brother' *irmã* 'sister']'

371b: o tratamento por *você* não é ofensivo. O mais usado é *vossemecê*. Tb. *o
senhor* quando é para alguém de certa ceremónia. Tb. usam *patrão*.

'Using *você* is not offensive. Most used is *vossemecê*. Also *o senhor* in formal contexts. Also use *patrão* 'boss''

Table 16: Forms of address used in Negrais (Lisbon).

Categories	<-> young	<-> equals	> parents	> older	> strangers	> superiors
appellative			ó pai	ó velh(inh)a		patrão
actantial		você	vossemecê	vossemecê		o senhor

ILB-2091/68_Negrais/Almargem do Bispo/Sintra/LISBOA [Q ²1962]

(13) Linhó (Lisbon)

371b: <vòsê>* é a forma de tratamento mais generalizada. Os filhos tratam os
pais pelos diminutivos – <pajziñu, mãjziña>*. O uso tratar-se os pais por *tu*
começa a infiltrar-se na gente simples o que escandaliza os mais antigos. O
tratamento de *mano* começa a ser dado aos cunhados talvez por influência
algarvia. Os enteados tratam o padrasto e a madrasta por *tio* e *tia*. O tratamento de *compadre* usa-se entre os pais e os padrinhos dos filhos daque-
les e ainda entre os festeiros [feStêruS]* – os que participam em festas dos
santos populares contribuindo com uma certa quantia de dinheiro.

'<vòsê>* (= *você*) is the most usual form of address. Children address their parents as <pajziñu, mãjziña>* (= *paizinho* 'father + diminutive', *mãezinha* 'mother + diminutive'). The custom of addressing their parents with *tu* starts to appear in lower status families, not without shocking the older people. *Mano* (short form of *irmão* 'brother') starts to be used amongst brothers-in-law – a possible influence from the Algarve. Stepchildren address their stepfather or stepmother with *tio* 'uncle' and *tia* 'aunt'. *Compadre* is used between parents and godfathers (it also denotes this relation), as well as between participants of local religious feasts who donate money for this purpose'

Table 17: Forms of address used in Linhó (Lisbon).

Categories	<-> young	<-> equals	> parents	> older	> strangers	> superiors
appellative			paizinho, mãezinha	tio/a		
actantial		você	você, tu		você	você?

ILB-2092/63_Linhó/São Pedro de Penaferrim/Sintra/LISBOA [Q ²1962]

(14) Pragal (Setúbal)

371: Quasi todas as crianças dizem: *paisinho, mãizinha*. É costume tratarem por *você*.

'Almost all children address their parents with *paizinho, mãezinha*. They habitually use *você*'

Table 18: Forms of address used in Pragal (Setúbal).

Categories	<-> young	<-> equals	> parents	> older	> strangers	> superiors
appellative			paizinho, mãezinha			
actantial			você			

ILB-2236/42_Pragal/Santiago/Almada/SETÚBAL [Q 1942]

(15) Madalena do Mar (Funchal)

371: Chamam: *mê pai* ou *mi-pai*, *mê padrinho*, etc. Quando falam com êles tratam-nos por *amecê*. [...] Não empregam *o senhor*. Para o povo é tudo *irmão*.

'Children use variants of 'my father', 'my godfather', etc. When they speak to them they use *amecê* (= reduced *vossamecê*). They do not use *o senhor*. For the general public everybody is called *irmão* 'brother''

Table 19: Forms of address used in Madalena do Mar (Funchal).

Categories	<-> young	<-> equals	> parents	> older	> strangers	> superiors
appellative		*irmão*	*mê-/mi-pai*			
actantial			*amecê*			

ILB-Ilhas 7/42_Madalena do Mar/M. do M./Ponta do Sol/FUNCHAL [Q 1942]

Table 20 provides a synthesis of the most common forms of address used in different districts of Portugal. Italics are used for the most commonly used forms.

Table 20: Synthesis: Common forms of address in the districts of Portugal.

North (1) to South (8) plus islands (9)	West	Middle	East
1	VIANA DO CASTELO		BRAGANÇA
	bocê/você		*bocê/você*
	bomecê/vomecê		*bomecê/vomecê*
	bossemecê/vossemecê		*bossemecê/vossemecê*
	buociê, buossameciê		bacê, bancê, boncê, bõucê
2	PORTO	BRAGA	VILA REAL
	bocê/você	*bocê/você*	*bocê/você*
	bomecê/vomecê	*bomecê/vomecê*	*bomecê/vomecê*
	bossemecê/vossemecê	*bossemecê/*	*bossemecê/vossemecê*
	bòcê	*vossemecê*	bocia
	bòmeciê	bòcê	boncê, vancê
		bòsjê	
3	AVEIRO	VISEU	GUARDA
	bocê/você	*bocê/você*	*bocê/você*
	bomecê/vomecê	*bomecê/vomecê*	*bomecê/vomecê*
	bossemecê/vossemecê	*bossemecê/*	*bossemecê/vossemecê*
	bocêê, boceia	*vossemecê*	bòcê
	bocemecê [= bossemecê]	bomcê [< bomecê]	
	\<bwòsnê\>*		
4	COIMBRA		
	bocê/você		
	bomecê/vomecê		
	bossemecê/vossemecê		
	bacê		
	bocês – bocêses		
	[= plural-extension]		
	bomecê, bomcê		
	vancê (Penacova)		

Table 20 (continued)

North (1) to South (8) plus islands (9)	West	Middle	East
5	LEIRIA *bocê/você* *bomecê/vomecê* *bossemecê/vossemecê* bacé		CASTELO BRANCO *bocê/você* *bomecê/vomecê* *bossemecê/vossemecê* bocé bossemecê vom'cê [< vomecê] vomessaj, vomessaji vossaj, vossaji vossamecé vossemecéj, vossemessöj vossomecê
6	LISBOA *bocê/você* *bomecê/vomecê* *bossemecê/vossemecê*	SANTARÉM *você* *vomecê* *vossemecê* vossemecê vomcêj vossemecêj	PORTALEGRE *bocê/você* *bomecê/vomecê* *bossemecê/vossemecê* bossemecê bossemê [ILB_R_2225/69] omecê [Simão 2011, 150] vossemecê
7	SETÚBAL *bocê/você* *bomecê/vomecê* *bossemecê/vossemecê* bocei – vocêí vossemecêia	ÉVORA *você* *vomecê* *vossemecê* vossemecej vossemeceia	BEJA *você* *vomecê* *vossemecê* vomecea vossemecea, vossemeceia
8		FARO *você, vomecê,* *vossemecê* abeceia, amecêa vocêa vomeceia vòssemecêa voumecê	
9	AÇORES (Horta) vomecêa		MADEIRA ---

Table 21 singles out the most commonly used terms. It thus provides an idea of what may be considered general tendencies of development.

Table 21: Summary of the main forms of address used in the dialects of Portugal.

Categories	Appellative Forms	Actantial Forms
<–> young	First name, e.g. *João, Maria*	*tu*, 2P
<–>equals	First name, e.g. *João, Maria; irmão*	*tu*, 2P, *você*, 3P
> parents	*(ó) (meu/mi-) (sr.) pai/mãe; paizinho*	*o pai/a mãe, você, vo(sse)mecê, amecê*
> older (in-group)	*ó velh(inh)a, tio/a*	*você, vo(sse)mecê*
> strangers	*senhor/a*	*você, v(osse)mecê, o senhor*
> superiors	*patrão, senhora*	*vo(sse)mecê, o senhor, Vossa Excelência*

4.3 Towards an onomasiological classification of address forms in the ILB

Table 22 includes more specific onomasiological concepts related to the types of address forms documented in the ILB. The concepts and abbreviations used are as follows:

a) The concept of *respect* is divided into *resp_1* in relation to older people (*resp_1a* specifying the group of parents and godparents, *resp_1b* all other older persons) and *resp_2* in relation to other superiors;

b) initial bilabial or labiodental consonants are mostly represented by their v-allomorphs;

c) the abbreviations *vc/vm/vmc* (here and elsewhere in this text) represent *você/vossemecê/vomecê* (or other graphic variations of these three);

d) further shorter forms are:

gen.x+1/2	one or 2 generations older
óP_vc	representing a typical context like *ó pai, você quer ...?*
oP_quer	representing a typical context like *o pai quer ...?*
oFul°/aFul^a	representing a typical context like *o João/a Maria*
ti/a Ful°/a	representing a typical context like *ti(o) João/ti(a) Maria*

Table 22: Classification of the address forms documented in the ILB.

FROM / TO	SAME CATEGORY equals	children > animals	youth	parents / godparents (=resp_1a)	ca. 30 years	ca. 60 years (resp_1b) (= +age)	higher status (=resp_2)	lower status	estrebaria (strong negative connotation)
All to in-group	tu vmc [oFulº/aFulª?] Sr/a	tu [oFulº/aFulª?] vcª	tu vc [oFulº/ aFulª]?	minha mãe óP_vc oP_quer Sr/a vc, vm/vmc (incl.vancê) vós	tu vc, vm, vmc ti/a_Fulº/ª Sr/a	vc vm, vmc compadre comadre ti/a_Fulº/ª Sr/a	vc (incl.bacê) vm, vmc Sr/a patrão	tu vc tiazinha santinha	**você** (< younger) ó home_vc vm (neg?)
All to out-group°	tu vc vmc Sr/a	tu menina/ menino vcª	tu	x x x x x x x x	ti/a_Fulº/ª vc, vm, vmc Sr/a o amigo_quer ó miga	vc vm, vmc Sr/a patrão amigo/a (incl. bôucê, bonsê)	vc (incl.bacê) vm, vmc Sr/a patrão; ó Mestre, vc... V.Exia minha Sra V.Sria	tu, vc vm, vmc menina santinha tiazinha Sr/a môSr	**você** ó home, vc/vm... (vc<younger)

Table 22 (continued)

FROM / TO	SAME CATEGORY equals	children > animals	youth	parents / godparents (=resp_1a)	ca. 30 years	ca. 60 years (resp_1b) (= +age)	higher status (=resp_2)	lower status	estrebaria (strong negative connotation)
children	tu	tu vc^a	tu vc (?)	vc, vm/vmc vós Sr/a óP_vc oP_quer minha mãe			[= supra?]		**você** (to older &/or to out-group)
youth (>out-group)	tu, vc vc°	tu vc^a	tu	[= supra?]			[= supra?]		**você** = "malcriados"
school-/workmates	tu (?)				tu, vc				**você** = "mal-criados"
parents (= gen. x+1) (>30 years) (>out-group)	tu (?) compadre / comadre	tu vc^a		[= supra?]	vc, vm vc°, vm°	vc, vm vc°, vm°	[= supra?]		**você** ó home_vc
60 years (= gen. x+2) (>out-group)	tu vc^a			[= supra?]	vc, vm vc°, vm°	vc, vm vc°, vm°	[= supra?]	menina° Sr/a, vm°	você

	mano/a vc, vm, vmc Sr/a Sr/aº	Tu	[= supra?]	vc	mano/a vc, vm, vmc Sr/a Sr/aº	você
rich/superior/ well-dressed (>in-group)	mano/a, vc, vm, vmc, Sr/a, Sr/aº					vc
(>out-group)				vc		santinha / vcº / tiazinhaº
poor (>in-group)	vm (?)		[= supra?]			
(>out-group)				vcº		santinha / vcº / tiazinhaº
old-fashioned (>in-group)	vm, vmc / santinha / tiazinha		[= supra?]			vm, vmc
(>out-group)	vm, vmc / Sr/a			vm		santinha / tiazinha

vc^a	representing use to animals
vc^o	representing use to outsiders (when necessary to be pointed out)
estrebaria[10]	serving as a label for common judgements classifying the use of *você* as "less educated/offensive".

Table 22 seeks to show as clearly as possible the varieties of Portuguese address forms in their conceptual positions, and especially the address form *você* evaluated according to the context of its use. In parallel with its etymological relatives *vossemecê* and *vomecê*, there mostly remains a positive, respectful evaluation when *você* is situated in a respect marking context like *ó pai, você/vo(sse)mecê*. However, *você* also acquires a special value of solidarity (in competition with the use of *tu*?) among (mostly younger) equals that prompted older generations and/ or many higher status individuals to label this use as *estrebaria*.[10]

5 From Late Latin VOSTRA MERCED to Pt. *você* – a pronominal pedigree

The geolinguistic distribution of the *você* forms (and their variants) in Table 20 will now be reconsidered in a pedigree, trying to establish the possible diachronic sequence of as much of the *vossa mercê* descendants as possible. For this purpose, Figure 1 presents historic types of VOSTRA MERCED (via *vossa mercê*) descendants belonging to the *vossemecê-você* family. The elements have been extracted from the available ILB corpora, and we can take them as a basis for a hypothetical pedigree in terms of diachronic reconstruction from the synchronic variationist data in the ILB. Some of the more or less generalized phonetic spellings of our examples have been normalized by bringing them close to standard (or at least near-standard) Portuguese written conventions (e.g. *vocemecê > vossemecê*). In order to graphically visualize this pedigree structure, uninterrupted lines are used to show the supposed mainstream, and dotted lines lead to some possible sideline evolutions. All forms in italics in Figure 1 stand for ILB-documented types; "ò" represents an open vowel and "ê" or "ô" a closed one; possible missing links are marked by "*[...]", and underlining is used to reinforce the distinctness of the forms in italics.

---

10 *Você é estrebaria* is a popular expression in Portugal's rural areas, meaning something like '*você* is crap'. The DLP (1996) defines *estrebaria* as follows: "lugar onde se recolhem bestas; cavalariça; (de *estrabo*, do lat. *stabûlu-, estábulo + -aria*)", that is, 'stable, barn'.

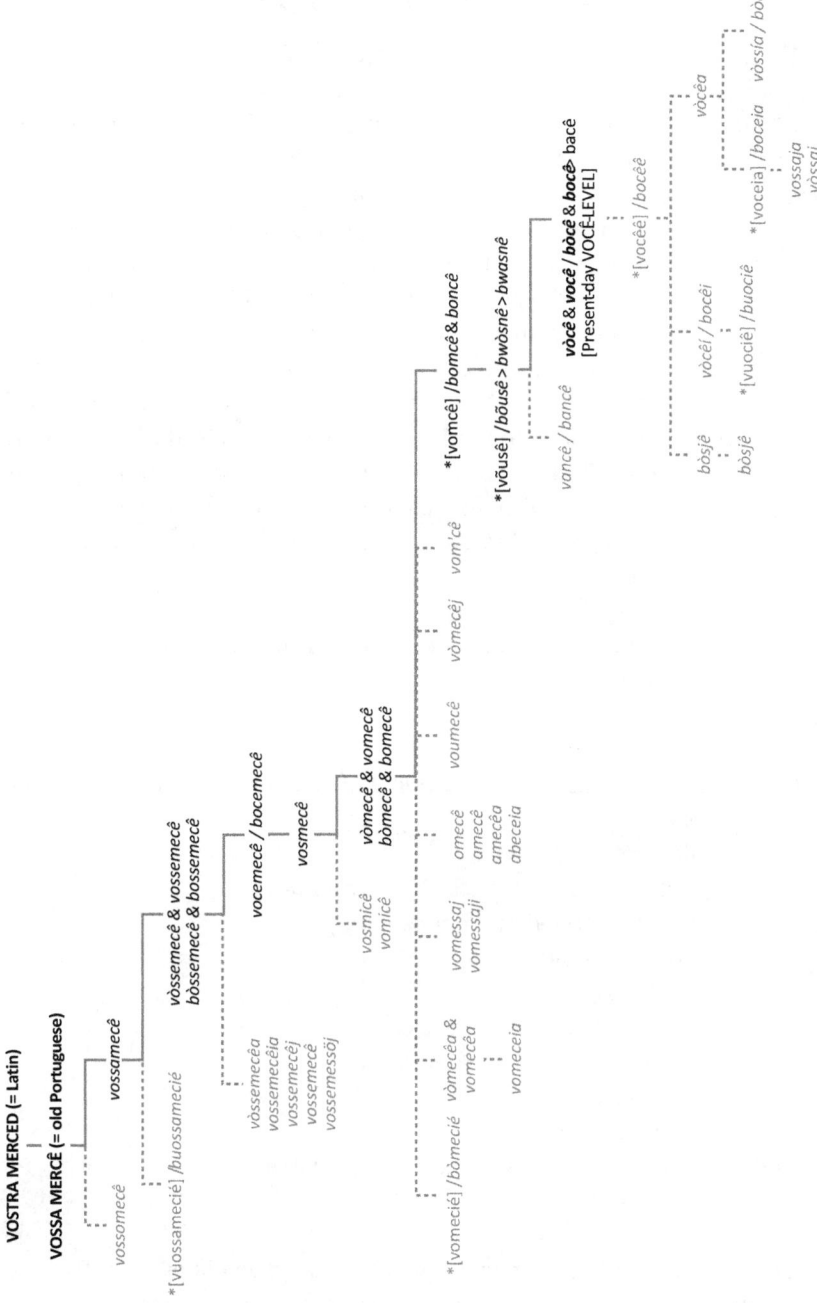

Figure 1: A pronominal pedigree of Portuguese VOSTRA MERCED descendants.

6 An example of address form choices documented for the District of Viseu

Table 23 groups the address forms documented in the ILB categorizing their respective use in the District of Viseu (Beira Alta). This District may be seen as representative of the surrounding areas. The Table presents relevant onomasiological categories that mainly separate in-group from out-group addressees (i.e. village insiders vs. outsiders). The documented types of address forms are mostly given by abbreviations which keep the regional marks of [v- : b-] as bilabial or labiodental initial consonants in order to shed light on the diatopic distribution of this phenomenon. Among the subjects asked to fill in the questionnaires, many (especially those completing questionnaires by correspondence from 1942) will have preferred to give the standard orthographic version instead of the genuine local phonetic variation. This means that the b-forms appearing in the answers to the questionnaires can be taken as valid evidence of this local phenomenon, while the v-spelling may hide b-pronunciation. The annotations used in the Table 23 are as follows:

xyz* (etc.)	"*" marking a possible use of the same item in a different context
vc/bc	*você/bocê*
vm/bm	*vossemecê/bossemecê*
vmc/bmc	*vomecê/bomecê*
estreb(aria)	comments like *<você é estrebaria; quando eu nascí já você palha roía>*
offs	offensive
-old	used to/expected by less old/younger people
+old	used to/expected by older people
old-	used by less old people
old+	used by older people
o_pai	context *o pai/a mãe quer*, etc.
óPai_vc	context *ó pai/mãe, você quer*, etc.
>stran(gers)	to strangers
>urban	to urban people
yng/young	younger people (when necessary, marked as *< = by, > = to, <-> = between*

Table 23 only contains data from questionnaires completed later than 1942 and their respective evaluation, which contain responses about address use in out-group relations. The original § 371 of the questionnaire was aimed explicitly at

Table 23: Address form use in the District of Viseu (Beira Alta).

= to:	IN-GROUP								OUT-GROUP		
+ characteristics:	children	equals	less distance / intimacy	(god-) parents (resp_1a)	+ reverence (resp_2a)	strong negative connotation offensive	lower status people condescending	equals equal standing	older people & strangers (resp_1b)	+ reverence richer p. (resp_2b)	repulsive estrebaria
1127/69[11]				vm	vm*			vm*	vm*		
1136a/71				bc					bc	Sr/a	
1139a/59				bm					bm*		
1142/65								vc, tu			
1145/65				vm, vmc; vc (neg)		vc (neg)			bm, Sr/a	Sr/a*	vc (neg)
1189/68				bc				bc*			
1196/68				vm					vm		
1207/58				bmc							
1223/65				vm				vc			
1224/57				vm, vmc					vm, vmc*		
1227n/71				vm, vmc					vm		
1238/69				óPai_vm					bc		

11 Code of the location/Year, e.g. 1127/69 = location + 1969

Table 23 (continued)

= to:	IN-GROUP						OUT-GROUP			
	children	equals	(god-)parents	+ reverence	strong negative connotation	lower status people	equals	older people & strangers	+ reverence	repulsive
1238a/71				vm*				vm*		
1253/62			bm, bc				bc*	bc, bm, Sr/a		
1253a/62			bm, vc				bc*	bc, bm, Sr/a		
1255/66							bc	bc, mc, Sr/a		vc (pos)
1258b/73	É Zé!							bc, bm, Sr/a		bc (pos)
1269a/70			vmc, vc					vc*		vc (pos)
1272a/69							bc	bmc		bc (pos)
1275/70			ó pai_vc					bc, bmc, vm*	vm*	bc (pos)
1280/65	tu*	bc	pai_bc/bm				bc*	bm		
1284/69			vmc					vmc*		
1288/67								bmc		bc (neg)
1290/68							vc	vc; vm	Sr/a	vm (neg)
1300/60			bm					bm, Sr/a	Sr/a*	
1301a/65			bmc, bm	vm*	vc (neg)			bm (+old)		bc (offs)
1312/66		bc (-old)	bmc				bc (-old)	bm/bmc (+old)		bc (-old)
1318/58			vm							vc (neg)
1326a/68			bmc					bmc, bm, Sr/a	Sr/a*	

Year			bc	bc (pos)	bm (+old)		bc (>inf)
1327/64		vm/vmc	bc				bc (>inf)
1352/69		vc (++pos.)		vc	vm		vc (pos)
1382/65		bc (>stran.)		bc*			vc (offs)
1394/65				bc >poor	Sr/a		
1395/71		Sr/a, bmc			bm, Sr/	Sr/a*	vc (offs)
1396/69					vm, Sr/a	Sr/a*	vc (neg)
1397/66				vc (-offs)	vm		
1401a/71		vm, vc (fam.)			Sr/a	V.Exia	vc (+/-)
1401n/73	vc (=young)	vc (>pais)	vm, vmc		vm, vmc	vc (neg)	vc (+/-)
1404/70				bc (pos)	bc, bm		
1405/70				bc (>stran)			
1406/64	tu (young)	bmc		tu; vc (+old)	bmc (++old)	Sr/a	
1410/65	tu*	vmc, Sr/a		tu	bc, Sr/a		
1415b/65		bc					
1417/68		(bc), vm	bc (=vc)	vc (>stran)	vm, patrão	Sr/a	vc (offs)
1418/63		bm	Santa	bc, bm	bc, bm*		
1424/72	vc*	vc & vm			Sr/a	Sr/a*	vc (offs)
1428/65		óPai_bc		bm, bc	bm*	bm*	bc (offs)

Table 23 (continued)

= to:	IN-GROUP						OUT-GROUP			
	children	equals	(god-)parents	+ reverence	strong negative connotation	lower status people	equals	older people & strangers	+ reverence	repulsive
1430/68			bmc				vc (neg.)			vc (offs)
1439/50			bm, bmc					bm, bmc*		
1442/62			bmc	bm	bc (offs)		bmc bm (+old)	Sr/a	Sr/a*	bc (offs)
1444/65		vc (young)	Sr/a, vc, vm, o pai	vm			vc (>young)	vm	Sr/a (>urban)	vc (>younger)
1448/69			bc	Sr/a			tu, bc (+old)	bm, Sr/a	Sr/a*	
1449/70		vc (-old)*	vm					vm (+old)		vc (offs)
1449a/72			bc; bm (old+)				bc (-neg.)	bm, Sr/a		bc (pos)

in-group relations, and very few questionnaires had any responses about out-group uses of address variants. However, Boléo added questions on address use in out-group relations in § 371b (see Table 3) in the first reprint of his second version of the questionnaire edited in 1962 (Boléo 1976: 25, fn. 2).

7 Diatopic survey of informants' evaluations of *você*

7.1 Informants' evaluations according to district

Table 24 outlines the most typical evaluations found within each district. In this table, a short characterization follows each district's name in "{...}". Negative evaluation of VOCÊ is marked by underlining (VOCÊ-neg.), and positive evaluation in bold (**VOCÊ-pos.**). These evaluations are (partially) marked by "(neg)" or "(pos)", but mostly using the following gradations: "++, +, +/-, –, --" (where "–" corre-

Table 24: *Você* evaluations by districts and sectors (see geographical description in Table 20).

West	Middle	East
VIANA DO CASTELO	BRAGA	BRAGANÇA
{positive in general}	{mixed evaluations}	{positive with young people}
0013/42: **bc (pos.) to parents**	0334/66_b: vc (–)	0480a/64_b: vc (–) (grumbling >
0017/64: **bc (pos.) to parents**	0177/66_b: **bc (+) (only equals**	children)
& strangers	**or inferiors)**	0640a/70_b: vc (–) (> aggressive
0026/69: **bc (pos.) to parents**	0297/63_b: **bc (+) (without**	answers)
& strangers	**great intimacy)**	0502/62_b: bc (+/–) (<bocê
0028/42: **bc (pos.) to parents**	0315/64_b: **bc (+) (very**	é estrebaria>?)
0032a/70: **bc (pos.) to**	**common)**	0509/64_b: vc (+/–) (seldom);
strangers	0232/70: bc (+/–)	0527a/71_b: **vc (+) (> equals)**
0053/42: **bc (pos.) to parents**	(ill-mannered to superior)	0580a/71_b: **bc (+) (among**
0059/42: **bc (pos.) to parents**	0241/69_b: vc (+/–) (offensive	**boys)**
0073/70: **bc (pos.) to**	to superiors)	0586/62_b: bc (–) (> animals)
strangers	0246/65_a: vc (to avoid when	0588a/71_b: bc (+/–) (> poor)
0112/64: **bc (pos.) to parents**	respectful)	0644a/71_b: **bc (+) (between**
0118/65: **bc (pos.) to parents**	0270/62_b: bc (+/–) (equals,	**younger speakers)**
& strangers	no intimacy)	0650/62_b: vc (–) (disrespect)
0128/65: **bc (pos.) to parents**	0146/68_b: bc (–) (<bòsê è	0561/65_b: **bc (+)**
0131/67: **bc (pos.) to parents**	burro 'stupid'>)	**(= most common)**
0132/69: **bc (pos.) to parents**		

Table 24 (continued)

West	Middle	East
PORTO {rather negative evaluations}	VISEU {mixed evaluations}	VILA REAL {reserved evaluations?}
0675/64_a/b: bc (−) 0896/67_a: **bc (++) <ò pài, bosê>** 0896/67_b: **bc (+)** 0730/42: **vc (+) = high status + <manos>** 0675/64_b: bc (−) 0675/64_b: bc (−)	1401n/73: vc (−) (> superiors); **vc (+) (preferred by younger speakers)** 1394/65_b: bc (> poor) 1395/71_b: vc (−) 1396/69_b: vc (−) 1401a/71_b: **vc (+) (family);** vc (−) (> strangers) 1373a/60: vc (−) (ill-mannered)	0381a/71: vc (−) (seldom)
AVEIRO {generally positive evaluations} 1026/65_b: bc (−) 0954/66_a: **bc (++)** 0955/63_b: **bc (> pais)** 0963/68_b: **bc/Sr (++)** 1067a/64_b: **vc (+) ó mestre, você = + 'familiar'** 0910a/71_b: **bc (+)** 0912/42: **vc (−) (> 'o pai')** 0954/66_a: **bc (++) (neta para mãe & avó)** 0977/42: **vc (++)** 1069/72_b: **vc (+/−)** 0977/42: **vc (++)**	1379a/71: **tu, vc, bmc, vm (+) (> equals)** vc (−) (<você é strebaria!>) 1449/70: vc (−) (> older superiors) 1444/65_b: **vc (+) (> younger)** 1449a/72: **bc (+) (general)** 1448/69_b: **bc (+) (older)** 1352/69: **vc (++) (> parents)** 1417/68_a: bc (−) (> + distance) 1338/64_b: vc (−) (offensive) 1346/63_b: vc (−) (<você, é burro/cão>) 1405/70_b: **bc (++) (to all strangers)** 1417/68: bc (−) (> distance) **vm (++) (> old & esteemed)** 1406/64_b: **vc (+) (> older)**	GUARDA {negative evaluations} 1474/65_b: vc (+/−) (less common; (sometimes kidding: 'você é um cão')* 1456/63_b: vc (−) (less educated/when angry) 1580a/70_b: vc (−) ('você na minha terra é <¡Struvaria>')* 1608/72_b: bc (+/−) (to inferiors)

Table 24 (continued)

West	Middle	East
COIMBRA		CASTELO BRANCO
{mixed evaluations}	1428/65_a: **bc (++) ('ó pai, bocê'**	{tendency rather negative}
1789/64_a: vc (–);	1428/65_b: bc (–) (in certain contexts)	1954/62_b: vc (–) ('malcriadeza')
1789/64_b: vc (+/–)	1301a/65_b: vc (–) (<você é strebaria> = disrespect)	1963a/72_b: vc (–) ('desrespeitoso' to all)
1622a/70_b: **vc (+)**/bc (> lavrador)	1288/67_b: vc (–) (<bocê è strebaría>)	1966a/70_b: vc (+/–) ('não se usa')
1631/68_b: **bc (+) (in-group)**/bc (–) (out-group)	1318/58: vc (–) ('não é muito empregado')	1977/63_b: vc (–)
1631/68_b: **bc (+) (in-group)**/bc (–) (out-group)	1327/64_b: bc (+/–) (> inferior)	1906/68: vc (–) (but: increasing use)
1679/65_b: vc (+/–)	1275/70: **bc (+) (> less intimity /superiors)**	1910/65_b: **vc (+)**
1683/66_b: bc (–) ('uma má palavra')	1312/66_b: **bc (+) (> younger)**	1913a/71_b: vc (–) (<Vòsöi è bürro>)
1683a/70_b: bc (+/–)	1288/67_b: '<bocê è strebaría>'	1913b/70_b: vc (–) ('é mais indelicado')
1687/55_b: bc (–) (<iStrubaria>)	1280/65: **bc (+) (confidential, less familiar)**	1914/72_b: **vc/vm (+) (> equals)**
1689b/54: **bc (++) (<bacê>)**		1918/68_b: vc (–)
1690/54: **bc (++) (<bacê>)**		1919a/70_b: vc (–)
1693/67_b: bc (–) (>estranhos)		1923/63_b: vc (–) ('na minha terra é burro')
		1924a/70_b: vc (+/–) ('só entrefamiliares')
		1931/62_b: **vc (+) (between superiors)**
1701/65_b: **bc (++) (>older, same class)**		I1946/72_b: vc (–) (= blaming young people)
1701a/68_b: **bc (+) (<bacê>) (friends)**		I1950/62_b: vc (–) ('nunca se usa')
1702/65_b: **bc (+) ('generalizado')**		1933a/72_b: bc (–) (<é a fidalgue ou zangado>)*
1631/68_b: **bc (+/–) (>known)**		2024/70_a: **vc (+)** ('fino para padrinho jovem')/vc (–) (never to older people)
1616b_b: bc (–)		2024/70_b: **vc (++)** ('para gente fina')

Table 24 (continued)

West	Middle	East
LEIRIA {rather positive evaluations}	SANTARÉM {rather positive evaluations (younger p.)}	2028a/71_b: **vc (++) ('é muito usual')** 1996/42: **vc (++) ('O meu pai você etc.' [?= ó meu pai, você])** 2004/69_a: vc (–) ('Você é estrebaria') 2004/69_b: vc (–) ('você é pouco usado') ("você é estrebaria"). 2037/63_b: **vc (+) (> 'pessoas+/– conhecidas')** 2039a/73_b: vc (–) (‚Revela falta de educação')
1862/64_b: vc (+/–) ('muito pouco usado') 1824/67_a: **bc;** 1824/67_b: **bc (+) (mais empregado)** 1839/64_b: **bc (> equal)** 1842/65_b: vc (<basé>) (shows disrespect) 1843/68_b: **vc (+) (boys & girls)** 1852/69_ b: **vc (+)** 1855/64_a: **vc (+)**	2144/64_b: vc (–) (seen by older) 2148/64_a: **vc (+)** (if not > very old) 2151/68_b: **vc (+)** 2152a/71_b: **vc (+)** 2135/48_b: **vc (+) (between friends)**	
LISBOA {rather positive evaluations?} 2091/68_a: **vc (+)**	ÉVORA {rather positive evaluations (younger p.)} 2288/72_b: vc (–) ('você é arte de escandalizar') 2279/72_b: vc (–) (offs. for older); **vc (+) (youth)**	PORTALEGRE {rather reserved evaluations?} 2225/69_b: **bc (+) ('empregam muito')** /bc ('as camadas mais idosas não gostam') 2196a/70_b: vc (–) (offs. > strangers)
SETÚBAL {rather positive evaluations?} 2238/42: **vc (+) (from young people)**	2295/64_b: vc (–) (when angry) 2308/70_b: <vocêi não se usa>* **2284/65_b: 'diz-se que você é estrebaria'**	BEJA {rather reserved evaluations?} 2337/70_b: vc (–) ('sentido depreciativo')
AÇORES	FARO {rather positive evaluations} 2395/63: **vc (+) (> same age)** 2399a/70: **vc (+) (> acquainted)**	MADEIRA

sponds to *algo provocante* 'middly offensive' and "−−" to *ofensivo* 'offensive'). We will use part of the original ILB differentiation (cf. ILB § 371 and 371b), but mark by "_a" comments belonging to § 371 (targeting insiders' use) and by "_b" those belonging to § 371b (added to the questionnaire only after 1942 and targeting address use with outsiders). As an illustration, "Bragança-0480a/64_a" refers to family/village in-group, and "Bragança-0480a/64_b" to strangers/village out-group.

Table 25: Synthesis of Table 24.

West Most typical features	Middle Most typical features	East Most typical features
{positive evaluations by younger}	{pos.: North = ó pai, você / South: younger people}	{positive evaluations by younger}
VIANA DO CASTELO **bc (pos.) to parents & strangers**	BRAGA bc (+/–) (to equals, no intimity).	BRAGANÇA bc (+/–) (<bocê é estrebaria>?) **bc (+) (between younger)**
PORTO **bc (++)= <ò pài bosê>**	VISEU a: **bc (++)** ('ó pai, bocê');	VILA REAL vc (–) (seldom)
AVEIRO **bc (++) (granddaughter to mother & grandmother)**	b: bc (–) (in certain contexts) SANTARÉM	GUARDA b: vc (+/–) (less common; (sometimes kidding: <você é
COIMBRA **bc (+) (in-group)** bc (–) (out-group)	a: **vc (+) (if not > very old).** b: vc (–) (seen by older).	um cão>)
LEIRIA **vc (+) (boys & girls)**	ÉVORA b: vc (–) (offs. for older); **vc**	CASTELO BRANCO vc (–) (but: increasing use)
LISBOA **vc (+)**	**(+) (youth)** FARO	PORTALEGRE b: **bc (+) ('empregam muito')**
SETÚBAL **vc (+) (young people)**	**vc (+) (> same age)**	bc (–) ('as camadas mais idosas não gostam') BEJA b: vc (–) ('sentido depreciativo')

It is challenging to give a concise survey of evaluations of the use of *você* when trying to base statements on the large amount of address evaluation data in the ILB documents. Thus we cannot design a simple map of a neat north–south and/ or east–west diatopic differentiation. Besides the phonetic (more or less north–south orientated) variation of initial bilabial vs. labiodental b-/v- (making *bocê* contrast with *você*), we can, however, identify a number of essential phenomena.

The more or less typical examples given seem to confirm the not uncommon tendency of younger people (sometimes already in 1942!) to use explicit *você* more generally than their older neighbors. The latter seem to have still been more orientated by presupposed respectful contexts such as *Ó pai, você já ouviu ...?* 'You Father, have you$_{VT}$ already seen...?' and their equivalents. This positive evaluation by younger people seems to be the case more in the western and southern parts of Portugal.

More exact statements about the present-day distribution of this phenomenon (its increase seems to be evident based on the author's own informal observations over the years) will certainly demand new and very detailed sociolinguistic research. The characteristic geolinguistic differences regarding salient *você* values results from the fact that, very often, in-group *você* usage (with family and neighborhood insiders) is evaluated more positively than out-group usage (with village outsiders and strangers).

Summing up and taking in account the ILB data reviewed here, I propose the following hypotheses:

1. The list of Portuguese address forms continues to comprise a large inventory ranging from an intimate *tu* to a very formal *Vossa Excelência*, together with different verb forms (second and third person to combine with singular and plural);
2. Not all forms are omnipresent, for all speakers or in all situations;
3. The forms may be used to express more or less polite address behavior;
4. Linguistic observation and fieldwork to describe the whole set of actively used Portuguese address forms will have to deal with a range of challenges. For example, when trying to interpret the actual meaning of a seemingly unambiguous statement like *Trato-o/a por você* 'I address him/her with *você*', two readings are possible:
    (a) *Trato-o/a por você* can actually refer to an explicit use of *você* as address pronoun;
    (b) In many regions, perhaps more in Northern regions neighboring the town of Porto, speakers saying *trato-o/a por você* may not imply the use of *você* itself at all.

In reading (a), we have to consider at least two possible explanations. Firstly, in a context where *você* takes over from its evolutionary predecessor *vossemecê* (or *vomecê* as its more colloquial and/or intimate realization), it will undoubtedly be accepted by everybody as respectful when it is presented, for example, as *Ó pai, você quer ...?* This respect marking context may moreover have been pronounced only once during an ongoing dialogue (or even not at all, but be presupposed as conventional background) to support the positive acceptation of *você*.

Secondly, apparently, the use of the address pronoun *você* (as had already been the case with *vossemecê* and *vomecê*, both of which did not lose – with very few exceptions – their positive values as a respectful address) was freed from an obligatory respect marking context (accompanied by a vocative like *ó Fulano, ...* or equivalents).

In some milieus, as represented, for example, by fishermen or muleteers,[12] besides the continuing intimate (or family bound) *tu* of solidarity, the use of *você* (besides or instead of *tu*?) seems to have become an expanding marker of solidarity not only for lower status workers. The same lower status speakers,

---

12 Pt. *almocreves* – for their historic professional conditions, see, e.g., the novel *Terras do Demo* by Aquilino Ribeiro (2012).

however, may have been disgusted when higher status representatives (excepting perhaps their direct superiors) addressed them by an explicit *você*. This specific solidarity-based value may find its echo in notorious address blaming formulas like *você é estrebaria*, still to be heard particularly in the northern parts of Portugal. As original sources for those statements we may imagine, among others, primary school teachers and clergymen ("their masters' voice") who were influenced by their own experience and pedagogical studies in urban centers (mostly orientated towards the standards of Lisbon/Coimbra/Porto). So they may have been propagating their respective cultural and language norms.

In reading (b), one has to bear in mind that nominal forms found their place in actantial positions, as in *O pai quer .../O senhor Fulano quer .../o João/a Maria quer ...*, etc., with their deictic function paralleling other paradigmatic elements that we commonly call pronouns. These nominal forms can most easily replace a *você* meant with disgust. This tendency seems to apply rather for certain higher middle-class individuals – who partly had also been used to addressing their siblings by *mano* 'brother' and *mana* 'sister'– and all those pupils influenced by their teachers' judgements. This use has presumably originally been established in and around the town of Porto.

8 Concluding remarks

Taking in account the rich ILB data and our attempts to discover diachrony within (a relative) synchrony with regard to special forms and modes of Portuguese address conventions, what sort of methodological approach can be proposed? We should perhaps not restrict our analysis to geolinguistic, sociolinguistic and transgenerational variation (see Endruschat & Schmidt-Radefeldt 2015: 214–240), and search instead for another type of explanation. This makes it difficult to find a way out of this complex and dynamic network – not least for the inhabitants of Portugal themselves: it is remarkable how easily Portuguese people speak about their address uncertainties or their experiences in general. Looking at heuristic categories such as *isoglosses,* traditionally delimiting language islands – based on phonetic, lexical, or other criteria – promises even better access to that multiplicity of rapidly expanding address subsystems that existed all over 20th century Portugal.

There are cultural observers who view as a special Portuguese phenomenon the impressive socio-cultural coexistence of different ages or historical periods up to the present day. The German journalist, author and poet Hans Magnus Enzensberger, alluding to the notorious synchronic coexistence of historical vestiges in present-day Portugal, proposed *Isochrones* to describe possible features of a topology of time. These should describe islands of time paralleling geographical topology (Enzensberger 1986: 49–50).

In accordance with this characterization, I would like to assert for 20th century Portugal (and probably not only as a phenomenon limited to Portugal) the existence of numerous many-layered islands of address-norm systems. These could be understood as being delimited by *socioglosses* defining address domains which are overlapping and exchanging with others, as individual speakers may, at least partly, participate in different address systems. My terminological proposal of *socioglosses* owes something to a similar effort in the domain of modality constructions by Franco Benucci, speaking of *faisceaux de chronoglosses* 'bundles of diachronic isoglosses' (Benucci 1988: 6).

These conventional address islands – delimited and perhaps connected by the respective socioglosses – are certainly subject to continuous conflicts with each other and with educational address standards suggested by teachers or other authorities. These authorities will have received their orientation from layers of society of so-called higher status. In any case, further, more detailed studies will be required to more fully analyze the address complexes (or islands) documented by ILB data.

References

Benucci, Franco. 1988. *Les constructions modales du français des Serments de Strasbourg à nos jours: une analyse syntaxique*. PhD thesis. University of Padova. Quoted from: Marc St-Pierre, Daniel Gosselin, Monique Lemieux & Marthe Faribault. 1991. Le temps recouvré: De la pertinence d'une constitution de corpus; méthodologie et usage. *Revue québécoise de linguistique* 202. 265. www.erudit.org. (21 June, 2017).

Boléo, Manuel Paiva. 1942/1974. *O estudo dos dialectos e falares portugueses. (Um inquérito linguístico)*. Coimbra. Reprinted in *Estudos de linguística portuguesa e românica*, 1974, vol.1,1, 1–43. Coimbra: Acta Universitatis Conimbrigensis.

Boléo, Manuel Paiva. 1959. *Amostra dos materiais do dicionário dos falares portugueses*. Coimbra: published by the author.

Boléo, Manuel Paiva. 1971a. *Materiais do "Dicionário dos falares portugueses modernos" e seu confronto com o "Grande dicionário da língua portuguesa" de Morais*. Coimbra: published by the author.

Boléo, Manuel Paiva. 1971b. *Lista das teses de licenciatura em linguística portuguesa (orientadas desde 1942 até 1971)*. Coimbra: Faculdade de Letras da Universidade de Coimbra – Instituto de Estudos Românicos.

Boléo, Manuel Paiva. 1974. *Estudos de linguística portuguesa e românica*, vol. 1,1. Coimbra: Acta Universitatis Conimbrigensis.

Boléo, Manuel Paiva. 1976. *Vida do Instituto de Estudos Românicos (1972–1974)*. *Revista de Filologia Portuguesa* 16, 1–2.
Boléo, Manuel Paiva. 1979. *Vida do Instituto de Estudos Românicos (1975–1979)*. *Revista de Filologia Portuguesa* 17.
Brown, Penelope & Stephen Levinson. 1987. *Politeness: Some universals in language use*. Cambridge: Cambridge University Press.
Bühler, Karl. 1967. El *yo* y el *tú*. In *Teoría del lenguaje*, 184–191. Madrid: Selecta de Revista de Occidente.
Clyne, Michael, Catrin Norrby & Jane Warren. 2009. *Language and human relations. Styles of address in contemporary language*. Cambridge: Cambridge University Press.
de Oliveira, Sandi Michele. 2009. Negotiating identity, conflict, and cooperation within a strategic model of address. In Ann Denis & Devorah Kalekin-Fishman (eds.), *Contemporary sociology. Conflict, competition, cooperation*, 416–432. Los Angeles: Sage.
DLP. 1996. *Dicionário [electrónico profissional] da Língua Portuguesa*. Porto: Porto Editora Multimédia.
Endruschat, Annette & Jürgen Schmidt-Radefeldt. 2015. *Introdução básica à linguística do português*. Lisbon: Colibri.
Enzensberger, Hans Magnus. 1986. Portugiesische Grübeleien. *Die Zeit* 40 (26.9.1986). 49–56.
Gibbons, John. 1984. *Não criei musgo. Retrato de uma aldeia transmontana*. Translated from: "I gathered no Moss", Coleja 1939. Bragança: Câmara de Carrazeda de Ansiães.
Glück, Helmut & Kristine Koch. 1998. Du oder Sie. Anredekonventionen in Deutschland und in anderen Ländern. *Der Sprachdienst* 1. 1–9.
Goffman, Erving. 1959. *The presentation of self in everyday life,* Garden City, N.Y.: Doubleday.
Hammermüller, Gunther. 1980. *Você* é estrubaria? *Iberoromania* 12. 30–40.
Hammermüller, Gunther. 1995. O I.L.B. à margem dum Atlas Linguístico de Portugal? In M. Fátima Viegas Brauer-Figueiredo (ed.), *Actas do 4⁰ Congresso da Associação Internacional de Lusitanistas*, 131–144. Lisbon/Porto/Coimbra: LIDEL.
Hammermüller, Gunther. 2010. Evolución de las formas de tratamiento del español medieval hasta el siglo XVI. In Martin Hummel, Bettina Kluge & María Eugenia Vásquez Laslop (eds.), *Formas y fórmulas de tratamiento en el mundo hispánico*, 507–529. México DF.: El Colegio de México/Universität Graz.
Hammermüller, Gunther. 2011. Insekten auf einem Datenfriedhof – Aufgespürt in den *Relatórios* des I.L.B. In Annette Endruschat & Vera Ferreira (eds.), *Sprachdokumentation und Korpuslinguistik – Forschungsstand und Anwendung*, 221–236. Munich: Martin Meidenbauer.
Heger, Klaus. 1965. Personale Deixis und grammatische Person. *Zeitschrift für Romanische Philologie* 81. 77–97.
Langenscheidt Online Wörterbücher. de.langenscheidt.com (11 June, 2017).
Lüdtke, Helmut. 2009. *Der Ursprung der romanischen Sprachen: eine Geschichte der sprachlichen Kommunikation*. Second edition. Kiel: Westensee-Verlag.
Matias, Fátima de Rezende. 1978. *Inquérito linguístico*. Questionário organizado por Manuel de Paiva Boléo. Third edition. Aveiro.
Ribeiro, Aquilino. 2012 [1905]. *Terras do Demo*. Lisbon: Bertrand.
Ribeiro, Aquilino. 2015 [1943]. *Volfrâmio*. Lisbon: Bertrand.
Simão, Teresa Susana Bengala. 2011. *O falar de Marvão. Pronúncia, vocabulário, alcunhas, ditados e provérbios populares*. Lisbon: Colibri.
Stanford encyclopedia of philosophy. plato.Stanford.edu (23 May, 2017).

Virginia Bertolotti
The loss of *vosotros* in American Spanish

Abstract: The use of a single pronominal and a single verbal form in the second person plural, *ustedes*, is one of the features that distinguishes the Spanish in the Americas from European Spanish, where in the domain of the plural informal *vosotros* still contrasts with formal *ustedes*. However, an explanation for the loss of *vosotros* forms in most communicative contexts in American Spanish has not been yet advanced. Based on a literature review and data from the *Corpus Dia-crónico y Diatópico del español de América* (CORDIAM), this chapter proposes a new dating of the loss of *vosotros* and corresponding verbal forms. It also suggests that the characteristics of the pronoun make it a good candidate for being lost, except in ceremonial formal situations.

Keywords: Spanish in the Americas, plural pronouns of address, loss of *vosotros*, diachrony

1 Introduction

The use of only one second person plural pronominal and verbal form of address is a well-known feature of spoken Spanish in the Americas that distinguishes it from European Spanish, in which two pronominal and verbal forms are used. As an illustration, a mother in Hispanic America speaking to her son and a friend of his with whom she is familiar will use a single form of address and say: Vengan *a tomar la merienda, yo la voy a tomar con* ustedes 'Come (neutral 2nd person plural) and have a snack, I´ll have it with you (neutral 2nd person plural)'. In the same situation, a mother in Spain will say: Venid *a tomar la merienda, yo la voy a tomar con* vosotros 'Come (2nd person plural) and have a snack, I´ll have it with you (informal 2nd person plural)', reserving the variants *vengan* and *ustedes* for polite/distant address.

A comprehensive historical explanation is yet to be given to account for two facts. The first one being that, in the Americas, *vosotros* has been virtually absent from situations of *communicative immediacy* since at least the 18th century, which has also been the case of its verb inflections *-ais/-eis/-is* and its pronominal

Note: I would like to thank Concepción Company Company, Sylvia Costa, and Marisa Malcuori for their feedback on preliminary versions of this manuscript and Irene Moyna for her help with the translation of some historical examples.

paradigm. The second fact is that in the 19th and 20th centuries (as well as in the 21st century) the pronouns and verbs corresponding to the *vosotros* paradigm, which disappeared from everyday life in the Americas, have been used in situations of *communicative distance* but only in a few genres.[1] These uses have a meaning of solemn deference that is diametrically opposed to the meaning of everyday familiarity that *vosotros* and its paradigm have in European Spanish, as the plural of *tú*.

In addition to elucidating these issues, this study makes two more contributions. The first is theoretical and consists of questioning the idea that some systems of address are more balanced than others. The second is historiographical and draws attention to a bias with which address – and certainly other linguistic phenomena – has been analyzed in American Spanish.

Section 2 opens with a brief overview of the state of the art on plural forms of address in Spanish, focusing in particular on American Spanish. Section 3 then presents a working hypothesis and describes the methodology. To substantiate this hypothesis, Section 4 reviews theoretical issues in address and the history of Spanish in the Americas. This is followed in Section 5 by a discussion of data drawn from the *Corpus Diacrónico y Diatópico del Español de América* (CORDIAM) 'Diachronic and Diatopic Corpus of American Spanish', which provide evidence that differs from data explored until now. Finally, in Section 6 I summarize the arguments and present the study's conclusions.

2 State of the art

2.1 Synchrony

The use of plural forms of address is one of the differences highlighted in both language manuals and reference works as distinguishing European Spanish from Spanish spoken in the Americas (see, among many others, Lapesa 1981: 579; Penny 2005: 38, 2004: 222). In this sense, Carricaburo (2015: 12), for example, notes:

> La primera distinción que surge cuando se intenta trazar un paradigma pronominal y verbal del español se deriva de una dicotomía de trato para la segunda persona plural que divide por un lado a la Península y por otro a Hispanoamérica y Canarias.

---

[1] I use the terms *communicative immediacy* and *communicative distance* as developed by Koch and Oesterreicher in the 1990s and 2000s (cf., for example, Oesterreicher 1996 or Koch & Oesterreicher 2007).

'The first difference observed when describing a pronominal and verbal paradigm in Spanish arises from a dichotomy in the form of address for the second person plural, which sets European Spain apart from American Spanish and the Canary Islands.'

According to the most widely held opinions, the parameters that govern the use of the two plural forms in European Spanish are social and interpersonal distance between the speakers, with less distance determining the selection of *vosotros* and greater distance determining the selection of *ustedes*. Given the overwhelming consensus on this point, a thorough review of Spanish manuals, teaching materials, and reference works is unnecessary. I will only cite here the latest reference grammar of the Spanish language published by the *Asociación de Academias de la Lengua Española* (ASALE) and the *Real Academia Española* (RAE). This grammar describes the distinction between *vosotros* and *ustedes* in the terms expressed above, in many cases qualifying the description with a geographical restriction for Europe. The section on morphology reads:

> No se hace distinción entre la variante de confianza y la de respeto en la segunda persona de plural (*ustedes trabajan*), salvo en el español europeo, excluidas la mayor parte de Andalucía occidental y Canarias. (RAE-ASALE 2009: § 4.4 e)

> 'No distinction is made between the variant that denotes familiarity and the variant that denotes respect in the second person plural (*ustedes trabajan*), except in European Spanish, excluding most of western Andalusia and the Canary Islands.'

In the section on syntax the text states:

> El pronombre de segunda persona de plural *vosotros/vosotras* es la forma común que se emplea en España para el trato de confianza, aunque alterna en Andalucía occidental con *ustedes*. El uso de *ustedes* como forma común para la segunda persona del plural, sin distinción de tratamiento, se extiende a toda América. En Europa se documenta también en las islas Canarias, aunque se ha observado que en las islas de La Gomera, El Hierro y La Palma se prefiere generalmente *vosotros* a *ustedes*, o se da alternancia entre ambas formas para el trato de confianza. (RAE-ASALE 2009: §16.15q)

> 'The second person plural pronoun *vosotros/vosotras* is the form commonly used in Spain for familiar address, although in western Andalusia it alternates with *ustedes*. *Ustedes* as a common form for the second personal plural, with no distinction in terms of address, is used throughout Hispanic America. In Europe it is also documented in the Canary Islands, although it has been observed that in the islands of La Gomera, El Hierro, and La Palma *vosotros* is generally preferred over *ustedes*, or else speakers alternate between both forms for familiar address.'

Thus, it is often held that the same parameters that determine the distinction between the plural forms determine the distinction between the singular forms, as set out in Table 1.

Table 1: Second person pronouns in Spain (Carricaburo 2015: 12).

Number	Informality/solidarity/familiarity/ closeness [less social distance]	Formality/power/politeness/ distance [greater social distance]
Singular	*tú*	*usted*
Plural	*vosotros/as*	*ustedes*

These few references illustrate the view that naturalizes a symmetrical system characterized by the combination of two features – social distance and number – which explain its four forms. In her classic article on the subject, Fontanella de Weinberg (1999: 1402) describes this system as "balanced", and other studies, such as Lara's (2010), continue along this line. After studying the use of *ustedes* in western Andalusia, Lara concludes that:

> el vacío de diferenciación social que deja la generalización de *ustedes* a todos los casos referidos a una pluralidad de interlocutores puede motivar, a la larga, el nacimiento eventual de nuevas distinciones en la escala de poder. (Lara 2010: 70)

> 'the absence of social distinction that is left by the generalization of *ustedes* for all cases referring to multiple addressees may eventually give way to the possible emergence of new distinctions in the scale of power'

A few sentences later, he stresses the idea that a symmetrical system is necessary, arguing: that a lack of distinction will likely give way to an innovation (Lara 2010: 69).

In addition to my own discordant voice, others have recently disagreed with this way of analyzing forms of address and with the need for symmetrical singular and plural forms. Morgan & Schwenter (2016) argue that symmetry in Castilian European Spanish is currently a myth, because the *vosotros/vosotras* form in European Spanish is actually the plural for both the singular *tú* and the singular *usted*, as they note in the following excerpt:

> *Vosotros* is, in fact, the only productive second person plural form for many Spaniards, for whom it serves as the plural of both *tú* and *usted*. Despite the universally expressed view that there exists symmetry in the Castilian system, such that *vosotros* is the plural of *tú* and *ustedes* the plural of *usted*, we show that there is in fact widespread asymmetry from singular to plural, i.e. a person might be addressed as *usted* in the singular while at the same time forming part of a group that is addressed as *vosotros* by the same speaker. (Morgan & Schwenter 2016: 264)

Table 1 is thus modified in Table 2 to reflect the above, with a single form used for the plural (*vosotros*) in Castilian Spanish, as occurs in American Spanish with *ustedes*, both in familiar or socially distant situations.

Table 2: Revision of second person pronouns in Spain by Morgan & Schwenter (2016).

Number	Informality/solidarity/ familiarity/closeness [less social distance]	Formality/power/ politeness/distancing [greater social distance]
Singular	*tú*	*usted*
Plural	*vosotros/as*	

European Castilian Spanish and American Spanish would differ in: (i) the form chosen for the plural (*ustedes* in American Spanish, or *vosotros* in (standard) Castilian Spanish), based on the studies by Morgan & Schwenter; and (ii) in the singular. In the Americas, the single plural form *ustedes* combines with five different singular forms (see Table 3). Since the varieties of American Spanish do not select and combine the same singular pronoun(s), we find five different systems of address are in use (Bertolotti 2015: 71).

Table 3: Second person pronouns in the Americas (Bertolotti 2015).

Number	With geolinguistic, social and situational variation				
Singular	*Tú*	*vos*	*usted*-T[2]	*su merced*	*usted*-V
Plural	*ustedes*				

2.2 Diachrony

2.2.1 The emergence of vosotros *in Europe*

The most thorough study to date on the emergence and spread of *vosotros* in the history of the Spanish language is by García, de Jonge, Nieuwenhuijsen & Lechner (1990). According to these authors, *vosotros* emerged and spread as a result of the communicative advantages it offered: *vos* was highly polysemous and the stressed form *vosotros* allowed for disambiguation (García et al. 1990:

---

2 Although it exceeds the scope of this chapter, I should note here that I distinguish two social meanings applied to *usted* in the Americas. I use the letter V – from the Latin *vos* – to code the various names given for social deixis indicating differences in *power*, for politeness, and for affective distance. I use the letter T to code the various names given for social deixis indicating symmetrical *power* relations, for non-reverential politeness, and for affective closeness. In both cases, I follow the classic study by Brown & Gilman (1960). The presence, the social variables, and the situations that govern singular forms are complex; they are described in Bertolotti (2015: 31–71).

75–76). In addition to this, they note the temporal predominance of *vosotros* over *nosotros* and the consequences of the tonic nature of *vosotros* compared to the unstressed *vos*.

With regard to dating, through references to grammarians García et al. (1990) observe that the use of *vosotros* had become widespread as early as the late 15th century and that by the 16th century it was the predominant form (García et al. 1990: 66). Years later, Nieuwenhuijsen (2006: 952) insists on the full integration of *vosotros* in the pronominal paradigm as of the 16th century.

There is very little research on the emergence of *ustedes*. However, the emergence of *vuestra merced* has been thoroughly studied and it is dated by De Jonge & Nieuwenhuijsen (2009: 1641–1642) at the end of the 14th century. They point out that the full integration of *vuestra(s) merced(es)* and their grammaticalized forms (*usted*, *ustedes*) are not firmly established until the end of the 17th century (De Jonge & Nieuwenhuijsen 2009: 1652).

This review of historical studies would not be complete without looking at works that focus on southern Spain. The characterizations of the values of *vosotros* and *ustedes* gathered by Calderón Campos (2015) in an analysis of a historical corpus from the Granada region provide useful insights. From the analysis of CORDEREGRA (Corpus of the Kingdom of Granada), Calderón Campos (2015: 74) concludes:

> *vosotros* es siempre una forma muy directa, usada en situaciones de tensión comunicativa, para insultar o denigrar a los destinatarios [...] o para dar órdenes. En el resto de los casos, se emplea *vuestras mercedes/ustedes*, que era la forma no marcada del plural.

> 'vosotros* is always a very direct form, used in situations of communicative tension to insult or belittle the addressees [...] or to issue orders. In all other cases, *vuestras mercedes/ustedes*, which was the unmarked plural form, is used.'

He does not date the emergence and spread of *vosotros* in the Granada corpus.

The study by Fernández Martín (2012) on the loss of the pronoun *vosotros* in western Andalusia is also particularly thought-provoking. She describes the sociolinguistic distribution of *vosotros* and dates the replacement of *vosotros* by *ustedes* to the first half of the 18th century:

> Se distinguen diversas pautas en el uso de *vosotros* en español entre 1700 y 1931. A nivel general, los hablantes de un estatus social bajo (rural y urbano) tenían muy limitado el uso de la 2ªPP y, por ende, mucho más el pronominal. Fuera del trato a los hijos, entre esposos, a los hermanos o de una amistad estrecha a los individuos del mismo estatus, dichas formas no tenían cabida. Esta restricción de usos y su carácter marcado revelaba una escasa aparición de la 2aPP/*vosotros*. (Fernández Martín, 2012: 564)

> 'Several patterns in the use of *vosotros* in Spanish can be distinguished between 1700 and 1931. Generally, for speakers of low social status (both rural and urban) the use of the second

person plural was very limited and, therefore, much more so the pronoun. These forms were not used other than to address one's children or between spouses, siblings, or close friends among individuals of the same social status. This restriction of uses and its marked nature revealed the limited appearance of the second person plural/*vosotros*'

In explaining how *vosotros* was abandoned, she turns to universal issues of address. She says that *ustedes* was more frequent than *vosotros* because of its inclusive and heterogeneous nature, so that *ustedes* could refer to a group in which there were both individuals who were addressed as *tú* and individuals who were addressed as *usted* (Fernández Martín, 2012: 564). I will come back to this below, in the section on theoretical considerations.

2.2.2 *The loss of* vosotros *in the Americas*

Historical studies on forms of address in the Americas have rarely focused on the history of the plural forms of address. This has already been noted by Moreno de Alba, who, in reference to the elimination of the pronoun *vosotros*, argues that there are no studies that fully account for this phenomenon (2011: 25).

In the bibliography by Fernández & Gerhalter (2017), only 20 entries in more than 1,500 (that is, less than 2%) include the term *vosotros*. Most of these texts are descriptions of the current use of *vosotros* (cf. Almasov 1974; Isaza Calderón 1976; Siciliano 1971, among others) and the diachronic aspect related to the loss of *vosotros* in the Americas is only considered in a few works (cf. Company Company 1997; Domínguez Hernández 2013; Nieuwenhuijsen 2006; Moreno de Alba 2010, 2011; Obediente Sosa 2011, 2013), most of which are examined in this study.

Moreno de Alba points out that an exception to the lack of historical analysis is the study by De Jonge & Nieuwenhuijsen (2009), which he understands offers relevant data regarding "the elimination of *vosotros*". Contrary to what Moreno de Alba notes, I see no new solid evidence on the history of *vosotros* in American Spanish in the above study, although it does provide excellent diachronic evidence of other forms of address. De Jonge & Nieuwenhuijsen (2009) summarize some of the literature concerning the disappearance of *vosotros* in the Americas that I review and assess here.

First of all, De Jonge & Nieuwenhuijsen (2009: 1607) point to the maintaining of *vos* as a possible cause for the disappearance of *vosotros*, given the high coincidence of the two paradigms. This has also been argued by Fontanella de Weinberg (1999). As a sole argument for the disappearance of *vosotros*, I find this is weak, for three reasons: (1) *vos* is maintained as a singular (not plural) form; *vos* as a plural form also disappeared, just like *vosotros*; (2) part of its paradigm – precisely the ambiguous forms – has been dropped; and (3) while the loss of *vosotros* has occurred throughout the Americas, *vos* has not been maintained throughout the entire continent.

De Jonge & Nieuwenhuijsen also attribute the decline of the form studied here to its use by not very prestigious speakers, and as an attempt at an explanation they also present the position put forward by Corominas & Pascual (1980–1983: 844):

> Corominas (1980–1983: s.v. vos) es el único que apunta hacia una explicación del fenómeno cuando señala que el pronombre *boso* del papiamento constituye la única huella de *vosotros* en América. El hecho de que el pronombre sobreviva en el papiamento, o sea el hecho de que fuera usado por los negros, sugiere, según Corominas, que el uso de *vosotros* llegó a considerarse en un momento dado como descortés, motivo por el cual fue rechazado o evitado primero por los blancos y más tarde por toda la población. (De Jonge & Nieuwenhuijsen 2009: 1606)

> 'Corominas (1980–1983: s.v. *vos*) is the only one who attempts an explanation of the phenomenon when he observes that the pronoun *boso* in Papiamento is the only trace of *vosotros* in the Americas. The fact that the pronoun survives in Papiamento, that is, the fact that it is used by black people, suggests, according to Corominas, that the use of *vosotros* came to be considered impolite, and for that reason it was rejected or avoided first by white people and later by the population as a whole.'

This argument has little basis given that in the early years of the 19th century *vosotros* and its paradigm were used extensively in national anthems, solemn declarations, and speeches.

In a previous work, Nieuwenhuijsen (2006) rules out the late emergence of *vosotros* as an explanation of its disappearance from the Americas. We must remember that this author dates the full integration of *vosotros* in the pronominal paradigm to the 16th century. She also rules out the idea of the absence of *vosotros* as an Andalusian attribute of American Spanish (Nieuwenhuijsen 2006: 952).

As for establishing when *vosotros* disappeared, Moreno de Alba identifies it as occurring in Mexico in the 19th century (Moreno de Alba 2011: 27). In his historical study about *vosotros*, Moreno de Alba also describes the process of the loss of the pronoun in American Spanish, noting the problems with the available data:

> *Vosotros* tiene vigencia, en el español americano, hasta fines del XVIII, cuando comienza a decrecer, proceso que se acelera notablemente en el XIX. Es probable, aunque por falta de documentación suficiente, no puede comprobarse que se empleara ya con normalidad *ustedes* sobre *vosotros* en los textos americanos de finales del XVIII, pues de otra manera sería difícil de explicar la proliferación de *ustedes* en textos americanos desde principios del XIX, ésta sí plenamente atestiguada en la documentación del CORDE. Esto permite suponer, asimismo, que *ustedes* venía compitiendo con *vosotros*, en lengua hablada, desde el mismo siglo XVIII y que, a lo largo del XIX, acabara por sustituirlo por completo en el registro oral. (Moreno de Alba 2011: 39)

'*Vosotros* remains in use in American Spanish until the late 18th century, when it starts to decline, a process that picks up significantly in the 19th century. While there is not sufficient documentation to prove it, it is likely that *ustedes* was already commonly chosen over *vosotros* in American Spanish texts of the late 18th century, since otherwise it would be difficult to explain the proliferation of *ustedes* in American Spanish texts starting in the early 19th century, a fact that is fully confirmed by CORDE documentation. This suggests, moreover, that *ustedes* had been competing with *vosotros*, in spoken language, from as early as the 18th century and that, in the 19th century, it would eventually replace it completely in spoken language'

Moreno de Alba (2011) observes the late division of the plural space into two in European Spanish, and, almost in passing, notes the numerous values of *vosotros*. According to this Mexican linguist, the *vosotros/ustedes* opposition, in European Spanish, operates from the 18th century (Moreno de Alba 2011: 28). In the 16th and 17th centuries the expression *vuestras mercedes* only competes [...] with *vos* and, especially, with *vosotros*, which, based on the figures he provides, was the preferred form (Moreno de Alba 2011: 29). Thus it is logical that in pre-18th century Spanish texts, the pronoun *vosotros* has both deferential and non-deferential value (Moreno de Alba 2011: 29).

Moreno de Alba's work suggests that there could have been an early single space for the plural, coded by different linguistic forms without a clear-cut closeness/distance division. However, although in the above study the author appears to have perceived this lack of division, he does not develop an explanation for it.

2.2.3 *Remnants of* vosotros *use in the Americas*

As noted above, the disappearance of *vosotros* is not absolute, since it is used in certain very specific – and therefore greatly restricted – contexts. Various authors have observed this and have highlighted the use of *vosotros* in proclamations, religious discourses, and speeches where reference is made to biblical figures or independence leaders (among them, Almasov 1974: 309; Caravedo 2005: 28–29; Frago 2011: 55 ff.; Moreno de Alba 2011: passim; Obediente 2011: passim; Rona 2014 [1958]: 112).

Caravedo (2015: 28) observes that the designative value of *vosotros* has been inverted and *vosotros* is used in contexts of great solemnity (proclamations, solemn discourses). She attributes this to the fact that it is learned through schooling as a form taken from artificial contexts.[3]

---

3 This can be illustrated with an anecdote of a girl in Uruguay who, after attending a ceremony in which she and other schoolchildren had to pledge allegiance to the national flag (an obligation

Frago (2011) documents *vosotros*, verbs with that inflection, and *vuestro* in the 19th century in the Americas. He highlights the importance of this century of independence, in which these forms appear almost exclusively in written language, especially in solemn linguistic contexts and doctrinal, political texts. As reasons for this, he suggests that the educated minority maintained for specific occasions the ancient prestige of the literary and administrative model of the old metropolis (Frago 2011: 69). Moreno de Alba also identifies the contextual restrictions and stylistic uses of *vosotros* in the Americas, but without venturing an explanation. He says that *vosotros* was still used during this century in historical, political, oratory, religious, theatrical texts and in certain contexts (when addressing one's children, when representing the speech of biblical or historical figures).

Obediente (2011) points out that his analysis of manifestos, decrees, discourses, proclamations, harangues, programs for public ceremonies, pamphlets, and brief tracts reveals that the form of address used in Venezuela throughout the 19th century to speak to citizens as a whole was *vosotros*, with some alternations with *ustedes* (Obediente 2011: 277).

The national anthems of Argentina (1), Uruguay (2) and Chile (3) address their intended audiences with forms of *vosotros* :

(1) ¡*Oíd*, mortales!, el grito sagrado:
     "¡libertad!, ¡libertad!, ¡libertad!"
     Oíd el ruido de rotas cadenas
     ved en trono a la noble igualdad.
     'Hear, mortals, the sacred cry:
     "Freedom! Freedom! Freedom!"
     Hear the noise of broken chains
     See noble equality on the throne'

(2) Tiranos, *temblad.*
     'Tyrants, tremble'

---

for all Uruguayan six-year-olds), remarked: "They spoke to us as if we were from another country, calling us **ustedéis**", in reference, surely, to verb endings. The call for children to pledge allegiance to the flag reads: ¿*Prometéis respetar y honrar esta Bandera que representa la dignidad, la soberanía y la gloriosa historia de nuestra Patria, la República Oriental del Uruguay?* 'Do you pledge to respect and honour this flag, which represents the dignity, the sovereignty and the glorious history of our homeland, the República Oriental del Uruguay?'

(3) *Vuestros* nombres valientes Soldados,
Que *habéis* sido de Chile el sostén,
Nuestros pechos los llevan grabados.

'In our chests we have engraved your names, brave soldiers, who have been Chile's support'

These forms were also present in political discourse in the 19th century. This can be illustrated with just one example from 1813, in which an independence leader addresses the representatives of various towns, during a time of strong anti-Spanish sentiment. The example below contains parts of the text in question:

(4) *Ciudadanos*: el resultado de la campaña pasada me puso al frente de *vosotros* por el voto sagrado de *vuestra* voluntad general. Hemos corrido 17 meses cubiertos de la gloria y la miseria y tengo la honra de volver a hablar*os* en la segunda vez que *hacéis* el uso de *vuestra* soberanía. [...]. Mi autoridad emana de *vosotros* y ella cesa ante *vuestra* presencia soberana. *Vosotros estáis* en el pleno goce de *vuestros* derechos: *ved* ahí el fruto de mis ansias y desvelos y *ved* ahí también todo el premio de mi afán. Ahora en *vosotros* está el conservarlo. (Near Montevideo, April 4, 1813. José Artigas).

'*Citizens*: The results of the last campaign and your sacred general vote will have gotten me to lead you. We went through seventeen months of glory and misery. I am so privileged to speak to *you*, on this second occasion in which *you enjoy your* sovereignty. My authority emanates from *you* and it stops in the face of *your* sovereign presence. *You are* fully enjoying *your* rights. *See* here the product of my anguish and wakefulness and *see* here the whole reward of my eagerness. Now *you have* to preserve it.'

As we can see, these examples are never accompanied by an explanation or a hypothesis stating why such remnants exist, except in Frago's statement about the prestige of the metropolis. The brief illustration in this section raises doubts as to whether the selection of the forms of *vosotros* was in any way related to an old literary prestige associated with Spain. There does not appear to be any firm data to support that claim. Instead there is ample evidence of anti-Spanish political sentiment among the local elites, for example, in their participation in the independence processes.

3 Working hypothesis

As I have shown above, no historical explanation has been provided for *vosotros* that would account for a dual situation in which, in the Americas, on the one hand, *vosotros* withdrew from the space of plurality, leaving it entirely to the more formal *ustedes*, and, on the other hand, *vosotros* was preserved as a very formal pronoun used in certain communicative contexts.

My working hypothesis is that a system with one plural form is not abnormal, despite the widespread assumption that considers the single form system an exception. In fact, there is abundant inter-linguistic evidence for languages using a single pronoun of address for the plural. That is the case of Albanian, Czech, Finnish, French, English, Tagalog, Turkish, and Yiddish, for example (cf. Helmbrecht 2013–45A). I argue that the assumption of abnormality derives from the general tendency to view (standard) European Spanish as the normal variety, with a symmetrical four-space paradigm – two for the singular and two for the plural. The discussion has thus been influenced by a strong research bias that leads us to explore the modes of Spanish spoken in Hispanic America using the categories and usage of Castilian Spanish. In fact, American Spanish has never really had a regulated system with two plural pronouns of address determined by social distance. Rather, it has had a single space for the plural, coded by different linguistic forms without a well-defined closeness/distance division.

4 Theoretical considerations

4.1 Homogeneity and heterogeneity of plural pronouns

Cross-linguistic evidence shows that there are languages with no pronoun distinctions based on distance (English, Irish, Ewe, Mapudungun), others in which such distinctions are binary (Basque, Turkish, Sango, Punjabi), and others that have more than two forms (Polish, Hungarian, Tagalog, and Nahuatl), as documented in *The World Atlas of Language Structures* (cf. Helmbrecht 2013–45A, chapter and map). There are several Romance languages that make no distinction at the level of allocative pronouns between closeness and distance in the plural or reduce it to a minimum (cf. French *vous*, Portuguese *vocês*, Italian *voi*). Nominal forms may also be used to introduce a formal/informal distinction, as for example Pt. *os senhores*. It is noteworthy that *ustedes* stems from such a nominal form: *vuestra(s) merced(es)*.

As for the referentiality of second person plural pronouns, Nowikow (1994) identifies two types: homogeneous (referential) plurality and heterogeneous (referential) plurality. He defines homogeneous plurality as that in which all class members belong to the same person, that is, *vosotros* is the sum of *tú* + *tú* + *tú*... This is the case, for example, of the pronoun *vosotros* used by a Madrid mother addressing all her children at the same time, as in example (2):

(2) [*vosotros* = *tú* + *tú* + *tú*]
     Niños, quiero que *vosotros* estéis todos acostados antes de las nueve los días de semana.
     'Kids, I want *you* in bed before nine every week day.'

Heterogeneous plurality occurs when all class members do not belong to the same grammatical person in the speech act, that is, *vosotros* is *tú* + not *tú* (Nowikow 1994: 285–286), as can be seen in example (3). In this example, a mother speaks to her daughter and refers at the same time to her daughter's friends (whom the mother would address individually with the familiar *tú* and therefore I mark them as *ella$_T$/ellas$_T$*), where the heterogeneity is *tú* + *ella$_T$* + *ella$_T$*.

(3) [*vosotros* = *tú* + *ella$_T$* ...or *ellas$_T$*]

     María, por favor, que alguna de *vosotras* tres me avise no bien lleguen a destino.

     'Mary, would one of *you* please let me know as soon as you arrive at *your* destination.'

In my opinion, heterogeneity could also refer to another situation: the difference in social deixis or respect, in addition to the difference in grammatical person. Besides the addressee, a second person plural may also refer to others who would receive a different form of address to reflect social distance or politeness. In that case, the plural pronoun is not the sum of heterogeneous persons in the speech act, but the sum of entities whose heterogeneity lies in that they are recipients of various forms of address in the singular, that is, considered individually. This heterogeneous plural occurs, for example, if an employee speaks simultaneously to a co-worker – whom he addresses as *tú* – and to his boss – whom he addresses as *usted* – as shown in example (4).

(4) [*ustedes* = *tú* +*usted*]

     – ¿Alguno de *ustedes* quisiera café?

     'Would anyone of *you* want coffee?'

Strictly speaking, we should identify a third type of heterogeneity, which emerges from the combination of the previous two, although it is not relevant for the purposes of my working hypothesis. The *not-tú* can be formed by third persons that, if addressed directly, would receive a distant address (*usted*, in current Spanish). It could be illustrated with the same characters from the previous example, but with an absent boss, who is therefore coded as third person and not second person, as shown in example (5).

(5) [*ustedes* = *tú* + *él$_V$*]
    −El jefe y yo terminaremos este trabajo mañana temprano.
    −¿Alguno de *ustedes* llegará mañana antes de las 7 a la oficina?
    '−The boss and I will finish this work tomorrow morning.
    −Will any of *you* get into the office tomorrow before 7?'

In sum, forms of address in second person plural can be homogeneous or heterogeneous. Heterogeneity can be determined by "the person – second or third", "the form of address – closeness and distance", or by both "the person and the form of address". Thus, it can be argued that the conditions of use of the plural forms for closeness are more complex than those of the plural forms for distance. That is because there only needs to be one addressee that requires social distance (or a third person requiring a distant form of address) to render inapplicable a not distant plural form (such as *vosotros* in the 17th to 20th centuries).

Based on these ideas, Fernández Martín (2012) explains the generalization of the plural *ustedes* in Andalusia as follows:

> El plural *ustedes* era más frecuente por su carácter inclusivo y heterogéneo, frente a *vosotros* exclusivo. Esto quiere decir que *ustedes*+3ª PP era el trato apropiado para aludir a un grupo en el que hubiese sujetos a los que se tutease y se tratase de usted. *Vosotros* exigía que a todos los miembros se los tutease independientemente. (Fernández Martín 2012: 564–5)

> 'The plural *ustedes* is more frequent because of its inclusive and heterogeneous nature, in contrast to the exclusive *vosotros*. This means that *ustedes* + third person plural was more appropriate to refer to a group composed of individuals who were addressed with *tú* and *usted*. *Vosotros* required that all members of the group were individually addressed as *tú*.'

These heterogeneities are not reflected in the current plural pronoun of address in Hispanic America, where speakers use a single form (*ustedes*). But they are reflected (or have been reflected) in Castilian Spanish, in which any heterogeneity in the form of address entails (or entailed) selecting *ustedes* instead of *vosotros*. That is, until recently. The study by Morgan & Schwenter (2016) cited above suggests there is a change in progress, with speakers tending to disregard this factor when choosing the plural pronoun.

It can also be asserted that plural forms are *critical* forms of address, as defined by Hummel, who uses the term to describe an inherent feature of address:

> Unlike in most linguistic domains, *crisis* is an everyday feature of address. Every time people meet, address is a latent problem that requires a solution. Crisis also affects the very system of address, that is, the verbal, pronominal, and nominal paradigms, especially the (subject) pronominal paradigm [...]. (Hummel, in this volume)

Plurals are, thus, so *hypercritical* because of their complex reference that they became *hypocritical*. They are governed by the parameters of person and social deixis. Speakers must consider both aspects in each of the referents that make up the plurality. This could be one of the reasons for the relative rarity of languages with two second person plural pronouns, as they have highly marked conditions of use, which are so algorithmic as to have a greater processing cost. In any case, I agree with Hummel (in this volume) in that the "plural seems to be perceived as less direct, at least with regard to the individuals who compose the group".

Some studies have pointed out the lack of distinction between closeness and distance in plural forms of address. In a literary corpus that spans over one century (from 1528 to 1640), Moreno (2006) finds no differentiated uses in terms of closeness/distance for the form *vosotros*. This suggests that during the time in which the Spanish language was massively exported to the Americas *vosotros* did not have a specialized use as a familiar form of address.

Fernández Martín (2012) observes that the lack of differentiation existed as late as the 18th century. She does note, however, that the scope of *vosotros* was limited to certain uses (Fernández Martín 2012: 187), which roughly coincide with those I suggested above for *tú*. Consequently, Spanish speakers leaving Spain for the Americas did not carry with them a specialized use as a familiar form of address.

Based on an analysis of the data provided by CORDE, Moreno de Alba also notes the difficulty in capturing the specificity of the use of *vosotros* in the Americas:

> Lógicamente, en textos españoles anteriores al XVIII, el pronombre *vosotros* al que, como dije, poca competencia ofrecían tanto el pronombre *vos* (plural) cuanto el sintagma *vuestras mercedes, tiene tanto valor deferencial cuanto no deferencial.* (Moreno de Alba 2011: 29).

> 'Logically, in pre-18th century Spanish texts the pronoun *vosotros*, which, as I said, presented little competition both to the pronoun *vos* (plural) and the syntagma *vuestras mercedes*, has both deferential and non-deferential value.'

4.2 Communication among the first people speaking Spanish in the Americas

To better understand the data from the Americas we need to consider not only the characteristics of plural forms of address, but also the characteristics of how address was regulated in the 16th and 17th centuries. Moreover, an analysis of such characteristics in the American Spanish communicative space, as previously noted by Zimmermann (2011: 14), that is, in the context in which speakers used and heard Spanish modes in the Americas, is also needed. It is important to take into account that, due to both the contact with native populations – the great disseminators of Spanish in the Americas – and the characteristics of the first settlers, conditions for interaction in the Americas were not conducive to familiar address.

The parameters that governed singular address in Spanish in the 16th and 17th centuries, as noted in Bertolotti (2015), were as follows: T-forms or familiar forms required (*a*) familiarity, closeness, or intra-group situations; (*b*) situations in which there was no need for regulated respect or any pragmatic need to mark distance; (*c*) that speaker and addressee knew each other well from an early age; (*d*) that speaker and addressee be of the same gender, and preferably related to one another; and (*e*) their use by older generations to address younger generations. Exceptionally T-forms could be used in out-group situations. In such cases, the speaker had to belong to a higher social class than the addressee, and, in general, it was used by masters to address their "familiar" servants. These parameters governed the use of *tú*. In the case of V-forms of address, their use was determined by two parameters: extra-group situations and deference in in-group situations. These parameters governed, roughly speaking, the use of *vuestra merced > usted*. All other situations were conveyed through *vos*, and this is one of the reasons for the survival of *vos* in the Americas, as I have shown in Bertolotti (2015). All the situations that were not covered by *tú* or by *vuestra merced > usted*, I argue, were covered by *vos*, and, therefore, *vos* was used in contexts of both closeness and distance, in both non-deferential and deferential contexts. Thus, *vos* satisfied most of the communication needs of the speakers regarding address. This explains the generalized presence of *voseo* in the Americas to this day, although with different social and situational distributions, with various social values, and with diverse morphological verbal manifestations.

It is reasonable to assume that the relevant conditions for selecting the singular were not substantially different from the conditions for selecting the plural, and the use of the familiar singular (*tú*) was limited by very strong restrictions. If we consider the conditions for communicating in the Americas, it is not difficult to see that the contexts where *tú* could be used were few and, therefore, the possible uses of *tú* would surely be combined with referents to which *vos* or *vuestra merced > usted* would apply. Intra-group situations, familiarity, long-lasting acquaintance with one another, and having a shared childhood were conditions that were improbably met among indigenous populations that interacted with Europeans, and even, to a great extent, among Spaniards in the Americas. These conditions were clearly not suitable for familiar address. Therefore, the low possibility of homogeneity in familiar social deixis strengthens the idea that a differentiated plural form of address was unnecessary.

If we combine the two issues discussed in this section (usage conditions for plurals and communication conditions in the Americas) we can easily accept the probability that two plurals were unnecessary (with one of them reserved for closeness) as their contexts of use would be very limited.

5 Analysis of the 16th to 18th centuries

5.1 The corpus

The data are taken from a corpus built specifically to research the history of Spanish in the Americas. CORDIAM-DOCUMENTS is a computerized corpus that consists of collections of texts taken from archives. It comprises four centuries (from 1494 to 1904) and all Spanish-speaking countries of the Americas. More than 3,500 texts were selected by researchers based on careful linguistic and philological criteria. Documents are predominantly characterized by their *communicative immediacy*.

5.2 Evidence from the *CORDIAM* corpus

5.2.1 Quantitative aspects

Let us now look at the information provided by American Spanish data from the 16th and 18th centuries, drawn from the CORDIAM corpus. Data from the 17th century were not included, as leaving out one century provides a clearer picture of change in progress.

A search for *vosotros* (and all its possible orthographical variants) produced 72 matches from the 16th century and eight from the 18th century. The searches for *vuestras mercedes* produced 243 matches from the 16th century and 91 from the 18th century. The contrast between *vosotros* and *ustedes* should be considered with great caution for reasons I discuss in Bertolotti (2010). I show that the presence of *usted* as a subject is not equivalent to its respective familiar form, and I attribute this to the fact that *usted* is a grammaticalization of an honorific form. Among other consequences, this results in a coincidence in the ending of the third person, which explains the "over-occurrence" for disambiguation. This could mean that the obligation to use *ustedes* was greater than the obligation to use *vosotros*, and this is something that must be taken into account. However, while it might be expected that the presence of *ustedes* as an explicit subject diminished as the grammaticalization process advanced, the data shows that *ustedes* increased its presence.

Again, these data, which are all from the Americas, do not support Moreno de Alba's claim that *ustedes* begins to predominate only from 1840. The CORDIAM corpus provides evidence that in the 16th century *vuestras mercedes > ustedes* was more frequent. Nevertheless, it must be pointed out that Moreno de Alba clarifies his claim by saying that unfortunately the documents in CORDE from the Americas are scarce for some decades, and they are far from being representative of the state of things in each of the various countries (Moreno de Alba 2011: 32).

Clearly, according to the newer data from CORDIAM, *vuestras mercedes*[4] predominates over *vosotros* as early as the 16th century, and this continues, more markedly in fact, into the 18th century.[5] Proportionally, the *vosotros/ustedes* ratio moves from 3.6 in the 16th century to 15.3 in the 18th century. That is, in the 16th century there is one instance of *vosotros* for every 3.6 instances of *vuestras mercedes > ustedes*. In the 18th century, however, there is one instance of *vosotros* for every 15 instances of *vuestras mercedes > ustedes*. It is important to bear in mind that I take these data as a general framework, and therefore rather than insisting on numerical contrast I focus on analyzing the contexts (with their nominal forms) in which each pronoun appears.

There is a single instance of *vosotros* in the 19th century. There are 18 uses of the corresponding verb inflections (-*ais*/-*eis*/-*is*) in the same century. All of them appear in formulaic or solemn contexts, which I do not analyze in this study. The *vosotros* form appears in a familiar context and was written by a woman from the countryside:

---

4 The number of matches results from the sum of the matches from searches for various abbreviations (*mercedes, mds, mrds*), combined with *vuestras* (or some of its possible abbreviations) and, excluding nouns and proper names, constructions with *sus*. It also includes matches for *vstedes, ustedes*.

5 It should be noted that the three periods have approximately the same number of words (around one million) and that in the 16th century there are 718 personal letters while in the 18th century there are only 308.

(6) {f.2v} *tu* padre esta deciando q*ue te bengas*/y atribullendo los trabajos
/⁵ de sus ijos a los desordenes/de su bida pasada dise q*ue*/ci **bosotras**
padeceis es por el/desareglo q*ue* hubo el Maria [...] la/cri[a]da esta cada bes
mas famosa /¹⁰ aquí pasan lo mas del tiempo/porque no nos ayamos cin/
eyos *Recibi* esperciones de/todos y se las *daras* a todos/y *manda* a *tu* mas
afetisima /¹⁵ tia q*ue* de corazon *te* quiere/Pascuala Albarez de Martinez/(Year
1816, Uruguay, correspondence, CORDIAM)

'*Your* father is looking forward to seeing *you* here. He considers that the
problems of his children are due to their previous life. He says that **you suffer**
because of this disorder. Maria, the maid, is increasingly famous. They spend
most of the time here in order to keep us company. *Receive* greetings from
all of us and *send* greetings to everybody there and *order your* most devoted
aunt who loves *you*. Pascuala Albarez de Martínez'[6]

Based on our data, then, we can argue that the generalization of *ustedes*, or more
precisely the shift from the older form *vosotros* to the more modern form *ustedes*,
had been underway since the beginning of the incorporation of the Spanish language in the Americas, and not since the 19th century.

5.2.2 Qualitative aspects

In this section, I present a qualitative analysis of the data and their communicative context. I consider social deixis, situation (familiar or social), and context
(formal or informal).

The analysis shows that in the 16th century *vosotros* has no restrictions determined by either social deixis, situation, or context. We find the use in an administrative text in which instructions are given, and, therefore, in a text from the
formal sphere, as can be seen in example (7).

(7) no **consyntireys** que los yndios se entremetan entre los españoles A lo menos
muchos syno que Antes vayan e esten por su parte haziendoles entender
que lo **hazeys** porque no **quereys** que ningun español les haga ni diga cosa
de que Resçiban enojo porque metiendose entre **vosotros** muchos yndios
pueden ten[d]er çelada para en abraçandose los vnos con **vos otros** salir los

---

6 In the examples and in the translation of examples (6)–(16) I coded pronominal and verbal *tú*
or *vos* in italics, pronominal and verbal **vosotros** in **bold italics**, pronominal and verbal *usted*
(vmd and similar) and *ustedes* (vs. ms. and similar) underlined.

otros e como son muchos **podriades** correr peligro y pereçer y **dexareys** muy Aperçibidos. (Year 1518, Cuba, administrative text, CORDIAM)

'**you cannot accept** that the Indians mix with the Spaniards, at least not so many of them. You have to convey to them that **you do** that because **you don´t want** any Spaniard to do or tell them anything that can make them feel angry. Because mixing with **you**, lots of Indians may set **you** up. Some of them can embrace **you** and others can go out. As they are so numerous, **you could be** in danger, and **you** may die.'

The use of *vosotros* to address parents is also found in family letters, where it alternates with *vuestra mercedes and* abbreviated alternative forms *vsms* as can be seen in example (8), and also with *vmd* [*vuestra merced* abbreviated form]).

(8) deseados padres salbeh**os** dios/con mas de[j]o de ber a <u>vs ms</u> que no de escriuy<u>lles</u>/<u>les</u> hago sauer como gloria a dios nuestro señor/estauamos en el peru yo e my hermano/ [...] yo/<u>les</u> ruego/que el vno o [en]tranbos <u>se vengan</u>/ para que aca <u>lleuen</u> algun descanso/para la bejez y de aca podemos prober {f.13} a nuestras hermanas y cuñados/e deudos y sy juan bonyllo nuestro/ primo quisyere benyr **dalde** mys besamanos/e **dezilde** que hare tanto por el/como por qualquiera de **vosotros**/[...] a todos <u>les</u> veso las manos [...] (Year 1568, Panama, correspondence, CORDIAM)

'Dear parents, God save **you**. Although I don´t see <u>you</u>, I write to <u>you</u>. I tell <u>you</u>, thank God that my brother and I, we are in Peru. I beg <u>you</u> that one or both of <u>you</u> <u>come</u> here. So *you* can bring some money here for your old age. From here we can support our sisters and brothers in law and the bereaved. If Juan Bonillo our cousin wants to come, **give** him my greetings and **tell** him that I will do anything for him as well as for any of **you**. To everyone I kiss <u>your</u> hands'

In the 16th century, the plural *vosotros* was also the plural of *vos*, as shown in example (9) in a letter addressed to a nephew.

(9) sobrino muchas vezes *os* e escripto que *vos* y *vuestra* muger y/hijos **os viniesedes** a estas partes para que gozásemos/de **vosotros** pues dios nos a dado para poder**os** haçer/vien y estamos en tierra donde no ay las necesidades/que en españa que lo que dios me a dado todo lo quiero/para *vos* y para mi sobrina. (Year 1590, Bolivia, correspondence, CORDIAM)

'My nephew, I have often written to *you* that *you* and *your* wife and children **should come** here so we can enjoy being with **you**. God has provided for us so we can help **you**. We live in a land that doesn't suffer the scarcity of Spain. What I have received from God, I want to share with *you* and my niece'

Finally, we find it as the plural of *tú* in a father's letter to his son in example (10).

(10) hijo/vna carta *tuya* reçibi que parecia mas/cartel de desafio que no carta de hijo a/padre estoy espantado de *ti* y de *tu* madre que *ayas*/querido ser tan contumaçis de no aver querido venir aca/donde **vuieredes** dadome a mi descanso y a **vosotros.** (Year 1570, Peru, correspondence, CORDIAM)

'My son, I have received a letter from *you* (sg.). It seemed more like a challenge billboard than a letter from a son to his father. I am appalled at *you* and *your* mother's stubborn refusal to come here, where **you** (pl.) **would have** given me solace as well as receiving it yourselves.'

This broad range of uses is similarly observed in the use of *vuestras mercedes* > *ustedes*. Considering only the extreme ends of the formal-informal continuum, we can see its use in a letter to the Council of the Indies (example (11)), a situation that requires the utmost formality.

(11) Manjficos señores./Por la carta que va con ésta he escrito tan largo a vs.mercedes, aunque a mi pareçer/corto, y en sumas lo que ha pasado, que temo que ya estaran ynportunados de/leer. (Year 1526, Mexico, administrative text, CORDIAM)

'Magnificent gentlemen, In a letter that I am sending with this one, I have written to you a great deal (although I think it is still a short letter) summarizing what has happened, to the point that I´m afraid you must be bored of reading.'

At the other extreme, we find the use of *vuesas mds* in a family letter to a sister, who is close to the writer in terms of affection and who is addressed alternatively with *vm(d)* and *vos*, pointing to no distinctin in terms of formality (example (12)).

(12) e querido/hacer esto para que la una u la otra tubiesen bentura/de llegar a manos de vmd [en] [e]l qual abiso a vmd de mi/salud y de *buestra* tia ysabel rodrigez de como estamos /buenos y de salud y ansi *bos* suplicamos nos aga/vmd merced [...] *entende* que yo deseo casar*os*/y poner*os* [en] cobro de maner[a] que *podays* estar/onradamente yo por no tener hijo ni hija ni parientes/mas llegados que vuesasmds e tenido por/bien y lo tengo de que *bengays* s a estar [en] mi conpania/y de *vuestra* tia porque tengo yo y ella con

que poder/remediar<u>les</u>. (Year 1590, Dominican Republic, correspondence, CORDIAM)

'I did this in the hope that at least one or the other letter would reach <u>your</u> hands. In these letters, I tell <u>you</u> about my health and about *your* aunt Isabel Rodríguez as well, we are healthy. We beg *you* to tell us about your health. *You* have to understand that I want *you* to be married, so that *you can live* honestly. I have no son or daughter or relatives closer than <u>you (pl.)</u>. I have wanted and still want for **you to come** and stay here with me and with *your* aunt. We can support <u>you (pl.)</u>.'

The results of the analysis of *vosotros* in the 18th century are not substantially different in qualitative terms, but there are quantitative differences, as there are only eight matches, as seen above, four of which are found in texts by the same writer. The very limited number of matches allows us, nonetheless, to say that *vosotros* was still used in a broad range of texts, from public announcements (example (13)) to family letters addressed to siblings (example (14)).

(13) Yo, verídico informante, **os** digo lo/mismo que **vosotros sabéis** por el padre Torres, padre Días, /[10] cabo de escuadra, padre Granado, sargento, y el padre Maldonado,/que éstos no hacen verdadero baptismo, verdadero/ sacramento de penitencia, verdadera extremaunción,/ni verdadera missa. (Year 1774, Mexico, legal texts, CORDIAM)

'As a truthful informant, I tell **you** what **you** already **know** through Father Torres, Father Díaz, squadron corporal, Father Granado, sargent, and Father Maldonado. They don´t baptize honestly, they don´t administer the sacrament of penance, they don´t really give the last rites, they don´t really say mass.'

(14) Hoy el objetto de mi attención es Andresitto, por sí y su buena madre, a quien tantto debí. Quiero saber si vive con **vosotros**, con su mujer o separados, y el porqué. [...]/Hermanos, desengañémonos que estto puede durar...También *te* escribí (*conttigo* abló Pepe) pregunttando el esttado y oficio que seguía el muchacho que esttá en León, nada *dices, haces* bien callar./(Year 1772, Peru, correspondance, CORDIAM)

'Today it is Andresito who needs attention, to whom and to whose good mother I owe so much. I want to know if he is living with **you** (pl.), with his wife or if he is separated and why. [...] Brothers, we have to accept that this can last. I also wrote to *you* (Pepe I spoke to you) asking *you* about

the situation and the occupation of the young man living in León. *You say
nothing. You* are right to keep quiet.'

This is also the case with *vuestras mercedes* > *ustedes*, which we find used both
in legal reports and in a letter to a brother (examples (15) and (16)) in which dramatic news is conveyed.

(15) vuestras mercedes/me sean testtigos cómo, aviéndole mandado al gobierno/
      que llevase preso a dicho Cárdenas, no quiso ovedezer, lo/qual se justtifica
      puestto que no está en dicha cárzel, antes/sí, como aziendo mofa y donaire
      de dichos mandattos,/se está, como ven vuestras mercedes, sentado en su
      puerta./ (Year 1716, Mexico, legal texts, CORDIAM)

      'I want you to be my witnessess that, although the government ordered
      him to detain Cárdenas, he refused to obey, which I can prove because he is
      not in jail. Instead, he is mocking and flouting the orders he received, he is
      sitting at his front door, as you can see.'

(16) Y a San Juan de Sahagún le pido encaresidamente me aiude para poderle
      mandar alguna cosa y vuestras mercedes se lo rogarán por mí./El cuñado
      de Pedro de Vega, llamado Manuel, se mantiene aquí conmigo. (Year 1737,
      Panama, correspondence, CORDIAM)

      'I beg San Juan de Sahagún to help me send you something. And I trust you
      will ask him in my name. Pedro de Vega's brother in law, called Miguel, is
      here with me.'

This analysis leads to the following five findings:
(a) It is reasonable to assume that in American Spanish there has always been
     (as there is today) basically a single space for plurality at the level of pro-
     nouns, expressed either through *vosotros* or through *vuestras mercedes* >
     ustedes, but that a *vosotros*/*ustedes* opposition never took root;
(b) This "non-division" of the space of plurality is explained by the difficult con-
     ditions of a homogeneous plurality that would justify a specialized pronoun
     of address;
(c) The "non-division" of the space of plurality is also explained by the very
     strong restrictions that existed in the 16th and 17th centuries on the use of
     familiar or closeness forms in Spanish, further limited by the communicative
     contexts in the Americas;
(d) It is possible that the use of *vosotros* was abandoned in everyday interaction
     in the 18th rather than in the 19th century;

(e) The remnants of *vosotros* use in the Americas can be explained because it is an old form, extinct in common speech and therefore more prestigious. As noted above, in the absence of good reasons to divide the space of plurality, it is reasonable to assume that the use of one of the two forms would decline.

6 Conclusion

In this chapter, I have explored theoretical, historiographical, and descriptive and explanatory issues. First, the theoretical issue involves questioning the idea that some systems of address are more balanced than others, in terms of the regularity of the parameters that explain the use of plural forms of address. I have argued that, due to homogeneity/heterogeneity problems, the divisions between the singular forms do not necessarily correspond to divisions between the plural forms.

Second, the historiographical issue lies in pointing out the research bias in the analysis of address – and most probably other linguistic phenomena – in American Spanish, whereby the Castilian system is taken as the norm. Third, in descriptive and explanatory terms, the disappearance of *vosotros* is not associated with the prestige of the speakers (Corominas' hypothesis); rather, it has to do with the *hypercritical* condition of the plurals in the communicative space of the Americas. I have also argued that a division of the plural based on social closeness and distance never took root in the Americas.

The data studied place the loss of *vosotros* in the 18th century and not in the 19th century (Moreno de Alba's hypothesis). These data correspond with those analyzed by Fernández Martín (2012) on the loss of the pronoun *vosotros* in western Andalusia in Spain.

As for the preservation of *vosotros* in formal discourse, the fact that *vosotros* and *ustedes* were two forms that competed for the space of plurality, with *vosotros* being the conservative form and *ustedes* the innovative form, explains why the former was chosen in formal and solemn contexts.

The explanation provided – namely, that in Hispanic America there was no division between plural address and that forms were contextually specialized – fully accounts for the two facts: loss of *vosotros* with only marginal traces of *vosotros* remaining.

References

Almasov, Alexey. 1974. *Vos* y *vosotros* as formal address in modern Spanish. *Hispania* 57,2. 304–310.

Bertolotti, Virginia. 2010. La gramaticalización de *usted*. Un cambio lingüístico en proceso. *Filologia e linguística portuguesa* 12,1. 149–177.

Bertolotti, Virginia. 2015. A mí de vos no me trata ni usted ni nadie. *Sistemas e historia de las formas de tratamiento en la lengua española en América*. Mexico City/Montevideo: UNAM/ UdelaR.

Brown, Roger & Albert Gilman. 1960. The pronouns of power and solidarity. In Thomas A. Sebeok (ed.), *Style in language*, 253–276. Cambridge: MIT Press.

Calderón Campos, Miguel. 2015. *El español del reino de Granada en sus documentos (1492–1833). Oralidad y escritura*. Bern: Peter Lang.

Caravedo, Rocío. 2005. La realidad subjetiva en el estudio del español de América. In Ingrid Neumann-Holzschuh, Volker Noll & Klaus Zimmermann (eds.), *El español en América. Aspectos teóricos, particularidades, contactos*, 17–32. Madrid/Frankfurt: Iberoamericana/Vervuert.

Carricaburo, Norma. 2015. *Las fórmulas de tratamiento en el español actual*. Second edition. Madrid: Arco/Libros.

Company Company, Concepción. 1997. El costo gramatical de las cortesías en el español americano. Consecuencias sintácticas de la pérdida de *vosotros*. *Anuario de Letras* 35. 167–191.

CORDIAM = Academia Mexicana de la Lengua. *Corpus Diacrónico y Diatópico del Español de América*. www.cordiam.org.

Corominas, Joan & Juan Antonio Pascual. 1983. *Diccionario crítico etimológico castellano e hispánico*. Madrid: Gredos.

De Jonge, Bob & Dorien Nieuwenhuijsen. 2009. *Formación del paradigma pronominal de las formas de tratamiento*. In Concepción Company Company (ed.), *Sintaxis histórica de la lengua española. Segunda parte: La frase nominal*, 1593–1671. Mexico City: Universidad Nacional Autónoma de México/Fondo de Cultura Económica.

Domínguez Hernández, Marlen. 2013. Tratamiento de *vos*/*vosotros* en una muestra de José Martí. *Moenia* 19. 481–495.

Fernández Martín, Elizabeth. 2012. *Vosotros*/*ustedes*. Estudios del tratamiento plural en el español dieciochesco. In María Teresa García Godoy (ed.), *El español del siglo XVIII. Cambios diacrónicos en el primer español moderno*, 153–194. Berlin: Peter Lang.

Fernández, Mauro & Katharina Gerhalter. 2017. Pronombres de segunda persona y formas de tratamiento en español. Una nueva bibliografía (1867–2016). *LinRed* 14. http://www. linred.es/numero14_info_2.html.

Fontanella de Weinberg, Beatriz. 1999. Sistemas pronominales de tratamiento usados en el mundo hispánico. In I. Bosque & V. Demonte (eds.), *Gramática descriptiva de la lengua Española*, vol. 1. Madrid: Espasa-Calpe. 1402–1452.

Frago Gracia, Juan Antonio. 2011. El español de América en la Independencia. Adiciones gramaticales. *Boletín de Filología* 46,1. 47–74.

García, Érica, Bob de Jonge, Dorien Nieuwenhuijsen & Carlos Lechner. 1990. (V)os-(otros): ¿dos y el mismo cambio? *Nueva Revista de Filología Hispánica* 38,1. 63–132.

Helmbrecht, Johannes. 2013. Politeness distinctions in pronouns. In *WALS. The World Atlas of Language Structures*. http://wals.info/feature/45A#2/25.7/137.

Isaza Calderón, Baltasar. 1976. La ausencia hispanoamericana del pronombre *vosotros* y de su concordancia verbal. In Baltazar Isaza Calderón (ed.), *El español de América: enfoques y perspectivas de futuro*, 47–49. Panama City: Editorial Universitaria.

Koch, Peter & Wulf Oesterreicher. 2007. *Lengua hablada en la Romania: español, francés, italiano*. Madrid: Gredos.

Lapesa, Rafael. 1981. *Historia de la lengua española*. Madrid: Gredos.

Lara, Víctor. 2010. *El uso de* ustedes *por* vosotros *en Andalucía occidental*. MA thesis. Madrid: Universidad Autónoma de Madrid.

Moreno de Alba, José. 2010. Notas sobre la cronología de la eliminación de *vosotros* en América. In Rosa María Castañer Martín & Vicente Lagüéns Gracia (eds.), *De moneda nunca usada: Estudios dedicados a José Mª Enguita Utrilla*, 461–470. Zaragoza: Institución Fernando el Católico.

Moreno de Alba, José. 2011. Sobre la eliminación del pronombre *vosotros* en el español americano. *Lingüística*. 25–39.

Moreno, María Cristobalina. 2006. La sociolingüística de los pronombres de tratamiento con referente plural en los siglos XVI y XVII. In José Jesús Bustos Tovar & José Luis Girón Alconchel (eds.), *Actas del VI Congreso Internacional de Historia de la Lengua Española*, vol. 3, 281–289. Madrid: Arco/Libros.

Morgan, Terrell A. & Scott A. Schwenter. 2016. Vosotros, ustedes, and the myth of the symmetrical Castilian pronoun system. In Alejandro Cuza, Lori Czerwionka & Daniel Olson (eds.), *Inquiries in Hispanic linguistics. From theory to empirical* evidence, 263–280. Amsterdam/New York: John Benjamins.

Nieuwenhuijsen, Dorien. 2006. *Vosotros*: surgimiento y pérdida de un pronombre en perspectiva diacrónica y diatópica. In José Jesús Bustos Tovar & José Luis Girón Alconchel (eds.), *Actas del VI Congreso Internacional de Historia de la Lengua Española*, vol. 1, 949–960. Madrid: Arco/Libros.

Nowikow, Wiaczesław. 1994. Sobre la pluralización de personas gramaticales en las lenguas románicas: *nos, vos/nos alteros, vos alteros. Anuario de lingüística hispánica* 10. 283–300.

Obediente Sosa, Enrique. 2013. Discurso de incorporación como "Individuo de Número" de la Academia Venezolana de la Lengua. *Lengua y habla* 13. 267–288.

Obediente Sosa, Enrique. 2011. Uso de *vosotros* en la historia del español de Venezuela. In José Luis Ramírez Luengo (ed.), *Por sendas ignoradas. Estudios sobre el español del siglo* XIX, 131–143. Lugo: Axac.

Oesterreicher, Wulf. 1996. Lo hablado en lo escrito. Reflexiones metodológicas y aproximación a una tipología. In Thomas Kotschi, Wulf Oesterreicher & Klaus Zimmermann (eds.), *El español hablado y la cultura oral en España e Hispanoamérica*, 317–340. Frankfurt/Madrid: Vervuert/Iberaomericana.

Penny, Ralph. 2004. *Variación y cambio en español*. Madrid: Gredos.

Penny, Ralph. 2005. *Gramática histórica del español*. Barcelona: Ariel.

RAE-ASALE. Real Academia Española/Asociación de Academias de la Lengua Española. 2009. *Nueva gramática de la lengua española*. Madrid: Espasa-Calpe.

Rona, José Pedro. 2014 [1958]. Aspectos metodológicos de la dialectología hispanoamericana. In Adolfo Elizaincín (ed.), *José Pedro Rona. Dialectología general e hispanoamericana*, 99–163. Montevideo: Ministerio de Educación y Cultura.

Siciliano, Ernest. 1971. The *vosotros* form again. *Hispania* 54,4. 915–916.

Zimmermann, Klaus. 2011. La construcción de la historia del español de América: propuestas y análisis crítico. *Cuadernos de ALFAL* 2. 8–24.

Philipp Dankel and Miguel Gutiérrez Maté

Vuestra atención, por favor 'your attention, please'. Some remarks on the usage and history of plural *vuestro/a* in Cusco Spanish (Peru)

Abstract: This chapter documents and explains the use of the possessive form *vuestro/a* 'your-PL' in Cusco Spanish. This phenomenon, which has gone mostly unnoticed by scholars so far, is very unusual in American Spanish. We distinguish between a formulaic use (e.g. *vuestra atención, por favor*) and a highly productive strategic one, which highlights a contrastive relationship between the actions/states of the plural addressee and those from the group in which the speaker positions himself. We then discuss three hypotheses on the origins of *vuestro/a* in Cusco Spanish related to colonial and early post-independence Spanish, examine the role of a notional transfer (Quechua → Spanish) and contextualize this development within the frame of *Cusqueño* society and its idiosyncratic *mestizo* identity.

Keywords: pronouns of address, cultural contact, notional transfer, possessives, linguistic identity, Andean Spanish

1 Introduction

The aim of this chapter is to provide a complete description of the use of the possessive form *vuestro/a* 'your-PL' in Cusco Spanish (Peru) and a tentative explanation about its origins (in tackling this problem, we will take a holistic approach). Every Spanish-speaking visitor to the city of Cusco (or its surrounding area) will wonder at the occasional use of *vuestro/a* instead of *su* (as expected from American Spanish) in contexts like *deseamos agradecerles por **vuestra** comunicación* 'we wish to thank you for *your* communication', in a local radio program, or

Note: We would like to thank the participants of the *Linguistisches Kolloquium* at the University of Erlangen-Nuremberg (21 January 2016) and the participants of the Workshop on *Spanish as a pluricentric language* at the Freiburg Research Institute for Advanced Studies (FRIAS), University of Freiburg (23-24 February 2017), for their comments and productive criticism on the core ideas presented in this chapter. Furthermore, we thank Lilli Geyer-Schuch for her help in compiling and preparing the corpus for this study and Christine Wabersich for her proofreading and formatting. Last but not least, we thank Lawrence Davies for patiently correcting our non-native English.

espero que haya sido de **vuestro** *agrado* 'I hope it has been to your liking', in the mouth of a tourist guide. This use has remained unstudied so far, and it seems to be only Caravedo (1996: 161, 2005: 28–29) and Rivarola (2005: 36) who mention it by making passing references to its presence in the Cusco area in highly formal or ceremonial contexts like public speeches or sermons.

This chapter will fill this gap by analyzing the different uses of *vuestro/a* in today's Cusco Spanish. It is based on a corpus of 23 hours of spoken interaction, recorded from local radio and TV stations between September 2016 and January 2017, as well as on a collection of 12 hours of YouTube videos, posted by local TV stations and official institutions between 2006 and 2017 (with the majority from 2014). The text types include moderated discussions, call-in programs, commercials, interviews, documentaries, press conferences, discussions and public speeches. They are all spoken texts, but following Koch & Oesterreicher's terminology, they tend to be characterized by *communicative distance* (Koch & Oesterreicher 1985, 2001, 2011, see below). As selection criteria, we determined that the different formats needed to be local productions from the Cusco region with local participants and largely addressed to a local audience. This empirical basis was complemented by a selection of written examples taken from Peruvian internet forums; despite the fact that such texts are not essentially formal and may even get closer to *communicative immediacy*, most instances of *vuestro/a* correspond to cases in which the writer still maintains a certain level of formality.[1] Finally, we present a diachronic explanation of the various uses of *vuestro/a* that relates them not only to some uses well attested throughout colonial texts but also to language contact and specific sociocultural factors.

In what follows, we will consider this 'formal *vuestro/a*' to be primarily related to linguistic varieties (in a general way, speech styles, but see below) and to discursive aspects (more precisely, the expression of contrast, which we understand here as a semantic category that is actually shaped discursively and is continuously updated as the linguistic interaction between speaker/s and hearer/s progresses). "Deference" may certainly play a role in the usage of *vuestro/a*, since this takes place in speech acts that actually show respect to the addressee, including some "intrinsically polite speech acts" like giving thanks (Haverkate 1994), but the preference of *vuestro/a* over *su* is rather a question of linguistic varieties. Its selection is the result of the adaptation of actual speech to the sit-

---

1 These examples were accessed via the *RomWeb* Corpus, compiled by Stefan Pfänder and his team for the project *Pf699/4-RomWeb Spanisch in den Anden und Französisch in Westafrika als Kontaktvarietäten unter den Bedingungen globalisierter und computergestützter Kommunikation* (funded by the DFG). As an associate member of the research group, one of the authors has access to this database.

uation in which the conversation takes place; more specifically, it depends on factors such as the public character of the speech, the distance between speaker and hearer (they usually don't know each other), the fixed character of the conversation (with little room for improvisation, or for switching quickly from one conversational topic to another) – in other words, on those factors that constitute the so-called *language of distance* (as defined by the above-mentioned German tradition of Koch & Oesterreicher (2011: 7), which goes far beyond the selection of the appropriate second person (2P) pronouns). We are aware, however, that there are some overlapping areas between the non-structural dimension of "formality" and the semantic/pragmatic category "deference", since both are determined contextually, but nothing justifies the intertwining of variationist and semantic – that is, structural – criteria for our linguistic descriptions. In other words, we do not consider *vuestro/a* to be necessarily more or less "polite" than *su*, which can convey both solidarity and politeness as much in Cusco as elsewhere in Hispanic America; we consider that *vuestro/a* fits better than *su* into some formal contexts that we will define and illustrate in this chapter. In one sense, however, formality is combined with semantics and especially with referentiality, since the use of *vuestro/a* is often related to the expression of contrast between speech act participants.

The chapter is structured as follows: Section 2 will present two different uses of *vuestro/a* that are common in Cusco Spanish – the strategic use being the most striking – and discuss them against the background of other reported uses of *vuestro/a* in the specialist literature, whereas Section 3 will be devoted to their possible origins. In this section, we will bring to the fore some general aspects of the history of American Spanish, including some methodological problems, and will formulate three hypotheses about the origin of *vuestro/a* in Cusco Spanish. These will need to be checked against more colonial texts in future research, as the size and availability of historical corpora continues to increase. We will postulate that several factors may have contributed altogether to the maintenance of *vuestro/a* in Cusco Spanish. Section 4 will account for the productivity of the use of *vuestro/a* and the fact that this seems to be restricted to the Cusco region. Section 4.1 will deal with language contact and introduce the concept of discursive or *notional transfer*; more specifically, we suggest that the kind of contrast that is regularly conveyed by means of the inclusive/exclusive distinction in Quechua – with a clear discourse structuring role in this language – kept being expressed by means of the distinction between different plural address forms in Spanish. Section 4.2 will relate the linguistic feature analyzed here, and more generally the linguistic idiosyncrasy of Cusco, to the idiosyncrasy of *Cusqueño* society and the shaping of its specific identity. Finally, a summary of the major findings will close the chapter.

2 The specificity of *vuestro/a* in Cusco Spanish

2.1 Formulaic vs. strategic uses

The possessive *vuestro/a* 'your', which, etymologically, belongs to the paradigm of *vos*, was brought to colonial Spanish America with both a singular and a plural meaning. However, the singular form was replaced by *tu* quite quickly (Díaz Collazos 2016) in those regions making use of the so-called *voseo* (i.e. the use of SG *vos* instead of *tú*) and the plural form was replaced by *su* everywhere in Hispanic America (and in the Canary Islands and some parts of Andalusia) at some point in the late colonial era (see Section 3 for further historical details). Consequently, the phenomenon analyzed here cannot be related to *voseo*, which is not even found in the Cusco region, even though it is widespread in many parts of Hispanic America (Bertolotti 2015: 281). In addition, the use of *vuestro/a* in Cusco is not reminiscent of that of European Spanish either. In Spain, it is integrated into the grammatical paradigm of the pronoun *vosotros* 'you-PL', which conveys solidarity as opposed to *ustedes* 'you-PL', which conveys politeness (Fontanella de Weinberg 1999). In Cusco, *vuestro/a* is always integrated into the paradigm of *ustedes*, so it neither combines with the object clitic *os* nor with the verb endings *-áis/éis*, which are never attested in Cusco (nor anywhere else in Hispanic America) with a plural meaning, except in some liturgical and ceremonial discourses (see Section 2.2).

In addition, *vuestro/a* is always attested in the function of a determiner in Cusco Spanish (it does not seem to be possible as a pronoun, e.g. **el vuestro, *las vuestras*). Even so, it is quantitatively far less frequent than the possessive *su*, which belongs etymologically to the paradigm of *ustedes*. *Vuestro/a* is attested before abstract nouns such as *preferencia, comunicación, presencia*, being mostly restricted to formulaic expressions such as *vuestra atención, por favor* 'your attention, please', *con vuestro permiso* 'with your permission', *gracias por vuestra deferencia* 'thank you for your deference', that can be heard in formal public speeches with a plural addressee. These uses consist of routinized speech acts that serve mostly as a phatic signal, as the expression of gratitude, as farewell, and so on.[2] The following examples illustrate this formulaic *vuestro/a*. Example (1) is taken from a pre-recorded sign-off of a radio program, a fixed formula, untied to any specific speech event which would allow for spontaneous composition and production. Example (2) contains the words that an Indigenous leader addresses to

---

2 Therefore, it could also be described as the fixed part of a partially schematic construction in the sense of construction grammar (e.g. Croft 2001; Goldberg 1995, 2003; Hopper 2004) with restricted productivity in the noun-slot.

other members of the community during a protest demonstration, where part of the demonstration was the raising of the Cusco flag as a symbolic move, which is announced by the speaker (taken from an uncommented livestream of CTC television). The formality of his speech is clearly instantiated by him from the very beginning by addressing the various groups of authorities with *señores* 'gentlemen'.

(1) 06 H: erre ese a: n:oTIcias[3]
    07 Com: <<music>>
    08 H: <<music fading out> red de comunicaciones ANTA> noticias
    09 Com: <<music>>
    10 H: <<music in the background> GRAcias por **vuestra** preferencia (-)
    11   dios mediante (.) ha:sta la próxima>
    12 Com: <<music>>
    13 H: <<music in the background> la mejor música variada>
    11   EN RAdio IMPACTO
    12   <<percussion in the background> PA:ra TO:do el SUR:>

'RSA-news, communication network ANTA-news, thank you for **your** preference [= thank you for choosing us]! God willing, see you next time. The best mixed music in Radio IMPACTO for all the South'

(2) 02 S: °°señores°° (-)
    03   señores autoridades (--)
    04   señores_e:h dirigentes (--)
    05   señores_e:h (---)
    06   maestros (.) kuraxkuna varayuxkuna (1.2)
    07   pueblo en general/ (--)
    08   con **vuestro** permiso (--)
    09   vamos a hacer (-)
    10   el izamiento (-)
    11   del pabellón de nuestro bandera del tawantinsuyu/ (-)
    12   que va corresponder/ (.)

'Gentlemen! Authorities, directors, teachers, superior and community authorities, people in general! With **your** permission, we are going to raise the flag of our banner of tawantinsuyu, which will be appropriate'

---

3 Transcription conventions can be found at the end.

However, the use of *vuestro/a* in Cusco Spanish goes far beyond this kind of formulaic expression. Always used in formal speech, it is also possible whenever the speaker wants to make clear the contrast between the actions of the plural addressee (indicated by *vuestro*) and those of the group in which the speaker positions himself (usually indicated by *nosotros* or *nuestro*). We are going to call this use, which turns out to be especially productive, contrastive or strategic. Example (3) is taken from a press conference of the regional government. In the excerpt, the governor opens the floor for questions after welcoming the audience and reading his statements.

```
(3)  01 C:  señores perioDIstas (1.3)
     02      estamos resueltos (.) nosotros (.) a respondER (-)
     03      a vuestras iniciaTIvas (-)
     04      a vuestras interroGANtes (--)
     05      que lo haREmos (-) en las mejores instancias
             posibles
     06      muchísimas gracias
```

'Ladies and Gentlemen of the media, we are determined to respond to **your** initiatives, **your** questions, which we will do in the best possible way. Thank you so much'

The speaker (the regional governor) makes this public appearance to report to the public opinion that the attendant media stand in for. The subject pronoun in line 02 *nosotros* 'we/us' is not only placed in the postverbal position – itself considered to be especially prominent for subjects in Spanish (Adli 2011) – but also appears right-dislocated, both syntactically and phonetically (between pauses). The use of *vuestras* shortly after (lines 03-04) complements this (contrastive) emphatic use. Even within the general willingness to help, we could still catch a glimpse of defiance or, at least, self-sufficiency in these words. Interestingly, although the use of *vuestro/a* in this case clearly surpasses the kind of formulaic expressions we saw in the first examples, its appearance at the end of the governor's turn, that is, at the transition point to the questions section, still resembles the formulaic use at the end of leave-taking sequences, yet it gained a lot more combinatorial autonomy.[4]

---

4 The same observation is true for some other cases in our data. The placement of strategic *vuestro/a* in leave-taking (or opening) sequences is certainly not by chance. Hence, as regards its syntactic distribution, this use might consist of an intersection between the formulaic and the strategic use. We cannot go deeply into these questions, but further diachronic research on this

In other cases, speakers try to distance themselves from the hearers – from the groups that the latter belong to or from what these groups represent – by using *vuestro/a* in contexts that are anything but formulaic. The following examples are taken from internet forums. In example (4) we notice the contrast of the speaker's family rules with those of the hearer, accused of belonging to a new generation of Peruvian youngsters who lack respect for their parents (*vuestra casa* vs. *mi familia*). In example (5) the reading is markedly exclusive: not only does the speaker distance himself from the hearers' states and/or actions, as in many other examples, but he also points out the fact that the hearers have to do something by themselves (*por ustedes mismas*):

(4) O sea que por que tu papá es viejito y te llama la atención le metes un ******
a viva voz y lo mandas callar, pues no se como [*sic*] funciona en **vuestras**
casas, pero en **mi familia** la palabra de los padres se respeta_así uno sea
presidente de la república los padres son los padres, y ese respeto intrínseco
e inalienable se mantiene hasta el último minuto de sus vidas, así me criaron
vertical. (Motorheadperu, 2008-09-15, 09:37:00; www.forosenperu.com)

'So just because your dad is old and reprimands you, you give him a loud
******* and make him shut up? Well, I don't know how it works in **your**
homes, but in **my family** the parent's words are respected, even if one is
the republic's president! Parents are parents, and that kind of essential and
inalienable respect must be maintained until the very last minute of our
lives. I was raised this way'

(5) Ahora, ¿en qué contexto es asesinado Pedro Huillca?, bueno ésa es una tarea
que te dejo a ti y a Nike para que la desarrollen fuera de las aulas de **vuestras**
universidades, pero, háganla racionalmente como si estuvieran preparando
vuestras tesis **por uds. mismas** (no vayan a Wilson)... (Tanotelo, 2008-03-
18, 19:25:00; www.forosperu.net)

'Now, in which context was Pedro Huillca murdered? Well, this is a task I'd
better leave you and Nike to carry out outside **your** university classes, but...
do it rationally, as if you were preparing **your** doctoral theses **by yourselves**
(don't ask Wilson)'

---

topic may be interesting to the extent that it relates to constructionalization and constructional
change (e.g. Smirnova 2015).

It has to be noted that the contrast between speech act participants conveyed by the strategic use of *vuestro/a* can adopt very different nuances in discourse. Sometimes, for instance, setting up some kind of confrontation at the beginning (lines 07 and 08 in example (6)) is used as a rhetorical discourse strategy and is therefore just a means to emphasize the consensus reached at the end. In example (6), a commissioner of the *Dirección General de Comercio Exterior y Turismo* publicly thanks the managers of several companies dedicated to regional tourism. Here, the contrast between the hearers and the organization that the speaker represents is used strategically to pave the way to the conclusion that they are all in the same business and share the same interests (at the end of the example, *nuestro sector* 'our sector' is intended to mean 'the sector of all of us'). Thus, *vuestro/a* is part of a rhetorical strategy by which the speaker begins by delimiting two different groups – which also allows him to praise the efforts made by the addressed group – and goes on to highlight the collaboration between speakers and hearers (line 12) – clearly trying to strengthen it for the future.

(6) 01 P: seGUro estoy/ (-)
    02   que durante TOdo el año/ (1.1)
    03   han hecho esfuerzos (.) INcreíbles
    04   dentro del sector priVAdo (1.3)
    05   con esos dine::ros (.)
    06   de poco a po:co (--)
    07   han ido construYENdo (.) **VUEStras** empresas en faVOR del turismo (--)
    08   y en faVOR (.) de **VUEStras** familias (---)
    09   el día de hoy/ (-)
    10   la dirección/ (1.0)
    11   tiene un ÚNico proposito (--)
    12   REconocER ESE esFUERzo que hacen (.) TOdos los días por nuestro sector\ (1.2)

'I am sure that you have made incredible efforts in the private sector throughout the whole year. With this money, bit by bit, you have been building **your** businesses for tourism and for **your** families. Today, the management has only one goal: recognizing this effort you are making every day for our sector'

As opposed to examples (1) and (2), and partially to example (3) (compare fn. 4), examples (4) to (6) provide clear evidence that *vuestro/a* can be placed outside of leave-taking or turn-final expressions. This illustrates its emancipation in Cusco

Spanish from the formulaic use which has occasionally been (and might still be) observed in some other parts of Hispanic America, though this is much more restricted. Thus, before we go any further in analyzing both formulaic and strategic *vuestro/a* in terms of their potential origins, some remarks are necessary in order to make clear the specificity of these uses when compared to other varieties of American Spanish. In the following sub-section, we will therefore describe the geolinguistic and diachronic background of plural address forms in Hispanic America. We will then identify the sources that served as discourse patterns in Cusco and determine which historical processes have shaped the use of a linguistic form that, etymologically, belongs to the paradigm of *vos(otros)*. All in all, these considerations will prevent us from simplistic, aprioristic explanations about the history of *vuestro/a* and make our subsequent proposal about Cusco Spanish more understandable.

2.2 *Other uses of* vuestro/a *reported in the literature on American Spanish*

Cusco Spanish is not the only variety in Hispanic America making use of *vuestro/a*. Yet, the specificity of the phenomenon we analyze in this contribution clearly stands out – in both frequency and quality – among the uses of the same form in other varieties.

Firstly, we have to note that *vuestro/a* in address formulae such as *Vuestra Señoría* 'Your Honor', *Vuestra Excelencia* 'Your Excellency', was an integral part of the very first Hispanic American parliamentary interactions (Vázquez Laslop 2012: 136) and can still be found in some institutional contexts (Fontanella de Weinberg 1999: 1419). However, in these uses, it is not a real referential possessive, that is, a possessive that relates the hearer to something that is possessed, but a part of a lexicalized deictic expression ("possessive + noun") used to directly address the hearer. Regarding possessive *vuestro/a* in Cusco, this means that we cannot rule out the possibility that these formulae had contributed to keeping the possessive form more accessible to speakers than any other form from the paradigm of *vosotros*. In point of fact, we do not yet completely understand why the possessive form is somewhat productive, whereas nothing remains from all of the other forms (i.e. the free pronoun *vosotros*, the object clitic *os* and the verbal endings *-á(i)s/-é(i)s*) – the functional characterization of possessives itself accounting only for part of the whole picture.[5]

---

5 We assume possessives to have a complex meaning: a relational one (linking the possessed to the possessor) and a deictic one (referring to the possessor), whereas free pronouns are only

Secondly, we have to pay special attention to the data presented by Bertolotti (2007) for Uruguay and by Wagner (1996/1997) for Chile. The latter points out the use of *vuestro/a* in formal contexts such as *Señor director: Junto con saludarlo solicito a Ud. publicar mi carta en vuestro diario* 'To the Director: Dear Sir, besides greeting you, I beg you to publish my letter in your newspaper'.[6] These uses are quite close to our formulaic one, but, in these examples, we can find *vuestro/a* with both a plural and a singular meaning (in fact, according to the diachronic explanation of Bertolotti 2007: 38–39, *vuestro/a* was first integrated into the paradigm of the SG deferential pronoun *usted* and expanded later as a plural form), whereas SG *vuestro/a* is never attested in Cusco.[7]

Finally, some exceptional examples presented by Morgan & Schwenter (2016) are also of special interest, for example in a Chilean greeting card for a wedding, which on the outside says *Mil Felicidades en **Vuestro*** [emphasis added] *Matrimonio* 'Congratulations on *your* Marriage' but inside switches to *su*: *Que la vida que hoy inician traiga a **su*** [emphasis added] *hogar la alegría de un sueño compartido* 'I hope the life you start today will bring your home the happiness of a shared dream'. The use of *vuestro/a* in Cusco, however, is not only restricted to a few specific discourse traditions but seems instead to be accessible to any educated speaker under formal circumstances.

The abovementioned uses of *vuestro/a* have usually been related to an extra nuance of formality – as opposed to *su* – and especially to semantic disambiguation. Whatever historical factors account for the use of *vuestro/a* in the Cusco region (see Section 3), speakers may have actually wanted to take some advantage of it in order to avoid the referential ambiguity of possessive *su*, which can indeed refer to *él/ella* (3SG), *usted* (2SG, V), *ellos/ellas* (3PL) and *ustedes* (2PL,

---

deictic, and object clitics and verbal endings are strictly grammatical (agreement markers). To the extent that possessives/relationals are not as grammatical (nor as formally bound) as, for instance, verbal endings, they are more easily perceived by speakers and therefore could be more easily adapted from other varieties (i.e. replaced by the corresponding forms in these varieties) (compare Hypothesis 2) or, for the very same reason, more easily retained (compare Hypothesis 1) – see Section 3.

6 Wagner (1996/1997: 855, 859) argues that the use of *vuestro/a* is a recent innovation, but he does not attempt to check this hypothesis diachronically, and it does not seem consistent with what we know about other Spanish varieties (as depicted by Bertolotti 2007).

7 From a synchronic point of view, it seems plausible to think that the formal resemblance of 1PL *nuestro/a* and 2P *vuestro/a* makes somewhat more natural the plural interpretation of the latter as well. This is especially the case if we accept that the usage of *vuestro/a* is not restricted to routinized speech acts and formulaic expressions (in this respect, we could still think that speakers can rely on another archetypical use of SG *vuestro/a*, the one in singular address formulae like *Vuestra Señoría*, with which they might associate any innovative use of *vuestro/a*).

T&V).[8] The other method for disambiguation is the reduplication of the possessor by a prepositional phrase "*de* + SN", as in *su casa de usetedes* (Fontanella de Weinberg 1999: 1403). As a matter of fact, this would not be the first time that the paradigm of third person pronouns in American Spanish has been considered to be functionally overloaded and, consequently, a place where linguistic change can occur more quickly. For example, the referential ambiguity of the clitic *se* has been pointed out as the main trigger for the overt marking of plural agreement between the object clitic *lo* and the lexical dative, as in the example *ya se los dije (a ustedes)* 'I already told you (2PL)'(Company Company 1997). However, since our historical knowledge about *vosotros/ustedes* in Hispanic America is quite limited (see further discussion below), we cannot even decide whether avoiding referential ambiguity was really a trigger for linguistic change (contributing to the spread of *vuestro/a* at some point when it might have been reinserted in the language; see Section 3, Hypothesis 3) or rather an obstacle for linguistic change (here, the alleged overgeneralization of *ustedes* over *vosotros*). In the latter case, *vuestro/a* should then be considered a linguistic remnant of the colonial era.

Be that as it may, referential ambiguity is by no means the main factor accounting for the presence of *vuestro/a* in Cusco Spanish, but may have helped it take root, especially in the case of the strategic or contrastive use. This is because disambiguation also conveys an intrinsically contrastive relationship between the real referent and the other potential referents; in fact, both categories have been traditionally considered alongside one other to explain some uses of emphatic personal pronouns like overt subject pronouns in Spanish (Gili Gaya 1993: 228–229). However, *vuestro/a* in Cusco Spanish keeps standing out inasmuch as it is mostly used to emphasize the psychological distance with 1PL *nuestro/a* (be this explicit or just somehow prominent in discourse) and not with the persons that *su* can potentially refer to.

One last aprioristic explanation of the success of *vuestro/a* in Cusco should be precluded. To the best of our knowledge, the alternation between different 2PL pronouns in Spanish has never been clearly related to the semantic category of "clusivity" (Simon 2005),[9] as attested in some languages that distinguish between two kinds of plural addressees: the hearers that the speaker is directly talking to

---

8 We follow the well-known convention of Brown & Gilman (1960), according to which T stands for address forms meaning proximity/solidarity and V stands for address forms meaning distance/politeness.

9 Eberenz (2000) is aware of these two possible meanings of 2PL pronouns. Even though it may seem, at first, quite intuitive to postulate such a semantic difference in order to account for the alternation between *vos* 'you-PL' and *vos otros* (lit. 'you (and) others' in Late Middle Age Spanish), the linguistic data do not support such a hypothesis (Eberenz 2000: 74-83).

(or even watching) during his/her speech act (exclusive reading) and the hearers as a semantic class, i.e. being associated with other people that the speaker considers he/she shares some properties with (generalizing or inclusive reading), as when a teacher speaks to his/her students, referring not only to them but also to any student in general. There is nothing in our data about Cusco Spanish suggesting such a relation either. Clusivity will play an important role in our argument, but this will be related to the inclusion of the speaker him/herself and not to the inclusion of absent addressees.

Consequently, until otherwise proven, we will continue to consider the usage of *vuestro/a* in the Cusco region to be unique in Spanish dialectology, even more clearly as regards its strategic use. Perhaps we should mention, however, that the example below from Fontanella de Weinberg (1999: 1404) rendering the words of the governor of Tucumán (Argentina) resembles our examples from Cusco:

> He bajado para dar la cara y hablar con ustedes como corresponde. Quiero manifestarles mi absoluta solidaridad con **vuestra** situación.
> 'I came down to face up to you and talk to you as it is good custom. I want to express my absolute solidarity with your situation'

3 Why was *vuestro/a* preserved in/brought to Cusco? Three diachronic hypotheses

Second person plural pronouns are notoriously understudied in Hispanic Linguistics, as they certainly are in many other linguistic traditions. The prevalence of both synchronic and diachronic studies about singular forms of address in the specialized literature is overwhelming. As regards Historical Linguistics, this problem may relate, amongst other factors, to the fact that 2PL forms are not so easy to find in historical sources (for instance, if we seek for private letters in the archives, we will predominantly find texts with a singular addressee). Thus, it is important to note that we still lack precise knowledge about the specific functions of the several competing 2PL pronouns during the whole colonial era. Linguists would therefore do well to ask themselves if there was ever really a clearcut distinction between T and V within the 2PL pronouns in colonial Spanish America, as there is in today's Spain (but see Morgan & Schwenter 2016). At least for now, there is no evidence supporting this claim and it seems to be, again, speech styles – perhaps alongside variation in speech acts – that have played an important role in the history of *vosotros* and *ustedes*, both during the colonial era and after independence.

As for the nominative pronouns, we know that there were five different forms throughout long periods of the colonial era. Indeed, we find not only *vosotros* and *ustedes* – the latter is documented in colonial texts in 1662 for the first time – as a plural of singular *vos* (Gutiérrez Maté 2013: 262), but three more forms: (1) plural *vos* (i.e. the form without -*otros*), which is still attested in the 17th century, even though its use has been sometimes considered to be marginal since the late 15th century (Eberenz 2000: 59, 75, 79); (2) third person plural *ellos/as* used for addressing (Gutiérrez Maté 2013: 254); and (3) *vuestras mercedes* (the etymological source of the newer pronoun *ustedes*) which did not disappear immediately after *ustedes* appeared).

PL *vos* seems to function as a variant of *vosotros*, which was used much more frequently in the colonial texts. In Huamán Poma we find some fragments in direct speech with both *vos* and *vosotros*. In example (7) the author is rendering what an *encomendero*[10] said to a group of Indians:

(7) **Bos**, curacas, a **buestro** padre y comendero aués de oyrme. Bibamos bien que el padre y corregidor, soy más mejor. Soys **bosotros** del conquistador mi padre. Y ací me aués de dar china y muchacho yanacona para que en las estancias hagáys bu[e]nas paredes y hagáys casas y me deys yndios ganaderos, pastores. (Huamán Poma 1615, Ch. 26, f. 713, Ed. of R. Navarro Gala 2000. CORDIAM).

'**You**, Indian chiefs, you have to listen to me as **your** father and *encomendero*. Let's live well, because I am better than a father and a magistrate. **You** belong to my father the Conqueror. That is why you have to give me servants who make good walls in the *estancias* and good houses and you have to give me Indians for work as ranchers and shepherds.'

The variety illustrated here can be considered very close to that of Cusco (see also example (8a)).

The use of each pronoun must have undergone some kind of social and/or discursive specialization, but there was also some space for interchangeability, an *envelope of variation* (Labov 1994) that has remained undescribed to this day. Let us consider two excerpts (examples (8a) and (8b)) from a Colombian document (written in Cartagena de Indias, 1694), which consists of the court order against a freed mixed heritage slave (*mulato*) supposed to have conspired with Black slaves

---

10 In the colonial period, the *encomendero* was the holder of a plot of land granted by the king, the so-called *encomienda*. The grant also included a given number of Indigenous people supposed to work for the *encomendero*.

against the local authorities (this unedited document is partially transcribed and commented in Gutiérrez Maté 2013: 463–473). In both cases, the scribe renders what the *mulato* admits to have said to a group of Black slaves. Thus, the speaker and the addressees are the same in both cases, and so is the general speech act (advice – more specifically, advice to stay quiet – even though it is mixed with a reproval in the first case and with a commissive act in the second):

(8) a. PL **vos** → ¡no **seáis** locos! ¡**quitáos** de eso! porque **vos tenéis** buen amo y si **avéis** de ser libres, a de ser cuando Dios quiera.

'Don't be silly and forget about it! Because you have a good master and if you are supposed to get your freedom sometime, it will just be when God wants it.'

  b. **ustedes** → ¡no es tiempo aora de esso! yo avisaré a **ustedes**.

'This is not the right time for it! I will let you know'

The possessive referential system consisted of only two forms: *su* (the possessive form of the free variants *ustedes*, *vuestras mercedes* and *ellos/as*) and *vuestro/a* (the possessive form of *vosotros* and PL *vos*). However, if we consider examples (8a) and (8b), we can also expect the same kind of (almost free) variation to happen as regards possessives.

Recent research tends to concede that *ustedes* was never marked for formality in colonial Spanish (Bertolotti, in this volume, 309, 311). In fact, even SG *usted* seems to have been used for a wide spectrum of functions that do not always fit well into the general label of "formality" since it is first documented in 17th century American Spanish (Gutiérrez Maté 2013: 251–253; Moser 2010). Likewise, we do not know either to what (if any) extent *vosotros* was ever really marked for "solidarity". Even though it is obvious that at some point in the history of American Spanish – most notably during the first decades of the 20th century – *ustedes* finally positioned itself as the only plural pronoun of address (with the exceptions explained above), the use of *vosotros* may have been very different from what we find in current European Spanish. Consequently, the alleged "neutralization" of T and V in the plural may have never happened in American Spanish (see also García Godoy 2012: 130–131, 140).

In what follows, we will introduce three potential diachronic explanations, without expressing a preference for any of them. They are, to some extent, compatible with one another but none of them (not even all three altogether) would on its own be enough to account for the success of *vuestro/a* in Cusco without paying attention to language contact and to the cultural aspects that will be outlined in Section 4.

3.1 Hypothesis 1: The use of PL vuestro/a results from its resistance to the overgeneralization/paradigmaticization of ustedes, possibly after SG vuestro/a had resisted the paradigmaticization of tú for some time

The scarcity of texts showing references to a plural addressee leads us first to take a look at 2SG pronouns in other texts that were written in colonial Cusco. Here, what stands out most is the frequent use of SG *vuestro/a*. Let us consider the following private letter (example (9)) written by a father to his daughter in 1655 (the linguistic forms belonging to the paradigm of *tú* are in italics, while those belonging to SG *vos* are in bold):

(9) Hija de mi corasón: Holgaréme en el alma ésta *te* alle con mui entera salud. La mía es buena para seruir*te* en todo lo que me **quisiéredes** mandar. Digo, hija mía Vrsula de Orellana, *te* doi parte y auisso de que **vuestro** marido al cabo de quinse años a venido a mi cassa a pedirme perdón, que le ha corrido [sic!] tantas desdichas, deue de ser permissión de Dios, pues que por mis puertas se dentró con **vuestro** padrino que *te* cassó, Mateo Arenas, señora Catalina Salinas, *tu* madrina, y assí quiero por uida **buestra** qu[e] *estés* con cuidado, que no me *des* más pesadumbres que las que me *as dado*. Como están cogiendo gente para Chile, por esso quiere ir **vuestro** marido a buscar*te*, si Dios le da salud. Si acasso *te* succediere algo, que ai va el nombre del cura que *te* cassó, don Pedro Cisneros, cura de la yglecia mayor del Cusco. Por la Virgen que *estés* con cuidado; e sauido como muxer fráxil *ayas caído* en alguna desdicha. **Guardaos**, por uida **vuestra**, que me tienes avejentado con las cosas que e [oí]do [de] **vuestra** madre Juana Quispe. *Tu* hermano se metió en San Juan de Dios, el otro *tu* hermano quiere ir a buscar*te*. Ya se fue a Copacabana Antonio Emandes, **vuestro** marido: si acasso *te* hallare **vuestro** marido **agasajaldo** qu'es *tu* espos[o], por la virgen santissima, que los arrieros que venían de Lima me decían que *[e]stauas* [...] no *tenías* **vos** la culpa sino es yo que *te* auía echo cassar tan criatura y assi *te* pido no m[e] eches maldición en algún trabaxo, que yo quissiera allarme en algún lado **vuestro** para seruir*te* como hixa mía con lo que vbiere. *Escríbe*me en el primer chasque, a veinte y ciete de dicienbre escreví esta carta de 1655, y con esto a Dios que *te* me guarde Dios muchos años./A mi hija Vrsula de Orillana. *(Ed. of J.L. Rivarola 2009, Documentos lingüísticos del Perú. Siglos XVI y XVII. Edición y comentario. CORDIAM)*

'Beloved Daughter of My Heart: My soul will become relieved if this letter gets to *you* in good health. My health is good and is ready to serve *you* in everything

you want to command. I say, My Dear Daughter Úrsula de Orellana, I give *you* notice and advice that, after 15 years, **your** husband has come to my home to beg for my pardon. He has struggled so much. It must be God's will, because he came in through the door of my house with **your** godfather Mateo Arenas, who married *you*, and with *your* godmother, Catalina Salinas. For **your** own life's sake! I want *you* to be careful, don't cause more pain than *you* already caused me. Since many people are getting enrolled now to go to Chile, **your** husband wants to search for *you*, if God gives him good health. If something happened to *you*, here is the name of the priest who married *you*: Pedro Cisnero, priest of the main church of Cusco. For Maria's sake, I beg *you* to be careful! I know, as weak as *you* are as a woman, *you* have struggled. Watch **yourself**, for **your** own life's sake! I have gotten older after hearing what **your** mother Juana Quispe says about you. *Your* brother became a monk at San Juan de Dios and *your* other brother wants to go to search for *you*. Antonio Emandes, **your** husband, already went to Copacabana: if **your** husband happened to find *you*, serve him well because he is *your* husband, for the Most Holy Virgin's sake! The muleteers from Lima told me that *you* were [...] It was not **your** fault, but mine, because I made *you* marry at such a young age. I beg *you* not to curse me in any business of mine, because I would love to be at **your** side as the beloved daughter of mine, in order to serve *you* in any possible matter. Write me in the first messenger station you come across. 27th, December 1655 I wrote this letter, and good bye. May God watch over *you* many years. To my daughter Úrsula de Orellana'

In this letter, we find 13 verb forms in the second person: ten of these seem to agree with *tú*, whereas only three agree with *vos*. Due to the lack of graphic accents in the manuscripts, there are no certain grounds, however, for deciding whether these verbs are conjugated in agreement with *tú* or with *vos* (*des* could also descend from the second person plural form, i.e. from *dedes* – after lost of intervocalic /d/ – or from an hypothetical intermediate form *déis* – thus, via monophthongization). The only exceptions are the forms *as dado* and *escríbeme*, whose morphology undoubtedly points towards the 2SG *tú*. There are 12 object clitics *te* and only one *os* (*guardaos*), which is used to introduce an important part of the letter (the main admonition). There is only one explicit subject pronoun, *vos*, which is placed postverbally and, as regards its role in information structure, carries a contrastive focus: *no tenías vos la culpa, sino es yo* (see also Octavio de Toledo y Huerta 2008, about the adversative connector *sino es*, which became quite common in Spanish during the 17th century).

The data commented on so far lead to the following conclusion: the use of SG *vos* (and the other forms of its paradigm) is much less frequent, and consequently much more marked, than the use of *tú*; when *vos* does appear in the text, it is clearly emphatic. This state of affairs looks consistent with a variety that we assume to be transitioning from *voseo* to *tuteo*. We know that the former had spread out as a T-pronoun all over the Spanish-speaking world during the 16th century, when *tú* started to be restricted to just a few social functions like when addressing children or slaves (compare Anipa 2001; Bentivoglio 2003; Carrera de la Red & Álvarez Muro 2004), whereas the latter must have prevailed in Cusco at a later stage of the colonial era (the Cusco region, unlike some enclaves of Southern Peru, has no remnants of SG *vos* today). However, the possessive *tu* is used only four times in the entire text, against nine instances of *vuestro/a(s)*, which is employed more frequently both with an emphatic function (such as when the possessive is postnominal: *por vida vuestra*) and, most importantly, in its neutral use (as in *vuestra madre*).

Elucidating the motivation for the partial alternation between (the forms belonging to the paradigm of) *tú* and (those belonging to the paradigm of) *vos* becomes a challenge for which we do not yet have a clear response.[11] Be that as it may, it is clear that, even when the use of *tú* had already become generalized, the possessive *vuestro/a* could still show up in some discourses. We could, thus, postulate a longer survival of possessives when the functional sphere of the pronominal paradigm they belong to is "invaded" by other pronouns, as when *tú* gained ground over *vos* and finally pushed it back in Colonial Peruvian Spanish. We wonder, then, whether PL *vuestro/a* paralleled SG *vuestro/a* in its longer resistance to a process of pronominal substitution: in our case, the pronoun *ustedes*, which is increasingly used from the second half of the 17th century onwards. As a matter of fact, the possessive form has already been proven to also persist longer in the process of displacement of *vosotros* by *ustedes* in Andalusian Spanish (Lara Bermejo 2015: 438). Another example of possessives resisting the invasion of other pronominal forms for some time is the use of 1PL *nuestro/a* in the letters written by the king to the colonial governors at a time when the subject pronouns, object clitics and verbal endings had already adopted the grammatical paradigm of *yo* (see Gutiérrez Maté 2013: 189–192 about the remnants of the so-called *majestatic plural*). Lastly, we

---

11 As has become clear, emphasis cannot be the only reason. Utterances like *Si acasso te hallare vuestro marido, agasajaldo, qu'es tu espos[o]* 'If your husband happened to find you, serve him well because he is your husband', may give us an additional hint to understand the variation between *tú* and *vos*. The first part of this utterance (a conditional clause followed by its apodosis) conveys a supposition, a possible scenario that can or cannot be realized in the future, whereas the second clause conveys an already proven fact 'he is *actually* your husband'. If we now read the rest of the text from this perspective, we discover that, in other cases, the utterances including the forms of *vos* contain conditionals, actions/states that are oriented to the future or reflect the speaker's wishes (the modal verb *querer* 'to want' is especially present in the text). This kind of modal reading seems to be absent in the actions rendered with *tú*.

cannot exclude the possibility that *vuestro/a* expanded from SG to PL, as happened in 19th and 20th century Uruguayan Spanish (Bertolotti 2007), the main objection being the fact that the colonial use of SG *vuestro/a* in Cusco (as in example (9) above, a letter written by a father to his daughter) was not marked for formality.

3.2 Hypothesis 2: The use of vuestro/a results from its idiomaticization from legal dispositions and other official directive documents

Throughout the entire colonial period we find *vos* in directive documents (*documentos dispositivos*, in the tradition of Hispanic Diplomatics), that is, in the official documents written from a superior position or institution to an inferior one (Real Díaz 1991) – for instance, when the king writes to governors or *Audiencias* (i.e. in the so-called *cédulas reales* 'royal decrees'), when governors write to mayors or to local commissioners, or when the *cabildos* (town councils) promote someone to an official position (Fontanella de Weinberg 1989: 114; Gutiérrez Maté 2013: 236–237). This leads us to two different types of *vos* that have to be studied separately. Fontanella de Weinberg (1992) refers to the polysemy of *vos*, whereas other authors speak of the "formal" or "reverential" *vos* as opposed to the common *vos*, although without further theoretical discussion. We consider the best way to catch these differences is to distinguish, according to the testimony in example (10) below, a "personal" *vos*, which was used in everyday's linguistic interactions, from an "official" *vos*, which was determined by the institutional role of the speakers and their addressees and found in very specific discourse traditions, such as those that belong to the institutional dialogue in the Hispanic colonial world. This differentiation between the interpersonal and the institutional dimensions of *vos* was perfectly known and explicitly regulated in the most important exponent of Spanish Colonial Law, the so-called *Laws of the Indies*, published in 1681 (Gutiérrez Maté 2013: 237; 2014: 69–72):

(10) Qvando Las Audiencias despacharen mandamientos por Nos el Presidente y Oidores, traten en ellos de **vos** á los Iuezes de Provincia, por hablar de Tribunal superior á Iuez Inferior, porque no se ha de considerar esto segun las **personas**, sino á los **oficios**, que exercen.

'When the courts passed writs on behalf of Ours, President and Hearers, they must address provincial judges with **vos**, since a superior court is speaking to an inferior judge, because this must not be related to the **person** but to the **person's position**.'

Both types of *vos* also differed formally in three important aspects: (1) the object counterpart of subject *vos* in its institutional use was always *(v)os* (the change to *te* took place only in the case of personal *vos*: Díaz Collazos 2016: 35–61); (2) possessives remained in their etymological form as well *(vuestro/a)*, without changing to *tu*, as occurred in the case of personal *vos*; and (3) most importantly, official *vos* could be used both with a singular and a plural meaning. To illustrate the latter, we reproduce here an excerpt of a royal disposition (1561) addressed to the religious authorities of the Andean provinces of Cusco, La Plata (today's Sucre) and Quito (example (11)); in addition, to specifically show the use of PL *vuestro/a*, we cite the beginning of a royal letter to the authorities of the City of The Kings (current Lima) (1564) (example (12)):

(11) Muy Reverendo y Reverendos in Cristo padres Arzobispo de la ciudad de los Reyes y Obispos de las ciudades del Cuzco y la Plata y Quito de las provincias del Perú. A nos se ha hecho relación [...]. Lo cual visto por los de nuestro Consejo de las Indias, fue acordado que debía mandar dar esta mi cédula para **vos** y yo túvelo por bien, por ende yo **vos** ruego y encargo que [...] (Konetzke 1958: 390)

'Very Reverend Archbishop and Bishops of the cities of Cusco, La Plata and Quito, in the provinces of Peru. We have been informed that [...]. This having been seen by our Council of the Indies, it was agreed that this letter of mine was given to **you**, which I considered to be good, so I ask and order **you** now to [...]'

(12) El Rey. Presidente y Oidores de la nuestra Audiencia Real de la ciudad de los Reyes de las provincias del Perú. Vi **vuestra** letra de 12 de abril del año pasado, y en lo que **decís** que [...] (Konetzke 1958: 412)

'The King. To the President and Hearers of Our Royal Audience in the City of the Kings, in the provinces of Peru. I saw **your** letter of April 12th from last year, and regarding what **you** say about [...]'

The formal characteristics of official *vos* were maintained throughout the entire colonial period, as can be easily confirmed by looking at the *cédulas* (legal orders on behalf of the king) written during the 18th century (Muro Orejón 1969), including those written to the *Audiencia Real* of Cusco, which became independent from Lima at the very end of the colonial era (1787) (Mejías Álvarez 1995).

These different types of dispositive documents influenced each other in such a way that the documents written by the king to the civil and religious authorities such as bishops, regional governors and the *Real Audiencias* served as a model for the latter when they had themselves to write legal directives to other subordinated local authorities, and so on. That is why several burocratic expressions were repeated and transmitted throughout the entire official correspondence in the Hispanic colonies. Finally, this sort of "officialese" was, to some extent, received by ordinary people, as when municipal edicts were read in public in the town squares. In addition, all over the Hispanic colonies, some critical *cédulas* were expected to be read in public:

(13) y para que lo susodicho sea público y notorio y ninguno pueda pretender ignorancia, se pregone públicamente esta nuestra cédula en las ciudades y pueblos que pareciere de la dicha provincia de Tierra Firme, y de la publicación de ella se tome testimonio en manera que haga fe. (Konetzke 1958: 490).

'and in order for all the aforesaid to be public and well-known and in order for no one to be able to pretend unawareness, I command this royal disposition to be publicly read in all affected cities and towns of the aforementioned province of Tierra Firme and I command this public reading to be registered by official scribe.'

The hypothesis, that some expressions that were first typical in official documents later became widespread in American Spanish, has been mentioned, though not really explained, by Cuervo (1954: 553, 557) and Guitarte (1969) (compare Carrera de la Red & Gutiérrez Maté 2009: 44). In our view, the expansion of elements whose usage was originally restricted to officialese has to be seen as an *idiomaticization* process (Ger. *Idiomatisierung*) in the sense of Koch (1997), that is, a process according to which a given linguistic expression (word, structure, etc.) escapes from one specific discourse tradition (or from a reduced set of discourse traditions) and becomes widespread in the language, thus becoming an integral part of the "historical-idomatic" rules of a given language (Coseriu 1982). To put it more simply, an expression that was formerly used only in texts with very specific characteristics becomes widely idiomatic (even though it may still be stylistically marked). To cite another example, in Gutiérrez Maté (2015: 189) it was postulated that the construction *servirse (de)* + INF (lit. 'to be served to do something'), which is used in many parts of Hispanic America, including the Cusco region, for polite requests in public speeches or in different formal circumstances with the meaning of 'to do the favor of doing something' (or just 'do something, please'),[12] was the result of another idiomaticization from colonial documents

---

12 One example (also from the Cusco region) will suffice to illustrate this use: *Señores pasajeros, sírvanse abordar su tren por las puertas de embarque señaladas en su boleto* 'Dear Passengers, please get on your train through the boarding gate as specified on your ticket'.

3.3 Hypothesis 3: The use of vuestro/a results from the revitalization of vosotros (and its entire paradigm) in 19th century American Spanish

The revitalization of *vosotros* (and its etymological paradigm) in (post-)independence American Spanish has been pointed out before (for a short summary, see Bertolotti, in this volume, 299–301), as has been the idea that *ustedes* was never a real V-pronoun in Colonial Spanish but a pronoun of address with a wider spectrum of uses (See above, 330). As regards the distribution of *vosotros* and *vuestro/a*, Frago Gracia (2011: 57) states that these forms can be found in almost any text type at the time of independence, most especially in official texts – generally written in a very traditional style, in doctrinal books or those characterized by erudition, and in those marked by solemnity, which, interestingly, may also strive for an emotional approach to the addressees, trying to encourage and persuade them.[13] Our claim is that prior to that time (say, during the last decades of the colonial era) the use of *vosotros* and its entire paradigm had become restricted to very few discourse types but had not disappeared completely, so it could experience a more or less ephemeral "revitalization" during the 19th century. This was partly because of an imitative and reinterpretative process of some linguistic patterns from European Spanish (see further below), partly because of the need for new linguistic strategies in order to shape the new discourses (most especially, at the political level) that were brought about by the birth of the new Hispanic American nations.

Unfortunately, our knowledge of Colonial Spanish at the turn of the 19th century is still limited, but it seems plausible to assume that the use of *vosotros* was, at best, obsolescent in ordinary conversation and had become restricted to just a few types of formal discourses. Amongst these, we find not only official documents but also some other texts that we consider to be paradigmatic such as the catechism *Explicación de la doctrina cristiana acomodada a la capacidad de los negros bozales* (1797), written by Nicolás Duque de Estrada in Cuba. In the preface

---

13 "Aunque el pronombre *vosotros*, y correlativamente el posesivo *vuestro*, puede encontrarse en no importa qué texto de la época de la Independencia, lo cierto es que su aparición se da con mayor profusión, incluso con regularidad, en los de carácter oficial, de estilo por lo general muy tradicional, en los doctrinales o marcados por la erudición, y en aquellos envueltos de solemnidad, que también pueden buscar, curiosamente, el acercamiento emocional a los destinatarios cuyos ánimos se desea enfervorizar y conquistar [...]". 'Although the pronoun *vosotros*, and in correlation the possessive *vuestro*, can appear in no matter what text of the Independence era, it is certain that its use is more common, even regular, in texts with official character, which in general have a very traditional style, in doctrines or in texts characterized by their erudition, and in such texts involved in ceremonial situations, which curiously can also achieve emotional reconciliation to the addressees, seeking to lift and conquer their spirit' (Frago Gracia 2011: 57).

to the edition of 1823, which is addressed to other priests working in the evangelization of Black slaves in Cuba, the author constantly uses *vosotros* (example (14)), whereas he only uses *ustedes* in the dialogues rendering prototypical interactions with slaves (example (15)).[14] Since the main stylistic principle governing these dialogues is, as the author states, to abandon "el uso de discursos elevados, de palabras cultas y rebuscadas" 'the use of elaborated discourses and erudite, stilted words' (*Dedicatoria*, iv), which he even accomplishes by using *foreigner talk*, it becomes clear that *ustedes* was not stylistically high, while *vosotros* was valid for at least some formal contexts. Interestingly, for the most stereotyped discourses like the final reverential words, he employs the abbreviation *Vds.*, which, since the letter *m* is lacking (as opposed to the abbreviation *Vmds.*), we tend to read as *ustedes* rather than as *vuestras mercedes* (compare García Godoy 2012: 122, 143) (example (16)). If this is correct, we might be obliged to distinguish between an idiomatic, ordinary use of *ustedes* and a formal or reverential use, which seems to be restricted to just a few formulaic expressions at the turn of the 19th century and, most importantly, already used with the possessive *vuestro/a* (see *vuestro siervo* in example (16)).

(14) Venerables sacerdotes, encargados de la instrucción de los negros esclavos, de los respectivos ingenios que se han puesto á **vuestro** cuidado. A **vosotros**, amados de mi alma, se dirige, como á su centro, este cuadernito. (p. 3)

'Venerable priests, you, who are devoted to the instruction of Black slaves in the different sugar factories **you** are taking care of. To **you**, my beloved in my soul, is addressed this booklet in its core.'

(15) **Ustedes** mismos no dicen "ese Hombre, esa Muger está loco"? Sí, porque solo una gente que tiene enfermo de loco puede facer así; pues **ustedes** también están locos, porque cuidan al cuerpo no más; y no cuida el Alma. Como Hijo son mejor que Perro, Alma mejor que Cuerpo. (p. 132)

'Don't **you** say, "that man, that woman is crazy"? Yes! Because only the people who have the illness of madness can do so; thus, **you** are crazy yourselves, because you take care of the body and not the soul. Just as sons are better than dogs, so [is the] soul better than [the] body.'

---

14 Perl & Große (1995: 205-221) were the first to note this asymmetry, even though they did not consider this dedicatory but only the final words of the catechism, in which Estrada again addresses the public who his work was addressed to.

(16) BLM [beso las manos] de **Vds** [=ustedes?]. **Vuestro** siervo en Señor Jesu-
cristo. (p. 8)
'I kiss **your** hands. **Your** servant in Jesus Christ.'

The use of *ustedes* in similar contexts to those of example (15) is also documented
in Andean Spanish around 1800. In a theater play written in 1799 (Arellano &
Eichmann 2005: 216) a white doctor addresses two Black protagonists in the following terms:

(17) Qué hacen **ustedes** aquí? [...] yo **les** mando a los dos que pronto **hagáis**
amistades.

'What are **you** doing here? I order **you** two to make friends soon'

To further complicate things, *ustedes* could occasionally combine with the paradigm of *vosotros* (in this example: *les... hagáis...*). However obsolescent the use of
vosotros (and the different forms of its grammatical paradigm) may have been,
it was still known to some extent, as the examples (14)-(17) have proven, so the
well-known impulse of *vosotros* during the early postcolonial era could take the
floor more easily. It is relatively common in several journals of the new American
nations (e.g. when editors address their readers) and it even passed into the most
patriotic texts such as national anthems. The following excerpt comes from the
Mexican anthem (written in 1853):

(18) Mexicanos, al grito de guerra   'Mexicans, at the cry of war,
el acero **aprestad** y el bridón.   make ready the steel and the bridle,
Y retiemble en sus centros la Tierra, and may the Earth tremble at its core
al sonoro rugir de el cañón.   at the resounding roar of the cannon.
Y retiemble en sus centros la Tierra, and may the Earth tremble at its core
al sonoro rugir de el cañón!   at the resounding roar of the cannon!'

Bertolotti (2007: 24–27) accurately explains how during the 19th century the
typically European pronoun *vosotros*[15] could have been considered somewhat
special and consequently reinterpreted for formality in at least some parts of Hispanic America. As we know, the manifold outlook of Hispanic America towards
the old metropole and its linguistic varieties from the very first decades after

---

15 The ultimate specialization of *vosotros* as a T-form might have taken place during the 19th
century as well, since we find its use as T just in an embryonic state during the 18th century
(Fernández Martín 2012: 153-199).

independence gave birth to different, even opposing, attitudes (Guitarte 1991) that, unfortunately, we do not yet really understand in their linguistic praxis. In other words, we do not know to what extent this process may have changed the linguistic profile of Hispanic America, that is, which linguistic features were involved[16] and, most importantly, how exactly the *architecture* (Coseriu 1982) of varieties (especially, as regards its situational marking and the opposition *language of immediacy/language of distance*) was reorganized at that time in the different Hispanic American nations.

4 Understanding the productivity and the geolinguistic distribution of *vuestro/a*

The three hypotheses introduced in the previous section are to a great extent compatible with one other. For instance, the idiomaticization of *vuestro/a* from official colonial documents (Hypothesis 2) looks even more plausible, as the SG possessive form had formerly become successful (at least for some time) in resisting the paradigmatization of *tú* (Hypothesis 1) and as the whole paradigm of *vosotros* was revitalized in postcolonial American Spanish (Hypothesis 3). However, even combining all three hypotheses, they fail to fully account for the fact that today's use of *vuestro/a*, as we have described it in Section 2, seems to be mostly limited to the Cusco region. It is therefore necessary to have a closer look at the

---

16 There are other linguistic features taking root in American Spanish that might have followed the pattern of European Spanish. Amongst these, we should mention the so-called *leísmo de cortesía* 'polite *le*'. The emergence of this use in American Spanish has not been clearly defined yet but it is supposed to be fairly old, even though it may have developed quite recently in some regions (Dumitrescu & Branza 2012). It consists of the use of *le(s)* instead of *lo(s)* as the object clitic counterpart of *usted(es)* (*NGLE* §16.8d). Despite its traditional designation (Lorenzo Ramos 1981), this feature seems to be related, first, to the stylistic dimension: Sedano (2011: 177), who describes this use in Venezuela, considers it to be "refinado". The sociostylistic history of this use in American Spanish resembles the history of the feature analyzed throughout this chapter; however, especially for the Andes, there are issues that would require further research. Just to mention one, the use of polite (or *refined*) *le* is very significant in Quito (Dumitrescu & Branza 2012: 679), but contrasts with the opposite use in other parts of Ecuador. Many Ecuadorians have overgeneralized the clitic *le* for all kinds of objects (also feminine); for these speakers, "in more prestigious registers, the use of *lo* (and *la*) in direct address, corresponding to *usted*, carries more respect than *le*, the inverse of trends found elsewhere in Latin America" (Lipski 1994: 251). In light of the above, special attention has to be paid to the clitic pronouns all over the Andes, since many vernaculars have been deeply restructured by language contact with Quechua, Aymara and other languages.

sociocultural idiosyncrasies of the Cusco Region in order to come closer to a valid explanation. In this section, we will analyze the linguistic feature described here from the perspective of cultural and language contact. More precisely, we claim that a notional transfer based on the Quechuan inclusive/exclusive distinction, which is deeply ingrained in Quechuan grammar (specifically, in the pronominal system, including possessives/relationals) and fully utilized by Quechua speakers to make discourse progress in one or another direction (Howard 2007), could have determined the success of *vuestro/a* in Cusco Spanish. In Section 4.2, we will elaborate on this explanation by adopting a more general perspective that discusses the emerging of an idiosyncratic *Cusqueño* identity, which is behind the linguistic idiosyncrasy of Cusco Spanish.

4.1 Language contact: notional transfer from Quechua

Interesting obervations on notional transfer have already been made in a significant number of studies on language contact, which show how languages can influence each other without borrowing any explicit forms, but transfering notional content. For example, Babel & Pfänder (2014) prove the effectiveness of this concept with a case study on the use of the past perfect (*había* + past participle) in Andean Spanish, which, aligning with comparable functions of Quechuan grammar, has incorporated a creative use as a mirative/deictic marker to the standard Spanish reading as past perfect tense. According to them, "[t]he effects of language contact are the accumulation of communicative routines or habits, which speakers play on as they engage in creative language use" (Babel & Pfänder 2014: 254).

This approach draws, to a great extent, on two other existing sources that we will also summarize here: (1) Jarvis & Pavlenko's (2008) plea for the importance of "subjective" similarity (similarity from an interlocutor's perspective) to facilitate transfer – also between typologically dissimilar languages ("objective" [dis-] similarity from a linguist's perspective); and (2) Johanson's code-copying framework (e.g. 2008). The first claims that the key to understanding language users' behaviour in language contact is to focus on the "similarities (and differences) that the L2 user *believes or perceives to exist* between the languages" (Jarvis & Pavlenko 2008: 178–179, our emphasis). Thus, speakers look out for forms, structures, meanings, functions or patterns in the target language that they perceive to be similar to a corresponding feature of the source language (perceived similarity). On the other hand, they assume the presence of a counterpart in the L2 of a linguistic feature that they know from the source language (assumed similarity). Jarvis & Pavlenko claim that such interlocutors' beliefs about the congruences between languages fuel language transfer, also between typologically distant languages like Quechua and Spanish.

The second, Johanson's code-copying model, provides a detailed framework for different possibilities on how parts of languages can be combined or copied selectively. He distinguishes between four types of copies: combinatorial, material, semantic and frequency-based (Johanson 2008). Typical cases of combinatorial copies are loan translations or syntactic calques, in which, generally speaking, a structure or pattern of the target language is partially rearranged to fit into a scheme from the model language: for example, whereas (S)OV word order would be considered exotic to the general Spanish grammar, speakers of Quechua-influenced Spanish frequently make use of it, though most especially in emphatic contexts (which does not fit perfectly into the Quechuan pattern, where SOV is the unmarked word-order) (Pfänder et al. 2009: 102–108). Material copies include not only loanwords but also phonological or morphological copies, for example, the incorporation of the Quechuan attenuative suffix *-ri* into the imperative paradigm of Bolivian Spanish (Pfänder et al. 2009: 242). Semantic (or functional) copies overlay the semantic content (in its broader sense) of one language with the semantics of the other, as when speakers of Andean Spanish, adapting the function of Quechua subordination suffixes, use the Spanish gerund construction mostly for adverbial subordination (Pfänder et al. 2009: 139–147; Soto Rodríguez & Dankel, in press). Lastly, frequency copies adopt the usage of a feature from the model code in the corresponding feature of the target code: a well-known example is the higher percentage of explicit subject pronouns in the Spanish spoken in the US because of language contact with English (Silva-Corvalán 1994). Furthermore, Johanson (2008: 62) stresses the fact that copies cannot, by definition, be identical to their models. Most typically, the semantic functions of copies have not reached the same stage of grammaticalization as their models and their use is often pragmatically determined (Johanson 2008: 70).

Finally, a complementary approach is the cognitive one adopted by Slobin (2016), who brings up the concept of "thinking for speaking". He considers contact phenomena as the long-term result of framing communicative interactions in different languages. He follows Levelt's (1989) psycholinguistic model, who distinguished a "conceptualizer" planning the forthcoming speech act from a "formulator" encoding the message on a lexical, grammatical and phonological level, and he further elaborates on this model by defining how it works in a language contact scenario. In this case, the conceptualizer becomes attentive to those meaning areas that are regularly marked in the contact languages and accomodates the linguistic outcome by providing formulation strategies in both languages. In other words, speakers who have to switch between languages frequently conceptualize the world in one language whilst speaking in another. This leads to contact-induced changes when speakers accommodate their "thinking for speaking" from the source language to the target language. To illustrate this, Slobin presents two contact scenarios (one of them being Spanish-Quechua language contact) where the language lacking grammatical marking for evidentiality has created new means for doing so out of the forms available in the target language.[17]

To sum up, whereas Johanson (2008) takes an empirical-observational perspective on a well-established contact variety, Jarvis & Pavlenko (2008) study the L2 accquisition process itself by focusing on speakers' assumptions and perceptions about the L2, and so does Slobin (2016) from a more cognitive viewpoint (more specifically, by focussing first on the dynamics in language processing mechanisms that enable contact-induced change). What is at stake in all of these approaches is the way in which speakers' communicative routines, which work on a cognitive level but have been shaped culturally, affect their understanding of how target languages work and give rise to linguistic outcomes in such a way that they are contextually and socially adequate. All approaches show how speakers creatively operationalize the potential of the available linguistic forms to convey their semantic and pragmatic needs in context-dependent ways. These studies relate to ours in that the strategic use of *vuestro/a* seems to be reflecting the same kind of contact-induced change: more specifically, the creative operationalization (reinterpretation) of a Spanish linguistic form to convey a communicative routine that is fully grammaticalized in Quechua.

As stated at the very beginning, scholars, even those working on Andean Spanish, have overlooked the use of *vuestro/a* in Cusco for several reasons.[18] However, some studies have already noticed a special (or strategic) use of other possessives and personal pronouns working as emphatic markers for delimiting/

---

17 For his Spanish-Quechua case study, Slobin (2016) limits himself to the already mentioned case of the Spanish pluperfect, which has been reinterpreted as an evidentiality/mirativity marker of unwitnessed information; however, a similar observation can be made for the development of the Andean Spanish reportative marker *dizque*, which is functionally modeled parallel to the Quechua reportative suffix (Dankel 2015).

18 Merma Molina (2007: 263), who studies language contact phenomena in Cusco Spanish, including possessives, cites an example of *vuestro*, but in her chapter on reported speech not possessives. However, it has to be noted that her account is selective, not exploratory (she mainly focuses on phenomena that already have broad recognition in the research community). Howard's (2007) approach to data collection (individual interview on community internal topics conducted by herself as an outsider) hardly allows for the appearance of 2PL personal or possessive determiners. In the case of Soto Rodríguez & Fernández Mallat (2012), the data collection contains a broader spectrum of text types, however the data is from the Bolivian variety of Andean Spanish, where, to the best of our knowledge, the phenomenon has not yet been documented.

confronting personal relations in the Cusco region, both as regards Spanish and Quechua. For example, Howard (2007), whose work is devoted to the cultural identities of Ecuador, Peru and Bolivia by means of a Critical Discourse Analysis of language attitudes, observes the use of *nosotros* 'we' as a strategy for opposing the voices of speakers and hearers amongst her informants from the Cusco region when speaking Spanish (Howard 2007: 76–77). This is even more true for regional Quechua, where the same discursive strategy is implemented by means of the grammatical differentiation of inclusive and exclusive 1PL pronouns and possessives (Howard 2007: 376–377). In fact, Southern Quechua, including the variety spoken in Cusco, happens to have the most elaborate system of personal reference markers within Quechuan dialectology (Adelaar & Muysken 2004: 212). If we now focus on possessives, we find the following distinctions (Table 1):

Table 1: The Southern Quechua possessive referential system; adapted from Soto Rodríguez & Fernández Mallat (2012: 83).

	SG	PL
1P	llaxta-**y** (*my* village; *mi* pueblo)	jak'u-**yku** (*our* flour, excl.; *nuestra* harina)
		suti-**nchis** (*our* man, incl.; *nuestro* hombre)
2P	llaxta-**yki** (*your* village; *tu* pueblo)	quwi-**ykichis** (*your* bunny; *vuestro* conejo)
3P	Wasi-**n** (*her*/*his* house; *su* casa)	chujcha-**nku** (*their* horse; *su* caballo)

Moreover, on a conceptual level, possessives actually convey a series of associations between persons and entities participating in a communicative event that contribute to shaping speakers' actual discourse, as Soto Rodríguez & Fernández Mallat (2012) have already shown on the basis of Quechua and Bolivian Spanish (they even prefer the label of *relationals* over *possessives*). Their analysis illustrates very clearly how Andean speakers use strategies of possessive/relational marking in the same way in both languages by relying on the same notional concepts and underlying cultural routines, even though the exact surface strategies are substantially different:

> las relaciones o vínculos indicados por estos morfemas pueden constituir recursos discursivos importantes para, según la situación, expresar la inclusión o la exclusión y el acercamiento o el alejamiento de un hablante respecto a determinados aspectos; lo cual, a su vez, permite a un hablante atribuir matices afectivos y despectivos a las asociaciones. [...] Todos estos valores y usos también se aplican a las muestras de español que hemos analizado. Este hecho nos hace pensar que parece tratarse de un concepto común para ambos grupos de hablantes y que lo único que cambia, según el caso, es la forma. Esta última está condicionada por las posibilidades y recursos que ofrece cada lengua. (Soto Rodríguez & Fernández Mallat 2012: 84)

'the relationships or connections conveyed by these morphemes turn out to be critical discursive means to express, according to the situation, the inclusion or exclusion [of the hearers] and the speakers' proximity or distance to different aspects, which, in addition, enables speakers to assign affective or derogatory nuances to the association process. [...] All these uses and nuances apply [not only to Quechua but also] to the Spanish samples we have analyzed. This fact makes us realize that there is just one concept for both speakers' groups and that the only thing that really changes is the [linguistic] form, which is strongly conditioned by the possibilities and expressive means of each language.'

Both Howard (2007) and Soto Rodríguez & Fernández Mallat (2012) emphasize the critical role of establishing clear relations and associations between persons and entities in order for speakers belonging to the Southern Andean culture to construct their discourse. These associations are formally conveyed by the Quechuan possessive/relational system with its clusivity distinction in the 1PL, but this kind of morphological distinction is not possible in Spanish. Nevertheless, the clusivity distinction could be transferred into (at least some varieties of) Andean Spanish on a notional level. Speakers unconsciously probed for available strategies in Spanish were able to emulate, to a certain extent, the original distinction. By so doing, they drew upon other fixed discursive routines in the target language (in our case, within the scope of address forms) that are also functional in the same context types (in our case, interactional discourses in which the relation between speech act participants has to be clear). The strategic use of *vuestro/a* in Cusco Spanish should be seen as one of these routines.

In fact, the communicative domain of inclusion/exclusion of the hearer and that of addressing belong together in the way that languages codify the involvement or the active role of hearers in speakers' actions or beliefs. Moreover, there might be some degree of correlation between both domains, which often seem to appear in inverse proportion: Southern Quechua displays the clusivity distinction but lacks the distinction based on politeness addressing,[19] whereas the opposite is true in the case of Spanish, which lacks any differentiation in clusivity but displays a relatively complex system of pronouns of address (even more so in colonial times). This correlation is not only characteristic of both languages from our contact scenario, but also of many other languages, as a look at the *World Atlas of Language Structures* (WALS) and more specifically at its features

---

19 Interestingly, according to the data of *WALS*, Northern Quechua shows the exact opposite realization of both variables: no clusivity in 1PL, but T-V distinctions in the addressing system.

39A ("inclusive/exclusive distinction in independent pronouns", Cysouw 2013) and 45A ("politeness distinctions in pronouns", Helmbrecht 2013) can quickly confirm.[20] If such a correlation between the two domains could be typologically confirmed, we could even think that they are somewhat associated in speakers' minds. In a language contact scenario, therefore, speakers could unconsciously consider a linguistic feature from one of these domains to be the natural replacement for a feature from the other domain or even, according to our understanding of notional transfer, adapt the linguistic forms of one of these domains in the L2 to the needs of the other domain in the L1.

These considerations allow us to think of the strategic use of *vuestro/a* in Cusco Spanish as an indirect compensation strategy for the missing differentiation between an inclusive and an exclusive form in Southern Quechua. Spanish has only one linguistic form for the 1PL POSS, which makes a direct transfer from Quechua impossible. Since speakers did feel the need to fill the functional gap left by the missing clusivity distinction in Spanish, they searched for an alternative way to keep on assessing their role by opposing the hearers and they found it in the linguistic variable 2PL. *Vuestro/a*, which had never disappeared completely from American Spanish, was then fully utilized to convey not only the meaning of 'your-PL' but also the meaning of 'not our'. Actually, *vuestro/a*'s informational role (in its strategic use) is that of a contrastive focus that makes explicit the opposition between the 2PL and the 1PL. Speakers took advantage of the variation in 2PL possessives between *vuestro/a* and *su* by using the former to convey the opposite meaning to the exclusive 1PL, whereas the latter remained in its canonical use as a referential 2PL (and as a 3PL, which could also be defined as the opposite of the inclusive 1PL). *Su* was itself not suitable for such a creative use, since it was already functionally overloaded and, when functioning as a 2PL, more widespread than *vuestro/a* (restricted to some discourse traditions).

---

20 The comparison of the maps for both features brings to light some interesting correspondences in several language areas: e.g. European languages systematically lack the inclusive/exclusive distinction and display the politeness distinction, whereas Australian languages regularly exhibit the first distinction but, in most cases, not the second. In addition, there are several languages with negative values for both variables and only a few with positive values for both of them (the Khoisan language Khoekhoe being one of these very few languages). The correlation between the two features (which we mention here only speculatively) is by no means perfect but it should not to be overlooked.

Table 2: Personal referential system (PL); Spanish variation *su – vuestro/a* as a compensation strategy for the inclusive/exclusive distinction.

Quechua			Cusco Spanish				Spanish	
/1PL inclusive/ [I, you, others]	-nchis	⮕	/1PL inclusive/ [I, you, others]	nuestro/a		/1PL/	nuestro/a	
/1PL exclusive/ [I, others]	-yku(na)		/– 1PL exclusive/ (=2PL contrastive)	vuestro/a				
/2PL/	-ykichis		/2PL/	suyo/a	⬅	/2PL/	vuestro/a (restricted) suyo/a (generalized)	
/3PL/	-nku		/– 1PL inclusive/ (=3PL)			/3PL/	suyo/a	

When speaking Spanish, the creative use of a contrastive 2PL meaning 'you' as opposed to 'us' enables speakers to structure their discourse on the basis of the contrast between them and their interlocutor/s (as regards actions, beliefs, opinions, and so on), that is, on the basis of the same discourse structuring principle for which speakers used the exclusive 1PL in Quechua.

We would surely go too far if we claimed that language contact is the main reason for the success of *vuestro/a* in Cusco, particularly as it does not account for the fact that this feature seems to be limited to just a small part of the contact zone between Spanish and Southern Quechua (although more empirical research about other varieties is still required). However, we do claim that the phenomenon described here would not have taken root in the region without language contact. To us, understanding properly how notional transfer works may solve, partially at least, the problem of the geographical spread of strategic *vuestro/a* (see Section 4.2 for a complementary explanation). As Dankel (2015) has already proven for the Spanish/Southern Quechua scenario, languages offer different structural potentialities to express a given notional category, so interlocutors in different regions – even when contact ingredients remain the same – find different ways to operationalize such a category out of the available linguistic forms. Experiences with categories in multilingual scenarios are first individual, used locally and, finally, may succeed in their bottom-up expansive process, but they may also remain restricted to a more or less local area. Therefore, it is *per se* natural for a contact phenomenon to be restricted to just a small area of the entire contact zone.

A final remark about the discursive meaning of *vuestro/a* has to be made: this form is often used in Cusco to shape social identity. In this regard, Howard's (2007) analysis had already proven, though mostly in reference to the 1PL, that the strategic use of personal pronouns plays a crucial role in speakers' creation of a local identity.

> Entre las estrategias discursivas que le sirven al hablante para posicionarse dentro del campo social, notamos el uso contextual de los pronombres personales de primera y tercera persona (*nosotros* versus *ellos*). El *nosotros* se vuelve sumamente ambivalente en algunos contextos: su uso estratégico sirve tanto para trazar como para borrar las fronteras socioculturales. (Howard 2007: 377)
>
>   'Among the discourse strategies used by speakers to position themselves in the social context, we notice the contextual use of first and third person pronouns (*we* vs. *they*). *We* becomes extremely ambivalent in some contexts: its strategic use allows speakers as much to draw as to erase sociocultural borders'

In a similar vein, Soto Rodríguez & Fernández Mallat (2012), while elaborating on their analysis of possessives (summarized here in the citation above), point out the importance of establishing social relations in the discourse of Andean speakers. In what follows, we will relate this to the singularity of *Cusqueño* social identity.

4.2 Cusqueño *(language) identity and the pride in being mestizo*

As the former capital of the Inca Empire and present-day touristic capital of Peru, Cusco has been constructing its own particular identity for centuries. Historically, this city has developed an actual mixed Hispano-Indigenous heritage (*mestizo*) identity since earlier colonial times, where the syncretism between Indigenous and European cultures is recognizable throughout different cultural manifestations. This mixture was always perceived and handled proudly by the local elites, amongst whom Spanish/Quechua bilingualism was quite common during the colonial era and far beyond. Spanish settlers and their descendants who turned into landlords around the city of Cusco often used Quechua and even claimed to be related to the Inca nobles (Mannheim 1991: 71–74). In this particular case, the rigidly stratified society during the colonial times resulted from an adaptation to Inca society, alongside the implementation of the archetypical colonial infrastructure. The pride amongst the ruling classes in thinking of themselves as *mestizos*, as opposed to other Spanish Creoles and most especially to the Indigenous people, who became stigmatized as illiterates, *provincianos* or *campesinos* 'peasants' (Brandt 2016; Delforge 2012), has remained to a great extent intact to this day.

In the last decades, tourism has entered this traditional scenario, altering it partially but also intensifying some previously existing tendencies. *Cusqueño* identity is currently fueled by a symbiotic relationship between ethnic tourism and nativist ideology (*incanismo*), where the latter authenticates the former as a product, while tourism itself (as a response to the international attention gained by Cusco in our global era) intensifies such an ideology (van den Berghe & Flores Ochoa 2000: 23; see also Silverman 2002), and thereby strengthens local pride (see below). Nevertheless, it has to be noted that tourism is not solely responsible for the success of *vuestro/a* in Cusco Spanish, as any amateur might claim if he/she thought, for instance, that the inhabitants of Cusco were trying to adapt their speech to those varieties spoken by the Spaniards that can occasionally be seen (and heard) on the streets of Cusco (mostly on their way to Machu Picchu). Among the languages of occasional migrants, European Spanish, that is, the only variety constantly using *vuestro/a*, is far less common than American Spanish (and, of course, less common than English and some other major languages).[21] However, tourism has definitely shaped the current linguistic identities of Cusco, since the city had to determine how to present itself to today's global world.

The local pride already mentioned results both in the cultivation of *Cusqueño* Quechua, which is usually considered to be Standard Quechua, and in a general tendency to use language as a means to stress the city's idiosyncrasy (most notoriously, as opposed to Lima). Niño-Murcia (1997: 156), whose research is focused on the linguistic purism in Cusco (especially, but not only, as regards Quechua), insists on the very same idea:

> In accordance with the regional attempt to define the characteristic features of its culture and in order to distance and enhance Cuzco's identity with respect to Lima, language is being used to stress its regional uniqueness within the country and also to create a social hierarchy within the city.

Such uniqueness is built to create a social hierarchy, distinguishing the urban elite from the rural groups of Quechua/Spanish bilinguals. Even though the situation is far more complex, we could state that, to a certain degree, the current opposition between (Spanish) monolingual speakers from the city and (Spanish/ Quechua) bilingual speakers from the rural areas parallels the opposition some authors have postulated for the colonial era between (Spanish/ Quechua) bilin-

---

21 The latest statistics of the *Dirección General de Comercio Exterior y Turismo* (Dircetur) of the Cusco regional government show that just 2.1% of all tourists are from Spain, whereas the percentage of tourists from Spanish-speaking American countries is 11% and national tourists account for 38% (numbers taken from the *Boletín Estadístico de Turismo* 2014 of the Dircetur: 8, 11).

gual speakers (i.e. the ruling *mestizos*) and the (Quechua) monolingual speakers (i.e. the Indigenous populations in and around Cusco).

In a study about the "recession" of unstressed vowel devoicing in Cusco Spanish, Delforge (2012: 331) introduces a new element in the formation of *Cusqueños'* self-consciousness and linguistic pride: getting rid of the cultural stereotypes of the Andean region (as seen from Lima and other parts of Peru):

> It has been suggested that Cusqueñans' tendency to view devoicing as typical of rural migrants has an attitudinal basis, reflecting their desire to escape the provincial perception of the region that has long existed in other parts of Peru and elsewhere.

Consequently, speakers negotiate their cultural and ethnic identity during their linguistic interactions (Howard 2007: 377), which means that their belonging to a given social group must also be conveyed by linguistic strategies. Amongst these, Howard (2007) – citing De la Cadena (2000: 30–33) – points out, again, the use of *nosotros*:

> Al observar los casos recurrentes de ambivalencia en torno al pronombre *nosotros* en los textos, me pregunto si se trata de un rasgo diagnóstico del discurso de un cierto tipo de actor social. Dicho de otro modo ¿podría afirmarse que la ambivalencia en el uso de este pronombre construye un campo discursivo socialmente definido? De hecho, el *nosotros* ambivalente suele tener el efecto de posicionar a los entrevistados a alguna distancia de una identidad indígena, por no decir que construye una **identidad amestizada**. (Howard 2007: 377, our emphasis)

> 'When we look at the recurring cases of ambivalence as regards the pronoun *we* in the texts, I wonder myself if this is a feature that signals a certain kind of social actor. In other words, would it be possible to state that the ambivalence of the usage of this pronoun builds a discursive field that is socially defined? As a matter of fact, ambivalent *we* usually has the effect for the interviewed speakers of positioning themselves at a certain distance from an Indigenous identity, if not creating a **mestizo identity**.'

We can now highlight the strategic use of *vuestro/a*, not just as a particular element in this setting that contributes to *Cusqueño* language identity, but as a prominent discourse strategy that is used in these negotiations. In a significant number of cases, the contrastive meaning conveyed by *vuestro/a* delimits the psychosocial role of speech act participants. We cannot decide, however, whether the creation of the contrastive use of *vuestro/a* in Cusco Spanish meets the culturally determined need of opposing the social role of speakers and hearers or if it is primarily devoted to the more general purpose of setting the conversational role of speakers and hearers without clear social implications (such as when a radio commentator speaks to his/her audience).

For now, we will just say that *vuestro/a*'s basic function is opposing (for whatever reason) the voices of speakers and hearers to each other and, in so doing, contributing to discourse structuring and progression. However, we cannot overlook the social conditioning of any discourse, which, most especially in Cusco, seems to serve a very specific set of interests and specifically social stratification. This aspect would solve, partially at least, the problem of the small geographical area of *vuestro/a*, even though we find many other cultural and linguistic features widespread all over the Spanish/Southern Quechua contact area.

In this regard, we would like to mention another linguistic feature (also related to the study of forms of address), whose use seems to have been widespread in this (transnational) contact area, being especially intense in the Cusco region. Readers familiar with the literature about forms of address in the Southern Andes may recall some studies by Granda (2004, 2005) about the usage of *su merced* in the same area. Interestingly, one of the main contributions of Granda's work is to describe how speakers of the upper social classes used to address each other with *su merced*. Putting aside other interesting uses of *su merced* that readers will surely be more familiar with, this form of address often carried a social identifying function as well. In the city of Cusco, this use seems to have been very common at least until the mid-20th century. Making use of it was an *acto de identidad lingüística* 'act of linguistic identity', with which speakers showed "su integración en dicha red social, constituida exclusivamente por las familias pertenecientes al estamento aristocrático cusqueño" 'their belonging to this social network, which consisted exclusively of families from Cusco's aristocracy' (Granda 2004: 252). Therefore, it seems plausible that these speakers were willing to assert their belonging to the upper classes both *in-group* (by using address forms like *su merced*) and *out-group* (by using address forms like *vuestro/a*, even though we do not preclude the possibility of this form being used *in-group* as well).

If we could confirm that the use of *vuestro/a* prevails amongst speakers of the upper classes (more precisely, again, amongst speakers willing to assert their belonging to the upper classes), we should then recall that, in Cusco, *upper class* relates to a *mestizo* identity and clarify that using *vuestro/a* is not meant to express disdain for the addressee nor to highlight any relation of *power* (in the sense of Brown & Gilman 1960). Quite the contrary, its use can protect the hearer's *face*; what really matters is that speakers, when using *vuestro/a*, bring to the fore their social background and position themselves as highly educated speakers and, more precisely, educated *mestizos*. In this regard, the use of *vuestro/a* in Cusco can also function as an "act of linguistic identity", but a type of act that does not necessarily rule out the hearers and may even serve as an invitation to the speaker's world, as our example (6) has already illustrated.

Elucidating the idiosyncratic sociological complexity of *Cusqueños* and their *mestizo* identity, which implies a particular adaptation and readjustment of an Indigenous culture, turns out to be a better way to understand why language contact (even at a notional level, see Section 4.1) is still a suitable explanation.

Otherwise, we could not account for a contact-induced change that, unlike the vast majority of changes resulting from the contact between Spanish and Indigenous languages in *Hispanic* America, started as a *change from above*.

5 Conclusion

In this chapter, we have analyzed the usage of *vuestro/a* in Cusco Spanish, which has never been studied in any depth, despite the fact that it is quite common in the region. *Vuestro/a* is always plural and takes part in the grammatical paradigm of *ustedes* (there is no *vosotros* or clitic *os* and no verbal endings of the etymological 2PL). We have distinguished two large groups of uses: formulaic and contrastive or strategic – the latter being especially striking, even though the former still deserve an analysis in much more depth.

Originating from our description of both uses of *vuestro/a*, we devoted the rest of the chapter to explaining how they arose in Cusco Spanish. First, we presented a heterogeneous group of problems that our research had to face: the existence of a semantic category of clusivity also in the 2PL, the survival of *vuestro/a* in other parts of Hispanic America, its use for referential disambiguation, and the fact that 2PL pronouns are generally understudied in Hispanic Linguistics. However, none of these problems preclude us from considering *vuestro/a* in Cusco Spanish a special phenomenon in its own right, as it actually is.

Second, we formulated three complementary hypotheses about its possible origins: (1) its parallelism to SG *vuestro/a* (as for its resistance to the overgeneralization of other personal pronouns) or even extension from SG to PL; (2) its *idiomaticization* from dispositive documents; and (3) the revitalization of *vosotros* in 19th century American Spanish. As these hypotheses did not account for the fact that *vuestro/a* is limited to Cusco Spanish, we claimed that language contact (specifically a notional transfer from Southern Quechua to Spanish) and the idiosyncrasy of *Cusqueño* society in the shaping of its specific identity provide the missing complementary explanation. Speakers with Quechua-L1, who were used to defining and constantly updating the relation between speakers and hearers during their verbal interactions and, for this purpose, relied on the clusivity distinction in 1PL pronouns, needed a way to keep on doing that when speaking Spanish. This language lacks, as is well known, such a clusivity distinction but does have (even more clearly so during the colonial era) an especially complex system of pronouns of address.

As regards the possessives, there were only two options: *su* and *vuestro/a* – the latter being more restricted in the diasystem (in a few discourse traditions, according to Hypothesis 2, and/or in foreign European varieties, according to Hypothesis 3). Speakers naturally adapted the variant that was felt to be more special (or salient) for the new special (or creative) use, which still shared some semantic characteristics with the canonical Spanish form. Of course, the creative use triggered by language contact also leads to convergence with Spanish, not only in form but also in meaning: for example, in the most plausible colonial source, that is, the so-called dispositive documents (cf. Hypothesis 2), *vuestro/a* was used from superior to inferior positions, which might still be recognizable, after some restructuring, in the use by speakers from the upper classes when they try to assert their belonging to the group of educated *Cusqueños*. Finally, we consider *vuestro/a* to be part of the broader discursive strategy of using personal reference markers as a means of sociocultural demarcation by speakers constantly positioning themselves as part of a (seemingly contradictory) social class of *mestizos*.

This kind of self-awareness on the basis of social criteria might prompt us to consider that the use of *vuestro/a* depends on sociolinguistic factors (literacy) or even geolinguistic factors (dichotomy "urban/rural"). This is partially true, particularly if we assume that the role of speakers' own perceptions is the basis for the interaction of linguistic varieties (see Koch & Oesterreicher 2011). However, it should then be noted that educated speakers use *vuestro/a* only in formal contexts (if we consider the so-called *Varietätenkette* 'variational chain', as defined by Koch & Oesterreicher 1985, the geographic and social markedness can be readjusted as speech styles or even as *communicative immediacy/distance*). On the other hand, as regards its strategic use, *vuestro/a* serves a very specific discursive function: contrast between speech act participants. That is why, as stated at the beginning, the usage of *vuestro/a* is related to variationist and discursive factors.

The centuries-old but constantly updating development of a very idiosyncratic cultural and linguistic identity in Cusco might allow us to predict a longer persistence of the phenomenon analyzed here. In the last few years, it seems to be increasingly perceived as stereotypically *Cusqueño* by other Peruvians: it has already entered the category of place-linked linguistic expectations (e.g. Carmichael 2016), and this is a sort of local flavor that *Cusqueños* may be willing to maintain for much longer – as shown by example (19) from an internet forum (our emphasis):

(19) La gente de cuzco usa el segundo pronombre plural: **VUESTRO (A) (S)** mientras que la gente de Lima usamos **USTEDES**. Me agrada la forma cuzquena. (sciffo, 27-ene-2008, 17:23, Lima; forosperu.net, thread: "Diferencias entre Lima y las provincias")

'People from Cusco use the second plural pronoun: **VUESTRO 'your'**, while we, the people from Lima, use **USTEDES**. I kinda like the form from Cuzco'

Our findings offer a rich compendium of possibilities. The availability of more historical corpora (especially from the 18th and 19th centuries) would be crucial to consolidate the diachronic paths we have laid out. Similarly, a broader database with more specific sociolinguistic information and more data from bilingual speakers is needed to be able to make a precise statement on the role of language contact. In this contribution, we have outlined sketches of a much more complex picture. Even though we consider that our analysis is on the right track, many questions remain and can only be addressed after a much larger amount of data has been gathered for every factor we have focused on. The expected rewards, however, seem to be promising and could contribute profoundly to our understanding of language variation, language contact and language change.

References

Academia Mexicana de la Lengua. 2017. *Corpus Diacrónico y Diatópico del Español de América* (CORDIAM). www.cordiam.org (March, 2017).

Adelaar, Willem F. H. & Pieter Muysken. 2004. *The languages of the Andes*. Cambridge: Cambridge University Press.

Adli, Aria. 2011. *Gradient acceptability and frequency effects in information structure: A quantitative study on Spanish, Catalan and Persian*. Habilitation thesis. Freiburg: Albert-Ludwigs-Universität Freiburg.

Anipa, Kormi. 2001. *A critical examination of linguistic variation in Golden-Age Spanish*. New York: Peter Lang.

Arellano, Ignacio & Andrés Eichmann (eds.). 2005. *Entremeses, loas y coloquios de Potosí (Colección del Convento de Santa Teresa)*. Frankfurt/Madrid: Iberoamericana/Vervuert.

Babel, Anna M. & Stefan Pfänder. 2014. Doing copying: Why typology doesn't matter to language speakers. In Juliane Besters-Dilger, Cynthia Dermarkar, Stefan Pfänder & Achim Rabus (eds.), *Congruence in contact-induced language change. Language families, typological resemblance, and perceived similarity*, 239–257. Berlin/Boston: De Gruyter.

Bentivoglio, Paola. 2003. Spanish forms of address in the sixteenth century. In Irma Taavitsainen & Andreas H. Jucker (eds.), *Diachronic perspectives on address term systems*, 177–191. Amsterdam/Philadelphia: John Benjamins.

Berghe, Pierre L. van den & Jorge Flores Ochoa. 2000. Tourism and nativistic ideology in Cuzco, Peru. *Annals of Tourism Research* 27,1. 7–26. doi:http://dx.doi.org/10.1016/S0160-7383(99)00043-2.

Bertolotti, Virginia. 2007. La cuestión de *vuestro/a(s)*: Vitalidad medieval y clásica en el español de Uruguay. In Virginia Bertolotti et al. (eds.), *Estudios de lingüística hispánica*, 17–41. Cádiz: Universidad de Cadiz.

Bertolotti, Virginia. 2015. *A mí de vos no me trata ni usted ni nadie: sistemas e historia de las formas de tratamiento en la lengua española en América*. Mexico City: Universidad Nacional Autónoma de México.

Bertolotti, Virginia. In this volume. The loss of *vosotros* in American Spanish.

Brandt, Hans-Jürgen. 2016. Campesinos und Indigene. In Iken Paap & Friedhelm Schmidt-Welle (eds.), *Peru heute. Politik-Wirtschaft-Kultur*, 261–286. Frankfurt/Madrid: Vervuert/ Iberoamericana.

Brown, Roger & Albert Gilman. 1960. The Pronouns of power and solidarity. In Thomas A. Sebeok (ed.), *Style in language*, 253–276. Cambridge, MA: MIT Press.

Cadena, Marisol de la. 2000. *Indigenous mestizos. The politics of race and culture in Cuzco, Peru, 1919–1991*. Durham: Duke University Press.

Caravedo, Rocío. 1996. Peru. In Manuel Alvar López (ed.), *Manual de dialectología hispánica: El español de América*, 152–168. Barcelona: Ariel.

Caravedo, Rocío. 2005. La realidad subjetiva en el estudio del español de América. In Volker Noll, Klaus Zimmermann & Eva Neumann-Holzschuh (eds.), *El español en América: Aspectos teóricos, particularidades, contactos*, 17–31. Frankfurt/Madrid: Iberoamericana/ Vervuert.

Carmichael, Katie. 2016. Place-linked expectations and listener awareness of regional accents. In Anna M. Babel (ed.), *Awareness and control in sociolinguistic research*, 152–176. Cambridge: Cambridge University Press.

Carrera de la Red, Micaela & Alexandra Álvarez Muro. 2004. Tratamientos y cortesía en la elaboración de fuentes documentales de la etapa fundacional de la provinica de Mérida. In Antonio Briz Gómez & Diana Bravo (eds.), *Pragmática sociocultural. Estudios sobre el discurso de la cortesía en español*, 227–244. Barcelona: Ariel.

Carrera de la Red, Micaela & Miguel Gutiérrez Maté. 2009. Los documentos americanos (o indianos) en la red CHARTA. In Andrés Enrique-Arias (ed.), *Diacronía de las lenguas iberor-románicas: Nuevas aportaciones desde la lingüística de corpus*, 39–54. Frankfurt/Madrid: Iberoamericana/Vervuert.

Company Company, Concepción. 1997. El costo gramatical de las cortesías en el español americano. Consecuencias sintácticas de la pérdida de *vosotros*. *Anuario de Letras* 35. 167–191.

Coseriu, Eugenio. 1982 [1958]. *Sentido y tareas de la dialectología*. Mexico City: Universidad Nacional Autónoma de México.

Croft, William. 2001. *Radical construction grammar: Syntactic theory in typological perspective*. Oxford: Oxford University Press.

Cuervo, Rufijo José. 1954. El castellano en América. *Obras* II, 522–560. Bogotá: Instituto Caro y Cuervo. [First published 1901. *Bulletin Hispanique* III. 35–62].

Cysouw, Michael. 2013. Inclusive/exclusive distinction in independent pronouns. In Matthew S. Dryer & Martin Haspelmath (eds.), *The World Atlas of Language Structures Online*. Leipzig: Max Planck Institute for Evolutionary Anthropology.http://wals.info/chapter/39 (28.8.2017).

Dankel, Philipp. 2015. *Strategien unter der Oberfläche*. Freiburg/Berlin/Vienna: Rombach.

Delforge, Ann Marie. 2012. *Nobody wants to sound like a provinciano*: The recession of unstressed vowel devoicing in the Spanish of Cusco, Perú. *Journal of Sociolinguistics* 16,3. 311–335. doi:10.1111/j.1467-9841.2012.00538.x.

Díaz Collazos, Ana María. 2016. Pragmatic forces in the evolution of *voseo* object pronouns from *os* to *te* in colonial Spanish. In María Irene Moyna & Susana Rivera-Mills (eds.), *Forms of address in the Spanish of the Americas*, 35–61. Amsterdam/Philadelphia: John Benjamins.

Dumitrescu, Domnita & Mircea-Doru Branza. 2012. Sobre el llamado *leísmo de cortesía* en Hispanoamérica. In Julio Escamilla Morales & Grandfield Henry Vega (eds.), *Miradas multidisciplinares a los fenómenos de cortesía y descortesía en el mundo hispánico*, 669–692. Barranquilla: Universidad del Atlántico.

Eberenz, Rolf. 2000. *El español en el otoño de la Edad Media. Sobre el artículo y los pronombres*. Madrid: Gredos.

Fernández Martín, Elisabeth. 2012. *Vosotros/ustedes*. Estudio del tratamiento plural en el español dieciochesco. In María Teresa García Godoy (ed.), *El español del siglo XVIII. Cambios diacrónicos en el primer español moderno*, 53–194. Bern: Peter Lang.

Fontanella de Weinberg, María Beatriz. 1989. Avances y rectificaciones en el estudio del voseo americano. *Thesaurus* 44,3. 521–533.

Fontanella de Weinberg, María Beatriz. 1992. La evolución de los usos americanos de segunda persona singular. *Lingüística (ALFAL)* 4. 7–25.

Fontanella de Weinberg, María Beatriz. 1999. Sistemas pronominales de tratamiento en el mundo hispánico. In Ignacio Bosque & Violeta Demonte (eds.), *Gramática descriptiva de la lengua española*, 1400–1425. Madrid: Espasa Calpe.

Frago Gracia, Juan Antonio. 2011. El español de América en la Independencia. Adiciones gramaticales I. *Boletín de Filología* 46,1. 47–74.

García Godoy, María Teresa. 2012. El tratamiento de *merced* en el español del siglo XVIII. In María Teresa García Godoy (ed.), *El español del siglo XVIII. Cambios diacrónicos en el primer español moderno*, 111–152. Berlin: Peter Lang.

Gili Gaya, Samuel. 1993 [1943]. *Curso superior de sintaxis española*. Barcelona: Vox.

Gobierno Regional Cusco, DIRCETUR. 2014. *Boletín Estadístico de Turismo 2014*. http://www.dirceturcusco.gob.pe/wp-content/uploads/2015/09/BOLETIN-ESTADÍSTICO-2014.pdf (2.2.2017).

Goldberg, Adele E. 1995. *Constructions: A construction grammar approach to argument structure*. Chicago: University of Chicago Press.

Goldberg, Adele E. 2003. Constructions: A new theoretical approach to language. *Trends in Cognitive Sciences* 7,5. 219–224.

Granda, Germán de. 2004. Una forma deferencial en el español peruano. *Lexis* 28,1–2. 447–459.

Granda, Germán de. 2005. La forma de tratamiento *su merced* en el área lingüística surandina. *Lexis* 29,2. 247–257.

Guitarte, Guillermo L. 1969. Para una historia del español de América basada en documentos: el seseo en el Nuevo Reino de Granada (1550–1650). *El Simposio de México. Enero 1968. Actas, informes y comunicaciones*, 191–199. Mexico City: Universidad Nacional Autónoma de México.

Guitarte, Guillermo L. 1991. Del español de España al español de veinte naciones. La integración de América al concepto de lengua española. In César Hernández et al. (eds.), *El español de América: Actas del III congreso internacional de el español en América: Valladolid, 3 a 9 de julio de 1989*, vol. 1, 65–86. Valladolid: Junta de Castilla y León/ Consejería de Cultura y Turismo.

Gutiérrez Maté, Miguel. 2013. *Pronombres personales sujeto en el español del Caribe: Variación e historia*. PhD thesis. Valladolid: University of Valladolid. http://uvadoc.uva.es/handle/10324/2517.

Gutiérrez Maté, Miguel. 2014. Hacia una tipología de variantes en documentos indianos. *Scriptum Digital* 3. 65–94.

Gutiérrez Maté, Miguel. 2015. Las "representaciones difusas" de los documentos dominicanos y su estudio lingüístico-variacional. In Juan Pedro Sánchez Méndez, Mariela de la Torre & Viorica Condita (eds.), *Temas, problemas y métodos para la edición y el estudio de documentos hispánicos antiguos*, 177–195. Valencia: Tirant Humanidades.

Haverkate, Wilhelm Hendrik. 1994. *La cortesia verbal. Estudio pragmalinguistico*. Madrid: Gredos.

Helmbrecht, Johannes. 2013. Politeness Distinctions in Pronouns. In Matthew S. Dryer & Martin Haspelmath (eds.), *The World Atlas of Language Structures Online*. Leipzig: Max Planck Institute for Evolutionary Anthropology. http://wals.info/chapter/45 (28.8.2017).

Hopper, Paul J. 2004. The openness of grammatical constructions. *Papers from the 40th Chicago Linguistic Society* 40. 239–256.

Howard, Rosaleen. 2007. *Por los linderos de la lengua*. Lima: IEP/IFEA/PUCOMPARE.

Groupe ICOR. 2013. *Conventions de transcription ICOR*. http://icar.univ-lyon2.fr/projets/corinte/documents/2013_Conv_ICOR_250313.pdf.

Jarvis, Scott & Aneta Pavlenko. 2008. *Crosslinguistic influence in language and cognition*. New York/London: Routledge.

Johanson, Lars. 2008. Remodeling grammar. Copying, conventionalization, grammaticalization. In Peter Siemund & Noemi Kintana (eds.), *Language contact and contact languages*, 61–79. Amsterdam/Philadelphia: John Benjamins.

Koch, Peter. 1997. Diskurstraditionen: Zu ihrem sprachtheoretischen Status und ihrer Dynamik. In Barbara Frank, Thomas Haye & Doris Tophinke (eds.), *Gattungen mittelalterlicher Schriftlichkeit*, 43–79. Tübingen: Gunter Narr.

Koch, Peter & Wulf Oesterreicher. 1985. Sprache der Nähe – Sprache der Distanz. Mündlichkeit und Schriftlichkeit im Spannungsfeld von Sprachtheorie und Sprachgebrauch. *Romanistisches Jahrbuch* 36. 15–43.

Koch, Peter & Wulf Oesterreicher. 2001. Gesprochene Sprache und geschriebene Sprache. Langage parlé et langage écrit. In Günter Holtus, Michael Metzelin & Christian Schmitt (eds.), *Lexikon der Romanistischen Linguistik*, vol. 1,2, 584–627. Tübingen: Niemeyer.

Koch, Peter & Wulf Oesterreicher. 2011 [1990]. *Gesprochene Sprache in der Romania: Französisch, Italienisch, Spanisch*. Second edition. Berlin/Boston: De Gruyter.

Konetzke, Richard. 1958. *Documentos para la historia social de Hispanoamérica 1492–1810*. Madrid: CSIC.

Labov, William. 1994. *Principles of linguistic change*, vol 1: *Internal factors*. Oxford: Blackwell.

Lara Bermejo, Víctor. 2015. *Los tratamientos de 2PL en Andalucía occidental y Portugal: estudio geo- y sociolingüístico de un proceso de gramaticalización*. PhD thesis. Madrid: Universidad Autónoma de Madrid. http://www.infoling.org/repository/PhDdiss-Infoling-22-7-2015.pdf (14.6.2017).

Levelt, Willem J. M. 1989. *Speaking: From intention to articulation*. Cambridge, MA: MIT Press.

Lipski, John M. 1994. *Latin American spanish*. New York: Longman.

Lorenzo Ramos, Antonio. 1981. Algunos datos sobre el leísmo en el español de Canarias. In Manuel Alvar (ed.), *I Simposio Internacional de Lengua Española*, 253–263. Las Palmas: Cabildo Insular de Gran Canaria.

Mannheim, Bruce. 1991. *The language of the Inka since the European invasion*. Austin: University of Texas Press.

Mejías Álvarez, María Jesús. 1995. El nacimiento de la última audiencia indiana. Sede, artistas y costes de la Audiencia del Cuzco. *Laboratorio de arte* 8. 193–206.

Merma Molina, Gladys. 2007. *Contacto lingüístico entre el español y el quechua: un enfoque cognitivo-pragmático de las transferencias morfosintácticas en el español andino peruano*. PhD thesis. Alicante: Universidad de Alicante. https://rua.ua.es/dspace/bitstream/10045/4114/1/tesis_doctoral_gladys_merma.pdf.

Morgan, Terrell A. & Scott A. Schwenter. 2016. *Vosotros, ustedes*, and the myth of the symmetrical Castilian pronoun system. In Alejandro Cuza, Lori Czerwionka & Daniel Olson (eds.), *Inquiries in Hispanic linguistics – from theory to empirical evidence*, 263–280. Amsterdam/Philadelphia: John Benjamins.

Moser, Karolin. 2010. San José (Costa Rica): Desde los significados pragmáticos del ustedeo en el registro coloquial actual hacia sus primeras manifestaciones en el Valle Central (siglo XVIII). In Martin Hummel, Bettina Kluge & María Eugenia Vázquez Laslop (eds.), *Formas y fórmulas de tratamiento en el mundo hispánico*, 671–713. México DF: El Colegio de México/Universität Graz.

Muro Orejón, Antonio (ed.). 1969. *Cedulario americano del siglo XVIII. Cédulas de Felipe V.* Sevilla: Escuela de Estudios Hispanoamericanos.

NGLE see Real Academia Española & Asociación de Academias de la Lengua Española.

Niño-Murcia, Mercedes. 1997. Linguistic purism in Cuzco, Peru. A historical perspective. *Language Problems and Language Planning* 21,2. 134–161.

Octavio de Toledo y Huerta, Álvaro S. 2008. Un nuevo esquema adversativo en el primer español moderno (ca. 1675–1825): la historia del nexo *sino es*. In José G. Moreno de Alba & Concepción Company Company (eds.), *Actas del VII Congreso Internacional de Historia de la Lengua Española*, I, 877–907. Madrid: Arco Libros.

Perl, Matthias & Sybille Große. 1995. Textos afro-hispánicos y criollos del siglo XIX. In Peter P. Konder, Matthias Perl & Klaus Pörtl (eds.), *Estudios de literatura y cultura colombianas y de lingüística afro-hispánica*, 205–221. Frankfurt: Peter Lang.

Pfänder, Stefan (in collaboration with Juan A. Ennis, Mario Soto Rodriguez & España Villegas Pinto). 2009. *Gramática Mestiza – Presencia del quechua en el castellano boliviano*, vol. 2. La Paz (Bolivia): IBLEL.

Real Academia Española & Asociación de Academias de la Lengua Española. 2009. *Nueva Gramática de la Lengua Española*, 2 vols. Madrid: Espasa Calpe.

Real Díaz, José Joaquín. 1991 [1970]. *Estudio diplomático del documento indiano*. Madrid: Dirección de Archivos Estatales.

Rivarola, José Luis. 2005. Sobre los orígenes y la evolución del español de América. In Volker Noll, Klaus Zimmermann & Ingrid Neumann-Holzschuh (eds.), *El español en América: Aspectos teóricos, particularidades, contactos*, 33–48. Frankfurt/Madrid: Vervuert/ Iberoamericana.

Sedano, Mercedes. 2011. *Manual de gramática del español, con especial referencia al español de Venezuela*. Caracas: Universidad Central de Venezuela.

Selting, Margret, et al. 2009. Gesprächsanalytisches Transkriptionssystem 2 (GAT 2). *Gesprächsforschung – Online-Zeitschrift zur verbalen Interaktion* 10, 353–402. www.gespraechsforschung-ozs.de (13.4.2012).

Silva-Corvalán, Carmen. 1994. *Language contact and change*. Oxford: Clarendon Press.

Silverman, Helaine. 2002. Touring ancient times: The present and presented past in contemporary Peru. *American Anthropologist* 104,3. 881–902.

Simon, Horst. 2005. *Only you?* Philological investigations into the alleged inclusive-exclusive distinction in the second person plural. In Elena Filimonova (ed.), *Clusivity. Typology and case studies of the inclusive-exlusive distinction*, 113–150. Amsterdam/Philadelphia: John Benjamins.

Slobin, Dan I. 2016. Thinking for speaking and the construction of evidentiality in language contact. In Mine Güven, Didar Akar, Balkız Öztürk & Meltem Kelepir (eds.), *Exploring* the Turkish linguistic landscape: Essays in honor of Eser Erguvanlı-Taylan*, 105–120. Amsterdam/Philadelphia: John Benjamins.

Smirnova, Elena. 2015. Constructionalization and constructional change. In Jóhanna Barðdal, Elena Smirnova, Lotte Sommerer & Spike Gildea (eds.), *Diachronic construction grammar*, 81–106. Amsterdam/Philadelphia: John Benjamins.

Soto Rodríguez, Mario & Philipp Dankel. In press. Contacto, cambio multifactorial y dinámico en la zona andina – epistemicidad encubierta en construcciones con DECIR. In Álvaro Ezcurra & Carlos Garatea (eds.), *Español de América. Historia y Contactos*. Frankfurt/Lima: Peter Lang/Fondo Editorial de la Pontifica Universidad Católica del Perú.

Soto Rodríguez, Mario & Víctor Fernández Mallat. 2012. Marcando referencias y vínculos en el español andino: A propósito del llamado doble posesivo. In Philipp Dankel, Víctor Fernández Mallat, Juan Carlos Godenzzi & Stefan Pfänder (eds.), *Neue Romania 41 – El español de los Andes: Estrategias cognitivas en interacciones situadas*, 57–88. Munich: Lincom.

van den Berghe, Pierre L. see Berghe.

Vázquez Laslop, María Eugenia. 2012. Títulos nobiliarios e identidad a debate en el primer congreso mexicano (1822). In Sabine Pfleger, Joachim Steffen & Martina Steffen (eds.), *Alteridad y aliedad. La construcción de la identidad con el otro y frente al otro*, 167–191. México DF: Universidad Autónoma Nacional de México.

Wagner, Claudio. 1996/1997. Sobre el posesivo *vuestro* en el español de Chile. *Anuario de Lingüística Hispánica* 12–13. 855–861.

Appendix: Transcription Conventions

based on Selting et al. (2009) and ICOR (2013)

`(.)`	micropause (shorter than 0.2 sec)
`(-)`, `(--)`, `(---)`	pauses of 0.2–0.5, 0.5–0.7, 0.7–1.0 sec.
`(2.85)`	measured pause
`:`, `::`, `:::`	segmental lengthening, according to duration
`/`	pitch rising to high at end of intonation phrase
`\`	pitch falling to low at end of intonation phrase
`VUEStras`	strong, primary stress
`señores_e:h`	assimilation of words
`°°señores°°`	low voice volume
`<<percussion> >`	commentaries regarding voice and other sound qualities with scope
`<<music>>`	description of extralinguistic actions and sounds

María Marta García Negroni and Silvia Ramírez Gelbes

Prescriptive and descriptive norms in second person singular forms of address in Argentinean Spanish

vos, *usted*, *tú*

Abstract: In this chapter, we analyze and compare the use of second person singular terms of address (*vos/usted/tú*) in Argentinean mass-consumption audiovisual and printed texts from two different periods (1960 and 2015). Using the distinction between prescriptive and descriptive norms (axiological and objective in Blanco 2000), we show that the paradigm of the former has changed over the last fifty years and now overlaps with the latter. However, there is still a gap between both norms: the use of *tú/contigo* and the *voseo reforzado* ("double" *voseo*) in present subjunctive. We propose an explanation for both phenomena in terms of social proximity and symbolic identity.

Keywords: Argentinean *voseo*, prescriptive norm, descriptive norm, audiovisual corpus, social proximity, symbolic identity, *vos*, *usted*, *tú*, "double" *voseo*

1 Introduction

Considered a vulgar form of address throughout Hispanic America during the 19th and early 20th centuries, the use of second person singular pronoun *vos* (*voseo* in Spanish) was criticized by advocates promoting normalization – standardization throughout Spanish-speaking areas – who favored the use of second person singular pronoun *tú* (*tuteo* in Spanish) over *vos*. This position has been supported by well-known authors, such as Andrés Bello, who claimed:

> El *vos* de que se hace tanto uso en Chile en el diálogo familiar, es una vulgaridad que debe evitarse, y el construirlo con el singular de los verbos una corrupción insoportable.
>
> (Bello 1945 [1847]: 339 § 234)

> 'The pronoun *vos*, widely employed in Chilean colloquial conversation, is a vulgarity that must be avoided, and constructions including it together with the singular form of a verb are an unacceptable corruption.'

Note: We would like to thank José Negroni for his careful reading of the English version of this chapter.

Normalization turned out to be successful in Chile and Peru, but it did not have a decisive impact on Argentinean Spanish. In Argentina, the National Council of Education (*Consejo Nacional de Educación*) required over the years that primary and middle school teachers address their students by the pronoun *tú* (Kurlat 1941). However, no native Argentinean speaker would nowadays employ the pronoun *tú* or present indicative/imperative *tú* forms to address a compatriot in any communicative situation characterized by trust, intimacy, informality and familiarity (García Negroni & Ramírez Gelbes 2004, 2010). This has been the situation at least since the 1960s.

In this chapter, we will analyze the use of second person singular terms of address (*vos*/ *usted*/*tú* forms) in Argentinean mass-consumption audiovisual and printed texts from two different periods. Firstly, we will explore the use of second person singular forms in a 1960s corpus (which includes the Argentinean film *La patota* starring Mirtha Legrand in 1960, political TV programs, presidential interviews, newscasts, cooking shows and magazines). Secondly, we will compare these results with those obtained from a contemporary corpus (which includes the latest version of *La patota* starring Dolores Fonzi in 2015, political TV programs, interviews with the current president, newscasts, cooking shows and magazines).

According to Blanco (2000), two types of norms must be distinguished: objective (or descriptive), and axiological (or prescriptive). Objective norms are defined as the culturally established and socially validated realization of the abstract possibilities of a certain linguistic system. Prescriptive norms, on the other hand, correspond to the current model of exemplary language usage in any community and every prescription concerning it. The main hypothesis in this chapter is that the prescriptive normative paradigm has changed over the last fifty years and now corresponds to the descriptive norm. After giving a brief historical account of second person singular forms of address in Argentinean Spanish, we will attempt to confirm our hypothesis by analyzing some corpus-derived examples.

2 Brief historical overview: from Latin *vos* to Argentinean *vos*

As is widely known and from an epistemological point of view, Spanish *tú* has its roots in Latin second person singular pronoun *tu*. In Latin, there is originally no T-V distinction (Brown & Gilman 1960: 254). Spanish *vos* stems from Latin second person plural pronoun *vos*, which started being used in the 4th century to address the emperor, who embodied two roles simultaneously: the emperor of the Western Roman Empire (based in Rome) and the emperor of the Eastern

Roman Empire (based in Constantinople). Contemporary pronoun *vos* is therefore connected with power from a historical point of view as *pluralis maiestatis* ('royal we'). It is also the case that "plurality is a very old and ubiquitous metaphor of power" (Brown & Gillman 1960: 254). As time went by, the *vos* employed to address the emperor was assimilated by the nobility. Nobles began to employ *vos* among themselves and were addressed by *vos* by lower classes.

By the 16th century in Spain, *vos* was so widely used that it started losing its capacity to discriminate among different situations. This encouraged the resurgence of a substitute for conveying formality and social distance, *vuestra merced,* which eventually became *usted.* According to different specialists, such as Fontanella de Weinberg (1999), the use of *vos* at that time was restricted to two very different scenarios. On the one hand, *vos* was a specific term for symmetrical communication between peers and asymmetrical interchanges between parents and children, or between uncles/aunts and nephews/nieces. On the other hand, it maintained "su valor de fórmula de respeto de alta formalidad en lo que en la época se conocía como su "uso antiguo", ya que conservaba el valor característico de vos en la Edad Media" 'the status of a respectful and formal term of address, which was considered "old-fashioned usage" at that time since it was close to the use of *vos* in the Middle Ages' (Fontanella de Weinberg 1999: 1412). Given that *vos* was becoming polysemic, the social strain of avoiding ambiguity encouraged the reassertion of *tú* in intimate, familiar contexts and *vuestra merced* in highly respectful and formal contexts.

This novel pronominal usage travelled from Spain to Mexican and Peruvian viceroyalties. The use of *vos* as a term of address, established in Hispanic America since the 15th century, prevailed in those areas far from the viceroyal courteous norm, where "faltó una clase social celosa de sus privilegios culturales" 'there was no social class protective about its cultural privileges' (Di Tullio 2006: 48). However, *vos* was uprooted from viceroyalty centers Mexico and Lima, "donde la lengua tenía un alto grado de estandarización" 'where language was highly standardized' (Fontanella de Weinberg 1999: 1414).

In fact, the overall use of *vos* in Hispanic America was progressively stigmatized, and during the 19th and early 20th centuries its use was criticized and considered vulgar. In present-day usage, however, in some Spanish-speaking areas both familiar terms of address *tú* and *vos* are employed to address a singular interlocutor, though rarely on an equal basis. In some regions, for example, in Chile, the use of *vos* forms – pronominal ones particularly – is limited and usually stigmatized, whereas the verbal and pronominal *tú* paradigm is considered the standard variety. In other areas such as Argentina, the pronominal *vos* paradigm no longer carries the stigma, and despite the criticisms, the *vos* paradigm is currently accepted as part of Argentine linguistic norms – both prescriptive and descriptive – and it is generally employed by Argentinean speakers. An illustrative example is the radio advertising slogan of the Argentinean women's magazine *Para Ti* in the late 1980s: "*Para Ti* quiere decir para vos" '*Para Ti* means for you'. The slogan is a play on words: the name of the magazine means 'for you' in Spanish but employs *ti* (oblique case for the *tú* paradigm) instead of *vos*. The use of *ti* in the magazine name was a "translation" of a formula crystallized by the prescriptive norm – not by the descriptive one – into Argentinean variety.

Nevertheless, the composition of the *vos* paradigm in Argentinean Spanish is not homogeneous. Indeed, second person familiar terms of address are realized by *vos* forms as much as by *tú* forms if we look at the whole paradigm. In the next section, we will consider this mixed *vos* paradigm in Argentinean Spanish.

3 The mixed *vos* paradigm in Argentinean Spanish

Table 1 sets out the pronominal paradigm for *voseo*.

Table 1: Pronominal paradigm in present-day Argentinean Spanish.

Oblique	Genitive	Accusative and dative	Nominative and vocative
vos	*tuyo*	*te*	*vos*

Examples (1) to (6) illustrate this paradigm, with pronominal and verbal *vos* forms highlighted.[1] The examples were all retrieved from Argentinean sources (CREA, Google sites, mass and social media, literature, ethnographic personal corpus), both oral and written. *Vos* forms appear in nominative (examples (1) and (6)), vocative (example (2)) and oblique (examples (3) and (5)). *Tú* forms appear in accusative (example (4)), dative (example (5)), and genitive (example (6)). Examples (4) to (6) show the coexistence of *vos* forms (pronominal and verbal) with *tú* forms: *sos* and *te* (example (4)), *sabes*, *te* and *vos* (example (5)), and *vos*, *hacé* and *tuya* (example (6)).

(1) Si *vos* te *vas*/Mi amor, si *vos* te *vas*/Nada más/Podemos decirnos, mi amor.

   'If you go away/My love, if you go away/Nothing else/can we say to each other, my love.'
   (Piero, *Si vos te vas*, http://www.musica.com/letras.asp?letra=1285562)

---

1 All the examples keep their original spelling – e.g. in example (5) written accents in *sabés* (verb 'know') and in *cómo* (interrogative pronoun 'how') are missing.

(2) Eh, *vos*, que *hacés* ahí/pegado contra la pared como una mosca/che, *vos*, que no *te movés*, no *te movés*/con esta música.

'Hey, you, what are you doing there/stuck to the wall like a fly/hey, you, who ain't moving, ain't moving/with this music.'
(Memphis la blusera, *Como una mosca*, http://www.musica.com/letras. asp?letra=825272)

(3) Para *vos* lo peor es la libertad. Para *vos* lo peor es la libertad.

'The worst thing for you is freedom. The worst thing for you is freedom.'
(Sumo, *Viejos vinagres*, https://www.youtube.com/watch?v=X4xwKh1fpFw)

(4) No puedo hacerlo, *sos* mi dios/*te* veo, me sonrojo y tiemblo/qué idiota *te* hace el amor.

'I can't do it, you're my God/I see you, I blush and tremble/Love makes you such an idiot.'
(Bersuit Vergarabat, *Un pacto*, http://www.musica.com/letras.asp?letra=116007)

(5) *Sabes* como *te* dicen *a vos*...

'You know what they call you'
(Taringa.net, http://www.taringa.net/comunidades/humortaringa/1265546/ Sabes-como-te-dicen-a-vos.html)

(6) *Vos hacé* la *tuya*, yo hago la mía, y cuando quieras hacemos la nuestra.

'Do what you want, I do what I want, and when you feel like it, we do what we both want.'
(Facebook, https://www.facebook.com/frasesforfree/posts/249434588506642)

There are some very specific contexts in Argentinean Spanish where *tú* forms can also be employed for the second person singular nominative case and in prepositional phrases acting as modifiers (*ti* and *contigo*). Thus, when speaking to a foreigner (example (7)), in prayers (example (8)) and in poetry and songs (example (9)) *tú* forms may be found.[2]

---

2 Rizzi (2002) includes *tú* as one of the three variants in the current Argentinean Spanish pronominal system (i.e. *tú*, *vos* and *usted*) and mentions the use of *tú* forms in funeral services, religious prayers, children games and some literary texts.

(7) Yo tengo algunas coincidencias *contigo* respecto del diagnóstico que *haces* en algunas cosas.

'I share certain similarities with you concerning the assessment you make in some things.'
(From Salta governor, J.M.Urtubey, to the Spanish journalist Pilar Rahola, in *Almorzando con Mirtha Legrand*, https://www.youtube.com/watch?v= VpOaGOTxLxs, 15 November, 2015)

(8) Dios te salve, María, llena *eres* de gracia./Bendita *tú eres* entre todas las mujeres.

'Hail Mary, full of grace./Blessed art thou among women.'
(Hail Mary, prayer)[3]

(9) Después de *ti* ya no hay nada/ya no queda más nada, nada de nada./Después de *ti* es el olvido/un recuerdo perdido, nada de nada.

'After you there is nothing left/there is nothing left, nothing at all./After you, there is oblivion/a lost memory, nothing at all.'
(Lerner, A., *Después de ti*, http://www.musica.com/letras.asp?letra=27995)

Similarly, in contexts where the familiar term of address *vos* could be felt too informal, some speakers may employ *tú* forms (example (10)) instead of *usted*, since they consider the latter too formal.

(10) Estoy de acuerdo *contigo*. 'I agree with you.'
(ethnographic personal corpus)

This was the case for the speaker of example (10), a university professor who after his lecture on the national elections in 2015 answered *Estoy de acuerdo contigo* 'I agree with you', to an interlocutor (a senior businessman) he had never met before. Once the conference finished, the professor was asked why he chose to use *tú* forms. He replied that he didn't want to be rude, which he felt he would have been if he had used *usted* – in a university context where most people employ a general *vos* – or *vos*, which he considered could be understood too intrusive or even daring.

---

3 Even though this is quite formulaic, in 1999 notebooks for clergymen the formulaic treatment "vosotros" (*La paz esté con vosotros* [May peace be with thou]) was changed into *ustedes* (*La paz esté con ustedes* [May peace be with you]), which suggests that only some formulae are changed.

According to Wainerman (1976: 5–6),

> Si actualmente en una tienda no somos tratados de vos sino de usted, sentimos que se nos percibe tan terriblemente viejos, y respetables, como para no merecer el tratamiento informal.

> 'Nowadays, if a shop attendant addresses us by *usted* instead of *vos*, we believe they considered us so terribly old and respectable that we cannot be addressed by an informal term of address.'

However, the use of *vos*, which has expanded over recent years, can still be considered excessively intimate in some contexts.

With regards to the verbal paradigm, present indicative and affirmative imperative forms take the stress on the last syllable (in Spanish, *formas agudas*), so that they belong exclusively to the *vos* paradigm, as in examples (11) and (12).[4]

(11) Cuando *vos empezás* a decir que habría que encontrar la unidad, yo entonces veo cosas muy hermosas pero muertas, flores disecadas y cosas así.

'When you start saying that unity should be found, I then see beautiful but dead things, dried flowers and things like that.'
(Julio Cortázar, 2004 [1963], *Rayuela*, Caracas: Biblioteca Ayacucho, p.86).

(12) *Descubrí* el teatro. *Viví* el teatro. *Vení* al teatro.

'Discover the theatre. Live the theatre. Come to the theatre.'
(http://www.venialteatro.org/)

In the case of other tenses, such as *pretérito perfecto simple* (example (13), similar to English simple past) and *futuro simple* (example (14), similar to English construction *will* + bare infinitive), standard verbal *vos* forms cannot be distinguished from verbal *tú* forms, even though they co-occur with *vos* nominative (see Table 2 below). However, there are two observations to make about the simple past (*pretérito perfecto simple*) and the present subjunctive for *vos*. Firstly, the simple past with *vos* has lost its etymological verb-final *-s* in standard Argentinean Spanish. According to different authors (Di Tullio 2006; RAE-ASALE 2009: 193, 208, among others), this loss may be due to the stigma that has been associated with the addition of a final *-s* in the *tú* simple past form.

---

4 In Spanish, words can be classified according to stress placement. Those words that take the stress on the last syllable are called *agudas,* those that take the stress on the penultimate syllable are called *graves* and those that take the stress on the syllable before the penultimate are called *esdrújulas.*

(13) *Vos dijiste* que Redrado era un golpeador y ahora volviste con él.

'You said Redrado was a [wife-]beater and now you are back with him.'
(Heated argument between Luciana Salazar and Yanina Latorre, https://www.primiciasya.com/yanina-latorre-luli-salazar-vos-dijiste-que-redrado-era-un-golpeador-y-ahora-volviste-el-n1173772)

(14) *Vos sabrás* lo que hacés arriba del escenario, pero abajo, siendo yo el técnico [...]

'You may know what to do on stage, but here, being myself the one in charge'
(Tinelli's warning to Soffritti, TKM, https://www.mundotkm.com/ar/hot-news/589801/el-reclamo-celoso-de-marcelo-tinelli-gaston-soffritti)

Secondly, the present subjunctive reveals a distinctive feature: when employed along with the pronoun *vos* (explicitly or implicitly), it can take the stress on the penultimate syllable (*formas graves*) which is typical of *tú* forms, as in examples (15) and (16), or on the last syllable (*formas agudas*) which is typical of *vos* forms, as in examples (17) and (18). This also occurs in the negative imperative form. We call this latter form *voseo reforzado* (García Negroni & Ramírez Gelbes 2003, 2004).

(15) Yo no quiero que vos *pienses*/Que esto es el final.

'I don't want you to think/That this is the end.'
(Los enanitos verdes, *Detrás de las ruinas*, http://www.letrasdecanciones.fm/los-enanitos-verdes/detras-de-las-ruinas#yo-no-quiero-que-vos-pienses)

(16) No te privaste de nada, buchón. Pero ahora la pagás.... No *mientas*.

'You didn't miss a thing, snitch. But now you will pay for it... Don't lie.'
(César Aira, "El criminal y el dibujante". *Relatos reunidos*, 2013, Barcelona: Mondadori, no pages)

(17) Igual, me chupa un huevo lo que vos *penses*[5] *[sic]*.

'Anyway, I don't give a damn about what you think.'
(Facebook. Concert gig, https://www.facebook.com/Igual-me-chupa-un-huevo-lo-que-vos-penses-283802138310302/)

---

5 The correct spelling would be *pensés*.

(18)   ¡No *mintás* más, Perro! 'Don't you lie again, Perro!'
(*Diario del fin del mundo*. Ushuaia, http://www.eldiariodelfindelmundo.
com/noticias/leer/50672/no-mintas-mas-perro.html)

Table 2 sets out the familiar second person singular verbal paradigm of Argentinean Spanish.

Table 2: The familiar second person singular verbal paradigm of Argentinean Spanish.[6]

	Typical *tú* forms	Typical *vos* forms
Present indicative	----	*empezás*; *querés*; *venís*
Present subjunctive	*empieces*; *quieras*; *vengas*	[*empecés*; *querás*; *vengás*]
Imperative	----	*empezá*; *queré*; *vení*
Simple past	*empezaste*; *quisiste*; *viniste*	[*empezastes*; *quisistes*; *vinistes*]
Future	*empezarás*; *querrás*; *vendrás*	-----

As it can be seen from Table 2, there are only four typical *vos* tenses. Whereas the present indicative and imperative are completely accepted as correct and do not compete with any alternative, typical *tú* forms may alternate with *vos* forms in the simple past (*pretérito perfecto simple*) and present subjunctive: as the latter are not registered in the *Diccionario de la lengua española (DLE)*, they are presented in square brackets in the Table.

4 Prescriptive and descriptive norms: historical context

As has already been mentioned, Blanco (2000) sets out two norms: the prescriptive or axiological norm, and the descriptive or objective norm. She defines the latter as the culturally established and socially validated realization of the abstract possibilities of a certain linguistic system. In other words, the descriptive norm is associated with how language is actually used at a given time as part of inherited habits (cf. Coseriu 1962), and it can be studied from a descriptive per-

---

6 The forms in square brackets are not registered in the *Diccionario de la lengua española*, and they are stigmatized, but they are the etymological *vos* forms in the simple past and present subjunctive.

spective. Blanco describes the prescriptive norm as including speakers' ideas of correct usage, the current model of standard language usage in a community and language prescriptions.

The prescriptivist perspective has exerted its influence on communication and educational public policies in Argentina. In 1934, for instance, the Instructions for Broadcasting Stations (*Instrucciones para las Estaciones de Radiodifusión*) were developed by Agustín P. Justo's *de facto* government. These instructions explicitly banned some Spanish varieties, such as *lunfardo* (Argentinian slang, which originated in the late 19th and early 20th centuries in the City of Buenos Aires due to immigrants' influence), *cocoliche* (Italian immigrants' creole, spoken in the City of Buenos Aires in the late 19th and early 20th centuries), *gauchesco* (spoken mainly in the Argentinean, Uruguayan and South-Brazilian countryside by peasants and *gauchos,* during colonial and postcolonial times) and *rioplatense* (spoken mainly in Buenos Aires, Rosario and Montevideo, and characterized by the use of *vos*). This ban was based on the idea that these varieties were not "in good taste". In 1943, the head of Telegraph and Post (*Correos y Telégrafos*) sent a memo in this regard, demanding the avoidance of 'every word belonging to slang and every idiom distorting the language that are so common in colloquial language, such as *salí, andá*, etc'[7] (Article 8, quoted by Vitale 1999).

General Edelmiro Farrell's *de facto* government developed these instructions further and in 1946 the *Manual de Instrucciones para las Estaciones de Radiodifusión* 'Instruction Manual for Broadcasting Stations' was published. This manual would be replaced by a less restrictive law during General Juan Domingo Peron's government. However, in 1957, during the Liberating Revolution (*Revolución Libertadora*),[8] this manual would be again replaced by its original form. Furthermore, these norms were echoed in public education of the time. For example, the National Council of Education banned the use of *vos* in every school under its government (Kurlat 1941; Vitale 1999). This meant that teachers had to address their students with *tú* and had to teach pronominal and verbal paradigms excluding *vos* forms.

---

7 In the original: "toda palabra del argot o bajofondo y de los modismos que desvirtúan el lenguaje y son tan comunes en el decir corriente, como *salí, andá*, etc."
8 This is the name given to the dictatorship that overthrew Juan Domingo Perón's constitutional government.

5 Corpus analysis: changes in prescriptive and descriptive norms from 1960 to 2015

The 1960s corpus we analyze here includes (a) examples where there is a gap between the prescriptive norm and the descriptive norm of the time;[9] (b) examples where the gap is closing between both norms; and (c) examples that do not respect the prescriptive norm.

The 2015 corpus, on the other hand, seems more homogeneous with regards to the identification of norms. Indeed, the recommendation of the Academia Argentina de Letras in 1982[10] and the standardization of the *vos* paradigm meant that the use of *vos* became part of the prescriptive norm in Argentina.

5.1 1960s: Gap between the prescriptive and descriptive norms

The 1960s corpus illustrates a certain respect for the prescriptive norm promoted by official spheres. The use of *tú* forms, both pronominal and verbal, and the limited direct address of the interlocutor are considered here as an illustration of the gap between the two norms.

Even though the use of *tú* (pronominal and verbal forms) is limited, it is employed, albeit non-systematically, and with a supplementary meaning: it contributes to the construction of specific scenarios. The use of *tú* in example (19) indicates an assumed, socially detached respect (it is the nursemaid who addresses the child with *tú*, demonstrating at the same time the close affective bond she has with the child who she has brought up).

(19) Nursemaid to Paulina
—Paulina, *tienes* que tomar el té. No *puedes* estar sin comer nada.
'—Paulina, you have to drink the tea. You must have something to eat.'
(*La patota*, film directed by D. Tinayre, 1960)

---

9 1960s TV programs on the Internet (e.g. *El amor tiene cara de mujer*, available at https://www. youtube.com/watch?v=RhgnlUUwLMs) can be visited for verification. Even though the objective norm also included the use of *tú*, it was restricted to written language, e.g. letters from parents to children, poems or songs. In oral language, this usage was even more limited, and it was restricted almost exclusively to elementary school teachers, due to ministerial guidelines (see Rizzi 2002).

10 As Carricaburo (2016) states, in 1982, the Argentinean Academy of Letters was the first academy in Hispanic America to accept the use of *vos* as an educated norm.

In examples (20) and (21), the use of *tú* contributes to the construction of a highly intersubjective and emotive situation, as in melodramas from previous decades.[11]

(20) Alberto to Paulina
　　　—Hay algo que no te deja resolver, Paulina, no sé qué. Una explicación, un extravío, algo que está en tu subconsciente. ¿Cómo *puedes* aceptar eso? ¡Ni siquiera pensarlo! Traer al mundo un hijo de no *sabes* quién... Nunca me separaré de *ti*.

　　　'—There is something that doesn't let you solve this, Paulina, and I don't know what it is. An explanation, a deviation, something in your subconscious. How can you accept that? No way! Having a child when you don't know who the father is... I will never separate from you.'
　　　(*La patota*, film directed by D. Tinayre, 1960)

(21)　Paulina to her father
　　　—Te quedaste solo muy joven y no buscaste otra mujer. Mamá murió al nacer yo. ¿*Piensas* que yo te la quité? ¿Que soy culpable de su muerte?

　　　'—You have been alone since you were very young and you didn't look for another woman. Mom died when I was born. Do you think I took her away from you? Do you think I'm responsible for her death?'
　　　(*La patota*, film directed by D. Tinayre, 1960)

In example (22), the *tú* forms maintain the original structure of the proverb alluded to (*Dime con quién andas y te diré quién eres*)[12] despite the construction of a familiar scenario between the participants (the reader and acquaintances alluded to) in the quoted discourse.

(22)　*Dime* qué hilo *usas*... ¡Y te diré como *coses*!

　　　'Tell me what kind of thread you use... And I will tell you how you sew!'
　　　(*Mucho gusto* magazine N° 176, June 1961)

---

11 One example is the film *La pródiga*, starring Eva Duarte in 1945 (available at https://www.youtube.com/watch?v=0eo26wYArYM, last accessed 31 January, 2017).
12 Literally, "Tell me who you hang out with, and I'll tell you who you are", that corresponds to the standard English proverb "Birds of a feather fly together".

The same respect for the prescriptive norm can be observed in the limited direct address of the interlocutor found in some of the examples, at least when compared to similar present-day situations. Pairs of hosts on TV shows, who addressed their audience with *usted* or *ustedes*, tended not to use the second singular form to each other in the 60s (cf. *Telenoche*, newscast of Canal 13).[13] We argue that this strategy is an attempt to follow the still prevailing prescriptive norms in the *Instructions for Broadcasting Stations*. Nowadays, *vos* forms are employed extensively in interactions among broadcast journalists.

5.2 1960s: Prescriptive norm closer to descriptive norm

The 1960s corpus includes some examples where the two norms become closer, relating to the use of *usted* and illustrated in examples (23) to (28). They show the extended use of *usted*, which corresponded to both the prescriptive and descriptive norms. The use of *usted* was extended to many different kinds of interchanges and situations. In the selected examples the use of *usted* reveals an acknowledgement of the social distance between interlocutors, either because of a lack of familiarity or to indicate social hierarchy.

(23) Headmaster to Paulina
　　 —¿De modo que *usted es* la Srta. Vidal?
　　 —Sí, señorita.
　　 —¿*Usted es* católica?
　　 —Sí, señorita.
　　 —Me alegro.

　　 '—So, you are Miss Vidal?
　　 —Yes, Miss.
　　 —Are you a Catholic?
　　 —Yes, Miss.
　　 —I'm glad to hear that.'
　　 (*La patota*, film directed by D. Tinayre, 1960)

---

13 An example of what is said here can be observed in https://www.youtube.com/watch?v= oYg2s8lLORc (1966). Even though one of the hosts uses *vos* and ¿*no te parece?* or the first name of the addressee, it is clear they tend to avoid the second person singular (verbal and pronominal) throughout the newscast.

(24) Student to Paulina
   —*Usted es* la que pone las reglas.

   —'You are the ruler here.'
   (*La patota*, film directed by D. Tinayre, 1960)

(25) Para que a *usted le* digan siempre "¡Qué bien coses!", *realice* todas sus costuras con hilos PBT.

   'So that everybody tells you "How well you sew!", make all your seams using PBT thread.'
   (*Mucho gusto* magazine N° 176, June 1961)

(26) Argentinean cook Doña Petrona to assistant and host:
   —Ana María, por favor, ¿les *pasa* los ingredientes?
   —Juanita, por favor, ¿me *levanta* la manga?

   '—Ana María, would you give them the ingredients, please?
   —Juanita, would you roll my sleeve up, please?'
   (*Buenas tardes, mucho gusto*, TV show for housewives, 1962)

(27) Argentine TV host Andrés Percivalle to the bar's owner:
   —¿*Usted está* contento de que este bar sea un centro de reuniones para estudiantes?

   '—Are you happy with this bar being a meeting point for students?'
   (*Telenoche*, newscast of Canal 13, 1966)

(28) A journalist to the president:
   —¿Qué significa para *usted*, Sr. Presidente?

   '—What does it mean to you, Mr. President?'
   (Interview with president Lanusse, along with his family in 1971)

We want to stress that, as in example (22), the use of *tú* in example (25) creates a familiar, intimate scenario (Maingueneau 1999), in opposition to the main advertising text that only employs *usted* to address the audience (readers). This form is much less used in present-day discourse, as we will show below.

5.3 1960s: Deviations from the prescriptive norm

Finally, we include some examples that do not fit the prescriptive norm of the time: the use of *vos* in examples (29) and (30) and *voseo reforzado* or *subjuntivo agudo* (subjunctive verbs with the stress on the last syllable) in examples (31) and (32).

(29) Paulina to his father:
—Lo que *vos hacés* es como el suicidio.
—¿Por qué no te *olvidás* de que fuiste juez? Me *tratás* muy duramente a veces.

'—What you are doing is like committing suicide.
—Why don't you forget your days as a judge? You sometimes treat me so harshly.'
(*La patota*, film directed by D. Tinayre, 1960)

(30) Argentine TV host Andrés Percivalle to a student, during an interview at don Celestino's bar:
—Y *vos*, ¿qué *estudiás*?
—*Mirá*, yo estudio Derecho.

'— And, what do you study?
—Well, I study Law.'
(*Telenoche*, newscast of Canal 13, 1966)

(31) Alberto to Paulina:
—He sido humillada, pero nunca... (llora)
—Por favor, Paulina, no *llorés*! Perdoname, te hago hablar de eso y te hago sufrir. Si te hubiese acompañado esa noche... Tenés que perdonarme.

'—I have been humiliated, but I never... (she cries)
—Paulina, please don't cry! Forgive me, I'm making you talk about it and I'm making you suffer. If I had joined you that night... You have to forgive me.'
(*La patota*, film directed by D. Tinayre, 1960)

(32) From one gang member (*patota*) to another:
—Contá ¿qué hace? Dale, Y ¿te gusta?
—Dame, no sabe, yo te cuento.
—No te *avivés*. Vos ya miraste.

'—Tell me, what is she doing? Come on, do you like it?
—Give it to me, I'll tell you about it.
—Don't be a know-it-all. You have already watched it.'
(*La patota*, film directed by D. Tinayre, 1960)

As can be seen, the 1960s corpus illustrates usage that did not suit the prescriptive norm from the time, such as the use of pronominal and verbal *vos* forms, typical of informal or intimate contexts.[14] Examples (29) and (30) exhibit typical *vos* forms of address (i.e. present indicative and imperative). Examples (31) and (32), on the other hand, reveal subjunctive forms with stress on the last syllable (typical *vos* forms or *formas agudas*). Even nowadays, many Argentinean speakers consider the latter forms incorrect but they occur in some contexts in alternation with typical *tú* forms or *formas graves* (stressed on the penultimate syllable) as will be shown below.

We have already suggested in previous studies (García Negroni & Ramírez Gelbes 2003, 2004) that subjunctive *formas agudas* must be regarded as a case of *voseo reforzado*. In fact, if typical subjunctive *tú* forms with the stress on the penultimate syllable (*formas graves*) are considered part of the *vos* paradigm – as they can be employed along with pronominal *vos* forms (*cf. vos amás, amá (vos), vos amaste, vos amarías, vos ames*), typical subjunctive *vos* forms with the stress on the last syllable (*formas agudas*) should be interpreted as double *voseantes* ("doubly" belonging to the *vos* paradigm). In fact, these forms are not only employed along with pronoun *vos*, but also take the stress on the last syllable, which is typical of present indicative and imperative *vos* forms. Just as last-syllable stress in enclitic constructions[15] (*cf. dámelo* vs. *dameló* 'give it to me' vs. 'give it to ME'), this "double" condition of the present subjunctive represents a stronger and closer bond between speaker and hearer by diminishing the social distance between them.

5.4 2015: Towards a convergence of prescriptive and descriptive norms

The 2015 corpus demonstrates that the use of *vos* has increased significantly, without underestimating those scenarios where other forms of address are

---

14 We should bear in mind that the Academia Argentina de Letras did not recommend the use of *vos* in every sphere of Argentinean high culture language until 1982.
15 The Spanish imperative requires postponing object pronouns. This position is called *enclitic*.

employed. This increase has led in particular to a decline in the use of *usted* and to an even greater reduction in the use of *tú* (close to become extinct), although the latter can still be found in the very specific situations we have already mentioned.

The following examples are organized from the smallest gap between prescriptive and descriptive norms to the greatest. The convergence of norms is manifested by the use of *vos* forms and *usted* forms in informal and formal contexts respectively (bearing in mind that informality is expanding in present-day exchanges). Examples (33) to (38) illustrate the use of *vos*.

(33) The person in charge of the educational program to Paulina:
—*Vení* así la saludamos.

'—Come here, to welcome her.'
(*La Patota*, directed by S. Mitre, 2015)

(34) A student to the person in charge of the educational program:
—*Vos sos* el Rubi?

'—Are you the Rubi?'
(*La Patota*, directed by S. Mitre, 2015)

(35) *Ahorrá* tiempo. *Comprá* tus entradas en TuEntrada.com
'Save time. Buy your tickets at TuEntrada.com'
(*La Nación* magazine, 30 April, 2016)

(36) Argentinean cook Narda Lepes to the audience:
—Te la presento. Tal vez, la *conocés* como jengibrillo.

'—I introduce it to you. Maybe you know it as *jengibrillo* [ginger + quince].'
(*Tres minutos con Narda*, cooking TV show, Fox, 2016)

(37) Argentinean TV journalist María Laura Santillán to another journalist (Santo Biasatti):
—¿Y? ¿Qué tal? ¿*Estás* contento?

'—So? How are you? Are you happy?'
(*Telenoche*, newscast from Canal 13, 2016)

(38) Argentinean TV host Santiago del Moro to the audience:
—¡Hay tanta actualidad, tanto para discutir! Un programa apasionante, cargado de información, cargado de voces, cargado de informes, por supuesto. Y *vos* que *sos* el/la protagonista de cada noche, muy buenas noches.

'—There is so much news, so much to discuss! A fascinating show, full of information, full of voices, full of reports, of course. And you are the one starring every night, good night.'
(*Intratables*, political TV show, Canal América, April 2016)

Even though these examples do not show how frequently *vos* is used, the form clearly occurs in most contexts in the 2015 corpus, in every situation examined and with all kinds of interlocutors, irrespective of their age or social background. This is illustrated in the shift in similar situations from *usted* to *vos* from the 1960s to 2015, as shown in examples (23) compared with example (33) or example (24) compared with example (34), and in the shift from limited direct address of the interlocutor to *vos* in TV newscasts as in example (37).

However, as examples (39) to (42) show below, the use of *usted* has not disappeared. Let's take, for instance, the film *La Patota*. Although some uses of *usted* in institutional, formal contexts were found in the latest version of the film (2015), this term of address is exclusively restricted to four scenes, one of which is presented in example (39), between a policeman and Paulina.[16] The rest of the scenes (i.e. between Paulina and her father, her boyfriend, her rapist, the doctor, the psychologist, the person in charge of the educational program, etc.) always include the reciprocal use of *vos*.

(39) Commissioner to Paulina, in the lineup:
—Señorita Vidal, están las personas para el reconocimiento. *Usted conoce* el procedimiento. Cuando *esté* en condiciones, por favor.

'—Miss Vidal, the people for the lineup are here. You know the procedure. When you are ready, please.'
(*La Patota*, directed by S. Mitre, 2015)

Restricted as they are in everyday use, *usted* forms still remain in some formal contexts: certain advertisements addressed to older addressees (example (40)), media talks with foreign or older people (example (41)), and interviews with certain representatives of the government. Example (42) is revealing because the exchange displays the tension between the previous relationship both interlocutors have (marked by *vos* forms) and the current political position of the interviewee (which calls for the use of *usted*).

---

16 The other three scenes with *usted* forms are between the commissioner and Paulina's father (the judge), between one of the students and his teacher, and between Paulina and a Government officer cross-examining her.

(40) BATIMAT. Expovivienda. *Agéndela!* 1 al 4 de junio 2016 La Rural. *Pre-acredítese* sin cargo en www.batev.com.ar

'BATIMAT. Expovivienda (home exposition). Put it in your diary! 1st to 4th of June 2016. La Rural. Register yourself for free at www.batev.com.ar'
(*Clarín* journal, 13 May, 2016)

(41) A journalist to an interviewee:
—Pilar, *déjeme* decir*le*, que afortunadamente en la Argentina desde antes de este gobierno han existido medios opositores al oficialismo.

'—Pilar, let me tell you that, fortunately, in Argentina before this government media opposed to the ruling party have existed.'
(*Intratables*, political TV show, Canal América, November 2015)

(42) A journalist to the president:
—Bueno, es la primera vez que *lo* entrevisto como presidente. Y además, en realidad, no *lo* puedo tutear, porque estoy entrevistando al presidente de la República Argentina. Me es hasta raro, porque yo a *usted* lo conozco de la época de Boca.

'—Well, this is the first time I have interviewed you as president. I actually can't address you by *vos*, because I'm interviewing the Argentinean president. It's strange, because I know you from the Boca days.'[17]
(*Animales sueltos*, political TV show, 21 July, 2016)

Even though they are not very frequent, the 2015 corpus has examples of alternation between *usted* and *vos* in the very same scene and produced by the same speaker, whenever he or she feels there is a change in the situation. In example (43) the shift marks a change in the audience (the speaker addresses the teacher but now in front of students), and in example (44) the change is provoked by the intimacy of the topic (the speaker reveals the name of her rapist to Paulina).

(43) The person in charge of the educational program to Paulina, in front of students:
—Profesora, *se* los dejo.

'—Miss, I leave you with them.'
(*La Patota*, directed by S. Mitre, 2015)

---

[17] The President of Argentina was previously the president of Boca Juniors Football Club, and the comment refers to that period.

In previous scenes, when the students were not present, *vos* forms were employed – see example (13).

(44) Ciro's former girlfriend to Paulina:
—Me dice la Laura que *usted está* embarazada... *Mire, señora,* yo no *la* conozco bien pero me imagino lo que *usted está pasando.* Si *quiere* que hable con la policía o que *le* salga de testigo o algo...
El que *te* violó *a vos* es el Ciro. Es el más grande de todos. No va a la escuela. Trabaja en el aserradero. Yo salí con él un par de veces.

'—Laura told me you're pregnant... Look, lady, I don't know you well, but I can imagine what you're going through. If you want me to talk to the police or to act as witness or anything...
The one who raped you is Ciro. He is the eldest. He doesn't go to school. He works in the sawmill. I went out with him a couple of times.'
(*La Patota*, directed by S. Mitre, 2015)

As a comparison, within the 48 scenes of 1960s version of *La patota*, *vos* forms were employed in 55% of dialogues and *usted* forms, in 48%. These figures show that, in practice, *vos* and *usted* were almost equally employed. This compares with the latest version of the film (71 scenes), where the use of *vos* rises to 82% and the use of *usted* drops to 15% – six times less than *vos*. Moreover, the same characters' linguistic choices in similar scenes (e.g. Paulina and the headmaster/ the person in charge, the doctor and Paulina) shift from *usted* to *vos* from one version to the other.

Although these figures relate to only two examples of one audiovisual genre, they can be analyzed along with the other audiovisual examples. In the 1960s, *usted* forms prevailed in TV cooking shows, TV political programs, print advertisements and in presidential interviews, either because of being generally chosen or because of limited direct address. This contrasts to 2015, where *vos* forms are the most frequent in all these contexts, even for addressing a president or the TV audience.

5.5 2015: Prescriptive norm farther from descriptive norm

The 2015 corpus also includes a few uses of *tú* and *voseo reforzado* (subjunctive forms with the stress on the last syllable) which exhibit a gap between the prescriptive and descriptive norms, as illustrated by examples (45) and (46) respectively.

(45) A TV host to the interviewee (a foreigner):
—Para recordarte, para acordarme de *ti*.

'—To remember you, to remember you.'
(*Intratables*, political TV show, Canal América, November 2015)

(46) Boyfriend to Paulina:
—Yo quiero que *hagás* lo que tengas ganas, pero que estés cerca de mí.

'—I want you to do whatever you like while you stand by me.'
(*La Patota*, directed by S. Mitre, 2015)

These examples deserve a different approach. Example (45), where an Argentin-ian addresses a foreigner, is a good example of the persistence of the old pre-scriptive norm. This phenomenon has already been studied from different per-spectives and by several authors (see, among others, Bein 1999; García Negroni & Ramírez Gelbes 2010; López García 2006; Ramírez Gelbes 2011). Argentinian speakers' perceptions of their own linguistic variety are typical of a substandard dialect, even though they do not consciously devalue it. This is why Argentinean speakers may switch from *vos* to *tú* forms when addressing a foreigner as if they believed they would not be properly understood.

On the other hand, example (46) is a subjunctive "double" *vos* form. Although it is not included in any grammar book or academic dictionary, this form conveys a closer intimacy – sometimes emphatic, sometimes aggressive – with the addressee. Indeed, while the use of *vos* indicates that interlocutors share a symbolic identity, the use of this subjunctive form (typical *vos* form or *forma aguda*) clearly reinforces the social proximity and reduces the symbolic gap between them, even physically – interlocutors get closer, either in a warm hug or in a physically hostile way.

6 Conclusion

In this chapter, we have demonstrated that the prescriptive normative paradigm of second person singular terms of address has been changing over the last fifty years in Argentina. Even though the chosen corpora (1960s and 2015) were col-lected from mass media, we consider them representative of the relationship between speaking norms in each period.

The paradigm that underlies the use of *vos/usted/tú* and limited direct address of the interlocutor in the first corpus differs considerably from that in the second corpus, which exclusively favors the use of *vos* in most contexts. In other words, a gap between the objective or descriptive norm – *vos* in familiar, intimate contexts and *usted* in respectful contexts marked by greater social distance – and the prescriptive norm – use of *usted/tú* and limited direct address of the interlocutor – was noted in the first corpus, whereas in the second corpus, the two norms were clearly becoming more closely identified. This identification between norms shows that the use of *vos* constitutes the main variant in most contexts, which has also been accepted, belatedly, by the Academia Argentina de Letras.

That said, there are two present-day examples that reveal a gap between the two norms. The first is the use of *tú* to address a foreigner or a compatriot, in order to convey greater social distance than the use of *vos* would convey but less than the use of *usted*. The second is the use of the present subjunctive with the stress on the last syllable (*forma aguda*), that responds to an attempt to reinforce social proximity and symbolic identity.

One last word concerning both corpora. There has also been a change in the frequency of use of the different terms of address that belong to the descriptive norm (*vos/usted*). Whereas in the 1960s corpus *vos* forms were employed similarly in proportional terms to *usted* forms, in the 2015 corpus the relative use of *vos* has increased significantly. The Argentinian president's response to the journalist quoted in example (42) is an eloquent illustration of this shift:

(47) Yo te desafío, a ver si lográs aguantar "no tratarme de vos" hasta el final, porque, después de tantos años de conocernos, para mí, se te va a escapar. [...] Bueno, pero convengamos que es una decisión tuya. Para mí es lo mismo: el respeto no pasa por si se tutea o no se tutea.

'I challenge you to keep on "not addressing me by *vos*" until the end; because, after so many years of knowing each other, I'm sure you won't be able to do it. [...] Well, let's agree that it's your decision. For me, it's the same: respect is not about addressing someone with *vos* or *usted*.'
(*Animales sueltos*, political TV show, Canal América, November 2015)

References

Bein, Roberto. 1999. El plurilingüismo como realidad lingüística, como representación sociolingüística y como estrategia glotopolítica. In Elvira Arnoux & Roberto Bein (eds.), *Prácticas y representaciones del lenguaje*, 191–216. Buenos Aires: Eudeba.

Bello, Andrés. 1945 [1847]. *Gramática de la lengua castellana*. Buenos Aires: Sopena.

Blanco, Mercedes. 2000. Norma y variedades: un problema de actitudes y políticas lingüísticas. In *Portal informativo sobre la lengua castellana*. http://www. unidadenladiversidad.com/historico/opinion/opinion_ant/2000/ mayo_2000/ opinion030500.htm (3 July, 2017).

Brown, Roger & Albert Gilman. 1960. The pronouns of power and solidarity. In Thomas Sebeok (ed.), *Style in language*, 253–276. Cambridge, MA: The MIT Press.

Carricaburo, Norma (2016). ¿Por qué algunos países de América Latina usan el *vos* en vez del *tú*? In *BBC News*. 30 August, 2016. http://www.bbc.com/mundo/noticias-america-latina-36928497 (18 June, 2018).

Coseriu, Eugenio. 1962. *Teoría del lenguaje y lingüística general*. Madrid: Gredos.

CREA = Corpus de Referencia del Español Actual. http://www.rae.es/recursos/banco-de-datos/ crea.

DEL = RAE 2014.

Di Tullio, Ángela. 2006. Antecedentes y derivaciones del voseo argentino. *Páginas de Guarda* 1. 41–54.

Fontanella de Weinberg, Beatriz. 1999. Sistemas pronominales de tratamiento usados en el mundo hispánico. In Ignacio Bosque & Violeta Demonte (eds.), *Gramática descriptiva de la lengua española*, 4 vols., 1399–1425. Madrid: Espasa.

García Negroni, María Marta & Silvia Ramírez Gelbes. 2003. Cortesía y alternancia *vos/tú* en el español de Río de la Plata. El caso del subjuntivo. In *Actas del Coloquio de París. Pronombres de segunda persona y formas de tratamiento en las lenguas de Europa*, 1–14. Paris : Instituto Cervantes. https://cvc.cervantes.es/lengua/coloquio_paris/ponencias/ garcia_ramirez.htm (4 March, 2020).

García Negroni, María Marta & Silvia Ramírez Gelbes. 2004. *No me hagas/hagás eso*: cortesía y subjetividad. *Proceedings of the I Congreso Argentino de la IADA: En torno al diálogo: interacción, contexto y representación social*, 464–470. La Plata: IADA.

García Negroni, María Marta & Silvia Ramírez Gelbes. 2010. Acerca del voseo en los manuales escolares argentinos (1970–2004). In Martin Hummel et al. (eds.), *Formas y fórmulas de tratamiento en el mundo hispano*, 1013–1032. México DF/Graz: Colegio de México/ Universität Graz.

Kurlat, Frida. 1941. Fórmulas de tratamiento en la lengua de Buenos Aires. *Revista de Filología Hispánica* 3,2. 105–139.

López García, María. 2006. La variedad geográfica en el género "manual escolar". *Lectura y vida* 27. 42–50.

Maingueneau, Dominique. 1999. *Ethos*, scénographie, incorporation. In Ruth Amossy (ed.), *Images de soi dans le discours. La construction de l'éthos*, 75–102. Paris: Delachaux/ Niestlé.

Ramírez Gelbes, Silvia. 2011. Correctores, periodistas y la Academia Argentina de Letras: amores y desamores. In Montserrat Alberte & Silvia Senz (eds.), *El dardo en la Academia*, 559–578. Barcelona: Melusina.

RAE-ASALE = Real Academia Española & Asociación de Academias de la Lengua Española. 2009. *Nueva gramática de la lengua española*, 2 vols. Madrid: Espasa.

RAE = Real Academia Española. 2014. *Diccionario de la lengua española*. http://dle.rae.es.

Rizzi, Laura. 2002. El voseo en el español de Buenos Aires: un sistema con dos variantes significativas. Confirmación en la poesía. In María M. García Negroni (ed.), *Actas del*

Congreso Internacional "La Argumentación", 994–999. Buenos Aires: Facultad de Filosofía y Letras.

Vitale, Alejandra. 1999. El problema de la lengua en la radiofonía argentina (1934–1946). In Elvira Arnoux & Roberto Bein (eds.). *Prácticas y representaciones del lenguaje,* 157–174. Buenos Aires: Eudeba.

Wainerman, Catalina. 1976. *Sociolingüística de la forma pronominal.* Mexico City: Trillas.

María Eugenia Vázquez Laslop

Addressing in two presidential election debates in Mexico (1994 and 2012)

Forms and functions

Abstract: The distribution of a corpus of Spanish forms of address (n = 3,548) in two Mexican presidential election debates (broadcast in 1994 and 2012) is organized according to two dimensions: *grammatical form* and *appellative function*. It is shown that while in the 2012 debate the candidates use an informal address system, which is almost non-existent in the 1994 debate, these forms are geared towards the citizens who are the candidates' target audience. In the 2012 debate the candidates are addressed with neutral nominal forms or formal grammatical forms. In 2012 horizontal configuration among the interlocutors is restricted to the candidates-citizens relationship. In 1994 there is a predominance of vertical configuration among the candidates and neutrality with citizens as a collective body.

Keywords: grammatical forms of address, nominal forms of address, appellative function of language, Spanish forms of address, presidential-election debates in Mexico

1 Introduction

At present, in the face of the demands of citizens in republican countries to encourage dialogic practices between those who govern and those governed, debates among candidates running for political positions in open elections have taken on a basic role in democratic processes. Moreover, these debates are broadcast over all multimedia spaces available to the community, mainly television, radio and the Internet.

Since their inception during the 1960s, presidential debates not only include the opposing candidates, but also one or more moderators, members of the press and, on occasions, voting citizens, which in turn means a complex network of interlocutors on different levels: those who are entitled to take the floor, the arbitrators, and the spectators who cannot speak but who in reality are the candidates' target

---

Note: I thank Georganne Weller Ford for the translation into English from the Spanish original. All errors are my sole responsibility.

audience. In addition to other concerns, the social deixis system of the language being spoken, including forms of address, plays a central role in the configuration of this network of participants during televised presidential election debates.

The objective of this study is to identify the deictic referents of the grammatical and nominal forms of address employed in two Mexican presidential election debates (1994 and 2012) and to contrast their use. The analysis is based on grammatical and pragmatic categories, specifically according to grammatical person, the nominal forms utilized, and the *appellative function* (Bühler 1982 [1934]).

The chapter is organized as follows: Section 2 describes the historical-political motivations that led to the inclusion of debates among candidates aspiring to positions of popular election in diverse electoral processes in Mexico. It also describes the circumstances under which the 1994 and 2012 debates selected for this study were carried out, as well as their discursive structure. Section 3 provides a brief overview of other studies on the referents of forms of address in political debates and defines the formal and functional categories involved, which form the basis of the quantitative aspects of this study. Sections 4 to 7 are devoted to the empirical study. Section 4 describes the corpus of the items included as forms of address in both debates, sets out the central issues to be covered in the study regarding who the referents were, and proposes how to cross some formal and functional variables of forms of address for the referents of these items. Sections 5 and 6 present the quantitative results according to formal and functional criteria respectively. Section 7 includes a contrastive analysis of both debates and a synthesis of the study's findings, followed by the conclusion.

2 The 1994 and 2012 presidential election debates

The Mexican political system is a republican model with three federal powers: the Executive, Legislative and Judicial branches. The Executive branch is composed of only one person, the president, who is elected directly by the citizens. The presidential term lasts for six years with no reelection allowed, as stipulated in Article 83 of the Mexican Constitution (*Constitución política de los Estados Unidos Mexicanos*). Non-reelection has always been respected since the promulgation of this 1917 Constitution, which is still the law of the country.

Nevertheless, during most of the 20th century, the presidents of the Republic were members of the same political party, the PRI (Institutional Revolutionary Party). Throughout history, this party gained power in most sectors of society, which in turn made it the party of the State. In fact, the Executive branch, with presidents in office for six years, extended its control to the Legislative and

Judicial powers as well (Cosío Villegas 1973, 1974, 1975a and 1975b). Political plurality barely began to gain ground in the decade of the sixties, when a shaky and slow process some called the 'transition to democracy' arose (Becerra, Salazar & Woldenberg 2005; Woldenberg 2012). Little by little, opposition political parties began to occupy seats in Congress and a few governorships in the states. Finally, by the year 2000, a candidate from an opposition party won the presidency (Ortega Ortiz 2010).

As part of its control in diverse arenas of social life, the State party enjoyed an exclusive presence in most of the mass media's broadcasts, especially television (Sánchez Ruiz 2005). Up until the 1980s, almost any candidate from an opposition party had appeared on screen and, if seen at all, it was only for a few seconds. However, by the 1990s, particularly in 1994, a year of presidential elections, the Mexican political system had fallen into a severe crisis, as attested, among other events, by the uprising of the *Ejército Zapatista de Liberación Nacional* ('Zapatista Army of National Liberation') – a movement against the Mexican Army by indigenous peoples from the state of Chiapas in the southeastern part of the country – and the assassination of the presidential candidate from the dominant party of the State.

In the face of a firm conviction by most citizens that there was electoral fraud in 1988, and the ensuing political and social events during these years, in 1994 the presidential candidates from opposing parties signed the 'Pact for Peace, Democracy and Justice', which included the following paragraph in addition to demands for establishing an impartial electoral institution to represent citizens:

> Nuestros acuerdos [...] son: [...] 3. Garantías de equidad en los medios de comunicación masiva, aprovechando los tiempos del estado y promoviendo que los medios concesionados contribuyan eficazmente al fortalecimiento del proceso democrático. Se propiciarán nuevos espacios e iniciativas que favorezcan la participación, objetividad y respeto de todas las fuerzas políticas. Esto garantizará la comunicación de los candidatos con los ciudadanos y la presentación de sus programas y puntos de vista sobre los asuntos más relevantes para la vida del país.　　　　　　　　　　(Pérez Fernández del Castillo et al. 2009, vol. 3: 188).

> 'Our agreements [...] are: [...] 3. Guarantees of equity in mass media communication, making use of the State´s time on the air and fostering licensed media to contribute efficiently to strengthening the democratic process. New spaces and initiatives will be created to favor participation, objectivity and respect for all political forces, which in turn will guarantee communication between the candidates and the citizens and the launching of their platforms and points of view on the most relevant concerns prevailing in the country.'

Given the presence of social and political pressure in 1994, it was possible to include in the General Board of the *Instituto Federal Electoral* (IFE) ordinary citizens who did not belong to any political party. Even though this body continued to be presided over by the Ministry of Internal Affairs – meaning the Executive power –, opposing political forces also managed to enter into an agreement with the Institute to organize the presidential debates and broadcast them on national television and radio. Finally, for the first time in Mexico, two debates of this nature were held on May 11 and 12, 1994. The first one was among the three candidates from minor parties and the second, among the three candidates from the major parties. Since then, and up until 2012, there were a total of eight televised presidential election debates, two per six-year period, which were mostly organized by electoral authorities (1994, 2000, 2006 and 2012). In 2012, for the first time, there was also a debate organized by a citizens' youth movement known as *#YoSoy132* ('I am 132'), which was transmitted over the Internet and provided an opportunity for the candidates to enter into a dialogue with university students.

2.1 The presidential election debate in Mexico on May 12, 1994

In the spirit of the 'Pact for Peace, Democracy and Justice', on January 27, 1994 leaders from various political groups held meetings with state authorities to reach an agreement on reforms in electoral laws. Within this framework two debates were organized among the presidential candidates. Due to the political and historical importance of these debates, I selected the second debate, which took place on May 12, 1994, and have contrasted it with one of the presidential election debates during the 2012 electoral process referred to in Section 2.2.

The presidential election debate in Mexico on May 12, 1994 was broadcast on the national network by the National Chamber of the Radio and Television Industry and was held at the Museum of Technology in Chapultepec, the most important public park in Mexico City. As already mentioned, at that time space available in the mass media was practically non-existent for opposition parties and their leaders. Thus the 1994 electoral debates were an excellent opportunity (almost the only one) for the presidential candidates to divulge their campaign platform to the citizens. They therefore did not limit their efforts to mere debating among themselves. Considerable interest was shown by the public. It was indeed estimated that some forty million spectators tuned in.[1]

On this particular occasion the participants of the debate were candidates Cuauhtémoc Cárdenas Solórzano from the PRD (Democratic Revolutionary Party), an opposition party from the left; Diego Fernández de Cevallos, from the PAN (National Action Party), an opposition party from the right; Ernesto Zedillo Ponce

---

[1] According to a poll carried out by Ricardo Peña and Rosario Toledo, published in May 1994 in the *Semanario de política y cultura "etcetera"* (in Becerra et al. 2000: 341–342).

de León, from the PRI (Institutional Revolutionary Party), the party in power, and the moderator, Mayté Noriega.

This debate lasted for 1h 26' 2" according to the structure shown in Table 1. In the left-hand column the discursive acts structure of the debate as agreed to by the political parties and electoral authorities is laid out. The last column, to the extreme right, sets out the discursive acts actually uttered. For example, while the second segment of the first part of the debate was supposed to be exclusively argumenta-

Table 1: Structure of the Mexican presidential election debate, May 12, 1994 (Vázquez Laslop 2014: 1882).

Regulated discursive act	Minutes	Speaker*-#Turn-talk	Discursive act(s) actually uttered
		Welcome	
	Preliminary (description of the rules of the debate by the moderator)		
		First part	
Proposal	8	CC-1	Proposal & Argumentation
	8	EZ-1	Proposal
	8	DF-1	Proposal & Argumentation
Argumentation	5	EZ-2	Proposal
	5	DF-2	Argumentation
	5	CC-2	Argumentation
Argumentation	3	DF-3	Argumentation
	3	CC-3	Argumentation
	3	EZ-3	Argumentation & Proposal
		Second part	
Proposal	5	CC-4	Proposal & Argumentation
	5	EZ-4	Proposal
	5	DF-4	Argumentation & Proposal
Argumentation	3	EZ-5	Proposal
	3	DF-5	Proposal
	3	CC-5	Argumentation
Argumentation	3	DF-6	Proposal
	3	CC-6	Argumentation
	3	EZ-6	Argumentation & Proposal
		Third part	
Conclusion	3	CC-7	Proposal
	2	EZ-7	Proposal
	1	EZ-8	Proposal
	3	DF-7	Argumentation & Proposal

*CC = Candidate Cuauhtémoc Cárdenas; EZ = Candidate Ernesto Zedillo Ponce de León; DF = Candidate Diego Fernández de Cevallos.

tive in nature (that is, debate style), candidate Ernesto Zedillo (EZ) decided to use his turn to set forth campaign promises. All turns were allocated by the moderator.

2.2 The presidential election debate in Mexico on June 10, 2012

The 2012 electoral process included three debates among the candidates for the presidency of the nation: two were organized by the previously existing IFE, according to electoral legislation, and one was organized by the citizens' youth movement *#YoSoy132* ('I am 132'). All four candidates participated in the official debates, but in the one organized by the citizens, only three took part, since the candidate from the PRI, which at that time was the opposition, refused to participate. By 2012 electoral legislation regulated the organization of these debates and their national dissemination in the mass media. As a matter of fact, in accordance with IFE guidelines, a special commission composed of electoral authorities and representatives of the candidates to the presidency was set up, in order to agree to the format of both debates (Otálora Malassis 2014: 16).

The second televised presidential election debate in 2012 – which is analyzed here – was broadcast on June 10, for the first time outside Mexico City, at the Expo Convention Center in Guadalajara, the capital of the state of Jalisco. This time the following candidates participated: Gabriel Quadri de la Torre, representing the New Alliance Party; Andrés Manuel López Obrador, for the coalition of the Democratic Revolutionary Party, the Workers Party, and Citizens' Movement Party; Enrique Peña Nieto, representing the coalition of the Institutional Revolutionary Party and the Green Ecological Party of Mexico; and Josefina Vázquez Mota, for the National Action Party.

This debate lasted 2h 32' 4" and adhered strictly to the structure outlined in Table 2. In comparison to the 1994 debate it was more complex. In Table 2, letters A to D correspond to each of the participating candidates according to the section in question. Assignment of the letters was by draw in the preliminary stage, both for the opening turns in the thematic sections of the debate, as well as in the order of turns in the closing phase. The results of the draw were the following.

– Opening and final turns of the thematic sections: A, Gabriel Quadri de la Torre; B, Enrique Peña Nieto; C, Andrés Manuel López Obrador; D, Josefina Vázquez Mota.
– Order in the conclusion turns: A, Andrés Manuel López Obrador; B, Gabriel Quadri de la Torre; C, Enrique Peña Nieto; D, Josefina Vázquez Mota.

Throughout the debate, each turn for the candidates could last up to 2' 30". During the thematic sections of the debate, the total turn-taking time of each candidate

Table 2: Structure of the Mexican presidential election debate, June 10, 2012.

Preliminary: Salutation and description of the rules of the debate by the moderator.						
Section	Opening turn	Medial turn	Medial turn	Closing turn	Time per candidate	Time per section
Opening	A	B	C	D	2' 30"	10' 00"
Debate	B	A – B – C – D ↩		C	8' 30"	34' 00"
Debate	C	A – B – C – D ↩		B	8' 30"	34' 00"
Debate	D	A – B – C – D ↩		A	8' 30"	34' 00"
Conclusion	A	B	C	D	2' 30"	10' 00"
Closing: Thanks and farewell						

altogether could be up to 8' 30". For their turn in these sections, the candidates had to request the floor from the moderator by raising their hand. Once the moderator recognized him or her, the candidate could not speak for more than 2' 30" and this time allotment was subtracted from the 8' 30" they were entitled to in each thematic section. If the candidate did not use up the full-time allotment, the remaining time could not be used later. This dynamic aspect is represented by the curved arrow (↩) in the average turns of each thematic section of the debate.

3 The study of forms of address in electoral debates

3.1 The referents of the forms of address in electoral debates: some studies

Forms of address have been dealt with in various studies on political debates, some of which are electoral in nature. I would like to mention some of those that have paid special attention to the relationship between forms of address and their deictic referents.

It is common practice to take as a point of departure the principles governing deixis discussed in Jespersen (1924), Bühler (1982 [1934]), Jakobson (1971 [1957]) or Benveniste (1979). These principles assume that the meaning of personal pronouns only takes place in a communicative situation. *I* means the person who is speaking and *you* the interlocutor; in other words, the discourse participants in Jakobson's terms. What is understood as social deixis, following Levinson (1983), broadens the scope of study to all those forms that codify the identity of the discourse participants, their relationship to each other, or between one of them and other entities they refer to (1983: 89).

For example, Zupnik (1994) has designated what she calls the discursive space and situates within it the position of the participants in a communicative situation of political discourse, with poles for the opponents, the audience and the moderator. In this space, she adds to the 'discursive role' of the participants their 'political role' and their 'cultural role'. Within this framework, forms of address are linguistic indicators of the discursive space. She also analyzes persuasive strategies and image building used by the participants. Following a conversational analysis approach, Blas Arroyo (2000) also centers his attention on a presidential debate in Spain with three reference domains: the world of the speaker, the world of the interlocutor, and the world shared by them.

Reference as related to forms of address, seen as units of social deixis systems, moves within the realm of what Bühler (1982 [1934]) has called the demonstrative field of language, different from the symbolic field, which is more in keeping with the representative function of language. The demonstrative field is configured based on the subjective axes of the speaker and intersubjective considerations between him/her and the listener. Therefore the referential space is interpersonal (see Lyons 1995: Chap. 10). It follows that for the case of forms of address, reference is indicating or pointing to an interlocutor or discourse participant (see De Cock 2014).

We can add to this the fact that in electoral debates verbal strategies employed by the adversaries are aimed at attacking their opponents, defending themselves, and persuading electors to vote instead for them, offering acclaims that stress the benefit of such a decision (Benoit 2007, 2014; Blas Arroyo 2011; Kerbrat-Orecchioni 2017). Therefore, most researchers who analyze forms of address in these communicative situations attempt to account for their strategic uses.

On the one hand, it is important to mention those studies that revolve around the *transgressive* uses of grammatical paradigms as related to personal pronouns. For example, Bull & Fetzer (2006) believe that it is necessary to analyze the context of forms of address in political discourse since their reference is an inferred meaning. De Cock (2009) compares what she categorizes as subjective and intersubjective uses of the first and second persons in the singular and plural in colloquial and political discourse in Peninsular Spanish. Proctor & Su (2011) refer to political discourse in the United States and Roitman (2014) to the 2012 debate between Hollande and Sarkozy in France, and they also analyze the first person plural. In the case of Roitman, she examines it as a strategy to reinforce *ethos*, or the good image of the candidate who is speaking. Vertommen (2013) analyzes the inclusive and exclusive uses of *wij* ('we') in Flemish by government officials and by members of opposition parties on talk shows in Belgium. Kuo (2002) compares the use of the second person singular *ni* in two debates in China. She found that in the first debate this pronoun is directed at the audience with greater frequency, a sign of solidarity with the electorate, while in the second debate the pronoun is directed at the opponents, so it has a conflicting value.

On the other hand, several studies deal with nominal forms of address that are usually employed by politicians in debates, but they are less numerous than studies on grammatical forms. Beyond political discourse, the need to study nominal forms of address had been proposed in the mid-20th century by Brown & Ford (1964) in an attempt to understand the principles of use according to certain diads of interlocutors. Zwicky (1971) had already proposed a categorization of vocative functions. In fact, in principle one might think that reference to nominal forms belongs to the world of Bühler's (1982 [1934]) symbolic field of language. But Dickey (1997), for example, questioned why certain nominal forms become forms of address or forms that acquire a social meaning which is not necessarily associated with their literal meaning, particularly in a language such as English, which at present does not have a grammatical system that separates formal terms of address from informal ones. In her study she distinguishes three types of meanings: the "address meaning", determined by its usage as a form of address; the "referential meaning", determined by its usage when referring to people or things (that is, in "non-address contexts"), and the "lexical meaning", which includes the two previous meanings (Dickey 1997: 256). A specific study of the ideological use and legitimation of nominal forms in electoral debates was authored by Jaworski & Galasiński (2000).

For the study of reference in forms of address in electoral debates, I follow De Fina's recommendation (1995: 403). She argues that to understand the pragmatic implications of the selection of the pronouns used in a given text, it is necessary to take into account the totality of these forms used in the text. In this way it will be possible to first identify the stable referents that correspond to the consistent use of certain pronouns and later identify their connections with the other referents of other pronominal and non-pronominal forms.

3.2 Formal and functional categories

The quantitative study of forms of address used in the presidential election debates of 1994 and 2012 in Mexico is covered in Sections 4 through 7. I analyze absolute and relative frequencies of the data included, according to the categories referred to in this section and defined in Vázquez Laslop (2019a, 2019b) to answer the questions set out in Section 4.2 below. In general, these questions attempt to identify the referents of grammatical and nominal forms of address used in both debates and to determine if there are differences between these two political moments.

By *forms of address* I understand those linguistic forms whose meaning is in keeping with an indication or pointing to by the addresser of an interlocutor in a communicative situation and whose function is to address this interlocutor. An interlocutor can be the addresser him/herself.

By *referent* of a form of address item I understand the interlocutor pointed to by this item. The referent is therefore always a discourse participant, although s/he might never take the floor. I am thinking, in this case, of the spectators within the communicative situation known as a "televised debate", whose identity is configured as "citizens", "potential voters", "members of society" or "Mexicans", and so on by the participants entitled to take the floor (*ratified participants*, following Goffman 1981; i.e., the political candidates or the moderator of the debate).

I divide the analytical categories according to a formal criterion and a functional criterion of a pragmatic nature. Given that these are Mexican debates, the *formal categories* refer to those that form part of Mexican Spanish.

Person: first, second and third. All have number: singular and plural. In Mexican Spanish there are two systems for the second person, one of which is informal, and whose nominative pronoun is *tú* (T-forms hereafter) and a formal system, *usted* (V-forms hereafter). The form *ustedes* – the second person plural – neutralizes this opposition (T~V-forms hereafter). The system of person in Spanish is present in several grammatical categories and not exclusively with nominative, accusative and dative pronouns. It can also be found in possessives and in verbal inflection. Note that Spanish is a *pro-drop* language, where the governing subject may not be overtly expressed.

Nominal categories: proper and common names. Proper names are classified as "first name + last name", "title + name (first name + last name or only the last name)" and, finally, "first name".

The *appellative categories* as defined in Vázquez Laslop (2019a, 2019b), which I reproduce here, have been characterized and exemplified in the 1994 and 2012 debates. These include:

Vocative: any item (deictic or non-deictic) which functions as an appellative, with no syntactic function, as in example (1).

(1) *Usted*, no sólo eso, *señor*; usted además de que se presenta hoy como tolerante, respetuoso y, podríamos decirlo, simpático frente a los estudiantes, no les dice que usted hizo una ley, en Michoacán, que realmente vulnera la

dignidad, no sólo de los estudiantes, sino de todo un pueblo. (DF-016-0299-4/5, 1994)[2]

'*You*, not only that, *sir*. In addition to presenting yourself today as tolerant, respectful and, we might even add, likeable, to the students, you aren't telling them that you passed a law, in Michoacán, that truly violates the dignity, not only of students, but of an entire people.'

Second person: a second person item functioning as an appellative, with syntactic function, as in example (2).

(2)   Yo *te* pregunto a *ti* si a doce años de haber dado pasos en la transición democrática de nuestro país, hoy *estás* mejor y la respuesta, seguro estoy, es que no. (P-014-0292-1/2, 2012)

'I am asking *you* whether or not, twelve years after having taken steps in the democratic transition of our country, *you are* better off today. The answer, I am sure, is no.'

Deictic pro second person: a non-second deictic item functioning as second person, with appellative and syntactic functions, illustrated in example (3).

(3)   Le voy a pedir a Gabriel, Gabriel Quadri de Alatorre que haga lo propio. *Empezamos* de este lado, Gabriel, y *pasamos* inmediatamente a mostrarlo. Es la letra "A". Significa que es el primero que participa en este debate. (S-001-059-01, S-001-060-01, 2012)

'I'm going to ask Gabriel, Gabriel Quadri de Alatorre, to do it himself. *We start* on this side, Gabriel, and *we will go* right on to show it. It's the letter "A". That means he's the first to participate in this debate.'

Narrated[3] *pro-deictic:*[4] a non-deictic item functioning as an indirect appellative, with syntactic function, shown in example (4).

---

2 The code at the end of each example indicates: Speaker-Turn_talk-Line_number-Item_number, year of debate.
3 I take this term from Jakobson´s distinction between *participants of the speech event* versus *participants of the narrated event* (1971 [1957]: 133).
4 *Pro-deictic* is the term proposed by Hammermüller (2010: 514). See also Bühler (1982 [1934]: 147, footnote 1).

(4)   Yo sí le pediría a *Andrés Manuel* que nos *explicara* un poquito mejor la aritmética de todas estas a-ahorros que van a promover en México la inversión de manera casi mágica, porque a mí las cuentas, la verdad, no me salen. (Q-028-0496-02/04, Q-028-0497-01, 2012)

'I myself would ask *Andrés Manuel* to explain *his* math to us a little bit better, regarding all these savings that are going to be brought about in Mexico, almost magically through investment, because, according to my calculations, truthfully, they don't add up.'

Inclusive first person plural: a first person plural item functioning as appellative, with syntactic function, addressing the addresser and addressee(s), as illustrated in example (5).

(5)   Amigas y amigos. Buenas noches. *Estamos* a pocos días de lograr una gran transformación para la vida pública del país. (L-010-217-02, 2012)

'Friends, good evening. *We are* just days away from achieving a huge transformation in the public life of the country.'

Exclusive first person plural: a first person plural item, with syntactic function, meaning the addresser and other(s) individual(s), who are not the addressee(s), as in example (6).

(6)   Desde la oposición, compatriotas, *hemos* logrado en Acción Nacional que el gobierno rectifique. (DF-012-0222-02, 1994)

'From the opposition, my fellow countrymen, *we* at National Action *have gotten* the government to rectify.'

Pluralis maiestatis ('the royal we'): a first person plural item functioning as first person singular, with syntactic function, shown in example (7).

(7)   Todos los candidatos en algún momento, quienes estamos aquí, ahora, frente a ustedes, hemos hablado de limpieza electoral; sin embargo, *nosotros afirmamos* que las elecciones del seis de julio fueron las elecciones más sucias en la historia de nuestro país. (CC-018-0344-01/02, 1994)

'At some time or another, all of the candidates here right now, before you, have talked about a clean election; however, *we contend* that the elections of July 6 were the dirtiest elections in the history of our country.'

Based on these formal and functional categories, I have determined the variables to apply to configuring the data in the quantitative study of forms of address in the 1994 and 2012 debates and which are developed further in the following sections.

4 Forms of address in the 1994 and 2012 presidential election debates: corpus and variables

4.1 The corpus of grammatical and nominal forms of address

The corpus of forms of address in the presidential election debates in Mexico in 1994 and 2012 includes the grammatical system of the first, second and third singular and plural persons, as well as common and proper names with one of the interlocutors as referents. The total number of cases per debate is presented in Table 3. As is shown, more than 80% of the items are grammatical forms of address in a similar proportion in both debates.

Table 3: Corpus of the grammatical and nominal forms of address in the 1994 and 2012 presidential election debates.

Year	1994		2012		TOTAL	
	N	**%**	**N**	**%**	**N**	**%**
Grammatical items	1,218	84.7	1,734	82.2	2,952	83.2
Noun items	220	15.3	376	17.8	596	16.8
Total items	1,438	100.0	2,110	100.0	3,548	100.0

4.2 Questions and variables

In an exploratory study on the mapping of the distribution of forms of address in the second person and common and proper names (Vázquez Laslop 2019b), I have made the following observations.

Firstly, in the 1994 debate, the second person singular system is limited to the V-forms and nouns are mostly common nouns (59%) and proper nouns with title (26.8%). In contrast to this, in the 2012 debate, the *tú* system (T-forms) appears in 16.7% of the cases, with a relative frequency that is a little higher than the use of *usted* (V-form), which appears in 16.3% of the cases. In addition, in this debate proper nouns with a title are barely used (5.8%). In a good number of cases only the first and last names are used (39.4%) or only the first name (31.6%), and common nouns are less frequent than in 1994 (18.6%). These data suggest that the forms of address used in the 2012 debates are less formal than in the 1994 debates; therefore, the configuration of intended interpersonal relations by the candidates in the 2012 debate are more horizontal (when using T-forms and proper nouns without title), while the intended relations by the 1994 candidates are more vertical (mostly using V-forms and proper nouns with title).

Secondly, in spite of these results, the exploratory study in Vázquez Laslop (2019b) provided data that could qualify trends regarding the type of pretended interpersonal relations in both debates. By observing the distribution of second person forms of address according to discursive acts, it can be seen that almost half of the occurrences of *tú* in 2012 (48.8%) are used in commissive speech acts – mostly candidates campaign promises expressed as proposals – and a little over one third (36%) in argumentative speech acts. In both debates, more than half of the singular V-forms (*usted*) appears in argumentative speech acts (64.9% in 1994 and 51.6% in 2012). These comparisons suggest, on the one hand, that those addressed with *tú* are the citizens, to whom the candidates direct their campaign promises with commissive speech acts; on the other hand, that those addressed with *usted* are the candidates, who are involved in a verbal duel with argumentative speech acts.

These observations call for a closer look at the targets of the forms of address used in the 1994 and 2012 debates. To this end, I will cross-tabulate the following variables for each debate and contrast the results: a) the referent by grammatical person, which includes the first, second and third persons; b) the referent by noun category, which calls for common nouns and the types of proper nouns used, and c) the referent by appellative function.

5 Addressing referents in the 1994 and 2012 presidential election debates: the form

5.1 The referents of forms of address by grammatical person

Table 4 shows the absolute and relative frequency distribution of the items by debate (1994 and 2012) in the whole corpus, according to grammatical person. Remember that Spanish is a *pro-drop* language, so these items belong to diverse

Table 4: Grammatical person of forms of address in the 1994 and 2012 debates (N = 3,548).

	1994		2012	
	N	**%**	**N**	**%**
1SG	362	25.2	688	32.6
1PL	441	30.7	487	23.1
2SG-T	0	0.0	125	5.9
2SG-V	185	12.9	122	5.8
2PL-T~V	94	6.5	124	5.9
3SG	117	8.1	134	6.3
3PL	19	1.3	54	2.6
Noun	220	15.3	376	17.8
TOTAL	1,438	100.0	2,110	100.0

grammatical categories: pronouns in the nominative, accusative and dative cases, possessives, and verbal inflexions. Table 4 includes all the nominal forms.

The first person is by far the most frequent in both debates. In the 1994 debate, the plural includes a third of the overall number of items (30.7%) and the singular, a quarter (25.2%). The opposite pattern emerges in 2012, when the first person singular represents a little more than a third of all occurrences (32.6%) and the plural reaches almost a quarter (23.1%). One might think that in both debates the nominal forms would be the second most frequently used form of address (15.3% and 17.8%), but this only holds true for the 1994 debate, when the second person reaches a total of nearly a fifth of all occurrences (19.4%, all second person forms). In the 2012 debate, nominal items only surpass by a couple of decimals the total occurrences of the second person (17.8% and 17.6%, respectively). What is particularly noteworthy, contrasting both debates, is that the second person forms are more diversified in 2012 than in 1994. While usage in 1994 is relatively more frequent for the singular form, all the items are used exclusively with *usted* (V-forms), with 12.9%. In the 2012 debate – as though this percentage were split into two –, the singular forms of the second person represent 5.9% for T-forms and 5.8% for V-forms.

Tables 5 and 6 display the details of the referents of the grammatical forms of address employed in both debates. The percentages are calculated according to the total number of items found in each debate: 1,438 in 1994 and 2,110 in 2012.

Table 5, which refers to the 1994 debate, shows that the candidates and the moderator are referents for the first person singular in 40% or more of the items. We also observe that 'everybody' (mainly the Mexican people, including

Table 5: Referents and grammatical forms of address by person in the 1994 debate (N = 1,438).

	1SG	1PL	2SG-T	2SG-V	2PL-T~V	3SG	3PL
Candidate	53	63	0	179	2	101	6
(793)	44.5%	7.9%		22.6%	0.2%	12.7%	0.8%
Moderator	8	0	0	3	0	2	0
(20)	40.0%			15.0%		10.0%	
People	0	5	0	3	85	0	5
(159)		3.1%		1.9%	53.5%		3.1%
Candidates	0	25	0	0	6	11	8
(71)		35.2%			8.4%	15.5%	11.3%
Everybody	0	293	0	0	1	0	0
(332)		88.2%			0.3%		
Cand* & Party	0	54	0	0	0	0	3
(62)		87.1%					4.8%
IFE** et al.	0	1	0	0	0	0	0
(1)		100.0%					
TOTAL	362	441	0	185	94	117	19

*Candidate; **Instituto Federal Electoral.

Table 6: Referents and grammatical forms of address by person in the 2012 debate (N = 2,110).

	1SG	1PL	2SG-T	2SG-V	2PL-T~V	3SG	3PL
Candidate	635	88	10	104	1	117	0
(1241)	51.2%	7.1%	0.8%	8.4%	0.1%	9.4%	
Moderator	49	8	0	1	0	0	0
(81)	60.5%	9.9%		1.2%			
People	1	9	115	17	82	5	13
(271)	0.4%	3.3%	42.4%	6.3%	30.3%	1.8%	4.8%
Candidates	1	29	0	0	37	11	38
(137)	0.7%	21.2%			27.0%	8.0%	27.7%
Everybody	1	334	0	0	4	1	0
(356)	0.3%	93.8%			1.1%	0.3%	
Cand* & Party	1	16	0	0	0	0	3
(20)	5.0%	80.0%					15.0%
IFE** et al.	0	3	0	0	0	0	0
(4)		75.0%					
TOTAL	688	352	58	50	51	39	28

*Candidate; **Instituto Federal Electoral.

the participants in the debate) or the candidates as members of their political party, are referents for the first person plural in about 90% of the cases. To a lesser degree (35.2%), the participating candidates as a whole are also referents of the first person plural. With respect to the second person, the V-form mostly has as referent a candidate (179 cases out of 185; 97.0%). Thus, after the first person singular, each candidate with the second person singular is the intended interlocutor of one of the participants in the debate in a little over a fifth of the cases (22.6%). Finally, the referents of the second person plural are almost exclusively the electorate or Mexican people, with 85 out of the 94 items (90.4%). From another point of view, the people are considered to be the whole set of addressees (*ustedes*, T~V-form) in 53.5% of the cases, much higher than as referents of the other personal plural forms (first and third in both cases, with 3.1%).

The items belonging to grammatical forms of address in the 2012 debate are distributed by referent and by person in Table 6. Both the candidates and the moderator refer to themselves in the first person singular in more than half of the items (51.2% and 60.5%, respectively). Everybody and the candidates as members of their respective political parties are referents for the first person plural (93.8% and 80%, respectively). The electorate or Mexicans are individual referents for *tú* with 42.4% or, as a group, for *ustedes* to a lesser degree, in 30.3% of the cases. Each candidate is the addressee of some form of the second person singular at a much lower frequency: 8.4% with the V-form and 0.8% with the T-form. The candidates, taken as a whole, are categorized as the second person plural in 27% of the cases, as occurred with the third person plural (27.7% of the cases).

5.2 Referents and nominal forms of address

In this section I examine in greater detail the types of nominal forms of address used in both debates, which, as shown in Table 4, encompassed 15.3% of the total number of forms of address used in 1994 and 17.8% in 2012. Table 7 shows the absolute and relative frequencies of the items from the 1994 debate and Table 8, those from the 2012 debate. As in the categorization of grammatical forms of address, the percentages are calculated according to the total number of items found in each debate: 1,438 in 1994 and 2,110 in 2012.

In the 1994 debate, when nominal reference is made to one of the candidates, a title is included with the proper noun (first name plus last name or only last name, 6.7%), or even with a common noun (4%). On the other hand, the few nominal references made to the moderator are just first name, without a last name or title (30%). When a nominal reference is made to the people or the candidates as a whole, it is with a common noun above all (38.4% and 19.7%, respectively).

Table 7: Referents and nominal forms of address by category in the 1994 debate (N = 1,438).

	First name + last name		Title + proper noun		First name		Common noun	
	N	%	N	%	N	%	N	%
Candidate (793)	0	0	53	6.7	0	0	32	4.0
Moderator (20)	0	0	0	0	6	30.0	1	5.0
People (159)	0	0	0	0	0	0	61	38.4
Candidates (71)	0	0	5	7.0	0	0	14	19.7
Everybody (332)	0	0	1	0.3	0	0	22	6.6
Cand* & Party (62)	3	4.8	0	0	0	0	2	3.2
IFE** et al. (1)	0	0	0	0	0	0	0	0

*Candidate; **Instituto Federal Electoral.

Table 8: Referents and nominal forms of address by category in the 2012 debate (N = 2,110).

	First name + last name		Title + proper noun		First name		Common noun	
	N	%	N	%	N	%	N	%
Candidate (1241)	145	11.7	21	1.7	101	8.1	18	1.4
Moderator (81)	3	3.7	0	0	18	22.2	2	2.5
People (271)	0	0	0	0	0	0	29	10.7
Candidates (137)	0	0	0	0	0	0	16	11.7
Everybody (356)	0	0	1	0.3	0	0	9	2.5
Cand* & Party (20)	0	0	0	0	0	0	0	0
IFE** et al. (4)	0	0	0	0	0	0	1	25.0

*Candidate; **Instituto Federal Electoral.

In the 2012 debate, as shown in Table 8, a good part of nominal reference directed at each candidate involves use of the first and last name without a title (11.7%), or of simply the first name (8.1%). On the other hand, the moderator is most frequently called by his first name (22.2%) and only exceptionally by his first and last name (3.7%). Nominal reference directed at the people and the candidates as a whole is especially with the use of common nouns (10.7% and 11.7%, respectively).

6 Addressing referents in the 1994 and 2012 presidential election debates: the appellative function

This section provides details on the ways of addressing each type of referent in each of the presidential debates. Table 9 presents the absolute and relative frequencies of the items of grammatical and nominal forms of address used in the 1994 debate, and Table 10 shows the frequencies for the 2012 debate.

Table 9: Referents and forms of address by appellative functions in the 1994 debate (N= 1,438).

	Candidate	Moderator	People	Candidate(s)	Everybody	Cand* & Party	IFE** et al.
Vocative	40	6	52	2	3	0	0
	5.0%	30.0%	32.7%	2.8%	0.9%		
2nd	181	3	88	6	1	0	0
	22.8%	15.0%	55.3%	8.4%	0.3%		
Prodeixis	1	0	0	3	0	1	0
	0.1%			4.2%		1.6%	
Narrated	155	3	14	35	34	7	0
	19.6%	15.0%	8.8%	49.3%	10.2%	11.3%	
1SG	353	8	0	0	1	0	0
	44.5%	40.0%			0.3%		
1PL inclusive	0	0	5	10	268	5	0
			3.1%	14.1%	80.7%	8.1%	
1PL exclusive	0	0	0	15	25	49	1
				21.1%	7.5%	79.0%	100.0%
1PL maiestatic	63	0	0	0	0	0	0
	7.9%						
TOTAL	793	20	159	71	332	62	1

*Candidate; **Instituto Federal Electoral.

Table 10: Referents and forms of address by appellative functions in the 2012 debate (N= 2,110).

	Candidate	Moderator	People	Candidate(s)	Everybody	Cand*.& Party	IFE** et al.
Vocative	157	19	4	2	1	0	0
	12.6%	23.4%	1.5%	1.4%	0.3%		
2nd	115	1	214	37	4	0	0
	9.3%	1.2%	79%	27.0%	%		
Prodeixis	15	0	11	22	1	0	1
	1.2%		4.0%	16.1%	0.3%		25.0%
Narrated	233	4	32	46	14	1	1
	18.8%	4.9%	11.8%	33.6%	3.9%	5.0%	25.0%
1SG	635	49	1	1	1	1	0
	51.2%	60.5%	0.4%	0.7%	0.3%	5.0%	
1PL inclusive	0	0	8	5	327	0	0
			2.9%	3.7%	91.8%		
1PL exclusive	0	0	1	21	7	16	2
			0.4%	15.3%	2.0%	80%	50.0%
1PL maiestatic	81	8	0	1	0	0	0
	6.5%	9.9%		0.7%			
TOTAL	1241***	81	271	137*	356*	20*	4

*Candidate; **Instituto Federal Electoral; ***9 items, no data.

In both debates the most frequent items are the first person singular with respect to other grammatical persons (25.2% in 1994 and 32.6% in 2012; see Table 4 above); this is reflected in Tables 9 and 10 with 44.5% in 1994 and 51.2% in 2012 with regard to these items. In the 1994 debate each candidate is addressed in the second person with a syntactic function in 22.8% of the cases, and in 19.6% of cases, each candidate receives indirect treatment with pro-deictic narrated forms. In fact, when the appellation is to candidates as a group, they receive pro-deictic indirect treatment in 49.3% of the cases. Those who receive the most direct treatment in this debate are the citizens, with appellations in the second person (55.3%) or with vocatives (32.7%). As expected, the inclusive *nos* is directed at everybody (80.7%) and the exclusive *nos* to the candidate together with his political followers (79.0%).

In the 2012 debate, from the figures in Table 10, and without counting the singular first person, each candidate receives more indirect than direct appellations. Some 18.8% of the items are categorized as pro-deictic forms, while the direct items did not surpass this figure: 12.6% are vocatives and 9.3% represent the syntactic second person. The appellations to the candidates as a group account for more than a third of the pro-deictic narrated items (33.6%), followed by the second person with a syntactic function (27.0%) and pro-deictic accounting for 16.1% of the occurrences. The people are addressed predominantly in the second person with a syntactic function (79.0%). As was the case of the 1994 debate, the inclusive *nos* is reserved for everybody (91.8%) and the exclusive *nos*, for the candidate and his political faction (80.0%).

7 Contrasts in the uses of forms of address between the 1994 and 2012 presidential election debates

With these results we are closer to answering the question of whether or not there are differences between the 1994 and 2012 presidential election debates with regard to the nature of interpersonal relations the participants intended to project through forms of address. In other words, whether or not the more frequent use of informal addressing systems in the 2012 debate than in the 1994 debate can be taken as an indicator of the linguistic configuration of more horizontal versus vertical interpersonal relations, respectively.

Graphs 1 and 2 highlight some of the most noteworthy contrasts from the point of view of the form used in both debates.[5] According to Mexican culture, addressing someone by his or her title plus last name and with V-forms is more formal than by a proper noun without title and V-forms. However, addressing someone this latter way still suggests some formality. An informal approach is to address a person by only his or her first name combined with T-forms. Graph 1 focuses on grammatical items whose referents were the individual candidates. As the graph attests, T-forms are barely used to refer to any candidate in the 2012 debate. If in the 1994 debate the use of the V-forms is more frequent to address each candidate, in 2012 greater use is made of the first plus last name (proper noun). Thus, from a grammatical point of view each candidate in the 2012 debate is addressed in a less formal way than in 1994, but address practices are still formal, as candidates tend to be addressed more often by a proper noun than was the case in 1994, which is quite clearly very formal in nature, with the use of

---

5 This information may change pending the submission of the data to relevant statistical tests to establish significant differences between both debates. An inferential statistical study will be the subject of next phase of the overall study once the remaining data from 2000 and 2006 debates have been included.

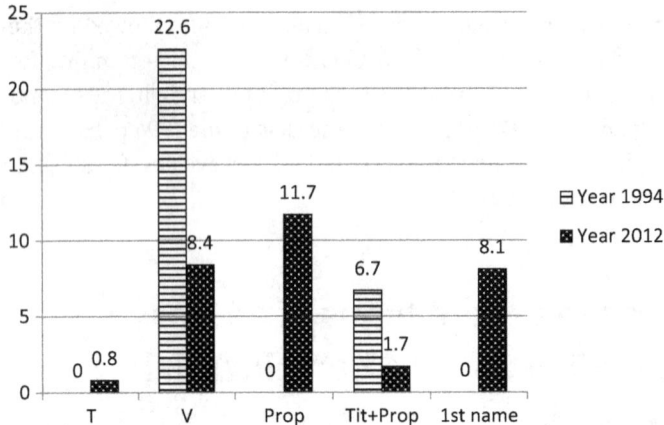

Graph 1: Candidates: Percent by grammatical person and nominal categories in the 1994 and 2012 debates.
Prop = Proper noun; Tit+Prop = Title plus proper noun.

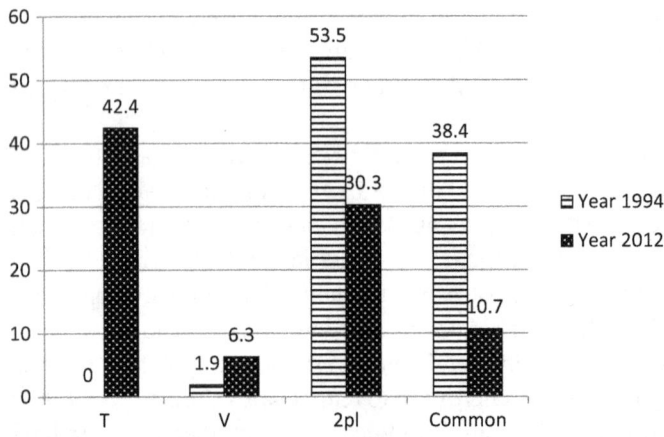

Graph 2: The people: Percent of grammatical persons and nominal categories in the 1994 and 2012 debates.
Common = common noun.

title plus last name and V-forms. I will come back to this issue at the end of this section.

Graph 2 compares ways of addressing citizens or the people in general (Mexicans, voters, women, youth, heads of family, etc.) in the two debates. In 2012 Mexicans are addressed with the T-form more often than the candidates involved in the debate. As a matter of fact, direct addressing is also more frequent in 1994 with the second person plural, which neutralizes the formal-informal opposition. Perhaps for this very reason it was frequent in the 2012 debate. In 1994, collective forms of address for the people are preferred, not only through the use of *ustedes* (second person plural), but also the frequent use of common nouns.

From a functional point of view, the use of forms of address in the 1994 and 2012 presidential debates does not show as much contrast as the grammatical perspective, as represented in Graphs 3 and 4.

The differences in the appellative functions to refer to each candidate between the 1994 and the 2012 debates are limited to direct addressing, that is, vocatives and second person. As shown in Graph 3, the most evident difference is appellation in the second person with a syntactic function, which is more frequent in 1994 than in 2012. On the other hand, in 2012 it is more common for each candidate to address others with vocatives than in 1994. Regarding the remaining appellative functions with reference to each candidate, the pattern is similar in both debates.

If we now observe the appellative functions in Graph 4 from the perspective of the people as a referent, we see a greater difference in the use of vocatives. While in both debates there is a preference to address the people in the second person with syntactic function, in 2012 individual citizens are addressed with deictics much more often than with other appellative functions.

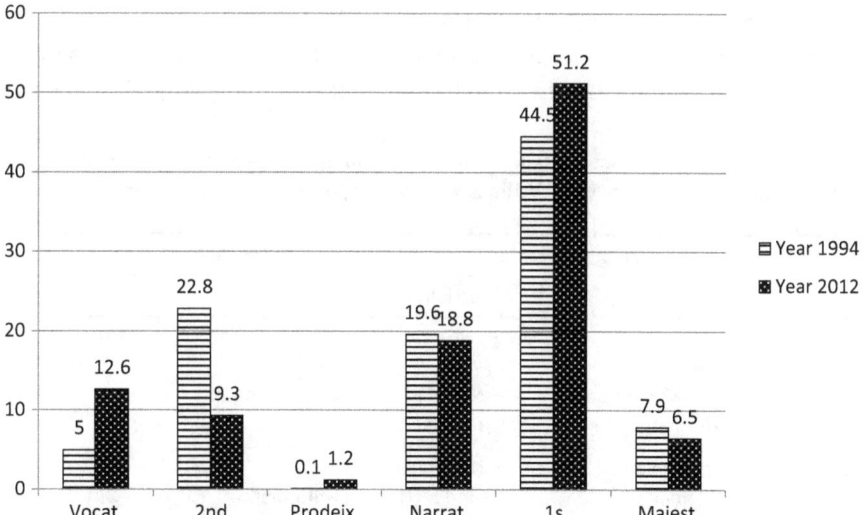

Graph 3: Candidates: Percent of appellative functions in the 1994 and 2012 debates.
Vocat. = Vocative; 2nd = second person with syntactic function; Prodeix. = Pro-deixis; Narrat. = Narrated; 1s = first person singular; Maiest.= maiestatic first person plural.

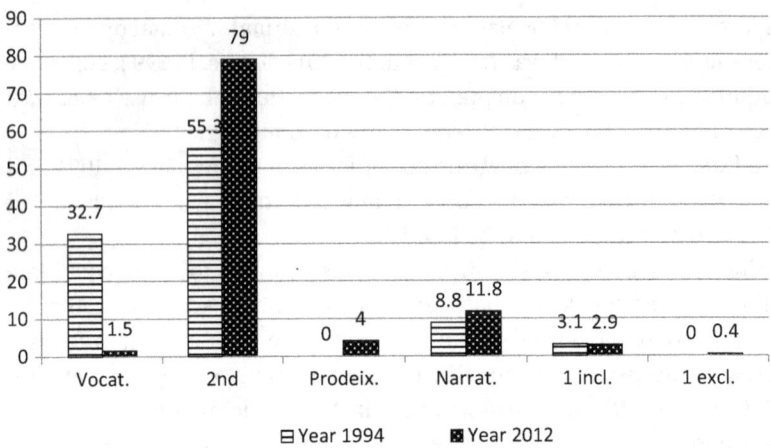

Graph 4: The people: Percent of appellative functions in the 1994 and 2012 debates.
Vocat. = Vocative; 2nd = second person with syntactic function; Prodeix. = Pro-deixis;
Narrat. = Narrated; 1 incl. = first person plural inclusive; 1 excl. = first person plural exclusive.

Table 11 gives a summary of the different ways in which the referents 'each candidate' and 'the people' are addressed in the 1994 and 2012 presidential election debates. The Table gives an outline with two addressing system parameters for the items I have mentioned in this section: one is a *direct-indirect* parameter by appellative function, and the other an *informal-formal* one by grammatical forms. On the appellative function parameter, the vocatives and the second person singular with syntactic function are found on the [+Direct] boundary;

Table 11: Summary of the form and function parameters for types of addressing the referents "each candidate" and "the people" in the 1994 and 2012 presidential-election debates.

	Each candidate		The people (individuals)	
	Form	Function	Form	Function
1994	– V [+Formal] – Title+Proper noun [+Formal]	– 2SG [+Direct] – Narrated [+Indirect]	– 2PL [I~F] – Common Noun	– Narrated [+Indirect]
2012	– Proper Noun [±Formal] – V [+Formal] – First name [+Informal]	– Narrated [+Indirect] – Vocative [+Direct]	– T [+Informal] – 2PL [I~F]	– 2SG [+Direct]

the plural deictic forms in the center, and the narrated pro-deictic forms on the [+Indirect] boundary. On the grammatical forms parameter, the T-forms and the first names are located on the [+Informal] boundary; proper nouns without a title in the center, tending toward formality [±Formal], and the V-forms together with proper nouns with a title on the [+Formal] boundary. From the point of view of formal addressing, the second person plural is neutral ([I~F]). Common nouns, given their meanings and connotations, can tend toward formality or informality; it is therefore not possible to arrive at a generalization in this category.

8 Conclusion

Debates among presidential candidates in Mexico were not incorporated into the electoral system until the last decade of the 20th century, but have now become an essential part of the democratic process. On the one hand, there is regulation for the organization of these debates in electoral legislation and, on the other, these rules were strictly applied to all electoral processes between 1994 and 2012.

The linguistic study of the forms of address used in the presidential election debates broadcast in 1994 and 2012 provides elements that allow us to identify the diversity of interpersonal configurations intended mainly by the ratified participants among the opposing candidates, the moderators, electoral authorities, citizens, the electorate and social groups. One of these linguistic elements are the referents of the forms of address, which match the addressees pointed to by the forms of address themselves, since they serve an appellative function each time they are used.

Given the study's objective to contrast the configuration of the interlocutors as referents by means of the forms of address used by the candidates in the 1994 and 2012 debates, consideration was given on the one hand to grammatical aspects of the forms of address, and on the other, to their appellative functions.

With regard to each candidate as a referent, the most important differences were in form, and there was a certain coincidence in functions. From the functional point of view, in both debates each candidate was predominantly addressed directly – in 1994 in the second person with a syntactic function, and in 2012 with vocatives. In both debates each candidate was also addressed indirectly. With respect to form, while in 1994 only the formal system was used to refer to each candidate, in 2012 neutral or informal forms emerged, especially nominal forms.

The most important formal and functional differences in the forms of address used in both debates were in the appellations used to address the people. While in 1994 Mexicans were addressed indirectly as a collectivity with common nouns or neutrally with second person plural forms, in 2012 they were predominantly addressed with the second person singular form as part of the informal system, or the neutral second person plural.

For the study of forms of address in any electoral debate it is important to include a multidimensional linguistic analysis of the addressees as referents, in order to obtain an extended panorama of the interpersonal relationships configured by the political participants, by means of these social deictic unities.

References

Becerra Ricardo, Pedro Salazar & José Woldenberg. 2005. *La mecánica del cambio político en México. Elecciones, partidos y reformas*. 3rd. ed. Mexico City: Cal y Arena.

Benoit, William L. 2007. *Communication in political campaigns*. New York: Peter Lang.

Benoit, William L. 2014. *Political election debates: Informing voters about policy and character*. Plymouth: Lexington Books.

Benveniste, Émile. 1979. *Problemas de lingüística general*. Translation by Juan Almela. 2 vols. Mexico City: Siglo XXI.

Blas Arroyo, José Luis. 1998. Funciones y estructuras discursivas del moderador en el debate político. *Langues et Linguistique* 24. 1–45.

Blas Arroyo, José Luis. 2000. 'Mire usted Sr. González...' Personal deixis in Spanish political-electoral debate. *Journal of Pragmatics* 32. 1–27.

Blas Arroyo, José Luis. 2011. *Políticos en conflicto: una aproximación pragmático-discursiva al debate electoral cara a cara*. Bern: Peter Lang.

Brown, Roger & Marguerite Ford. 1964. Address in American English. In Dell Hymes (ed.), *Language in Culture and Society*, 234–244. New York: Harper & Row Publishers.

Bühler, Karl. 1982 (1934). *Sprachtheorie*. Stuttgart: Gustav Fischer.

Bull, Peter & Annita Fetzer. 2006. Who are *we* and who are *you*? The strategic use of forms of address in political interviews. *Text & Talk* 26,1. 3–37.

Cosío Villegas, Daniel. 1973 [1972]. *El sistema político mexicano. Las posibilidades de cambio*. 4th. ed. Mexico City: Joaquín Mortiz.

Cosío Villegas, Daniel. 1974. *El estilo personal de gobernar*. Mexico City: Joaquín Mortiz.

Cosío Villegas, Daniel. 1975a. *La sucesión presidencial*. Mexico City: Joaquín Mortiz.

Cosío Villegas, Daniel. 1975b. *La sucesión: desenlace y perspectivas*. Mexico City: Joaquín Mortiz.

De Cock, Barbara. 2009. Funciones pragmáticas de la referencia de persona en el lenguaje coloquial y en el discurso político. *Oralia* 12. 247–266.

De Cock, Barbara. 2014. *Profiling discourse participants. Forms and functions in Spanish conversation and debates*. Amsterdam: John Benjamins.

De Fina, Anna. 1995. Pronominal choice, identity, and solidarity in political discourse. *Text* 15,3. 379–410.

Dickey, Eleanor. 1997. Forms of address and terms of reference. *Journal of Linguistics* 33. 255–274.

Gofmann, Erving. 1981. *Forms of talk*. Philadelphia: University of Pennsylvania Press.

Hammermüller, Gunther. 2010. Evolución de las formas de tratamiento del español medieval hasta el siglo XVI. In Martin Hummel, Bettina Kluge & María Eugenia Vázquez Laslop (eds.), *Formas y fórmulas de tratamiento en el mundo hispánico*, 507–529. México City: El Colegio de México/Universität Graz.

Jakobson, Roman. 1971 (1957). Shifters, verbal categories and the Russian verb. In *idem, Selected writings*, vol. 2: *Word and language*, 130–147. The Hague/Paris: Mouton.

Jaworski, Adam & Dariusz Galasiński. 2000. Vocative forms of address and ideological legitimization in political debates. *Discourse Studies* 2,1. 35–53.

Jespersen, Otto. 1924. *The Philosophy of Grammar*. Chicago: The University of Chicago Press.

Kerbrat-Orecchioni, Catherine. 2017. *Les débats de l'entre-deux-tours des élections présidentielles françaises. Constantes et évolutions d'un genre*. Paris: L'Harmattan.

Kuo, Sai-hua. 2002. From solidarity to antagonism: The uses of the second-person singular pronoun in Chinese political discourse. *Text* 22,1. 29–55.

Levinson, Stephen C. 1983. *Pragmatics*. Cambridge: Cambridge University Press.

Lyons, John. 1995. *Linguistic semantics. An introduction*. Cambridge: Cambridge University Press.

Ortega Ortiz, Reynaldo Yunuen. 2010. De la hegemonía al pluralismo: elecciones presidenciales y comportamiento electoral, 1976–2006. In Soledad Loaeza & Jean François Prud'homme (coords.), *Los grandes problemas de México*, vol. 14: *Instituciones y procesos políticos*, 405–447. Mexico City: El Colegio de México.

Otálora Malassis, Janine Madeline. 2014. *Debates políticos y medios de comunicación*. México City: Tribunal Electoral del Poder Judicial de la Federación.

Pérez Fernández del Castillo, Germán, Arnulfo Puga Cisneros & Héctor Díaz-Santana (comps.). 2009. *Memoria histórica de la transición democrática en México 1977–2007. Documentos básicos para entender el cambio político*, vol. 3. Mexico City: H. Cámara de Diputados LX Legislatura/Senado de la República LX Legislatura/UNAM/Miguel Ángel Porrúa.

Proctor, Katarzyna & Lilly I-Wen Su. 2011. The 1st person plural in political discourse—American politicians in interviews and in a debate. *Journal of Pragmatics* 43, 3251–3266. doi: 10.1016/j.pragma.2011.06.010.

Roitman, Malin. 2014. Presidential candidates' ethos of credibility: The case of the presidential pronoun *I* in the 2012 Hollande-Sarkozy debate. *Discourse & Society* 25;6. 741–765.

Sánchez Ruiz, Enrique. 2005. Los medios de comunicación masiva en México, 1968–2000. In Ilan Bizberg & Lorenzo Meyer (coords.), *Una historia contemporánea de México*, vol. 2: *Actores*, 403–454. Mexico City: Océano.

Vázquez Laslop, María Eugenia. 2014. El discurso político en México (1968–1994): la emergencia del diálogo. In Rebeca Barriga Villanueva & Pedro Martín Butragueño (dirs.), *Historia sociolingüística de México. Espacio, contacto y discurso político*, vol. 3, 1783–1895. Mexico City: El Colegio de México.

Vázquez Laslop, María Eugenia. 2019a. *Tú y yo en los debates de candidatos a la Presidencia en México (1994–2012). Un estudio de deixis política*. Mexico City: El Colegio de México.

Vázquez Laslop, María Eugenia. 2019b. Pragmatic and grammatical categories for the analysis of forms of address in presidential election debates. In Bettina Kluge & María Irene Moyna (eds.), *It's not all about you: New perspectives on address research*, 305–331. Amsterdam/Philadelphia: John Benjamins.

Vertommen, Bram. 2013. The strategic value of pronominal choice: Exclusive and inclusive *we* in political panel debates. *Pragmatics* 23,2. 361–383.

Woldenberg, José. 2012. *La transición democrática en México*. Mexico City: El Colegio de México.

Zupnik, Yael-Janette. 1994. A pragmatic analysis of the use of person deixis in political discourse. *Journal of Pragmatics* 21. 339–383.

Zwicky, Arnold. 1971. Hey, Whatsyourname! In Michael W. Le Galy, Robert A. Fox & Anthony Bruck (eds.), *Papers from the Tenth Regional Meeting. Chicago Linguistic Society*, 787–801. Chicago: Chicago Linguistic Society.

Calderon Campos, Miguel and Maria Teresa Garcia-Godoy

The European roots of the present-day Americanism *su merced*

Abstract: The allocutive *su merced* 'His Grace, His Worship' is currently regarded as a syntactic Americanism. In certain Hispanic American geolects, *su merced* is currently used for second person singular (2P *su merced*) deixis and may denote respect (V address) as well as intimacy (T address). The traditional hypothesis argues that these uses are only found in American Spanish, and that the allocutive *su merced* dates back to the Afro-Hispanic varieties of the colonial period. This chapter establishes, for the first time, the evolutionary connections of the current Americanism with the history of *su merced* usage in Spain. It also explores a new, non-literary database and argues for a new diachronic hypothesis on (2P) *su merced*, from a Pan-Hispanic perspective.

Keywords: history of the Spanish language, historical Morphosyntax, T-V distinction, diachrony of *su merced*

1 Introduction

Currently, *su merced* is a morphosyntactic feature of American Spanish, especially in the Colombian area (see *Diccionario de americanismos* (DA)). The 21st century, from the pluricentric perspective of the Real Academia Española, has seen two important new developments in the academic status of this second person (2P) form of address. First, the *su merced* form, which Kany had noted as an Americanism (1963: 92–94), has entered into the official grammar (RAE-ASALE 2009: 1257). Second, a new classification of Hispanic forms of address was proposed, which included (2P) *su merced* (Bertolotti 2015; Fontanella de Weinberg 1999 does not mention this form).

Contemporary corpora corroborate the relative currency in America of this address form in certain locations. For instance, CORPES XXI offers American Spanish examples of (2P) *su merced*, which can denote either the maximum (1) or minimum (2) communicative distance:

Note: The names of the two authors are mentioned in alphabetical order, without denoting a different level of involvement in this study. The level of authorship credit is totally equitable between the two authors. The research is financed by the reference project HISPATESD, FFI2017-83400-P, MINECO/AEI/FEDER/UE.

(1)   Decidí pasar la alambrada que me encerraba, cuando uno de los hombres de machete que me trajo al campamento apareció. Tenga *su merced* la ama-bilidad de seguirme. Era un campesino de ojos claros, curtido por el sol. (2003, Venezuela. Pedro Rangel Mora, *El enemigo*, CORPES XXI)

'I decided to cross the fence that enclosed me, when one of the machete-wielding men who brought me to the camp appeared. Would you be so kind as to follow me? He was a light-eyed *peasant*, weathered by the sun.'

(2)   Papá, ¿*su mercé* está seguro de que quiere ir? ¿No es mejor dejarlo para después cuando esté mejor? (2008, Colombia. Triana, *Antología de obras de teatro*, CORPES XXI)

'Dad, are you sure that you want to go? Is it not better to leave it until later when you are better?'

What are the historical roots of these American Spanish uses of (2P) *su merced* as a respectful (1) and intimate (2) form of address? Currently there is no com-plete answer to this question, given that a thorough history of (2P) *su merced* in European and American Spanish remains unfinished. However, it will be shown that the roots of this current Americanism can be found in European Spanish. In fact, (2P) *su merced* as a respectful form of social address must have been used in the Spanish spoken on the Iberian Peninsula, but today survives only in Hispanic America. The roots of example (1) in today's Venezuela can be traced back to Spain. By contrast, the use of (2P) *su merced* in the family context can be shown to be a particular evolutionary development of Hispanic America. The Colombian example (2), in which a daughter addresses her father as *su mercé*, shows a current drift in this use in Hispanic America towards inti-macy. In this regard, *su merced* appears to show a dual function in Hispanic America, analogous to the phenomenon of *ustedeo* (the overarching use of *usted* as a single pronoun of respect and intimacy) in Bogota or Costa Rica. The retrodating of this dual function, however, has yet to be determined. Accord-ingly, today's scientific perspective does not precisely clarify the question as to when (2P) *su merced* began to be used in Hispanic America as an intimate form of address.

Chronologically, the Spanish American history of (2P) *su merced* is quite imprecise, given that hardly any testimonial evidence has been found of this address form in the colonial era. Previous studies have largely focused on a bicentennial history of the phenomenon, based on literary sources from the 19th and 20th centuries. Starting around 1850, the use of (2P) *su merced* as a respectful form of address first emerges in Hispanic American *costumbrismo* (i.e. literature of local customs and manners), especially when Black servants address their masters.

Indeed, one of the main hypotheses posits the origin of the current Americanism in the linguistic contact between Spanish and African languages (Lipski 2005). According to this view, the *bozal* (or broken-Spanish) sociolect was the first to incorporate the *su merced* form of address. The label *bozal* refers to the group of Black African slaves and their descendants, who had difficulty speaking Spanish (Lipski 2005: 7). The *bozal* change revolves around the fact that *su merced* is not used to speak *of* the master (canonical use of the third person [3P]), but rather to speak *with* him or her ("non-canonical" use of 2P). Accordingly, the Caribbean would be the primary region in the history of this ethnolinguistic feature of Hispanic America.

In short, the current research outlook generally defends this literary history of the (2P) *su merced* Americanism, as derived from the speech of theatre characters of low socioeconomic status. As a consequence, we still do not know whether non-literary language confirms or refutes this Afro-Hispanic link to the form of address in question, a connection that is found in fiction genres. For this reason, the present study will explore a Hispanic American corpus of historical documents (from the 16th to 19th centuries; see Section 4), and will offer evidence of the non-literary use of *su merced*. In a diatopic sense, the study focuses on the Caribbean area, given that this was the territory usually chosen by the *costumbrista* authors to set their literary instances of Afro-Hispanic uses of *su merced*.

The main objective of this chapter is to trace the entire history of *su merced* in Hispanic America, and to connect it to its European roots, using as data archival documents that offer a wider social and regional perspective than that of the stereotypical 19th century *costumbrista* interpretation. It will present the first evidence of (2P) *su merced* in the colonial era, while chronologically specifying the history of this Americanism.

Section 2 presents the study's epistemological framework, hypothesis and objectives. This is followed by a bibliographical account of the diachrony of (2P) *su merced*, pointing out the weaknesses of the slavery hypothesis. Section 4 describes the document corpora, and Section 5 offers empirical evidence of *su merced* in the corpora, from a Pan-American perspective. An analysis of this evidence from the Caribbean region is presented in Section 6, followed by the conclusions.

2 Epistemological framework, hypothesis and objectives

Conceptually, a form of address is defined as a "linguistic macrostructure, the functioning of which implies the combined use of pronominal, verbal and nominal forms with which the speaker interacts with his or her interlocutor, refers to a third person or signals his or her own reference" (Rigatuso 2008: 354). The key role played by the nominal element in forms of address is often ignored. It has a decisive function in those cases in which a single pronoun handles all uses of the second person deixis, as with the pronoun *you* in contemporary English, in the plural of American Spanish (*ustedes*, example (3)), or in *ustedeo*, i.e. the use of *usted* with intimate friends or family members (see example (4)). In all these cases, nominal elements such as *chicos* 'guys' (intimacy) or *señores* (respect) codify the type of personal deixis (example (3)). This same pattern of the plural *ustedes* moves to the singular in Hispanic American regions using *ustedeo*, an instance of which is seen in example (4): the nominal elements *mija* (< *mi hija*) 'my daughter'[1] and *señor* indicate, respectively, intimacy and respect of a grand-mother *ustedeante* 'who uses *usted*' when speaking to her granddaughter or to a doctor.

(3)   ¿Qué sitio prefieren, *chicos*? ("intimacy")/¿Qué sitio prefieren, *señores*? ("respect")

'What place do you prefer, kids?/What place do you prefer, gentlemen?'

(4)   Aquí tiene, *mija* ("intimacy")/Aquí tiene, *señor*. ("respect")

'Here you are, little one/Here you are, sir'

The examples show that nominals are used to determine communicative distance. In order to research the deixis of the second person in Spanish diachrony, it was especially useful to combine the morphosyntactic dimension of the forms of address with the parameter of communicative distance. This parameter is

---

1 The *Diccionario de americanismos* (DA) lists *mijo, mija* as an allocutive formula applied to three possible recipients: a) a child; b) a friend or companion, and c) a sentimental partner. The three cases fall under the popular or affective type. As to the diatopic distribution, the three uses simultaneously coexist in the usage of three countries: Mexico, Chile and Colombia. Separately, each of these three uses is also currently used in other regions of Hispanic America (DA).

implicitly stated in the classic theory of power and solidarity of Brown & Gilman (1960). According to this first formulation regarding the listener, connections with a greater level of solidarity (symmetrical relations) are codified into forms of address with minimum distance. On the other hand, connections with a higher degree of power (asymmetrical relations) choose forms of address with maximum distance. This study coined the well-known terms "T forms" (+closeness -power) and "V forms" (+distance +power) (Brown & Gilman 1960: 257–259). The analysis in terms of power and solidarity is appropriate for stable binary pronominal systems, such as that found in the French language: *tu/vous* (T form/V form). The same theoretic paradigm, however, shows limitations in other Romance language systems that, through evolution, have distanced themselves from this binary prototype (see e.g. Hummel in this volume; Moyna & Rivera-Mills 2016: 2).

Spanish *ustedeo* serves as an example of extreme pronominal simplification. For these cases, Uber (1985) suggests adapting the parameter of communicative distance, such that the same pronoun functions as the V form (maximum distance) well as the T form (minimum distance). In line with Uber's (1985) proposal, in this study we propose that *su merced* functions as a V address (1) and as a T address (2) in certain areas of American Spanish.

Historically, *su merced* in solidarity relations (= *su merced*$_T$; see (2)) may represent the last evolutionary link of an Iberian-Romance language phenomenon that, from the end of the 16th century (example (6)), affected all honorary pronouns having the "*su* + abstract name" structure. In this study we propose, for the first time, connecting this Hispanic American link with the Romance language "chain" of the same linguistic phenomenon. Accordingly, here we defend the hypothesis that intralinguistic motivations led to the triggering of the change in (2P) *su merced* in different Spanish speaking areas, regardless of the fact that there were African migratory flows and *bozal* speakers in those geographic areas (we will treat this aspect more thoroughly in Section 3).

Before analysing the data, it is important to explain how the "*su* + abstract noun" structure evolved in the Romance language environment within the honorific address paradigm. As is well known, in Romance languages personal deixis is realised through pronouns and nominal groups (RAE-ASALE 2009: 1256). The latter include the honorific title, composed of a title name (e.g. *excelencia, señoría, merced*) preceded by the possessives *vuestra/su*. This subsystem (possessive *su/vuestro* + abstract noun) specialises in the honorific deixis – in the allocutive (e.g. *vuestra señoría*) as well as the delocutive (e.g. *su señoría*) uses. As such, from the end of the Middle Ages, each title has a form with *vuestra* for the second person (deixis in presence) and another form with *su* for the third person (deixis in absence). As an illustration, in 16th century Spanish, *vuestra excelencia*

'Your Excellency' is used to speak *with* a viceroy (2P), while (3P) *su excelencia* is employed to speak *of* or *about* a viceroy.[2]

All in all, it is possible to notice movements of the delocutive 3P forms towards 2P allocutives in the diachrony of the Romance languages (Coffen 2002; Mazzon 2010). For that reason, honorifics having the "*su* + title" structure can function not only as forms of address for the 3P deixis in absence (conservative use), but also as the 2P deixis in presence (innovative use) in the Romance language environment. In the viceroy examples above, at the end of the 16th and beginning of the 17th centuries, *su excelencia* begins to be used to speak *with* the viceroy (innovative 2P use), and not only to speak *about* the viceroy (conservative 3P use). Table 1 shows how the delocutive forms with *su* (3P deixis in absence) already enter the allocutive environment of forms with *vuestra* (2P deixis in presence) in the Spanish Golden Age.

Table 1: *Su merced* in the honorific subsystem (Golden Age).

DELOCUTIVE FORMS (3P)	ALLOCUTIVE FORMS (2P)
Su Excelencia ⇒	*Vuestra Excelencia* (>*vuecencia*)
	Su Excelencia
Su Señoría ⇒	*Vuestra Señoría* (> *usía*)
	Su Señoría
Su Merced ⇒	*Vuestra Merced* (>*usted*)
	Su Merced

This evolution of the honorific paradigm causes forms of address with the "*su* + abstract name" structure to take on a double personality: they preserve their delocutive (3P) status, while assuming a new allocutive (2P) status. With this double deixis, these honorifics become ambiguous forms of address: only contextual elements serve to disambiguate the delocutive or allocutive character of the "*su* + abstract noun" forms. The level of ambiguity is still higher in the specific case of *su merced*, given that historically this form of address has been able to express a triple personal deixis, which we attempt to illustrate in examples (5) to (8).

---

2 The legislation of the time determined that the honorific *excelencia* corresponded only to the viceroy in Italian states, while viceroys from the Indies should be addressed as *señoría* – a lower level (Sáez Rivera: 2013). Generally, the colonial documents show two usage guidelines for viceregal address in 16th century Hispanic America: the legal (*señoría*) and the factual (*excelencia*) (García-Godoy 2019).

(5)   E doña Leonor de Avendaño dixo que *su merced del señor corregidor* había mandado. (1513, Spain. *Notary documents of the San Bartolomé convent*, CORDE)

'And lady Leonor de Avendaño said that the honourable mayor had ordered.'

(6)   Margarita: Entremos en esta tienda, que es la más rica.
Mercader: ¿Qué manda v.m., señor caballero, qué ha menester?

Thomás: Yo ninguna cosa; esta señora, muchas.

Mercader: Pues pida *su merced*, que todo se le dará aquí a buen precio.

Margarita: Muéstreme acá algunos tocados, guirnaldillas. (1599, Spain. Misheu, *Diálogos gramaticales*. CORDE. See García-Godoy 2011: 237)

'Margarita: Let's go into this shop, it is the finest. Merchant: What does the good gentleman command, what does he need? Thomás: I do not need anything, but this lady needs a lot. Mercader: Well, ask then, and you will receive at a good price. Margarita: Show me those headdresses and *guirnaldillas*.'

(7)   Padre y Sor Dn Domingo de Basavilbaso. Padre y muy S.^{or} mío, por la adjunta esquela reconocerá *Smd.* el triste estado en q$^{.e}$ me hallo. (1762, Buenos Aires. Letter from Francisco Antonio de Basavilbaso to his father, *apud* Rigatuso 2009: 85)

'Father and Sir Domingo de Basavilbaso. Father and sir, by the attached notice, you will recognise the sad state in which I find myself.'

(8)   Mi adorada Blanca: Estoy con la pena de no haber recibido carta de *su merced* [...] me haces, amorcito, mucha falta. (1950, Guatemala. Love letter from Miguel Ángel Asturias to Blanca de Mora. CORDE)

'My dear Blanca: I am saddened not to have received your letter [...] I miss you, my little love.'

Examples (5) to (8) potentially illustrate the slow gestation of this triple deixis, as set out in Table 2. The starting point (stage A, example (5)) is a delocutive form (deixis 1 = 3P *su merced*) that brings in second person values of respect marked by subscript $_V$ (deixis 2 = *su merced$_V$*), in the social (stage B1, c. 1599; see example (6)), as well as family domains (stage B2, c. 1762, example (7)). From this position, it could finally foster the definitive movement towards the sphere of maximum intimacy (stage C, example (8), deixis 3 = *su merced$_T$*, where $_T$ marks intimacy. This

Table 2: Proposed evolution of *su merced*.

STAGE A 3P *su merced*	STAGE B1 (social) 2P *su merced*	STAGE B2 (family) 2P *su merced*	STAGE C 2P *su merced*
Deixis 1 "él" (5)	Deixis 2 "vuestra merced > usted" (6)–(7) FORM OF ADDRESSV		Deixis 3 "tú" (8) FORM OF ADDRESST

third deixis can only be found in contemporary Hispanic America, at least since 1950, according to the RAE corpora. Given that conservative (3P) and innovative (2P) uses may have coexisted at certain historical moments, it is not unreasonable to think that some Hispanic geolects simultaneously employed the triple deixis of *su merced*: "él" (example (5)), "usted" (example 7) and "tú" (example (8)).

The history of this phenomenon must be based on these three evolutionary stages. It is important to stress the fact that examples (6) and (7) are evidence of this innovative use (stages B1 and B2) before the 19th century in the non-literary language, and that they all illustrate urban uses by the White elite. Thus, we can cast doubt on the Caribbean slavery hypothesis, which we will describe in the following section, given that it dates the emergence of (2P) *su merced* to an excessively late period (19th century), while also lacking non-literary evidence from before the 19th century.

3 From the "external" slavery hypothesis to the "internal" Romance language hypothesis

This section presents two explanatory models covering the origin of the (2P) *su merced* form of address. We will start by analysing the traditional hypothesis which, as noted above, is based on Afro-Hispanic linguistic contact (external factors), and is exclusively contextualised in American Spanish. We then present our new hypothesis, which interprets the same linguistic change as a development within the Spanish language itself (internal factors), in Spain as well as in Hispanic America.

3.1 External factors in the traditional hypothesis

The Hispanic American history of *su merced* remains enigmatic. Although it is claimed that the *su merced*V innovation originated with the migratory movements of Africans to vice-regal Hispanic America, empirically this Afro-Hispanic trait is only seen in literature starting from the mid-19th century (Álvarez-López & Bertolotti 2013). Indeed, without furnishing any historical documentation, it is argued that in the present-day countries of Peru (De Granda 2004: 488–489), the Dominican Republic (Pérez Guerra 1988, 1989), Cuba (Pérez Guerra 1988, 1989) and the Commonwealth of Puerto Rico (Álvarez Narario 1982) *su merced*$_V$ existed due to the slavery system and to the linguistic contact between Spanish and African languages. It is also claimed that in these three countries and commonwealth, the "feudal" form of address *su merced*$_V$ constituted a sociolinguistic marker of the Black slaves subject to severe social abuse in colonial society. For that matter, it is also posited – from this same study perspective, and without any demonstration whatsoever – that this Black African form of address disappeared from common usage upon the end of slavery in those countries, with the exception of the Dominican Republic (Pérez Guerra 1988, 1989; see Hummel 2010: 305–306).

Accordingly, the slavery hypothesis implicitly assumes that, before the period of political emancipation, Hispanic America only saw the use of *su merced*$_V$ in markedly asymmetrical relations of power. It is only in the 20th century that new patterns of Hispanic American use of equal power solidarity relations begin to develop (Álvarez-López & Bertolotti 2013: 23). In this way, the old colonial form of address would have "democratised" – a fact that would make it possible to explain the familiar use of *su merced*$_T$ in solidarity relations of equal power, although the geolects of countries currently using *su merced*$_T$, the so-called "países sumercedeantes" (the Colombian and Ecuadorian Andes, Venezuela), would differ from the abovementioned countries in order to contextualise the Afro-Hispanic linguistic contact hypothesis. The latest formulations of this slavery hypothesis ignore or minimise the most recent documented discoveries of 2P *su merced* in the last colonial century. We are referring to documented 18th century evidence of the form of address in slavery, as well as non-slavery contexts in such varied Hispanic American locations as Buenos Aires (Rigatuso 2008), Merida, Venezuela (Obediente 2009, 2010), Cartagena de Indias, Colombia (Gutiérrez Maté 2013: 258) and the Dominican Republic (Gutiérrez Maté 2013: 258).

Despite these advances, there are currently no documented diachronic studies covering the entire history of (2P) *su merced* in Hispanic America, from its colonial origins as a reverent form of address – supposedly linked to slavery (*su merced*$_V$) – to the present as an overarching form of address (*su merced*$_V$ + *su merced*$_T$).

The main research gap in prior studies can be found in the colonial era: in the 17th and 18th centuries the innovative use of (2P) *su merced* does not seem to appear in the vice-regal literature. For this reason, the fact that *su merced* in literature only emerges in the post-colonial era in the speech of Black slaves or mixed heritage (Sp. *mulato*)[3] characters stands out. The hypothesis concerning the slavery origin of the current Americanism is based solely on this Hispanic American contextualisation of the phenomenon, linguistically set in Afro-Hispanic contexts. As previously mentioned, this hypothesis assumes that extralinguistic factors (contact of languages) triggered the change of *su merced* towards the second person. Accordingly, if this contact of languages occurred only in the New World, the genesis of (2P) *su merced* would be historically linked with the Afro-Hispanic varieties in Hispanic America. There this phenomenon would have emerged as an ethnolinguistic feature of the language spoken by the Black slave minority.

This slavery hypothesis, which as we have seen has not been empirically confirmed in the colonial era, is a common denominator in diachronic studies of American Spanish in general, and the Caribbean area in particular. These studies ignore the key fact that the mother country Spain also witnessed the use of the form of address (2P) *su merced* for no less than three centuries (16th to 19th) (Lapesa 2000; García-Godoy 2011).

3.2 Internal factors of the new hypothesis

Our hypothesis is based on the fact that the first use of (2P) *su merced* is historically documented in 16th century European Spanish, which we previously mentioned in the bridging example (6) (García-Godoy 2011). The context for this example is a commercial exchange between two strangers (seller-customer dyad), included in a colloquial Spanish conversation. In this early example from 1599, *su merced* is used to speak with a customer (deixis in presence). In these first commercial uses of (2P) *su merced*, there does not appear to be any hierarchical relation between the seller and the customer.

In Spanish Golden Age theatre, however, we begin to see another, different use of (2P) *su merced* in work contexts with asymmetrical relations (servant-master dyads). This use increasingly appears in Spanish literature in the 18th and 19th centuries as a form of address used by White servants (Lapesa 2000). Similarly, literary evidence of (2P) *su merced* in analogous contexts can be found in 18th century Sephardic texts (García Moreno 2004). Moreover, 19th century Hispanic American (Álvarez-López & Bertolotti 2013) as well as Portuguese-Brazilian *costumbrismo* (Alkmim 1996) provide documented examples of the most extreme version of this servitude relation: the slave-master dyad. A look at the wide range

---

3 The Spanish term *mulato* is used in the original citations.

of documented examples of the phenomenon in the Spanish speaking world would indicate that in the first stage of the change, *su merced*$_V$ only appears in the social environment between strangers (commercial contexts) or between acquaintances with asymmetrical relations (work contexts of White servitude or Black slavery). This first stage of the change is found exclusively in European Spanish from the 16th to 18th centuries (Lapesa 2000), although in the following century the literary context of servitude will spread throughout the Spanish speaking world.

In short, in this section we have seen that there are two opposing explanations for the movement of *su merced* towards the second person in the historical map of the Spanish language. As we have seen, in the New World external factors of language contact are invoked. In the Old World, by contrast, intralinguistic factors are brought in. Delocutives of the (3P) "*su* + title" structure begin to take on their (2P) functional load in the Golden Age, and can also be used as forms of address in a colloquial manner. Consequently, *su merced*$_V$ in Spain is, in our opinion, the history of a colloquialism that emerges in the 16th century and begins to fade away in the 19th. According to the slavery hypothesis, *su merced*$_V$ is the history of a *bozalismo* used by the Black minority as a slavery form of address in Afro-Hispanic varieties until the 19th century.

In the following sections, we will examine in more detail the corpora upon which we base our hypothesis of the origin and evolution of *su merced*.

4 The corpora

In this study we use two corpora of historical Hispanic American documentation, covering the same time span (16th to 18th centuries), and from identical textual genres (administrative and legal documents, and private letters). The main corpus is CORDIAM (Company & Bertolotti 2015), which comprises a new evidence base of historical, non-literary Hispanic American documents. In addition, we have created an additional corpus specifically for this study. This second corpus brings together a set of documents[4] which have yet to be incorporated into the current version of CORDIAM (see Section 8 on sources).

---

4 Similarly to the main corpus, the additional corpus is made up of archival documents, except the "Crónica Perú" (see references for this document in the "Additional Corpus" section at the end of the chapter). This is the chronicle of the Creole Juan Meléndez, printed in 1681. The first edition of this work was included in the corpus for its relevant linguistic interest: this is where the first historical evidence of American Spanish use of *su merced* at issue was found.

5 Evidence of *su merced* in the corpora (16th to 19th centuries)

This section provides an overall Pan-American perspective of *su merced* in the two corpora (see Section 6 for a specific analysis of the Caribbean region). It opens with a count of all occurrences of *su merced* in the new evidence base (Section 5.1) – conservative (3P) as well as innovative (2P) uses. It then separately explores the innovative trend in the corpora and shows the first evidence of the innovative pattern (2P *su merced*, Section 5.2). It closes with an analysis of the proportion of slavery contexts (social and family domains) in which this innovative trend is seen (Section 5.3).

5.1 *The double personality of* su merced: *conservative (3P) and innovative (2P) uses*

The initial evaluation of the occurrences of *su merced* in both corpora shows the omnipresence of the conservative delocutive (3P), clearly predominant in the four centuries under study. On the other hand, the (2P) *su merced* innovation is underrepresented in this new evidence base: in CORDIAM it comprises 2.7 % of the occurrences, although in the additional corpus that figure reaches 7.4% (Table 3).

Table 3: *Su merced* in the corpora: conservative (3P) and innovative (2P) use.

	3P *su merced*	2P *su merced*
CORDIAM	97.03% (621/640)	2.7% (19/640)
ADDITIONAL CORPUS	92.6% (253/273)	7.4% (20/273)

Considering the large size of the empirical base studied, the very limited number of instances of 2P *su merced* (39 examples) is telling. All would appear to indicate that this pattern of use that was recommended for the spoken language[5] in 1714 (García-Godoy 2011, 2016) had little impact in the written language tradition.

---

5 L'Abbé de Vayrac, in his *Grammaire espagnole* (1714), associates the use of (2P) *su merced* with the spoken language: "surquoi il faut remarquer que quand on l'employe dans les Lettres, on dit *vuestra Merced*, & que quand on l'employe dans la conversation, on dit *su Merced*" 'whereto it should be added that *vuestra Merced* is used for writing, whereas *su Merced* is preferred in conversation' (see García-Godoy 2011: 247). In the previous (17th) century, the grammarian

Thus, the Hispanic American history of the phenomenon still remains an enigma. In view of this, these thirty-nine Hispanic American examples represent a true documental discovery for the task of outlining the first non-literary history of (2P) *su merced* based on corpora data.

Note how, empirically, the corpora show that the (2P) *su merced* change occurs alongside the persistent maintenance of the conservative (3P) *su merced* pattern. In the period under study, the coexistence of conservative and innovative uses occurs between the 17th and 19th centuries, if we consider the chronology of the two corpora (Tables 4 and 5).

Table 4: *Su merced* in CORDIAM (16th to 19th centuries).

FORM	16TH CENT.	17TH CENT.	18TH CENT.	19TH CENT.	TOTAL	
3P *su merced*	194/194	78/78	322/341	27/27	621/640	97.03%
2P *su merced*	—	—	19/341	—	19/640	2.7 %

Table 5: *Su merced* in the Additional Corpus (16th to 19th centuries).

FORM	16TH CENT.	17TH CENT.	18TH CENT.	19TH CENT.	TOTAL	
3P *su merced*	3/3	219/226	21/27	10/17	253/273	92.6%
2P *su merced*	—/—	7/226	6/27	7/17	20/273	7.4%

It is striking that, for approximately two hundred and fifty years, the coexistence of the conservative patterns together with the neological uses made *su merced* a thoroughly ambiguous form of address in large areas of Hispanic America. Table 6 sets out the geographical origins of (2P) *su merced* in the corpora, which represent nine Hispanic American varieties.

In the history of these nine Hispanic American varieties, the emergence of the innovative (allocutive) form of address does not coincide with a decline in the conservative (delocutive) use of the form– on the contrary. It is logical to think that, in such a prolonged evolutionary state, only the context would provide the keys for disambiguating the personal deixis of *su merced* – a form that is formally third person, but grammatically has a double personality (delocutive 3P and allocutive 2P). For our analysis, the co-reference of *su merced* with other linguistic elements has allowed us to identify the predominant conservative (3P) uses

---

Correas had already described the vacillation in the use of *vuestra merced/su merced* as allocutive second person forms (Lapesa 2000: 321).

Table 6: Geographical origins of (2P) *su merced* in the corpora.

	CORDIAM	ADDITIONAL CORPUS
Buenos Aires (Argentina)	+	–
Cartagena de Indias (Colombia)	–	+
Havana (Cuba)	–	+
Lima (Peru)	–	+
Merida (Venezuela)	–	+
Mexico	+	–
Santo Domingo (Dominican Republic)	–	+
Santa Lucia (Venezuela)	+	–
Puerto Rico	–	+

vis-à-vis the minority, innovative (2P) uses. The former are found in the corpora, in prototypical form, in duplicate possessive constructions of the *su merced del señor alcalde* type. Uses of the second person, however, are most often found in direct discourse, and are usually combined with highly disambiguating, vocative nominal enhancements such as *su merced* + *amigo, señor* (+*provisor, alcalde, padre*), *mi amo, hermano* ('religious'), *mamita*, etc.

5.2 Chronology of the (2P) su merced change in the corpora: first indications of the innovative trend

Hispanic American *costumbrista* literature systematically shows (2P) *su merced* as an innovative form of address from 1850, although in the previous century an isolated example of this innovation was already used in the Creole farce *El amor de la estanciera* (García-Godoy 2011). Thus it would seem that the dramatic representations of the allocutive form constitute a phenomenon of the modern era. Yet the non-literary language allows us to pre-date the same phenomenon to the classic period. Examples (9) to (12) present the first documentary evidence found in the two corpora of the innovative trend:

(9) Amigo, Hermano, perdone *su merced* (le decía) no me hallo con lo que pide, bien sabe Dios, que quisiera darle el hábito. (1681, Lima. Priest → parishioner. *Crónica Perú*. Additional Corpus)

'Friend, brother, pardon me (he said), but I do not have what you want, yet if it were up to me, as God knows, I would give you even the frock that I am wearing.'

(10) Por fin señor valga el ser *Su merced* Padre y con posibles, o ser yo hijo y sin ninguno; y si todo esto no basta para que consiga el mejorar de suerte, tenga *su merced* piedad de un inocente. (1762, Buenos Aires. Son → father. *Apud* Rigatuso 2009. Also in CORDIAM 2015)

'Finally, sir, it is a fact that you are a father with economic resources, and I am a son with no resources whatsoever. And if this is not enough, so that with your help I may improve my situation, I beg you have pity, father sir, on an innocent such as myself.'

(11) Señor[6] *general* don Gav[r]iel Gutieres de Ruvalcava. Mui se*ñ*or mío por esta le notisio a v.md. cómo el preso q*u*e v.md. despachó con los de Soquitlán se huyó de esta cársel timprano [...] Él se fue con grillos y dejó su ropa que se la remito a v.md.: una manta, unos sapatos, el sombrero y su devastimento. Su m*erce*d verá lo que determina a este otro preso hoy irá a dormir [...] besa la mano de v.md. su humilde criado. (1767, Ojotolapa, México. Governor → general. CORDIAM)

'Mr. general Gav[r]iel Gutieres de Ruvalcava. My good sir, I hereby inform you that the prisoner that you sent with those of Soquitlán escaped from this prison early [...] He left in shackles, and left his clothes, which I forward to you – a blanket, some shoes, a hat and his provisions. You will see where this other prisoner sleeps today [...] your humble servant kisses your hand.'

(12) Ilustrísimo Señor vicario [...] Hago presente a *su merced* todos mis trabajos [...] su más humilde esclavo. (1784, Merida, Andean Venezuela. Slave → vicar. *Apud Cartas de Mérida*. Additional Corpus)

'Illustrious Mr. Vicar [...] I herein present you with my work [...] your most humble slave.'

In the historical documents under analysis, the earliest examples of (2P) *su merced* date to the 17th century in the additional corpus (Table 5) and to the 18th century in CORDIAM (Table 4). Note how in the main corpus the innovative trend is quite short lived, given that it hardly amounts to a generation (thirty-three years) in the second half of the 18th century (1762–1795). Yet if we look at the chronological indicators in both CORDIAM and the additional corpus, we find evidence of (2P) *su merced* in Hispanic America from 1681 until 1823. This documented retro-dating

---

6 We use italicized letters to represent reconstructed letters (e.g. Se*ñ*or for Sr, or m*erce*d for md).

of the innovative form of address substantially modifies the status of previous knowledge.

This would all seem to indicate that the type of source consulted provides different chronologies of the innovative trend. A look at fiction genres clearly indicates the change occurring only in the postcolonial period. However, the non-literary genres show the same phenomenon appearing from the 17th century, in chronicles, letters and witness statements from the colonial era until the period of independence. This new, earlier dating of (2P) *su merced* in Hispanic American usage allows us to venture that the beginning of the change is more synchronised on both sides of the Atlantic than was previously thought. In non-literary language, (2P) *su merced* is an innovation that begins to take its place in European grammar from 1605, while there is evidence of the same innovation in the New World in the same century.

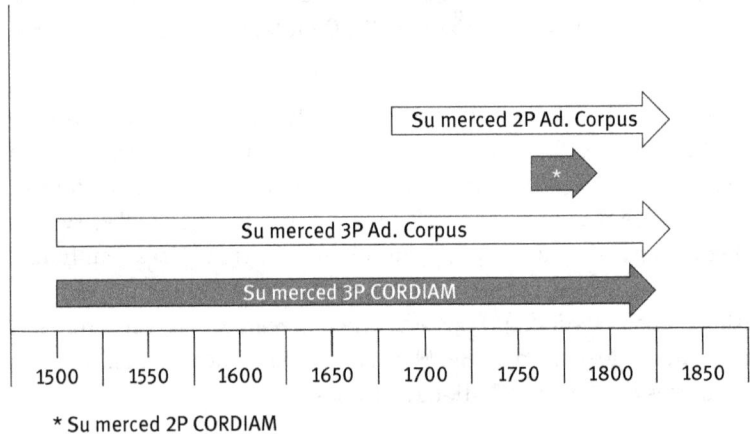

Figure 1: Development of *su merced* as observed in the corpora.

5.3 The innovative trend in Hispanic America: areas of usage and slavery-related contexts

As previously shown, the additional corpus more fully reflects the diachrony of the innovative phenomenon in Hispanic America (1681–1830). During this time period of approximately a century and a half, (2P) *su merced* is found in the social context. Yet this form of address is historically less common in the family domain; the corpora only provide examples of (2P) *su merced* within families from 1762 until 1830 (approximately three generations). On the other hand, if we count the occurrences of the innovative use in those two domains, we see that the corpora provide a greater number of examples in family relations than in non-family social relations.

In light of the appearance of the phenomenon in non-literary language, fiction genres could provide a more skewed perspective of (2P) *su merced* in American Spanish. These literary genres partially represent the "social life" of this form of address in the slave-master dyad, but minimise the "private life" of this innovation in the child-parent relation. As we have seen, the literaturisation of (2P) *su merced* shows a positive correlation between the use of the new form of address and slavery contexts, limited exclusively to the social environment.

However, the new evidence base under study does not confirm this positive correlation, although it does show the use of (2P) *su merced* in the slave-master dyad. Indeed, only the additional corpus offers Afro-Hispanic American contexts of *su merced* (+*mi amo*), yet they comprise only a small minority in the social context (1/13) and do not exist in the family setting (Table 7). A comprehensive examination of all the occurrences of the new form of address in both the family and social contexts shows that there is only one use of (2P) *su merced* in the slave-master dyad (1/39, 2.56 %) in the corpora (Tables 7–8).

Table 7: CORDIAM: Social and family context usage. 2P *su merced* in the slave-master / other dyads.

DOMAINS OF USE	16TH CENT.	17TH CENT.	18TH CENT.	19TH CENT.	TOTAL	
Social context	—	—	0/1	—	0/1	0%
Family context	—	—	0/18	—	0/18	0%

Table 8: Additional Corpus: Social and family context usage. Examples of 2P *su merced* in the slave-master / other dyads.

DOMAINS OF USE	16TH CENT.	17TH CENT.	18TH CENT.	19TH CENT.	TOTAL	
Social context	—	0/7	1/6	—	1/13	7.69%
Family context	—	—	—	0/7	0/7	0 %

6 Diachrony of (2P) *su merced* in Afro-Hispanic varieties: the Caribbean region

In a diatopic, i.e. geographical, sense, the slavery hypothesis has almost always been contextualised in the Caribbean region. From the pioneering work of Álvarez Nazario (1982) until the most recent work of Álvarez-López & Bertolotti (2013), researchers have stressed that, diachronically, the contact between African languages and Spanish in this geolect triggered some of the morphosyntactic characteristics of this region. These researchers have historically resorted to this extra-linguistic process as a linguistic identity element that brings together a region that is dialectally heterogeneous, yet geographically united by the Caribbean Sea.

In the Caribbean region, the development of the institution of slavery and that of the Americanism under study are chronologically quite different, in spite of the fact that earlier studies have magnified the historical parallel between both processes. Moreover, while the historical process covers four centuries (1503–1886), the dialectal phenomenon of (2P) *su merced* in prior studies is basically documented in the last century of that time period. Regarding the Black African usage of (2P) *su merced* in the Caribbean, there are few studies that provide evidence of the historical use in Caribbean locations in the 18th century. The Caribbean retro-dating of (2P) *su merced* is mostly set in the second half of the 19th century, and has a literary source. In this regard, Álvarez-López & Bertolotti (2013) offer the most complete panoramic view of fiction genres (based on Lipski's written legacy), set linguistically in two Caribbean locations – Puerto Rico and Cuba. Evidence is given for a positive correlation in both islands of the 19th century use of *su merced* (and its variants) + *mi amo* among the Black slave population.

In short, these literary uses set in Cuba and Puerto Rico in the second half of the 19th century are the first instances of the slave usage of *su merced* in both islands.[7] Note the fact that slavery existed in that region from the 16th century, and that in the same century the (2P) *su merced* linguistic change appears in the mother country – with no link whatsoever with African migration to the West Indies.

Furthermore, given that the allocutive (2P) *su merced* has not survived to the present day in the Caribbean geolect, the claim is made that the extinction process in the area must be connected to the abolition of slavery. Yet as we know, abolition movements occurred at a different rate in the Caribbean. Slavery was

---

7 There are striking differences in the polymorphism of the *su merced* form of address in Caribbean usage between the examples appearing in literary genres and those in the archival corpora under study. Álvarez-López & Bertolotti (2013: 15) document fourteen formal variants in the literature: *su mé, su mecé, su melcé, su mercé, su merced, su mesé, su messé, su miecé, sumasé, sumacé, sumelcé, sumece, sumercé, sumesé*. This extensive inventory of literary variants contrasts with the formal stability of the form of address in the non-literary corpora. There, four variants have been documented – two in complete writing forms (*su merced, su mercé*) and two in abbreviated forms (*S md, S mrd*). Concerning the phenomenon of literary polymorphism in the diachrony of the *merced* honorific, see García-Godoy (2016).

abolished throughout Hispanic America between 1810 and 1850, except in Puerto Rico and Cuba, where it was not abolished until 1870 and 1873 respectively.

In this section we analyse the twenty Caribbean instances of (2P) *su merced* appearing in the corpora, for the five locations listed in Table 9. First, we will explore the innovative uses in the social context, and calculate the percentage of Afro-Hispanic American contexts. Secondly, we will analyse the evolution of (2P) *su merced* in Caribbean family environments. Finally, we will show whether the Caribbean history of *su merced* in areas of late abolition (Cuba) confirms or refutes the slavery-based history of this form of address.

Table 9: Caribbean usage of (2P) *su merced* in the corpora.

	CORDIAM	ADDITIONAL CORPUS
DATE/LOCATION	1795/Santa Lucia	1700/Santo Domingo 1762/Cartagena de Indias 1810/Puerto Rico 1829/Havana
NUMBER OF INSTANCES	1	19

6.1 *The social context in the Caribbean history of* su merced

In the corpora, the Caribbean region shows the greatest number of innovative instances of (2P) *su merced*, over a period of 129 years (1700–1829). Surprisingly, however, only a minority of these Caribbean instances are documented in the social context. An examination of Table 10 shows that the most extensive corpus (CORDIAM) does not even reflect this social phenomenon in this geolect. Only the additional corpus, albeit in a minority of cases, offers these five instances of the "social life" of (2P) *su merced* in the Caribbean (examples (13) to (17)), dated between 1700 and 1763:

Table 10: Caribbean instances of (2P) *su merced* in the social context: slave-master/other dyads.

CORPUS	16TH CENT.	17TH CENT.	18TH CENT.	19TH CENT.	N. OF SLAVE-MASTER INSTANCES
CORDIAM	—	—	0/1	—	0
ADDITIONAL CORPUS	—	—	1/5	—	1

(13) Señor, pregúntele *su mrd* al lizenciado don Francisco de Manzaneda qué viene a buscar a mi casa. (1700, Santo Domingo. Neighbour → graduate. *Pleito1, Santo Domingo*. Additional Corpus)

'Sir, ask the graduate Francisco de Manzaneda what he is coming to look for at my home.'

(14) Mi señor, justicia, que me ha venido a matar a mi casa este perrito de este mulatico de Pedro de Almonte, porque habiéndome echado a perder a mi hija Juana Enriques y preservando en su maldad y reprehendiéndola yo y tratando de castigarla por ello, viéndola inquieta, se me apareció este dicho mulato con el machete que *su mrd* le vée. (1720, Santo Domingo. Mixed heritage (Sp. *mulato*) slave of the church → ordinary mayor of Santiago de los Caballeros. *Pleito2, Santo Domingo*. Additional Corpus)

'My lord, I ask for justice, because this "mulatto" dog Pedro de Almonte came to my house to kill me, because having caused the loss of my daughter Juana Enriques, in all his evil, and my having scolded her and trying to punish her, for that reason, seeing that she was upset, this "mulatto" dog appeared with the machete you see.'

(15) ¿Qué tiene *su md* mi amo? ¿qué le duele o aflige?
(1762, Cartagega de Indias, Colombia. Slave → master. *Pleito, Cartagena de Indias*. Additional Corpus)

'What do you have, my master? What hurts or afflicts you?'

(16) No me acuerde *su mercé* que tuve mi primer hijo.
(1763, Santo Domingo. Black slave → mixed heritage (Sp. *mulato*) neighbour. *Crónica, Santo Domingo*. Additional Corpus, II: 109)

'Do not remind me, sir, that I had my first son.'

(17) Y dixo al Obispo: "señor vea *su mercé* que son travesuras de Antonillo."
(1763, Santo Domingo. Servant → bishop. *Crónica, Santo Domingo*. Additional Corpus, II: 109)

'And said to the Bishop: sir, see that these are the antics of Antonillo'

The Afro-Hispanic American contexts in Cartagena de Indias and Santo Domingo are unequivocal in three of the five examples. (2P) *su merced* is mostly documented in the speech of Black Dominicans during the period from 1700 to 1763. Yet it is quite interesting to note that in these historical instances of innovative (2P) usage, interlocutors of different ethnic backgrounds receive the same *su merced*$_V$ form of address from Black speakers, whether or not they are their masters.

It should be noted that of the five interlocutors receiving the *su merced*$_V$ form of address, only one fits the slave servitude prototype: "*su merced mi amo*" (example (15); see Table 10). In the other examples, a governor (White), an ordinary mayor (White), a bishop (White) and a simple neighbour (*mulato*) are also addressed with *su merced*$_V$, either as a bare form of reference, or in coreference with other elements.

Regarding the social context, the innovative form of address in the 18th century Caribbean would appear to show a "social life" similar to that described in the mother country Spain and in vice-regal Lima a century earlier – interlocutors with or without a hierarchical relation to the speaker can receive *su merced*$_V$.

6.2 The family context of (2P) su merced in the Caribbean

As mentioned earlier, family usage of (2P) *su merced* has only been documented in Hispanic America. The first instances of this innovative use as a form of address from children to parents have been located in the Rio de Plata area in the last colonial century. In fact, in Buenos Aires in 1762, within a patrician family, the children address their father as *su merced* (+ (*ilustrísimo*) *señor padre*). This pattern of use among the White population is minimised in fiction genres, in favour of slavery contexts within the Black population.

In the Caribbean region, almost all instances of (2P) *su merced* in the corpora correspond to the family context (Table 11). This innovative use is documented in the Caribbean thirty years after it appears in Buenos Aires. From 1795 to 1830, *su merced* (+ *taita, madresita, mamita*) as a form of address from children to parents is found in three areas of this Afro-Hispanic region: Caribbean Venezuela (Santa Lucia), Cuba (Havana) and Puerto Rico.

As in the Southern Cone,[8] family usage of *su merced* in the Caribbean also develops in urban environments of the White elite. Afro-Hispanic American contexts are not seen in any of the family uses in the Caribbean.

Examples (18) to (20) are the first instances of the "family life" of 2P *su merced* in the Caribbean region. Here we offer the earliest evidence from both corpora for three Caribbean areas: Venezuela (18), Puerto Rico (19) and Cuba (20).

---

[8] The Southern Cone comprises South American countries around and south of the Tropic of Capricorn, traditionally viewed as Argentina, Chile and Uruguay.

Table 11: Caribbean instances of 2P *su merced* in the family context: slave-master/other dyads.

CORPUS	16TH CENT.	17TH CENT.	18TH CENT.	19TH CENT.	N. OF SLAVE-MASTER INSTANCES
CORDIAM	–	–	0/1	–	0
ADDITIONAL CORPUS	–	–	0/5	0/14	0

(18) Tayta, cómo puede decir que es falso, quando *Su merced* sabe que pasó como dije. (1795, Santa Lucia, Venezuela. Santa Lucia Lawsuit: daughter → father. *Apud* Tejera 2006. Also in CORDIAM 2015)

'Father, how can you say that it is false, when you know that it happened as I say.'

(19) Muy mi estimada madresita de mi corazón: [...] llegó a mis manos la carta que *su merced* se sirvió dirixirme en contestación de la que mandé con D[on] Manuel. (1810, Puerto Rico, place not indicated, Family letter, son → mother. *Cartas de llamada*. Additional Corpus)

'My dearest mother: the letter that you sent in response to that which I sent with D[on] Manuel has reached me.'

(20) Queredísima mamita: [...] Dígame *su merced* si está enteramente bien de la perlesía [...] Abrace *su merced* a mis hermanas. (1830, Havana. Family letter, son → mother. *Cartas familiares*. Additional Corpus)

'Dearest mommy: [...] Tell me if you are fully recovered from the palsy [...] Give a hug to my sisters.'

From a linguistic point of view, this new "family life" of (2P) *su merced* as a way of addressing parents evolved differently in the first uses in Buenos Aires in 1762 (examples (7) and (10)) and in the Caribbean instances (examples (18) to (20)) from later generations (1830). These idiomatic differences are found, once again, in the nominal enhancements that coappear with (2P) *su merced* – distant (*señor padre*) in the mid-18th century, and close (*mamita*) at the beginning of the 19th. As we know, the change in paternal and maternal appellations (*padre/madre* > *papá/mamá*) that dates to the first Spanish modern age (c. 1780–1835) is seen as a direct linguistic manifestation of the socio-educational change that took place during that time. In that period we begin to see a struggle between these two linguistic variants: a) *(señor) padre/(señora) madre* and b) *papá/mamá*. This last variant (b) represented a far reaching idiomatic innovation at the time, as it implied the definitive abandonment of the kinship terms *padre/madre*, and their replacement by the more prestigious Gallicisms (*papá* and *mamá*).

This abandonment highlights the evolution of the family educational model from a pattern that favours the hierarchical parent-child relation towards a new canon that fosters solidarity in the same parent-child relation. This innovation slowly appears in different Spanish speaking areas from the first third of the 19th century: Buenos Aires (Rigatuso 2005: 91–97), New Mexico (Balestra 2008: 82), Spain (Bustos & Iglesias Recuero 2003: 279–280; García-Godoy 2010: 597). In relation to this, there are a number of studies that associate the adoption of the neological nouns *papá/mamá* with the start of using of T-forms of address in the family context: *tuteo* (or the use of *tú*) in Spain (García-Godoy 2010: 604–608) and *voseo* (or the use of *vos*) in Argentina (Rigatuso 2005: 94). The first stage of this change can be dated to between 1830 and 1880 in both locations.

Within this perspective, the Cuban uses of *mamita* + *su merced* (20) could also be regarded as T-forms of address, given that they represent a similar change in the model of education for children in the Caribbean during the same period. It is the children of the White urban Caribbean elite who address their parents with (2P) *su merced* in coreference with the appellations that indicate this educational change in the family context (*mamita*).

Indeed, it is precisely in those areas of the Caribbean that were among the last to abolish slavery where it is possible to document the movement of (2P) *su merced* towards the domain of intimacy. As such, although Cuba continued with slavery until 1873, and Cuban *costumbrismo* only portrays the reverent use of *su merced*$_V$ in the speech of Black slaves, non-literary language confirms that 19th century Havana was among those Hispanic American locations in which *su merced* could have reached the triple deixis (Figure 2) – (3P) *su merced*, *su merced*$_V$ and *su merced*$_T$ – although none of the three have survived to the present.

The new evidence base therefore refutes the effect of ethnic factors on the history of (2P) *su merced* in Cuba. While (2P) *su merced* acts as a socio-racial marker of Black slaves in the Cuban *costumbrismo* of 1850, non-literary language in 1830 Cuba reflects the multiethnic character of the same form of address.

Finally, from the chronological viewpoint, the date of the abolition of slavery in Cuba (1873) clearly emerges as a crucial moment in the final stage of the change – the extinction of the form of address due to the extreme social stigmatisation of the *bozalismo su merced*$_V$. Yet the non-literary corpora provide conclusive evidence for another, different reality: Cuba saw both the social use of *su merced*$_V$ (stage B1) as well as the family usage of *su merced*$_T$ (stage C) before the abolition of slavery. Cuban *sumercedeante* usage is seen from at least as far back as 1813. These movements of (2P) *su merced* towards the domain of intimacy have come to be regarded

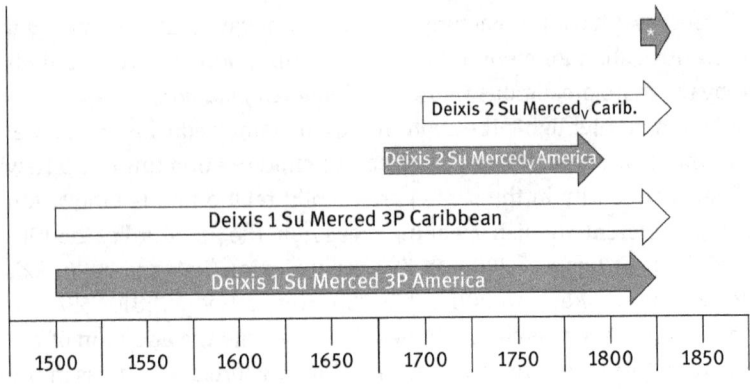

* Deixis 3 Su Merced$_T$ Carib.

Figure 2: The triple deixis of *su merced* in the corpora. The Caribbean region in the Hispanic American context.

as "liberating" evolutions belonging to the postcolonial era. In Hispanic America, however, the seed of *su merced*$_T$ was crystallising at the same time that the pronouns of respect were also moving towards the domain of informality and intimacy (Calderón Campos 2019; García-Godoy 2015). All of these extreme evolutions, which today distinguish the morphosyntax of American Spanish, begin to be seen at the end of the 19th century and beginning of the 20th (García-Godoy 2012). The unidimensional American Spanish systems of plural (*ustedes*) and singular (*ustedeo* and *sumercedeo*) address seem to have begun in the late colonial period (with slavery still in place), as the last stage of a phenomenon that originated in Iberian-Romance Spanish.

7 Conclusion

Literary and non-literary genres provide evidence for two distinct views of the Hispanic American history of the *su merced* form of address. These two views do not share the same chronology of the change from 3P *su merced* (delocutive) > 2P *su merced* (allocutive), social stratification of the phenomenon, or geographic area.

Chronologically, the literary history of (2P) *su merced* in Hispanic America generally falls into the independence period (from the second half of the 19th century), while the non-literary history dates back to the end of the 17th century – in the midst of the colonial period. From 1681, the corpora offer American

Spanish instances of the same change that was occurring in the mother country during the same century: the movement of the delocutive form to the allocutive domain. During the classic period, the use of *su merced* as the form of address$_V$ is a Pan-Hispanic phenomenon witnessed on both sides of the Atlantic.

In this first stage of the change – from the mid-18th century – the allocutive *su merced*$_V$ begins to show certain divergences in colonial Spanish. The differentiating element begins to be seen in the appearance of the same form of address in the family context. From 1762, the corpora used in this study provide instances of how the children of urban patrician families address their parents as (2P) *su merced*. At that time, children still use this as the V-form of address (*señor padre* + *su merced*$_V$), but starting in the first third of the 19th century, they use it as the T-form of address (*mamita* + *su merced*$_T$). The nominal enhancements are those that historically allow us to identify the seed of this dual deictic of (2P) *su merced* that distinguishes the current Americanism (respectful as well as intimate form of address). In line with this, we find evidence starting in 1823 of *sumercedeo* in Hispanic America. This *sumercedeo* (form of address$_T$) is a modern and exclusively American Spanish evolutionary trend, representing the last stage of an Iberian-Romance change witnessed since the 16th century. The dating of this *sumercedeo* as a morphosyntactic Americanism of the late colonial period suggests a new bicentennial history of a phenomenon that has been regarded as contemporary in the literature.

From a diastratic perspective, the American Spanish use of (2P) *su merced* exhibits opposing profiles in different kinds of contexts. *Su merced* is an ethnic (Black speech) and rural marker in Hispanic American fiction genres. By contrast, the historical documents reveal that the colonial use of (2P) *su merced* connects with Pan-Hispanic models of spoken language, as seen from the end of the 16th century in multiracial contexts. The history of the allocutive *su merced* in literary language is one of an ethno-linguistic vulgarism (mostly *bozal*). In non-literary language, however, it is the history of a Pan-Hispanic colloquialism. While diastratic factors determine the change in literary language (the ethnicity of the speaker), diaphasic factors (the colloquial communicative situation) are the most relevant in non-literary language. Therefore, in the historical documentation, listeners of any ethnicity can receive the (2P) *su merced* form of address in commercial and servitude contexts as well as within the family. Literary genres, however, portray only one part of this wide-ranging reality – usage of the form of address by Black slaves in a relation of servitude.

From a Pan-Hispanic perspective, this literary use of (2P) *su merced* by Black slaves could be regarded as the application of the theatrical rhetorical canon to the Hispanic American context. Masters are addressed as such by White servants in European Spanish from the 17th century onwards, while Black slaves use the same form of address starting in the 19th century. This usage by Black servants does not represent a divergence in colonial Spanish, but rather a mere transatlantic continuity of the same Hispanic literary pattern, which begins in classic comedy and emerges in 18th and 19th century *costumbrismo* on both sides of the Atlantic.

Diatopically, the historical regions of the (2P) *su merced* form of address are unknown. Currently, this overarching form of address survives in Andean Colombia (T- and V-form of address). Yet the origin of the phenomenon is not contextualised in this Andean region, but rather in the Afro-Caribbean geolect. The prevailing diachronic hypothesis connects the institution of Caribbean slavery with the birth of *su merced*$_V$ in the speech of *bozal* Blacks and their descendents in the West Indies. Yet once again, the non-literary corpora refute this traditional hypothesis, because from the 17th century *su merced*$_V$ is documented in numerous Hispanic American locations, and not only in the Afro-Hispanic varieties. *Su merced*$_V$ is evidenced as much in the vice-regal courts of Lima as it is in more peripheral areas (Southern Cone and the Caribbean), in convergence with the innovative trend in the mother country. The corpora also confirm that the Caribbean geolect witnessed the use of *su merced*$_T$ before the abolition of slavery. For example, in the capital of Cuba – the last Spanish-speaking country to abolish slavery – White Creoles were using *su merced* in 1823, although this phenomenon no longer exists on that Caribbean island.

All this indicates that, in the history of the allocutive (2P) *su merced* form of address, the Old World witnessed only the first evolutionary link of the change (*su merced*$_V$, social context), while the New World witnessed the three links of the diachronic chain (*su merced*$_V$ social > *su merced*$_V$ family > *su merced*$_T$). The Hispanic American use of *su merced*, the historical map of which may possibly have included a greater number of locations than it does today, could have taken shape in regions where standardisation was latest to arrive, with less normative pressure.

Additional Corpus

[*Cartas de Mérida*] 3 cartas de particulares. Mérida (Venezuela) 1783–1784. In Obediente 2009, 100–101.

[*Cartas de llamada*] 938 cartas de particulares. In Werner Stangl. 2012. *Zwischen Authentizität und Fiktion: Die private Korrespondenz spanischer Emigranten aus Amerika, 1492–1824.* Köln/Weimar/Wien: Böhlau [Suplemento electrónico: Edición de las cartas de llamada, http://www.boehlau-verlag.com].

[*Cartas familiares*] Epistolario familiar (1800–1862) del cubano José de la Luz y Caballero. 2017. *Obras V*. Barcelona: Linkgua.

[*Crónica Perú*] Meléndez, Juan. 1681. *Tesoros verdaderos de las Yndias en la historia de la gran provincia de San Iuan Bautista del Perú de el Orden de Predicadores*. Roma: Imprenta de Nicolas Angel Tinassio.

[*Crónica Santo Domingo*] Peguero, José Luis. 1762. *Historia de la Conquista de la isla española de Santo Domingo* [manuscript]. Biblioteca Digital Hispánica: http://bdh-rd.bne.es/ viewer.vm?id=0000010189&page=1.

[*Pleito Cartagena de Indias* 1762] In Gutiérrez Maté 2013, 258.

[*Pleito1 Santo Domingo* 1700] In Gutiérrez Maté 2013, 258.

[*Pleito2 Santo Domingo* 1720] In Gutiérrez Maté 2013, 258.

References

Alkmin, Tânia. 1996. Linguagem de escravos: em busca de registros históricos. *Estudios portugueses e africanos* 28. 63–71.

Álvarez-López, Laura & Virginia Bertolotti. 2013. Usos americanos de *su merced* en el siglo XIX. *Lexis* 37. 5–32.

Álvarez Nazario, Manuel. 1982. *Orígenes y desarrollo del español de Puerto Rico (siglos XVI y XVII)*. Río Piedras, Puerto Rico: Editorial Universitaria.

Asociación de Academias de la Lengua Española. 2010. *Diccionario de americanismos*. Lima: Santillana.

Balestra, Alejandra. 2008. Formas de tratamiento en correspondencia en español: California y Nuevo México 1800–1900. In Alejandra Balestra, Glenn Martínez & María Irene Moyna (eds.), *Recovering the U.S. Hispanic linguistic heritage: Sociohistorical approaches to Spanish in the United States*, 75–88. Houston: Arte Público Press.

Bertolotti, Virginia. 2015. *A mí de vos no me trata ni usted, ni nadie. Sistemas e historia de las formas de tratamiento en la lengua española en América*. México DF: Universidad Nacional Autónoma de México/Universidad de la República de Uruguay.

Brown, Roger & Albert Gilman. 1960. The pronouns of power and solidarity. In Thomas Sebeok (ed.), *Style in language*, 253–276. New York: M.I.T. Press.

Bustos Gisbert, Eugenio & Silvia Iglesias Recuero. 2003. Relaciones familiares y formas de tratamiento en la novela realista del siglo XIX. In José Luis Girón Alconchel et al. (eds.), *Estudios ofrecidos al profesor José Jesús de Bustos Tovar*, vol. 1, 277–295. Madrid: Editorial Complutense.

Cabal Jiménez, Munia. 2013. *From deference to face: the evolution of* usted *in Costa Rican Spanish*. Ph.D. thesis. Champaign, IL: University of Illinois at Urbana-Champaign.

Calderón Campos, Miguel. 2010. Variantes formales y valores semánticos de *(v)os(otros)* en la diacronía del español. In Rosa María Castañer Martín & Vicente Lagüéns Gracia (eds.), *De moneda nunca usada. Estudios dedicados a José María Enguita Utrilla*, 135–149. Zaragoza: Fernando El Católico/CSIC.

Calderón Campos, Miguel. 2019. Pérdida del pronombre *vosotros* y su paradigma. In Juan Pedro Sánchez Méndez, Antonio Corredor Aveledo & Elena Padrón Castilla (eds.), *Estudios de morfosintaxis histórica hispanoamericana*, vol. 1: *El pronombre*, 125–162. Valencia: Tirant Humanidades.

Coffen, Béatrice. 2002. *Histoire culturelle des pronoms d'adresse. Vers une typologie des systèmes allocutoires dans les langues romanes.* Paris: Honoré Champion.

Company Company, Concepción & Virginia Bertolotti (eds.). 2015. *Corpus diacrónico y diatópico del español de América.* http://www.cordiam.org. (11 May, 2016).

CORDE = Real Academia Española. *Corpus diacrónico del español. http://*www.rae.es/recursos/banco-de-datos/corde (20 May, 2016).

CORDIAM, see Company & Bertolotti.

CORPES XXI = Real Academia Española. *Corpus del español del siglo XXI.* http://*www.rae.es/recursos/banco-de-datos/corpes-xxi* (15 May, 2016).

DA, see Asociación de Academias de la Lengua Española.

De Granda, Germán. 2004. Una forma deferencial en el español peruano: *Su merced. Lexis* 28,1–2. 447–459.

De Granda, Germán. 2005. La forma de tratamiento *su merced* en el área lingüística surandina. *Lexis* 31. 165–175.

De Granda, Germán. 2007. Hacia la diacronía de una forma de tratamiento en el español: *su merced. Lexis* 29,2. 247–257.

Díaz Collazos, Ana María. 2015. *Desarrollo sociolingüístico del voseo en la región andina de Colombia (1555–1976).* Berlin/Boston: De Gruyter.

Fontanella de Weinberg, María Beatriz. 1999. Sistemas pronominales de tratamiento usados en el mundo hispánico. In Ignacio Bosque & Violeta Demonte (eds.), *Gramática descriptiva de la lengua española*, 1401–1425. Madrid: Espasa.

García-Godoy, María Teresa. 2010. El tratamiento a los progenitores en el español peninsular (siglo XIX). Contraste de dos variedades geográficas. In Hummel et al. (eds.), 595–618.

García-Godoy, María Teresa. 2011. *Su merced* en la variedad andaluza dieciochesca: ¿un caracterizador dialectal? In Pilar Carrasco Cantos & Francisco Torres Montes (eds.), *Lengua, historia y sociedad en Andalucía. Teorías y textos*, 227–254. Frankfurt/Madrid: Vervuert/Iberoamericana.

García-Godoy, María Teresa. 2012. El tratamiento de *merced* en el español del siglo XVIII. In María Teresa García-Godoy (ed.), *El español del siglo XVIII. Cambios diacrónicos en el primer español moderno*, 111–152. Bern: Peter Lang.

García-Godoy, María Teresa. 2015. El cambio *vuestra merced > usted* desde la documentación archivística. In Juan Pedro Sánchez Méndez, Mariela de la Torre & Viorica Codita (eds.), *Temas, problemas y métodos para la edición y el estudio de documentos hispánicos antiguos*, 661–694. Valencia: Tirant Humanidades/Colección Diachronica Hispanica.

García-Godoy, María Teresa. 2016. ¿Fue vulgar y plebeyo el origen de *usted*? La diacronía del pronombre de respeto desde la interfaz oral/escrito. *Oralia* 19. 63–86.

García-Godoy, María Teresa. 2019. El tratamiento indirecto en el español colonial. Los títulos honoríficos. In Juan Pedro Sánchez Méndez, Antonio Corredor Aveledo & Elena Padrón Castilla (eds.), *Estudios de morfosintaxis histórica hispanoamericana*, vol. 1: *El pronombre*, 219–262. Valencia: Tirant Humanidades.

García Moreno, Aitor. 2004. *Relatos del pueblo ladinán (me'am lo'ez de éxodo).* Madrid: CSIC.

Gutiérrez Maté, Miguel. 2013. *Pronombres personales sujeto en el español del Caribe. Variación e historia.* PhD thesis. Valladolid: Universidad de Valladolid. http://uvadoc.uva.es/bitstream/10324/2517/1/TESIS258-130318.pdf. (23.05.2016)

Hummel, Martin. 2010. El estudio de las fórmulas de tratamiento en las Antillas hispano-hablantes. In Hummel et al. (eds.), 293–324.

Hummel, Martin, Bettina Kluge & María Eugenia Vásquez Laslop (eds.). 2010. *Formas y fórmulas de tratamiento en el mundo hispánico*. México DF: El Colegio de México/Karl-Franzens-Universität Graz.

Kany, Charles. 1963. *American-Spanish syntax*. Chicago: The University of Chicago Press.

Lapesa, Rafael. 2000. Personas gramaticales y tratamientos en español. In Rafael Cano Aguilar & María Teresa Echenique Elizondo (eds.), *Estudios de morfosintaxis histórica del español*, vol.1, 311–345. Madrid: Gredos.

Lipski, John. 2005. *A history of Afro-Hispanic language. Five centuries, five countries*. Cambridge: Cambridge University Press.

Mazzon, Gabriela. 2010. Terms of address. In Andreas H. Jucker & Irma Taavitsainen (eds.), *Historical pragmatics*, 351–376. Berlin/New York: Mouton de Gruyter.

Moyna, María Irene. 2016. Introduction. In María Irene Moyna & Susana Rivera-Mills (eds.), *Forms of address in the Spanish of the Americas*, 1–12. Amsterdam/Philadelphia: John Benjamins.

Obediente, Enrique. 2009. Formas de tratamiento en Mérida (Venezuela) durante el siglo XVIII. *Boletín de Lingüística* 21. 1–18.

Obediente, Enrique. 2010. Visión diacrónica y dialectal de las formas de tratamiento en los Andes Venezolanos. In Claudia Borgonovo, Manuel Español-Echevarría & Philippe Prévost (eds.), *Selected proceedings of the 12th Hispanic Linguistics Symposium*, 87–96. Somerville, MA: Cascadilla Proceedings Project.

Pérez Guerra, Irene. 1988. La forma alocutiva *su merced* en República Dominicana: usos y funciones. *Anuario de Lingüística Hispánica* 4. 241–248.

Pérez Guerra, Irene. 1989. El sistema alocutivo en el español dominicano. Nuevos materiales y precisiones. *Anuario de Lingüística Hispánica* 5. 143–204.

Quesada Pacheco, Miguel Ángel. 2010. Formas de tratamiento en Costa Rica (1561–2000). In Hummel et al. (eds.), 649–670.

RAE-ASALE, see Real Academia Española.

Real Academia Española & Asociación de Academias de la Lengua Española. 2009. *Nueva gramática de la lengua española*, vol. 1: *Morfología/sintaxis*. Madrid: Espasa Libros.

Sáez Rivera, Daniel M. 2013. Formación e historia de *vuecencia* en español como proceso de rutinización lingüística. *Iberoromania* 77. 108–129.

Rigatuso, Elizabeth. 2005. Las fórmulas de tratamiento del español bonaerense desde la perspectiva de la sociolingüística histórica. *Analecta Malacitana* 28,1. 77–100.

Rigatuso, Elizabeth. 2008. Discurso de incorporación a la Academia Argentina de Letras: *A su merced... de su más humilde hijo*. Asimetrías e identidades en construcción: fórmulas de tratamiento y cortesía verbal en el español de Buenos Aires en la etapa colonial. *Boletín de la Academia Argentina de Letras* 73. 297–298. 349–405.

Tejera, María Josefa. 2006. La segunda persona en el nuevo corpus histórico del español de Venezuela. In José Jesús de Bustos Tovar & José Luis Girón Alconchel (eds.), *Actas del VI Congreso Internacional de Historia de la Lengua Española (Madrid, 29 de septiembre-3 de octubre de 2003)*, vol. 3, 2355–2368. Madrid: Arco Libros.

Uber, Diane R. 1985. The dual function of *usted*: forms of address in Bogotá: Colombia. *Hispania* 68,2. 388–392.

Isabel Molina Martos

Linguistic change and social transformation

The spread of *tuteo* in Restoration Spain and the Second Republic (1875–1939)

Abstract: This chapter investigates the spread of *tuteo* in a period of constant innovations which broke with hitherto apparently invulnerable social conventions. This spirit of innovation emerged at a particular moment in Spain's social and political history which was marked by far-reaching social upheavals: the Restoration (1875–1931), the Second Republic (1931–1936) and the Civil War (1936–1939). An analysis of an extensive corpus of private letters written between 1875 and 1939, expressing relations of friendship and affection, shows when and how changes occurred in the parameters of power and solidarity in dealings between interlocutors from the same social group and generation.

Keywords: Spanish sociolinguistics, linguistic and social change, *tuteo* in Spain, private letters corpus

1 Introduction

This chapter deals with the spread of *tuteo*, a wholesale linguistic change which affects the Spanish language's grammatical structure and gives linguistic codification to interpersonal relations. *Tuteo* is defined as the use of informal second person pronouns, e.g. *tú*, instead of polite pronouns, e.g. *usted*. Throughout the 20th century Spain stood out in the Hispanic world as a particularly innovative community in its use of pronouns to express politeness. This spirit of innovation emerged at a particular moment in Spain's social and political history which was marked by far-reaching social upheavals: the Restoration (1875–1931), the Second Republic (1931–1936), and the Civil War (1936–1939). The evolution of *tú* is explored during a historical period rife with innovations which broke with previous traditions.

Given such a complex period of change, the analysis follows the chronological order of the political and social events that had an impact on the pronoun system. The spread of innovation is considered over three distinct periods of Spanish history, in the course of which *tuteo* became the predominant form of address used in family relations and between friends and acquaintances of the same social status. These periods are:

- 1800–1860: young aristocrats in Madrid initiated the expansion of *tuteo* (García Godoy 2008, 2010; Calderón 2010). The pronoun of solidarity, used first in family address among the upper classes, had spread to the middle classes by the middle of the 19th century.
- 1860–1930: the innovation spread across society at large, driven by the lower classes and by the intellectuals of the age, or "institutionists".
- 1930–1940: the decade's political events – the Second Republic (1931–1936) and the Civil War (1936–1939) – led to the definitive consolidation of the pronoun of solidarity in Spanish society.

In order to trace the evolution of this innovation in the society of the time, an extensive corpus of private letters written between 1875 and 1940 has been analysed. All the letters that express relations of friendship and affection show how and when the perception of power and solidarity in the relationships between interlocutors of the same social group and the same generation began to change.

The evolving uses of pronouns among the lower classes are studied with the aid of a corpus containing letters from Asturians (López Álvarez 2000; Martínez Martín 2010) and Galicians (Soutelo 2003) who departed for the Americas as economic emigrants in the second half of the 19th century and the early decades of the 20th century. This collection of letters makes it clear how mutual use of *tuteo* developed over a lengthy period of time and makes it possible to explore how personal changes were being transformed at the start of the last century.

Secondly, the corpus reveals patterns of use among the better educated, the products of the movement of social renewal triggered by Spain's Free Educational Institutions of the period and their promoters, the "institutionists". Such letters are more easily available given the political and social prominence of their authors. The present study reviews the correspondence between a selection of interrelated intellectuals (Altolaguirre 2005; Anderson & Maurer 1997; Castillejo 1999; Cortés & García Perales 2009; Menéndez y Pelayo & Leopoldo Alas 1943).

The pattern of innovation traced in this study comes to a climax in the 1930s, the decade of the Second Republic and the Civil War. Most recent research into this period has uncovered important collections of letters written by Republican (Hinojosa 2009; Matthews 2015; Sierra 2008) and Francoist (Ramón & Ortiz 2003) soldiers during the war, as well as by the Republican prisoners (Fonseca 2014; Martínez Aguirre 2014; Sierra 2003) who would fill Spain's prisons from the outset of the Franco dictatorship. The analysis of these letters from the 1930s yields important evidence about linguistic change in Spain during the period.

In short, the aim of what follows is to reconstruct the historical context that enabled the spread of *tuteo*: the social conditions which facilitated it, the means by which it was propagated through the social fabric of Spain at the time, and the confluence of interests between different social sectors which encouraged the evolution of the system of solidarity.

2 1800–1860: the development of *tuteo* in the 19th century, a linguistic change from above

Available data (García Godoy 2008, 2010; Calderón Campos 2010) about the appearance of *tuteo* in horizontal relations, that is, between equals, situates this pronominal change in aristocratic circles of the early 19th century. With a view to making the analysis clearer, we separate the spread of *tuteo* in the family from its spread in horizontal relations between friends and acquaintances. *Tuteo* as addressed to one or other of these two groups had different social consequences which need to be viewed as catalysts of its diffusion in Spain in the early decades of the 20th century.

The *tuteo of parents by offspring* in place of a previous non-reciprocal *ustedeo*,[1] was the most significant change in the pronominal system in the early 19th century; by the end of the century the use of *tú* in imitation of high society was starting to be widespread among the younger generations of the middle class:

> Addressing parents as *tú* was a distinguishing feature of high society. This glamorous formula began to become more widespread in Restoration Spain, when the new pattern starts to be the preferred form among Madrid's urban, middle-class young people, who were under 20 in 1890.
>
> (García Godoy 2010: 603)

According to García Godoy (2010: 613), "the new elocutional pattern amounts to a *change from above*, initiated by the aristocratic classes and imitated intentionally by the affluent upper-middle classes". Women "under 35 from the middle and upper levels of the urban bourgeoisie" were responsible for the change and the epicentre of the innovation was Madrid, which was more advanced than Andalusia, where modes of address were slower to develop than in the cities.

As for relations outside the family between friends and acqaintances from the same social class, it was the *younger generation with high economic status and aristocratic tastes* – the so-called *pollería* 'gathering of young people, chickens' – which made *tuteo* fashionable. García Godoy (2008: 44) explains the main traits of the *lechuguino* 'dandy', the archetypal member of this social group, with

---

1 *Ustedeo* means use of *usted*.

reference to a sketch published in the Madrileñian weekly periodical, *Semanario Pintoresco*, with the title *Spanish types. The enthusiast*:[2]

> El aficionado moderno es un hijo maleducado [...] apunta en la cartera el nombre del último sastre que ha llegado de París [...] prefiere las telas impermeables al paraguas. Reprueba el V[3]. de buenas a primeras porque *entre personas que se encuentran, como él dice a una misma altura, es una palabra muy fraternal ese tú* que forma el encanto y la delicadeza de los enamorados.
> (Semanario pintoresco 1846: 404)

> 'The modern enthusiast is a spoilt child [...] [who] jots down the name of the latest tailor to have arrived from Paris [...] prefers waterproof cloths to umbrellas. They quite simply scoff at *usted* because *when people of, so to speak, the same standing meet, this tú is a very fraternal word* which gives form to the charm and delicacy of the lovestruck.'

García Godoy concludes her explanation by also highlighting the role of women as prime movers of the innovation, as may be deduced from the courtesy manuals which "reprove the fashion for *tuteo* in Restoration Spain, and point to young upper-class women as the main exponents of the change" (García Godoy 2008: 46).

Mutual *tuteo* (T ←→ T) among the upper classes implied class solidarity and peer complicity, while also marking a separation from the rest of society, with which the old assymetrical system of hierarchical address was maintained: V (*usted(es)*) for the superior, T (*tú/vosotros*) for the inferior.

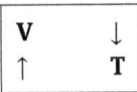

The familiar and the aristocratic forms of *tuteo* were motivated by different social conditioning factors. The family was the basic unit of society which presupposed ties of solidarity. However, this solidarity was projected onto a hierarchical structure which only admitted the innovation gradually: *tuteo* first began to be used among relatives of the same generation (siblings, cousins, siblings-in-law), while the *tuteo* of parents by young aristocrats became fashionable later. By promoting affection over respect, the relations between parents and children were transformed in a way that created a space for affective proximity in pre-existing relationships of solidarity, but without eliminating any social barriers.

---

2 In the citations, all forms of address and sociolinguistic comments referring to forms of address are in italics. The emphasis is always the author's.
3 V stands for *usted(es)* and T for *tú/vosotros*.

3 1860–1930: urban development, modernity and political evolution

The new century ushered in an acceleration in the transformation of 19th-century modes of address. This was a reflection of social changes: migrations from the country to the towns and cities, a fall in illiteracy rates, a second phase of industrialisation, the growth of the third sector in the economy, the consolidation of political parties and trade unions representing the masses, and the rise in living standards (Otero 2015: 18).

This social development was founded on the metropolitisation of cities such as Madrid, Barcelona and Bilbao. The steps towards modernity taken by Madrid in the 1930s led to levels of progress comparable to those of other European capitals of the age. Spatial expansion and demographic growth altered the period's economic, political, social and cultural coordinates and fostered the emergence of the *new urban middle classes* composed of professionals, tradesmen, salaried and qualified workers whose standards of living, habits of consumption and leisure, system of values and social practices signalled the arrival of modernity. The new century saw how the parties of the masses came to take centre stage (Otero 2015: 16).

3.1 Tuteo popular: a change from below. The letters of Asturian and Galician emigrants

In order to identify the use of pronouns among the lower classes, we have analysed three corpora of letters written by Asturian and Galician emigrants to America, where they hoped to improve their economic condition. The letters written by the Asturian emigrants and contained in two letter collections span a broad period of time: the letters of the first collection were written between 1863–1936 (Martínez Martín 2010), and those of the second between 1864–1925 (López Álvarez 2000). For their part, the corpus of letters written by Galician emigrants covers only the decade of the 1930s (Soutelo Vázquez 2003). From the three collections a total of 105 letters involving 210 different interlocutors have been analysed.

The letters studied still retain a traditional letter structure, with fixed greetings (*mi estimado amigo, mi buen amigo, queridos padres* 'my dear friend, my good friend, dear parents' and farewells). The greetings are always followed by a paragraph enquiring after the health of the interlocutor or relative by means of conventional formulas, as illustrated in examples (1) to (9).

(1) [*tuteo*]
Estimado hermano: deseará que al recibo de ésta te encuentres con saluz [sic] en compañía de nuestros padres y hermanos, pues la mía y la de todos es buena, a D[ios] g[raci]as./*Hermano*, he recibido *tu* apreciable y deseada carta con fecha del 16 de agosto y en ella veo el buen estado de saluz [sic] [...]" (Letter from Luis Carrera (Silao, México) to his brother José Carrera (Posada, Llanes), 12.10.1888)

'Dear brother: I hope that you are well when you get this, along with our parents and the rest of the family, just as I'm well and so is everybody else, thank God./Brother, I received your [*tu*] kind and eagerly awaited card dated 16th August, and I can see from that you're well [...]'

(2) [*tuteo*]
Mi estimado amigo: la presente tiene por objeto el participar*te* que lo mismo Fabián que yo tenemos pensado embarcar el 21 ó 22 del prósimo [sic] noviembre en La Coruña, vien [sic] en el Correo o en el Francés, es decir, si el Correo lleva mucha tropa iremos en el Francés, según veamos haremos [...]" (Letter from Aurelio Arango (Cañedo, Pravia) to his friend Indalecio del Río (La Habana, Cuba), 30.10.1895)

'My dear friend: This is to let you know that Fabian and I are both thinking of embarking next 21 or 22 November in La Coruña, either on *El Correo* or on *El Francés*, I mean, if *El Correo* is too crowded we'll go on *El Francés*, it all depends [...]'

(3) [*usted*]
Querido padre: me alegro que al recibo de ésta *se* halle vueno [sic] en compañía de nuestra madre y hermanos [...] Querido padre, la presente es para manifestar*le* que *le* mando el viaje para mi hermano [...]" (Letter from José Fernández (Buenos Aires) to his father Ramón Fernández (Villamar de Abajo, Salas), 18.8.1909)

'Dear father: I hope you're well, along with mother and the rest of the family, when you receive this [...] Dear father, this is to tell you that I'm sending you the ticket for my brother [...]'

(4) [*tuteo*]
Querido amigo: tengo en mi poder *tu* estimada carta y por ella beo [sic] que estás bueno, yo sin nobedaz [sic]./Pues *Manuel*, refiriendo acerca de

lo que *tú* mi [sic] dices de que *tú* tienes miedo binir [sic] para aquí porque tienes miedo hir [sic] para Triscornia, pues chico sobre ese particular no tengas miedo porque para eso estoy yo aquí [...] (Letter from Amado García (La Habana) to his friend Manuel Suárez Roza (Cancienes, Corvera de Asturias), 17.12.1919**)**

'Dear friend: I've got your kind letter here and I see that you're well. No news for my part./Anyway Manuel, about what you say about being afraid to come here because you're afraid to go by way of Triscornia, well, mate, there's no need to be afraid about that because that's what I'm here for [...]'

(5) [*usted*]

Mi querida mamá:/Deseo que al recibo de ésta *se* allen [sic] disfrutando de buena salud, yo bien a Dios gracias./*Sabrán* como llegamos a ésta sin novedad el jueves por la mañana y desembarcamos a la tarde [...] (Letter from Ricardo Ruiz Balbín (Ciego de Ávila, Cuba) to his mother Bernarda Ruiz Balbín (Lué, Colunga), 13.12.1920)

'My dear mama:/I hope this find you all in good health. I'm well, thank God./ Just to let you know that we arrive safely on Thursday morning and disembark in the afternoon [...]'

(6) [*tuteo*]

Mi inolvidable Alfredo:/Para que en ningún concepto tengas *tú* mucho a decir que notas en mí cierta indiferencia *te* escribiré muy extenso y bastante frecuente [...] (Letter from Antonia M. Abrahantes (Colonia La Florida, Cuba) to her boyfriend Alfredo Rodríguez (Cuba), 20.11.1923)

'My unforgettable Alfredo:/So that you don't have the slightest reason to say that I seem a bit indifferent, I'll write to you at length and quite often [...]'

(7) [*tuteo*]

Amor mío:/Prometí escribir*te* y así lo cumplo, quizás impulsada tal vez por causas que yo misma no sé explicarme, como no tengo la seguridad que *tú* vengas el jueves según son mis deseos [...] (Letter from Ana Mª Cruz (Peñasco, Cuba) to her boyfriend José Manuel Rodríguez (Cruces, Cuba), 15.12.1930)

'My dear:/I promised to write to you and I'm keeping my promise, perhaps driven by reasons that not even I can explain, as I'm not sure you'll come on Thursday, as it is my wish [...]'

(8) [*tuteo*]

Mi más querida amiga: hace días reciví [sic] *tu* atenta carta la que me llenó de satisfacción y por ser *tú* la más íntima amiga y que con más gusto me pones al corriente de todo lo de por hay [sic] [...] (Letter from Honorina (Caibarien, Cuba) to her friend Domitila Rodríguez (Inclán, Pravia), 15.12.1924)

'My dearest friend: I got your kind letter some days ago and I really liked it, and as you're the closest friend and you take pleasure in keeping me up to date with everything that's going on there [...]'

(9) [*tuteo*]

Mi buen amigo Herminio: poseo *tu* carta fecha 5 y seis días antes de las elecciones de ésa de lo cual ya *te* felicité por el triunfo alcanzado en ellas, y hoy *te* felicito a *ti* y al amigo Riestra como así mismo a los amigos Arizaya, Ramonín y demás por el advenimiento de la República consagrada a un nuevo régimen de gobierno [...] (Letter from Bernardo Antuña (Tenafly, New Jersey) to his friend Herminio Fernández (Noreña, Gijón), 27.4.1931)

'My dear friend Herminio: I am in receipt of your letter of the 5th, six days before the elections on your success for which I already congratulated you, and today I congratulate you and friend Riestra as well as friends Arizaya, Ramonín and the rest for the advent of the Republic, committed to a new governmental regime [...]'

Table 1 shows that in 73% of the letters studied the emigrants used *tuteo*, whereas 27% used *usted*: this means that between the later 19th and the early 20th centuries, *tuteo* was firmly established among this social grouping in horizontal relationships between siblings, cousins or brothers/sisters-in-law, as well as in the egalitarian address between friends, partners and acquaintances of both sexes.

Table 1: Pronominal use in emigrant letters (1860–1930). T= *tú*; V = *usted*.

	Family relationships				Non-family relationships		Total
	Offspring to parents	Father/ mother to offspring	Siblings, cousins	Brothers/ sisters-in-law	Friends	Acquaintances	
usted	22 V		2 V	1 V	2 V	1 V	28 V (27%)
tú	2 T	6 T	42 T	6 T	21 T		77 T (73%)

The emigrants' correspondence reveals how intensively *tuteo* was propagated in relations between equals. The bulk of the correspondence written between

1860 and 1900 was between relatives, but some was also addressed to friends, which demonstrates that *tuteo* was already habitual in horizontal non-family relationships (21 instances of *tú* against three of *usted*). In contrast, for addressing parents or other members of the family in a position of hierarchical superiority (aunts and uncles, grandparents), it was only later that *tuteo* came to be employed (22 instances of *usted* and only two of *tú*), and this was usually after *tuteo* had defined the egalitarian address between friends and acquaintances. It was, therefore, frequent for Asturian emigrants to use *tuteo* to address their friends, while continuing to favour *usted* for fathers, mothers and grandparents.

Except for parents addressing offspring or acquaintances, in all the cases reflected in the table the two pronouns *tú* and *usted* co-exist side by side. This alternation between two forms as co-variants when addressing the same type of interlocutor indicates a change in progress from below where *tuteo*, present in 73% of the letters analysed, has taken over as the first-choice option.

3.2 The Free Educational Institution (FEI) and the reformist project of the Second Republic: The Silver Age of Spanish science and culture

In the vanguard of these currents of renewal, the so-called "institutionists" played a key role in the social transformation which characterised turn-of-the-century Spain. Since the foundation in 1876 of the *Free Educational Institution* (*Institución Libre de Enseñanza*), and until its demise in 1936, intellectuals on the national political scene took up the cause of liberal and progressive ideals. With the freedom of education and science as its banner, the FEI inspired moves to open the university to society (Moreno & Martínez 2012, I: 18–19). For the institutionists, if the breach separating Spain from the most advanced European nations was to be closed, the education system had to be reformed, an opinion that was to become part of the creed of the reformist intelligentsia during the first three decades of the 20th century (Otero 2014).

In harmony with institutionist principles, in 1907 the *Junta de Ampliación de Estudios* 'Council for Advanced Studies' came into being, the brainchild of Francisco Giner de los Ríos, whose goal was to modernise education and scientific research in Spain (Otero 2014).[4] The leading scientists of the age were asso-

---

4 The Council created the Centre for Historical Studies and the National Institute of Physical and Natural Sciences. The former organised the Humanities into sections such as Philology, under the direction of Ramón Menéndez Pidal, and History, directed by leading lights like Claudio Sánchez-Albornoz or Américo Castro (Otero 2014).

ciated with the Council while at the same time holding university chairs, most of them in the Central University of Madrid. A generation of young researchers was nurtured around them, researchers who had been trained abroad thanks to the grants scheme before joining scientific institutions. With the proclamation of the Second Republic in April 1931, the Council's activities were given a new boost and university access was opened to the newly emergent middle classes.

The forging of this alliance between science and politics during the Second Republic permitted the development of the schemes to renew education which the Free Educational Institution and the reformist sectors had been campaigning for since the turn of the century. If the nation, whose illiteracy rates were high, was to be regenerated, its education had to be revamped and universalised (Otero 2015: 33, 35). The Council's achievements during the barely thirty years of its brief existence amounted to a genuine *Silver Age* of Spanish science, the fulfilment of a dream which, like the modernising project as a whole, would be cut short by the Civil War.

3.2.1 The usted of the institutionists (first generation)

The forms of address favoured by the institutionists, an educated bourgeoisie composed of leading social, political or cultural figures, may be determined by reviewing countless letter collections. For our study we selected the correspondence between 33 interlocutors belonging to the social circle of the institutionists (Altolaguirre 2005; Anderson & Maurer 1997; Castillejo 1999; Cortés y García Perales 2009).

The *first generation of institutionists* includes intellectuals such as Giner de los Ríos, Ramón y Cajal, Ramón Menéndez Pidal, Manuel Bartolomé Cossio, Juan Ramón Jiménez, Antonio Machado, Américo Castro, María de Maeztu, Navarro Tomás, Ortega y Gasset among many others. They were the teachers of the *second generation* (1890–1910), who had already received training under the modernising aegis of the Council for Advanced Studies.

In their correspondence, the intellectuals born before 1890 preserve *usted* despite the affectionate relations that may often be read into their letters. This is because for the generation of Menéndez Pidal and Antonio Machado forms of politeness and respect were too deeply rooted in their conception of personal relationships. It is striking that even Américo Castro, Juan Ramón Jiménez, María de Maeztu or Navarro Tomás, all of whom were in their forties and therefore relatively young at the start of the Second Republic, never depart from using *usted* to address colleagues or friends, regardless of their ages, as can be seen in examples (10 to (18).

(10) [*usted*]

Sr. D. Leopoldo Alas/Mi querido amigo: Perdone *Vd.* que hasta hoy haya dilatado el contestar a su muy grata, pero de fijo me ha de disculpar *usted* si recuerda las mil molestias y pesadeces de esta vida que llaman política, a la cual mis pecados me han traído, aunque sea por accidente [...] (Letter from Marcelino Menéndez y Pelayo to Leopoldo Alas "Clarín" (Madrid), 23.2.1885)

'Leopoldo Alas, Esq./My dear friend: please forgive me for not having taken time until today to reply to your kind letter, but I'm sure you'll pardon me once you recall the thousands of trials and tribulations associated with what they call a life in politics, a life to which my sins have brought me, albeit by accident [...]'

(11) [*usted*]

Mi querido amigo y condiscípulo: Acabo ahora mismo de leer con muchísimo gusto y provecho, *su* prólogo de la *Proaladia*, y *le* doy por él las gracias y la enhorabuena [...] (Letter from Leopoldo Alas "Clarín" to Marcelino Menéndez y Pelayo (Madrid), 23.3.1900)

'My dear friend and co-student: I've just read with the utmost pleasure and benefit your prologue to *Proaladia*, for which I thank and congratulate you [...]'

(12) [*usted*]

Mi distinguido amigo: Recibí la *suya* a la que no he contestado antes por quererlo hacer a Madrid y cuando hubiera *V.* reanudado sus trabajos [...] (Letter from Elvira Alonso to José Castillejo (Paris), 14.8.1907)

'My distinguished friend: I haven't replied to your latest since I wished to write to you in Madrid, and once you had returned to work [...]'

(13) [*usted*]

Querido Cossío: Recibiría *Vd.* la mía de ayer. Ya se figurará lo que damos vuelta a *su* asunto: D. Francisco, Posada, Azcárate, Uña y yo [...] (Letter from José Castillejo to M. B. Cossío (London), 28.1.1908)

'Dear Cossío: You must have received my letter of yesterday. You'll already be able to imagine all the thought we're giving to your affair: D. Francisco, Posada, Azcárate, Uña and I [...]'

(14) [*usted*]

Sr. D. Miguel de Unamuno/Mi querido amigo y compañero: mucho hubiera querido que durante mi estancia ahí hubiésemos hablado algo, ya que hace tanto tiempo que no tenía ese gusto, y que éste hubiese sido mayor siendo nuestras conversaciones dentro de esa ciudad que *Vd.* ha hecho su segunda patria. Ojalá podamos vernos en otra ocasión por acá [...] (Letter from Ramón Menéndez Pidal to Miguel de Unamuno (Madrid), 9.10.1910).

'Miguel de Unamuno, Esq./My dear friend and colleague: I would dearly like to have conversed with you during my stay since I haven't had the pleasure for such a long time, and the pleasure would have been all the greater for our conversations taking place in that city which you have made your second home. I hope we can meet up another time over here [...]'

(15) [*usted*]

Querido D. Ramón: Llegó la carta de *V.* y se me admitió a trabajar en el Laboratorio. He encontrado además una pensión buena y barata. Estoy, pues, en buenas circunstancias para poder aprovechar aquí un poco el tiempo./El Laboratorio me ha dejado admirado; hay en él todo lo que se puede desear, todos los aparatos de física, de medicina y puramente de fonética que suelen emplearse en este estudio. La instalación de muebles, electricidad, gas, agua, etc., está hecha con un gran sentido práctico y además con una riqueza casi suntuosa [...] (Letter from Tomás Navarro Tomás to Ramón Menéndez Pidal (Hamburg), 4.8.1913)

'Dear D. Ramón: Your letter arrived and I was admitted to work in the laboratory. I've also found a decent and cheap boarding house. I am, then, well set to be able to make something of my time here./The laboratory impressed me; it has all one could wish for, all the apparatus for physics, medicine and pure phonetics that are normally employed in this field of study. The furnishings, electricity, gas, water, etc. have all been fitted with good practical sense and almost to the point of luxury [...]'

(16) [*usted*]

Sr. Don Ramón Menéndez Pidal/Muy Sr. mío y apreciado amigo: Aprovecho el viaje de mi amigo Mosén Llauró para escribir*le* dos palabras. En primer lugar para felicitar*le* por haber sido propuesto para la presidencia de la Société de Linguistique Romane [...] (Letter from Antoni Griera to Ramón Menéndez Pidal (Barcelona), October 1927)

'Ramón Menéndez Pidal, Esq./My dear Sir and valued friend: I take the opportunity presented by the journey of my friend Mosén Llauró to write you a couple of words. Firstly, to congratulate you on being nominated to the presidency of the Société de Linguistique Romane [...]'

(17) [*usted*]

Querido Alonso: [...] Del Atlas Lingüístico hay una esperanza de empezar, pero sólo una esperanza. La ausencia de *usted* es irreparable. Estoy haciendo un cursillo de preparación fonética para tres jóvenes que parecen dispuestos a viajar; no sé si *usted* les conocerá: Lapesa, Lacalle y Ortega Lamadrid. El primero es el mejor. El Ministerio de Estado nos ha dado 5.000 pesetas para los primeros viajes. Tal vez hagamos unas salidas de tanteo esta primavera [...] (Letter from Tomás Navarro Tomás to Amado Alonso (Madrid), 2.3.1929)

'Dear Alonso: [...] À propos the *Atlas Lingüístico*, there's a chance, but only a slim one, that work may commence. There is no brooking your absence. I'm running a small course in phonetic training for three young men who seem willing to travel; I don't know if you know them: Lapesa, Lacalle and Ortega Lamadrid. The first is the best. The Ministry of State has given us 5,000 pesetas for the first trips. We may do some reconnoitring this spring [...]'

(18) [*usted*]

Sr. D. Felipe Gil Casares/Rector de la Universidad de Santiago/Mi distinguido amigo y compañero: me entero aquí casualmente de que fue entregado en la frontera a las autoridades de Tuy por la policía portuguesa el Sr. Otero [...] Yo, invocando la buena amistad que me une al primo de *V. D.* José Casares Gil, acudo a *Vd.* rogándo*le* intervenga, si lo cree oportuno, para librar a un inocente y salvar un trabajo de alto interés para la cultura y la historia españolas [...] (Letter from Menéndez Pidal to F. Gil Casares (La Habana), 18.2.1937)

'D. Felipe Gil Casares, Esq./Rector of the University of Santiago/My distinguished friend and colleague: I happen to have been informed here that the Portuguese police delivered Mr Otero over at the border to the Tuy authorities [...] May I appeal to the close friendship that connects me to your cousin, José Casares Gil, and ask you to intervene, should you think it opportune, to free an innocent man and to salvage a work of great interest for Spanish history and culture?'

In turn, and in reciprocation, in this generation the senders are always addressed as *usted* by all their interlocutors, regardless of status, age or gender.

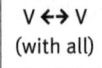

The nominal forms employed in letters also kept a respectful distance: *señor don* + NP and surname (*Sr. Don Ramón Menéndez Pidal*; *Sr. D. Miguel de Unamuno*); *don* + NP (*Querido D. Ramón*); surname (*Querido Alonso; Querido Cossío*). The *usted* address in the letters was established from the outset of the relationship and remains unchanged thereafter. It comes as something of a surprise to see how these intellectuals, many of whom lived well into their nineties and wrote hundreds of letters, preserved the 19th-century system of address throughout the 20th century.

An analysis of this group's letters provides evidence of a generational gap separating those born between 1860 and 1890 (*first generation*), and their disciples, born around the turn of the century, between 1890 and 1910 (*second generation*). In relations with their peers, the first generation institutionists always addressed their interlocutors as *usted*, regardless of age or sex (see Table 2). This respectful form of address was unaltered by the degree of personal affection;

Table 2: First generation institutionists (1850–1889).

First Generation Institutionists, born between 1850–1889 PRONOMINAL ADDRESS: V ↔ V (with all interlocutors)		
Born 1840–1869 61–70 years old in 1930s	**Born 1870–1879** 51–60 years old in 1930s	**Born 1880–1889** 41–50 years old in 1930s
Ramón Menéndez Pidal (1869–1968)	Antonio Machado (1875–1939)	Tomás Navarro Tomás (1884–1979)
Miguel de Unamuno (1864–1936)	José Castillejo (1877–1945)	Antoni Griera (1887–1973)
Francisco Giner de los Ríos (1839–1915)	Felipe Gil Casares (1877–1953)	Juan Ramón Jiménez (1881–1958)
Manuel Bartolomé Cossío (1857– 1935)		Américo Castro (1885–1972)
Santiago Ramón y Cajal (1852–1934)		María de Maeztu (1881–1948)
Marcelino Menéndez y Pelayo (1856–1912)		José Ortega y Gasset (1883–1955)
Leopoldo Alas (Clarín) (1852–1901)		

rather, it was the custom to address teacher, disciple, colleague, acquaintance and friend as *usted*. In this generation, the pronouns used in address show no variation: quite categorically, *usted* is the form to be employed, which leads to the conclusion that the intellectuals of the 19th century never adapted to the change in egalitarian, non-family relations.

3.2.2 Spread of *tuteo* popular among institutionists (second generation)

This second group of institutionists also comprised some of the leading scientists, thinkers, writers, teachers, artists or philologists of the period, such as Dámaso Alonso, Gerardo Diego, Jorge Guillén, Rafael Lapesa, Federico García Lorca, Miguel Hernández, María Zambrano, Rafael Alberti, Lorenzo Rodríguez Castellano, Aurelio M. Espinosa, Vicente Aleixandre, Amado Alonso and many others. It is a generation which came of age under the Second Republic: in 1930 its members were all aged between twenty and thirty, while in the same year the ages of their mentors, the instituionists of the *first generation*, ranged from 40 to 70. Table 3 shows the names of some representatives of this second generation whose letters have been analysed.

Table 3: Second generation institutionists (1890–1910).

Second Generation: Born between 1890–1910 PRONOMINAL ADDRESS: T ↔ T (with own generation) V↔ V (with their elders)	
Born in the 1890s **In their 30s in 1930s**	**Born in the 1900s** **In their 20s in 1930s**
Dámaso Alonso (1898–1990) Amado Alonso (1896–1952) Federico García Lorca (1898–1936) Vicente Aleixandre (1898–1984) Gerardo Diego (1896–1987) Jorge Guillén (1893–1984)	Rafael Lapesa (1908–2001) Aurelio M. Espinosa (1907–2004) Lorenzo Rodríguez Castellano (1905–1986) M. Sanchis Guarner (1911–1981) Aníbal Otero (1911–1974) Miguel Hernández (1910–1942) Salvador Dalí (1904–1989) Manuel Altolaguirre (1905–1959) Luis Cernuda (1902–1963) María Zambrano (1904–1991) Rafael Alberti (1902–1999)

While the letter collections offer a conservative picture of the 19th-century institutionists, with *the new century* the convergence of cultural elites and lower classes became increasingly evident: the generation that enrolled in Madrid's university in the 1920s and 1930s adopted *tuteo* to address companions, colleagues, friends and acquaintances of the same age and of both sexes. Some of the period's major figures offer testimony to the new uses. Lapesa (1996: 357) explains how, in the early 20th century:

> En el trato familiar se había aflojado ya la respetuosa rigidez en la relación entre padres e hijos: el galicismo *papá* y *mamá* y el *tuteo* entre padres e hijos se habían generalizado en los estratos sociales alto y medio, mientras el *padre* y *madre* y el *usted*, *ustedes* de hijos a progenitores se mantenían en los ambientes populares y rústicos [...]. El tratamiento recíproco de *usted* entre jóvenes fue disminuyendo: si en 1923–1925 podía darse todavía entre varones compañeros de estudios o de oficina, en los años treinta el *tuteo* se había impuesto incluso entre ambos sexos. (Lapesa 1996: 357)

> 'Address within the family had by now loosened the relationship of stiff respect between parents and offspring: the gallicisms *papá* and *mamá* and *tuteo* between parents and offspring had spread throughout the middle and upper social strata, while the use of *padre* and *madre* and *usted* or *ustedes* between offspring and parents was retained in lower and rural spheres [...] The reciprocal use of *usted* between young people was in decline: if between 1923–1925 it could still be heard among male fellow students and officeworkers, by the 1930s *tuteo* had won the day even between members of both sexes.'

Those born around the turn of the century continued to use *usted* to address colleagues, acquaintances and friends from the previous generation (V←→V), but had already adopted *tuteo* for friends and acquaintances of their own age or younger (T←→T). The nominal forms in their letters exhibit the same pattern of reciprocal respect towards elders but of solidarity with members of their own generation. When addressing their seniors, the younger institutionists used such formulas of respect such as: *don* + NP (*don Ramón*); *señor* 'Mr' + surname (e.g. *Sr. Navarro*); *distinguido profesor* 'distinguished professor'; *muy distinguido señor mío* 'my most distinguished Sir'. In contrast, they used surname or forename to address those of the same age or younger. And this is due precisely to the second generation, students at Madrid's Central University in the 1920s and 1930s where they were educated based on Krausist[5] ideals which combined quality training with social awareness. For they set the seal on *tuteo popular* which was being propagated by the lower classes. When using *tuteo* amongst themselves, the

---

5 Krausism is a doctrine which defended quality training and academic freedom against dogmatism. It takes its name from Karl Christian Friedrich Kraus. His philosophy was spread in Spain by Julián Sanz del Río and the *Institución Libre de Enseñanza* (*Free Educational Institution*).

young university students were not trying to emulate the fashion of the young 19th-century aristocrats, but were adopting the form of address that had taken root among the lower classes whose interests the enlightened bourgeoisie had made their own. By adopting *tuteo* in this way, the intellectuals were instrumental in the final dismantling of the 19th-century system of address; for in the first three decades of the 20th century, Spain underwent root and branch social transformation, whose catalysts included a Republic and a Civil War.

Before the war, Dámaso Alonso recalled how *tuteo* between peers – whether in age, gender or social class – had caught on in the university classrooms of the 1920s:

> ya por aquellos años de antes de 1936 eran evidentes los avances del tuteo. *La juventud de ambos sexos lo admite como una de las formas naturales de su concepción de vida.* Otras causas, no políticas, van a colaborar [...] (Dámaso Alonso 1962: 264)

> 'the onward march of *tuteo* was apparent even in the years before 1936. *Young people of both sexes accepted it as one of the natural forms their view of life took.* Other, non-political causes played a part [...]'

This process accelerated throughout the 1920s, was propagated across society under the Second Republic, and was consolidated during the war. The young institutionists adopted *tuteo popular* with enthusiasm, but only when addressing other young people. When addressing their seniors or teachers, with whom they were often united in friendship or by father-son relationships, they still preserved reciprocal *usted*, which the former insisted on in all non-family relations.

Examples (19) to (21) from letters written by students to their teachers illustrate reciprocal *usted* (V⟵→V) between institutionists from different generations.

(19) [*usted*]

> *Querido Sr. Navarro*: Diversas circunstancias han retrasado considerablemente el envío de noticias nuestras. Las distancias entre punto y punto han resultado grandes, y por consiguiente hemos tenido poco tiempo para escribir [...] Recuerdos a Vallelado y Aguilera, y a *Ud.* le aprecian siempre/Aurelio Espinosa y L. Rodríguez (Letter from A. M. Espinosa and L. Rodríguez Castellano to Tomás Navarro Tomás (Molina de Aragón), 1.5.1932)

> 'Dear Mr. Navarro: A variety of circumstances have delayed considerably the despatch of our news. The distances between one place and another have proven to be great, and we have therefore had little time to write. Greetings to Vallelado and Aguilera, and you are always greatly appreciated/Aurelio Espinosa y L. Rodríguez'

(20) [usted]

Sr. D. T. Navarro Tomás. Madrid./*Muy distinguido señor mío*:/El estado de salud de mi esposa ha mejorado mucho, pero el médico le ha ordenado un par de meses de absoluto reposo [...] Creo que a pesar de ello podría aprovechar el tiempo en beneficio de los trabajos del Atlas, si *Vdes*. me mandasen las primeras instrucciones [...] (Letter from F. de B. Moll to Tomás Navarro Tomás (Palma), 23.1.1934)

'T. Navarro Tomás, Esq. Madrid./My distinguished Sir:/My wife's health has improved greatly, but the doctor has prescribed her a couple of months of absolute rest [...] I think that she might, nonetheless, make use of the time to the advantage of the atlas, if you were to send me the initial set of instructions [...]'

(21) [usted]

Querido señor Castro: muchas gracias por *su* carta. De Rosenblat no sé nada; supongo que sigue en París, ya que lo del Ecuador, como *usted* le previno, es cosa más que problemática [...] (Letter from Luis Cernuda to Américo Castro (Surrey), 24.10.1938)

'Dear Mr. Castro: Many thanks for your letter. I have no news of Rosenblat; I presume he is still in Paris, since the Ecuador business is, as you anticipated, freighted with problems [...]'

In what amounts to a radical break from the previous generation, the younger institutionists show no variance in the forms they use. In the letters exchanged between friends and colleagues from their own generation, *tuteo* is reciprocal and systematic: (T←→T), as examples (22) to (24) illustrate.

(22) [tuteo]

Querido Federico:/*Te* escribo lleno de una gran serenidad y de *tu* santa calma; veras: ya hace un poco de mal tiempo en este bendito septiembre, llueve, hace viento, ancla un barco en el puerto [...] (Letter from Salvador Dalí to Federico García Lorca (Cadaqués), September 1926)

'Dear Federico:/I write to you full of great serenity and your own saintly calm: the weather is already a little rough this blessed September; it's wet and windy, a boat is dropping anchor in the harbour [...]'

(23) [tuteo]

Querido Sijé:/He quedado tristemente impresionado desde cuando recibí y leí *tu* carta: Dices que ahí no tienes más recursos. Pero *tú* debes intentarlo

y porque tenga remedio. Madrid es cruel [...] (Letter from Miguel Hernández
to Ramón Sijé (Madrid), 22.3.1932)

'Dear Sijé:/I have been all of a commotion since I received and read your
letter: You say that you have run out of resources there. But you must make
the attempt and find some remedy. Madrid is cruel [...]'

(24)   [*tuteo*]
Queridísimo Federico:/Con muchísima alegría, recibí, en Madrid, *tu* carta.
Me la entregó Gustavo. No *te* he contestado antes por falta de tiempo./Hace
tres días llegué aquí, a Rute. Ahora con toda tranquilidad *te* contesto [...]
(Letter from Rafael Alberti to Federico García Lorca (Rute), 1.12.1925)

'Dearest Federico:/I was overjoyed to receive, in Madrid, your letter. Gustavo gave it to me. I haven't replied earlier for lack of time./I arrived here,
Rute, three days ago. Now I am at complete leisure to answer you [...]'

Far from abrupt, this generational change from *usted* to the categorical use of
tuteo was a gradual process. The seeds of social change had been sown in the
second half of the 19th century and came to bear fruit among the generations
born around the turn of the century, before finally spreading among the educated
republican classes between 1920 and 1930.

Testimony from the likes of Rafael Lapesa or his contemporaries Zamora
Vicente and Dámaso Alonso is emphatic that it was during this period that a
system of address in harmony with the progressive tendencies of the period
caught on quite visibly in Madrid society. From the opening decades of the
century until the outbreak of the Civil War in 1936, Madrid was the epicentre
of a democratising sociolinguistic change which enjoyed the backing of university students, intellectuals, thinkers and artists who had been trained in
republican ideals and converged in Madrid at a time of great social and political ferment.

4 1930–1940: precipitation of social and linguistic change.

Republican theoretical premises were the basis of a linguistic change which codified a new conception of personal relations. Freedom as an inalienable right,
democracy as a system of government by the people, and the disappearance of
the great social inequalities made up the republican scheme of things. Lapesa

provides an eyewitness's explanation of the spread of *tuteo* on the coattails of new political tendencies:

> Bien es verdad que la extensión del *tú* no es cosa de la última hornada, pues cundió en el decenio 1930–1940 con *la camaradería reglamentaria en partidos políticos de diverso signo*, y se afianzó con la sacudida de la guerra. (Lapesa 1996a: 407)

> 'True enough, the spread of *tú* was not the work of the latest generation alone; rather it took root in the decade 1930–1940 and its *regulatory camaraderie in political parties of diverse hues*, and it was consolidated in the cataclysm of war.'

Social change found its reflection in a wholesale overhaul of customs that had traditionally served to underscore class difference: dress, language, manners and even headwear underwent substantial modifications. Lapesa (1996a: 363) recalls how in films of the period, the poets of the '27 generation doffed their hats in greeting until *sinsombrerismo* – the vogue for not wearing hats at all – "[e]mpezó entre la juventud y en el desahogo veraniego, pero cundió rápidamente según fueron llegando la amenaza y la efectividad de la guerra incivil". [6] *Sinsombrerismo* signified the prosperous classes' renunciation of wearing hats, a fashion that had traditionally distinguished them from the lower classes.

When there are substantial changes in the political system, above all if they are of a revolutionary nature, the linguistic repercussions fail to penetrate into the structure of the language, although they may be reflected in the lexicon.[7] During the Spanish Civil War (1936–1939), everything was in tumult and people's fates hung in the balance until the conclusion of the conflict. The cities like Madrid, Barcelona or Valencia that remained in the Republican zone were for a time under the spell of a classless society, which proved the ideal context for the spread of egalitarian forms of address. In such circumstances, the way people related to each other underwent drastic, albeit ephemeral, changes, which would not become consolidated once the totalitarian regime had been installed in Spain at the end of the war. These passing changes were commented upon by eyewitnesses to them. Passing through Barcelona, Orwell in *Homage to Catalonia*, which was first published in 1938, made express mention of the disappearance of formal expressions of address as well as of other aspects related to alterations to personal appearance and social behaviour as a result of the war:

---

6 'started among the young during carefree summers but gathered pace with the threat of the uncivil war and then the war itself'

7 Various studies have investigated in depth the change in nominal forms of address during this period. Cf. Fernández Lagunilla (1985) and García Santos (1980).

Waiters and shop-walkers looked you in the face and treated you as an equal. Servile and even ceremonial forms of speech had temporarily disappeared. Nobody said *Señor* or *Don* or even *Usted*; everyone called everyone else *comrade* and *Thou*, and said *Salud!* instead of *Buenos días* [...] When I first reached Barcelona I had thought it a town where class distinctions and great differences of wealth hardly existed. Certainly that was what it looked like. Smart clothes were an abnormality, nobody cringed or took tips, waiters and flower-women and bootblacks looked you in the eye and called you *comrade*.

(Orwell 1938: 48; cf. Rodríguez González 1989: 236)

Orwell perceived a similar state of affairs on the Aragon front:

In the strip of Aragon controlled by Anarchist and P.O.U.M.[8] troops, the same conditions persisted, at least outwardly. The revolutionary atmosphere remained as I had first known it. General and private, peasant and militiaman, still met as equals; *everyone drew the same pay, wore the same clothes, ate the same food, and called everyone else* thou *and* comrade; *there was no boss-class, no menial-class, no beggars, no prostitutes, no boot-licking, no cap-touching*. I was breathing the air of equality, and I was simple enough to imagine that it existed all over Spain.

(Orwell 1938: 103)

As for Zamora Vicente, his words paint a similar picture as he relates how in November 1936, four months after war was declared, the Republican Government had ordered the works of art housed in the Prado Museum to be removed to Valencia, where it too was to relocate, in order to protect them against bombardments. A photograph captured the moment the *Meninas* by Velázquez was carried out of the museum:

En esa imagen, aparecen las Meninas, tensas, sacadas de su refugio en las Torres de Serrano. Hay mucha gente en esa fotografía. A un lado, junto al cuadro, está Tomás Navarro [Tomás], *serio, grave, encorbatado, clamoroso su traje frente a los monos de faena*, los equipos seudomilitares, el visible calor del mediodía valenciano. *Quizá es la única persona que, en ese momento, trata de usted a los soldados, obreros, carpinteros, funcionarios, curiosos...* La foto corrió por todas partes. El contraste de Tomás Navarro con los demás retratados marcaba muy bien el paso del tiempo, el violento hiato que dividía nuestra sociedad.

(Zamora Vicente 1979: 426)

'The picture shows the Meninas, tense, removed from their refuge in the Torres de Serrano. There are many people in the photograph. To one side, next to the painting, is Tomás Navarro [Tomás], *serious, grave, wearing a tie, his suit conspicuous amongst the workmen's overalls*, the pseudo-military teams, the visible heat of Valencia at midday. *He may be the only person who, at that moment, addresses the soldiers, workmen, carpenters, functionaries, bystanders as* usted... The photo was circulated everywhere. The contrast between Tomás Navarro and the other people in the picture was eloquent of the passage of time, of the violent rupture that divided our society.'

---

8 Partido Obrero de Unificación Marxista 'Workers' Party of Marxist Unification'

But as fast as the changes had spread, so they were reversed months later as one defeat on the battlefield followed another:

> *The "revolutionary" forms of speech were dropping out of use.* Strangers seldom addressed you as *tú* and *camarada* nowadays; it was usually *señor* and *usted*. *Buenos días* was beginning to replace *salud*.
> (Orwell 1938: 48)

4.1 Letters from the trenches

The analysis of letters written from the front during the Civil War (1936–1939) is particularly fruitful when gauging the extent of *tuteo popular*. This corpus of letters corresponds in part to Republican soldiers writing from different fronts. The largest group of letters is from the Extremadura front, but other letter collections from the Avila, Ebro, Alicante and other fronts have also been examined. Where known, and frequently they are not, the origins of the soldiers are completely heterogeneous.

In addition to the letters written by Republican soldiers, we have also reviewed a corpus of letters written by Francoist troops to their *madrinas de Guerra* 'war godmothers', a practice that was widespread on the Francoist front as a means to keeping the combatants' morale high. The significance of this collection is twofold: on the one hand, it allows cross-checking to determine whether there were ideologically conditioned differences in the use of *tuteo*. On the other hand, it reflects address outside family relationships and in the sphere of communication between men and women who were at first unknown to each other, then became acquaintances and sometimes even friends, that is to say, in the sphere of egalitarian relations between people of the same generation. Examples (25) to (29) illustrate the letters from soldiers on the front.

(25) [*tuteo*]
Nena, me dices en la *tuya* que no me enfade porque no me pongas besos ni abrazos en las cartas porque *te* da mucha vergüenza de poner eso en las cartas, pues *te* digo que a mí me gusta y quiero que me los pongas. (Miguel Romero to Pepa Lozano)[9]

---

9 Where some of the letters reproduced here were written and the relationship between sender and receiver are sometimes unknown. In each case we provide all available data.

'*Babe,* in your letter you tell me not to be angry if you don't put kisses or hugs in your letters because you find it embarrassing to put them in your letters. But what I say is that I like it and I want you to put them.'

(26) [*tuteo*]

Luis, en esta carta yo tengo que conta*r*te algo y es que ya no soy herrador, que no quiero ganar la guerra poniendo clavos, pues he venido otra vez a la trinchera como soldado [...] y de lo que me dices que no véis a las mujeres nada más que en los periódicos, pues yo *te* digo que yo al pueblo hace un mes que no bajo. (Efigenio Gallego to his friend Luis Martín, both from Don Benito (Badajoz), from the Extremadura front)

'*Luis,* I've got to tell you something in this letter, and the thing is I'm not a farrier, I don't want to win the war by hammering nails, but I'm back in the trenches as a soldier [...] and as for what you tell me about not seeing women except in the newspapers, for my part, I haven't been down to the village in more than a month.'

(27) [*tuteo*]

Juan, me dices que *te* cuente algo de la familia, pues no *te* puedo decir más que a mi hermana Paca no le pagan la pensión que le pertenece de su marido muerto en campaña, a mi Ángeles no le pagan la pensión perteneciente a la mía y a mí tampoco me pagan lo que me pertenece de mi accidente. (Antonio Vicente to his friend Juan Camacho Ferré, from the Avila front)

'*Juan,* you ask me to tell you something about the family, and all I can tell you is that they haven't paid my sister Paca the pension she's entitled to for her husband killed in action, they haven't paid my Angeles the pension she's entitled to for mine, and they haven't paid me what I'm entitled to for my accident.'

(28) [*tuteo*]

Pedro, sabrás cómo hemos estado unos días de jaleo pero a mí no me ha pasado nada; también *te* digo que quisiera que lo hubieras visto *tú* obuses donde estábamos nosotros, que nosotros estábamos a unos 200 o 300 metros y ya hubieras visto el tangai que se lio [...] (Emilio Quiles to Pedro Pardo (Granada), from the Avila front)

'*Pedro,* as you must know, we've had a few days of rumpus, but I'm all right; I can also tell you that I wish you'd seen the shells where we were, I mean, we were 200 or 300 metres away and you'd have seen the mess it all caused [...]'

(29) [*tuteo*]

José en este momento silban los proyectiles facciosos y caen aquí en la huerta mía, fíja*te* si arrastraremos miedo. (Manolita Paredes to José Corner)

'*José*, right now the rebels' missiles are whistling and landing in my vegetable plot. Imagine how afraid we are.'

The first great difference between the 19th-century emigrants' letters and those written by soldiers on the front is the change in register that characterises the soldiers' writing, which does without traditional letter structure and adopts an often colloquial tone lacking all formality. *Tuteo* was the dominant mode of address among the Republican soldiers: of the 62 letters, 54 use *tuteo*, while the remaining eight, six of which are addressed to parents, employ *usted*. Using *tuteo* for friends of either sex and even for acquaintances was the norm among these soldiers, and it was often accompanied with terms of endearment and colloquial words. It is significant that occasionally, and always between men, bad language is used, as illustrated in examples (30) and (31). This anticipates the trend towards colloquialism across Spanish society as a whole in the latter decades of the 20th century.

(30) [*tuteo*]

[...] Sobre lo de la comida *las estamos pasando más que putas*, ya que en Intendencia cada vez van desquitando la ración de carne [...] (Letter from Juan Gri Rovira to Eduardo Valle (Mataró))

'As for the food *we're going through hell*, as the quartermasters are always taking the meat ration from us [...]'

(31) [*tuteo*]

también *te* digo que he recibido el pitillo que me has mandado pues *por aquí jodíamente del tabaco*, pues *tú* no sabes lo bien que me sentó cuando me lo estaba fumando, no hacía nada más que acordarme de *ti* en que si fumabas. (Letter from Germán, on the Teruel front, to his nephew Virgilio)

'I can also tell you that I received the fag you sent me, because cigarettes are few and bloody far between here, and you can't imagine how good it felt when I smoked it, all I could do was think about you and whether you were smoking'

The collection of letters written by Francoist soldiers includes letters from 37 different authors addressed to the war godmothers. 31 of the letters reviewed were written during the Civil War (1936–1939) and a further six between 1941–1943, by Francoist soldiers serving with the Blue Division.[10] These letters frequently commence or conclude with phrases like *Arriba España, Arriba Franco* or *Viva la Falange* 'Up with Spain!', 'Up with Franco!' or 'Long live the Phalange!', although it should be pointed out that *camarada* was used by communists and Phalangists alike, as can be seen in examples (32) to (36).

(32) [*tuteo*]

Queridos *camaradas* del PC, *os* mando un saludo revolucionario a todos en general. Me acuerdo de *vosotros* en el segundo aniversario de la guerra de España que han declarado unos generales traidores a la patria [...] (Comissaire Anselmo Ruiz to the members of UGT and PCE (Orellana la Vieja))

'*Dear comrades* of the C[ommunist] P[arty], I send you all a revolutionary salute. You are all in my thoughts on the second anniversary of the war in Spain, declared by a group of generals who have betrayed their country'

(33) [*tuteo*]

Camarada Delegada de la Sección Femenina de F.E.T. y de las J.O.N.S."/ *Distinguida camarada:* No hay derecho a que por no ser uno andaluz se vea privado de tener una madrina sevillana./*Tú* bien sabes que en Navarra no falta el valor en los hombres, pero en cambio falta la sal en las mujeres [...] Espero no me negarás la gracia de tener una madrina sevillana, por lo que quedo a tu incondicional disposición con un fuerte "*Arriba España*": Jesús Fortún (Letter from Jesús Fortún to his war godmother, 1938)

'Fellow Delegate of the Women's Section of the F.E.T. and the J.O.N.S.[11]/ "*Dear Comrade:* It's not fair that just because someone isn't Andalusian he can't have a godmother from Seville./As you know, while men from Navarre are not lacking in courage, its women are short of spice [...] I trust you won't begrudge me a Sevillan godmother, and I, remaining entirely at your service, I greet you with a loud "*Up with Spain!*": Jesús Fortún'

---

10 The *División Azul*, or Blue Division, was the unit of the Spanish army which fought alongside Nazi troops during the Second World War.

11 F.E.T. and the J.O.N.S.: Falange Española Tradicionalista and the Juntas de Ofensiva Nacional Sindicalistas were two right-wing organisations which merged in 1934 and became known simply as the Phalange.

(34) [*tuteo*]
Arriba España/Viva la Falange Femenina de Sevilla, ele./Maria Lª Laffite le
escribe a mi amigo Vizcaino y le dice que si no tiene algún compañero que
quiera Madrina de Guerra y yo inmediatamente acepté y a toda prisa me
apresuro a comunicar*te*lo, no sea que haya alguno que haya leido la carta y
quiera anticiparseme porque entonces las bofetadas se van a oír en Campa-
na [...] Supongo que me contestareis a toda velocidad para que digais el lugar
de la cita mientras tanto me despido de *tí* con un fuerte./*Arriba España*/José
Andrés (First letter from José Andrés to his war godmother, 13.8.1937)

'*Up with Spain!/Long live the Women's Phalange* of Seville, ele./Maria Lª Laffite writes to her Biscayan friend she asks him if he doesn't know anyone
who wants a War Godmother and I accepted at once and hurry to tell you in
case someone else has read his letter and wants to beat me to it, in which
case the thumping will ring out to high heaven [...] I suppose you'll answer
me without delay to tell me where we meet. In the meantime I bid you farewell with a loud./*Up with Spain*'

(35) [*tuteo*]
¡Saludo a Franco! ¡¡Arriba España!!/Porcuna (Jaén) 22 marzo 1938/II Año
Triunfal./Srta. Carmina Sánchez Sevilla/Simpatíca madrinita:/Hace ya una
enormidad de tiempo que *te* escribí, enviando*te* al mismo tiempo una foto,
y hasta la fecha no he tenido el gusto, ni el placer, ni el honor de recibir contestación, alguna, aunque solo hubiesen sido unas lineas. *Tu* silencio me
demuestra que [...] Sin otro particular y pendiente de *tús* prontas y agrada-
bles? noticias, recibe *un afectuoso Saludo nacional-Sindicalista* de *tu* ahijado,/José Romera (First letter from José Romera to his war godmother)

'*Hail Franco! Up with Spain!!*/Porcuna (Jaén) March 22th, 1938/II Triumphal
Year./Miss. Carmina Sánchez Sevilla/Dear little godmother:/I wrote to you
an absolute age ago, enclosing a photo too, and up till now I haven't had the
privilege, the pleasure or the honour to receive any reply, not even just a few
lines. Your silence shows me that [...] Looking forward to your prompt and
pleasant? news, please accept *a warm National-Syndicalist greeting* from
your godson,/José Romera'

(36) [*tuteo*]
¡Ea! Ya tienes un ahijado mujer, y un ahijado como *tu* lo querías. Has tenido la suerte que *tus* deseos encajaran perfectamente en mi fisico [...] *¡Viva
La Muerte!/¡Viva La Legión!* (First letter from Víctor to his war godmother,
19.1.1939)

'Blow me! Now you've got a godson, lady, and a godson just as you wanted. It's your good luck that your wishes fit my physique perfectly [...] *Long live death!/Long live the Legion!*'

In the letters to war godmothers, *tuteo* is the most habitual form address used. The only difference is whether *tuteo* commences with the first letter, when both interlocutors are still completely unknown to each other, or from the second, when an agreement has been reached to start an epistolary relationship. Of the 37 soldiers comprising this part of the corpus, 29 (79%) start using *tuteo* from the very first letter despite not knowing their potential war godmother; in contrast, only 8 (21%) employ *usted* in their first letter, as in examples (37) and (38).

(37) [*usted*]

Apreciable Srta:/Mucho *le* agradezco que se haya dignado escogerme por ahijado, máxime teniendo en cuenta que mi nombre no es de los que atraen o hacen propaganda por si mismo [...] (First letter from Ramón Vega to his war godmother (Madrid), 1937)

'Dear miss:/I'm very grateful that you've been good enough to choose me to be your godson, above all bearing in mind that my name isn't the most attractive or the best advertisement [...]'

(38) [*tuteo*]

Estimada madrinita:/Hoy he recibido *tu* simpática carta [...] (Second letter from Ramón Vega to his war godmother)

'Dear little godmother:/Today I received your kind letter [...]'

Thus soldiers on both sides not only shared a new paradigm of pronominal address, but also similar dreams of equality, which were also countenanced in the ideology of the Spanish Phalange,[12] expressed in example (39).

(39) [*tuteo*]

Simpática madrinita:/Aunque la lectura de *tu* carta ha sido un poco accidentada debido a que la mitad la he tenido que suspender para echarle una bronca al Furriel de la compañía, después cuando la he leído por segunda

---

12 Traditionalist Spanish Phalanx of the Committees of the National Syndicalist Offensive (FET and the JONS).

vez, la he asimilado y me ha alegrado mucho. *Lo de tratarme de tu, lejos de enfadarme me ha gustado mucho, soy falangista hasta la médula y me honra el que en España se vaya generalizando la costumbre de tratarnos familiarmente que nuestro querido "Ausente" deseaba* [...] (Letter from José Lardiés Bosque to his war godmother. (Zaragoza), aged 22, 1938)

'Dear little godmother:/Although I had to interrupt my reading of your letter halfway through in order to give a ticking off to the company's quartermaster sergeant, afterwards, when I read it a second time, I was able to take it all in and it made me very happy. *As for addressing me as tu, far from making me angry, it made me feel pleased as I'm a Phalangist to the marrow and proud of the fact that the custom of addressing each other in this familiar way is becoming widespread, much as our dear "Absent One"*[13] *wished* [...]'

Although the corpus of letters studied does not provide sufficient data for any categorical assertion, there seems to be a relationship between level of education and use of *tuteo*, for the soldiers who employed *usted* in their first letter were usually those who had received the least education. One extreme case of a barely educated letter writer is Manuel Fernández Barbosa, who adopts *usted* and whose multiple spelling mistakes impede any easy reading (example (40)).

(40) [*usted*]
Miqueridisima Madrina es taes para decirle que oi dia 1 e caido en san lucar con mucho dis gusto poravel me venido y no avel la visto y ave y do que es ta talde pensava de aver y do alla a los pita [...] (Letter from Manuel Fernández Barbosa to his war godmother)

'My dearest godmother, this is to tell you that today I've been in Sanlucar and am so upset for coming and for going without seeing you that this afternoon I thought I could have gone to the hospital [...]'

Another is Fernando Giménez Fernández, barely literate like Manuel Fernández who writes only two letters and in both uses *usted* (example (41)).

---

13 José Antonio Primo de Rivera, founder of the Phalange in 1934 and executed in Alicante in November 1936.

(41) [*usted*]

Distingida Señorita:/Sunonbre ast haora pormi des conocido, ha llegao-
hastami trinchera Enel montos en qe la nostagia por la ausencia de to da mi-
familia, esmenos lle vadera [...] (Letter from Fernando Giménez Fernández
to his war godmother)

'Esteemed miss:/Your name, till now unknown to me, has reached me in my
trench at a time when my I'm finding it hardest to take missing all my family
[...]'

Table 4 sums up the usage of *tú* and *usted* in the Republican and Francoist soldiers' letters.

4.2 Letters from prison

The last groups of letters analysed were written by republican prisoners, male
and female, in Francoist prisons. These are mainly *authorised* letters exchanged
between the prisoners and their families, although there are also some *clandestine notes* written in highly colloquial, lower class language, often with spelling
mistakes, since this group of letters is characterised by the low educational level
of their writers.[14] Table 5 gives a summary of *tú* and *usted* use in this set of letters.

Among the prisoners, *tuteo* is almost completely consolidated. Of the 33
letters produced by different writers, 32 employ *tuteo* against only one, addressed
to a mother, using *usted* (examples (42) and (43)).

(42) [*tuteo*]

Maruja, ves a ver a Engracia, vive en Artista 7, es familia de Carmen Barrero,
di que está bien y poneros de acuerdo vosotros, nosotras hacemos la vida
juntas. No os digo más por no poder. Dar muchos recuerdos a todos de mi
parte y recibir un fuerte abrazo y un millón de besos de vuestra hija y hermana. Dionisia (Dionisia Manzanero, aged 20, (Madrilenian district of Cu-
atro Caminos), member of PCE[15], one of the *thirteen roses*).

---

14 Prison correspondence also included the so-called *letters of supplication* written by the in-
mates of Francoist prisons from a position of subordination to the authorities responsible for
their imprisonment and therefore not quantified in our study. In these letters *usted* is the only
form of address used within a rigid formal structure where the nominal address is V.S. (*Vuestra
Señoría*).
15 PCE: Spanish Communist Party.

Table 4: Letters from soldiers on the frontline (1936–39); (1941–43). T= *tú*; V=*usted*.

		Family relationships					Non-family relationships			Total
		Offspring to parents, grandparents	Parent to offspring	Siblings, cousins	Wife	Partner	Friend	Acquaintance	Stranger	
Republican soldiers	*usted*	6V						1V	1V	8V (13%)
	tú	1T	3T	5T	16T	3T	25T		1T	54T (87%)
Francoist soldiers	*usted*								8V	8V (11%)
	tú							37 T	29T	66T (89%)

Table 5: Letters from Republican prisoners in Francoist prisons (1939–1945). T=*tú*; V=*usted.*

	Family relationships				Non-family relationships		Total
	Offspring to parents, grandparents	Parents to offspring	Siblings/ cousins	Wife	Partners	Friends	
usted	1V						1V
tú	3T	2T	3T	7T	4T	13T	32T

'Maruja, pop in on Engracia, calle Artista 7, relative of Carmen Barrero, and tell her it's all right and come to an agreement. We're getting on with life together. I can't tell you more. Pass on my Greetings to everyone and a big hug and a million kisses from your daughter and sister. Dionisia'

(43) [*tuteo*]
Mamá, el día 1 vienes con la madre de Loli. Darás muchos recuerdos a mis hermanos y sobrinos y a todos, y *tú* recibes lo que quieras de *tu* Juli, que no te olvida. Julia". "Mamá, ánimo y no llores, que tú has sido siempre muy fuerte, y no te vayas a poner mala". (Julia Conesa Conesa, aged 19 (Madrid), member of JSU[16], one of the *thirteen roses*).

'Mama, come the 1st with Loli's mother. Please give my regards to my brothers, sisters and cousins, and to everybody, and for you, everything you could wish from your Julie, who never forgets you. Julia". "Mama, cheer up and don't cry, after all you've always been very strong, and you're not going to make yourself ill now".'

In the clandestine notes, where the level of colloquialism and informality is greater, *tuteo* is once again the norm, as illustrated in examples (44) to (47).

(44) [*tuteo*]
Las niñas están bien corriendo por lacalle [sic] pina es mui [sic] simpatica el dia que medieron [sic] las tarjetas me dice trai [sic] mana yo yo *te*las [sic] leo y me acen [sic] gracia que dicen UHp *saluz camarada* y alcan [sic] el puño que eslarisa [sic] con ellas. (Prisión del Dueso (Santoña, Santander), note written by the wife of prisoner José Peña Quintanal)

16 JSU: Unified Socialist Youth.

'The girls are well, dashing about the street. Pina's very nice. The day they gave me the cards, she says give them to me, mum, and I'll read them for you, and it's funny when they say UHp *Hail comrade* and raise their fists – it makes you laugh.'

(45) [*tuteo*]

Querido hijo emos [sic] recibido la tarjeta y por ella beemos [sic] que disfrutas de saluz [sic] nosotros todos buenos/Sin mas por hoy recibes muchos recuerdos de toda la familia de *tus* hermanos y de estos *tus* Padres que de corazon *te* quieren, Julia y Vicente.

'Dear son, we got your card and we see that you're well; we all are too./ That's all for today. Greetings from all the family, from your brothers and sisters and from these parents of yours who love you with all their heart, Julia and Vicente.'

(46) [*tuteo*]

Jose tu carta tenia que haber benido [sic] el Jueves y a llegado oy [sic] Sabado, figura*te* que dos dias mas penosos y tristes para mi [...]

'Jose, your letter should have arrived on Thursday but it came today, Saturday. Just imagine what a few sad and painful days I've had [...]'

(47) [*tuteo*]

Me dices lo mucho que sufres moralmente por mi y nuestra separacion tan larga y asi *Paco mio* sucede en mi, que es un continuo pensar y sufrir con el recuerdo constante de cuanto *tu* sufres y una separacion que se me hace inmensa [...]

'You tell me how much you're suffering for me in your soul on account of our endless separation, and the same happens to me, Paco. I'm endlessly thinking and suffering at the constant recollection of how much you're suffering and this being apart which is overwhelming me'

5 Conclusion: the development of a linguistic change in the social structure

The letters studied have enabled us to reconstruct the socio-political context which facilitated the rise of *tuteo* in Spain around the turn of the century, to trace its spread through Spain's social fabric of the time and, in sociolinguistic terms, to determine which interests common to the different social sectors led to the development of an egalitarian system of pronoun use.

In the last few decades of the 19th century and the first decades of the 20th, testimony from diverse sources demonstrates how *tuteo* in Spanish society began to spread beyond the family sphere and into relations between friends and acquaintances of either sex. The correspondence of the Galician and Asturian emigrants to America shows how from at least the second half of the 19th century the use of *tuteo* among the lower and fledgling middle classes had spread beyond family circles. Nonetheless, the shift towards *tú* for non-family relationships occurred before its consolidation as the term of address used for parents. The coexistence of *tuteo* for friends with *usted* for parents leads to the conclusion that in social terms relationships with friends were perceived as closer than those with parents, in relation to whom traditional hierarchies were preserved for much longer.

Once the *linguistic change* was set in train, its spread was simultaneously *from below* and *from above*. In the same period the new usage was propagated among society's lower classes (*tuteo popular*) and in the higher echelons (*upper class tuteo*) which had witnessed the evolution since the 19th century of egalitarian, non-hierarchical relationships with interlocutors from the same social group.

All this occurred at a time of far-reaching social, political, economic and cultural transformations which found expression in the growth of workers' organisations and the flowering of the institutionist spirit among leading sectors of the political class. The innovation was able to triumph because new actors emerged in the social fabric whose interests converged: the lower class, the new urban middle classes, and the cultural and political elites all shared an urge to modernise which found an outlet in the reformist project of the Second Republic. University students took up *tuteo popular* which was by then already widespread among the lower classes, whose interests were shared by the republican bourgeoisie. But that common ground was shared not only by the different social groups but also by ideological opponents, since both Phalangist doctrine and left-wing ideology advocated a political project of popular appeal which favoured an egalitarian conception of social relations. When intellectuals aligned themselves with the *change from below* in the early decades of the 20th century, the writing was on the wall for the 19th-century system of address.

This innovative development can be given, so to speak, names and surnames since it was the second generation of institutionists who gave the definitive push *from above* to a change which was being spread *from below* by the lower classes. Although this scenarios might imply an abrupt change, the process was in fact gradual. The seeds of social change which had been planted in the second half of the 19th century came to fruition among the generations born around the turn of the century and were propagated among the educated republican classes between 1920 and 1930; their correspondence is plain testimony to the abrupt consolidation of the change in its final stages.

During the Civil War, the markedly colloquial letters written by members of the lower classes show the fully consolidated use of *tuteo* in relationships between peers. In none of the letters written from the frontline or the prisons are friends addressed as *usted*. On the contrary, there is a marked tendency towards the "bad" language that was to impregnate everyday language in the second half of the 20th century.

Although the end of the war represented a turning point in the development of Spanish society, the letter collections show that there was no retreat in the use of *tuteo*, which in fact survived unchanged in egalitarian intragroup relations among the new generations born around the turn of the century. It may well be that this huge impulse given to the system of pronouns in the early 20th century is part of the explanation for today's differences between the Spanish system of address and its equivalents in Spanish-speaking America.

References

Epistolaries

Altolaguirre, Manuel. 2005. *Epistolario 1925–1959*. Madrid: Residencia de Estudiantes.

Anderson, Andrew A. & Christopher Maurer (eds.). 1997. *Federico García Lorca. Epistolario completo*. Madrid: Cátedra.

Castillejo, David. 1999. *Epistolario de José Castillejo*. 3 vols. Madrid: Castalia.

Castillo, Antonio & Feliciano Montero (eds.). 2003. *Franquismo y memoria popular*. Madrid: Siete Mares.

Castillo, Antonio & Verónica Sierra (eds.). 2014. *Cinco siglos de cartas. Historia y prácticas epistolares en las épocas moderna y contemporánea*. Huelva: Universidad de Huelva Publicaciones.

Cortés Carreres, Santi & Vicent García Perales. 2009. *La historia interna del Atlas Lingüístico de la Península Ibérica (ALPI). Correspondencia (1910–1976)*. València: Universitat de València.

Fonseca, Carlos. 2014. *Trece rosas rojas y la rosa 14*. Madrid: Temas de hoy.

Hinojosa Durán, José. 2009. *Tropas en un frente olvidado. El ejército republicano en Extremadura durante la Guerra Civil*, 316–344. Mérida: Editora Regional de Extremadura.

López Álvarez, Juaco. 2000. Cartas desde América. La emigración de asturianos a través de la correspondencia. 1864–1925. *Revista de Dialectología y Tradiciones Populares* 55,1. 81–120.

Martínez Aguirre, Rebeca. 2014. La escritura de cartas en las cárceles de mujeres durante el franquismo. In Antonio Castillo & Verónica Sierra (eds.), 391–410.

Martínez Martín, Laura. 2010. *"Asturias que perdimos, no nos pierdas"*. *Cartas de emigrantes asturianos en América (1863–1936)*. Gijón: Muséu del Pueblu d'Asturies.

Matthews, James. 2015. *Voces de la trinchera*. *Cartas de combatientes republicanos en la guerra civil española*. Madrid: Alianza.

Menéndez y Pelayo, Marcelino & Leopoldo Alas Clarín. 1943. *Epistolario. Prólogo de G. Marañón*. Madrid: Ediciones Escorial.

Ramón, Manuel de & Carmen Ortiz. 2003. *Madrina de guerra. Cartas desde el frente*. Madrid: La Esfera de los Libros.

Sierra Blas, Verónica. 2003. Al otro lado de las rejas. Correspondencia a los presos del Centro Penitenciario de El Dueso (Santander, 1936). In Antonio Castillo Gómez & Feliciano Montero García (eds.), 55–97. Madrid: Siete Mares.

Sierra Blas, Verónica. 2005. En espera de su bondad, comprensión y piedad. Cartas de súplica en los centros de reclusión de la guerra y posguerra españolas (1936–1945). In Antonio Castillo & Verónica Sierra (eds.), *Letra bajo sospecha*, 165–200. Gijón: Ediciones Trea.

Sierra Blas, Verónica. 2008. Palabras en la nieve. Una carta desde el frente de Aragón. *El Filandar. O Fiadeiro* 18. 12–15.

Soutelo Vázquez, Raúl. 2003. La correspondencia de los emigrantes gallegos. In Antonio Castillo Gómez & Feliciano Montero García (eds.), *Franquismo y memoria popular. Escrituras, voces y representaciones*, 123–176. Madrid: Siete Mares.

References to linguistic and social studies

Alba de Diego, Vidal & Jesús Sánchez Lobato. 1980. Tratamiento y juventud en la lengua hablada. Aspectos sociolingüísticos. *Boletín de la Real Academia Española* 60, 219. 95–129.

Alonso, Dámaso. 1962. La muerte del *usted*. In idem, *Del siglo de oro a este siglo de siglas*, 264–267. Madrid: Gredos.

Beascoechea Gangoiti, José María & Luis Enrique Otero Carvajal (eds.). 2015. *Las nuevas clases medias urbanas. Transformación y cambio social en España, 1900–1936*. Madrid: Catarata.

Bustos Gisbert, Eugenio & Silvia Iglesias Recuero. 2003. Relaciones familiares y formas de tratamiento en la novela realista del siglo XIX. In José Luis Girón Alconchel et al. (eds.), *Estudios ofrecidos al profesor José J. de Bustos Tovar*, vol. 1, 277–295, Madrid: Servicio de publicaciones de la Universidad Complutense.

Calderón Campos, Miguel. 2010. Los elementos nominales en el sistema de tratamientos del español de Andalucía durante la Restauración (1875–1931). Historia y situación actual de los pronombres de tratamiento en el español peninsular. In Hummel et al. (eds.), 531–549.

Fernández Lagunilla, Marina. 1985. *Aportación al estudio semántico del léxico político: el vocabulario de los republicanos*. Hamburg: Helmut Buske.

Fox, Jeremy. 1969. The pronouns of address in Spanish. In Alexandru Graur (ed.), *Actes du Xᵉ Congrès International des Linguistes (Bucarest 28 août-2 Septembre 1967)*, vol. 1, 685–693. Bucharest: Académie de la République Socialiste de Roumanie.

García Godoy, María Teresa. 2008. La reconstrucción del sistema de tratamientos en el español de Andalucía (s. XIX). In Esteban Montoro del Arco, María A. López Vallejo, Francisco José

Sánchez García (eds.), *Nuevas perspectivas en torno a la diacronía lingüística. Actas del VI Congreso Nacional de la Asociación de Jóvenes Investigadores de Historiografía e Historia de la Lengua Española (Granada, 29–31 de marzo de 2006)*, 31–65. Granada: Servicio de Publicaciones de la Universidad de Granada.

García Godoy, María Teresa. 2010. El tratamiento a los progenitores en el español peninsular (siglo XIX). Contraste de dos variedades geográficas. Historia y situación actual de los pronombres de tratamiento en el español peninsular. In Hummel et al. (eds.), 595–617.

García Santos, Juan E. 1980. *Léxico y política de la segunda República*. Salamanca: Universidad de Salamanca.

Hummel, Martin, Bettina Kluge & María Eugenia Vázquez Laslop (eds.). *Formas y fórmulas de tratamiento en el mundo hispánico*. México DF/Graz: El Colegio de México/Karl-Franzens-Universität Graz.

Lapesa, Rafael. 1996a. Nuestra lengua en la España de 1898 a 1936. In *idem, El español moderno y contemporáneo. Estudios lingüísticos*, 343–396. Barcelona: Crítica Grijalbo Mondadori.

Lapesa, Rafael. 1996b. La lengua entre 1923 y 1963. In *idem, El español moderno y contemporáneo. Estudios lingüísticos*, 397–413. Barcelona: Crítica Grijalbo Mondadori.

Moreno Luzón, Javier & Fernando Martínez López. 2012. *La Institución Libre de Enseñanza y Francisco Giner de los Ríos: nuevas perspectivas*, 3 vols. Madrid: Fundación Francisco Giner de los Ríos/Acción Cultural Española.

Otero Carvajal, Luis Enrique. 2014. La edad de plata y la renovación de la universidad española. In idem (ed.), *La universidad nacionalcatólica. La reacción antimoderna*, 15–67. Madrid: Universidad Carlos III.

Otero Carvajal, Luis Enrique. 2015. La sociedad urbana en España, vanguardia de la modernidad, 1900–1936. In José María Beascoechea & Luis Enrique Otero (eds), *Las nuevas clases medias urbanas. Transformación y cambio social en España, 1900–1936*, 15–38. Madrid: Catarata.

Rodríguez González, Félix. 1989. Sociolingüística del tratamiento político: a propósito de Orwell. *Revista de Estudios Políticos* (Nueva Época) 63. 233–249.

Zamora Vicente, Alonso. 1979. Necrológica. Tomás Navarro Tomás, por su último discípulo en España. *Boletín de la Real Academia Española* 59,218. 413–431.

9 783110 690262